D1878626

INDIA'S CRIES

TO

BRITISH HUMANITY,

RELATIVE TO
INFANTICIDE, BRITISH CONNECTION WITH IDOLATRY,
GHAUT MURDERS, SUTTEE, SLAVERY AND
COLONIZATION IN INDIA

INDIA'S CRIES
TO
BRITISH HUMANITY,

RELATIVE TO
INFANTICIDE, BRITISH CONNECTION WITH IDOLATRY,
GHAUT MURDERS, SUTTEE, SLAVERY AND
COLONIZATION IN INDIA;
TO WHICH ARE ADDED,

HUMANE HINTS

FOR THE
MELIORATION OF THE STATE OF SOCIETY
IN

BRITISH INDIA.

JAMES PEGGS

GYAN

Published by

Gyan Publishing House
5, Ansari Road
Daryaganj, New Delhi-110002
Phone: 011-47034999, 9811692060
E-mail: books@gyanbooks.com

Distribution Network
gyanbooks.com
India, USA, Canada, UK, Australia, France

ISBN: 978-81-212-8726-5 (PB)
First Published, 1830

2nd Impression 2023

Printed at: Gyan Press, Delhi.

INDIA'S CRIES TO BRITISH HUMANITY, RELATIVE TO INFANTICIDE, BRITISH CONNECTION WITH IDOLATRY, GHAUT MURDERS, SUTTEE, SLAVERY AND COLONIZATION IN INDIA

Author: JAMES PEGGS

INDIA'S CRIES

TO

BRITISH HUMANITY,

RELATIVE TO THE

SUTTEE, INFANTICIDE, BRITISH CONNEXION WITH IDOLATRY, GHAUT MURDERS, AND SLAVERY IN INDIA;

TO WHICH IS ADDED

HUMANE HINTS

FOR THE

MELIORATION OF THE STATE OF SOCIETY

IN

BRITISH INDIA.

BY J. PEGGS,

LATE MISSIONARY AT CUTTACK, ORISSA.

Second Edition, revised and enlarged,

WITH AN ACCOUNT OF THE PRESENT STATE OF INFANTICIDE AND OF SLAVERY IN INDIA.

"In childhood, must a female be dependent on her father; in youth, on her husband; *her lord being dead, on her sons*; if she have no sons, on the near kinsmen of her husband; if he left no kinsmen, on those of her father; if he have no paternal kinsmen, on the sovereign." *Menu.*

"I imagine that the ceremony (the Car Festival of Juggernaut) would soon cease to be conducted on its present scale, if the institution were left entirely to its own fate, and to its own resources, by the officers of the British Government." *Stirling.*

"When we reflect on those evils that are inseparable from even the mildest state of Slavery, and consider how large a portion of our most industrious subjects are at present totally deprived of a free market for their labour, restricted by inheritance to a mere subsistence, and sold and transferred with the land which they till,---policy no less than humanity would appear to dictate the propriety of gradually relieving them from those restrictions, which have reduced them, and must otherwise continue to confine them, to a condition scarcely superior to that of the cattle, which they follow at the plough." *Madras Board of Revenue*, 1819.

LONDON:

PUBLISHED FOR THE AUTHOR,

BY SEELY AND SON, FLEET STREET,

SOLD ALSO BY WIGHTMAN, PATERNOSTER ROW: WAUGH AND INNES, EDINBURGH: AND KEENE, DUBLIN.

1830.

PREFACE

TO THE SECOND EDITION.

THE Author, during his residence in India, having witnessed the horrid rite of burning a widow with the body of her deceased husband,—the miseries of pilgrimage to the great Temple of Juggernaut in Orissa (the celebrity of which is increased by British regulation and support),—the exposure of the sick and the dead on the banks of the Ganges,—and other cruelties of Hindoism, has, since his return to his native country in 1826, laboured to diffuse information respecting these things and to urge the propriety and facility of their suppression. In prosecution of this object the Author has published two editions of a Pamphlet entitled "The Suttees' Cry to Britain;"* two editions of "Pilgrim Tax in India;" an edition of "Ghaut Murders in India;" and a small edition of "Infanticide in India."—The principal part of these Pamphlets have been put in circulation. Through the liberal exertions of numerous friends, a considerable number have been circulated gratuitously in this country, and also in the different Presidencies of India, among the various Functionaries of Government. To show the propriety of these exertions, and to encourage similar and extended efforts, the Author (though with much hesitation) is induced to refer to an extract of a letter from the private Secretary of the present

* The Coventry Society for the abolition of Human Sacrifices in India has published an abridgment of this Pamphlet, entitled "A Voice from India."

Governor General of India, Lord W. Bentinck, dated Dec. 1828, acknowledging the receipt of the Suttee and Pilgrim Tax Pamphlets, which had been forwarded to his Lordship. —"I am directed to acknowledge the receipt of your letter to the Governor General, dated the 7th of April last. His Lordship desires me, at the same time, to present his best thanks for the copies of your Pamphlets which accompanied it; and to assure you that the one on the Suttee question relates to a subject which has engaged his particular attention."* In perfect accordance with these sentiments is the following notice, which, says a correspondent in India, in March, 1829, appears daily in the Papers:—"The Governor General invites the communication of all suggestions tending to promote any branch of national industry; to improve the commercial intercourse by land or water; to amend the defects in the existing establishments; to encourage the diffusion of education and useful knowledge; and to advance the general prosperity and happiness of the British empire in India." Surely a brighter day has dawned on the East.

To this edition is added—'The present State of Infanticide and of Slavery in British India.' Upon these subjects but little correct information appears to be possessed. A very general impression prevails that Infanticide is abolished; and a late celebrated writer on India has stated—"No slavery legally exists in the British territories at this moment;" with what surprise will the reader hear that there are two volumes of Parliamentary Papers on

* It appears that some steps have been taken by the Governor General to abolish the Suttee. Mr. Smith, a Missionary at Benares, writes Feb. 13, 1829:—"Went out by the river side and conversed with a number of Brahmuns on religious subjects, and also brought in the order respecting the prohibition of Suttees. On hearing which, a Brahmun exclaimed, "What has Government now arisen from sleep? So many years has this cruel practice been carried on, and has compassion at last entered into their breasts? They ought to have prevented this horrid practice many years ago." "It astonished me," says Mr. S., "to hear such expressions from a Hindoo." An interesting statement is also given by him, of this prohibitory order being read by the Daroga at *Gopee gunj*, before more than 200 Brahmuns and pundits: after which, the whole listened to his preaching the gospel, and some individuals seemed to be much affected by it. "The English," say they, "now wish to enlighten us." (World Paper, Jan. 20, 1830.) Letters from Calcutta and Serampore, in July, do not mention this subject; and hence it is probable that the measure is of a *limited nature*. The fact, as an *experiment*, is peculiarly encouraging.

Infanticide, and that a very voluminous collection of Papers, of nearly 1,000 folio pages, on Slavery in India, were "ordered to be printed by the Hon. House of Commons, Mar. 12, 1828."—From these valuable documents full and accurate information may be procured.

For the Parliamentary Papers on the Burning of Hindoo Widows, which now contain six volumes, and the Papers relative to Infanticide, the Temple of Juggernaut and Slavery in India, the Author is under the highest obligation to T. F. Buxton, Esq., M.P., and to W. Smith, Esq., M. P. If this volume contain information of a nature calculated to promote the welfare of British India, it is chiefly to be attributed to the important materials supplied by these valuable Papers. The Author's labour, in a considerable part of the work, has been little more than selection and arrangement; and, without such important materials, he should never have presumed to publish upon the different topics discussed in these pages. The necessity of circulating information respecting the state of India, for the purpose of promoting the abolition of the cruelties of heathenism, appears evident. "Shall superstition be suffered to issue her decrees, from year to year, and from age to age, against the lives of poor defenceless and disconsolate widows (and, it may be added, of female infants, pilgrims, and the sick exposed by the Ganges),—hundreds of whom are annually sacrificed to its relentless cruelty, and yet no voice be lifted up on their behalf? Then where are human sympathies? and what are nature's claims? But no: humanity can refrain no longer. A cry has at length been raised for the daughters of sorrow on the plains of India. It has reached the British Isle and reverberated from her shores: it has sounded in the ears of her Legislature:—it is heard in the midst of our city:—it is a loud and bitter cry!"

It is hoped that this revised, uniform, and enlarged edition, of the various piercing plaints of India to British humanity, will be encouraged by a humane and liberal public. The infatuated Suttee,—the murdered female Infant,—the perishing Pilgrim (allured to the shrines of Idolatry, rendered more celebrated by British connexion and support),—the sick exposed by the Ganges,—and the degraded Slave, present their cry to Britain; and shall not that cry be heard and reiterated, from "Dan to Beersheba," till the Senate and the Throne hear, and feel, and redress their wrongs?—"The continued sanction of these enormities is *one of those national delinquencies which press like an incubus, with intolerable weight, on the propriety and stability of our country;* while it opposes an almost insurmountable barrier to the free progress of the gospel." (Mis. Reg. Aug. 1929.) The proceeds of the editions of those parts of the volume which have been published in Pamphets, have been devoted to gratuitous circulation and missionary exertions in India. The profits of this edition are to be devoted to liquidate the debt on the Sabbath School Rooms belonging to the Author's friends in Coventry. It is a source of the highest gratification to him, still to labour for the welfare of the millions of India; and the promotion of this great object, in connexion with those of a more local nature in Britain, is peculiarly grateful to the writer's feelings. With great diffidence, and humble dependence on Divine Providence, this work is sent forth into the world. May the Father of the fatherless and the Judge of the widow, even "God in his holy habitation," incline those who hold in their hands the destinies of India to regard "India's Cries to British Humanity;" and thus bring upon themselves "the blessing of them that were ready to perish, and cause the widow's heart to sing for joy."

Coventry,
Charter House Leys,
Feb. 15, 1830.

CONTENTS.

BOOK. I.

SUTTEES.

CHAP. I.

CHAP. II.

CHAP. III.

CHAP. IV.

CHAP. V.

CHAP. VI.

Page.

CHAP. II.

CHAP. III.

CHAP. IV.

CHAP. V.

BOOK IV.

GHAUT MURDERS.

CHAP. I.

CHAP. II.

CHAP. III.

BOOK V.

SLAVERY.

CHAP. I.

EXTRACTS FROM REVIEWS.

THE SUTTEES' CRY.—"We strongly recommend the perusal of Mr. Peggs' Pamphlet, which, to the feeling testimony of AN EYE-WITNESS of the horrible practice he describes, adds a mass of information, and documents of the most valuable and decisive nature."—*Eclec. Rev. June*, 1827.

"This interesting Pamphlet is every way deserving of serious perusal and extensive circulation."—*Chris. Guardian, June.*

"To this publication we solicit the attention of such readers as desire to make themselves acquainted with the farther details of this important question" (the Suttee).—*Orient. Her. May*, 1829.

"Mr. Peggs' Appeal is forcible, but dispassionate; and we hope that, in behalf of the widows in India, he will not plead in vain."—*Imp. Mag. July*, 1827, *and May*, 1828.

"A valuable collection of papers."—*Evan. Mag. Aug.* 1828.

"The able Pamphlet before us contains much information, collected from the most authentic sources."—*Wes. Mag. June*, 1827.

"This excellent Pamphlet is evidently the result of much labour and research."—*Bap. Mag. June.*

See also "Congregat. Mag." Jan. 1828—"Missionary Reg.," "Asiatic Journal," "Sailors," "Part. Bap. Mag.," "Gen. Bap. Repos.," 1827—"The World Paper," April, 1829.

BRITISH CONNEXION WITH IDOLATRY IN INDIA.—"We earnestly recommend the perusal of these facts and observations to the consideration of the Christian public."—*Eclec. Rev. March*, 1828.

"The Pilgrim Tax levied by the Indian Government on idolaters going on pilgrimages, whatever was its design, has had the acknowledged effect of sanctioning and legalizing this destructive and wicked superstition. The Rev. J. Peggs, late a Missionary near the Temple of Juggernaut, has recently published a Pamphlet, in which he has collected abundant testimony to the duty, facility, and advantages of the entire and immediate abandonment of this pernicious system."—*Mis. Reg. Feb.*

"This Pamphlet relates to a subject which appears to have received a very inadequate share of public attention, and with the details of which, we suspect, many of the best informed and most influential members of society are very imperfectly acquainted. We cordially recommend it to the attention of our readers."—*Bap. Miscellany, Oct.*

"Great credit is due to the excellent Author of these two Pamphlets (the Suttees' Cry and Pilgrim Tax), for the pains which he has taken in collecting information concerning some of the most cruel and destructive superstitions of India, and in presenting it to the British public in *a cheap form*. We know of no publications in the English language, which, in so small a compass, contain so much information on these subjects, so interesting to every friend of humanity and religion."—*Wes. Mag. May.*

"We believe that the Pamphlet before us is the only exposure of the system which has found its way through the press to the English public. We hope it will be widely circulated, and followed by others, in increasing numbers, until the evil is at an end, and the disgrace wiped away."—*Month. Rep. Dec.* 1829.

See also "Congregat. Magazine," Jan. and Feb.—"Bap. Magazine," "Gen. Bap. Repository," "The World," April, 1828.

Ghaut Murders in India.—" We are sorry we have lost even an hour in introducing this cheap, important, and stirring Pamphlet to the notice of our readers. We have gone through it with astonishment and shame;—*astonishment*, that a practice, like that on which this work principally treats, should be allowed by the British Government; and *shame*, that Christians, so much alive to the very name of oppression in England, should not have arisen as one man to 'appeal to British humanity and justice' in the senate of our land. We implore Christians to make a determined effort on this subject; and we entreat Mr. Peggs to allow the Christian public no rest till the great object of his desires is accomplished."—*Bap. Mag. Apr.* 1829.

" If there be the least spark of benevolence yet alive in the breasts of Englishmen, this appeal will not be in vain.—*The World, June.*

See " Imp. Mag." April, " Gen. Bap. Rep." Jan. 1829.

" Infanticide.—The author has brought an abundance of matter into a small compass; by carefully selecting the best articles written on the subject, from the pens of those best qualified to treat of it, he has compiled a work which will be read with interest, by all who are not sntirely indifferent to the interests of their fellow-creatures. He is evidently impressed with the magnitude and importance of the subject, and we sincerely hope he will not labour unsuccessfuly, in making it as evident to the minds of others."—*Ori. Quar. Rev. Jan.* 1830.

India's Cries to British Humanity (First Edition).—" This volume furnishes on this subject (the safety of the abolition of Suttees), and on the several subjects to which its title-page refers, the most accurate and ample information. Mr. Peggs has entitled himself to the thanks of the British public for his reiterated appeals. We beseech our readers to acquaint themselves with his statements, and to let no opportunity be neglected of advancing his benevolent aim."—*The World, July*, 29, 1829.

" These publications are the fruits of Mr. P.'s observation and reading, and demand attention from all who desire to free their country from the guilt of conniving at the atrocious practices therein exposed."—*Mis. Register, March.*

" A very interesting little work."—*J. S. Buckingham, Esq.*

" The public are much indebted to Mr. P., for his enlightened and indefatigable labours in the cause of humanity. He has fairly made out his premises, that *all the murderous customs now practised by the Hindoos, may be abolished with safety and honour to the British Government.* We earnestly entreat our readers to peruse these Tracts. They are altogether resistless in their appeals."—*Evan. Mag. March*, 1829.

" Those who, like Mr. Peggs, furnish us with a faithful representation of facts, on which to ground our efforts for the melioration of the state of the Hindoos, deserve the thanks, not of India alone, but every friend of humanity in the country which governs India. For the zeal and industry with which this gentleman has been enabled to lay before the public so large a body of important facts, and for the benevolence with which he has long laboured to redress the miseries of the heathen population of India, his Christian brethren, of every denomination, must feel deeply indebted to him. We hope that his exertions will result in success; and that his appeal, to the natural sympathies and benevolent principles of his countrymen, will not be unheard or disregarded."—*Month. Rep. Dec.* 1829.

See " Asiatic Journal," March, " Imp. Mag." May, 1829.

INDIA'S CRIES

TO

BRITISH HUMANITY.

BOOK I.

SUTTEES.

CHAPTER I.

Origin—nature—number—cause of principal prevalence in Bengal—and atrocity of Suttees.

SUTTEE is the name given in India to a woman who immolates herself on the funeral pile of her husband, and denotes that the female is considered true or faithful to him, even unto death; the term is also applied to the rite itself.

Diodorus Siculus, who twice refers to the practice of Suttee, in the 103rd and 106th Olympiad, or B. C. 327 and 314 years, supposes the practice to have originated in the unfaithfulness of the women to their husbands, and their taking them off by mixing deadly plants with their food. "This wicked practice," says he, "increasing, and many falling victims to it, and the punishment of the guilty not serving to deter others from the commission of the crime, a law was passed, that wives should be burned with their deceased husbands, except such as were pregnant and had children; and that any individual who refused to comply with this law should be compelled to remain a widow, and be for ever excluded from all rights and privileges, as guilty of impiety. This measure being adopted, it followed that the abominable disposition to which the wives were addicted was converted into an opposite feeling. For, in order to avoid that climax of disgrace, every wife being obliged to die, they not only took all possible care of their husband's safety, but emulated each other in promoting his glory and renown."* Strabo is of the same opinion.† Mandello, a German, who witnessed a Suttee at Cambay, in 1638, accounts for the rise of this singular custom in the same manner.‡ It is possible that this practice may have originated in a mistaken idea of the import of the injunction of the shastra, addressed by the priest to the bride in marriage: "Be thou the companion of thy husband in life and in death;"—or from the following passage in the Rigvad:—"Let those women, no longer widows, excellent wives, anointed with collyrium and ghee, enter, without tears, without complaints, excellent jewels, let them ascend before the source of beings." It is supposed that these words are addressed to fire, as a god, and that they justify the burning of widows. They appear to recommend it, but not with that clearness which the importance of the case requires. Since their meaning is doubtful, it cannot be a good cause which rests upon them as its chief authority, particularly when there are other passages which afford a refuge from the extreme into which they lead.

"The origin of the custom," says an intelligent magistrate in India, "will most probably be found in the voluntary sacrifice of a widow inconsolable for the loss of her husband, and who resolved to accompany him on the funeral pile; not with any idea that such an act could be acceptable to the gods, or any way beneficial to herself in a future existence; but solely because her affection for the deceased made her regard life as a burden no longer to be borne. The example of this heroine, if it remained the only incentive to Suttee, would have been rarely followed; but it of course excited admiration as a novelty; and in a short time the Brahmuns began to perceive, that, if properly managed, Suttee might be made a very productive source of emolument;§ and the most esteemed authors of

---

* Lib. xix. c. 32, 33.

† Geogr. lib. xv. See Asiat. Journ. May, 1827.

‡ Asiat. Journ. Jan. 1823.

§ The expense of the Suttee witnessed by the author at Cuttack, Aug. 19, 1824, was, according to the pundit, as follows:—"Ghee, three rupees; cloth, one rupee; woman's new cloth, two rupees and a half; wood, three rupees; adawlut pundit, three rupees; the woman gave one rupee for some purpose; rice, one anna; betel nut, two pice; flowers, one anna; cocoa, one anna; hemp, four annas; haldee, one anna; mateeanlet, chundun, doop, cocoa nut, one anna, one pice; carrier, five annas; musicians, half a rupee; paring nails, four annas; cutting wood, three annas; total, fifteen rupees, five annas, three pice. Intended shradda (funeral feast), fifteen or twenty rupees." Thus thirty rupees

the age were induced to recommmend it as a most meritorious act, productive of good effects to the soul of the widow and her husband, and to those of the surviving members of their families: they also prescribed forms and ceremonies, in which the attendance of Brahmuns was of course indispensable. Menu, and the most ancient and respectable writers, do not notice Suttee; it was therefore, in their time, either unknown or not approved. If the former, how comes it to be recommended in the more modern shasters, if the custom was not of the nature supposed? No modern lawgiver would have ventured to praise an act not mentioned by his predecessors, if an example had not occurred, and been received with universal praise, though a novelty and an innovation. If known, but not mentioned because not approved by Menu, the authority of the modern shaster is not sufficient to give any merit to the sacrifice. In the first case we do not find that the practice originated in the law, but that the law is the consequence of the practice; and that sacred authority is subsequently produced to enforce the merit of an act originating in the mortal feelings of affection, grief, despair, or some other passion of the mind, equally incapable of affording a hope that it would be acceptable in the eyes of the Deity."* It is a painful circumstance, that this barbarous custom, which existed prior to the Christian era, should not, before this period, have been annihilated by the progress of civilization, and especially the diffusion of the salutary influence of Christianity in the East.

Various detailed accounts of Suttees have been communicated to the public through the periodical publications of Missionary Societies, the six volumes of Parliamentary Papers on Hindoo Immolations, and the Newspapers of the Presidencies in India. A few instances only of the nature of this inhuman rite are here given.

The "Friend of India," for September, 1824, published at Serampore, contains an account of a Suttee at Cuttack, in Orissa, which the author and some of his friends witnessed:

"On Aug. 19, 1824, this place was defiled with innocent blood. About twelve o'clock the Judge sent a note to the Mission House, in-

---

(value 2s. 6d. at par) were expended. Occasionally considerable sums must be realized by the Brahmuns and their adherents.

* Par. Papers on the Immolation of Hindoo Widows, 1821, vol. i. p. 231.

forming us of the intended Suttee. The woman was a Telinga, the wife of a Brahmun who died that morning about daybreak. Her reply to the several questions proposed to her through the Telinga interpreter was, "What have I any more to do with the world? I must go to my husband." Support for life, and a conveyance to her own home, were offered, but they were rejected. From my pundit I have gathered some particulars which cast light upon this dreadful rite. He stated, that it is customary to lament the dead with crying and noise, but she did not; saying, she was going to her husband. She said, she was a stranger and had nothing, and therefore desired the neighbours to provide what was necessary for a Suttee. She said also, that she had been a Suttee in *three former births*, and must be so *four times more*, and then she should attain endless felicity. Those who should dare to prevent her, by confining her in a house or jail, their seed should die, and they should descend into hell. Some approved of this, others said, that as she had no son nor daughter therefore she wished to die. To this she replied, she had a brother and sister, and in her own country many friends, but she wished to go to her husband. From joog to joog (age to age), in this manner, with the same husband, she was to be born and die.

"About half-past three o'clock she proceeded to the pile. I was then too unwell to venture out. Mrs. P. saw her on the way and talked with her. About six o'clock in the evening I went to the spot, expecting the tragical business to be closed. I was, however, surprised to find nothing more done than the pile partly prepared. The Judge and three other gentlemen, with some of our English congregation, were present, and a great number of Natives. Frequent and persevering efforts were made by the above gentlemen to dissuade her from her purpose, assisted by the members of the Mission who were present. She was sitting near the pile with the corpse of her husband covered with a cloth lying near her. I knew two Telinga Brahmuns present, and, taking them, endeavoured to speak to the woman. I told her I was a Padree; that God had sent me and others to teach the people the true Incarnation, Jesus Christ, who died for our sins: that if she would go with me to my house she would be able to learn this knowledge; and that I would send her in a palkee to her own country: but if she ate fire and died now, how could she gain this knowledge, without which she could not be saved? I told her, thus to destroy herself was not God's will. I fear my translators were not faithful; but all the poor woman said was, 'Narayun, Narayun.' This she repeated with a stupidity of mind truly indescribable. Mr. B., one of the gentlemen present, was desirous to convince her, by some ordeal, that she could not burn; but the infatuated woman played with a piece of fire like a child, though when her hand was pressed upon a coal she showed no resolution. He lifted up one of her eye-lids, and affirmed that she was *intoxicated*. This was stated to the Judge, and urged as a sufficient reason to forbid the horrid murder; but he thought it wanted evidence, and hesitated to use his authority to save her. The pile, which was slowly preparing, was about eight feet long, four feet wide, and about two feet high. At each corner was a piece of wood which supported the roof; three sides of the pile were blocked up. Raw flax was laid on the wood, upon which the corpse was placed. Ghee was forbidden to be put on the pile by the Judge, that the woman might have the opportunity to escape, by feeling the effects of the fire gradually: a practice which, if the Suttee were always, according to ancient custom, to ascend the funeral pile while burning, or if, previous to its being lighted, she were left unbound and unincumbered, might prevent the shedding of much innocent blood. As she had been touched by several persons after her first bathing, she went to the river and bathed again. I saw her enter the pile as a person would get into bed, and lay herself down by the left side of her husband and farthest from the entrance of the pile. The wood under the corpse, after a short time, burned fiercely; and it was horrible to see it consuming the head and elevated stiffened hand of the deceased, while the poor woman was scarcely touched by the devouring element. I stopped about a quarter of an hour, hoping the unhappy sufferer might labour to escape; but, alas! no signs of it appeared; and, after viewing the burning of the dead and the living, till my feelings and concern for my health determined me to go away, I left the horrid circle and hastened home. All such outrages upon the principles of society are unnatural and inhuman, and, when said to be from religious motives, a species of insanity; and hence may properly be suppressed by the powerful voice of reason and authority. When shall these murders cease? Where does the salutary godlike power lie, or from what quarter will it originate to abolish them?"

The following account was communicated, from the temple of Juggernaut in Orissa, in July, 1824, by the author's colleague, the Rev. W. Bampton:—

"The infatuated woman, whose death I witnessed, was the widow of a Brahmun who had died in the morning. The man's age seems to have been about forty and the woman's thirty-five. The place where the Suttee took place was called Swurgu Dwar, which signifies the gate of heaven; and when I reached it I found the coolies employed in digging the hole, which was circular, about six feet deep, its diameter at bottom perhaps a little less than its depth, and at top twice as much. Soon after my arrival, about twelve persons came, each bringing a load of wood on his or her head, for several of them were women. I charged the labourers with being accessary to the crime about to be committed, and the general reply was, that they worked for money, and did this work as they did other work, because they were paid for it. Carelessness or cheerfulness characterised all the Hindoos near or on the spot. The pit being finished, a quantity of water was mixed with cow-dung and sprinkled on the margin about one-third of the way down; two ropes were also well wetted with the same mixture. Inquiring the use of two bamboos which lay near, I was told that they were *to stir the fire and turn about the bodies!* The bits of wood prepared for the occasion were between twelve and eighteen inches long, and on an average five or six in circumference; a quantity of them were thrown into the pit, and a man at the bottom proceeded to set them up on their ends two or three thick round the sides; upon this he placed a second tier; and on the second, a third; he also covered the bottom perhaps five or six inches thick, so that the pit was now two-thirds lined with wood. Soon after all was finished, the dead man was brought on a rough bier, which I suppose might have been made in less than a quarter of an hour. I soon saw the procession (if it may be called one), halting a few hundred yards before me: the crowd was kept off the woman by a square made of four pieces of wood, five or six feet long. The rabble were preceded by some of their rude music. Unwilling to see her burn herself, my worthy companions, Lieut. W. and T. B. Esq., tried several times to prevent the horrid deed, and I lent my feeble assistance, but all to no purpose. They halted twenty or thirty yards from the flaming pit, where the last effort was made, and, that failing, her infamous coadjutors gave her a lighted lamp, which I think she put into an earthen pot under her arm. In a little time all was confusion; and a scene, the most perfectly hellish that we ever saw, was presented; a way was made for the woman to the pit, and its margin was left clear; she advanced to the edge facing her husband, and two or three times waved her right hand; she then hastily walked round the pit, and in one place I thought the flames caught her legs; having completed the circle, she again waved her hand as before, and then jumped into the fire * * * * * *

At this moment I believe the drums beat, and an infernal shout rent the air, but I can scarcely say I know,—all was confusion. A dense smoke issued from the pit, intermixed at intervals with partial bursts of flame, occasioned by quantities of powdered resin thrown into the pit by handfuls. In a little time they allowed the fire to clear itself, and we then saw the wretched woman in the midst of it: I think her posture was that of sitting on her heels; she sometimes moved gently backward and forward, as if she bowed. The poor creature still kept an erect posture; but at length seemed partially to rise, and pitched forward with her head against the side of the pit, about two feet from her husband's left hand. The motion of her head in this position indicated pain, and she continued to live two or three minutes longer. The gentlemen then went home, but I staid a little longer and saw the bodies taken out: for, though the women are burnt in these pits, the bodies are taken out while they are distinguishable, and consumed in two different fires (at least that is the case here), and we are told it is done that *the son may make sure of some fragments of both his parents to be thrown into the Ganges.* Now the ropes came into use; one was doubled and the middle thrown down to catch the man's chin, one or two bamboo levers were put under his head to raise it and get the rope round his neck; the rope was then twisted, in order to fasten it, and they began to draw, but they failed, for the rope slipped off. Another man then attempted to fasten the rope; he succeeded, and they drew up the body, with the exception, I think, of the legs; but it was quite dark, and nothing could be seen but by the light of the fire. They then tried to raise the woman, but could not easily get the rope round her neck, so they put it on her arm, which projected in such a way as to favour their doing so; and, after twisting it well, they drew her nearly to the top of the pit: but they seemed afraid that they should lose her again if they trusted entirely to her arm, so she was held just below the edge of the pit till another man put the other rope under her chin, and she was then drawn quite up. Some of the people employed themselves in arranging the wood for the fires to consume the bodies, and I staid perhaps ten minutes longer, finally leaving the bodies on the brink of the pit. Such are the facts, and I leave them to produce their proper effect."

The Suttee represented in the engraving is narrated by the Rev. J. England, of Bangalore, in the Madras Presidency, in a letter, dated June, 1826. He says—

"I received a note from a gentleman that a *Suttee* was about to take place near his house. On hastening to the spot, I found the preparations considerably advanced, and a large concourse of spectators assembled. On my left, stood the horrid pile; it was an oblong bed of dry cow-dung cakes, about ten feet long, and seven wide, and three high. At each corner of it, a rough stake about eight feet in length was driven into the ground; and at about a foot from the top of these supporters was fastened, by cords, a frame of the same dimensions as the bed, and forming a flat canopy. This frame must have been of considerable weight; it was covered with very dry small faggots, which the officiating Brahmuns continued to throw upon it, till they rose two feet above the frame-work. On my right, sat the poor deluded widow, who was to be the victim of this heart-rending display of Hindoo *purity* and *gentleness;* she was attended by a dozen or more Brahmuns; her mother, sister, and *son* (an interesting boy about three years of age), and other relatives, were also with her. *Her own infant, not twelve months old, was craftily kept from her by the Brahmuns.* She had already performed a number of preparatory ceremonies; one of which was washing herself in a strong decoction of saffron, which is supposed to have a purifying effect. It imparted to her a horrid ghastliness;—her eyes indicated a degree of melancholy wildness; a forced and unnatural smile now and then played on her countenance: and every thing about her person and her conduct indicated that *narcotics* had been administered in no small quantities. Close by me stood the *Fousdar,* a native officer, who, besides regulating the police, is the chief military officer at the station. So heartily did he engage in this murderous work, that he gave the poor widow twenty pagodas (between six and seven pounds sterling), *to confirm her resolution to be burned!* The Rev. Mr. Campbell addressed her in the Carnatic language, but the effect of his address was counteracted by the influence of the Brahmuns. The pile being completed, a quantity of straw was spread on the top. An increase of activity was soon visible among the men whose "*feet are swift to shed blood.*" Muntrams (prayers or incantations) having been repeated over the pile, and the woman and every thing being in readiness, the hurdle to which the corpse of the husband had been fastened was now raised by six of the officiating Brahmuns; the end of a cord about two yards long, attached at the other end to the head of the bier, was taken by the widow, and the whole moved slowly towards the pile. The corpse was laid on the right side, and four men furnished with sharp swords, one stationed at each corner, now drew them from their scabbards. The trembling, ghastly offering to the Moloch of Hindooism, then began her seven circuits round the fatal pile, and finally halted opposite to her husband's corpse, at the left side of it, where she was evidently greatly agitated. Five or six Brahmuns began to talk to her with much vehemence, till, in a paroxysm of desperation, *assisted by the Brahmuns,* the hapless widow ascended the bed of destruction. *Her mother and her sister,* too, stood by, weeping and agonized; but all was in vain—the blood-thirsty men prevailed. The devoted woman then proceeded to disengage the rings from her fingers, wrists, and ears; her murderers stretching out their greedy hands to receive them: afterwards all her trinkets, &c., were produced, and distributed among the same relentless and rapacious priests. While in the act of taking a ring from her ear, her *mother* and *sister,* unable any longer to sustain the extremity of their anguish, went up to the side of the pile, and *entreated that the horrid purpose might be abandoned;* but the woman fearing the encounter, and the strength of her resolution, without uttering a word, or even casting a *parting glance* at her supplicating parent and sister, threw herself down on the pile, and clasped the half-putrid corpse in her arms. Straw in abundance was heaped on the dead and the *living;* gums, resins, and other inflammable substances were thrown upon the straw which covered the bodies, while muntrams were repeated at their heads: six or eight pieces of kindled cow-dung cake were introduced among the straw, at different parts of the pile; ghee and inflammable materials were applied, and the whole blazed in as many places. The men with swords at each corner then hacked the cords which supported the canopy of faggots—it fell and covered the lifeless corpse and the living woman! A piercing sound caught my ear; I listened a few seconds, and, notwithstanding the noise of the multitude, heard the shrieks of misery which issued from the burning pile. In an agony of feeling, we directed the attention of the Brahmuns to this; and, *while so doing,* again—still louder and more piercing than before—the burning woman rent the air with her shrieks! Several of the Brahmuns called out to the *half-consumed, still conscious and imploring widow,* TO COMFORT HER. The pile was now enveloped in flames, and so intense was the heat, that, as by one consent, the Brahmuns and spectators retreated several paces: they then sang a Sanscrit hymn; the hymn ended, but not the shrieks and groans of the agonized sufferer; *they* still pierced our ears, and almost rent our hearts! Scarcely conscious of what I did, in the midst of these vain repetitions, I left this scene of fiendish barbarity?"

The number of widows who annually perish, the victims of this appalling superstition, has in former years been variously stated, and it appears (though doubtless undesignedly) exaggerated. The following information may be relied on, being extracted from the official reports of the Magistrates in India, and printed in England by order of the House of Commons, from 1821 to 1828. It is probable, that Suttees are occasionally perpetrated, without being officially announced to the police; and no correct idea can be formed of the number that occur in the territories of tributary, allied, and independent Chiefs, whose subjects are not under the laws and regulations of the British Government, but who are doubtless encouraged in the sanction of this cruel custom, by British apathy and legislation.

The following facts show that several widows are sometimes burned with the body of their husband:—

"Goopeenaut, a Brahmun employed in the Serampore printing office in 1799, saw *twenty-two females* burnt alive with the remains of Ununtu, a Brahmun of Bagnapore, near Nuddeya. This Kooleen Brahmun had more than a hundred wives. At the first kindling of the fire only three of these wives had arrived. *The fire was kept kindled three days!* On the first day *three* were burnt, on the second and third days *nineteen* more. Some of these women were as much as forty years old, and others as young as sixteen. The first three had lived with the Brahmun, the others had seldom seen him. He married in one house four sisters; two of these were burnt."—*Buch. Apol. for Christ. in India,* pp. 14—16.

"When Row Lacka, grandfather of the present chief of Cutch, died, *fifteen concubines* burned at his funeral pile, but not one of his wives performed the sacrifice."—*Hamilton's Hindostan*, vol. i. p. 638.

"It is consolatory to state," says Sir John Malcolm, "that those shocking scenes which *still occur on the death of the princes of Jaypore, Joudpore, and Oudipore, to swell whose funeral honours numbers of unwilling females are forcibly thrown upon the pile, have long been unknown in Malwa.*"*

Though the number of Suttees in India is not so great as to preclude the possibility of the abolition of the practice, yet it is so considerable as to call aloud for Britain to stretch forth her hand, and save those who are "drawn unto death and ready to be slain."

Number of Suttees in the different Districts of the Bengal Presidency, from 1815 *to* 1824.

	1815	1816	1817	1818	1819	1820	1821	1822	1823	1824
Calcutta Division	244	280	428	533	388	337	364	300	309	348
Cuttack Ditto....	9	9	14	11	33	33	28	28	31	25
Dacca Ditto	31	24	52	58	55	51	52	45	40	40
Moorshedabad ...	11	22	42	30	25	21	12	22	13	14
Patna Ditto......	20	29	49	57	40	42	69	70	49	42
Bareilly Ditto....	15	13	19	13	17	20	15	16	12	10
Benares Ditto. ..	48	65	103	137	92	93	114	102	121	93
Total ..	378	442	707	839	650	598	653	583	575	572

Total in the Presidency of Bengal in ten years	5997
In eight years in the Madras Presidency	287
In nine years in the Bombay Presidency	248
There being no returns for Tanjore, from 1814 to 1819 inslusive (17 being returned for 1820), lowest possible estimate for six years	40
In the Par. Papers, May, 1827, no regular returns are given for Madras. In the Southern Concan (Bombay) in 1824, 27; in 1825, 32. Northern Concan in 1825, 1 Suttee .	60
Total in ten years, for the three Presidencies .	6632
Bengal Presidency, 1825, 639; 1826, 518	1157
	7789†

As it may be interesting to see at one view the extent of the practice under the Bengal Presidency,‡ where it chiefly prevails, the following abstract is given from the Parliamentary Papers, May, 1827, p. 124:—

* Report on Malwa, Feb. 1821. Par. Papers, vol. v. p. 44.

† Par. Papers, 6 vols. Poynder's Speech, p. 4. The Parliamentary Papers, July 18, 1828, contain no regular returns.

‡ The average number of Suttees under the Madras Presidency, from 1820 to 1823 inclusive, was 50; and under that of Bombay, from 1819 to 1823, 49. How easily might these few poor widows have been saved!

ABSTRACT STATEMENT

Of the Number of Hindoo Widows burnt or buried alive in the Zillah and City Courts of the Bengal Presidency, in the year 1824.

	Courts.	No. of Suttees.
Calcutta Division.	Burdwan	56
	Hooghly	91
	Jessore	30
	Jungle Mehals	16
	Midnapore	22
	Nuddyah	73
	Suburbs of Calcutta	34
	Twenty-four Pergunnahs	22
	Baraset	4
	Total	348
Cuttack Com.	Cuttack	11
	Khoordah	13
	Balasore	1
	Total	25
Dacca Division.	Buckergunge	23
	Chittagong	2
	Noacolly	—
	City Dacca	7
	Dacca Jelalpore	2
	Mymmensing	—
	Sylhet	—
	Tipperah	6
	Total	40
Moorshedabad Division.	Beerbhoom	3
	Bhaugulpore	—
	Monghyr	—
	Dinagepore	—
	Maldah	1
	City Moorshedabad	8
	Purneah	1
	Rajshahye	—
	Rungpore	1
	Rungpore Commissioner	—
	Total	14

	Courts.	No. of Suttees.
Patna Division.	Behar	1
	Monghyr	—
	City Patna	—
	Ramghur	10
	Sarum	12
	Shahabad	18
	Tirhoot	1
	Monghyr	—
	Total	42
Bareilly Division.	Agrah	—
	Alligurh	1
	Barelly	—
	Shahjehanpore	1
	Peelebheet	—
	Cawnpore	5
	Bhitowra	1
	Etawar	—
	Joint Ditto	—
	Furrackabad	—
	Mooradabad	—
	Nuygeena	—
	Meerut	—
	Boolunshuhur	1
	Saharunpore	1
	Muzuffer Nugger	—
	Deyrah Door	—
	Sirpoorah	—
	Total	10
Benares Division.	Allahabad	5
	Bithora	—
	Bundlecund, S. Div.	5
	Bundlecund, N. Div.	2
	City Benares	16
	Ghazeepore	33
	Gorukpore	17
	Juanpore	1
	Azimgurh	8
	Mirzapore	6
	Total	93
	Grand Total	572

The cause of *the principal prevalence of this inhuman custom in Bengal, and especially in the vicinity of Calcutta*, is thus stated by H. Oakley, Esq., Magistrate of Hooghly, December, 1818 :—" The Suttee is supposed by some to be an act enjoined by the religon of the Hindoos ; but, if so, why does it prevail in one part more than another ? and why in the immediate neighbourhood of the Presidency? The worship of the Hindoo deities is tolerably equal, wherever the religion extends, and the pilgrimages by which they are to be propitiated are the same throughout India ; and, if Suttee were really an act enjoined by religion, it would be universally meritorious, and equally observed wherever that religion is followed ; but, as it is not, we must account for its prevalence among the Hindoos in the neighbourhood of Calcutta, *not by their peculiar strictness in the observance of religious and moral duties, but by some peculiar circumstances affecting their moral character*. It is notorious that the natives of Calcutta and its vicinity exceed all others in profligacy and immorality of conduct. The idol of the drunkard and the thief (Kalee) is scarcely to be met with in the distant provinces, and none but the most abandoned will confess that he is a follower of Kalee. In Calcutta we find few that are not. Her worship must harden the hearts of her followers, to whom scenes of blood and crime must become familiar. By such men a Suttee is not regarded as a religious act, but a choice entertainment ; and we may conclude, that the vicious propensities of the Hindoos in the vicinity of Calcutta are a cause of the comparative prevalence of the custom. But I am utterly unable to assign a cause for *this local depravity*, and for the prevalence of a worship despised and abhorred by every Hindoo of respectable character."*

Ram Mohun Roy, in a Tract entitled " *Brief Remarks regarding modern encroachments on the ancient rights of Females, according to the Hindoo law of inheritance*," supposes the prevalence of Suttee in Bengal to arise from the existence of polygamy, and the dependent and unhappy circumstances in which widows are left. He says—" All the ancient lawgivers unanimously award to a mother an equal share with her son in the property left by her deceased husband, in order that she may spend her remaining days independently of her children." But modern expounders,

* Par. Papers, vol. v. p. 237.

"whose opinions are considered by the natives of Bengal as standard authority in the division of property among heirs," have thus explained away this ancient law:—"A widow can receive nothing when her husband has no issue by her; and in case he dies leaving only one son by his wife, or having had more sons, one of whom has happened to die leaving issue, she shall in these cases have no claim to the property: again, should any one leave more than one surviving son, and they, being unwilling to allow a share to the widow, keep the property undivided, the mother can claim nothing in this instance; but when a person dies leaving two or more sons, and all of them survive, and are inclined to allot a share to their mother, her right is in this case only valid. Under these expositions, and with such limitation, both step-mothers and mothers have, in reality, been left destitute in the division of their husbands' property; and the right of a widow exists in theory only among the learned, but unknown to the populace.

"It is not from religious prejudices and early impressions only that Hindoo widows burn themselves on the piles of their deceased husbands; but also *from their witnessing the distress in which widows of the same rank in life are involved, and the insults and slights to which they are daily subjected*, that they become in a great measure regardless of existence after the death of their husbands; and this indifference, accompanied with hope of future reward held out to them, leads them to the horrible act of suicide. It cannot pass unnoticed, by those who are acquainted with the state of society in India, that the number of female suicides in the single province of Bengal, when compared with those of any other British provinces, is almost ten to one;* we may safely attribute this disproportion, chiefly to *the greater frequency of a plurality of wives among the natives of Bengal, and to their total neglect in providing for the maintenance of females*."—Referring to a practice of disinheriting the daughters, throwing the expense of their marriage upon their brothers, and the sordid principle from which many are given in marriage, he adds—"The humane and liberal among Hindoos trust that the humane attention of Government will be directed to those evils which are chief sources of vice and misery, and even of suicide among women; and to this they are

* This appears too great a proportion.—AUTH.

encouraged to look forward, by what has already been done in modifying, in criminal cases, some parts of the law enacted by Mahomedan legislators, to the *happy prevention of many cruel practices formerly established.*"*

It is humiliating to the national character of Britain to reflect that the horrid rite of Suttee " occurs not in a remote corner of Hindostan, where the eye of authority penetrates with difficulty; but principally in Bengal and in that portion which is *the seat of Supreme Government—where Christianity is professed—and where laws becoming the character of a civil community and of an enlightened nation are presumed to be administered.* More than half of the total amount of Suttees in the Presidency occur in the Calcutta division. The dignity of Government is insulted by a spectacle so avowedly in opposition to all the provisions of civil law and justice; while the honour of religion is compromised by the want of a more visible impression on the surrounding idolatry and superstition."†

The subject of this cruel custom can rarely be considered voluntary. This is very forcibly stated by W. Ewer, Esq., Sup. of Police, Lower Provinces Bengal Presidency:— " It is generally supposed that a Suttee takes place with the free will and consent of the widow, and that she frequently persists in her intention to burn, in spite of the arguments and intreaties of her relations. But there are many reasons for thinking that such an event as a voluntary Suttee very rarely occurs: few widows would think of sacrificing themselves unless overpowered by force or persuasion; very little of either being sufficient to overcome the physical or mental powers of the majority of Hindoo

---

* Miss. Regis. 1823, p. 187—190. Oriental Herald, vol. x. p. 251—258. " Dr. M.," observes the late Bishop Heber, " said that; these horrors (Suttees) are of more frequent occurrence within these last few years than when he first knew Bengal, an increase which he imputes to *the increasing luxury of the higher and middling classes, and to their expensive imitation of European habits,* which makes many families needy, and anxious to get rid, by any means, of the necessity of supporting their mothers or the widows of their relations. Another frequent cause is, he thinks, the jealousy of old men, who, having married young wives, still cling to their exclusive possession even in death, and leave injunctions, either with their wives themselves to make the offering, or with their heirs to urge them to it. He is strongly of opinion that the practice might be forbidden in Bengal, where it is of most frequent occurrence, without exciting any serious inconveniences."—*Journ.* vol. i. p. 37.—Auth.

† Grimshawe's " Appeal on behalf of Hindoo Widows."—Hatchard, p. 3.

females. A widow, who would turn with natural instinctive horror from the first hint of sharing her husband's pile, will be at length gradually brought to pronounce a reluctant consent; because, *distracted with grief at the event, without one friend to advise or protect her, she is little prepared to oppose the surrounding crowd of hungry Brahmuns and interested relations, either by argument or force.* Accustomed to look on the former with the highest veneration, and to attach implicit belief to all their assertions, she dares not, if she were able to make herself heard, deny the certainty of the various advantages which are supposed to attend the sacrifice:—that by becoming a Suttee she will remain so many years in heaven, rescue her husband from hell, and purify the family of her father, mother, and husband; while, on the other hand, that disgrace in this life, and continual transmigration into the body of a female animal, will be the certain consequence of refusal. In this state of confusion, *a few hours quickly pass, and the widow is burnt before she has had time even to think on the subject.* Should utter indifference for her husband, and superior sense, enable her to preserve her judgment, and to resist the arguments of those about her, it will avail her little,—the people will not be disappointed of their show; and the entire population of a village will turn out to assist in dragging her to the bank of the river, and in keeping her down on the pile. Under these circumstances *nine out of ten widows are burnt to death.**

A letter from a lady who has resided in India, dated Salisbury, Dec. 1827, contains the following afflicting account:—

"At a Ghaut near Serampore I witnessed the burning of a respectable woman about thirty years of age, whom I found with *five* children, the eldest a fine boy about thirteen, As soon as she saw me, she asked *if I were come to deliver her.* I told her I had no power to deliver her, but was come to persuade her not to burn. She shook her head and said, '*I will burn! How can I go back? However, the servant is gone to the English Magistrate,*† *at his return my fate will be decided.*' Two hours elapsed before he returned, the greater part of which I spent in conversation with her. She often turned to her children, and with affection pressed her hand upon the face of her youngest child, who

---

* Par. Papers, vol. i. p. 227. See vol. v. p. 17.

† "During my residence at Serampore *many widows applied for permission to burn, but were not permitted.* Those who did burn were obliged to get permission of an English Magistrate, and go out of the bounds of Serampore."

could just lisp *ma, ma.* At length the servant returned with permission for her to burn. As soon as she saw him, her countenance changed, her eyes sunk into her head, the furrows deepened in her face, and when she heard her fate, resolution failed, and *nature took possession of her breast.* When the eldest son saw that his mother was so timid, he said, *he would not set fire to her head.* But her brother-in-law said, '*Now she must burn; for the boro Sahab* (the great Gentleman) *has sent her permission to burn!*' He then began to anoint her, and put a little oil into her hand to pour over her children as her blessing. The eldest son refused the oil, and persisted that he could not set fire to her. But neither the tears nor the screams of the boy, nor the agonizing fear of the mother, prevented her *being bound to the dead body of her husband, and pressed down with two bamboos.* If I had had any authority *merely to have said, 'you are not to burn,' all this would have been prevented.* I am sure both the people and the Brahmuns would have dispersed without a murmuring word. Many call it *a bad custom, and are quite tired of it.*"

The description of a Suttee, the motives which generally lead to it, and the objects for which the victim is sacrificed, abundantly prove that the Suttee is miscalled *suicide*, or voluntary self-immolation. This idea receives confirmation from the fact, that in the annual list of Suttees, in the years 1815 to 1820 inclusive, it appears sixty-two widows were burnt, most of whom were mere children in years.*

Years	17	16½	16	15	14	13	12	10	8
Number	14	1	22	6	2	2	10	1	3

A Bengalee Newspaper, named Kowmoody, published in Calcutta, under date August, 1825, contains the following account:—

"Ramchundea Mitto, an inhabitant of Boydbooty, who generally lived at Calcutta, being attacked with the Cholera Morbus, was taken home by his relations, and on the night of the 29th he died, aged twenty-five years. His young and beautiful widow, *only about fourteen or fifteen years of age*, thinking herself altogether worthless in the world on the death of her husband, and *anticipating the many distresses she would have to suffer if she survived him*, absolutely burnt herself on the funeral pile.'

The same paper, in October, 1825, contains a similar relation:—

"We are astonished to hear that Muddon Mohun Chuckrobutty, *about fifteen years of age*, inhabitant of the twenty-four Purgunnahs (Calcutta), having lately died, his widow, *a little girl about twelve years of age!* no longer willing to inhabit this transitory world, obstinately burnt herself on the funeral pile."

Of juvenile and aged Suttees, the Asiatic Journal for September, 1827, justly remarks:—"It is lamentable to

* Par. Papers, vol. ii. p. 45; vol. v. p. 17.

find, that of the twenty-four young creatures under twenty years of age, who underwent this cruel rite in 1824, one was aged *thirteen*, another *eleven*, and another only *nine*. In all these cases, the Suttees were decidedly illegal; the last especially. The widow was a Brahmunee, and she burnt, upon receiving intelligence of her husband's death, with his turban and other clothes. Two persons who appeared to have assisted at this *murder* were committed to take their trial at the sessions. Of aged Suttees there are many examples in the Returns (Par. Papers, vol. v. 1827), several having burned who were *eighty* and upwards, some aged *ninety*, and one at the great age of *ninety-five*. Surely these poor creatures ought to have been assumed to be *irrational*, and their anticipation of an event which must be so near, prevented on that ground."

The indifference frequently manifested, by the unhappy mothers, to their orphan children, confirms the propriety of the rather singular reply of a Magistrate to an official inquiry relative to the act of Suttees being voluntary or not:—"*The act, I apprehend, is always voluntary, provided a being in a state of stupefaction and delusion can be said to possess the power of volition.** The aggregate of Suttees in India in ten years, according to the official documents, is 6632; allowing two children only to each widow, here are 13,264 orphans, "left to the mercy of those who have decoyed their mothers to the fathers' funeral pile." The misery of a Hindoo orphan was thus pathetically described by a writer in a Calcutta paper, while the author was in India:—

THE INFANT HINDOO MOURNER.

"Upon a woody bank I roamed at eve,
Close to the Ganges gliding stilly on;
And through a glade the sun's last beams I saw,
And o'er the golden tide their radiance streamed.
It was a sweetly pensive hour of calm;
The Myna chirped upon the Mango bough,
And gently coo'd the Ring-dove 'midst the leaves.
I heard a fretful cry of infant wail,
Tremulous, floating on the breeze of eve,
And paused to listen, when these words I caught:
"Mother! mother! Oh my dearest mother!"
I hurried onward to the sandy waste
That edged the water. On the ground there sat,
Near to a heap of ashes mould'ring drear,
Weary and desolate, a little child:

---

* Par. Papers, vol. v. p. 26.

One tiny hand a drooping flower held fast,
Emblem most meet of that unhappy child;
The other wiped away the scalding tears
That from her dim black orbs came trickling down,
As on that ashy heap she gazed intent,
Repeating still her cry of infant wail,
" Mother! mother! Oh my dearest mother!"
" Stranger!" exclaimed the aged peasant near,
" The story of that orphan soon is told:
Child of my child, her father paid the debt
Which awful nature claims, nor recked his babe,
Who deemed him sleeping in a heavy sleep:—
' And wont you wake my father?' she would say,
' And wont you speak, nor take me on your knee?'
The Brahmun came—a garland in his hand—
And hung it round the victim mother's neck:
And then the living with the dead went forth.
The drear procession reached the fated ground
Where wood and fire as meet convenient lay:
The child her mother followed, laughing still,
Or skipped before her, sportive as a lamb;
Or grasp'd the hand whose soft caress was life.
At last the parent stoop'd and kiss'd the child,
And, as she kissed her, down a truant tear
Trickled away, and from her quiv'ring lips,
The pangs she spoke not, breath'd upon her child.
A quick presentiment appear'd to cast
Its instant gloom upon the little one:
Unto her mother's bosom fast she clung,
And sobbed and wept. The mother, soothing, placed
Yon flower, now faded, in her infant hand.
The frail pledge remains, but O the giver!
One last long kiss she gave, then tore away;
And then the pile she mounted by the side
Of him who pressed that bridal couch of death.
Her infant fain would follow; but we held
The little struggler, while her piercing cries
In vain reached her, who soon could hear no more.
' Come back, my mother! mother! mother! mother!'
The din of direful discord rose, and smoke
Ascended blackly through the sunny air.
The crowd dispersed, but still the babe remains,
And has remained since that dread morning hour,
Weeping, and gazing for her mother there;
And nothing finds but loneliness and ashes.—
Mark the said wildness of her young despair,
As on the ashy heap her gaze is fix'd,
With bitter tears and thick convulsive sobs;
And hark again! her cry of infant wail,
' Mother! mother! Oh my dearest mother!' "*

* This was most probably written on reading the following account:—
" As a party were proceeding up the river, in passing Isharah, near

The frequent inability of the widow to escape, arising from the binding of the living and the dead together, the quantity of wood laid upon them, and the administration of intoxicating opiates (circumstances frequently stated in relations of this appalling rite), show the real character of this sanguinary superstition.

The Author's colleague at Cuttack, the Rev. C. Lacey, describing a Suttee that occurred in that city, March 21, 1826, says,—

"The young woman was about seventeen years of age, the wife of a Bengalee Brahmun, and was accompanying her husband on a pilgrimage to Juggernaut. Having performed her perambulations round the pile of death, she laid herself by the corpse of her husband amidst the approving cries of the Bengalees present, 'O mother, Juggernaut save thee! Juggernaut save thee! O happy and blessed! The pile seems to have been unusually high; plenty of ghee and other inflammable materials were thrown upon it, and, after she had laid down, a quantity of wood was heaped upon her. The proper authorities were present. How they were allowed to lay a pile of wood upon her, and thereby render her escape impossible had she been inclined, I cannot imagine; it could not be because there was not sufficient to consume the bodies without it; and it was quite inconsistent with a voluntary sacrifice; because in the time of trial, when infatuation is most likely to yield to the love of life, the poor victim could not act according to her own wishes, nor could any one judge of her change of resolution, as the fire must have diminished her strength, and rendered her quite unable to raise herself from under twenty or thirty seers (forty or sixty pounds!) weight of wood. Thus confined, the poor creature was consumed to ashes. Oh! when shall we wash our hands from human blood!"—*Friend of India, Ap.* 1826.

The levity, apathy, and brutality which characterize these immolations, demonstrate that the practice is any thing rather than a religious rite; and hence the imperious duty of the Legislature to abolish them as fanaticism and murder. A correspondent in the West of England, who resided several years in India, in a letter dated October, 1827, thus describes what he had witnessed:—

Serampore, their attention was attracted by the cries of a child, and on drawing to the shore they were redoubled. Near her was lying a heap of ashes, not quite extinquished, and which appeared like the remains of a recent concremation. A number of children were standing near her, and at a little distance three or four grown up people looking on very contentedly. An inquiry was made by a humane individual whence the cause of her distress proceeded, and it was some time before an answer could be obtained. At length it was ascertained that the *ashes were those of the funeral pile on which the mother of this unfortunate child had immolated herself with the body of her husband, and the lamentations of the child were occasioned by this cause.*" *Bengal Hurkaru, August*, 1823.

"I have seen two Suttees, and might have seen many others, but the effect was too powerful for my feelings. The first was an aged female; she appeared to go through the ceremonies connected with her burning with extreme agitation; her own daughter, about twenty years of age, applied the blazing torch to the pile which consumed at once the bodies of her aged father and widowed mother. The circumstances of the other widow were different; she was about *sixteen years of age*, young and beautiful. The dreadful scene had not the least appearance of a religious ceremony; it resembled an abandoned rabble assembled for the purpose of worrying to death some tame animal, or a company of fiends rejoicing over the accumulated misery of human beings. Such were the confusion and levity of the people, while the poor woman was burning before their eyes, that all humanity appeared extinct in their breasts."

The following relation is from the Parliamentary Papers, relative to Suttees, vol. ii. p. 68:—

"One Seetloo, a Brahmun, died when absent from his family. A fortnight afterwards his widow Hoomuleea, *a girl about fourteen years of age*, proceeded to burn herself, the pile being prepared by her nearest relations, then at the village in which she resided. Her father Puttun Terwarry was in another part of the country, and does not appear to have been made acquainted with what was passing. Whether the sacrifice was originally a voluntary one has not been ascertained; it must be presumed it was so.

"The preparatory rites being completed, Hoomuleea ascended the pile, which was fired by her uncle the prisoner Sheolol. The agony was soon beyond endurance, and she leaped from the flames; but seized by Sheolol, Bhichhook, and others, she was taken up by the hands and feet and again thrown upon it, much burnt, and her clothes quite consumed; she again sprang from the pile, and running to a well hard by laid herself down in the watercourse, weeping bitterly. Sheolol now took a sheet offered for the occasion by Roosa, and, spreading it on the ground, desired her to seat herself upon it. *No*, she said, *she would not do this; he would again carry her to the fire, and she would not submit to this; she would quit the family and live by beggary; any thing, if they would have mercy upon her.* Sheolol, upon this, swore by the Ganges, that, if she would seat herself on the cloth, he would convey her to her home. She did so; they bound her up in it, sent for a bamboo which was passed through the loops formed by tying it together, and carrying it thus to the pile, now fiercely burning, threw it bodily into the flames. The wretched victim once more made an effort to save herself, when, at the instigation of the rest, the Moosulman Buraichee approached near enough to reach her with his sword, and cutting her through the head she fell back, and was released from further trial by death. The number of spectators before whom this diabolical and most lamentable sacrifice was exhibited is variously stated; about 200 persons were probably witnesses of it. A trial ensued, and the following was the sentence:—'Making allowances for the superstitious prejudices of the Hindoos concerned, and for the ignorance of the Moosulman, the Court do not discern in any of them the guilt of murder; and, viewing the case as culpable homicide, sentence the prisoner Buraichee to be imprisoned with labour for five years; and the prisoners Sheolol, Bhichhook, Hurrepal, and Ijrail, to be imprisoned without labour for two years, from this date.'"—Goruckpoore, May 1821. Such an account needs no comment.

When, when shall the British Government see and feel the true nature of this most barbarous custom, and by one merciful act of legislation abolish it for ever? Thus saith the Lord, "Learn to do well, seek judgment, relieve the oppressed, judge the fatherless, plead for the widow."

CHAP. II.

Remarks on the nature of the practice of Suttee, and on the causes that occasion its perpetration, or prevent its suppression.

THE enormity of the practice of burning widows with their deceased husbands would strike even the Hindoos themselves, did not a blind attachment to the vices of their forefathers overcome every natural feeling. In all the annals of human depravity it will be difficult to discover a custom so horrible in its nature, or so destructive in its consequences on individual and public happiness. This is not the case of a patriot relinquishing life to establish the freedom of his country,—it is not a martyr braving the flames to maintain the rights of conscience,—it is not a noble mind sacrificing even life itself on some occasion of exalted virtue to secure to posterity the benefit of its high example. On these occassions we feel a melancholy pleasure in applauding a voluntary resignation of life. But it is the helpless and disconsolate widow torn from her family at the very climax of her grief, and hurried to the flames amidst the shouts of an unfeeling multitude. She must stifle every feeling of compassion for the offspring of her womb, she must renounce them at a period when they stand most in need of her care, and, when weighed down with sorrow, she must take a last look on all mortal things, and enter the flames. Surely this is a case of unparalleled barbarity, and tends almost beyond any thing else to develope the extent of the depravity to which Hindooism owes its origin.

How then is it possible that the murder of the amiable and defenceless should have continued so long? How is it that common humanity has not overleaped every bound, and constrained superstition to desist from a course so inhuman? Among other reasons which might be mentioned, this certainly has its share, that *the whole of the horrible deed is really concealed from view.* The victim being brought before the multitude in a state which scarcely leaves her the power of reflection, being hastily led through certain ceremonies, and hurried to the pile by those whose countenances wear the appearance of hilarity; covered instantly with the fuel, *held down by a pressure which renders all resistance totally unavailing*, all the horrors of death are hid from the sight; while the shouts of the unthinking crowd, which begin to rend the air the moment the torch is applied to the fatal pile, no less effectually conceal from the ear those agonizing shrieks, from which it is scarcely in nature to refrain at the touch of the flames. The agonies, and shrieks, and dying groans of the unhappy victim are witnessed by no one,—but by Him who is the Avenger of blood.

Those who are doomed to undergo these agonies, unpitied, because never beheld, are *the most amiable part of the Hindoo race!* If there be any thing to be found of conjugal fidelity, it resides among these, since an extraordinary degree of conjugal affection, real or ascribed, is made the lure by which these unhappy victims are betrayed to death. Those who are thus cruelly murdered year by year are, in most instances, the most amiable and the most virtuous of the Hindoos.

If we turn to the *unhappy offsprings* who are abandoned, we behold a sight of still deeper woe!—Scarcely recovered from the blow inflicted on them by the death of their father, they are hurried from their once peaceful home to the funeral pile, to witness the death of their mother! A state of the deepest misery succeeds to a state of the highest happiness with such rapidity as almost to deprive them of the exercise of their mental faculties.—The family compact is destroyed with the suddenness of an earthquake. The corpse of the father is scarcely cold before their only living parent is consumed in their presence. But there are circumstances of still greater enormity attached to this system; the funeral pile must be lighted by the eldest son! He accompanies his mother to the banks of the Ganges; he beholds his mother, endeared to him by the recollection of a thousand acts of kindness, thrown on the funeral pile like a beast of sacrifice; and, surrounded by his brothers and sisters, he lights up the pile which consumes the living parent with the dead. Every circumstance which can aggravate this scene of woe is here combined; nor is it possible to conceive of any thing which could add a deeper tinge of barbarity.

The influence of this system is *very destructive to the general happiness of society.*—It aggravates every natural calamity, and gives additional horror to every disease. In other countries the prevalence of an epidemic only serves to increase the energies of benevolence. In India there are no attempts made to stem the current of disease, or to console the afflicted and bereaved. Those of the family whom the disease has spared are only reserved for accumulated misery—the survivors, instead of receiving assistance, are deprived of that parent who could most effectually have afforded it. Every epidemic assumes an aspect of tenfold horror. When therefore the country is afflicted with a destructive epidemic, the numerous victims to disease, the augmented number of female immolations, the number of relatives who tremble for their sisters or their daughters, added to the number of children who stand exposed by the ravages of superstition and death to the loss of all parental aid, form a consummation of misery to which no country on earth presents a parallel.

By whom this crime is perpetrated is worthy of the strictest inquiry. With the victims themselves it can scarcely be said to originate; for, a few days previously, they are often as void of all desire to destroy themselves as to destroy others; and they are generally averse to the deed till their minds are completely deluded by fallacious representations. The *deed is generally encouraged by the relatives of the husband;* those of the wife, on the contrary, being generally on the side for which nature pleads; although her own son, if old enough, *is obliged to kindle the pile prepared for his mother's destruction.* It is therefore on the husband's relatives that the fate of every female is suspended the moment her husband dies: and, when it is considered that they are bound to her by none of the ties of consanguinity, it will not appear strange if some one or all of the following reasons should, in general, so preponderate, as to doom to the flames one for whom they can have little or no personal feeling.

The honour of the family.—This is supposed to arise in proportion to the number of unhappy victims who can be mentioned as having devoted themselves to the flames.

The husband's relatives of course claim to themselves a certain degree of credit for having surmounted feelings of affection, which they never possessed; while the number of widows in their families devoting themselves to the flames, apparently from love to their husbands, gives rise to the idea that these relatives of theirs possessed that excellence of character which rendered it impossible to survive their loss. *The wish to get rid of a burden.*—If her own relatives be unwilling to support her, or not sufficiently opulent, she must live with the surviving relatives of the husband. And, although her life is far from being an affluent one, a certain degree of expense is entailed on the family. The consideration of an expense, though small, yet scarcely terminable within the space of their own lives, added to the vexation often arising from female relatives living together, may possibly make them wish to rid themselves at once of a heavy burden, when it can be done in a way which, instead of being esteemed dishonourable, or any proof of the want of affection, reflects a high degree of lustre on the character of the family. At least this is a temptation which humanity would not throw in the way of a Hindoo, who sets so little value on human life. While impurity reigns among these very relatives of the husband, perhaps in such a degree as to attach to itself no kind of disgrace, *a deviation from purity of conduct* in a widow would, in the public estimation, fix an indelible stain on the family of the deceased husband. When the hazard of this dishonour, through perhaps a long life, is present to minds in which no natural affection towards a brother's widow is supposed to exist, it will excite little surprise that they should, on the death of her husband, decide also on the death of his relict.

The death of the mother deprives the children of their natural guardian.—It sometimes happens that a man who is opulent dies, and leaves children in a state of mere infancy. That their wealth should never be desired by the surviving relatives is what no one will expect who is acquainted with the history of human nature, and much less those who are aware with what earnestness one brother among the Hindoos will labour to supplant another. That, in cases of infancy, an affectionate mother should stand in the way of the surviving relatives of her husband, is only what might be naturally expected. The history of orphans, even in Christian countries, sufficiently shows us how dangerous, in the hands of presumptive heirs, would be such a power of removing, under a religious pretence, the mother of rich but helpless orphans.* All these are so many temptations to the destruction of a widow, which, through this dreadful practice, may be accomplished without the least suspicion being excited of the real views of those interested in her death.

Although the husband's relatives affect to dissuade her from the deed, it cannot be difficult to discern which way their minds really lean. From them the slightest hint, *that they wish her to die*, must operate on a widow of delicacy like a sentence of death pronounced by a judge. With what feelings could she commit herself for life to the mercy of those who had discovered this wish, and felt in the least disappointed by her refusing to precipitate herself into the flames? The law itself, indeed, insists that, while she is never to marry again, she is also to lay aside every thing like ornament for the rest of her days, and every sign of cheerfulness; that she is never to make a full meal, and that one day in every week she is to devote wholly to fasting and grief. In these circumstances it is almost impossible that any degree of ill-treatment, which the resentment of her husband's relatives might dispose them to inflict on her, could interest her neighbours in her sufferings so as to procure her redress; particularly when the interior of a Hindoo habitation, surrounded as it often is with walls, is nearly as impervious as an ancient castle, and the female relatives are scarcely more in the public view than were formerly the unhappy inmates of its dungeon. It is not strange, if, at the most distant intimation of this nature, from those on whose kindness depends every future mitigation of her lot, a widow of sensibility should feel almost distracted, and prefer a speedy death to the unknown horrors of her future destiny.

Certain Brahmuns perform the ceremonies observed at the funeral pile on which a widow sacrifices herself. *These Brahmuns receive even from the most indigent families something on a widow's devoting herself to the flames*; and

* In the only case of Suttee in the Rungpore district (Moorshedabad), in 1824, the magistrate committed for trial all the parties concerned, thinking there was a strong suspicion, corroborated by the inability or refusal of the parties to explain, that the object of the ceremony was *to get rid of the widow in order to secure some property left by the deceased to his brother in the event of her death.*—*Asiat. Journ. Sept.* 1827.

from some wealthy families as much as *two hundred rupees on these occasions.* While it is the obvious interest of these Brahmuns that the wife should be induced to destroy herself when the husband dies, they have access to every family, and are acquainted with the circumstances of the various inhabitants. In what circumstances must a helpless female stand, who has for her spiritual adviser, on the subject of her living or dying, a man who has every kindness to expect from those who are presumptive heirs to the property of her infant son, or who may merely dread her devolving on them as a burden to the end of life! Nor is it necessary to suppose that Brahmuns, in forwarding the views of an infirm husband's relatives, and preparing the mind of the wife for self-destruction, should consider themselves as auxiliaries in the murder of a fellow-creature. They must be supposed to be as much habituated to the employment from which they derive their gain, as a slave-captain to kidnapping and selling slaves, of whom probably a third die in the middle passage through ill treatment and want of air. They may possibly regard the act as meritorious, and admire those relatives who thus wish to raise the reputation of their families. The distant prospect of a large remuneration may urge them so to work on the mind of a simple, artless female, whose age is perhaps under twenty, that, at the moment of her husband's death, no persuasions shall be needed to induce her to make the fatal declaration—beyond the *insidious dissuasions* of her husband's relatives, increasing her desire by affectedly doubting her resolution, and really inflaming her vanity. Were these relatives, however, sincere in these dissuasions, *they have it always in their power to prevent the act,* as the preparation of the funeral pile, and all the expenses of the widow's destruction, devolve wholly on them.

That other feelings than those of unconquerable affection for a husband, often twice their own age, or than any inspired by a steady belief in those wonderful tales of conjugal felicity to be enjoyed with him for boundless ages, influence the minds of the greater part of these unhappy victims, might be shown by numerous instances wherein widows have been prevented by accident from burning.

A man of the writer cast, at Kon-nugur, about four miles from Serampore, between twenty and thirty years of age, died in December, 1817, leaving two wives, one about thirteen years of age and the other about sixteen. Both of these, in the usual manner, expressed their wish to burn with their deceased husband. The elder, being pregnant, was advised to delay till after her confinement, and then to burn herself with something belonging to her husband. The younger, not being prevented, was burned with the corpse. The elder solemnly engaged to burn herself a month after her confinement, till which period she was taken home by her own parents. She at first expressed such displeasure, at being thus denied the opportunity of burning, as to beat herself severely and possibly accelerate her confinement; but at the expiration of the month after that period, when called upon to fulfil her engagement, she had considered the subject more at leisure, and, being at home in the house of her own parents, she positively refused to destroy herself; nor could all the appeals made to her feelings, all the threats and reproaches poured upon her, alter her resolution. She was in the house of her parents, and completely independent of her husband's relatives; and, as every thing which could be done was confined to verbal exertion, she determined to remain with her parents.

As this instance is by no means a solitary one, we have little reason to conclude that the desire to destroy themselves is more firmly fixed in the minds of multitudes than it was in the mind of this young woman. The apparent wish to die, which is thus factitiously produced, is in most instances the mere effect of circumstances created by others; and therefore no more exculpatory of the guilt of deliberate murder, than would be a man's intoxicating another with wine, or any deleterious drug, so as to deprive him of the power of resistance that he might secure his destruction.*

If these circumstances be carefully weighed, it will appear that this inhuman practice has not even those pretentions to its being *a religious ceremony*, which most people have been ready to imagine. *It has no foundation in any peculiar command given in the shastras.* Nor indeed is there in the ceremony any thing that marks it as being peculiarly of a religious nature. The woman devotes herself to no deity; her professed object is merely that of rejoining her husband in a state of happiness. Certain Brahmuns officiate and obtain a sum of money on the occasion; but this is not peculiar to this ceremony; in almost every concern of life Brahmuns are called in, and there are few which are not to them a source of profit.†

There is in this act a violation of the laws of nature, not only on the part of the widow, but also on that of her son, who sets on fire the funeral pile. All civilized nations have agreed that it is the duty of a child to honour its parents: hence, when a Grecian lawgiver was asked why he had

* Friend of India, vol. i. p. 301—304. † Vol. ii. p. 319—330.

specified no punishment for the murderer of a parent, he replied that he did not believe such a monster could ever exist; and hence the Romans erected a temple in honour of one who had, in an extraordinary manner, supported a parent, when dying in a dungeon. The writer very well recollects, that an English child, when he heard the relation of the Bengalees burning their own mothers, very gravely asked: "*And, Sir, don't they hang them for it?*" The unnatural friends who urge the mother and son to the perpetration of the murderous deed, the Brahmuns who officiate, and the multitude who applaud the act, are all guilty of murder, according to the laws of Menu; for he states that, in any crime, the instigator, the perpetrator, and the encourager, are equally criminal. If we view things in this light, we shall find that there is no country in all the world so full of murderers and murder as Bengal. It has generally been considered that the burning of a widow is a simple act, which affects only the individual who suffers; but it is not so. How many urge her to it; how many assist her at it; and how many rejoice at it! This swells the enormity of the crime more than a hundred fold.

The shastras have attempted to extol the practice very highly in reference to the persons immediately concerned, and have asserted that the merit of the deed is so great, that its influence will extend to the individuals and their ancestors for an almost indefinite period. The very words, however, which they have used to celebrate this conduct, afford the plainest proofs of its demoralizing effects. While the consequences which result from this system to the bereaved families are passed over in silence, those which result to society in general are calculated with no degree of precision. Ungira affirms that this deed will expiate any crime.

"If the man has been the murderer of a Brahmun, or ungrateful, or the murderer of his friend, the woman purifies him."

Menu has declared that killing a Brahmun is an unpardonable sin, for which there is no expiation. Passing by these gross contradictions, we would solicit attention to the moral tendency of these words. We should not have supposed that a people so mild and so averse to murder, as the Hindoos, would have trifled so strangely with the subject as to suppose that it could be atoned for by the burning of a widow. If one murder can thus expiate another, we may conclude that any vice will produce its opposite virtue. It is happy for this country that the general disposition of the natives prevents them from turning such ideas to the mischievous purposes of which they are capable. We had heard it asserted by some, that gratitude was a thing so little known among the natives of Bengal, that they had not a word to express such an idea. This is a mistake; yet what must we think of the extent to which ingratitude prevails, when it is maintained not to be ungrateful for a son to set fire to his own mother? And how are we to account for the extent of this bad principle but by attributing it to that spurious morality which teaches that any crime may be expiated by the murder of a helpless widow?

It appears that the shastras do not require or command a widow to burn; in recommending it they have not taken into consideration whether it is murderous or not, but have expressed themselves so unguardedly as to leave the subject fairly open, on their own grounds, to this objection:—in case the woman does not choose to burn, they prescribe methods by which she may obtain future bliss, without the pain of burning; should the widow burn, upon the supposition that she is a self-murderer, they involve also, in the charge of murder, the son and the Brahmuns that assist her; they do not, in the least degree, countenance the cruelties which are now practised, in binding the widow to the dead body, and holding her down with bamboos; the rewards, though apparently great, are little more than are attainable by offering *a single flower or plantain;* since, according to the shastras, the Brahmuns and their families do not go to hell when they die, there cannot be the least need of the widow's suffering to deliver them; and the considerations on which this practice is recommended are such as tend to destroy all morality, and open the door to the commission of the most enormous crimes.*

Such is the real state of the case respecting the burning of widows, which so many have been ready to tolerate under the idea of its being a most sacred religious ceremony, with which it would be sacrilege to interfere. With almost as much justice might the Slave Trade have been regarded with veneration, as a sacred relict of antiquity; or the prac-

---

* See Asiatic Observer (Jan.—April, 1824), No. V. VI. pp. 21—24; No. VII. pp. 111—120.

tice of killing all prisoners taken in war; or that of sacrificing hecatombs of men at the funeral of a favourite chief; or the conduct of certain banditti in India, who are said to seize men and immolate them at the shrine of their imagined deity. *It has scarcely enough of religious ceremony connected with it to varnish it over with the name of religion.* Instead of being a deed of mere superstition, there is reason to fear it is too often the offspring of the meanest self-interest. *It is not binding on all.* It falls only on one sex, while the deed is perpetrated by the other, whom it can never reach; and of that sex it affects only one description of persons, and with these it is professedly optional; were it a religious ceremony, it would be binding on all. It is never equally the interest of the husband's relatives that the widow should live, as that she should be burnt to death. With the former there is connected a certain loss of reputation, and the expenses of maintaining a person to the end of life; with the latter, the full removal of this burden, and a high degree of reputation to their families. Is it right that in a country so richly endowed with the bounties of Providence, the mere question of interest should be suffered to doom the most amiable of our Hindoo subjects to the most cruel death, merely because their being uninformed in mind renders them liable to the grossest deceptions, and their being unable to support themselves renders them dependent? We would entreat all to remember, *murder concealed from public view is murder still*; and that our not actually witnessing the dreadful deed, when we are certain that it is committed, will do little towards exonerating us from guilt.*

CHAP. III.

The rite of Suttee not enjoined by the most authoritative of the Hindoo legislators, and opposed to their views of eminent virtue. Force forbidden by the shastras, yet frequently employed.

A learned native, named Ram Mohun Roy, well known by his luminous examination of the Hindoo Theology and

* Friend of India, vol. ii. pp. 330—332.

Philosophy, in 1818 printed and widely circulated a tract in the Bengalee language, the object of which is to dissuade his countrymen from the practice of this horrid rite: he also published a translation of the tract in English. It is in the form of a dialogue between an advocate and an opponent of the system. The advocate cites various passages from Ungira, Vyas, Hareet, and the Rig-ved, which enjoin or applaud the practice of self-immolation. Against these passages the opponent produces an extract from Menu, the great Hindoo legislator, of whom the Veda itself says, "Whatever Menu has said is wholesome:" which Vrihuspute corroborates by adding, "Whatever is contrary to the law of Menu is not commendable." The extract is as follows: "Let a widow emaciate her body, by living voluntarily on pure flowers, roots, and fruits; but let her not, when her lord is deceased, even pronounce the name of another man. Let her continue till death, forgiving all injuries, performing harsh duties, avoiding every sensual pleasure, and cheerfully practising the incomparable rules of virtue which have been followed by such women as were devoted to one husband."

From this passage the opponent infers, that, as Menu directs the widow to pass her whole life as an ascetic, he intended she should *remain alive* for this purpose; and that this direction of Menu is totally opposed to the directions of the other sages; and that their authority must bend to that of this great legislator. The opponent adduces as his next argument, the disesteem in which the generality of the Hindoo sages regard works of merit or demerit, or, more properly, works done with the interested motive of gaining future happiness; and to show that these are not necessary to the attainment of what the Hindoos esteem the highest state of felicity, absorption in Brumhu, he quotes the following passage from the Veda: "By living in the practice of regular and occasional duties, the mind may be purified. Thereafter by hearing, reflecting, and constantly meditating on the Supreme Being, absorption in Brumhu may be attained. Therefore, from a desire during life of future fruition, life ought not to be destroyed." The immolation of the widow being urged wholly on interested motives, that of enjoying numerous ages of happiness with her deceased husband as its fruit, is therefore opposed to that system, which magnifies the value of divine knowledge as leading to absorption in Brumhu.

The advocate for the practice replies—that the later authorities, in directing the woman to burn herself, do not contradict this law of Menu; and supports this idea by saying Menu directs the performance of Sundhya or evening worship, but is silent as to worshipping Huri, by calling aloud on his name; while Vyas prescribes calling on the name of Huri, and adds that the words of Vyas do not contradict those of Menu. He therefore infers, when Vishnoo and others command the widow to follow her husband through the flame, they do not contradict the command of Menu. This the opponent meets with the utmost ease by showing that there is no analogy in the cases, the performance of Sundhya not preventing any one invoking the name of Huri during another part of the day, while a woman burning herself with her husband will infallibly prevent her living the life of an ascetic; and completely fixes the charge of *contradicting the immutable laws of Menu* on those who have prescribed this practice. The advocate for the practice endeavours to justify it further by quoting the Rig-ved and Hareet, as commending it. This the opponent confutes by various passages esteemed sacred by the Hindoos, which reprobate men performing religious rites merely from interested motives, and among the rest the following from the Bhagvut-Geet, which he terms the essence of all the Smritees, Poorans, and Itahases: "All those ignorant persons who attach themselves to the words of the Vedas that convey promises of fruition, consider those falsely alluring passages as leading to real happiness, and say that besides them there is no other reality. Agitated in their minds by these desires, they believe the abodes of the celestial gods to be the chief object; and they devote themselves to those texts which treat of ceremonies and their fruits, and entice by promises of enjoyment. Such people can have no real confidence in the Supreme Being." These passages the advocate at length acknowledges to be indeed consistent with the Vedas, with Menu, and with the Bhagvut-Geet, adding, however: "But from this I fear that the passages of the Vedas and other shastras, that prescribe Concremation and Postcremation as the means of attaining heavenly enjoyments, must be considered as *only means to deceive*." This the opponent of the practice very dextrously obviates, by urging that these could intend no deception: they only set before mankind two methods of obtaining happiness, the one excellent, the other mean and unworthy for those who are enveloped in desire, passion, and cupidity, who, if they had no shastras holding out rewards, would reject all shastras, and follow their own inclinations like an elephant unguided by the hook.

Unable to urge any thing better, its advocate insists that, after all, a practice handed down to them by Hareet and others ought not to be set aside. This his opponent meets not only by saying that this argument is inconsistent with justice, but by urging the violation of their own rule in the very act of burning. The direction is, that "the widow shall voluntarily quit life ascending *the flaming pile* of her husband." Now, says he, "You first bind down the widow along with the corpse of her husband, and then heap over her such a quantity of wood that she cannot rise. At the time too of setting fire to the pile, you press her down with large bamboos. In what passage of Hareet or the rest do you find authority for thus binding the woman according to your practice? This is in fact deliberate female murder." The advocate urges as an excuse for this horrid practice, that were the woman to shrink back terrified with the flames, after having recited the usual incantations, it would be sinful, and be considered disgraceful by others. The sin his opponent treats with due contempt, by saying that according to themselves it could be expiated by bestowing the value of *three kahuns of cowries* (three-fourths of a rupee); and justly reprobates the idea of esteeming the prevention of murder a disgrace. The advocate, driven to his last resort, defends the binding down the afflicted widow merely on the ground of its being a custom observed throughout Hindostan. This his opponent denies, and then justly reprobates, even were it thus universal.

In some parts of Hindostan, however voluntary the widow may be in her determination, force is occasionally employed in the act of immolation. After she has circumambulated and ascended the pile, several natives bind her to the corpse of her husband, and instantly throw over the bodies, thus bound to each other, a large bamboo or two, which prevent the possibility of her extricating herself when the flames reach her. Logs of wood are also thrown on the pile, which is then set in flames in an instant. Scarcely a moment is left to the spectator to contemplate the scene before the unhappy woman is writhing in the agonies of death. The author of the pamphlet under review states, that this practice has been recently introduced, and that it is confined almost exclusively to Bengal. This information, we have reason to believe, is perfectly correct. The use of force by means of bamboos is, we believe, not unfrequent in Bengal; it is intended to prevent the possibility of the widow's escape from the flames, as such an act would be thought to reflect indelible disgrace on the family.* The number of widows burnt in Bengal, however, exceeds, by nearly three times, the number burnt in all the other provinces of Hindostan. Thus in numerous cases that force is used which renders all resistance on the part of the unhappy sufferer vain. This is totally contrary to the rules even of those shastras which commend the practice; they strictly enjoin that the sacrifice shall be perfectly voluntary in every stage of its progress. Constraint is forbidden by the very nature of the sacrifice. It is called a Suttee, because a woman devotes herself to the flames to prove that she has continued immovably faithful to her husband. Not only therefore must the intention be voluntary, but, to evince this, the act of immolation must not include the most distant idea of constraint.

The Supreme Government has for several years issued various regulations to the magistrates, strictly forbidding the immolation of widows in cases where the Hindoo shastras have forbidden it. Under the influence of these regulations, some females of tender age have been rescued from destruction, yet not a single murmur has been heard. Were the use of bamboos forbidden, we feel assured that the tranquillity of the country would not be disturbed for a moment. And if the apprehension that the widow, unable to ascend the *burning pile*, might possibly reflect disgrace on the family by a change of mind, should in any case induce the relatives to dissuade a female from incurring the

---

* "It is a notorious fact, that, especially in Bengal, in opposition to the express ordinance of the shastra, which forbids any restraint whatever upon the widow to prevent her escape from the funeral pile, and provides for her being lifted off in the event of her being terrified, she is often bound down with cords to the pile, with the body of her deceased husband, or fastened by bamboos placed over her, so that she cannot possibly escape, notwithstanding a change of resolution." J. H. Harrington's Minute on the Suttee, June 28th, 1823. Par. Papers. Vol. iv. p. 14. Bishop Heber refers to this practice, Jour. Vol. i. p. 56. AUTH.

risk, the advantage would be entirely on the side of humanity and justice. Considering the British Government to be the greatest temporal blessing which Providence has conferred on this country, we cannot give up the hope that, ultimately, Government will abolish entirely a custom which involves the murder of the helpless and the innocent, almost without the shadow of support from the Hindoo superstition.*

CHAP. IV.

Review of a Pamphlet in defence of the burning of Hindoo Widows, written in Bengalee by a Pundit.

To the pamphlet addressed by Ram Mohun Roy to his countrymen on the subject of the Suttee, noticed in the former chapter, this work is an answer drawn up by some of the pundits in Calcutta. It is sent forth without a name and without a title page; but from private information, as well as from the pamphlet itself, we find that it is the work of men by no means deficient in learning. It is written in the form of a dialogue between an advocate for the system of burning widows, under the term "Bidhaok," and an opponent, termed "Nishedhok." In the work every authority supposed to countenance the inhuman custom, and every scrap of Sunscrit found on its side among Hindoo writers, is given in the original text, and translated into Bengalee. It is valuable from its containing every thing found in the Hindoo shastras in favour of this practice, and, if all this fall short of *an absolute and indispensable injunction,* the practice will be found to be as illegal according to the Hindoo shastras, as it is inhuman in itself. It is evidently intended for the perusal of Europeans also; as an English translation is prefixed. In our extracts from this pamphlet we prefer quoting its own language for the sake of doing it every degree of justice. The work commences by the advocate urging the claims of his cause in the following sweeping declaration:—

---

* Friend of India. Vol. i. p. 305—311.

"It is ordained by Srutee, Smrtee, Pooranas, and other sacred books, that the women, on the death of their husbands, should die in Shuhu-murun, that is to burn (should burn) themselves alive with the corpse of their respective husbands; and that, in want of the corpse, they should die in Unoo-murun, that is to burn (should burn) with something belonging to their husbands: which usages the great sages during all the four ages of the world, viz. Suttwa, Treta, Dwapur, and Kalee, have regularly maintained in their codes. It is very improper that you throw obstacles to prevent such a matter." To this the opponent replies: "You say this is improper for want of knowledge of the shastras or law, but, when you know the shastra, you will no more say so."

This forms the signal for the advocate to pour forth on the opponent every scrap of Sunscrit, in support of the practice, which he had been able to collect. The chief of these authorities is that of *Ungeera*, who, however, does little more than *recommend* the practice. We give his opinion in the advocate's translation:—"The woman that mounts the funeral pile of her deceased husband equals herself to Uroondhootee the wife of Vushisht'ha, and enjoys bliss in heaven with her own husband. She that accompanies her husband to the other world dwells in heaven for three and a half cootee years (thirty-five millions),* which is equal to the number of hairs on a human body, and with her own power taking her husband up, in the same manner as a snake-catcher would have taken a snake out of its hole, remains with him in diversion. She that goes with her husband to the other world purifies three generations, that is, the generations of her mother's side, father's side, and husband's side; and so she, being reckoned the purest and best in fame among women, becomes too dear to her husband, and continues to divert herself with him for a period equal to the reign of fourteen

---

* "He who offers a single ripe plantain to Seeb, shall, with his relations, be exalted to heaven for thirty millions of years." Asiatic Obs. (Ap. 1824.) "If," says Ram Mohun Roy, "in defiance of all the shastras, you maintain that such promises of reward are to be understood literally and not merely as incitements, still there can be no occasion for so harsh a sacrifice as burning people to death in order to save the lives of progenitors; for, *by making an offering of one ripe plantain to Seeb, or a single flower of kurubeer either to Seeb or Vishnoo, thirty millions of lives of progenitors may be saved!*"

Indras; and, although the husband be guilty of slaying a Brahmun or friend, or be ungrateful of the past deeds, yet the said woman is capable of purifying him from all these sins. Hence," says the advocate, "Ungeera affirms, that after the demise of a husband, there can be no other duty for a chaste wife than to destroy herself in the fire."

Purasura is then quoted as confirming part of this recommendation:—"The woman that goes with her husband to the other world, dwells in heaven for three and a half cootee years, which is equal to the number of hairs on a human body." *Hareeta* is, after this, introduced as enjoining it by consequence in the following observation: "After the death of a husband, until his wife does burn herself in the fire, she cannot get rid of her feminine body." The *Muhabharut* is then adduced as declaring that a woman burning herself on her husband's funeral pile, atones for her having been a scold or even unfaithful through life, and secures her accompanying him in the other world, maugre all unwillingness on his part: and this although she burn herself from "amours, wrath, fear, or affection." The highest countenance given to the practice therefore, by their own writers (and these appear but four, Ungeera, Purasura, Hareeta, and Vyas), *amounts only to a recommendation of it* from certain advantages the widow is deluded with the hope of obtaining; that is, enjoyment of happiness with her husband—by no means to eternity, but for as many years as there are hairs on the human body; *after which she must descend to the earth again, and undergo all that vicissitude of birth which, in the opinion of the Hindoos, constitutes future punishment.*

The advocate for the burning of widows goes on to notice another authority, that of *Vishnoo-Risee*, who, however, leaves burning *perfectly optional*, in the following language:—"After the demise of a husband, his wife shall either devote herself to Brumhachurya (a life of austerity), or mount the funeral pile of her husband." To remove the force of this option, the advocate adds, that the choice of a life of austerity would involve in it eight faults or crimes (but which he has not mentioned that the reader might judge of their nature), and that even this option is therefore to be rejected. He then goes on to state the authority for Unoo-murun (a woman burning herself after her husband's death with something belonging to him), a practice by no means uncommon at the present day. For this he adduces the authority of *only a solitary writer*, the author of the Mutsya-Pooran:—"In case of the demise of a husband in a distant country, the chaste wife should purify her person by bathing, and then, taking her husband's shoes or another thing, enter into a burning pile to be prepared on purpose." This he justifies by saying, that the Rig-veda declares such women not to be guilty of self-murder; which plainly indicates, if this be self-murder, in the opinion of the Hindoos, it would be condemned. Such is the whole of the countenance this advocate has been able to adduce from the Hindoo writers themselves; and this, one quotation from *Oosuna* condemns in the gross,—it is the voice of nature involuntary speaking:—"*Let not Brahmunees, or wives of Brahmuns, suffer death by entering into a separate pile; but, for the rest of the women, this law is most preferable.*" If it be meritorious to ascend the separate funeral pile, why deny this privilege to the daughters of Brahmuns? *Nature spoke in the breast of this writer.* He was a Brahmun, and he shuddered at the idea of the immolation of his daughter, for the sake of a husband, who might perhaps have treated her with neglect and cruelty all his life. The Brahmuns of the present day consign them to the flames precisely as they do others; a plain proof *that a regard for the authority of their own shastras has little to do in continuing this practice.*

To these quotations from Ungeera, Hareeta, and Purasura, the advocates for this practice are well aware, are opposed authorities of far greater weight, and such as completely nullify them and forbid this inhuman custom. The opponent is now made to quote these, that the advocate for the burning system may obtain an opportunity of invalidating them. He first adduces the famous legislator *Menu*, whose authority is paramount to that of every succeeding writer, as prescribing an opposite course for widows:—"Listen to the law which Menu has prescribed for the husbandless woman. 'After the death of husbands their wives should make themselves lean, by living upon sweet flowers, roots, and fruits; never mind the name of a man, and, until the time of their respective death, with resignation and restriction continue to observe the laws prescribed for Ekputnees (those who have married but one husband); that is, they should, with the desire of obtaining the state of chaste women, devote themselves to the law prescribed for Brumhachurya. As thousands of young Brahmuns, who, before their arriving at full age, devoted themselves to Brumhachurya and begat no children, have gone to Surga or Heaven; the chaste women in like manner, who, after their husband's death, devote themselves to the law of Brumhachurya, may obtain bliss in heaven though issueless.' Hence, says the opponent, Menu has ordained, that women, after their husband's death, should spend the remaining part of their lives in Brumhachurya. This decision of Menu the opponent confirms by adducing the following corroborative declaration from one of the Vedas: 'Know that whatever Menu pronounced is a medicine for the soul;' and another from *Vrihusputee*, 'A Sreeti inconsistent with that of Menu is not praiseworthy.'"

To remove this decision of Menu, which *completely forbids the practice*, is the grand object of this work, and for the sake of this alone it is quoted. This the advocate, knowing that no commentator can erect himself into a lawgiver, and abolish the law itself, first attempts by affirming, that it is only the Smritee *inconsistent* with Menu which is unworthy of regard; but, as a woman can live a life of abstinence and chastity after burning herself, these two of course are not inconsistent! Feeling ashamed of this argument, he quits it, and adducing the following sentence from *Juyminee*, "where there arises an inconsistency among laws, that maintained by many is preferable," attempts to infer, that the *recommendation* of Ungeera, Purasura, and Hareeta, ought to outweigh *the law itself*, enacted by Menu. Deserting this argument as untenable, he quotes a passage from the Rig-veda, recommending the practice of burning, and affirms that the law of Menu on the subject means nothing more than that a woman who may by any accident be *prevented* from burning herself with her husband, or afterwards with one of his shoes, ought to devote herself to a life of austerity. The author of this pamphlet, while he professes to set the authority of the Rig-veda against that of the great Hindoo legislator, is however well aware that *the Vedas contradict each other on this very point*. That he may in some way or other obviate this discrepancy, so fatal to his argument, he now introduces the opponent as quoting a well known passage from the Veda which forbids the burning of widows in the following words:—"As by means of living still, the duties usual and occasional can be performed to purify the mind, and as by hearing of, fixing our mind and devoting our soul to Brumhu or the Supreme Spirit, we can attain it (absorption in Brumhu), no woman should therefore spend her life, that is, suffer death, in hopes of attaining Surga or bliss in heaven."

This is the doctrine which it is the object of the writer of this pamphlet to overthrow. After the opponent has stated it, the advocate urges, first, that to infer from the authority of Menu and the Veda, that a woman, instead of burning herself, ought to embrace a life of abstinence and chastity, would strip the writings of those who recommend her burning herself of all authority! an overwhelming argument truly. He then adduces a sentence from Menu, to show that when one Smriti appears to have one meaning, and another a different one, *both are to be held as law!* The plain inference from this would be, that a widow ought to immolate herself on her husband's funeral pile, and to embrace a life of austerity too! To confirm this exposition the advocate quotes the following contradictory sentence by way of illustration: "In the Otirata, or the oblations of clarified butter, offered to the consecrated fire, the Shorassee is to be taken; and in the Otiratra the Shorassee is *not* to be taken." The just meaning of which contrary Sutras, says he, is, that if in this sacrifice the Shorassee be taken or received, the sacrifice is superlatively meritorious; but, if it be not, the deed is still complete. From this illustration the writer infers, that if a widow wishes to attain connubial bliss in heaven, she may burn herself; but if she wishes final beatitude, she may embrace a life of self-denial; and then adds triumphantly, "See therefore that a woman's burning herself for the sake of connubial bliss in heaven has no way been forbidden." This only goes to say, that even by these authorities, if a widow desires final beatitude she is not commanded to burn herself; and that, according to them, all *is merely matter of option.* But a further examination of the subject will show that this recommendation, while viewed by themselves as degrading in the highest degree, is subversive of the whole system of Hindooism.

The Hindoos throughout India believe the human soul to form an integral part of Brumhu, or the Deity, and hence esteem the summit of future bliss to consist in what they deem final beatitude, or absorption into Brumhu. To the attainment of this all their endeavours are directed; for the sake of it the most tremendous austerities are performed; and nothing beyond this is supposed to be within the wish of man. There are, according to their ideas, many heavens or inferior stages of bliss, to be obtained by certain meritorious deeds. None of these, however, is considered lasting; but the duration of every state of bliss is, according to them, proportioned to the merit of the deed of which it is esteemed the reward. Their state of misery indeed is esteemed no more lasting than that of happiness; but every kind of suffering therein is supposed to be proportioned in duration to the demerits of the sufferers; after which they also are said to be born again on the earth, and there to undergo all the vicissitudes of transmigration till they become sufficiently pure to obtain absorption. Hence a woman who may burn herself for the sake of living with her husband in heaven for a certain period, on its expiration, descends to the earth, and, according to the Hindoos, may be found in hell in the course of years.

The opponent is represented as approving this decision; but, for the sake of its being answered, he is made to urge another objection in the following words:—"As in various shastras contempt has been poured on actions done from cupidity, a woman's burning herself from such motives is by no means proper." He then quotes the *Kuthopunishut* as declaring, that while the pursuit of the system of sacred wisdom is considered safe, he who pursues the other system, which includes a widow's burning herself, degrades his own nature. This he further corroborates by a long quotation from the *Bhaguvut Geet*, which charges such as follow the system with acting only from cupidity and ambition. The whole of this system, therefore, is, by their best writers, regarded as having nothing in it of the nature of virtue; but as being in reality the indulgence of cupidity, ambition, and malice. Among these the opponent properly classes a widow's burning herself with her husband's corpse, with the view of enjoying connubial bliss in heaven; and intimates that, if actions of this kind are not evil, they are at least unnecessary. This fires the advocate, who, to overwhelm his adversary at once, exclaims, "Listen then to Srutee, 'A man wishing heaven for himself, shall perform Ushwameda-jauga' (the sacrifice of a horse); and again, 'a man wishing heaven for himself, shall perform Jotisuma-jauga.' These, and other Srutees, are they to lose their *spirits?* (that is, to have no effect). Say what is your answer? The opponent humbly bows beneath the weight of this rebuke, and acknowledges that the Srutees which commend selfish actions are not useless, but intended for those who, previously filled with "amours, wrath, and covetousness," are not inclined to enter disinterestedly into the service of the Supreme God; and that, without these Srutees enjoining them thus to sacrifice from cupidity or malice, they would be like an elephant without his guide. To prevent this, says he, certain jaugas were ordained to be performed by them; as, *sena-jauga*, by one wishing the death of his enemy; *pootrosti-jauga*, by one longing for a son; and *jotistuma-jauga*, by one wishing bliss in heaven. This concession is made with the view of enabling the opponent to bring forward the last objection he has left, that the advocate may demolish it like a man of straw. This is couched in the following words:—"If you maintain that the disinterested actions are better than those self-interested, why do you then, instead of permitting husbandless women to adopt the law of Brumhachurya, which gives final beatitude, endeavour to preserve the system of self-interested actions of Shuhu-murun and Onoo-murun, which produce bliss in heaven?"

This argument, which the advocate was aware must appear on the face of the subject, and must weigh in favour of a life of abstinence and chastity in preference to burning, he attempts to obviate by urging that a woman, in embracing a life of chastity, would still do it with a view to final beatitude, and therefore from self-interested motives: hence as burning herself would also rescue her husband from the pit he might be driven into for slaying a Brahmun, or friend, or being ungrateful, together with the three generations before mentioned, and enable the woman to "get herself rid of her feminine sex," he esteems it far more desirable that she should burn."

To this conclusive argument the opponent replies:—"Now your sayings are consonant with the shastras." Still, however, he suggests the *probability* of women's attaining the state of final beatitude, were they, after the death of their husbands, "to be disciplined in sacred wisdom, which, by burning themselves, they can never attain." To this the advocate has an unanswerable argument ready, that all instruction would be totally vain; for, says he, "it would be attended with no other success than to condemn them for both the one and the other;" in other words, either they would not live the life of chastity recommended, or they would be too dull to do it from proper motives. He concludes the argument with saying, "It is therefore very improper that the women who have never been conscious of so much as the meaning of the word wisdom, should be desired to follow the system of sacred knowledge."

These are the grounds on which those who oppose the abolition of the practice still desire to preserve this privilege of *burning alive their mothers, their sisters, and their daughters.* It is not because it is sanctioned by the Hindoo law; for their greatest legislator *positively forbids it* by enjoining on widows a contrary course. But this *unparalleled course of murder* is practised *wholly* as a PREVENTATIVE! As a preventative of what? the effects of their dulness! their inability to comprehend "the instructions of sacred Wisdom!" What would be these effects? That they would live a life of abstinence and chastity from improper motives, from a desire after final beatitude! and thus, losing final beatitude, only obtain heaven. Yet what does this burning system itself profess to hold out to the poor widow? Only a little evanescent bliss for a limited time. As for the other part, the poor widow's dragging her murderous or ungrateful husband out of the hands of Yum (death), as a snake-catcher drags a snake out of his hold, it were much better not done. If he have died under the dominion of such barbarous or ungrateful dispositions, it were better far to leave him in the hands of Yum for a season, to be taught better principles, than to take him with her to heaven with these feelings remaining in him. A wretched heaven indeed she would be likely to experience during these thirty-five millions of years. If he did not *murder* her there, it would be merely because she could not become mortal again. What then is even pretended as the superior advantage of burning? *Nothing:* while on their own principles it is optional, the option is quite against the widow's interests.

This honest declaration, that their chief motive for supporting this system of burning is furnished by women's stupidity, brings to light a part of the creed of these advocates for matricide which few ever suspected to belong to Hindooism. The whole of the sex are hereby doomed to *interminable misery,* since they are declared to be such that it would be improper for them even *to be desired* to follow that system of sacred knowledge universally esteemed by the Hindoo writers *the only path* to final beatitude. Astonishing! To what absurdity—to what contradiction even of the whole system of Hindooism, have these advocates for burning their mothers and sisters reduced themselves! After all their pleadings for tenderness to their religious prejudices, it appears evident that *this murderous practice is not more contrary to humanity than it is subversive of their own religious dogmas.*

The advocate evidently states, that, *as they would not live a life of chastity, their burning themselves is the only preventive of their condemnation.* And have they then this shocking idea of their female relations? Will nothing preserve them in widowhood from a life of lewdness but being burnt alive? Then a Suttee at once loses its name and its nature. It is no longer the effect of chaste affection; it is *the highest dishonour to every family in which it may happen.* It proclaims in the loudest manner, that the victim *is so corrupt in her disposition that there is no method of keeping her from a life of unchastity but that of burning her alive.* But is it right that this *preventive measure* should be adopted with any one, much less with such near relatives? Is it agreeable to natural equity that a person should be burnt alive, not *for* impurity of conduct, but *to prevent it?* If it be, ought it to be confined to one sex? If this *preventive course* be allowable at all, it ought not to be confined to the most virtuous, merely because they are the most defenceless; it ought to be extended to the *advocates* of the measure themselves. If they do not discover an equal disposition to impurity, they may to other vices equally injurious to society, and, according to their own creed, equally punishable in the other world. The same *preventive* might with equal benevolence be exercised on them, or at least on such as seem most likely to perpetrate vice; and, if they were less fond of the burning system than they say the poor widow is, they might be permitted to choose any other mode of dying, and thus the country would, in due time, be purified in the most effectual manner.

The author having thus far silenced the opponent, now attempts to justify binding the poor widow fast to the corpse of her deceased husband, heaping wood upon her, and pressing her down with bamboos. For this purpose he makes the opponent, after acknowledging that the advocate for the system had given the "just sense of various shastras," observe, that instead of causing the women to mount the burning pile, as the laws direct, they make them first mount the pile, and then, having tied the widows to the corpse of their husbands, heap over them wood and large bamboos, and, setting fire thereon, burn them to death. "We proclaim," adds he, "that you must not slay women in such a manner." The advocate does not reply by denying the truth of this shocking fact, or by urging that it is too strongly stated; but he defends it by saying, "in whatever country the practice is to mount the full burning pile, there it is indisputable; but that in those countries where this is not the practice, this following of local custom is not inconsistent with the shastras, quoting several authors to show that the usages and customs of a country ought to be observed. The opponent is then made to reply: By this rule, those who, residing in forests and mountains, make it their profession to kill living creatures, are to be held blameless. "By no means," says the advocate, "for the actions of these rude foresters are not approved by men of fidelity, and the laws on the head of Shuhu murun have been regularly maintained by the holy sages, philosophers, and the learned." The plain meaning is, that the learned have introduced into Bengal this custom of binding women to the corpse of the deceased husband, heaping wood on them, and pressing them down with large bamboos from a regard to the custom of the country, when no such custom existed till created by them!

The manner in which the advocate justifies their violating the woman's promise to *mount the burning pile*, is still more singular. The woman, before she burns, pronounces what is termed the Sunkulpa, which is couched in the following terms—"*I will mount the* BURNING *pile*." Adverting to this the Opponent says, "How can the Sunkulpa be completed, because it is pronounced with a promise to mount a burning pile? instead of which they mount it before it touches fire." This difficulty the advocate removes in a moment. Says he, "Whatever you say regarding the incompletion of the Sunkulpa arises from your inattention; for, should a little part of a village or a cloth be consumed by fire, it is then said, even by learned men, that the village or cloth was burnt. In the same manner a little burning pile is also called a burning pile, and in that case the Sunkulpa was not incomplete." As much as to say, if a single twig be set on fire, this constitutes a burning pile! In this manner do these men *sport the violating even their own most sacred formulas, for the sake of securing the destruction of a poor defenceless widow.*

The next reply, for its *levity* and *falsehood*, is, if possible, *still more disgusting.* The opponent is made to answer:—"I approve of your saying this; but from what instances do the people attending funeral ceremonies tie up the women that are about to mount the burning pile? and why are they not guilty of the sin of slaying women?" To this the advocate replies:—"In the aforesaid text of *Hareeta* it was expressed, that until the women themselves cause their bodies to be consumed in the fire, they cannot finally get rid of their sex. In which case, should any part of their bodies, while burning asunder in the piles, *be slipped out thereof, it cannot be wholly consumed.*" It is difficult to say, whether the *indelicacy*, the *shocking levity*, or the *impudent falsehood* of this reply be most to be detested. For men *thus to sport with decency, humanity, and truth, in defence of* MURDER, *is of itself sufficient to condemn for ever the* INHUMAN CUSTOM. The opponent having expressed his approbation of this reason for binding women, has only one scruple left, which is, whether those who assist in burning the widow are not guilty of sin. To this the advocate replies, that it rather exalts them to glory than renders them guilty of sin, which he confirms by reciting the following example from the *Mutsya-poorana.*—"There was a prostitute, named Leelavutee, who, having resolved to make an offering of an artificial salt-hill, a goldsmith undertook the work, and perceiving it to be a divine action he took nothing from the girl for his hire, but constructed for her a salt-hill with so much elegance that afterwards, in reward thereof, the said poor and theological goldsmith, together with his wife, was endowed with immense riches, and became himself the monarch of the seven-dweep universe, with a shining form equal to the rays of ten thousand suns." Hence he gives the opponent to understand, that whoever assists in burning a widow is likely to reap glory, as well as this theological goldsmith for assisting the prostitute in her devout offering. Thus do the supporters of this system, by the *most idle fables,* as well as the most *indecent examples,* trifle with the *real murder* of their female relatives.

We subjoin extracts from a document drawn up in Sunskrit, by Mrityoonjuy-Vidyalunkur (the chief pundit successively in the college of Fort William, and in the Supreme Court), at the request of the chief Judge in the Sudder Dewanee Adawlut, who wished him to ascertain, from a comparison of all the works extant on the subject, the precise point of law relative to burning widows, according to those who recommend the practice. This document, as the compiler of it, from his own extensive learning and the assistance of his friends, had an opportunity of consulting more works on the subject than almost any pundit in this presidency, may be regarded as possessing the highest legal authority according to the Hindoos. After having consulted nearly thirty works on the subject, current in Bengal and the northern, western, and southern parts of Hindostan, among which are all those quoted for the practice by the author of this pamphlet, he says:—“ Having examined all these works, and weighed their meaning, I thus reply to the questions I have been desired to answer.—The Juttee Mullah Bilas shastra directs the following formula to be addressed to the bride by the priest at the time of marriage: ‘be thou perpetually the companion of thy husband, in life and in death.’ Hareeta, *a later writer,* says that it is the inheritance of every woman belonging to the four casts, not being pregnant or not having a little child, to burn herself with her husband.” The compiler afterwards quotes *Vishnoo-moonee,* as speaking thus,—“ let the wife either embrace a life of abstinence and chastity, or mount the burning pile;’ but he forbids the latter to the unchaste.” He then enumerates particularly the various rules laid down by him and others who have followed him on the same side of the question, relative to the time and circumstances in which a woman is permitted to burn herself, and in what cases she is even by them absolutely forbidden. These extracts show that binding the woman, and the other acts of additional cruelty which the author of this pamphlet justifies, are totally forbidden. The *Soodheekoumoodee,* as quoted by the compiler, says,—“ Let the mother enter the fire after the son has kindled it around his father's corpse; but to the father's corpse and the mother let him not set fire; *if the son set fire to the living mother he has on him the guilt of murdering both a woman and a mother.*" Thus the possibility of a woman being bound to her husband's corpse is taken away: *the son is not to be, in the least degree, accessary to the mother's death;* if she burn herself at all, it must be by throwing herself into the flames already kindled. And the *Nirnuya-sindoo* forbids the use of any bandage, bamboos, or wood, by way of confining the woman on the funeral pile; nor before she enters it must the least persuasion be used, nor must she be placed on the fire by others. Thus the practice as existing in Bengal *is deliberate murder,* even according to the legal authorities which recommend burning as optional.

Mrityoonjuy shows, from various authors, that though burning is termed optional, it is not to be *recommended.* To this effect he quotes the *Vijuyuntee:*—" While Brumhachurya and burning are perfectly optional, burning may arise from concupiscence, but Brumhachurya cannot; hence they are not equally worthy, how then can they be equally optional? By Brumhachurya the widow obtains bliss, though she have no son." He then quotes several authors, as declaring that women ought not to burn, because it is merely a work of concupiscence; the *Julwa mala-vilas* and others as declaring that the practice is merely the effect of cupidity, and not the fruit of a virtuous and constant mind; and the *Mitakshura* as declaring that by embracing a life of abstinence the widow, by means of divine wisdom, may obtain beatitude; and hence, a woman's burning herself is improper: adding, that *in former ages nothing was heard of women's burning themselves: it is found only in this corrupt age.*

The following is the conclusion drawn by this able pundit and jurist:—" After perusing many works on this subject, the following are my deliberate ideas. Vishnoo-moonee and various others say, that, the husband being dead, the wife may either embrace a life of abstinence and chastity, or mount the burning pile; but, *on viewing the whole, I esteem a life of abstinence and chastity to accord best with the law;* the preference appears evidently to be on that side. Vyas, Sungkoo, Ungeera, and Hareeta, speaking of a widow burning, say, that by burning herself with her husband she may obtain connubial bliss in heaven; while, by a life of abstinence and chastity, she, attaining sacred wisdom, may certainly obtain final beatitude. Hence to destroy herself, for the sake of a little evanescent bliss, cannot be her duty; burning is for none but those who, despising final beatitude, desire nothing beyond a little short-lived pleasure. Hence *I regard a woman's burning herself as an unworthy act, and a life of abstinence and chastity as highly excellent. In the shastras appear many prohibitions of a woman's dying with her husband, but against a life of abstinence and chastity there is no prohibition.* Against her burning herself the following authorities are found:—In the Meemangshadurshun it is declared that every kind of self-inflicted injury is sin. The Sankhya says, that a useless death is absolutely sinful. The killing for sacrifice commanded by the shastras has a reasonable cause, and is yet sinful in a certain degree, because it destroys life. And while, by the Meemangsha, either of the two may be chosen; by the Sunkhya, a life of abstinence and chastity is alone esteemed lawful. But, by the Vedanta, all works springing from concupiscence are to be abhorred and forsaken; hence a woman's burning herself from the desire of connubial bliss ought certainly to be rejected with abhorrence.

" No blame whatever is attached to those who prevent a woman burning. In the shastras it is said that Kundurpa being consumed to ashes by the eye of Shiva, his wife, Rutee, determined to burn herself; and commanded her husband's friend, Mudhoo, to prepare the funeral pile. Upon this the gods forbade her; on which account she desisted, but by Kalee-das no blame is attached to them for this conduct. Thus also in the *Shree-Bhagubut*; a woman, named Kripee, had a son, a mighty hero, from love to whom she forbore to burn herself with her husband; yet she was deemed guilty of no sin therein. Now also we hear of sons and other relatives attempting to dissuade a woman from burning; yet they are esteemed guilty of no crime. It is also evident that a woman, in thus burning herself, dies merely from her own self-will, and from no regard to any shastra; such *the command of a thousand shastras would not induce to die*. They merely reason thus: ' By the death of my husband I have sustained an irreparable loss; it is better for me to die than to live;' hence a woman determines to die: and her relatives, seeing this mind in her, provide the funeral pile, and say, ' if you are determined to die, to die by falling from a precipice would be tedious, die in this manner:' thus a father who has a son determined to go to a distant country, finding all dissuasion vain, at length sends a guide with him who knows all the rivers and dangerous places. The various shastras therefore describe this action as being merely that of one who, having received an incurable wound, is determined to die, whether by falling from a precipice, by fire, or by water."

After this full investigation, by one so able and possessing such opportunities, the subject, as far as relates to the law of the Hindoos, or to the countenance it receives from the Hindoo system, may well be supposed to be fully before the public.

While the practice is allowed to have been recommended by certain writers, it is evident that it was never considered as a *law*, or as a religious injunction essential to the duty of a good Hindoo. If it be a law, the greater part of India must have lived in a state of direct disobedience to the laws of their own religion; for, as the recommendation is directed to widows of every cast, it must have been imperative on all, at least as matter of conscience. Yet, if the number of widows burnt in Bengal annually does not exceed five hundred, it cannot be obeyed even in Bengal, where it is most prevalent, by at least ninety-nine out of a hundred of the population, and in the western part of Hindostan by a still greater proportion;* while, in the southern part of the British dominions, it is scarcely regarded at all.

But many have condemned the *very principle* on which it has been recommended. Those who contend for the burning of widows hold that certain deeds, though done from the most unworthy motives, are in themselves so available as to merit a certain degree of recompense. All these deeds the more learned treat with the greatest contempt, declaring them to be nothing more than vice in another shape. These writers, therefore, view a woman's burning herself as perfectly unlawful. Thus those who form *the great support of the Hindoo system totally condemn the very PRINCIPLE on which the practice is at all recommended, while they insist that the law commands a widow to live a life of abstinence and chastity.* That these compose the greater

* "Supposing the entire Hindoo population of the Bengal Presidency to be 50,000,000, and the annual deaths to be 1 in 33, or above 1,500,000; a sixth of this number, or 250,000, might, on a general computation, be assumed as the number of Hindoo females becoming widows, of whom little more than 600 devote themselves on the death of their husbands." (Par. Papers, July, 1825, p. 11.) How easily might these be saved by Britain's paternal arm! AUTH.

part of the Hindoos, may be inferred from the proportion of widows burnt alive when compared with the whole population of Hindostan.

Such is the state of things relative to this practice, even when described by its most strenuous advocates. As a *command* it has not the least foundation in the Hindoo system. As a *recommendation* it has not been supported by one-fifth of the Hindoo writers on ethics or jurisprudence, nor practically regarded by a thousandth part of those who profess Hindooism. It is in *direct opposition* to the command of the great Hindoo lawgiver, grounded on principles completely subversive of the Hindoo system, and opposed to that course which the Hindoos believe to be the only path to final happiness. Yet this practice, *thus opposed to their great legislator's command—to the very nature of their religious system—and to all their best ideas of virtue, is kept alive in the metropolis and its vicinity by acts of unfeeling coercion;* while in those provinces of Hindostan, which are held to have been the chief seat of every important transaction detailed in their mythology, the practice has nearly expired beneath the feelings of common humanity.

When it is considered that this practice causes the death of a greater number of persons in one year (who, *if they ought not to be thus burnt alive, involve the country in all the guilt of innocent blood)* than are publicly executed for their crimes throughout the whole of India in the course of twenty years, it cannot be wrong to call to this momentous subject the attention of every friend to his country. How would Britain feel if within herself a hundred innocent persons suffered death by some mistake of the law in the course of a year! How then ought she to feel when, in her dominions in the East, *seven or eight hundred innocent widows are every year burnt to death?* Were this inhuman persecution (which, in the number of its annual victims, exceeds all that papal superstition ever brought to the stake in Britain in the course of a century) directed by the supporters of this practice against any particular *sect*, or class of men, they would long ago have appealed to their rulers for redress, or they would have left the spot where they were treated with such cruelty. But how can mothers and sisters make an appeal against their own relatives? How can a wife, a mother, withdraw from her own family? They may endure continual agony under the apprehension of the dreadful doom which they know awaits them—they may feel their anguish renewed at the sight of every female neighbour they behold led forth to the flames—they may tremble at every touch of disease that affects their husbands, and weep at every recollection of their hapless children—but can they leave the scene of suffering? can they make known their sorrows? dare they betray the anguish which preys on their vitals? They lie bound as sheep for the slaughter;—and thus they must remain, suffering in silence, till *British sympathy shall duly realize their hitherto unknown, unpitied misery.**

CHAP. V.

The present partial interference of the British Government tends to promote the CELEBRITY *and* SUPPOSED LEGALITY *of Suttees.*

THE sentiment of the poet, " 'Tis but lame kindness that does its work by halves," applies with peculiar force to the regulations adopted in British India relative to the burning of widows. This will appear by the following extracts from the six volumes of Parliamentary Papers relating to Hindoo widows: printed July, 1821; June, 1823; June, 1824; July, 1825; May, 1827; and July, 1828. The "*Draft of Directions to be issued by Magistrates to the Public Darogahs,*" sufficiently exhibits the nature of the system adopted by the British Government in India, for the regulation of Suttees, appears from the following:—

" Whereas, it appears that, during the ceremony denominated 'Suttee,' certain acts have been occasionally committed in direct opposition to the rules laid down in the religious institutes of the Hindoos, by which that practice is authorised, and forbidden in particular cases; as, for instance, at several places pregnant women, and girls not yet arrived at their full age, have been burnt alive; and people, after having intoxicated women by administering intoxicating substances, have burnt them without their assent whilst insensible; and, inasmuch as this conduct is contrary to the shastras, and perfectly inconsistent with every principle of humanity (it appearing, from the expositions of the Hindoo law delivered by pundits, that the burning a woman pregnant, or one having a child of tender years, or a girl not yet arrived at full age, is expressly forbidden in the shasters; and also that intoxicating a woman, for the purpose of burning her without her assent or against her will, is highly illegal, and contrary to established usage), the police darogahs are hereby

---

* Friend of India (monthly series), Vol. ii. page 453—483.

accordingly, under the sanction of government, strictly enjoined to use the utmost care, and make every effort to prevent the forbidden practices above-mentioned from taking place within the limits of their thannahs. And they are further required, on all occasions, immediately on receiving intelligence that this ceremony is likely to occur, either themselves to proceed to the spot, or send their mohurrir or jemadar, accompanied by a burkundaz of the Hindoo religion, to learn of the woman who is to be burnt whether she has given her assent, and ascertain the other particulars above-mentioned relative to her age, &c. &c. In the event of the female who is going to be burnt being less than *sixteen* years of age, or there being signs of her pregnancy, or on her declaring herself in that situation, or should the people be preparing to burn her after having intoxicated her, without her assent, or against her will (the burning a woman under any of these circumstances being in direct opposition to what is enjoined in the shasters and manifestly an act of illegal violence), it will be then their duty to prevent the ceremony thus forbidden, and contrary to established usage, from taking place, and require those prepared to perform it to refrain from so doing; also to explain to them that in their persisting to commit an act forbidden they would involve themselves in a crime and become subject to retribution and punishment. But, in the case of the woman being of full age, and no other impediment existing, they will nevertheless remain on the spot, and not allow the most minute particular to escape observation. And, in the case of people preparing to burn a woman by compulsion, or after having made her insensible by administering spiritous liquors or narcotic drugs, it will be then their duty to exert themselves in restraining them; and, at the same time, to let them know that it is not the intention of the government to check or forbid any act authorised by the tenets of the religion of the inhabitants of these dominions, or even to require that any express leave or permission be obtained previously to the performance of the act of Suttee, and the police-officers are not to interfere or prevent any such act from taking place. And, lastly, it will be their duty to transmit immediately, for the information of the magistrate, a full detail of any measures which they may have adopted on this subject. And also, on every occasion, when, within the limits of their thannahs, this ceremony of 'Suttee' may take place, the same being lawfully conducted, they will insert it in the monthly reports."*

Calcutta, Oct. 9th, 1813.

N. B. Instructions were subsequently communicated that a Brahmunee must not burn on a separate pile; and a child under three years was not to be left without a written security from some one that it should be provided for.†

The nature and tendency of the system of legalizing the Suttee will appear by the following extracts from the Parliamentary Papers:—

"It appears to me," says W. Ewer, Esq., Act. Sup. of Police, Lower Provinces, Calcutta, Nov. 1818, "that, if the practice is allowed to exist at all, the less notice we take of it the better. The interference of the police may, in

* Par. Papers, vol. v. p. 38, 39. † Par. Papers, vol. i. p. 41—43. See p. 137, 144.

some cases, have induced compliance with the rules of the shastras; but *the official attendance of the darogah stamps every regular Suttee with the sanction of Government;* and I must humbly submit that authorising a practice is not the way to effect its gradual abolition."*

"Previous to 1813 no interference on the part of the police was authorized, and widows were sacrificed legally or illegally as it might happen; but the Hindoos were then aware that the Government regarded the custom with natural horror, and would do any thing short of direct prohibition to discourage and gradually to abolish it. The case is now altered. The police-officers are ordered to interfere, for the purpose of ascertaining that the ceremony is performed in conformity with the rules of the shastras, and in that event to allow its completion. *This is granting the authority of Government for the burning of widows; and it can scarcely be a matter of astonishment that the number of the sacrifices should be doubled when the sanction of the ruling power is added to the recommendation of the shastra.*"† (H. Oakley, Esq., Mag. Hooghly, Dec. 1818).

"The Governor General in Council is reluctantly led to express his apprehension that the greater confidence with which the people perform this rite under the sanction of Government, as implied or avowed in the circular orders already in force, combined with the excitement of religious bigotry by the continual agitation of the question, may have tended to augment, rather than diminish, the frequency of these sacrifices."‡ (Calcutta, Dec. 1819).

The increase here referred to was evident from the returns of Suttees in the several districts subordinate to the Presidency of Fort William, viz. in the year

"1815 378
1816 442
1817 707
1818 . . . . . 839."§

Relative to the increase of Suttees the magistrates in the Allypore district remark,—"The abstract statement of the number of Suttees exhibits the frequency of these abominable sacrifices so progressively and materially increased since the period referred to (from 1815 to 1818), as to justify our being confirmed in the belief, before more than

* Par. Papers, vol. i. p. 229. See p. 232. † p. 236. ‡ p. 241, 242. § p. 241.

once expressed by this to the superior court, that any interference, save that of *a total prohibition under the severest penalties*, will ever be productive of a mistaken spirit of jealousy and opposition, which will hope, by encouraging the prevalence of this superstitious usage, to induce us to discontinue altogether our interference."* (Allypore, March, 1819). To the same effect are the following extracts:—

"As far as my observation goes, I shall say that the humane intentions of the framers of the Regulations regarding these ceremonies will not be fully answered. Some few widows, perhaps, escape, as falling under exceptions specified in the Bengal pundit's reports, whilst, on the other hand, it can hardly be doubted but that the necessary presence of the police-officers of Government, at these immolations, stamps on them that character of *strict legality*, and seems to afford them *that degree of countenance on the part of Government, which must produce an evil effect*."† (J. F. Petty, Esq., Mag. Southern Concan).

"After having weighed, with every deliberation, the mode of carrying into effect the intention of Government, I became most fully satisfied *that if the prohibitory points to the sacrifice were to be determined by native police-officers, the practice of this awful rite would shortly multiply manifold*."‡ (J. Marriott, Esq., Mag. Tannah, Sep. 1819).

"Our Government," says C. Smith, Esq., Second Judge, Calcutta, "by modifying the thing and issuing orders about it—orders which even the Government and the Sudder Judges themselves do not appear clearly to comprehend—have thrown the ideas of the Hindoos upon the subject into a complete state of confusion. They know not what is allowed and what interdicted; but, upon the whole, they have a persuasion that our government, whom they most erroneously suppose to be indifferent about the lives of the natives, are rather favourable to Suttees than otherwise. *They will then believe that we abhor the usage when we prohibit it in toto by an absolute and peremptory law. They have no idea that we might not do so with the most perfect safety. They conceive our power and our will to be commensurate*."§ Aug. 1821.

The Court of Directors of the Honourable East India Company, in a letter to the Governor General in Council, in June, 1823, express their opinion upon the subject of

* Par. Papers, vol. i. p. 218. † p. 254. ‡ p. 255, 256. § Vol. ii. p. 67

partial interference :—" To us it appears very doubtful (and we are confirmed in this doubt by respectable authority) whether the measures which have been already taken have not tended rather *to increase than to diminish the frequency of the practice.* Such a tendency is, at least, not unnaturally ascribed to a regulation which, *prohibiting a practice only in certain cases, appears to sanction it in all others.* It is to be apprehended that, where the people have not previously a very enthusiastic attachment to the custom, a law which shall explain to them the cases in which it ought not to be followed may be taken as a direction for adopting it in all others. It is, moreover, with much reluctance that we can consent to make the British Government, by a specific permission of the Suttee, *an ostensible party to the sacrifice ;* we are averse also to the practice of making British Courts expounders and vindicators of the Hindoo religion, when it leads to acts which, not less as legislators than as Christians, we abominate."*

The opinions of the second, third, and fifth judges of the Nizamut Adawlut in Calcutta, are as follows :—

" The second judge cannot subscribe to any instructions that have a tendency to *modify, systematize, or legalize the usage,* or that appear to regard a legal Suttee as at all better than an illegal one. He is convinced that, if this mode of issuing orders under the sanction of Government to regulate Suttees, is continued, *the practice will take such deep root, under the authority of the supreme power of the country, that to eradicate it will become impossible.* The usage will be much more likely to fall into disuse under a total neglect on the part of Government than under the present system of attention and inquiry, which serves but to keep the feelings of the Hindoo population alive upon the point, and to give a sort of interest and celebrity to the sacrifice, which is in the highest degree favourable to its continuance and extension."† (C. Smith, Esq.)

" I conceive that we have already done a great deal of mischief in this way, and that instead of diminishing we have increased the evil."‡ (J. T. Shakespear, Esq.)

" I confess that my own opinion inclines me to impute to the regulations a positively pernicious tendency, in proportion to the degree in which they have brought the

---

* Par. Papers, vol. iii. p. 45 and 48. † Vol. iv. p. 149. ‡ p. 148.

sacrifices under the more immediate cognizance of the officers of Government, whose presence at the ceremony, instead of operating as a restraint, has, I am afraid, contributed to invest it with additional solemnity, and to confer on the performance of it, in the mistaken views of the natives, a species of *authoritative sanction* which it was not before considered to possess."* (W. B. Martin, Esq.)

The officiating Registrar addresses the Chief Secretary of Government, W. B. Bayley, Esq.:—"From these minutes it will be seen by his lordship in council, that the majority of the court do not concur in the expediency of the measures suggested by the officiating chief judge, and that they are of opinion *it would be preferable to enact a regulation for the future prohibition of Suttees throughout the country.*†"—Fort William, July 23, 1824. It is deeply to be regretted that such a regulation has not been enacted.

J. H. Harington, while officiating as chief judge of the Nizamut Adawlut in 1825, proposed a circular letter to the courts of circuit, containing a recommendation of measures for insuring a timely notice to the police of any intended Suttee. This circular was opposed by three of the judges of the court, and the officiating chief judge, as inconsistent with the object of Government, that of refraining from measures that would *constructively legalize this abominable practice.* In this opinion the supreme Government coincided, observing,—"The governor-general in council is duly sensible of the humane motives by which Mr. Harington is actuated in urging the points noticed in his minute, but being of opinion that the measure proposed for requiring the zemindars, and others, to give previous information of all cases of Suttee, though varying in form, would be substantially the same as those which government has before declined to adopt, and that they would in fact be open to nearly all the same objections, he concurs with the majority of the court in thinking it inexpedient to circulate the orders proposed by the officiating judge."‡

"It can hardly be doubted but that the printed work regarding Suttees has given the ceremony, in the eyes of the natives, *a stamp of legality which in our provinces it never before possessed,* and it may therefore be ques-

---

* Par. Papers, vol. iv. p. 149. † Vol. iv. p. 85.
‡ Vol. v. p. 51. Asi. Journ. Sept. 1827.

tioned whether, upon the whole, more harm than good may not have followed its publication."* (Bombay, Jud. Cons. June 1820.)

"This permission (says a correspondent in the Bombay Courier), I found that the people most ignorantly and perversely abused; and at every stage of my argument with them an appeal was made to *the order of government*, as a vindication of their conduct. There can be no doubt of the benevolent intention of government in issuing such an order, and as little of its beneficial influence in many instances, as it prevents the employment of force; but the people construe it into *a direct approval of the dreadful act*; and for a long time '*the order of government*' seemed to form a triumphant answer to all my arguments." And again:—"The only answer they attempted to give was, 'It is the custom, and we have got the government order for so doing.' †" Oct. 1824.

The Parliamentary Papers on the immolation of Hindoo widows, ordered to be printed May 1827, contain additional confirmation of these sentiments.

E. L. Warner, Esq., Act. Mag. 24 Pergunnahs, states, that he "finds it difficult to account for the increase of the Sutttees, unless it may be attributed to *the orders of Government*; for the attendance of the police officers gives *a legal sanction to the practice*, and, by so doing, enhances the reputation of the family of the person who devotes herself."‡.

"It seems undeniable that in tolerating the practice, under any *regulations and restrictions whatsoever*, you tolerate what you have virtually forbidden in those regulations, and afford the natives ground for concluding that the practice of Suttee was to be expected from their operation."§ (Bombay Regulations.)

S. Marriott, Esq., magistrate in the Northern Concan, says,—"It was the prevalent opinion among the natives, that *this sacrifice would not be tolerated by the British Government*; under these circumstances, to have given instructions to my people would at once have informed the community that the sacrifice of the Suttee is allowed by the British Government, and that therefore it might have been performed with impunity. It would have opened

---

* Par. Papers, vol. iv. p. 156. † 212, 213. See the account, Asi. Journal, Aug. 1825, p. 145—148.

‡ Par. Papers. vol. v. p. 2. § p. 4.

a source of emolument to such native officers as are corrupt enough to sell their authority at the expense of a human victim. With the confidence which would have been thus given to its performance, and with the inducements which I have mentioned to the police officers to encourage the practice, *I am certain the number of victims would have greatly increased!*" The conduct of this magistrate in not giving publicity to the regulations, but keeping them merely for his own direction, was approved by the Hon. E. Nepean, governor of Bombay:—"It appears to me that he exercised a sound judgment, in refraining to place the power to which he alludes in the hands of his native establishment, which, if done, would, in my opinion, have been attended with the consequences he anticipated." Oct. 1819.—F. Warden, Esq., member of council, concurred in this opinion:—"I also think that the collector has exercised a sound judgment in not promulgating the circular orders regarding the performance of Suttee." A. Bell, Esq., another member, was of the same opinion; but G. L. Prendergast, Esq., the other member, adopted the contrary, and appears very strenuous for the permission of this cruel rite, so replete with every evil predominating in the Hindoo character.*

J. H. Harington, Esq., officiating chief judge in Calcutta, in a minute upon the Suttee Reports, dated Feb. 4, 1825, candidly acknowledges that the present regulations relative to Suttees make them legal. 'It seems now to be too late to examine the general question adverted to by the Hon. Court, whether a prohibition of the practice, in certain cases only, may not appear to give it public sanction in others; in truth *such sanction is virtually and effectually given by the circular orders in force*, for these alone exempt the parties concerned in the performance of even a voluntary immolation from the operation of the regulation already noticed."†

Another judge in Calcutta, C. T. Sealy, Esq., under date Jan. 1825, declares: "I have always been of opinion that *we increased the number of Suttees by sanctioning them*."‡

The governor of Bombay, the Hon. M. Elphinstone, in a minute, dated June, 1825, relative to the presence of a magistrate at a Suttee, remarks:—"In general such at-

* Par. Papers, vol. i. p. 256. 260, 261. † Vol. v. p. 46.
‡ Vol. v. p. 50. See 135.

tendance is inexpedient, as tending to give more dignity to the ceremony and to render the merit of the sufferer more conspicuous."*

F. Warden, Esq., member of council, Bombay, in a minute at the same time, states:—"We ought either to issue a positive prohibition, or abstain altogether from manifesting the slightest anxiety on the subject: the attendance of European functionaries, where the efforts are unavailing to prevent the ceremony, appears rather calculated to inspire the Suttee with a greater degree of resolution, in affording Europeans a proof of the firmness with which the victim seeks and endures the sacrifice. Fanaticism can be successfully combated only by neglect and indifference. Any intermediate measure between a positive prohibition and perfect neglect and indifference appears to me to be most impolitic."†

The speech of J. Poynder, Esq., on human sacrifices in India, at the court of East India proprietors, March, 1827, contains some important confirmation of the statements contained in this section.—This gentleman gives his own opinion of the nature of the present regulations relative to Suttees:—"It was impossible that any government could promise itself that the correction of the abuses of any given system could of itself produce the abolition of the system. It is to be greatly deplored that the inevitable consequences of permitting certain sacrifices as legal went *virtually to sanction and set the broad seal of Government upon all that was not prohibited. Nine* instances out of 654 (in 1821), which appear to have been saved by the retraction of the vow, or by the police, afford matter of congratulation to the authorities; but it does not seem to have been considered that probably *the greater number of those who perished are to be referred to the sanction afforded by the regulations to the performance of the rite.*"‡

The Rev. T. Thomason, chaplain in Calcutta, in a letter dated Feb. 1827, speaking of the Bengal Government requiring that the Suttee should be performed agreeably to certain regulations, observes,—"The measure actually legalized it by British authority, to the great joy and benefit of the Brahmuns, securing to them and even increasing their fees by multiplying the formalities. Every

---

* Par. Papers, vol. v. p. 144. † p. 149. See 153.
‡ Poynder's Speech (Hatchard), p. 32. 99.

evil might have been anticipated from this unwise act. This regulation legalized the Suttees. The Government became by it, without intending it, *particeps criminis.* It pronounced that to be legal (under certain circumstances) which ought never, under any circumstances, to be deemed legal. If the Government interfere at all, their interference should be to abolish, not to limit or sanction such an abomination. This I very strenuously maintained in argument with some persons *officially* concerned in the regulation. The question has often been asked, whether this regulation did in fact increase or diminish the number of Suttees. On a deliberate review of the whole case, I rest in the conviction *that the number has been increased rather than diminished.*"*

A chaplain of the Hon. Company, in a letter dated Calcutta, Dec. 1820, addressed to a member of parliament, states to the same effect:—" In this respect the wisdom of our Government appears to the great body of judicious people amongst us to be *rather timidity, or even guilty apathy.* It is notorious that these abominable sacrifices might be stopped *without exciting the least opposition,* and even with the general approbation of the natives. Yet we have, *in an evil hour,* sanctioned them, in a manner, by pronouncing them legal if performed under certain circumstances."†

W. Sherar, Esq., late accomptant-general in Bengal, in a letter written March, 1827, gives his unqualified disapprobation of the present system:—" I consider the evil of the restrictive regulation of 1812, respecting Suttees, *so great and lamentable as to require the earliest possible redress.* As things now stand, all the Suttees in Bengal are sanctioned by the presence and acquiescence of the police officers of the British Government! This evil, to the disgrace of our Government, has now been going on for fifteen years, and surely requires to be stopped without further delay."‡

The Eclectic Review of Bishop Heber's Journal in India contains the following reference to the subject of this section:—" The increased frequency of these infernal sacrifices in Bengal is clearly chargeable upon the Calcutta Government, whose mischievous half measures have legalized the practice 'to the great joy and benefit of the Brahmuns,

* Poynder's Speech, p. 66—69. † p. 68. ‡ p. 70.

securing to them and even increasing their fees by multiplying the formalities.' And here we have (vol. i. p. 267) the testimony of the bishop, that, for its professed object, the securing of the publicity of Suttees, that measure has proved both abortive and delusive;—so much so as to bring into question the *intention of its framers*. For any good purpose it has been absolutely insufficient and useless. Its only operation has been to systematize, legalize, and extend the practice; to make it more popular and more respectable, and to increase indefinitely the difficulty of abolishing it at any future period." (May, 1828.)

The Asiatic Journal for October, 1827, in a brief notice of the pamphlet, candidly acknowledges:—"This writer, in common with many of the best authorities in India, thinks that partial interference increases the evil; he has devoted a division of his work to show that 'the present partial interference of the British Government promotes the *increase, celebrity,* and *supposed legality* of the Suttee.' Mr. Poynder is also of opinion, 'that the prohibitory regulations have been practically only productive of evil, and that nothing short of abolition will suffice.' In this opinion we are disposed to concur: the question then is, whether we ought immediately to abolish the practice or to wait till the slow influence of education and more correct habits of thinking, which cannot be denied to be now gaining ground in India, extinguish a custom not kept alive by persecuting and irritating measures.'"

"If such practices," says R. Jackson, Esq., "were continued longer under the authority of the Company, there was not a man in the court who did not become *accessary to the crime of murder!* He that refrained from doing all in his power to prevent it, *on his head be the guilt of the sanction he gave.*"*

To give but one more extract taken from the Par. Papers of the session of 1828, contained in a letter of the Hon. Court of Directors to the Governor of Bombay:—"A minute interference in the details of Suttee, such as it is the purpose of the new rules to assume, is likewise liable to *the obvious objection of virtually extending the sanction of the British Government to the performance of the rite when conducted in the prescribed form.* We are aware, however, that as long as the burning of widows shall be tolerated

---

* Speech of R. Jackson, Esq. (Parbury), relative to Suttees, p. 9.

under some circumstances and prohibited in others, interference of some kind or other cannot be altogether avoided. With the exception to which we have already adverted, we do not feel that we should be justified in prohibiting the adoption of the rule as an experiment for checking the practice of Suttee, as every measure tending to the infrequency of the custom must necessarily afford increased facilities towards its ultimate suppression."*

From these observations, in which most of the magistrates concur, it is presumed that partial interference with the burning of Hindoo widows has not been attended with the desired end—the discountenance and decrease of the practice. May Britain "awake to righteousness," nor fear to spread her shield over the head of the deluded and oppressed widows daily appointed to death by this unnatural and suicidal custom, and "the blessing of those who were ready to perish will come upon her, and she will cause the widow's heart to sing for joy."

CHAP. VI.

Authorities to confirm the propriety, safety, facility, and success of efforts for the suppression of Suttees.

The volumes of parliamentary papers, relating to the burning of Hindoo widows, printed by order of the Hon. House of Commons, from 1821 to 1828, contain numerous authorities for the immediate suppression of this dreadful rite. The following appear in an investigation of these valuable documents:—

"From what I have heard of several very respectable Brahmuns, I am almost satisfied that the exercise of a very trifling degree of authority would put a stop to this perversion of reason and humanity. It appears that the late *Peishwa* frequently *personally exerted himself* to dissuade women from becoming Suttees; and that he always took upon himself the charge of supporting those who attended to this advice. I shall be glad to use my influence at this place, in a similar manner, and have little doubt of the

---

* Par. Papers, vol. vi. p. 28.

success of my interposition in the majority of cases that may occur, when I have it in my power to assure the women of the means of subsistence."* (H. Pottinger, Esq., collector, addressed to the Hon. M. Elphinstone, Governor of Bombay, Oct. 1818.)

"The letter from the Magistrate of Chinsurah," says E. Watson, Esq., Alypore, "deserves the serious attention of the Nizamut Adawlut and the Government. It appears that this abhorrent, and often utterly illegal practice, was forbidden by the foreign governments of those settlements; and that the prohibition was obeyed without a murmur. So little do the people appear to have interested themselves in the affair, that we find, from Mr. Forbes' letter, that the mere publication of an order from himself, prohibiting the practice, effectually prevented it, and that no single instance of a woman burning herself has occurred since."† The Court of Nizamut Adawlut in June, 1817, endeavoured to overturn Mr. Watson's reasoning, as far as applied to the analogy of the cases cited, but it appears without success. They express in concurrence with him that "There is a strong presumption that *little resistance would be opposed to the suppression of a practice so repugnant to the common feelings of humanity*, if from experience of continued abuses on the investigation or performance of female sacrifices, as now tolerated, it should at any time be *deemed necessary* to enact a Regulation, prohibiting the priesthood and kindred of the deceased, as well as all others from assisting in such sacrifices."‡ "I feel disposed," says the late J. H. Harington, Esq., May, 1822, "to concur with Mr. Forbes and the local judicial officers consulted by him, on the facility and safety with which a practice so repugnant to humanity may be suppressed by law—*if it should be deemed indispensably necessary*."§ Surely it is *necessary* to endeavour to rescue six or seven hundred deluded women from a most horrid death. How many Europeans in India imbibe, imperceptibly, a degree of the apathy of the Hindoos!

"If the British, *in imitation of the Mogul Government*, were to lay an immediate and positive inhibition upon it, and would declare the parties aiding in the ceremony indictable for murder, and proceed against them accordingly, *it must totally die away*; but if tolerated, under whatever

* Par Papers, Vol. i. p. 65. † p. 99, 100. ‡ p. 107. Vol. iv. p. 20.

restrictions, I do not hesitate to pronounce that it will, in a short time, become nearly as prevalent as it now is in Bengal."* (W. Wright, Esq., Mag. Furruckabad, April, 1819.)

W. Ewer, Esq., Act. Superintendent of Police, Lower Provinces, Nov. 1818, acknowledges, "I have offered the grounds of my opinion that the barbarous custom of Suttee may be prohibited without exciting any serious or general dissatisfaction among our Hindoo subjects."†

"I do not hesitate in offering my opinion," says H. Oakley, Esq., Mag. of Hooghley, Dec. 1818, "that a law for its abolition would be objected to only by *the heirs,* who derive worldly profit from the custom,—by Brahmuns, who partly exist by it,—and by those whose depraved nature leads them to look on a sacrifice as a highly entertaining show; at any rate the sanction of Government should be withdrawn without delay. The adoption of this measure will most likely be followed by a decrease in the number of Suttees, and the *Magistrate's feelings will not be outraged, as they frequently are at present, by compelling him to so barbarous a custom.*"‡

"The interference of Government is well understood to be the Christian wish of humanity. The Rajah of this place is a Moosulman; and the Hindoos seem generally willing to embrace the excuse of the will of the reigning power to evade the Suttee, believed of their little read and less understood shastra."§ (R. Morrieson, Esq , Sory Burthom, Dec. 1813.)

C. Chapman, Esq., Magistrate in Jessore, under date Dec. 1818, thus addresses the Acting Superintendent of Police, Lower Provinces, Calcutta:—"Any law abolishing the Suttee would be attended with no other effect than it should have under every good system of Government—*the immediate and due observance of its enactments.* I would most willingly undertake to promulgate any orders regarding its abolition, throughout the district under my charge, *without dread of any ill consequences arising from the interference of Government.*"||

G. Forbes, Esq., first Judge of the Calcutta Court of Circuit, thus writes to the Registrar of the Nizamut Adawlut, Aug. 1819:—"I take this opportunity to express my concurrence in the opinion which I found to prevail with

---

* Par. Papers, Vol. i. p. 212. † p. 229. See p. 233. ‡ p. 237. § p. 338. See p. 239. || p. 241.

the judicial Officers at the several stations, with whom I conversed on the subject, that the practice of Hindoo women burning themselves on the funeral pile of their deceased husbands, if prohibited by Government, might be effectually suppressed without apprehension of any serious obstacles. I am happy in being able to adduce an instance of effectual interference in the suppression of this barbarous custom under British authority. In the territory of Delhi, the late Resident, Mr. Metcalfe, *never* (when apprized of the intention) *permitted the burning of a widow to take place, and was prepared to prevent the practice, whenever necessary, by forcible interference, but which was requisite* ONLY ON ONE OCCASION *that came under his immediate observation.* I have been induced to mention the instance of successful interference by the Resident of Delhi, as affording an example which I believe nearly every magistrate in the country would, if authorised, be most happy to follow; and in order to show that there appears no insurmountable obstacle to a measure, with regard to the existency of which, if shown to be practicable, there can be but one sentiment."*

"I am convinced," says F. Warden, Esq., Member of Council in Bombay, "of the practicability of abolishing not only *this*, but also *every other sanguinary practice of the Hindoos*, and without endangering either the popularity or the security of our supremacy."†

C. H. Higginson, Esq., Judge at Trichinopoly, writes in Feb. 1820:—"If I were required to give my opinion as to the best means of putting a stop to the Suttee in future, I should say, that the collector and magistrate ought to be authorised to issue a Proclamation prohibiting altogether a custom so unnatural, which, though permitted, does not by any means appear to be insisted upon by the shastras. I would authorise the magistrate to declare, by Proclamation, any person or persons assisting in the self-immolation of a widow, liable to be brought to trial as an accessary in homicide; and would issue strict orders to all heads of villages and officers of police, to put an immediate stop to any attempt at preparation for an "anugamanum" (Suttee). In the present times the good sense and humane feelings of the Brahmuns, as well as of the greater proportion of the Hindoo inhabitants, would point out to them the benevolent

* Par. Papers, vol. i. p. 243. † p. 261. See vol. ii. p. 85.

motive of Government, in prohibiting a practice which has originated in ignorance and infatuation, and which must be reflected upon with abhorrence by every mind capable of distinguishing good from evil."*

The third Volume of Parliamentary Papers, printed June, 1824, contains little besides a detail of the number, names, castes, &c., of Suttees in 1821. The following expression of public opinion, favourable to the abolition of the burning of widows, appears important:—

"As far as every information I can obtain, this revolting ceremony could be altogether prevented, by a short prohibitory enactment of the legislature."† (R. C. Plowden, Esq., Barripore, June, 1822, to C. H. Hopper, Esq., Mag. of the 24 Pergunnahs, Calcutta.)

J. H. Harington, Esq., officiating Chief Judge in Calcutta, in a minute relative to the Suttee, of considerable length and interest, written June, 1823, and which was forwarded to the Court of Directors by the Governor General, Dec. 1824, declares:—"I am desirous of putting upon record some considerations which appear to merit attention in any future deliberation upon this important question, and which, I acknowledge, have produced in my own mind a strong belief, if not a full conviction, that whenever it may be judged expedient to suppress this barbarous practice by legal prohibition, instead of restricting it to what is sanctioned by the shastra, as at present, *it will not be found impracticable, nor, as far as I can judge, attended with any political danger.* On a deliberate view of all those instances in which the laws, customs, and prejudices of the Hindoos, when found to be at variance with the principles of justice and good society, have been necessarily superseded and abrogated by the laws and regulations of the British Government,‡ and the whole of which supercession has

* Vol. ii. p. 101. † Vol. iii. p. 4. See p. 51.

‡ Such as the execution of the Brahmuns; suppressing the sacrifice of children at Saugur; preventing women and children, in the provinces of Benares, from burning in a *koorh,* or circular inclosure, on the approach of a public officer to serve any judicial process on Brahmuns; abolishing Dhurna; Infanticide among the Rajkoomars; burying widows alive; cruel ordeals, &c. The late Bishop Heber thus describes the custom of Dhurna. "How little a female death is cared for may appear by a circumstance which occurred a short time ago at a small distance from Ghazeepore. In consequence of a dispute which had taken place between two small freeholders about some land, one of the contending parties, an old man of seventy and upwards, brought his wife of the same age to the field, forced her, with the assistance of their children and relations, into

been quietly submitted to, *as obviously and exclusively originating in motives of equity and humanity, unconnected with any degree of religious intolerance*, we may, I think, safely conclude that a similar result will attend the enactment of a legislative provision to prevent the yearly sacrifice of several hundreds of deluded unoffending females, born and living under the protection of the British Govenment." This document thus closes. Referring to certain probable excesses in the perpetration of Suttees, it is added, "In such a state of things I could not hesitate to adopt the opinion expressed by the second Judge of the Court of the Nizamut Adawlut, that the toleration of the practice of Suttees is a reproach to our Government; and *even now* I am disposed to agree with him, '*that the entire and immediate abolition of it would be attended with no sort of danger.*'"*

Among the papers forwarded to the Hon. Court of Directors is one containing, says Mr. Harington, "An extract from a well-written paper, '*On female Immolation,*' published in the valuable periodical work entitled '*The Friend of India,*' which the late Sir Henry Blossett and myself read on our voyage to India, and which appeared to both of us a powerful and convincing statement of the real facts and circumstances of the case."† A few paragraphs only are given.

"We are confident that the continuance of the practice stands on the doctrine of *expediency alone.* This is its only prop; of which could it once be deprived it would fall beneath the weight of justice and humanity. It cannot therefore be improper to weigh the question of expediency, and to collect into one focus all the light which can be obtained on the subject from our preceding transactions in

---

a little straw hut, built for the purpose, and burned her and the hut together: in order that her death might bring a curse on the soil and her spirit haunt it after death, so that his successful antagonist might never derive any advantage from it. On some horror and surprise being expressed by the gentleman who told me the case, one of the officers of his court, (the same indeed who had reported it to him, not as a horrible occurrence, but as a proof how spiteful the parties had been against each other), said very coolly: "*Why not?—she was a very old woman,—what use was she?* The old murderer was in prison; but my friend said he had no doubt that his interference in such case, *between man and wife*, was regarded as singularly vexatious and oppressive."—See Asiatic Researches, vol. i. p. 268—9. Vol. iv. p. 330. Evan. Mag. 1816. p. 518.

* Par. Papers, vol. iv. p. 8—18. † p. 13.

India. And if it should appear that we have not been arrested in our career of justice by the prejudices of the natives, that on the contrary the Hindoos have already gone hand in hand with us, without discovering any hostility to our authority; there can be no reason to apprehend that, in the abolition of female immolation, we shall experience the least interruption. To prove this we will adduce three examples:—

"In the province of Guzerat the deluded parents had been for a long series of years in the habit of destroying their female infants as soon as they were born. Whether the custom was sanctioned by the shastras or not is irrelevant; it was enough that it was deeply rooted in the practice and prejudices of the natives. These unnatural murders at length attracted the attention of Government, and *they were abolished by an order of the supreme power*.*

"From time immemorial it was the custom of mothers to sacrifice their children to the Ganges at the annual festival held at Gunga Saugur. The British Government regarded the practice with those feelings of horror which such unnatural murders are calculated to inspire; as persuasion would have been unavailing with those who had parted with every parental feeling, *the practice was prohibited by a public regulation, and the prohibition enforced by public authority*. This order was promulgated in the presence of thousands assembled at a public festival, in the highest excitement of superstitious frenzy. What was the consequence? Not one instance of resistance was attempted by that immense crowd! The mothers who had brought their children to this funeral sacrifice were constrained to carry them back unhurt; and many, perhaps, to whom the heinousness of the crime had never appeared, were, by this interposition, awakened to a sense of its enormity.

"The Hindoo laws absolutely prohibit the execution of a Brahmun; they forbid the Magistrate even to imagine evil against him. Thus fenced by the laws, and extolled by their sacred books, they are still more powerfully guarded by the respect and veneration of the people. When our Government commenced in the East, we were reduced to the most serious dilemma. To have inflicted punishment on Brahmuns would have been to violate the most awful sanctions of Hindoo law, and the dearest prejudices of the

---

‡ See "Infanticide in India," Book ii.

people; to have exempted them from punishment would have been to deliver over the country to desolation, ravage, and murder. The reign of equity which we were about to introduce was stopped at the threshold; the destiny of millions hung in suspense. How did we act on this occasion? Did we lay the laws of justice at the feet of the sacred tribe? Did we abrogate our code of jurisprudence, and adopt the Vedas for our guide? Did we deprive the country of our protection, because the Hindoo shastras forbid the punishment of the aggressors, if they happen to be Brahmuns? We boldly stepped forward in vindication of the rights of society; and in spite of a formidable phalanx of Hindoo juris-consults, and of the strongest prejudices, caused these delinquents to pay the forfeit of their lives to the laws of offended justice. Have the natives complained of this outrage on the sanctity of their priesthood, or considered it as an infringement of our toleration? Have they, in any one instance, petitioned us to disregard their welfare and exempt their spiritual guides from death? or have they not on the contrary tacitly sanctioned every act of punishment, and applauded the inflexible tenor of our proceedings."*

The opinion of J. H. Harington, Esq., officiating chief Judge in the Nizamut Adawlut, Calcutta, on the expediency of abolishing the Suttee, has been given. The second Judge, C. Smith, Esq., declares:—"The practice of Suttee OUGHT TO BE ABOLISHED, and it may be abolished with PERFECT SAFETY." The third Judge, J. T. Shakespear, Esq., likewise states:—"I am prepared to concur in a recommendation to Government, that a regulation be promulgated prohibiting Suttees throughout the country." The fifth Judge, W. B. Martin, Esq., at the same time stated:—"The toleration of the practice by our Government, and its disposition to interfere no further than was necessary to guard it from abuse, has been misconstrued into a tacit recognition of the principle of a usage, the legality of which, within certain limits, it has formally acknowledged." The minute of the officiating Judge, J. Ahmuty, Esq., is as follows:—"I feel satisfied that it would be far preferable to enact a regulation *prohibiting the practice of Suttees at once, and rendering it punishable by law*, than having recourse to any partial or indirect means to repress it gra-

* Par. Papers, vol. iv. p. 22—24.

dually, if even such a result could be reasonably expected to ensue."*

The Magistrate of Poona, under the Bombay Presidency (Captain H. D. Robertson), thus states the nature of the popular feeling relative to the Suttees:—"The feeling, I might almost say, *is general to stop them;* it was hinted to me, through various respectable channels, that although a show of discontent would be exhibited, an order of Government to prevent their continuance would be a palatable measure."†

Another Magistrate in Bombay (J. Barnard, Esq.) observes:—"The circumstances under which Suttees prevail, the classes interested therein, the number of instances, and the conduct of the community in their communications both with the Magistrate and with each other, on such occasions, as well as the impressions generally entertained by those not concerned, convince me that there are few cases in which *evil would ensue from prohibition and coercive prevention.*"‡

"All religions," says Colonel Dow, in his History of Hindostan, "must be tolerated in Bengal, except the practice of *some inhuman customs which the Mahomedans have already, in a great measure, destroyed.* There are particular usages, established by time into a law, which *our humanity must destroy.* Let no women burn themselves with their husbands, no dying person be exposed by his friends. To leave the natives entirely to their own laws would be to consign them to anarchy and confusion."§ Vol. iii. p. 128, 143.

The Commentaries of Bras de Albuquerque, the son of the Great Albuquerque, one of those extraordinary men who, nearly three hundred years ago, raised to the highest pitch of glory the Portuguese name in India, contains the following passage:—"When Alf. de Albuquerque took the kingdom of Goa he would not permit that any woman thenceforward should burn herself; and, although to change their custom is equal to death, nevertheless they rejoiced in life, and said great good of him, because he commanded that they should not burn themselves. Long after his death, when a Moor or Hindoo had received wrong and

---

* Par. Papers, vol. iv. p. 148, 149, 153. † p. 167. ‡ p. 209.

§ "Collection of Facts and Opinions relative to the Burning of Hindoo Widows," by Dr. Johns, p. 89.

could obtain no redress from the Governor, the aggrieved person would go to Goa, to Albuquerque's tomb, and make an offering of oil at the lamp which burned before it, and call upon him for justice."* Wilberforce's Speech, 1813, 8vo. p. 93, 94.

The Rev. T. S. Grimshawe, in his valuable pamphlet, "An earnest Appeal to British Humanity in behalf of Hindoo Widows" (1825, Hatchard), refers to the suppression of Suttees by other powers:—"The Mogul Government has uniformly discountenanced the practice of burning widows alive; and the extent of the benefits thus conferred may be estimated by the remarkable fact that *in no part of Hindostan is the rite less known than under this sway; and in none is it more common than in that which is the centre of British power, and ascendency!* This example was humanely followed by the Portuguese. The Dutch, the Danish, and the French Governments, uniformly refused to sanction the custom. Why is the name of Britain alone excluded from this honourable list of competitors? Is it that policy and duty in our case are irreconcilable, however blended in that of others? The conviction is most humiliating that *the British Government is the only European power in India that tolerates the practice of burning widows alive on the funeral pile!!*" pp. 17, 18.

In the Par. Papers on the Suttees, printed in 1827, are some *proposed paragraphs* for Bengal in the judicial department (pp. 2—31), containing a very lucid and powerful representation of the facility of abolishing Suttees. This important document was, on March 19, 1824, referred to the consideration of the Committee of Correspondence, but it does not appear, from the Papers now published, that it has been approved and sent to India. This copious and interesting document contains a comprehensive statement of the facts and correspondence contained in the Papers on Suttees, printed by the Honourable House of Commons. Its general publicity in Britain, and the adoption of its principles in India, are very desirable. The following recapitulation gives a distinct and connected view of its contents, and of the position established by it:—

1. "That the practice of Suttee is not founded in Hindoo law, and only recommended, but not enjoined in the shastras.

---

* "Collection of Facts and Opinions relative to the Burning of Hindoo Widows," by Dr. Johns, p. 103, 104.

2. " That every other inhuman Hindoo practice has been prohibited under severe penalties under your Government, not only without resistance, but apparently without exciting disapprobation; although those practices had their support in what is certainly the main support of the practice of Suttee, namely, superstitious custom and prejudice.

3. " That your Government having contravened a fundamental principle of Hindoo law, held sacred by all Hindoos, by abolishing the impunity of Brahmuns, and making them amenable to the British laws, without its having been followed by any evil consequence, there can be no serious grounds for apprehending that prohibiting a practice which *is not founded in Hindoo law, nor recognized by Hindoos in general, and prevailing only among certain tribes or castes of Hindoos, few in number compared with the mass of the population*, and the only object of which prohibition would be the protection of the wives and daughters of Hindoos from perishing in flames, would produce any serious opposition to British rule, or even a permanent dissatisfaction.

4. " That there is a great and acknowledged diversity of sentiment among the Hindoos on the subject of Suttees; that the practice chiefly, if not exclusively, prevails among the lowest and most ignorant, and is discountenanced by the upper and educated classes; that even in Bengal, though prevalent in the vicinity of Calcutta, the practice is far from general, and in the extensive territories on the Madras side of India, reaching from Cape Comorin to Orissa, it is by no means general. That in some districts it is unknown, and in others of rare occurrence; and that in the territories subject to the Bombay Government the prevalence of it is far from being general; in some of its districts, particularly in Guzerat, scarcely known; and that in the Concan, comprising the Mahratta countries conquered from the Peishwa, in which it was very prevalent, the people, on becoming subject to the British rule, *voluntarily discontinued the practice, in consequence of understanding that it was repugnant to the British laws*, a fact which proves at least that in their attachment to the practice enthusiasm had no share, and obviously points to the conclusion, that a public declaration confirming that impression, and announcing the punishment of death in whomsoever should assist at any of those ceremonies, would have been implicitly and quietly acquiesced in.

5. " That the practice was not permitted by the Foreign States when they had power and territory in India.

6. " And which we think conclusive of the practicability of abolishing the practice, or at least of the safety with which it might be prohibited, that in many instances it has been prevented from taking place without exciting even a murmur, by either direct interference on the part of the local authority, by refusal of permission, or by a procedure similar to that which was adopted by the criminal Judge of the Zillah of Masalipatam.*

" The officers who acted in these instances of prevention, it was well known, acted in virtue of the authority they held under Government. It might be considered that, in each instance, an experiment was made as to the consequence of a prevention, and as not one of them appears to have been resisted, or even to have excited any feelings of dissatisfac-

---

* Threatening to commit as accomplices in the murder all persons who should any way assist to destroy the woman.

tion, we find it difficult to imagine that *a general prohibition by the Government itself would be less efficacious, or produce any serious opposition or discontent.* The very utmost we should apprehend from it would be temporary clamour or agitation among the lowest and most ignorant of the people in insulated districts, where the practice prevails, and where venal Brahmuns may have influence, but would be discountenanced and reprobated by the higher and more educated classes of the community.

7. "And lastly, is the equally satisfactory and important fact, that a great number of the most able and experienced servants of the Company, employed under the immediate authority of your Government, and the Presidencies of Fort St. George and Bombay, in the stations which afford the best means of forming a correct judgment on the subject, including members of your court of Nizamut Adawlut and superintendents of police, have voluntarily, and some of them nearly in the same terms, recommended the abolition of the horrid practice, and recorded their confident opinions and belief, that it might be abolished without any evil consequence whatever."*

John Hudlestone and William Taylor Money, Esqrs., signed a dissent to the motion which referred the proposed paragraphs for Bengal to the Committee of Correspondence, stating—"As they could not possibly be productive of *harm*, we regret the *indefinite delay of any good* which the immediate adoption of them might eventually have produced, reflecting that *probably no day passes on which some victims are not sacrificed to the horrid practice in India, and more especially in the Bengal provinces.*" They further observe,—"However necessary the toleration of the horrid enormity alluded to in Mr. C. Grant's work (written in 1792) might have been, when he so ardently deprecated its continuance, we think ample grounds are laid (in the proposed dispatch) for doubting if that necessity any longer exists; and whether the British Government in India, with the power it now possesses, would find greater difficulty or danger in putting down the most revolting of all the Hindoo practices, than it experienced in prohibiting all their other, but less cruel practices, and especially in annulling the Hindoo law which gave impunity to Brahmuns, and making them, in common with the inferior casts, amenable to the British laws."†—(East India House, March, 31, 1824).

The late Rev. T. Thomason, chaplain in Calcutta, expresses his convictions of the propriety and safety of the abolition of Suttees, Feb. 1827:—"Of the practicability of the abolition of these sacrifices with the most perfect safety—without the interception of the peace of the country for a moment—and even with the thanks of multitudes, I have not

---

* Par. Papers, vol. v. p. 29, 30. † See 33, 34. See p. 111, 130.

the least doubt. It is a great mistake to say that this is one of the deep-rooted general customs of the country, which on that account it would be dangerous to meddle with. It has been voluntarily discontinued over a very large part of India. As to the *practicability* of abolishing the custom, there is, I believe, but one opinion with well-informed persons. Nothing would be easier. The Government has only to frame a regulation prohibiting the practice under proper penalties—the highest penalties—and the local magistrate would then be empowered to act. I do not apprehend the smallest political risk, and this I know to be the opinion of some of the ablest and most experienced magistrates in Bengal. I could have wished the odious practice were abolished by the Government *there*; but, as this is hopeless, it will rejoice my heart to find it done by authority from *home*."*

"I cannot refrain from giving it as my decided opinion," says the Rev. W. Ward, in a letter to the Earl of Clarendon, "that this dreadful practice might easily be abridged, and finally abolished by the British Government, without creating any alarm among the Hindoos."

Dr. Marshman expresses the same opinion: "It is only for the British Government to say—*the murder of your widows is contrary to reason and revolting to humanity—We forbid it*,—and the practice will cease without giving birth to the slightest tumult. Forty years after the prohibition our Indian empire will be found, as far as this interference could effect it, equally unimpaired in its vigour and more deeply fixed in the enlightened attachment of its subjects."†

In reviewing the annual statement of Suttees, presented to the Indian Government, while it is distressing to see with what frequency and brutality the widow is hurried to the pile, it is grateful *to see humanity sometimes triumph, and the infatuated victim rescued*; affording demonstration how easily—

"*One mild effort* of the conqu'ring hand
Might free the earth from this detested blot,
And lead in blest religion to withstand,
By her meek precepts, what has dimmed the lot
Of man, and wrought such deeds as cannot be forgot."

The success of efforts to discountenance the perpetration of this practice under the Presidencies of Madras and

---

* Poynder's Speech, pp. 182—185. † p. 184.

Bombay, has been very considerable, and shows the facility of entirely suppressing this unnatural rite. The return of Suttees for the Madras Presidency, from 1817 to 1819, was 183; in 1820, 66; 1821, 50; 1822, 47; 1823, 38; total in seven years, 384; *average per annum*, 56. Under the Bombay Presidency, from 1819 to 1823, 245; *average per annum* 49. Who can doubt whether these few individuals, sacrificed every year, could not have been saved in those extensive territories without exciting the least commotion? Nor is the evil under the Bengal Presidency (containing probably a population of 50,000,000) so great as to deter exertions for its suppression; the number of Suttees being, from 1815 to 1826, 7154; *average per annum* 596.* Might not British humanity and magnanimity have rescued these poor widows without the least danger to the state? The multitude of counsellors reply in the affirmative.

In the Bareilly division it is reported that, in 1815, three women were prevented from becoming Suttees. In the Patna division, in 1817, twenty-five Suttees took place, but five women were prevented who "were saved from burning by the interference of the people of the village, or by the arrival of the police-officers." In the same year five Suttees are stated to have been prevented in the city of Benares. In the following year three other Suttees were prevented in the same city, and "one woman, cast a Brahmun, ran away from the pile after it was set fire to, and is still living." Four widows were saved at Cuddapah in 1820.†

The magistrate of the Patna division, in his returns of Suttees for 1822, writes,—"It is with satisfaction that I have noted that TWELVE WIDOWS have been either prevented or dissuaded from becoming Suttees; in nine of which they were dissuaded by the police officers; in one the widow was prevented by a police officer, on account of a legal impediment, and in the two remaining cases the widows were dissuaded, one by the zemindar of the village and the other by her friends." In the returns from the same division for 1823 is the following interesting statement:—"It will probably be considered the most remarkable feature of the present report that, on *nine occasions* of intended Suttees, at which alone the police-officers had an opportunity of

---

* See Account of the York Meeting for the Suppression of Suttees, Jan. 1827, p. 21. Jackson's Speech, p. 24.

† Par. Papers, vol. i. p. 167, 173; vol. iv. and v. p. 22—24.

being present, *they succeeded, without difficulty or opposition, in dissuading the widows from sacrificing themselves.* From the enquiries that I have been able to make on the subject of Suttees during the last two years, I do not hesitate to offer an opinion that, in this district, it would not be attended with any dissatisfaction of a dangerous nature, if the Government should deem it proper *to prohibit this lamentable custom altogether*; it even appears to me that the inhabitants of the district generally are prepared to hear of such a prohibition."† When shall suffering humanity in India hear the voice of mercy saying, kindle these horrid fires no more!

In some parts of Orissa a pit is used for this dreadful sacrifice, and the woman, after circumambulating it three or seven times, throws herself into the fire. The author saw one of these pits at Juggernaut's temple, in May 1824, but did not hear of the Suttee in time to be present. Even from this pit the victim sometimes escapes. In the Par. Papers of 1825, p. 109 and 150, is the following account:—"Rahang, in the thannah of Pooree (Juggernaut), died Aug. 25, 1823, and his widow, Mussumut Munee, aged fifty declared her intention of becoming a Suttee, and repeated the declaration in the presence of the police officers. In pursuance of this intention, the day following she went through the usual ceremonies, and *threw herself into a burning pit, where the body of her husband was consuming*, but almost immediately leapt out and made her escape. She was severely but not dangerously burnt, and an engagement was taken from the managers of the village binding themselves that she should be taken care of and proper remedies applied. She returned to her family and was received by them as usual."

W. Brooke, Esq., collector at Shahabad, in 1789, refused his consent to a widow's burning herself on application made to him; but no bad consequences followed. In 1805, J. R. Elphinstone, Esq., magistrate of Behar, prevented a Suttee, *a girl of twelve years of age!* He was afterwards "given to understand that the girl and her friends were extremely grateful for his interposition." J. Hodgson, Esq., magistrate of Midnapore, and the magistrate of Goruckpore, in 1817, prevented Suttees; and it is added, "in both cases the intended Suttees were *eighteen years of age.*" W.

---

† Par. papers, vol. iv. p. 122. See also Par. Papers, 1828, p. 18.

BURYING ALIVE A HINDOO WIDOW. *Page* 77.

Bird, Esq. magistrate of Benares, in 1815, prevented two women from destroying themselves. He observes: " both these Suttees were prevented by means of force; and by this means no less than *five Suttees* have been prevented within the space of two years at this place, without the slightest inconvenience resulting from it." J. Haig, Esq., acting judge in the Zillah Tinnevelly, in 1819, writes: " I am confident that the people are aware that the practice will never be sanctioned by the magistrate, and am happy that the accompanying documents enable me to afford a proof of the successful interposition of authority on a late occasion, in preventing the immolation of two females of high rank."*

A regulation, prohibiting widows of the Jogee tribe *burying themselves alive*, was promulgated Sep. 1817, which appears interesting, as indicating the influence of the British Government in India. It is as follows:—

1. " It having been ascertained that the shastra contains no authority for a practice which has prevailed amongst the Jogee tribe in some parts of the country, especially in the district of Tipperah, of burying alive the widows of persons of that tribe who desire to be interred with the bodies of their deceased husbands, such practice must necessarily be regarded as a criminal offence uuder the general laws and regulations of Government.

2. " The magistrates and police-officers, in every district where the practice above-mentioned has been known to exist, shall be careful to make the present prohibition as publicly known as possible; and if any person, after being advised of it, shall appear to have been concerned in burying a woman alive in opposition thereto, he shall be apprehended and brought to trial for the offence before the Court of Circuit.

3. " The magistrates and police-officers are farther directed to use all practicable means for preventing any such illegal act: and an attempt to commit the same, after the promulgation of these rules, though not carried completely into effect, will, on conviction, be punishable by the city magistrate, or by the Court of Circuit, according to the degree of criminality and circumstance of the case."†

Burying alive appears still to be permitted! The magistrate of Burdwan, in March, 1820, is commended for not using his authority to save the widow of a jogee.‡ The Somachar Durpun, a newspaper in Bengalee, contains the following account:—" A certain jogee, or weaver, inhabitant of Somrah, died; his wife, according to the custom

* Par. Papers, vol. v. p. 18, 19, 28. For an interesting account of the rescue of a Suttee at Juggernaut, see the Gen. Baptist Missionary Report for 1826.

† Par. Papers, vol. i. p. 141. Mis. Reg. Dec. 1824.

‡ Par. Papers, vol. ii. p. 27.

of her own caste, went down to the grave with her deceased husband. Her friends and relatives instantly covered the victim and the corpse with earth, and in this inhuman manner made an end of her existence." (Asi. Journ. Feb. 1827.)

"Human sacrifices, as of children, (says the late Bishop Heber, when at Ghazeepore, Aug. 1824), are never heard of now in these provinces, but it still sometimes happens that a leper is burnt or buried alive; and as these murders are somewhat blended with religious feeling, a leper being supposed to be accursed of the gods, the Sudder Dewannee, acting on the same principle, discourages, as I am told, all interference with the practice. The best way to abolish it would be to establish *Lazar houses*, where these poor wretches should be maintained, and, if possible, cured; or at all events kept separate from the rest of the people, a policy 'by which more than any thing else this hideous disease has been extirpated in Europe."* Why is Britain so timid to prevent the ravages of this murderous superstition?

Before the late Marquis of Hastings left India, in Jan. 1823, the following "*Supplicatory Lines*" were addressed to him in a Calcutta Paper. They are expressive of the public opinion in India upon the subject of Suttees:—

"Ere thy benignant power retires
From India, bless'd beneath thy care,
O quench those foul unhallow'd fires,
Which hell's own flame has kindled here,
The stain of earth and upper air!
Then o'er the sea,
The orphan's blessing and the widow's prayer
Shall follow thee.
O ne'er to man has pitying Heaven
A power so blest, so glorious given,
Say but a single word and save
Ten thousand mothers from a flaming grave,
And tens of thousands from the source of woe,
That ever must to orphan'd children flow!
Save from the flame the infant's place of rest,
The couch by nature given—a mother's breast;
O bid the mother live—the babe caress her,
And sweeter still its hoping accents bless her.
India with tearful eye and bended knee,
Hastings, her lord and judge, presents her plaint to thee."

* Jour. vol. i. p. 269.

O Britain, "plead for the widow!"—Let petitions pour into Parliament from every quarter, which, like the streams of the east, may quench these dreadful fires. Let the rulers of India, who hold its destinies in their hands, hear the appeal of a writer in that country:—"Let us freely look at the practicability of its abolition, and number both its friends and its foes. We may calculate on the support of all the humane, the wise, and the good throughout India. We may depend on the great majority of the people who have prevented every village in India from being lighted up monthly with these infernal fires. Those who have used all their influence to liberate their country from the stigma of this guilt, by preventing their mothers and sisters from ascending the funeral pile, will undoubtedly support us in discountenancing the practice. We shall enlist on our side all those tender feelings which, though now dormant, will then be roused into new vigour, but above all, we shall surround ourselves with the protection of that Almighty Power, whose command is, 'Thou shalt do no murder;' who defends the weak and succours the injured; who, when the cries of oppressed India had pierced his throne, selected us of all other nations to break its chains and restore it to happiness."*

CHAP. VII.

A collection of European and Native testimony to the position that the Suttee is not absolutely enjoined by the Hindoo shastras, and hence should be suppressed—methods proposed for its abolition — objections answered—concluding appeal.

Sir W. Jones, in his translation of the Institutes of Menu, the great Indian legislator, thus describes the work:—"This system of duties, religious and civil, and of law in all its branches, the Hindoos firmly believe to have been promulgated in the beginning of time by Menu, son or grandson of Brahma, or in plain language the first of created beings, and not the oldest only, but the holiest

* Par. Papers, vol. iv. p. 26.

of legislators." His high character is described in the following terms:—"Menu sat reclined with his attention fixed on one object, the Supreme God; when the divine sages approached him, and after mutual salutations, in due form, delivered the following address:—'Deign sovereign ruler to apprize us of the sacred laws in their order, as they must be followed by all the classes, and by each of them, in their several degrees, together with the duties of every mixed class; for thou, lord, and thou only among mortals, knowest the true sense, the first principle, and the prescribed ceremonies of this universal, supernatural Veda, unlimited in extent, and unequalled in authority.'" After a careful perusal of this work, not the slightest reference to the custom of the Suttee has been found. It contains various laws relative to females; a few extracts, in addition to what has been already quoted, may be interesting:—"In his passage to the next world, neither his father, nor his mother, *nor his wife*, nor his son, nor his kinsmen, will remain in his company: his virtue alone will adhere to him. When he leaves his corse, like a log or a lump of clay on the ground, his kindred retire with averted faces: but his virtue accompanies his soul. Equal care must be taken of barren women, of women without sons, of women without kindred, of *widows* true to their lords, &c. A widow, who, from a wish to bear children, slights her deceased husband, by marrying again, brings disgrace on herself here below, and shall be excluded from the seat of her lord. Like those abstemious men (unmarried Brahmuns) a virtuous wife ascends to heaven, though she have no child, if after the decease of her lord she devote herself to pious austerity."* The duty of Hindoo widows is evidently a life of austere devotion till death, and the custom of Suttee is unknown in the institutes of this great legislator.

The following extracts from the Parliamentary Papers, stating that the Suttee is not positively enjoined by the Hindoo shastras, and may therefore be suppressed, according to the opinion of many Europeans high in office in India, appear very important:—

"We really think (say the judge and registrar of Allypore, Ap. 1818) there is as little justification for a woman to burn herself with the remains of her deceased husband,

---

* Sir W. Jones' Works, vol. vii. p. 240. 334. 271.

as for a rájkoomor to destroy his daughters at their birth; burying alive for the leprosy where the party is desirous to die; human sacrifices at Saugur; putting sorcerers to death, or killing a human creature by any other means, without justification or excuse: *all of which are made capital offences by the regulations.* The killing in all these instances has quite as much in its favour (on the score of prejudice and superstition) as the practice of Suttee: but we do not find the punishment of death, denounced against these crimes, has at all been considered by the people as an infringement of that complete toleration, in matters of religion, which it has been a fundamental principle of the British Government to allow. *And there can be no doubt that the practice of Suttee might be as easily prevented throughout the British territories as any of the murderous practices above referred to.*"*

"The suicide in these cases is not indeed a religious act, nor *has it the sanction of Menu and other ancient legislators revered by the Hindoos.* On the contrary, Menu declares that a virtuous wife ascends to heaven, though she have no child, if after the decease of her lord she devote herself to pious austerity.† The texts of Yama and Catyayana, quoted in the *Vivada Bhangarnana* (digest of Hindoo law), "on the duties of widows choosing to survive their husbands," are also to the same effect;‡ and Vrihaspate adds,§ "whether she ascends the pile, or survive for the benefit of her husband, she is a faithful wife." Some authors have condemned the suicide of widows altogether, as coming within a general prohibition against the wilful abridgement of human life; and proceeding from a desire of future sensual enjoyment, in preference to the more pure and perfect state of beatitude promised for a life of virtue and piety."|| (Govt. Regulations relative to Suttees).

"I submit," says W. Ewer, Esq., Sup. of Police, Calcutta, Jan. 1819, "that *it has little or no connexion with their religion.* The practice is strongly recommended by the shastras, but nothing more, and Menu (with other authorities of great respectability) prescribes the duties of a widow,

* Par. Papers, vol. i. p. 99.
† Text, 141, "Digest of Hindoo Law," book iv. ch. 3, sec. 2.
‡ Texts, 144, 145, "Digest of Hindoo Law." § Text, 130.
|| p. 126.

without *hinting* that burning herself is one of the most important. In permitting, or indeed *authorizing* Suttees, we are by no means showing a proper forbearance to the religious customs, or long established prejudices of the Hindoos; *an act no where enjoined by any of the shastras;* on the contrary a crime which their own laws would punish with death; and only tolerated by our Government because we overlook the impudent imposition which has transformed a *recommendation* to the widow to accompany her husband, into *an order*, which the relations must carry into effect if she should evince symptoms of disobedience. I cannot attempt to account for the great prevalence of Suttees in some districts and the rarity of them in others; but it is a proof that it is a custom seldom thought of in the greater proportion of our dominions."*

"I feel emboldened, in the cause of humanity, to state, that the practice (of Suttee) *is neither prescribed by the shastra, nor encouraged by persons of education or influence.* I can speak, from positive authority, that his Highness the Rajah of Tanjore has ever discouraged it; and I feel assured that, with the exception of a few Brahmuns, who derive a nefarious reward for presiding at this infernal rite, the prohibition of the practice would give universal satisfaction."† (C. M. Lushington, Esq., Mag. at Combaconum, Sept, 1813.)

C. Smith, Esq., second Judge in Calcutta, thus expresses his convictions of the necessity of suppressing this custom:— "My opinion is that *the toleration of the practice of Suttee is a reproach to our Government, and that the entire and immediate abolition of it would be attended with no sort of danger.* I would suggest a short regulation on the subject, somewhat in the style of the regulation against the sacrifice of children at Saugur:—Whereas the practice of Suttee is shocking to humanity and contrary to nature; and whereas the British Government, after the most careful inquiry, and the most mature consideration, feels it impossible to be satisfied that this commission of self-murder can ever be in truth the voluntary and unbiassed act of the female who is sacrificed; and whereas to interfere with a vigorous hand for the protection of the weak against the strong, of the simple against the artful classes of its subjects, is one of the most impe-

* Par. Papers, vol. i. p. 228. † p. 270. 258.—Account of York Meeting, p. 26.

rious and paramount duties of every civilized state; a duty from which it cannot shrink without a manifest diminution of its dignity, and an essential degradation of its character among nations, &c. &c."* (May, 1821.)

"The ordinances of Menu," says S. Newnham, Esq., Cuddapah, April, 1820, "which are one of the principal law authorities in this part of India, do not encourage the sacrifice in the same manner as others quoted in the Vivade Changamana, translated by Mr. Colebrook. 'Let him not wish for death! Let him not wish for life! Let him expect his appointed time, as a hired servant expects his wages,' are doctrines more agreeable to the Institutes of the oldest Hindoo legislator, who mentions doctrines very averse from self-immolation of widows; such as the raising up a son to the deceased by the widow. Here the marriage of widows is now deemed illegal, but not so in some of the most southern parts of the Peninsula. The Hindoo shastra lays down rules for securing proper provision for the widow, and confidence on the uninterrupted validity of such claims has probably proved, as a solace to their afflictions, one of the most efficacious considerations to the prevention of the practice; while the persuasion which the priesthood use to widows, to induce them to devote their bodies to this sacrifice, have the greatest influence on those, *who, being without future protection and maintenance, regard a future sojourn in this world with despair.*"†

The Hon. Court of Directors, in a letter addressed to the Governor General in Council, at Fort William, June, 1823, thus express their views of the obligatory nature of Suttee, and the means of its abolition:—"Connected with the opinions expressed by many intelligent men, that *the practice of Suttee is not a tenet of religion to which the people are enthusiastically attached, but rather an abuse, fostered by interested priests and relations*, these instances of partial success lead us to regard the notion of *prohibition*, modified according to circumstances, of this barbarous custom, with rather less apprehension than it has generally produced. Assuredly the most acceptable form of success would be that which would be brought about by such an increase of intelligence among the people as should show them the wickedness and absurdity of the practice; next to this, we should rejoice to see the abolition effected by the

---

* Par. Papers, vol. ii. p. 63. † p. 93. See p. 103, 104.

influence and the co-operation of the higher order of natives."* It is gratifying to see this interesting subject discussed by different classes of society, and there can be no doubt that the abolition of the Suttee would be hailed in India as an act expected from the British Government, and reflecting lustre upon its administration.

"Whatever opinion may be entertained," says J. H. Harington, Esq., in a paper addressed to the Right Hon. the President of the Board of Control, in May, 1822, "on the policy which has hitherto induced the British Government to tolerate the immolation of Hindoo widows, as considered to be in some degree a religious observance, *although it is not a prescribed duty,* as may be seen in Mr. H. Colebrook's Translation of Original Texts on the subject (Vol. iv. of the Transactions of the Asiatic Society), there can be no sufficient or legitimate reason for permitting a practice so repugnant to every feeling and principle of humanity, *in opposition to the only laws which can be pleaded in justification of it.*"†

"It is worthy of remark," says the Asiatic Journal, "that the practice seems to prevail most in particular districts. In so considerable a degree is it of a local character, that there is just ground for regarding it as a rite not considered by the Hindoos in general as enforced by any *positive obligatory rule* (which is not the fact), but owing its prevalence to local prejudices, to the effect of example, and perhaps to the disingenuous efforts of interested individuals. Were such the fact, the danger of resolute interference would be materially lessened." Asiat. Jour., Dec., 1825.

R. Jackson, Esq., in the debate on the subject of the Suttees, at the General Court of Proprietors, March, 1827, said, "He relied upon the opinion of near *sixty of their most eminent servants,* such as residents, judges, and magistrates, that it might easily be subdued by a mixture of firm and conciliatory measures, who founded their opinions upon at least as many instances in which such conduct had been successful. Should it now fail, he would not hesitate at coercion—they must obey God rather than man!" Asiatic Journal, May, 1827, p. 732.

"The Suttee," says Charles Marsh, Esq., in the House of Commons, in 1813, "*is enjoined by no positive precept*

---

* Par. Papers, vol. iii. p. 45. † Vol. iv. p. 20. See p. 155, 156. Also p. 181, 182.

of the Hindoo religion. It is a species of overstrained interpretation of its duties: and the offspring of that fanaticism which will inevitably grow up, and has more or less grown up, under every system of religion."* Ought not such fanaticism to be corrected?

The late C. Grant, Esq., in his "Observations on the manners of the natives of British India," adverts to this custom, and intimates that to say we should continue to allow of these great disorders in "all time to come would be too daring a conclusion." "It may indeed appear surprising that in the long period during which we have held these territories, we have made no serious attempt to recal the Hindoos to the dictates of truth and morality. This is a mortifying truth how little it has been considered that the ends of Government and the good of Society have an inseparable connexion with right principles. We have been satisfied with the apparent submissiveness of these people, and have attended chiefly to the maintenance of our authority over the country, and the augmentation of our commerce and revenue; but have never, with a view to the promotion of their happiness, looked thoroughly into their internal state."†

The philanthropic and eloquent Wilberforce thus pleaded the cause of benighted India, in the British Senate, in 1813:—"Oh, Sir, if we lived nearer these unfortunate people, their distressed situation would exact from us more prompt relief. It was formerly my task to plead the cause of a people whose woes affected every heart, who were finally rescued from the situation in which they groaned by the abolition of the Slave Trade. That cause was doubtless the cause of suffering humanity; but I declare that, even if we exclude the consideration of religion, *humanity appears to me to be still more concerned in the cause I am now pleading, than in that of which I was formerly the advocate.*"

The Rev. T. Scott of Aston Sandford, in his valuable Commentary, has the following remarks on Numbers xxxv. 33:—"So ye shall not pollute the land wherein ye are; for blood it defileth the land: and the land cannot be cleansed of the blood that is shed therein but by the blood of him that shed it." "The *connivance* of our Government in the burning of widows, and in human sacrifices, and in other species of murder committed in our East Indian do-

* Dr. Johns's Pamphlet respecting the Suttee, p. 96. † Par. Papers, vol. v. p. 33. Townley's Answer to the Abbey Dubois, p. 109.

minions, under the pretext of an idolatrous religion, is wholly unjustifiable, and *burdens our land, and all connected with those distant regions, with the guilt of blood not expiated by that of those who shed it.*"—The blood of Suttees cries to Britain. O may she soon " make inquisition for blood," that " the blood of the souls of the poor innocents" may not be " found upon her skirts!"

The Rev. H. Shepherd, late senior chaplain in Calcutta, in a pamphlet " On the Inefficiency of the Ecclesiastical Establishment of India," justly remarks,—" These dreadful sacrifices (Suttees) form *no essential part of the Hindoo system of religion;* and that these burnings alive, amidst the horrid din of discordant instruments and the unhallowed shouts of enthusiastic thousands, proceed from the force of education, or perhaps from an organised system of an intolerant priesthood. If it were a system of religion, as shedding of human blood, it would have no claim to toleration from any Government; but, as a system of priestcraft, it may more consistently be considered as a system of murder; and as such it ought, even by the strong arm of power, to be suppressed."—p. 66, 67.

The editor of the Missionary Register (Feb. 1828), referring to the Suttee and the pilgrim tax in India, very justly observes,—" There are two topics of a very distressing nature, because they are putting to hazard the fidelity of this country in the discharge of that high trust which has been committed to it in its delegated stewardship in India." On the suppression of the Suttee, it is said, " opinions are circulated, in the face of the overwhelming weight of authorities to the contrary, that it would not be safe (to abolish it), and that, therefore, it is not the duty of Government to put an end to the practice. We are painfully convinced, in reading the declarations and arguments of almost all those who make these assertions, whether persons in office in India or such as attempt to influence the public opinion at home, that they understand and feel neither the real nature nor the exclusive obligation of Christianity. It will be nothing short of odious hypocrisy in the sight of Almighty God to refrain, under the notion of danger, to carry into effect a solemn resolution which has in view the advancement of his glory and of the acknowledged good of the natives placed under our charge, when no such apprehension of danger prevents the attainment, even by force, of any object deemed important to political welfare."—p. 75.

It appears very important to ascertain *the opinion of the Hindoos themselves upon the obligation of the rite of Suttee.* In the Bewasta, received from Mutoonjoy, pundit of the Supreme Court, in 1817, respecting the burning of Hindoo widows and other sacrifices among the Hindoos, Menu is not mentioned among the various authorities quoted; and it is acknowledged "on the subject of anoogamun (Suttee) the shastras exhibit a great variety of opinions; but no difference prevails with regard to the propriety of leading a life of austerity."*

"The judge of the Southern Concan, V. Hale, Esq., in Oct. 1819, says,—'In the neighbouring state of Sawunt Warree these restrictions (adopted by the Peishwa) were carried at one time to much greater length than mere persuasion, since we find during the reign of Kem Sawunt *a positive prohibition against the practice,* which existed for ten or twelve years, and that too *without creating any disturbance or any outward marks of discontent,* affording (if the tradition be not greatly exaggerated), a most favourable instance of what might be done, and to what the people would submit without considering their religious prejudices too much shocked."†

"I can speak from positive authority," says C. M. Lushington, Esq., acting magistrate of Combaconum, in 1813, "that his highness the Rajah of Tanjore has ever discouraged it." Mr. Lushington alludes to Serfagee, the present rajah, who had succeeded his uncle Ameer Sing, and we understand that the late Rajah Tuljajee, of whom the present Rajah is the adopted son, discouraged the practice; and, as a proof of his disapprobation of it, a very few hours before his death, gave positive orders to his wives not to burn on his funeral pile, and to his principal officer not to permit them, and the orders were obeyed without opposition and apparently without exciting any dissatisfaction."‡

W. Chaplin, Esq., Commissioner in the Deccan, in 1825, observes,—"The Brahmuns appear to be far from satisfied with the mode of our interposition, and some have suggested to me, that in preference to continuing it, *the community would be infinitely better pleased were Government absolutely to prohibit women altogether from becoming Suttee.*"§ Upon which F. Warden, Esq., member of coun-

---

* Par. Papers, vol. i. p. 124. † Vol. v. p. 23. ‡ p. 25. See p. 131, 132. § p. 146.

cil, Bombay, justly observes,—"The remark contained in the Commissioner's letter affords an opening for considering the expediency of exercising a more decided interference by absolutely prohibiting the practice of Suttee: I have already recorded an opinion that *all the sanguinary customs of the Hindoos might be prohibited, without affecting either the security or popularity of our supremacy.* Many of the most intelligent Brahmuns view the custom with abhorrence; from the Mahrattas, I conclude, we need apprehend no opposition, nor from the Mahomedans; and we may safely calculate on the forbearance of a majority of those who possess influence over the minds of the Brahmunee females."*

The late Rev. W. Ward, in a letter to the Earl of Clarendon, relates the following remarkable facts:—"In 1817 I was riding near Serampore, where there had been a Suttee: after making inquiries respecting the family and rank of the widow, I addressed a few individuals on the crime in which they had been assisting. One of these men answered,—*Sir, whatever the act now committed may be, we have nothing to fear. You* (the English Government) *must see to that; for the police magistrate has been here and given the order, and according to that order the woman has been burnt.*"†

The judge of Chittor, in 1823, declares—"The best informed and most respectable part of the natives would themselves have often prevented this ceremony, if they had had the power."‡

In Malabar a summary of the laws of the shastra was drawn up by the natives, from which they actually conclude against the practice in the following terms:—"From these texts it is clear that the rules relative to the observance of Anugamanum (Suttee) does not extend to the Keroola, and cannot be admitted to be performed there, even if a person is willing to do so."§

Bruja Mohun, in his Strictures on the present system of Hindoo Polytheism, written in the Bengalee language and printed in Calcutta, 1818, reprobates the practice of Suttee. "Promising heaven to your elder or younger sister—to your mother or grandmother—or daughter or friend—you bind them down with ropes and bamboos, and burn them on

---

* Par. Papers, vol. v. p. 149.

† Poynder's Speech on Human Sacrifices in India, p. 65. See 114.

‡ p. 216. § p. 217.

the funeral pile. When we witness the perpetration of these murders, does not nature itself move us to forbid them? Some of you consider the drinking of wine, and the extinction of life, and the shedding of blood, as conducive to salvation—we do not. To burn defenceless women, to murder an aged father and mother, by immersing them in water, you esteem holy—we esteem these deeds unholy."*

In 1819 a petition was presented to the late Marquis of Hastings, from the Hindoo inhabitants of Calcutta, praying for the abolition of Suttees. An extract only is given:—"Your petitioners beg leave to submit, to the benevolent attention of your Lordship's Government, that in the opinion of many of the most learned Brahmuns, founded upon the shastras, all kinds of voluntary death are prohibited; that Menu, whose authority is admitted to be equal to that of the Vedas, positively enjoins widows to lead a life of virtue and abstinence from sensual gratifications; that the Vedant which contains the essence of the Vedas, as well as the Geeta, forbids all acts done with the view of future temporary reward; and that amongst the inferior authorities, while some, as the Smritee shastras, actually prohibit all violent death: others, Mitakshura, declare the leading of a virtuous life preferable to dying on the pile of the husband; and a few only insist on the superior merit of concremation."†

"When the meeting was held by the Hindoo gentlemen of Calcutta to vote an address of thanks to Lord Hastings on his leaving Bengal, in 1823, Rhadacant Deb proposed, as an amendment, that Lord Hastings should be particularly thanked for 'the protection and encouragement which he had afforded to the ancient and orthodox practice of widows burning themselves with their husbands' bodies:' a proposal which was seconded by Hurree Mohun Thakoor, another wealthy baboo. *It was lost, however; the cry of the meeting, though all Hindoos, being decidedly against it.*—(Heber's Journ. vol. i. p. 72.)

Ram Mohun Roy, in his pamphlet entitled "A Conference between an advocate and an opponent of the practice of burning widows," states the sentiments of the humane and enlightened among the Hindoos on this subject:—The Veda declares,—'By living in the practice of regular and occasional duties the mind may be purified. By hear-

* Friend of India, Dec. 1818.

† Poynder's Speech, p. 220. See p. 222—224.

ing and reflecting and constantly meditating on the Supreme Being, absorption in Brumhu may be attained. Therefore, from a desire during life of future fruition, life ought not to be destroyed!' Menu, Yagnyuvulkyu, and others, have, in their respective codes of law, prescribed to widows the duties of ascetics only. The ancient saints and holy teachers and their commentators and yourselves (advocates of the Suttee), as well as we and all others, agree that Menu is better acquainted than any other lawgivers with the spirit of the Vedas. He has directed widows to spend their lives as ascetics." It is thus closed:—"It is to me a source of great satisfaction that you (the advocates) are now ready to take this matter into your serious consideration. By forsaking prejudice, and reflecting on the shastra, what is really conformable to its precepts may be perceived, and the *evil and disgrace brought on this community, by the crime of female murder, will cease.*"

"I have heard," says the Rev. H. Townley, in his "Answer to the Abbe Dubois," of the reply being repeatedly given to the expostulations of Europeans:—"*If there is any blame in our proceedings, it belongs to yourselves; for we are acting under British sanction.*" He adds, "The native who instructed me in the Bengalee language (who was a Brahmun of more than ordinary intelligence), *frequently expressed his surprise* to me that Government did not issue an order that no more Suttees should be permitted; intimating his conviction that no commotion whatever would ensue."*

The Rev. E. Carey, late missionary in Calcutta, at a public meeting at Manchester, in Aug. 1828, observed,—"As the subject of Suttees had been mentioned, he would state his conviction that *all the real obstacles to the practice of burning widows existed at home.* He did not mean to say that obstacles were to be found in the wishes of any party, but in their misconception of the case. He had conversed with a Brahmun and pundit on the subject, who said, '*If the practice is so heinous, why not suppress it?*' They fear (Mr. C. observed) to hurt their religious scruples. "What! (replied the Brahmun). We have compulsory taxes on the brahminical lands, and will it go nearer to our consciences to save our daughters from the flames?"

* Townley's Answer to the Abbe Dubois, p. 180. 190.

When Dr. Johns was in India (in 1812), the principal Brahmuns at the Mission Press, Serampore, were asked, whether the interference of the Government to suppress so horrid a custom would be objected to by the natives. They promptly answered "*that it would not*, and encouraged the idea of such an interference."* "It ought to be considered, that some of the most respectable pundits do not approve the practice, and would be happy if it were abolished: while many others *reproach us for permitting it to exist*.'"†

Why is Britain afraid to do justice upon those who shed innocent blood?—"Where are the bowels of our mercy? —Where our fears of the retributive justice of heaven?—How long shall this scourge continue to desolate India, and dishonour Britain? We may answer in the memorable language of a Brahmun, '*till the British Government shall think proper to abolish it*."‡

While some of the authorities in India hesitate relative to the propriety of suppressing Suttees, it must be interesting to know the *methods proposed for the abolition of this horrid rite*.

In 1805 the Court of Nizamut Adawlut, Calcutta, expressed themselves as follows:—"After information has been obtained of the extent to which the practice prevails, and of the districts in which it has fallen into disuse, or in which it is discountenanced by the most respectable classes, it may be *immediately abolished in particular districts*, and be checked and ultimately prohibited in the other parts of these provinces." But "since this time the inhuman practice, instead of its abolition being effected or any prohibition of it issued, appears to have gradually increased!"§

The late J. H. Harington, Esq., member of council, Calcutta, in a very important minute on the Suttee, June, 1823, states,—"With respect to the impracticability of putting a stop to the immolation of Hindoo widows by a legal prohibition and penal enactments, if the assistance of Brahmuns and others be requisite to enable the widow to devote herself in the prescribed mode, it would surely be possible to prevent such aid being given by a public

* See Dr. Johns's pamphlet, p. 92.—Account of York Meeting, p. 23, 24.

† Asiatic Observer, No. viii. Oct. 1824, p. 371.

‡ Grimshaw's Appeal, p. 24. § Par. Papers, vol. v. 1827, p. 6.

interdiction, with a declaration that any person hereafter promoting a female sacrifice shall be liable to a criminal prosecution, as principals or accomplices, for homicide; and that, on conviction, it will not be held any justification that the person was desired by the deceased to cause, aid, or in any manner to promote her death; or that the deceased became a Suttee by a voluntary act of self-devotion. This, in fact, is already in force (Sec. 3, regula. viii. 1799), although the intention of the regulation has not been considered applicable to Suttees. It would I conceive be sufficient to issue a proclamation through the country, declaring the section applicable to all persons convicted as principals or accomplices in wilful homicide, in the instance of a woman sacrificed by *sahamaran* or *anoomaran*.* It is probable that a proclamation to this effect would not at once prove completely effectual; secret immolations would still take place occasionally, and in some instances the widow, under a paroxysm of grief and the delusion of superstition, might be expected to devote herself on her husband's pile, or otherwise even without brahminical assistance; but such cases would be rare; and, after a few examples of wilful deviation from the rule, I *have no doubt the practice would be soon abandoned, as unsanctioned by Government, and subjecting the abettors to punishment in our criminal courts*."† It is deeply to be regretted that this judicious plan has not been adopted. The author has heard of a magistrate at Ganjam preventing a Suttee by prohibiting the sale of the materials requisite for the dreadful sacrifice.

The magistrate at Gazeepore, W. L. Melville, Esq., addressed a letter to the judges of the provincial court circuit, Benares, in July, 1823, in which he says,—"I wish to obtain the sanction of the superior authorities to a plan for checking the practice of Suttee. It appears to me desirable to attempt to carry this object, in the first instance, *in particular districts*, and not simultaneously throughout the country.‡ I do not think any new regulations upon

* Burning with or without the body of her husband.

† Vol. iv. 1825, p. 10.

‡ In a discussion respecting Suttees in the House of Commons, June 6, 1825, C. W. Wynne, Esq., M. P., said, "he would give his consent to its being wholly prohibited in those districts where it had already fallen into disuse; but he thought that going any farther would not be attended with the effect the friends of humanity anticipated."

the subject are requisite. Under the Mahometan law I conceive any person aiding or abetting another in committing suicide would be punishable: all I wish for is *permission to carry into execution laws which have been dormant.* I would begin by endeavouring to induce the *principal people in the district to unite among themselves to abandon and discourage the practice;* should they consent to this, little further difficulty would, I hope, be experienced; should I be mistaken, and meet with decided opposition, I doubt whether it would be expedient to proceed farther at present; from what I have heard I am inclined to think the people would be very well pleased to have so good a reason as an order of Government would afford for entirely giving up the performance of the rite." On this communication it is remarked:—"The court have no observations, in addition to what has been already advanced, to offer on the present occasion."* Fort William, July 25, 1823.

It is to be deeply regretted that these judicious measures have not been tried.

Captain H. Pottinger, collector of Ahmednauger, speaking of a Suttee that occurred in that city in Aug. 1818, says,—"I tacitly consented to the sacrifice, but at the same time positively *refused any assistance towards defraying the expenses for the requisite clothes for the woman or for the wood to form the pyre, and likewise declined to sanction the proceeding by my presence or that of any person on my part.* I have little doubt of the success of my interposition, in the majority of cases that may occur, when I have it in my power *to assure the woman of the means of subsistence.*"† A former volume of the papers (vol. iii. p. 47) remarks:—"An encouragement seems at one time to have been held out to Suttees, by granting to the family of the victim a portion of free land, similar to the provisions of the descendants of sepoys killed on service. The instances are far from numerous." Chandgurgh, Bombay Presidency, July, 1821. It is to be hoped that such instances of the encouragement of this custom are not numerous!

In the Par. Papers, vol. i. p. 264—268, relative to the Bombay Presidency, reference is made to making provision for the widow who was prevailed upon to decline immo-

* Par. Papers, vol. iv. p. 84, 85. † Vol. v. p. 20. Vol. i. p. 244.

lating herself. But this plan, like every other, short of entire prohibition, is defective, as it may have (to use the language of W. Chaplin, Esq., Commissioner of the Deccan) "the injurious effect of leading persons to feign a resolution to burn themselves in the hope of being paid for desisting."

J. H. Harington, Esq., suggested that magistrates should be authorized "to hold out some public encouragement, as an honorary dress, title, or other rewards, to any landholder or other person of local influence, who should distinguish himself by active and successful endeavours to discourage and suppress the sacrifice of Hindoo widows." The chief secretary to Government replied under date, Ap. 14, 1825:—"His lordship in council will be happy to notice by a suitable mark of his approbation any Zemindar, or other native of rank or respectability, who may have caused or may cause the discontinuance of the practice where it was before prevalent among his own relations and connexions, and may have successfully exerted himself in procuring the general relinquishment of it in his own estate, or to any considerable extent within the sphere of his influence."*

The nature of the system of discountenancing Suttees pursued on the Madras side of India is as follows:—"Where (says the writer of the following article in a Calcutta paper) the immolation of widows, *though once frequent, is now seldom known.* Before any woman can destroy herself by burning, permission must be obtained of the magistrate. On the request being preferred the applicant is directed to wait a little for an answer; the magistrate in the mean time sends for his cutwal and instructs him to proclaim that a certain woman intends burning herself, but should any Bunian or Bukall be discovered selling any article required for the purpose to the said woman, or any cooly offering his assistance by carrying oil, wood, &c., to the spot appointed, the former shall be turned out of the bazar, and the latter otherwise punished. It is also proclaimed that, should any crowd collect, the police peons are to disperse it, and to confine to the Cutwal's Choultry all persons resisting the police authority; should any Brahmun belonging to any public offices be seen in the crowd, or any of his relations be found aiding the ceremony, *such*

---

* Par. Papers, vol. i. p. 51.

servant shall be discharged from his situation. The whole of this being proclaimed, the applicant is desired to take leave. As may be expected, it has been observed, that *with these restrictions no burning has taken place!—Prevent a crowd from collecting to witness the immolation, and rest assured no such ceremony proceeds!* Mark the disappointment of the Brahmun when he discovers that a crowd cannot be collected; mortified, he abandons the victim of his persuasion to shift for herself. His zeal is exerted in proportion to his expected popularity, or to the worldly advantage he is to derive. So it is with the poor deluded widows; harassed into assent to they know not what, ninety-nine out of a hundred of them secretly rejoice that their attempt at self-destruction has been, by the above means, frustrated. As the remedy can hardly be said to be attended with coercion, it appears no difficult undertaking to introduce the practice of it in Bengal, and hereby render an essential service to the Hindoo community." (R. S. Moligaipore, March, 1823.)

The Rev. H. Shepherd, late of Calcutta, in his pamphlet "On the inefficiency of the Ecclesiastical Establishment of India," suggests the following steps to suppress Suttees:—that "An edict be published, declaratory that Suttees shall continue to be allowed to take place under the regulations now in force, but that, as the Government cannot refrain from expressing their utter abhorrence of such proceedings, they do for the future determine *that no son, brother, or cousin, of the first or second degree, of any female so burning, shall be permitted to hold any situation or renew any leases under Government.* Such a decree would so effectually operate in deterring many from their atrocious practices, who employ artifice to entrap the widow into the fatal declaration which consigns her to death; that thousands in after-times will live to bless the Government who have had the power and the will to deliver them from the despotic dominion of a sanguinary priesthood."* This measure would doubtless save many widows, but would not annihilate the cruel custom.

"Were second marriages," says the editor of the 'Friend of India,' esteemed honourable, and the children born of them permitted to inherit equally with those of a first marriage; a practice sanctioned not merely by the laws of all

* Shepherd's Inef. of Ecc. Esta. of India, 2d edition (London), p. 67, 68.

Christian countries, but even those of Greece and Rome notwithstanding their idolatry; many think that this alone would gradually extinguish the practice."* The importance of such a change in the circumstances of Hindoo widows must be self-evident.

In the debate at the India House, on the subject of Suttees, March 1827, Captain Maxfield suggested "that a woman applying to burn herself with the body of her husband should be obliged to wait *three months;* and that in all cases the application for such license should be made in person; this he had no doubt would, in a vast majority of cases, be an effectual prevention, as it would afford time for reflection." Dr. Gilchrist said—"He thought there was a way by which the abolition of the practice might be effected without danger to the Company's interest. That way, as an author, he had pointed out to their governor-general in India *forty years ago.* His plan was that any Hindoo *in any way connected with a Suttee, not merely instrumental to the burning, but any relation or connexion of a woman who had burned herself, should be declared for ever incapable of holding any place of office, authority, or emolument, in the Company's service.* It would be a stain upon their character, as sovereigns, as legislators, and as men, if they did not take some steps to check a practice repugnant to the laws of nature and of civil society."†

In the Asiatic Journal for July, 1826, are three letters in English, written by Bengalees, on the subject of Suttees, extracted from a Calcutta Newspaper, which are very curious compositions, and show the sentiments of sensible natives on the nature of this appalling rite. We can give but a short extract or two.—"Her brother Roopnarain Gosaul, who is supposed to be a wealthy man, and being so long in the Honourable Company's service ought to be discharged from his place, and prosecuted in the Supreme Court for giving countenance to such an inhuman act. *No body anger could be minded when a life is concerned; she ought to be prevented to burn. If Governor General gives orders to remove the woman from her relations, at her pronouncing that she will burn, and allow her to remain one day in a comfortable place with English Ladies that understand*

---

* Vol. ii. 332. † Asi. Journ. May, 1827.

the country's language, there is not doubt her mind shall be purified, and her foolish thoughts shall be removed, and will not be anxious to do such a base act as to burn with the dead person." (Muddunmohun Mullick, Calcutta, Jan. 27, 1827.)

"I fully agree with the sentiments contained in Muddunmohun's letter. If the Government in Council give orders to remove all the women on pronouncing that they will burn, to be placed with an intelligent English person to persuade them to the contrary, and not allow any of the relations to converse, or make them take *intoxicating drugs*, they will never die in such an inhuman manner. I have lost my wife these *six years*, and have not married again for fear she may burn with my body at my death.—The Hindoo women have no sense; they hear from their superiors the cremation is an holy act, and they are fools enough to listen to it, which only induces them to express their sentiments that they will burn; and as soon as such a declaration is obtained, all the unfeeling relations use all their exertions to induce the poor unfortunate widows to suffer such a cruel death. I hope you will not refuse to have this appeared in your interesting Paper, and oblige me." (Sunchurn Sill, Calcutta, Jan. 31, 1826.)

A writer in the Asiatic Observer, No. 8 (published in Calcutta, Oct. 1824), very forcibly remarks upon this subject,—'Let *one man of influence in society* take the object into consideration, deliberately, and with a determination to find out some plan to which he can solicit the attention of the public, and we have as little doubt of his success as we have of the disposition of the public to assist him. It has been thought that it would be advisable for the inhabitants of Calcutta to present a petition to the Supreme Government, or through them to *our own Legislators at home*. It would certainly be an honourable thing to those who made it, and entitle them to *a place among the friends of India to the latest age*. It has been suggested that it would be very honourable to the ladies in Calcutta, were they all to unite in presenting a petition and soliciting the Lady of the Governor General, to do them the honour of putting her name first. This would display the humanity and sympathy of the Calcutta Ladies, and have a great practical effect, by leading many to impress on their husbands the importance of rescuing a degraded part of the female sex.* If all *the Knights* of the present day could be persuaded to undertake the rescuing of Bengalee widows from the flames, they would attempt a nobler deed than was ever achieved since the order was instituted; and, should they be successful, would transmit to posterity a name more honourable than any or all of their brethren. Another plan that has been proposed, and acted upon in part, is, that houses of agency, mercantile houses, &c., would set ther faces against this practice, by dismissing from their employment any person who has been brutal enough *to burn his own mother*. This would teach the natives the abhorrence that Europeans have of the crime, and would, in many instances, prevent it from being committed. We are encouraged, from the spirit of the British Nation, and the prophecies of Scripture, confidently to anticipate an end of the miseries we now deplore. That a Parliament which has abolished the Slave Trade will for ever permit the burning of widows, we can never believe. Slavery did not receive its death-blow at once; many blows were aimed at the monster before its head was broken; and its carcase is not even yet all consumed. So it may be in the case under discussion: it may be brought forward several times before all objections to it, real and fictitious, are answered; but, *unless humanity and wisdom perish from the British Senate, we are certain that sooner or later they will put an end to this horrid practice.*"

The nature and extent of human sacrifices in British India present 'a tale whose lightest word might harrow up the soul.'† *What objections to the abolition of these sacrifices* (particularly to the Suttee) *can be urged sufficient to justify a Christian Government in the permission of such sanguinary practices?* "The importance of this inquiry, either with reference to the sacrifice of human life, or to the

* Would not petitions to the British parliament, signed by females from the principal cities and towns in Great Britain and Ireland, have a similar effect? Should it be objected—this is an unprecedented method of expressing public opinion; it may be replied, "Is not the destruction of so many hundred unhappy widows annually in British India, a sufficient justification of it?" In the session of 1829 three female petitions were presented and were favourably received. AUTH.

† See Address of the Society for the Abolition of Human Sacrifices in India. Evan., Bap., and Cong. Magazine, January, 1829. And also Meth. Mag. and Month. Repos.

character of British rule in India, cannot be overrated."* The following appear to be *the principal objections to the immediate suppression of the burning of Hindoo widows.*

It is considered an *ancient custom or religious rite, and its abolition intolerance to the Hindoo religion.* "Those who deny," says the Asiatic Journal, "that it is expressly enjoined by ancient law, admit that it is countenanced and commended by its expositors; and custom itself, as of so long standing as can be pleaded in favour of this kind of sacrifice, is, perhaps, of superior weight as an authority, than any positive law, where no absolute prohibition can be shown."† "I should consider," says the magistrate of Zillah Behar, Dec. 1818, "the prohibition by law of a ceremony which is encouraged by the shastra as an infringement of that system of complete toleration in matters of religion declared to be a fundamental principle of the British Government in India."‡ That this custom is ancient cannot be denied, but probably its antiquity has been overrated. Menu makes no mention of Suttee, and among the numerous Hindoo authors whose names are mentioned by Mutonjoy, the pundit of the Supreme court in his Bewasta respecting the Suttee, this great legislator is not named.§

J. Adam, Esq., secretary to the governor-general, in Oct. 1817, referring to the regulations respecting the Suttee, observed—"It is trusted they will have a beneficial influence, by lessening a sense of obligation under which there is reason to believe many are induced to make this sacrifice of their lives, and showing that *the practice is far from being inculcated as such by the most approved authorities of the Hindoo law.*"‖

"I look upon this inhuman custom," says C. M. Lushington, Esq., magistrate of Trichinopoly, "as one tolerated to the disgrace of the British Government; *it is ever abominated by the better sort of natives themselves, and no where is it enjoined by Hindoo law.* The authorities against self-immolation are Menu, Bhooraspattee, and several others. The weight of authority is in favour of a rigid practice of austerities, because it is that prescribed by Menu, revered by the Hindoos as the first and greatest law of authority. *Custom* can only be legally upheld when it does

* Par. Papers, vol. v. p. 31. † Oct. 1827.

‡ Par. Papers, vol. i. p. 240. § p. 119.

‖ Digest of Hindoo Law; Text, Par. Papers, vol. i. p. 147.

not militate against *law* ; '*consuetudo pro lege servator,*' will only extend to cases where no specific law exists. In the present instance there is a specific law, sanctioned by Menu, in direct opposition to authorities of inferior weight. I apprehend, the obvious absurdity of the law (exempting Brahmuns from death) and the impossibility of reconciling it with our notions of justice induced its abolition. If, then, a *law* can be repealed from its inconsonancy with reason, the same arguments exist in a stronger degree against an inhuman, barbarous, and unjust custom." *

From the numerous extracts given of the sentiments of the great majority of the European functionaries of Government in India, and even of the natives, when writing in defence of the practice, it appears evident that the Suttee is not an integral part of the religion of the Hindoos, but a cruel rite, subversive of its principles and of the natural dictates of humanity.

A second objection to its abolition is, *the rite being supposed a voluntary act, and an attempt to suppress it calculated to increase its reputation*. That these unhappy women are frequently involuntary sacrifices to this horrid custom numerous facts abundantly testify. The dispatch, hurry, and confusion, by which the rite is characterised, are opposed to the calm exercise of mind requisite in a voluntary sufferer. The husband frequently dies in the morning, sometimes at noon, and, before the evening shades are closed, the dreadful rite is consummated. Where delay is occasioned, the woman not unfrequently takes stupifying and intoxicating drugs, and remains without food, generally sitting near the body. In the instance witnessed by the author the woman appeared so stupid that one of the functionaries of Government declared her intoxicated. Her husband died that morning at day-break, and she was burnt in the evening. "No fair judgment," says L. Warner, Esq., magistrate of 24 Pergunnahs, Calcutta, in 1818, "can be passed upon a person *non compos mentis*, assenting to the performance of this act; for can a person be called actually in a sound state of mind under the agitation of grief? Would a person's deposition, under this state of mind, be received in a court of justice in a cause where life and death are at stake?"† "The act," says C. M. Lushington, Esq., Magistrate at Trichinopoly, "I apprehend is always voluntary,

* Par. Papers, vol. ii. p. 103, 104. Vol. v. p. 4. ‡ Vol. i. p. 147.

provided a being in a state of stupefaction and delusion can be said to possess the power of volition !!"* A magistrate at Bhooj, Guzerat, in Oct. 1819, writes,—" There has been only one instance of a woman desiring to burn herself in our district, in Cutch, since 1816. In that instance I proceeded to her house; and, as she appeared firm in her resolution, I could only persuade her to delay the ceremony for a few days, promising that at the expiration of that time, if she persisted in her wish, she should meet with no hindrance. As might be expected, *twenty-four hours produced a total change!* Instead of the hysterical grief with which she was affected, tears came to her relief, and she declared her resolution not to burn. Her friends were very anxious that she should be dissuaded from burning."†

On the latter part of this very common objection it is stated, in the late Bishop Heber's Journal,—" Some members of Government conceive that the likeliest method to make the custom more popular than it is, would be to forbid it, and make it a point of honour with the natives: and that, if we desire to convert the Hindoos, we must above all things be careful to keep Government entirely out of sight in all the means which we employ, and to be even, if possible, *over scrupulous* in not meddling with or impeding those customs which, however horrid, are become sacred in their estimation; and are only to be destroyed by convincing and changing the public mind."—(Vol. i. p. 58.) To this it may be replied—the experience of the British Government in India for the last fifty years is directly opposed to these sentiments. Have not the Hindoo and Mahomedan laws been changed in several important parts—cruel ordeals abolished—infanticide at Saugur and Guzerat suppressed—the Brahmun, though esteemed an incarnation of Brumha, every year executed, like the degraded Soodra, &c.? Have the absurd, cruel, and sanguinary customs thus suppressed been held in higher estimation by the people—or the popularity of the Government decreased? Bishop Heber here gives the opinions of others; his *own opinion* we have in the following words:—"All these stories (respecting the Suttee, dhurna, and burying alive of lepers) have made a very painful impression on me. If I live to return to Calcutta, it is possible that, by conversation with such of my friends as have influence, and by the help of what addi-

---

* Par. Papers, vol. i. p. 239. Vol. v. p. 26. † vol. i. p. 260.

tional knowledge I may have acquired, I may obtain a remedy for some of them."*

A third objection is, that *its abolition might promote disaffection in the Native army and insurrection in the country.* This objection has been well met by Sir C. Forbes, on the discussion of the subject of Suttees, Mar. 1827:—"If the British Government," says this eloquent gentleman, "did all in their power to put down this practice, it would soon disappear. They could not view it in any other light but as a horrible rite that ought not to be tolerated; and in his opinion it might be put down, and could be put down, without delay and without danger."

"He was sorry to hear, on a question of this kind, insinuations thrown out, that, if an attempt were made to remove this evil, it would be attended with danger from the army. He viewed such insinuations as a libel on that army. He had no doubt that the army of India would rather feel themselves called on to support all just and lawful commands issued by the Government, for putting down such abominable rites. He would ask, did they ever hear of one sacrifice in a British camp in India? Never; and he would contend that the suppression of this practice did not involve the feelings of the native army in India. They every day heard of Brahmuns brought to punishment for different crimes. If, on their behalf, an appeal was made to the army, they would at once be told, 'You do not deserve to be assisted; you may thank your own crimes for your punishment.' Why should not their native army, who were just in other affairs, be just also with reference to this? For his own part he had not the least apprehension of their tried fidelity."†

"It has been said that the point which appeared to be of more importance and delicacy than any other,—the probable effect of our interference on our native army, had not been touched on in any of the opinions given by the Government abroad. It was very true that the judges, magistrates, residents, collectors, and all the various persons he had quoted, never touched on such an argument; and they had abstained from doing so, because such an idea never entered their minds. Living, as they did, in the country, and having every opportunity for observing the conduct of the army, it was wholly impossible that they

* Journal, vol. i. p. 269.

† Asiat. Journ. May, 1829.

could anticipate danger. 'The time had been,' said Mr. Burke, 'when 10,000 swords would have leaped from their scabbards to avenge a threatening look against a royal female;' and were they to suppose that their whole army would be weak and wicked enough simultaneously to unsheath their swords for the very opposite purpose? Would that army array itself against the British power, because that power humanely attempted to prevent mothers and sisters (persons united to this very soldiery by the ties of blood) from sacrificing themselves on the funeral pile."*

The late J. H. Harington, Esq., refers to this subject, and states:—"The register has, at my request, carefully examined the Suttee reports for 1823 (the first in which the possessions of the deceased husband has been generally stated), and can find *only one instance of a native soldier's wife having sacrificed herself in the year.* The case occurred in the district of Shahabad, which furnishes many recruits to our native army; but in Bengal and Orissa, where so large a proportion of the total number of Suttees annually take place, very few of our sepoys are raised, insomuch that I have good reason to believe, on inquiry, that there are not at present in our whole regular army (gun Lascars excepted) above 1000 men who are natives of those provinces.† (Feb. 1825.) The fallacy of this objection appears very evident.

Another objection to the suppression of these atrocities is the supposition *that we are bound by treaty not to interfere in the abolition of this custom.* The Marquis Wellesley, in 1805, stated the principles of our Government in India:—"It is," said the Governor General, "one of the fundamental maxims of the British Government to consult the religious opinions, customs, and prejudices of the natives in all cases in which it has been practicable, *consistently with the principles of morality, reason, and humanity.*" Locke very justly observes, "No opinions contrary to human society, or to those moral rules which are necessary to the preservation of civil society, are to be tolerated by the magistrate." Upon this principle is the letter of Lord Wellesley and his council founded,—a principle only to be shaken when the elements of society shall

---

* Asiat. Journ. May, 1827, p. 703. See also Jackson's Speech, as above, p. 23—25.

† Par. Papers, vol. v. p. 47.

sustain an overthrow, but not before; for according to the principle of all natural law, and of our own in particular, "*Jura naturæ immutabilia sunt.*" The letter recognizes the amplest toleration, so far as is consistent with "the principles of morality, reason, and humanity," but no further; and it affords a complete answer to all those who argue that we cannot act as we are required, because we have made a treaty or compact with India, to respect her religion. I contend we are not bound hand and foot by any supposed compact, which is at variance with principles as old as the creation, and the obligation of which principles had force long antecedent even to the moral law. "When," says Colonel Walker, "the custom and rites of any people are harmless, whatever form they assume, and from whatever source they may be derived, they are entitled to toleration and protection; but they ought to be punished or amended, when their evident tendency is to diminish population, and to alienate the natural affections of mankind."* To the same effect are the remarks of the late C. Grant, Esq., in 1792, see Par. Papers, vol. v. p. 33.

"*Neglect,*" by some, "*is thought better than immediate abolition, and the annihilation of the practice by the progress of knowledge and establishment of Christianity preferable to coercion.*" To this it may be replied, in the language of Dr. Johnson,—"He that voluntarily continues in ignorance is guilty of all the crimes which ignorance produces; as to him that should extinguish the tapers of a light-house might justly be imputed the calamities of shipwreck. Christianity is the highest perfection of humanity; and, as no man is good but as he wishes the good of others; no man can be good, in the highest degree, who wishes not to others the largest measure of the greatest good. To omit for a year or a day the most efficacious method of advancing Christianity (and consequently the amelioration of society), in compliance with any purpose that terminates on this side the grave, is a crime of which I know not that the world has an example, except in the planters of America, a race of mortals whom I suppose no other man wishes to resemble."† "The argument that we may ultimately look for the cure of this evil in the gradual

* Poynder's Speech, p. 14, 15.

† Cormack's Infanticide, p. 343.

increase of intelligence, which is beginning to develope itself in India, might have some weight, if the progress of intelligence were of a more accelerated character than circumstances allow us to suppose, or if the immediate abolition of the rite were not proved to be both safe and practicable. But, this fact once satisfactorily established, to delay the enjoyment of an acknowledged good, because at some future time we anticipate its attainment by the operation of other causes,—what is this but to procrastinate a happiness already within our reach, and to be justly responsible for all the misery of the intervening period of a long and criminal delay?"*

What shall arouse British humanity, magnanimity, justice, and piety, to abolish without delay the bloody rite of Suttee? Behold *the magnitude of the evil.* The official returns of the widows buried or burnt alive in the Bengal Presidency, from 1815 to 1826, inclusive, were 7154, which with the returns from the other Presidencies of Madras and Bombay, where the custom is much less frequent than in Bengal, would amount to 7789. (p. 13.) Here is a sacrifice in twelve years, to the Moloch of superstition in India, before whom Britain is seen to tremble, and her arm become nerveless in the protection of the unhappy widow. Oh Britain, I blush for thee! Will it be believed a century hence that, "We the British people—the advocates of every thing humane—the natural opponents of every thing cruel and oppressive—we the protectors of innocence, the avengers of wrong! that we the British people *sanctioned by our own authority* this diabolical custom! nay, that we went further; for *by our neglect we permitted the practice, in many cases which, even according to the barbarous doctrines of the shastra itself, were illegal!* Was it possible that the Court would not make some effort to wipe out this stain upon our country?" (Jackson's Speech, p. 13.) How injurious must be our influence upon the tributary, allied, and independent princes, in whose territories this most unnatural custom exists?† Are there a thousand

* Grimshawe's Appeal on behalf of Hindoo Widows, p. 26, 28.

† "By accounts lately received from the Hill country twenty-eight *females were burnt with the remains of one of the Rajahs*; there appear to have been two other women who escaped; one was pregnant, the other resisted all importunity to be burnt. How can we expect that these horrid practices will cease among the neighbouring heathen princes, while they are countenanced by the British Government!" Proceedings

widows annually sacrificed in British India? how many thousands must have perished since the rise of the British power after the decisive battle of Plassey in 1756.* *Seventy thousand* widows thus cruelly murdered! "Murder most foul, strange, and unnatural." What a tragic history would a comple detail of these burnings make! Imagination fails in attempting to describe the horrors of these ravages of superstition; the mind recoils from the subject: but as the philanthropic Wilberforce pleaded for India in the British Parliament, in 1813:—"True humanity does not consist in a squeamish ear, but in a humane heart; it consists in feeling for the miseries of our fellow creatures and endeavouring to put an end to them—not in turning away from the view of them, or denying their existence when they are feelingly stated."

The responsibility of Britain to exert her influence in abolishing this practice should be seriously considered. Britain delays to speak the decisive word that shall save ten thousand widows from death, but (how important the inquiry!) "*On whom will the blood of the many thousand victims that are destined to perish be visited?* This is a solemn question, before which we may well pause and weigh all the present and the future consequences. It cannot be dissembled, that the charge of guilt attaches primarily to the *Government of India*, who are the conscious spectators of the act, and, possessing the means, are yet deterred from employing those means for its suppression. It next attaches to the *British Government* at home, who acquiesce in the motives that influence this reluctance.

---

of Manchester Meeting for the Abolition of Suttees, May, 1827. "General Bheem Syre's eldest nephew, Vizier Singh, arrived at Nepal in November, and died on the 3d of December. The following day the body was burned and along with it *two of his wives and three slave girls!* the latter had not the honour of being burned on the same pile, but had one to themselves. The brother of the deceased, with his nephew in his arms, lighted the funeral fires—such being the custom! *Suttees are not unfrequent in the valley.* A curious one took place some months ago, of a woman burning herself with her seducer, who had been killed by her husband. *So much for religious ordinances!*" Cal. John Bull, Jan. 19, 1824.

* It is a fact worthy of being generally known, as demonstrating even in the infancy of British power in the East, the practicability and success of humane exertions on behalf of Hindoos, that, Mr. Job Carnock, who founded Calcutta, in 1694, rescued a native woman from the funeral pile, and made her his wife. Ought not Calcutta thus founded in mercy to promulgate the law which shall abolish the Suttee?

And finally, the *whole British people become parties to this moral guilt*, if, knowing as they do, the existence of the crime, they do not consider themselves pledged to use all lawful means for abolishing a rite, derogatory to the British character, forming an anomaly in the administration of civil law, and involving a flagrant breach of the law of God."* May those in whose hands are the lives of these myriads of helpless females, "accounted as sheep for the slaughter," and the destinies of the millions of Hindostan, consider the impressive language of the Word of God: "If thou forbear to deliver them that are drawn unto death and ready to be slain: if thou sayest, behold we knew it not; doth not He that pondereth the heart consider? and He that keepeth thy soul doth not He know? and shall not He render to man according to his works?" Prov. xxiv. 11, 12.

The general expression of public opinion by petitions to Parliament for the abolition of the burning of widows is important. The attention of the Legislature will be awakened and directed to the subject, and encouraged to act worthy of their high character. "In an account of the York Meeting, for petitioning Parliament on the subject of the Immolation of Hindoo widows, held in Jan. 1827," it is stated, "the importance of petitioning Parliament will be duly appreciated, when it is understood that the late Marquis of Hastings said *he would at once have put down the atrocious practice, if he could have relied upon the popular feeling being in his favour in our own country, and that* THE DANGER WAS FELT—NOT IN INDIA BUT ONLY IN ENGLAND!"—Why has not Britain long since removed this unaccountable suspicion of her abhorrence of shedding innocent blood? Let the inhabitants of Great Britain and Ireland speak, and supplicate, that no more of these horrid murders defile our country. And shall this cause want advocates in the British Senate? "Every question brought before a British House of Parliament seems to require, to a certain degree, to be supported and urged by some distinguished advocate, and blessings be upon the head of him who shall step boldly forward in this cause. Let some glorious Hero come forward to this voluntary martyrdom, and like another *Curtius* plunge, if necessary, into the gulf of personal destruction for the general good! But no, he will invest his

* Grimshawe's Appeal, p. 20, 26.

brow with immortal laurels! a million of mothers and mother's sons will celebrate his name; the records of history will perpetuate it; but above all God and his own conscience will approve his efforts! Still, we venture to predict, whether with or without a popular advocate, in concurrence with or in defiance of political parties and prejudices, the deed will be done! There is a voice that must be heard, that will require it,—*the voice of an enlightened and Christian people:*—a voice that will be heard by the Parliament and the Prince: that voice (Oh, let it be loud and solemn!) must, we are confident, awaken a power and move an arm that, sooner or later, will extinguish the Suttee fires of India!"*

Bedford, in 1823, and Crail, near Edinburgh, in 1825, took the lead in this work of justice and mercy. In the year 1827 the author heard of petitions to Parliament relative to this object from

Ashbourn	East Retford	Newark	Sutton Ashfield
Belper	Hinckley	Newbury	Staines
Belfast	Hinton	Northampton	York
Chester	Loughborough	Reading	
Colchester	Manchester	Rochdale	
Derby	Melbourn	Salisbury	

In the two succeeding Sessions less public attention appears to be directed to this subject, as fewer petitions were presented. "We are astonished (says a writer in the Evangelical Magazine, Aug., 1828) that Britain, so justly famed for humanity, does not more powerfully plead for the widow, and that petitions more numerous than those against the sacramental test do not flow into Parliament from all quarters." Since the important discussions on the Suttee, in the Court of Proprietors, in March, 1827, the subject has been brought forward again, but little progress appears to be made. R. Jackson, Esq., in a letter to the author, in Oct., 1828, declares—"With regard to the Suttee question, I believe I expressed to you, some time back, *my despair of any material alteration for many years to come!* unless the religious part of the public shall come forward in a manner so decided as to induce attention from His Majesty's Government, and from the House of Commons. They seem ignorant, notwithstanding the Papers printed by Parliament, and other publications, that *the average of these murders has been for many years from*

* See Review of "India's Cries," 1st edit., in The World, July, 29, 1829.

forty to fifty per month!! I fear litle more can be done in the General Court." When will the friends of humanity and religion, in a manner becoming the importance of the object, "plead for the widow," and thus deliver the land "from blood guiltiness?"

The following petition, which may serve as a specimen, was adopted at a very respectable meeting at Manchester:—

To the Right Honourable the Lords Spiritual and Temporal of the United Kingdom of Great Britain and Ireland, in Parliament assembled.

The humble Petition of the Inhabitants of Manchester and its Vicinity, adopted at a Public Meeting, convened by the Boroughreeve and Constables of Manchester, and held in the Town Hall, on the 9th of May, 1827.

Showeth,—That your Petitioners have learned with the greatest regret that the Burning of Widows with the dead Bodies of their Husbands, and other customs by which human life is wantonly sacrificed, continue to be practised in various parts of British India, with undiminished frequency, in gross violation of the Law of God, and of the rights and feelings of humanity.

That it further appears to your Petitioners that the existing regulations of the Suttee, circulated by the Bengal Government, in one thousand eight hundred and fifteen, have rather tended to increase than to diminish the number of human sacrifices, it being understood by the Natives, that by those regulations the sanction of the ruling power is now added to the recommendation of the shastra.

That it appears from documents submitted to your Right Honourable House, and since laid before the public, that the practice of Burning Hindoo Women alive, if prohibited by Government, might be effectually suppressed, without any ground for apprehension of evil consequences.

That your Petitioners deeply impressed with the obligation of the Inhabitants of Britain to promote the civilization and improvement of their fellow-subjects in India, as expressed by a resolution of your Right Honourable House, in the year one thousand eight hundred and thirteen, most earnestly implore your Right Honourable House to adopt such measures as may be deemed most expedient and effectual for the suppression of customs so abhorrent from the British character, and so opposed to the welfare of our Indian possessions, and thus to remove the stigma which at present attaches to our national character, and relieve the Inhabitants of British India from this cruel scourge.

And your Petitioners will ever pray.

A similar one was presented to the Hon. House of Commons.

The degraded state of India is most apparent, and the consequent duty of Britain to promote its melioration and evangelization. Its Suttees, Infanticides, Pilgrimages, swinging festivals, murder of the sick by the Ganges, innumerable destructive austerities, show that as it respects its intellectual and moral condition the people are "sitting in darkness and the region of the shadow of death." The appalling description of Job appears almost literally applicable to it:—"A land of darkness, as darkness itself; and of the shadow of death, without any order, and where the light is as darkness.' Job, x. 22. Bible, Missionary, and Education Societies are dispelling the darkness.

"The day has broke which never more shall close."

The author has seen a Bengalee Christian and a Preacher, who, when a boy, set fire to the pile that consumed the body of his father and his living mother to ashes! Behold the triumph of Christianity. In humble dependence on the Divine blessing, let means adequate to the great work of the illumination of India and the East be applied, and all the atrocity of heathenism—its idols—its temples, will ere long be seen no more. Let the friends of humanity and religion prosecute their arduous work; for their "labour is not in vain in the Lord,"

It is not unfrequently asked by some—Has not Britain formed a connexion with India, and agreed to govern it upon such terms as to admit the perpetration of these evils? Does not such a contract with India exist? The late C. Grant, Esq., in his "Observations on the state of Society among the Asiatic Subjects of Great Britain," written in 1792, and submitted to the Hon. Court of Directors in 1797, thus answers these enquiries:—"Are we bound for ever to preserve all the enormities in the Hindoo system? Have we become the guardians of every monstrous principle and practice which it contains? Are we pledged to support for all generations by the authority of our Government, and the power of our arms, the miseries which ignorance and knavery have so long entailed upon a large portion of the human race? Is this the part which a free, a humane, and an enlightened people, a nation itself professing principles diametrically opposite to those in question, has engaged to act towards its own subjects. It would be too absurd to maintain that any engagement of this kind exists;—that Great Britain is under any obligation, direct or implied, to uphold errors and usages, gross and fundamentally subversive of *the first principles of reason, morality, and religion. In Hindostan, mothers of families are taken from the midst of their children, who have* *just lost their father also, and by a most diabolical complication of force and fraud are driven into the flames! Shall we be in all time to come as we have hitherto been, passive spectators of this unnatural wickedness?** In the suppression of infanticide at Saugur; sitting Dhurna; exempting Brahmuns from the penalty of the law, &c., we have acted according to just sentiments, and the abolition of Suttees may be accomplished with equal facility and safety. This has been shown from the concurrent testimony of many Europeans resident in India, and from the Natives themselves. The rite is not an integral part of Hindoism, but an abuse fostered by the ignorant, superstitious, and unprincipled. It is the evident and imperious duty of Britain to spread her protecting shield over these defenceless widows and orphans.

"Who that sees Great Britain yet upon her throne, after a conflict in which she has survived the united assaults of the European nations, and has equally triumphed over the arts and arms of her oriental enemies—who that beholds her 'sitting as a queen,' and, after having humbled the Tyrant of Europe and raised the nations he had oppressed, now legislating in peace, for her own remote empire in the East;—who that beholds her enriched by commerce, and ennobled by conquest, will hesitate to pronounce that this is peculiarly the time to interpose for the deliverance of her own subjects from the oppression of a sanguinary superstition, and to prove to the world that she has herself been preserved amidst surrounding ruin, for no ordinary purposes."† And what are those purposes, but being the eminently honoured means of promoting the universal diffusion of the principles of that Gospel, by which the language of prophecy shall be fulfilled:—"All the ends of the world shall remember and turn unto the Lord: and all the kindreds of the nations shall worship before Thee. They shall not hurt nor destroy in all my holy mountain: for the earth shall be full of the knowledge of the Lord, as the waters cover the sea."

* Par. Papers, vol. v. 1827, p. 33. † Poynder's Speech, p. 214.

A VOICE FROM INDIA;

OR

THE HORRORS OF A SUTTEE.

WHAT means that gloomy funeral pyre,
 On Ganges' banks its tall head raising,
And those red gleams of murky fire,
 E'en now around its broad base blazing?
What mean those wild and frantic yells,
 As from a thousand throats resounding,
With drums and trumpet's awful peals,
 From distant hills and woods rebounding?

Ah! 'tis a dark and murd'rous deed,
 Which cruel Brahmuns there are doing,
Well may the heart turn sick, and bleed,
 While such a dreadful theme pursuing!
For see! on that detested pile,
 By her lord's corpse the widow lying,
While Moloch, with a fiendish smile,
 Looks on, and views his victim dying.

See how she writhes! hark to her screams,
 As now the lurid flames enfold her!
But all is vain, no pity gleams
 In the stern face of one beholder!
Her kindred stand with hearts of stone,
 Cased by the demon Superstition;
Hear her last agonizing groan,
 Nor heave a sigh at her condition!

Ye British matrons, husbands, sires,
 Your souls with soft compassion glowing,
O! haste to quench the horrid fires
 Whence human blood is daily flowing!
With your loved King and Country plead,
 Implore the Senate of your nation,
That British India may be freed
 From scenes of such abomination.

And send, O! send the Gospel forth
 To the dark haunts of superstition!
That they may learn a Saviour's worth,
 And find in him sin's true remission.
Arise, thou Sun of Righteousness!
 On heathen lands pour forth thy splendour;
Then love and peace their homes shall bless,
 And their steeled hearts grow soft and tender.

Matlock Bath. ELLEN.

DESTRUCTION AND PRESERVATION OF INFANTS IN INDIA. *Page* 113.

BOOK II.

INFANTICIDE.

CHAP. I.

Introductory remarks—sketch of the early and extensive prevalence of Infanticide and Human Sacrifices in various countries.

THE abolition of Infanticide in India has been the triumph of the philanthropist and the subject of history. "Moor's Hindoo Infanticide" was published in 1811, and in 1815 appeared "Cormack's Account of the Abolition of Female Infanticide in Guzerat, with Considerations on the question of promoting the Gospel in India." Through the circulation of these publications, the well-known suppression of the destruction of children at Saugur by the Marquis of Wellesley in 1802, and the little that is known in this country respecting the Peninsula of Guzerat, a very general impression prevails that Infanticide is abolished in India. It is a painful but necessary task to remove this impression—to show that the evil still exists to a considerable extent, and to rouse the friends of humanity and religion to prosecute the abolition of this and every sanguinary custom in British India. The Parliamentary Papers on Hindoo Infanticide, printed by order of the Honourable House of Commons June 1824, and July 1828, fully substantiate the fact, that, notwithstanding the philanthropic and successful efforts of Colonel Walker and Governor Duncan to abolish this unnatural custom, it has revived; and that the most decisive measures are requisite to effect its entire and speedy abolition. When shall every cruel custom in India be abolished, and thus the progress of Christianity in that country be facilitated? Let the sentiments of the eloquent Burke be known and considered:—"The blood of man should never be shed but to redeem the blood of man. It is well shed for our family, for our friends, for our God, for our kind. The rest is vanity—the rest is crime."

"The prevalence of Human Sacrifices, and the continuance of such in human customs in the nineteenth century of the Christian era, and in the British Dominions, is a fact deeply interesting to every philanthropic mind. The learned Jacob Bryant has given a comprehensive view of the nature and extent of these sacrifices in different ages and countries. "One would think it scarcely possible," says he, "that so unnatural a custom as that of human sacrifices could have existed in the world; but it is very certain that it not only existed, but almost universally prevailed. The Egyptians of old brought no victims to their temples, nor shed any blood at their altars. But human victims, and the blood of men, must here be excepted, which at one period they certainly offered to their gods. The Cretans had the same custom, and adhered to it a much longer time. The nations of Arabia did the same. The people of Duma in particular sacrificed *every year a child*, and buried it beneath an altar, which they made use of instead of an idol; for they did not admit of images. The Persians buried people alive. Amestris, the wife of Xerxes, entombed twelve persons alive, under ground for the good of her soul. It would be endless to enumerate every city, or every province, where these practices obtained. The Cyprians, the Rhodians, the Phœcians, those of Chios, Lesbos, Tenedos, all had human sacrifices. The natives of the Tauric Chersonesus offered to Diana every stranger whom chance threw upon their coasts. Hence arose that just expostulation in Euripides, upon the inconsistency of the proceeding wherein much good reasoning is implied. Iphigenia wonders, as the goddess delighted in the blood of men, that every villain and murderer should be privileged to escape; nay be driven from the threshold of the temple; whereas, if an honest man chanced to stray thither, he was seized and put to death. The Pelasgi in a time of scarcity vowed that they would give *the tenth of all that should be born to them for a sacrifice*, in order to procure plenty! Aristomenes, the Messenian, slew three hundred noble Lacedemonians, among whom was Theopompus, the king of Sparta, at the altar of Jupiter, at Ithome; without doubt the Lacedemonians did not fail to make ample returns, for they were a severe and revengeful people, and offered the like victims to Mars. Their festival of the Deamastigosis is well known, when the Spartan boys were whipped, in the sight of their parents, with such severity before the altar of Diana Orthia that they often expired under the torture. Phylarchus affirms, as he is quoted by Porphyry, that of old every Grecian state made it a rule, before they marched towards an enemy, to solicit a blessing on their undertakings by the sacrifice of human victims.

"The Romans were accustomed to the like sacrifices. They devoted themselves to the infernal gods, and constrained others to submit to the same horrid doom. Hence we read in Titus Livius that in the consulate of Omilius Paulus and Terentius Varro, two Gauls, a man and woman, and two in like manner of Greece, were *buried alive at Rome*, in the ox-market, where was a place under ground walled round to receive them, which had before been made use of for such cruel purposes. He says it was a sacrifice not properly Roman, that is, not originally of Roman institution, yet it was frequently practised there, and that too by public authority! Plutarch makes mention of a like instance a few years before in the consulship of Flaminius and Furius. There is reason to think that all the principal captives who graced the triumphs of the Romans were, at the close of that cruel pageantry, put to death at the altar of Jupiter Capitolinus! Caius Marius offered up his *own daughter for a victim to the Dii Aversunce*, to procure success in a battle against the Cimbri, as we are informed by Dorotheus, quoted by Clemens; it is likewise attested by Plutarch, who says her name was Calpurnia. Cicero, making mention of this custom being common in Gaul, adds, that it prevailed among that people even at the time he was speaking; whence we may be led to infer that it was then discontinued among the Romans; and we are told by Pliny that it had then and not very long been discouraged. There was a law enacted, when Lentulus and Crassus were consuls, so late as the 657th year of Rome, that there should be no more human sacrifices; for till that time these horrid rites had been celebrated in open day, without any mask or control, which, had we not the best evidence for the fact, would appear scarcely credible. And, however discontinued they may have been for a time, we find that they were again renewed, though they became not so public, nor so general; for, not very long after this, it is reported of Augustus Cæsar, when Persia surrendered in the time of the second triumvirate, that besides multitudes executed in a military manner, he offered up upon the Ides of March *three hundred chosen persons*, both of the equestrian and senatorian order, at an altar dedicated to the manes of his uncle Julius. Even at Rome itself this custom was revived; and Porphyry assures us that in his time a man was every year sacrificed at the shrine of Jupiter Latiaris. Heliogabalus offered the like victims to the Syrian deity, which he introduced among the Romans. The same is said of Aurelian.*

"The Gauls and the Germans were so devoted to this shocking custom that no business of any moment was transacted among them without being prefaced by the blood of men. They were offered to various gods, but particularly to Hesus, Taranis, and Shautates. These deities are mentioned by Lucan, where he enumerates the various nations who followed the fortunes of Cæsar. The altars of these gods were far removed from the common resort of men, being generally situated in the depth of woods, that the gloom might add to the horror of the operation, and give a reverence to the place and proceeding. The persons devoted were led thither by the Druids, who presided at the solemnity, and performed the cruel offices of the sacrifice. Tacitus takes notice of the cruelty of the Hermunduri in a war with the Catti, wherein they had greatly the advantages, at the close of which they made one general sacrifice of all that were taken in battle. The poor remains of the legions under Varrus suffered, in some degree, the same fate. There were many places destined for this purpose all over Gaul and Germany, but especially in the mighty woods of Arduenna, and the greater Hercinian forest, a wild that extended above thirty days' journey in length. The places set apart for this solemnity were held in the utmost reverence, and only approached at particular seasons. Lucan mentions a grove of this sort near Masselea, which even

---

* "In Homer and Virgil, we have accounts of human sacrifices, communicated in such a way as indicates no abhorrence in the poet, and was meant to inspire none on the part of the reader. Cæsar informs us that it was a prevalent maxim among the Gauls, that the deity could not be appeased unless the life of one man, which had been forfeited by guilt, were atoned by the life of another who was innocent." (De Bel. Gal. L. vi. c. 15.)

the Roman soldiers were afraid to violate, though commanded by Cæsar. Claudian compliments Stillico that, among other advantages accruing to the Roman armies through his conduct, they could now venture into the awful forest of Hercinia, and follow the chase in those so much dreaded woods, and otherwise make use of them.

"These practices prevailed among all the people of the North, of whatever denomination. The Massageta, the Scythians, the Getes, the Sarmatians, all the various nations upon the Baltic, particularly the Suevi and Scandinavians, held it as a fixed principle that their happiness and security could not be obtained but at the expense of the lives of others. Their chief gods were Thor and Woden, whom they thought they could never sufficiently glut with blood. They had many celebrated places of worship, especially in the island of Rugen, near the mouth of the Oder, and in Zealand. Some, too, very famous among the Sumnones and Nahanvalli. But the most reverenced, and the most frequented, was at Upsal, where there was every year a grand celebrity, which continued for *nine days.* During this term they sacrificed animals of all sorts, but *the most acceptable victims, and the most numerous, were men!*

"Of these sacrifices none were esteemed so auspicious and salutary as a sacrifice of the prince of the country. When the lot fell for the king to die it was received with universal acclamations and every expression of joy; this once happened in the time of a famine, when they cast lots, and it fell to the king Domalder to be the people's victim, and he was accordingly put to death. Olaus Triliger, another prince, was burnt alive to Woden. *They did not spare their own children!* Harold, the son of Gunild, the first of that name, slew two of his children to obtain a storm of wind. 'He did not let,' says Verstegan, 'to sacrifice two of his sons unto these idols, to the end he might obtain such a tempest at sea as should break and disperse the shipping of Harold, king of Denmark.' Saxo Grammaticus mentions a like fact; he calls the king Haquin, and speaks of the persons put to death as two hopeful young princes. Another king slew *nine sons in order to prolong his own life,* in hopes, probably, that what they were abridged of would, in a great measure, be added to himself; such instances did not often occur; but the common victims were very numerous. Adam Bremensis, speaking of the awful grove of Upsal, where these horrid rites were celebrated, says, that there was not a single tree but what was reverenced, as if it were gifted with some portion of divinity. And all this because they were stained with gore, and foul with human putrefaction! The same is observed by Scheffer in his account of this place.

" *The manner in which the victims were slaughtered was diverse in different places.* Some of the Gaulish nations chined them with the stroke of an axe. The Celts placed the man who was to be offered for a sacrifice upon a block or an altar, with his breast upwards, and with a sword struck him forcibly across the sternum ; then, tumbling him to the ground, from his agonies and convulsions, as well as from the effusion of blood, they formed a judgment of future events. The Cimbri ripped open the bowels, and from them they pretended to divine. In Norway they beat men's brains out with an ox-yoke. The same operation was performed in Iceland by dashing them against an altar of stone. In many places they transfixed them with arrows. After they were dead they suspended them upon the trees, and left them to putrefy. One of the writers above quoted mentions that in his time seventy carcases of this sort were found in the wood of the Suevi! Dithmar, of Mursburgh, an author of nearly the same age, speaks of a place called Sedu, in Zealand, where there were *every year ninety and nine persons sacrificed to the god Swantowite.* During these bloody festivals a general joy prevailed, and banquets were most royally served. They fed, and gave a loose to indulgence, which at other times was not permitted!

" They imagined that there was something mysterious in the number nine, for which reason these feasts were in some places celebrated every ninth year, in others every ninth month, and continued for nine days; when all was ended they washed the image of the deity in a pool, on account, it is supposed, of its being stained with blood, and then dismissed the assembly. Their servants were numerous, who attended during the term of their feasting, and partook of the banquet. At the close of all *they were smothered in the same pool, or otherwise made away with!* On which Tacitus remarks, how great an awe this circumstance must necessarily infuse into those who were not admitted to these mysteries. These accounts are handed down from a variety of authors, in different ages. Many of whom were natives of the countries which they describe, and to which they seem strongly attached. They would not, therefore, have brought so foul an imputation on the part of the world of which each were writing; nor could there be that concurrence of testimony were not the history in general true.

"The like custom prevailed in a great degree in Mexico, and even under the mild government of the Peruvians, and in most parts of America. In Africa it is still kept up, where, in the inland parts, they sacrifice some of the captives taken in war to their fetiches, in order to secure their favour. Snelgrave was in the king of Dahoomi's camp, after his inroad into the countries of Adra and Whidaw, and was a witness to the cruelty of this prince, whom he saw sacrifice multitudes to the deity of his nation. The sacrifices, if we except some few instances, consisted of persons doomed by the chance of war, or assigned by lot to be offered. But, among the nations of Canaan, the victims were peculiarly chosen. Their own children, and whatever was nearest and dearest to them, were deemed the most worthy offering to their god.

"The Carthaginians, a colony from Tyre, carried with them the religion of their mother country, and instituted the same worship in the parts where they settled. It consisted in the adoration of several deities, but particularly of Kronus; to whom they offered human sacrifices, and especially the blood of children! If the parents were not at hand to make an immediate offer, the magistrates did not fail to make choice of what was most fair and promising, that the god might not be defrauded of his dues! Upon a check being received in Sicily, and some other alarming circumstances happening, Hamilcar, without any hesitation, laid hold of a boy and offered him on the spot to Kronus, and at the same time drowned a number of priests to appease the deity of the sea. The Carthaginians, upon a great defeat of their army by Agathocles, imputed the miscarriage to the anger of this god, whose services had been neglected. Touched with this, and seeing the enemy at their gates, they seized at once *two hundred children of the chief nobility, and offered them in public for a sacrifice. Three hundred persons, who were somehow obnoxious, offered themselves voluntarily, and were put to death with the others!* The neglect of which they accused themselves, consisted in sacrificing children purchased of parents among the poorer sort, who reared them for that purpose! and not selecting the most promising and the most honourable, as had been the custom of old. In short, *there were particular children brought up for the altar, as sheep are fattened for the shambles;* and they were brought and butchered in the same manner; but this indiscriminate way of proceeding was thought to have given offence. It is remarkable that the Egyptians looked for the most handsome person to be sacrificed. The Albanians pitched upon the best man of the community, and made him pay for the wickedness of the rest. The Carthaginians chose what they thought the most excellent, and at the same time most dear to them, which made the lot fall heavy upon their children. This is taken notice of by Silius Italius in his fourth book. Kronus, to whom those sacrifices were exhibited, was an oriental deity, the god of light and fire; and therefore always worshipped with some reference to that element. The Carthaginians first introduced him into Africa; he was the same as the Orus of the Egyptians, and the Alorus of the eastern nations.

"He was universally adored in Cyprus, but particularly in this part, which Porphyry supposes to have been Salamis. This deity was the Moloch of the Tyrians and Canaanites, and the Melech of the east; that is, the great and principal god, the god of light, of whom fire was esteemed a symbol; and at whose shrine, instead of viler victims, they offered the blood of men.

"Such was the Kronus of the Greeks, and the Moloch of the Phœnicians, and nothing can appear more shocking than the sacrifices of the Tyrians and Carthaginians which they performed to the idol. In all emergencies of state, and times of general calamity, they devoted that which was most necessary and valuable to them for an offering to the gods, particularly to Moloch. Besides these undetermined times of bloodshed, they had particular and prescribed seasons every year, when *children were chosen out of the most noble and reputable families.* If a person had an *only child,* it was the more liable to be put to death, as being esteemed more acceptable to the deity, and more efficacious of the general good. Those who were sacrificed to Kronus were thrown into the arms of a molten idol which stood in the midst of a large fire, and was red with heat. The arms of it were stretched out with the hands turned upwards, as it were to receive them, yet sloping downwards, so that they dropt from thence into a glowing furnace below. To other gods they were otherwise slaughtered, and, as it is implied, by the very hands of their parents. What can be more horrid to the imagination than to suppose a father leading the dearest of all his sons to such an infernal shrine? Or a mother, the most engaging and affectionate of her daughters, just rising to maturity, to be slaughtered at the altar of Ashtaroth, or Baal? Justin describes this unnatural custom very pathetically. Such was their blind zeal, that this was continually practised, and so much of natural affection still left unextinguished, as to render the scene ten times more shocking from the tenderness which they seemed to express. They embraced their children with great fondness, and encouraged them in the gentlest terms that they might not be appalled at the sight of the hellish process; begging of them to submit with cheerfulness to this fearful operation. If there was any appearance of a tear rising, or a cry unawares escaping, the mother smothered it with her kisses, that there might not be any show of backwardness or constraint, but that the whole might be a free-will offering! These cruel endearments over, they stabbed them to the heart, or otherwise opened the sluices of life, and with the blood, warm as it ran, besmeared the altar and the grim visage of the idol. These were the customs which the Israelites learned of the people of Canaan, and for which they are upbraided by the Psalmist: 'They did not destroy the nations concerning whom the Lord commanded them, but were mingled among the heathen, and learned their works; yea, they sacrificed their sons and their daughters unto devils, and shed innocent blood, even the blood of their sons and of their daughters, whom they sacrificed unto the idols of Canaan, and the land was polluted with blood: thus were they defiled with their own works, and went a whoring with their own inventions.'

"These cruel rites, practised in so many nations, made Plutarch debate with himself, 'Whether it would not have been better for the Galato, or for the Scythians, to have had no tradition or conception of any superior beings, than to have formed to themselves notions of gods who delighted in the blood of men;—of gods who esteemed human victims the most acceptable and perfect sacrifice? Would it not,' says he, 'have been more eligible for the Carthaginians to have had the atheist Critias, or Diagoras, their lawgiver at the commencement of their polity, and to have been taught that there was neither God nor demon, than to have sacrificed in the manner they were wont to the god which they adored? Wherein they acted not as the person did whom Empedocles describes in some poetry, where he exposes this unnatural custom. The father, with many idle vows, offers up unwillingly his son for a sacrifice, but the youth was so changed in feature and figure that his father did not know him. These people used wilfully to go through this bloody work, and slaughter their own offspring. Even they who were childless would not be exempted from this cursed tribute, but purchased children at a price, of the poorer sort, and put them to death. The mother who sacrificed her child stood by, without any seeming sense of what she was losing, and without uttering a groan. If a sigh did by chance escape, she lost all the honour which she proposed to herself in the offering, and the child was notwithstanding slain. All the time of this celebrity, while the children were murdering, there was a noise of clarions and tambors sounding before the idol, that the cries and shrieks of the victims might not be heard.' 'Tell me,' said Plutarch, 'if the monsters of old, the Typhons and the Giants, were to expel the gods, and to rule the world in their stead, could they require a service more horrid than these infernal rites and sacrifices.'"*

"Mr. Bryant," says Colonel Walker, "does not appear to be aware of the existence of human sacrifices among the Hindoos; and it is melancholy to add to the list of human infirmity by citing the translation of the Rudheradhyaya from the Calican Puran, by Mr. Blaquiere, as an evidence of this barbarous rite being sanctioned by the Hindoo Legislature. It was not only enjoined, but in the ancient rites of the Hindoos was frequently practised, under the denomination of Mer Med, or Wud, the sacrifice of a man. There is at this day a numerous class of Brahmuns who are accused of this practice. They are called Kurrada, and are inhabitants of the Conkan. The object of their worship is Maha Lukshmee, to whom human sacrifices are acceptable; and the more so if the victim is a Brahmun, learned in the shastras.

"The public performance of this sacrifice has long since fallen into disuse; but a sect of the Kurrada Brahmuns are accused of effecting, by the secret operation of poison, that object which they dare not avow. 'I know several Kurrada Brahmuns in respectable public situations, intel-

* Annual Register, vol. x. 1767. Par. Papers on Hindoo Infanticide, June 1824, p. 53—58.

ligent, charitable, and humane, who would abhor the commission of this detestable crime, and who, though they admit the former existence, most strongly deny its present practice; but the power of prejudice is sometimes stronger than the most complete evidence of moral conduct; and many people, under the influence of this passion, would decline to eat of food prepared by a Brahmun of this tribe, of which he himself should not at the same time partake.' "*

" However shocking," says the late Rev. W. Ward, " it may be, *it is generally reported among the natives, that human sacrifices are to this day offered in some places in Bengal.* At a village called Ksheeru, near the town of Burdwan, it is positively affirmed that human sacrifices are still offered to the goddess Yoogadya, a form of Doorga; at Kireetukona, near Moorshedabad, to Kalee; and at many other places. The discovery of these murders in the name of religion is made by finding the bodies with the heads cut off near these images; and, though no one acknowledges the act, yet the natives well know that these people have been offered in sacrifice. About seven years ago, at the village of Serampore, near Cutwa, before the temple of the goddess Tara, a human body was found without a head; and in the inside of the temple different offerings, as ornaments, food, flowers, spirituous liquors, &c. All who saw it knew that a human victim had been slaughtered in the night; and search was made after the murderers, but in vain. At Brumha-neetula, near Nudeeya, is an image of Munusa, before which the worship of Doorga is performed. It is currently reported, that at this place human victims are occasionally offered as decapitated bodies are found there. Ram-naut Vachusputee, the second Sunskrit pundit in the College of Fort William, assured me that about the year 1770, at the village of Soomura, near Gooptipara, he saw the head of a man, with a lamp placed on it, lying in the temple before the image of the goddess Sidheshwuree, and the body lying in the road opposite the temple. A similar fact is related respecting an image of Bhurga-Bheema at Tumlook, where a decapitated body was found. At Chit-poor, and at Kaleeghaut, near Calcutta, it is said that human sacrifices have

* Par. Papers on Hindoo Infanticide, 1824, p. 52. On this subject see Asiatic Journal, May 1823, p. 680.

been occasionally offered. A respectable native assured me that at Chit-poor, near the image of Chittreshwuree, about the year 1788, a decapitated body was found; which, in the opinion of the spectators, had been evidently offered on the preceding night to this goddess.

The following story respecting Rajah Krishnu-chundru-ray is believed by many respectable natives of Bengal:—A Brumhucharee of Kritukona, after repeating the name of his guardian deity for a long time, till he had established a great name as a religious devotee, at length had a dream, in which he supposed that his guardian deity told him to make a number of offerings to her, which he understood to mean *human sacrifices;* and that then she would become visible to him, and grant him all his desires. He was now very much perplexed about obtaining the necessary victims; and, as the only resource, he applied to Krishnu-chundru-ray, and promised that, if he would supply the victims, he should share in the benefits to be derived from this great act of holiness! The Rajah consented to this, and built a house in the midst of a large plain, where he placed this brumhucharee; and directed some chosen servants to seize persons of such and such a description, and forward them to the brumhucharee. This was done for a considerable time (some say for two or three years), till at length the brumhucharee became weak and emaciated through the perpetration of so many murders; and the Rajah began to suspect that there must be *some mistake in the business!* He consulted a learned man or two near him, who declared that the brumhucharee had very likely mistaken the words spoken to him in his dream; for that these words might mean simple offerings of food, &c. A thousand victims are said to have been thus butchered."*

* View of the Hindoos, vol. ii. pp. 49—52. The late Bishop Heber having visited a temple at Umeer, in Jeypore, observes, "The guide told us in our way back that the tradition was that in ancient times, *a man was sacrificed here every day;* that the custom had been laid aside till Jye Singh had a frightful dream, in which the destroying power appeared to him, and asked him why her image was suffered to be dry? The Raja, afraid to disobey, and reluctant to fulfil the requisition to its ancient extent of horror, took counsel and substituted a goat for the human victim, with which the

"Dark goddess of the azure flood,
Whose robes are wet with infant tears,
Scull-chaplet wearer, whom the blood
Of man delights three thousand years,
Was pleased to be contented."

The Preliminary Discourse of Sale's Koran (p. 174) affords information of the existence of these sacrifices in Arabia. "The law of Mahomed put a stop to the inhuman custom which had been long practised by Pagan Arabs, of *burying their daughters alive*, lest they should be reduced to poverty by providing for them, or else to avoid the displeasure and disgrace which would follow, if they should be made captives, or become scandalous by their behaviour; the birth of a daughter being, for these reasons, reckoned a great misfortune, and the death of one as great a happiness! The manner of their doing this is differently related:—some say that, when an Arab had a daughter born, if he intended to bring her up, he sent her clothed in a garment of wool or hair, to keep camels or sheep in the desert; but, if he designed to put her to death, he let her live till she became six years old, and then said to her mother, '*Perfume her and adorn her, that I may carry her to her mothers!*' which being done, the father led her to a well, or a pit dug for that purpose, and, having bid her to look down into it, pushed her in headlong as he stood behind; and then, filling up the pit, levelled it with the rest of the ground. But others say that, when a woman was ready to fall in labour, they dug a pit, on the brink whereof she was to be delivered; and, if the child happened to be a daughter, they threw it into the pit; but if a son they saved it alive. This custom, though not observed by all the Arabs in general, was yet very common among several of their tribes; and particularly those of Koreith and Kendeh; the former using to bury their daughters alive in Mount Abu Dalama, near Mecca. In the time of ignorance, while they used this method to get rid of their daughters, Sasaa, grandfather to the celebrated poet Al Farazdak, frequently redeemed female children from death, giving for every one two she-camels big with young, and a he-camel; and hereto Al Farazdak alluded, when, vaunting himself before one of the Kalifs of the family of Meya, he said, '*I am the son of the giver of life to the dead!*' For which expression, being

"It is not generally known that persons now alive remember human sacrifices in the holy places near Calcutta. A very respectable man of my acquaintance, himself by accident, and without the means of interfering, *witnessed one of a boy of fourteen or fifteen*, in which nothing was so terrible as the perfect indifference with which the tears, prayers, and caresses, which the poor victim lavished, even on his murderers, were regarded." Journ. vol. ii. p. 150. 315.

censured, he excused himself by alleging the words of the Koran, 'He who saved a soul alive shall be as if he had saved the lives of all mankind.' The Arabs, in murdering their children, were far from being singular, the practice of exposing infants and putting them to death being so common among the ancients, that it is remarked as a thing very extraordinary in the Egyptians that they brought up all their children; and by the laws of Lycurgus no child was allowed to be brought up without the approbation of public officers. At this day, it is said, in China the poorer sort of people frequently put their children, the females especially, to death with impunity."*

Colonel Walker, in a highly interesting document repecting Infanticide, of considerable length, addressed to the Bombay Government, March, 1808, states upon this subject,—"However extraordinary the practice of Female Infanticide among the Jahreja Rajpoots may appear, it is not confined to the Jahrejas. The practice of female Infanticide prevails with the Rajkoomars and other tribes in Bengal. The custom of putting their infant daughters to death has also been discovered to exist with the Rhatore Rajpoots of Jeypore and Jhoodpoor; but this fact, when reported in Europe, was doubted and denied to be possible. It is confirmed, however, by every intelligent and well informed native of that country; nor does there appear any ground whatever for questioning its existence. The existtence of the custom is traced to other tribes of Hindostan, and in particular to the Jauts and Mewats, which latter are a sect of Mussulmans. It would be interesting to trace and develope the laws and customs of the most distinguished people of antiquity which sanctioned Infanticide. If we except the fabulous history of the Amazons, I am not aware that we have any account of a positive law or custom for the regular and invariable destruction of children of either sex. The Amazons are said to have formed a state from which they excluded men. They held a commerce only with strangers, and for the purpose merely of having daughters. They killed their male children, and cut off the right breast of their females, to render them more fit for war. The method of the ancients in exposing their children was a very general practice, and they do not appear to have considered it as either cruel or barbarous. Romulus is said

* Par. Papers, as above, pp. 58, 59.

to have laid the citizens under an obligation to educate all their male children, and *the eldest of their daughters!* The requiring of this obligation from the citizens must have been suggested by *the necessity of restraining the practice of Infanticide;* and Romulus probably trusted in procuring wives for his males from the other tribes in his neighbourhood, with as little difficulty as the Jahrejas do at present.

" Montesquieu proves that the same motives prevailed with the Roman fathers for exposing their children as with the nations of India, who commit Infanticide. 'We find not any Roman law that permitted the exposing of children. This was, without doubt, an abuse introduced towards the decline of the Republic, when luxury robbed them of their freedom; when wealth divided was called poverty; when the father believed all was lost which he gave to his family and when the family was distinct from his property.' It appears that infants newly born were placed on the ground: those who were agreeable to the father he took up, or educated; but those who were displeasing to him he neglected and exposed. In Greece, Infanticide, or the exposure of children, appears to have formed a part of the policy of those states. *Solon gave permission by the law to parents to kill their children!* Aristotle appears an advocate for the exposing of children; and conceives, where this is not the case, that the number of those brought forth ought to be limited. He proposes expedients for this purpose more barbarous than any usage of the Jahrejas! The Greeks appear to have been led to expose their offspring from the sterility of their territory, and the apprehension of want, excited by a redundant population. The same motive, arising from a fear of famine, has induced the government of China, if not to permit, at least to tolerate, parents to sell and expose their children.

" In Robertson's history of America we are informed that the difficulty of training up an infant to maturity, amidst the hardships of savage life, often stifles the voice of nature among the Americans, and suppresses the strong emotions of parental tenderness. Some of these women are stated, in particular, to destroy their female children in their infancy. At Otaheite, and other islands of the Pacific, a peculiar society exists who destroy their children;* and

---

* This has been happily abolished: see Ellis's Tour in Hawaii, pp. 303—305. The Rev. Mr. Knott, a missionary in the South Sea Islands,

other nations in a rude state have been found, who do not suffer those to live who are born with any natural defect or deformity. However disgusting it may be to human nature, we find that many nations have tolerated or permitted parents to destroy their own offspring, and we are certain that parents have deprived their children of life by availing themselves of this privilege; but the custom of exclusively murdering females (although the regulations of Romulus evidently point to their destruction in preference to that of the males), and a *systematical Infanticide, seem to be confined to the Rajpoots of India.*"*

"The missionaries in New Zealand had repeatedly heard that female infanticide was practised among its inhabitants; and one day in August, 1824, the melancholy fact was confirmed by a chief, who a short time previously had saved his own child from this fate, out of the hands of its inhuman mother! She had twice attempted to put it to death soon after it was born. The brethren entered into a free conversation with the natives on the subject, and they spoke of it with pleasure rather than otherwise, and referred them to several of the most respectable females with whom they were acquainted, who had thus destroyed their children. The manner of putting them to death is, by what they call *ro-mea*, or squeezing the nose, as soon as they are born; then the hypocritical mother cuts herself with shells, and makes a great outcry about her dead child. The reasons which they assigned for this practice were two:—The first, and perhaps the principal one, was that they were no good to them in war; for they would only shout and make a noise, but not fight. The other was, that where the offspring is numerous, they make the mother too much work, &c., therefore she kills the girls, but saves the boys. We endeavoured to show them the impolicy and wickedness of such proceedings, telling them that it was murder, in the sight of God; but they said it was not, it was only *ro-mea*, or squeezing the nose. Oh when will the bright rays of the gospel chase away their gloom, and deliver them from their wickedness."†

"The Jahrejas," says Colonel Walker in a letter to the

---

stated that a female presented to him a child, and said that it was indebted to him for its life: she had had *five children and murdered them all!*

* Par. Papers, vol. i. p. 44, 45.

† Smith's History of Missions, vol. ii. p. 748.

Court of Directors in August, 1819, "are aware that the custom of Infanticide is followed by other tribes besides their own. Although we have not discovered the motive that has led so many people to adopt this unnatural and remarkable custom, it is probably among them all to be ascribed to the same event, and to the same origin. The sacrifice is confined, it would appear, to females, and to Rajpoots, or such as claim their descent from that military race. Among a people devoted to war, and peculiarly exposed to danger, the rearing of their daughters may often have been an object of great difficulty, and in some situations they may have proved an impediment to the profession of arms. They may therefore have made this sacrifice on some emergency, to their convenience and even to their safety; or, if we choose to ascribe it to a dreadful superstition very prevalent in ancient times, as the means of appeasing the wrath or of propitiating the favour of the gods. We are told that the ancient nations assigned this as their reason for having recourse to similar sacrifices: 'They thought nothing,' says Polybius, 'sordid or dishonourable that is employed in that design.' The senate of Carthage proposed to sacrifice the infant son of Hannibal, after he had gained the battles of Teeinus and Trebia.

We may assume it is an unquestionable fact, that the existence of female Infanticide prevails to a greater extent in India than has yet come under the observation of the British Government. The knowledge of this fact would, until lately, have been productive of little more than to gratify a melancholy and speculative curiosity. It might have added to the list of those offences which are contrary to the common course of nature, without affording an opportunity of correcting this particular departure from duty and affection. The case is now very much altered; and the same inquiry at this moment might be attended, not merely with the discovery of the existence of the fact, but enable us, *by the means we possess at present, to suppress every where this revolting crime within the region of Hindostan.* Many of the Districts in which the practice is supposed to prevail have either fallen under the influence or the actual Government of Great Britain. Many of those people are become our subjects, and *we are bound in duty, as well as honour, to reclaim them from the reproach of killing their own children!* I am certain that the Company's Government requires no other excitement nor encouragement for undertakiug this humane work, than would result from the probability of their success."*

Who does not blush for the degradation and depravity of human nature? In civilized countries these well authenticated statements appear almost beyond credibility: but the ancient prevalence of human sacrifices may dispose the reader to receive with painful credence the affecting accounts of the present state of Infanticide in India contained in this book.

CHAP. II.

Infanticide in India.—Origin—nature—crime—extent—present state—demoralizing influence.

Infanticide appears principally to exist at the present period in India and China. Of its prevalence in China a Missionary writes:—"A man came to me for medicine, with whom I conversed awhile privately. I asked him how long he had left China, and whether he ever thought upon his family there? He said he frequently thought on them, and intended next year to return and visit them, for he had three sons, and one daughter who was married. 'I had another daughter,' he added, 'but I did not bring her up.' 'Not bring her up,' said I; 'what then did you do with her?' 'I smothered her,' said he. 'This year also, I heard by letter, that another daughter was born: I sent word to have that smothered also, but the mother has preserved her alive.' I was shocked at this speech; and still more at the indifference with which he uttered it. 'What!' said I, 'murder your own children! Do you not shudder at such an act?' 'Oh no,' said he; 'it is a very common thing in China; we put the female children out of the way to save the trouble of bringing them up: some people

---

* Par. Papers, 1824, p. 127, 128. For farther information upon this subject, see *Grotius' de Satisfi Christi, c. x. Dr. J. Owen, de Nat. Veræ Theol.* c. viii. *p.* 33—41. *Magee's work on Atonement and Sacrifice, Dis.* v. *p.* 3.

have smothered five or six daughters !' My horror was increased by his continued indifference, and the lightness with which such crimes are perpetrated in China with impunity. What an awful view does this present of the 'Celestial Empire, loaded with crime, deluged with blood, and ripe for destruction!"

Of the internal state of China, little is known in Europe, but the paramount influence of Great Britain in Hindostan, renders the subject, under discussion, peculiarly interesting in this country.

"The people in some parts of India," says the late Rev. W. Ward, "particularly the inhabitants of Orissa, and of the eastern parts of Bengal, frequently offer their children to the goddess Gunga. The following reason is assigned for this practice :—When a woman has been long married, and has no children, it is common for the man, or his wife, or both of them, to make a vow to the goddess Gunga, that, if she will bestow the blessing of children upon them, they will devote the first-born to her. If after this vow they have children, the eldest is nourished till a proper age, which may be three, four, or more years, according to circumstances, when, on a particular day appointed for bathing in any holy part of the river, they take the child with them, and offer it to this goddess: the child is encouraged to go farther and farther into the water till it is carried away by the stream, or is pushed off by its inhuman parents. Sometimes a stranger seizes the child, and brings it up; but it is abandoned by its parents from the moment it floats in the water, and, if no one be found more humane than they, it infallibly perishes! The principal places in Bengal where this species of murder is practised are, Gunga, Saugur, where the river Hooghly disembogues itself into the sea; Voidyuvatee, a town about fourteen miles to the north of Calcutta; Trivinee, Nudeeya, Chakduh, and Prayag or Allahabad.*

"The following shocking custom appears to prevail principally in the northern Districts of Bengal. If an infant refuse the mother's breast, and decline in health, it is said to be under the influence of some malignant spirit. Such a child is sometimes put into a basket, and hung up in a tree where the evil spirit is supposed to reside. It is

* See the proceedings of the British Government with regard to Infanticide at these places in the latter part of this book.

dren were born; and as, among the Hindoos, it is incumbent to provide husbands for their daughters whilst they are in their non-age, the Jahreja chieftain applied accordingly to his family Brahmun to pursue the necessary measures for getting the said female children contracted in marriage with the sons of his equals in the tribe, and of like valour and power. The Brahmun, after making every inquiry, and going about to every place in quest of suitable matches for these children, returned without effecting his object; reporting it to the chieftain that, although he had exerted all his endeavours to find proper alliances for his female children, still he had not traced any one who was of competent qualifications to be his son-in-law: wherefore (said the Brahmun), since to retain these, your female offspring, in the family house, after their arriving at the age of womanhood, is contrary to the rules of religion, I will take them with me, and will burn them in the fire, on condition that it be stipulated on your part, to destroy, at their birth, all issue of the same sex that shall be born in your family. I now lay my solemn malediction, both here and hereafter, on you and yours, if you fail to perform the same; in such manner, that, if you shall preserve any of your future daughters, they shall pass their lives in penury and want; nor shall good attend the father or mother of such children. It is further reported that the Brahmun took away those innocent girls, and consumed them in the flames; and that, in conformity to the stipulation and denunciation aforesaid, the people of the Jahreja tribes, dwelling in the country of Cutch, and in the Pergunnahs of Hallar, and other places within the Peninsula of Guzerat, have to the present day continued to adhere to the practice in question; whereby, whenever a daughter is born, they put these helpless babes, without compassion, to death; without allowing their surviving for the shortest space."

Being interrogated respecting Adeeba, the daughter of Ralakjee, former Rajah of Cutch, who was married to one of the Guicowar Rajahs, he replied,—" It is true Adeeba is still surviving at Booj, the capital of Cutch, yet there are but few exceptions, such as in this instance, to the general rule, because, from the effect of the malediction pronounced, no good ensues from their preservation; insomuch that if any daughters of this tribe get married into other houses, the grain in such houses becomes less plentiful; nor do such women produce sons, but are the occasion of feuds arising in the families into which they are thus transplanted! Throughout all the country of Cutch there may be six or eight houses wherein the Jahreja masters of families bring up their daughters; or otherwise, the practice is general; and, besides what happens within the limits of that country, the Jahreja chieftains of Moorvee, Goondul, and Jamnagur, in the Peninsula of Guzerat, also kill their female infants. Those who occasionally preserve their daughters are induced by the consideration of thereby acquiring the merit of having sons born to them; as, for instance, when a man has a succession of female children in his family, he will, at the suggestion of any one, be induced to believe that, by bringing them up, sons will also be born to him; whence chiefly Jahreja daughters are sometimes met with, of whom there is within my recollection another instance, in the case of the Roe chieftain of Cutch, by name Vijrajee, who has married a daughter of his to the son of Attabye, the Rajah of Bhownaguth; that lady may now be about twenty or twenty-two years of age, but I have not heard that she has yet had any male issue, but that, on the contrary, her husband and she do not agree."*

Colonel Walker endeavours to account for the rise of this singular practice as follows:—"Before I proceed to detail its progress and circumstances, I shall endeavour to ascertain the origin and history of a practice, the most barbarous that ever owed its existence either to the wickedness or weakness of human nature. The early customs and history of every people are obscure and fabulous. The Hindoos, with a facility proportionate to their credulity, generally ascribe their peculiar institutions to a divine origin: and, by connecting their observance with religious duties, they have passed inviolate through many ages. This, probably more than any other cause, has maintained that great distinction which is evident between the Hindoos and other nations, and also between their own castes. When the customs or rites of any people are harmless, whatever form they assume, and from whatever source they may be derived, they are entitled to toleration and protection; *but they ought to be punished or amended when their evident tendency is to diminish population, and to alienate the natural affections of mankind.* Of this description is the custom of female Infanticide, which prevails among the tribe of Rajputes, denominated Jahrejas. The

---

* Par. Papers, 1824, p. 23.

traditionary and legendary accounts of the Hindoos, although sometimes ingenious, are often the extravagant fictions of a rude and superstitious people; but the oral accounts of the atrocious custom of Infanticide are comprised in a simple narrative, and exhibit under a slight disguise a remote historical event.

"The Jahrejas relate that a powerful Rajah of their caste, who had a daughter of singular beauty and accomplishments, desired his rajgor, or family Brahmun, to affiance her to a prince of desert and rank equal to her own. The rajgor travelled over many countries without discovering a chief who possessed the requisite qualities; for, where wealth and power were combined, personal accomplishments and virtue were defective; in like manner, where the advantages of the mind and the body were united, those of fortune and rank were wanting. The rajgor returned and reported to the prince that his mission had not proved successful. This intelligence gave the Rajah much concern, as the Hindoos reckon it to be the first duty of parents to provide suitable husbands for their daughters; and it is reproachful that they should pass the age of puberty without having been affianced, and under the necessity of living in a state of celibacy. The Rajah, however, strongly reprobated every match for his daughter which he conceived inferior to her high rank and perfection. In this dilemma the Rajah consulted his rajgor, and he advised him to avoid the disgrace which would attend the princess's remaining unmarried, by having recourse to the desperate expedient of putting his daughter to death. The Rajah was long averse to this expedient, and remonstrated against the murder of a woman, which, enormous as it is represented in the shastras, would be aggravated when committed on his own offspring. The rajgor at length removed the Rajah's scruples by consenting to load himself with the guilt, and to become in his own person responsible for all the consequences of the sin. Accordingly the princess was put to death, and female Infanticide was from that time practised by the Jahrejas. From this narrative curiosity receives little gratification. It resembles the tales of infancy, rather than the grave history of a transaction involving the fate of a numerous portion of the human race. This, however, comprises all the information which the Jahrejas possess of the origin of a custom so contrary to the dictates of nature, and which is justifiable on no plea, as it gratifies no reasonable passion. Notwithstanding this unsatisfactory account of the origin of Infanticide, many absurd institutions like this are dependent less on reason than on particular circumstances, which in the course of many ages, give them importance and influence."*

"I have met with an account of Infanticide," the Colonel further observes, "which ascribes its origin to a circumstance more probable than the disappointment felt by the Rajah at not finding a suitable match for his daughter. It is said that one of the early Mussalman invaders of the Jahrejas' country, who experienced the determination with which they defended their liberties, united policy to arms, and sought to consolidate their interests in the country, by demanding the daughters of the Rajahs in marriage. The high-spirited Jahrejas would not brook the disgrace, and pretended they did not preserve their daughters; but, fearful of the consequences, and that force would be resorted to in order to obtain what was refused to entreaty, they listened to the advice of their Rajgors in this extremity, and, deluded by the fictitious responsibility which they accepted, the practice of Infanticide originated, and has since been confirmed. In consistency with this relation is an account which I have heard of one of the Rajahs of Noanuggur, whose daughter was demanded in marriage by the Emperor of Delhi, and which also throws some light upon the doubtful point, whether a grown-up daughter is ever put to death. It appears that although much discredit would attach to a Jehreja who killed his daughter, after having preserved her for any time, yet that such occurrences, however unfrequent, are not without precedent. In some period of the history of the Jahrejas, it is said that one of the Jams was despoiled of his country by the king of Delhi, who promised to restore it, provided Jam gave him a daughter, whom he had preserved, in marriage. This must have been a legitimate daughter, as Jam disdainfully rejected the alliance, and transmitted his refusal through the governor of Ahmedabad, who was the medium of the proposal on the part of his sovereign. After some time was given to reflection, Jam was counselled by his friends apparently to comply and to depart for Delhi, accompanied by his daughter; when he might evade the disgrace, save his honour, and recover his country, by putting his daughter to death, and give out that she died of sick-

* Par. Papers on Infan., 1824, p. 31, 32.

ness or fatigue during the journey. The plan was put into execution, and this conduct does not appear to have received the disapprobation of the caste; probably it was applauded."*

The nature of Infanticide, or the manner in which the horrid practice is perpetrated, like its origin, is involved in considerable obscurity. J. Duncan, Esq., Resident at Benares, in 1789, in his enquiries upon the subject, was informed that the Rajkoomars "killed their infant daughters, or allowed them to die, by denying them all sustenance from their birth."† The same gentleman, when Governor of Bombay, in a conversation with Gajra Bye, daughter of one of the Guicowar Princes, of Guzerat, in February, 1804, incidentally ascertained the existence of Infanticide in Cutch. On enquiry from Captain Seton, stationed at Mandavee, it was stated,—"The custom mentioned in Gajra Bye's relation is in force to this day. Every female infant born in the Rajah's family, if of a Ranne or lawful wife, is immediately dropped into a hole dug in the earth and filled with milk, where it is drowned."‡

"Curiosity," says Colonel Walker, "will naturally be excited to learn the methods observed in committing these Infanticides; and whether they were attended by any compunction and ceremony. The common expressions for Infanticide are "*Deekree Marne ne Chal,*" or "the custom of killing daughters;" and "*Naree Deekree Marne ne Chal,*" or "the custom of killing young daughters." In conversation, and in discussing the subject with the Jahrejas, the term used was "*Deekree Babut,*" or "the article of girls." The subject is disgusting, and I shall endeavour to state briefly the result of my enquiries. Although the Jahrejas spoke freely of the custom of putting their daughters to death, without delicacy, and without pain, they were more reserved on the mode of their execution, and appeared at first unwilling to be questioned on the subject. They usually replied that *it was an affair of the women; it belonged to the nursery, and made no part of the business of the men.* They at last threw off this reserve.

"The following is the translation of a memorandum from Wassonjee Eswarjee, a Nagur Brahmun, who attended the camp in the quality of Vakeel from the Gondul Chief.

* Par. Papers, p. 52, 53. † p. 7. ‡ p. 20.

'When the wives of the Jahreja Rajputes are delivered of daughters, the women, who may be with the mother, repair to the oldest man in the house; this person desires them to go to him who is the father of the infant, and do as he directs. On this the women go to the father, who desires them *to do as is customary,* and so to inform the mother. The women then repair to the mother, and tell her to act in conformity with their usages. The mother next puts opium on the nipple of her breast, which the child inhaling with its milk, dies! The above is one custom, and the following is another: When the child is born, they place the navel-string on its mouth, and it expires.' From the conversations of the Jahrejas, it appears that the opium is put into the mouth of the child; but the mode of administering this drug, described by Wassongee, may have given rise to the opinion that the Jahrejas drown their daughters by throwing them, as soon as they are born, into a vessel of milk. From every enquiry, I could not understand that the Jahrejas ever put their daughters to death after this manner; but the story may have had its origin in the idea of the infant's imbibing poisoned milk, or from an expression which is ascribed to the father, who, when the birth of a daughter is announced, with brutal equivocation, says to the attendants '*Dhood Pillana.*' This is but a popular story; and, independently of the circumstance of few infants sucking immediately on their birth, the placing of opium on the nipple would effectually prevent it. The true manner by which the Jahrejas kill their daughters, as received from the chieftains of Rajkote and Jallia, is subsequently related.

"If a father wishes to preserve a daughter, he previously apprises his wife and family, and his commands are obeyed. If a mother entertains a wish of preserving a daughter, and her husband is averse to it, the infant must be put to death! There are, however, instances where the blandishments and influence of the mother have succeeded in saving the infant, by obtaining the revocation of the decree for its destruction, but these instances of maternal solicitude are either unfrequent or but seldom successful. The father sometimes expressly orders the infant to be put to death, probably when he suspects some intention of the mother to preserve it; but in general this sanguinary intimation is unnecessary; *a total silence on the part of the husband*

is considered to imply his unalterable resolution that the child, if a female, should perish!

"To render this deed if possible more horrible, ***the mother is commonly the executioner of her own offspring!*** Women of rank may have their slaves and attendants, who perform this office; but the far greater number execute it with their own hands. This compliance of the women must appear the more extraordinary, as they belong to castes who rear their females, and are brought up in families where their own existence is evidence against the unnatural practice: but as they are betrothed at an early age they imbibe the superstition of their husbands, and some of them appeared even as advocates for this custom. They have been known to pride themselves like the Jahrejas, and to consider their murder as an act of duty; an act which these females, who are mild, modest, and affectionate, would, if married into any other caste, hold in detestation. They appear to have several methods of destroying the infant, but two are prevalent. Immediately after the birth of a female, they put into its mouth some opinm, or draw the umbilical cord over its face, which prevents its respiration. But the destruction of so young and tender a subject is not difficult, and it is probably effected without a struggle. The natural weakness of the infant, when neglected and left uncleaned some time, causes its death, without the necessity of actual violence; and sometimes it is laid on the ground, or on a plank, and left to expire! These accounts I learned in conversation with Jahrejas, and prefer them to the information of the translated memorandum. The infant, after it is destroyed, is placed in a small basket entirely naked, and in this state carried out and interred. In Kattywar any of the female attendants of the family perform this office; but in Cutch it is done by the domestic Rajgor. The Rajgors who bury the infants that perish receive a fee of one koree, which is a coin equivalent in value to one-third of a rupee (about ten pence sterling), and a meal. In Cutch the female Rajgors are the executioners of the infant instead of the mother, and this seems to approach nearer to the origin of the custom.

"The birth of a daughter is considered by the Hindoos of every description as an inferior event, and they rarely make it the subject of congratulation; while the birth of a son is celebrated with great ostentation and hilarity. It is not, therefore, surprising, that on the birth of a daughter, which they may have even preserved, and predetermined to bring up, a Jahreja family should discover no demonstration of joy. The event is allowed to pass over in silence, as if they were ashamed of it. Should any inquisitive person ask a Jahreja the result of the pregnancy of his wife, if it were a female, he would answer '*nothing;*' and this expression, in the idiom of the country, is sufficiently significant. *The infant is invariably put to death immediately on its birth, and it would be considered a cruel and barbarous action to deprive it of life after it had been allowed to live a day or two.* Although instances of this deliberate murder may be very rare, yet from the examination of a Jahreja, who was reported to me as having been guilty of this deed, I have reason to believe they sometimes occur. The death of a daughter is generally viewed by a Jahreja as an infallible consequence after its birth; and it is considered to be an event of such insignificance that he is seldom apprized of it! The occurrence excites neither surprise nor enquiry: and is never made a subject even of conversation. It is attended by no ceremony, and publicity is avoided. Jussajee, of Jallia, has had *three daughters;* they were all put to death at the time of their birth. Jussajee attended the camp; he is a man of intelligence, and served the detachment as a guide. His character and disposition, both for humanity and propriety, are favourable; but he has not the least compunction for the murder of these children, and considers the deed to be, in every respect, justifiable."*

The following is the statement of Jahreja Dadajee, chief of Rajcote; "Many of the Jahrejas of Cutch preserve their daughters, and, previous to the birth of a child, the father, if he wishes to preserve the child, signifies such a wish, and his will is invariably obeyed; if the mother wishes, and the father is averse to preserve his daughter, it is killed! Exceptions to this take place now and then, when the mother has great influence over the father. When the daughters are killed, they are almost invariably put to death immediately after their birth. On the birth of a daughter, the mothers very seldom apprize the father, but put it to death at once. Daughters, when put to death, are always buried in the state in which they are born, without any purification, or being wrapped in any clothes. Dadajee

* Par. Papers, 1824, p. 35—37.

has a daughter alive. He states that he expressed a wish to preserve it previously to its birth. Some Jahrejas preserve their daughters that may be born within the space of six months after the death of a chief: though this is little observed, it is still reckoned proper; but he says that avarice, or other passions of the parent, make them disregard this practice. He says there is no uniform mode of killing the infants. Sometimes they terminate their life by opium, sometimes by placing the navel-string on their mouth and suffocating them. Dadajee, on being interrogated as to any other mode, said, in reply, '*What difficulty is there in blasting a flower?*' He observes, there is no impropriety in Jahrejas' preserving their daughters. Sometimes the mothers, if there are no female attendants, kill their infants themselves; but, in general, women of station never perform this unnatural office. In allusion to this subject, as descriptive of the motives for Infanticide, he states, that in Kattywar and Hallaur the rubbaries or goatherds allow their male kids to die when there are many of them brought forth; and the charons follow the same practice with their male buffaloes, both being reckoned unproductive, in a country where little flesh is consumed, and the only profit which arises from these animals is from their milk!"*

In Zillah Furruckabad, Bareilly Division, in Sep. 1806, a man was tried for the murder of his child. The atrocious act is thus described by the murderer:—"About twenty days ago a daughter was born in my house, about a little time before sun-set. On the same day, in the evening, I, the deponent, on account of the ancient customs of my tribe of not contracting our daughters in marriage with any one, as well as from my ignorance of the regulations of justice, and the contents of the proclamation made with respect to refraining from murdering of daughters, and likewise from my dwelling in the jageer, depending upon the Nawab of Khurudmund Khan; on this account I took out of my house some of the juice of the Ag tree (a deadly poison) and caused my new-born child to drink it. At about ten o'clock at night my daughter expired. I was not acquainted with the Company's regulations, if I had, I should never have committed this crime: now, that I am acquainted with them, I will never again commit the same crime." He was ultimately pardoned on the ground of his ignorance.†

* Par. Papers, 1824, p. 68. † Par. Papers on Infan. 1828, p. 33, 34.

The crime of female murder is very great according to the Hindoo shastras.—" The doctrines of the Hindoo religion have been singularly careful to protect the female sex and infants from violence; and it is unlawful to put a woman to death for any offence whatever. In support of this opinion they quote the following sloke or verse:—

Shut gao wudhe vepra
Shut vepra wudhe istreea
Shut istreea wudhe bala
Shut bala wudhe muresha.

'To kill one Brahmun is equal to one hundred cows:
'To kill one woman is equal to one hundred Brahmuns:
'To kill one child is equal to one hundred women:
'To kill one hundred children is an offence too heinous for comparison.'

The crime therefore of killing a woman is considered as great a sin as killing a hundred Brahmuns; and the sin of killing a young child of either sex is equal to killing a hundred women."*

J. Duncan, Esq., while Resident at Benares procured a translation of an extract from a Hindoo shastra, in which the same sentiments are expressed.—" Let all the four castes of Brahmun, Khetry, Bys, and Sooder, know that *the killing of a woman is the greatest of crimes.* The person guilty of such act, having gone into the nerk or hill called Kal Sooter, shall remain there without nourishment, and be gnawed by worms for as many years as there are hairs on the woman's body, and shall remain there always in pain and misery; and afterwards, being born again in the lesser castes, shall become a leper for the same number of years; and thereafter, becoming of the cast of Sooder, shall be afflicted with the zukhma, or vomiting of blood. Being again born of that cast, he becomes the servant or valet of a Brahmun, by which he is exonerated. In the same Pooran it is written, that causing abortion is equal to killing a Brahmun. It is distinguished by the name of broon hettea."† How ignorant of, or inattentive to, their own shastras must these people be, to perpetrate these inhuman acts of cruel murder! Can there be any impropriety in the British Government abolishing the *Suttee*, by which practice hundreds of women are annually murdered?

---

* Par. Papers, 1824, p. 42. † Par. Papers, 1824, pp. 7, 8.

The extent and present state of this cruel custom appear by the following extracts from the Par. Papers on Infanticide of 1824 and 1828. The Papers of 1828 contain the most recent account of the state of Infanticide in the districts of Cutch and Cattywar, in Benares and other parts of the territories under the Bengal Presidency, and also under the Presidency of Fort St. George. The Papers of 1824, which contain the most information, are divided into four parts.

Part the first contains "*Papers relating to Infanticide, practised by the Rajkoomars, Rajevanses, &c., in Benares and other parts of the territories under the Bengal Presidency, and in the state of Oude:* 1789 *to* 1820, pp. 5—16.

Of the Rajkoomars, Rajevansees, &c., J. Duncan, Esq. in April, 1789 (referring to the favourable description of the country), observes,—"The only very unfavourable instance of this kind that has come before me has happened in the Mehal of Juanpoor, and its immediate dependencies, which comprehend the Purgunnah of Juanpoor proper. The small ones of Raury and Augle; the Salt Mehal of Zufferabad; together with two distinct Talooks, called Kereeat Dowst and Kereeat Mhera, and the independent frontier Talooka, of Singramow. The people I mean to describe consist of at least three distinct classes, which it is my duty in this address to bring to the knowledge of Government, that they may hereafter be treated as your Lordship in Council may think fit. The first class is the tribe of Rajekoomars, who deduce their descent from Rajah Pethawra (in whom about 600 years ago ended the Chowhan dynasty of the Princes of Delhi), and from whose stock the present race of the Rajkoomars (who then assumed this new family denomination) is believed to be sprung. It is said their numbers do not altogether exceed 40,000, most of whom inhabit, in nearly one society, the opposite line of our boundary, in his Excellency the Vixier's dominions; but unfortunately for the quiet of both countries they possess lands that pay about 20,000 rupees revenue in Augle and Rereeat Mhera, on our side. They were originally Rajpoots; and even exceeded that tribe in the wildness of their notions, and peculiarity of their manners, scarcely owing any allegiance either to the Nabobs or our Government, and always ready to betake themselves to arms, to which they are inured from infancy, either in resentment of public or private wrongs, real or imaginary; at the same time, I am assured, they have a point of honour from which they do not deviate, and are famous for faithfully adhering to those engagements into which they are pleased to enter."*

Sir John Shore (now Lord Teignmouth), in a Paper on the Customs and Practices of the Hindoos, has the following observations on the subject:—"That the practice of Infanticide should ever be so general as to become a custom with any sect or race of people requires the most unexceptionable evidence to gain belief; and I am sorry to say that the general practice, as far as regards female infants, is fully substantiated with respect to a particular tribe on the frontiers of Juanpore, a district of the province of Benares, adjoining to the country of Oude. A race of Hindoos, called Rajkoomars, reside here; and it was discovered in 1789 only, that the custom of putting to death the female offspring, by causing the mothers to starve them, had long subsisted, and did actually then very generally prevail among them. The Resident at Benares, in a circuit which he made through the country where the Rajkoomars dwell, had an opportunity of authenticating the existence of the custom from their own confessions; he conversed with several; all unequivocally admitted it, but all did not fully acknowledge its atrocity; and the only reason which they assigned for the inhuman practice was the great expense of procuring suitable matches for their daughters if they allowed them to grow up! It is some satisfaction to add that the custom, though general, was not universal, as natural affection, or some other motive, had induced the fathers of some Rajkoomar families to bring up one or more of their female issue; but the instances *where more than one daughter had been spared were very rare!* One village only furnished a complete exception to the general custom; and the Rajkoomar informant, who noticed it, supposed that the inhabitants had sworn, or solemnly pledged themselves to each other, to bring up their females; in proof of his assertion in favour of the village in question, he added, that several old maids of the Rajkoomar tribe then actually existed there, and that their celibacy proceeded from the difficulty of procuring husbands for them, in consequence of the great expenses attending the marriages of this class of people."†

---

* Par. Papers, 1824, p. 5. † Asi. Res. vol. iv. p. 5.

E. Smith, Esq., Second Judge of the Benares Circuit Court, Jan. 1813, observes,—"Juanpore is a district which requires a most vigorous hand; indeed there is no keeping it in order, perhaps, but by a vigour somewhat beyond the law. The most turbulent of the Pergunnahs is Unglee, inhabited principally by the Rajkoomar Rajpoots, *the daughter-killing-race*, who are supposed to carry on that practice in spite of Regulation XXI. of 1795. Indeed it is said not to be confined to the Rajkoomar Rajpoots, but to be common with the Raghoovansee bur, and other Rajpoots; it is now of course practised with much more secrecy than formerly, but it is still, I understand, by no means at an end."*

J. Shakspeare, Esq., Acting Superintendent of Police in the Western Provinces, thus speaks of the state of Infanticide in April, 1816: "Section XI. Regulation III., 1804, contains provisions for the prevention and punishment of the inhuman practice prevalent among the tribe of Rajkoomars, of causing their female infants to be strangled to death. There is reason to believe that *this practice still obtains among the Rajkoomars to nearly the same extent as formerly*, though a great degree of caution is observed to prevent detection. In the records of this office I find a few reports from Darogahs in former years of the murder of female children, by mixing their food with the milky juice of the plant *aselepias gigantica*, known in Bengal by the name of *akond*, and by that of *ack* in Hindostan. This mode of destroying their offspring is said to be still commonly practised. Some few instances have been reported, during the last year, of persons destroying their children with the intention of revenging themselves for actual or supposed injuries, under the impression that the sin of murder would be visited on the persons by whom they were aggrieved."†

W. Cracroft, Esq., Magistrate of Juanpore, in May, 1819, shows the existence of the practice at that period:— "Eight Rajkoomars, married men, whom I called before me, had among them *seventeen sons and only one daughter!* another mentioned that he had a wife whom her father had reared, but that her dowry had ruined the family. Surubdoween Singh, who is a Rajkoomar, of the Nawab's country, has a sister twelve years old, whose wedding has been settled in Bauswarrah; he has also a daughter three

---

* Par. Papers, p. 13. † p. 14.

months old, whom he has promised to rear. Talem Singh, his grandfather, also brought up a daughter, who is a widow, and lives in Busera. Soogreem Singh, his son, has also reared a daughter, who is eight years old, but her marriage has not been determined on. There are some families, therefore, among them who would willingly rear their daughters, but those are very few; and, if by any misfortune their circumstances should become reduced, they would not hesitate to have recourse to the practice of the caste. Should you require farther information respecting Unglee, or the Rajkoomars, I request you will do me the favour to state specifically the subjects on which you wish me to report."*

The Par. Papers respecting the Burning of Widows (vol. i. 1821): contain the following confirmation of this lamentable state of society: The magistrate of Agra, in the Suttee Report of 1816, remarks,—"The practice of burning women on the funeral piles of their husbands does not exist in this district in the same degree as in others; the reason of this may be ascribed to *the prevalence of female child murder*. It is well known that no Rajpoot allows a daughter to live: their wives are of other castes, and consequently not obliged to sacrifice themselves."† "The practice of the Rajkoomars (says W. Ewer, Esq., Act. Sup. of Police, Lower Provinces) is, I have reason to think, *but little checked by the enactment*."‡ Nov. 1818.

Part the second of the Par. Papers of 1824 relates to "*Infanticide practised by the Rajpoots in the District of Cutch and Kattywar, a District of Guzerat, within the Dominions of the Guikwar:* 1800 *to* 1808." pp. 17—70.

The subject is first noticed in a report from Kerpa Rama, minister of the Nawaub of Surat, received by J. Duncan, Esq., Governor of Bombay in 1800:—"I have heard people say," said the Minister, "that among the tribe of Rajpoots, and especially among the Rajahs of that class, the birth of a daughter in their houses was considered as disgraceful; on which account their women refuse to let their newly-born daughters have access to their milk, and do put them in any

* Par. Papers, p. 16.

† The Court of Nizamut Adawlut declare child murder to be contrary to the existing law of 1804, and wish to know how this can have been evaded.

‡ Par. Papers relative to Suttees, vol. i. p 104.

way to death; but this practice is not general through all the subdivisions of their tribe, though in several places they do thus stony-heartedly kill them."* The same gentleman received from Gajra Bye, a daughter of a Guicowar prince of Guzerat, the following intelligence, Feb. 1804: "Damaji Guikwar carried his arms as far as to Cutch, with the Rajah of which a reconciliation took place, on condition of one of the princesses, his daughters, being given in marriage to Damaji; which lady, named Dankur Bye, lived among the Guikwars till after Damaji's death; when, at her own request, the then Rajah Fatteh Sing permitted her to return to her own family in Cutch."† "This incidental narrative," says the Minute to Government, "from Gajra Bye leading to the question, Whether Dankur Bye had of this marriage any children? it was answered negatively; and Gajra Bye immediately followed up his answer by explaining, that, *among that Lady's caste in Cutch, the daughters are not brought up, but drowned immediately at their birth in a vessel of milk*. Being next questioned how this caste of people upheld their families, he observed, that they are only one of the numerous tribes of Rajpoots among the other subdivisions of which they find wives; and that Dankur Bye was spared in consequence of her extraordinary beauty having excited a particular affection in the breast of her mother."‡

The Honourable the Governor of Bombay delivered the following memorandum on this subject, Dec. 1806:—"A person desired to speak to me, saying he was come from the country of Cutch Boojh, and had something of a secret nature to impart from Roy Dhun, the Rajah of that territory. On this person being admitted he said his name was Sheojee Goorjee; that he is the confidential servant of Roy Dhun, the Rajah of Cutch, that he is sent by him to solicit our aid for his release from the restraint under which that chieftain labours, by being placed in a state of confinement by Futteh Mahomed, whom he states to have subjected the whole country to his will, not, however, from the dread of his power and influence. He admits that his master has no sons; but there is a male child of Prethy Rowjee, his late brother, seven years old, and who is called Luckput. *He confesses they never rear daughters in his master's fa-*

---

* Par. Papers on Infan. p. 19. † p. 19.
‡ Par. Papers, 1824, p. 19. See pp. 20, 21.

*mily; and, being asked the reason, he answers, 'Where have they an equal to whom to be bestowed in marriage?'"**

Colonel Walker in his important document on the subject, dated Baroda, March 1808, gives a full account of the extent of this custom among the Jahrejas:—"The practice of Infanticide appears to have been discontinued by the descendants of the Jahrejas who inhabit Scind, and who have become converts to the Mahomedan religion. I was told, however, of an exception, and that one of these converted tribes, or families, still follows the custom of their ancestors. A few of the Jahrejah tribes of Cutch have also discontinued Infanticide, or practice it but occasionally; for my information was not clear and positive on this point. The following Jahreja families in that country were mentioned as systematically refraining from Infanticide, and their names deserve to be recorded. The families of Bulach, Bottan, Sar Cubbur, Kotee, Ubra, Jarria, Guffun, Murasee, Mokarra, Kuya, Retreea, Mor, Row, Jessa, Dessa, Danrar, Detteea, Joreea, Adreea, Verac, Kunorde, and Veeur, are enumerated as rearing their daughters. Some of these families are of responsibility in Cutch; but the far greater part of the inhabitants follow the practice without the least remorse. In the Peninsula, although some individuals have occasionally preserved their daughters, it appears to have been the result of accidental circumstances and impressions, and not the effect of any steady resolution or principle. *The origin of Infanticide among the Jahrejas is not supposed to be more remote than 500 years.* As no disgrace or stigma is attached to the omission of this act, we might expect that natural affection would prevail over a barbarous custom; but this is overpowered by the influence of habits and prejudices, strengthened by little selfish views of economy and of domestic ease. I endeavoured to ascertain the motives of the Jahrejas who preserved their daughters; and, by their own confession, *this act of humanity did not proceed from parental feelings.* It appeared to be inspired, not by motives of affection for the object, so much as by personal considerations, arising from the ideas of Metempsychosis, which are so universally and rigidly observed by the Shavuch Banians, the followers of Jena. These people consider it a sin to deprive any being or creature, however mean or noxious, of

---

* Par. Papers, p. 27.

life; and their doctrines are said to have made an impression on a few of the Jahrejas.

"It would be an interesting inquiry to ascertain *the number of females who perish annually from this detestable practice of Infanticide.* This could only be effected by a careful research among the Jahreja families, which might determine their number, and obtain a tolerably correct estimate of the casualties. The result of my information was too vague and uncertain to afford any data of an accurate calculation; but it may be useful to state this information, as, although defective, it may convey some determinate notion of the extent of this offence against the first laws of human nature. I shall begin by stating an account which has the appearance of exaggeration. According to a loose computation, the number of Jahreja families inhabiting Cutch and Kattywar is estimated at 125,000, and the number of female infants yearly destroyed to amount to 20,000. Being desirous of reducing this inquiry to a state of greater certainty, I endeavoured to procure a particular list of the Jahrejas inhabiting these countries. I found it impracticable to obtain this information respecting Cutch; but the following is an account of the names and the number of Jahreja families inhabiting Hallaur aud Muchoo Khaunta, furnished by an intelligent native, well acquainted with that extraordinary race:—

A list of the families of the different tribes of Jahrejas who inhabit Hallaur and Muchoo Khaunta:—

Jam Zadeh, the descendants of the Jams	40	Bharanee	100
Hurdols	500	Bhananee	50
Doonguranee	500	Amrun	500
See Sungeea	100	Dil	600
Kubbur	100	Halla	100
Rewanee	100	Hapa	100
Weebanee	500	Khumanee	100
Lakanee	100	Kana	200
Moranee	500	Rao	400
Kunkerya	100	Batach	100
Ummur	100	And other castes	500
			5,390

"*It is supposed that the annual number of Infanticides in the Peninsula of Guzerat amounts to* 5000. The number of Jahrejas in Cutch, on the authority of the natives, is ten times as many as Hallaur and Muchoo Khanta, and this would give us a population of 150,000 men; for all these calculations are exclusive of women and children, who must, from the nature of the case, either be wives or boys. As a number of Jahrejas in that country have disused Infanticide, without any formal renunciation, however, of the practice, the number of deaths may be estimated at 30,000. I shall, lastly, state the lowest estimate that I received of those murders; and, although its moderation may appear in favour of its truth, I am disposed to think this account *as short of the number destroyed as the preceding is probably an exaggeration.* These accounts, it is to be observed, do not pretend to rest on calculation, but convey the opinions of persons well-informed respecting the state of the country. According to this authority, *the number of Infanticides annually in Hallaur and Muchoo Khanta are between* 1000 *and* 1100; *and in Cutch about* 2000! The disagreement of these estimates would probably defeat any attempt to reconcile them, but they are sufficient to establish the enormity and magnitude of the crime.

"Whenever a Jahreja saves his daughter he invariably exerts every means, sometimes to the impoverishment of his family, to obtain a respectable settlement for her in life. It is, perhaps, this strong desire that prevents the lower orders saving their daughters. The instances that were reported to me of Jahrejas who saved their daughters were of families of rank in the country; but these instances of humanity are few. I shall begin with stating the most remarkable of them, as it was the effect of conscience, although operating by a kind of double faculty. The Jahreja, Mokajee of Anundgur, one of the byaud or brotherhood of the Gondul chief, after a short period, renounced matrimonial intercourse with his wife, from the apprehension of having a daughter. This was persevered in for several years, and Mokajee during that period patiently resisted the scoffings and persuasions of his cast and relations, without being in the least diverted from his purpose. The case became serious, aud the family assembled to prevent the misfortune, if possible, of Mokajee dying childless. After every other expedient had failed of success, Koombajee, late chief of Gondul, in his capacity of Teelaat, or head of the family, was obliged to lay a solemn and public injunction on Mokajee, to preserve his daughters. On receiving the order of his superior, Mokajee returned to his wife, and had born to him in succession four daughters; a circumstance which exposed him again to the taunts of the Jahrejas, but which he appears to have supported with philosophical indifference. These daughters are still alive, and are married to the chiefs of Draugudra, Wudwan, Limree, and Wancaneer.

"The motives that led Mokajee to pursue this conduct deserve to be explained. He had become a Kubeer Punt. The Kubeer Punts form a sect of Biragees, who follow the tenets of Kubeer, a holy man who lived about 300 years ago. They deny, in general, the authenticity of the shastras and vedas; and assert that God is one and invisible, possessing in himself every attribute ascribed by the Hindoos to different deities. They deny the debtars or incarnations, and place no confidence in the efficacy of the ceremonies of worship and purification by washing in rivers; but put their whole trust in the sincerity of devotion, and in good works. Kubeer himself was a Mahomedan by cast, and a weaver by profession. His disciples may be either Mahomedans or Hindoos. On his death the Mahomedans claimed a right to bury him; in consequence of which they quarrelled, and placed a sheet over the corpse, which, when they withdrew, they found the upper part of his body to be metamorphosed into a toolsee plant, the favorite nymphæ of Krishna, the lower part into rehan, an odoriferous herb of green colour, the colour of the prophet Mahomed! As a zealous Jahreja, the honour and custom of his cast required that Mokajee should kill his daughters. As a Kubeer Punt, the principles of the sect rendered Infanticide unlawful and criminal. In this situation Mokajee could only avoid disgrace or sin by that course of celibacy which he prescribed for himself, and from which he was relieved by the commands of his chief.

"The chief of Kersura is the next instance of a Jahreja who has brought up his daughter, and who is now married to Wujee Sing, the eldest son of the Thakore of Bhownuggur. The whole merit of this act of humanity is due to an Arab Jemadar, who gave up to this sordid and mercenary chief all the arrears of pay which he had earned in his service, and which amounted to a considerable sum, on condition that he would preserve his daughter.

"It is more pleasing to relate the third instance, as it appears to have proceeded from the natural affections of a parent. Dadajee, the brother of the present chief of Rajkote, has preserved his daughter; and, from his conversation and manners, I was fully impressed that it was the effect of principle and duty. A similar instance occurs in the example of Hootajee, the chieftain of Kotara Sangani, who has preserved all his female offspring. Hootajee is a professed robber, to whom sentiment and feeling might be supposed to be strangers. The profession which he followed did not prevent me conversing with Hootajee, nor avoiding a pretty frequent intercourse with him. This man, with the aspect and manners of a barbarian, possessed all the feelings of natural affection, which led him to cherish his daughters in opposition to the usage and prejudices of his tribe. His daughters are between six and eight years of age, and he brought them to my camp, where they were vaccinated. I observed their father caressing them with pleasure, and exulting in them with true parental satisfaction. Their persons and manners are very interesting. It deserves remark, as exhibiting a strong feature in the character of the Jahrejas, and of their feeling with respect to their daughters, that these girls wore turbans, and were dressed and habited like boys. As if afraid or ashamed of acknowledging their sex, they assured me that they were not girls, and, with infantile simplicity, appealed to their father if it were not the case!

"The last instance which I shall mention of a Jahreja saving his daughter is the chief of Malia, and I believe this comprises *the whole number of existing cases that came to my knowledge*. The wife of this Thakore prevailed on him to rear his daughter; but, notwithstanding this, he was one of the last who subscribed to the instrument for abolishing the practice of Infanticide. My reports for the settlement of the revenue of this country have occasionally exhibited a solitary instance, wherein the Jahrejas have saved as well as destroyed their daughters, but my intercourse with the Jahrejas brought me acquainted with several who had caused *three or four of their female offspring to be put to death*; and they spoke of the circumstance with the indifference incident to the most ordinary transaction.

"Even the poorest and lowest Jahreja feels the utmost solicitude not to taint his blood by an improper alliance. It does not appear that the number of their wives is limited by any rule. The practice of concubinage is common among the Jahrejas, and in forming these connexions they are under little or no restraint with respect to cast. It will be observed that the settlement of their daughters born of rackelees, or mistresses, is attended with little expense or publicity; and the motives, therefore, which lead the Jahrejas to destroy their legitimate daughters, do not in the former case exist with equal force. It is remarkable that it is the practice of these rackelees, or mistresses, to perform Suttee with deceased Jahrejas, which is but rarely done by their wives. When Rao Lacka, the grandfather of Rao Raydim, the present chief of Cutch, died, *fifteen rackelees burnt at his funeral pile!* two of these women were Mahomedans of the country, and another a Seedeen; the rest were Hindoos of different casts, *but not one of Rao Lacka's wives sacrificed herself on this occasion.* This deviation from the general Hindoo practice is merely the effect of another habit or custom, as there is no law against a Jahreja wife burning with her husband, and they sometimes voluntarily devote themselves to the flames. This ceremony is less expected from the wife than the rackelee, and these unfortunate females conceive it a point of honour to consume themselves with their lords, being often inspired with a dreadful emulation to become the first victim. The Jahreja wives or rackelees are at liberty to follow this custom, or to abstain from it, and neither disgrace nor opprobrium is attached to those who may choose to survive. It may be mentioned as another extraordinary deviation from the general custom of Hindoos, that, in the district of Hulwud, *the wives of the lowest casts invariably burn with their husbands,* which may be the reason that the Jahreja women excuse themselves; and, as it is only people of rank who keep rackelees, instances of this nature are not frequent.

"The influence of example and communication is capable of procuring converts to the most flagitious courses. The Jaitwa Rajpoots, who rule over the division of Burrudda, have been accused of adopting the barbarous practice of the Jahrejas in destroying their daughters. The Jaitwas may have thought it no disgrace to follow a custom cherished by their conquerors; and, having lost the greater part of their possessions, they may have been desirous, like the Jahrejas, of relieving themselves from the burthen of portioning their daughters. They observe a silence on the subject, and the deed is performed in secrecy; but the singular fact, that the Ranas of Poorbunder have had *no grown up daughters for more than a hundred years*, would be sufficient evidence against them. Their chief executed the same instrument as the Jahrejas did for renouncing the custom; an unequivocal proof that it existed."*

The third part of the Parliamentary Papers relates to "*Infanticide practised by the Rajpoots in the Districts of Cutch and Kattywar, within the Dominions of the Guickwar:*" 1808 *to* 1820, pp. 71—128.

Colonel Walker, referring to the success of his endeavours to abolish Infanticide among the Jahrejas, remarks in his important document: "I was willing to think that the example might produce a favourable effect on the Jahrejas of Cutch, and in this expectation I addressed myself again to Futteh Mahomed. The Jemadar's answer contained a second defence of Infanticide, but in more moderate terms; and it disclosed a circumstance which is probably true, that his situation rendered it improper for him to say any thing on the subject to the Jahrejas. It appears that the Jahreja Byaud of Cutch could easily overturn the usurped authority of Futteh Mahomed; and that they only sanction or submit to it, because they have acquired thereby an extension of their own authority, and many illegal possessions. It is generally understood that if this Jemadar attempts to deprive them of any of their privileges, or to circumscribe their unjust acquisition, they could, without much difficulty, deprive him of his own power. Under these circumstances we cannot probably indulge any strong hope that the suppression of Infanticide will soon be attained in Cutch; and, in the actual state of affairs in that country, they may, perhaps, afford some apology for Futteh Mahomed's appearing as a constrained advocate for the unnatural crime of Infanticide."†

J. R. Carnack, Esq., Resident at Baroda, addressed the Chief Secretary of the Bombay Government, July, 1816, "I have the honour to report, in pursuance of the orders of the Right Honourable the Governor in Council, that the abolition of this inhuman practice in Cutch has not been accomplished. The urgent representations to that Government during the life of Futteh Mahomed, and our subsequent intercourse with his Highness Raidhum and his

* Par. Papers, 1824, pp. 37—42. † p. 50.

ministers, were attended with no effect; in the first case, from a declaration, that an interference with the religious prejudices of the country was incompatible with the situation of Futteh Mahomed; and latterly the impaired power of the Rao, and the internal revolutions of Cutch, have been made a pretext for paying no attention to the execution of our wishes. Circumstances have not enabled us therefore to carry our views, for the abolition of Female Infanticide in Cutch, beyond the measure of representation; and, considering that the prejudice which tolerates this atrocious practice is interwoven with the conceived notions of honour of families of Jahreja origin, it could not be expected, until our influence was established, that Female Infanticide could be suppressed. It may require also considerable exertions and discretion, now that we have obtained a political establishment in Cutch, before any progress is made in the success of our object. In the customs of the natives of India, but especially in their religious feelings, any spirit of reform must be introduced by taking advantage of occasional opportunities to offer advice or gentle remonstrance, and not by inculcating innovations or changes from the imposing appearance of our power. I should have been happy to announce that Female Infanticide was entirely eradicated from the Peninsula of Cattywar. Although there has lately been no evidence afforded to me, either by my assistant, or the Guicawar local authority, of any Jahreja having destroyed his offspring since the accession to the engagements by means of Colonel Walker; I have been disappointed in the result of the statement of those children who have been reported as preserved. The letter from Captain Ballantine seems to vouch *for only fifteen*, the disparity of which number is very great according to the ordinary progress of population."*

The Governor in Council writes to the Honourable Court of Directors, December, 1817, "To the last report from the Assistant to the Resident at Baroda, on this subject, we particularly wish to draw your attention, as submitting a register of the Talookas in Cattywar, where the Jahrejas reside, and showing how many female children have been saved (with the names and places of abode of the parents) since the introduction of Colonel Walker's arrangements, accompanied by his observations on the

* Par. Papers, p. 97, see p. 106.

register, and in regard to the adoption of measures which might be calculated to root out the evil. The report of Captain Ballantine, while it affords satisfactory proof that SIXTY-THREE *female children had been preserved by our interposition, exhibits a melancholy picture of the almost universal continuance of the horrid practice, and that to an extent beyond what we had anticipated.* It is observable that the preservation of no more than the above small number of children can be established throughout the Talookas specified by Captain Ballantine, where it is concluded the number of Jahrejas must be very considerable; since Draffa alone contains 400 families; nor can it escape your attention that the Jahrejas enumerated as having preserved their female children, have saved *only* ONE *of the number that must have been born according to the ordinary course of nature.*"*

Colonel Walker having retired from India, but still deeply interested in this philanthropic design of abolishing Infanticide, addressed the following letter to the Secretary of the Court of Directors, in 1819:—"In acknowledging your letter, and the documents to which it gave cover, I beg to enclose, for the Honourable the Court of Directors, a memorandum on the subject of Female Infanticide. I have found it impossible at present to give that important subject all the consideration which is due to it, and I shall probably avail myself of a future opportunity of transmitting, for the notice of the Honourable Court, some additional reflections which may occur to me.

"Although there can be no difference of opinion regarding the enormity of the crime of Infanticide, yet it is not to be considered as peculiar to the natives of India. In other parts of the earth the same practice has prevailed. In China it is not uncommon at this day; where it is permitted by the legislature, and where it is reckoned no disgrace nor dishonour to the individual. Every humane person, however, must agree that such a practice should be stopped by all the means which a wise Government can command; that we have the means in our power there cannot be a doubt; and I must beg leave to say that my own success is a proof of this. The means are, persuasion and reason. If these be wisely applied, by the agents of Government, they will be found to be quite sufficient without any inquisitorial

* Par. Papers, p. 106, 107.

institution, without any odious system of espionage, which no remote advantage can make necessary. The foundation of reform was laid. It was proved to the natives that this practice was against their sacred institutions, and it was revolting to the best feelings of the human heart. They agreed to it, and probably did sincerely mean to do so. *The Government, however, and the local authorities, became remiss, and the people returned by degrees to habits too long established.* I am convinced that it is necessary, by undeviating attention to the subject, to satisfy them that we are really sincere in our wish to abolish the crime. All depends on attention to the subject for a sufficient length of time, till the influence of custom is forgotten, and the natural affections have sprung up again in the hearts of parents. They are not wholly lost, although some unhappy circumstances have been able to cover them for the present. In attaining this object there cannot be a doubt of our success, for nature is working in our favour. All that is required is attention to the subject, and that for a sufficient length of time. *Naturam repellas furca, tamen usque recurret.*"*

Part the fourth, of the Papers of 1824, contains "*Papers relative to Infanticide, by drowning, practised by the Hindoos at Saugur, and other places:*" 1794 *to* 1820. pp. 129—144.

A case of Infanticide, and the punishment adjudged as stated in pages 131—133, is painfully descriptive of the moral state of the Hindoos.—"Mussumaut Jarlee, and Cumlee, are charged with murder, but under such circumstances as urge humanity to soften the rigour of the law. Jarlee's daughter was labouring under a loathsome disease, incurable in its nature, and which, by prejudices it were vain to oppose (but by erecting *native hospitals* for the reception of such objects) exposed the unhappy mother to the desertion and contempt of kindred and of friends, who artfully exhorted her to shorten a life which this growing malady was slowly and painfully extinguishing, and thus relieve a suffering child, whose desperate situation admitted no remedy, and secure to herself, oppressed by poverty and shunned as one visited by divine vengeance, an exemption from misery. Mercy pleads in behalf of a crime committed under the prevalence of long-established prejudices, and by

---

* Par. Papers, pp. 118, 119.

one, too, hopeless and deserted: and whom, if it be difficult, perhaps exceptionable, to defend, it is impossible not to commiserate. Little can be weighed in excuse for Cumlee's conduct to accompany the unfortunate mother, and not forcibly: such a deed of horror seems unnatural; and yet to dissuade her from the commitment of it was more than could be expected from ignorance and superstition."* Jarlee was confined for one year and then dismissed!

The Bombay Judicial Consultation, Jan. 1824, speak of the trial of Bheeme Mussalin by the magistrate of Poona, for the wilful murder of her female child, for which she was to be "imprisoned for, and during the term of, her natural life." The Monthly Return of Criminal Cases decided by the Judge, north of the Mahee, Nov. 1826, speak of a woman, "after having given birth to a child, exposing it on a dunghill, where it was destroyed by hogs. Sentence *six months imprisonment, with such labour as befits her sex!* If this heinous offence (says Mr. Goodwin) be not provided for by our code, I deem it a fit subject for legislation. In Bengal, such atrocities are, I fancy, punished capitally. The Honourable Governor of Bombay adds, the new regulation seems to provide for this offence."†

The first account of Infanticide at Saugur is introduced by a letter of the Calcutta magistrates to the Honourable G. H. Barlow, Vice-President of Council, Feb. 1802.

"We think it our duty to submit to your consideration the enclosed copy of a deposition delivered at the police-office, by Mr. C. Stirling. The deponent in substance states, that, being at Saugur on the day of the full moon, in the month of November last, he was a witness to several inhuman sacrifices, offered, as he represents, to the sharks, and that the victims consisted of *old men, old women, and children.* Other depositions have been taken, some on oath, and some without an oath, to the same effect. Having made the circumstances above-mentioned an object of our particular attention, it appears that the sacrifices are, as stated in the depositions, of two descriptions; of aged persons of both sexes, which are voluntary, and of children, which of course are involuntary; and that the periods fixed for the performance of them are at the full moon in November and in January. The custom of sacrificing children is confined to the people of the eastern districts. The practice arises from vows made by their parents, who, when apprehensive of not having issue, had promised, in the event of their having *five children, to devote the fifth in its infancy to the Ganges.* It might be supposed that superstition could not be carried father. The following, however, is an incident in which the dictates of bigotry appear to be still more strongly

---

* Par. Papers, p. 131.

† Par. Papers on Infanticide, 1828, p. 31, 32.

opposed to the sentiments and feelings of nature. Apprehensions being entertained lest these sacrifices might, at a future period, be prevented by the police, a boy of about twelve years of age, who, we have reason to believe, was not the fifth child, and who, consequently, according to the strict letter of the vow, was not liable to be sacrificed, was thrown into the Ganges. The boy having saved himself by swimming, a Gosayn endeavoured to extend to him his protection; but, singular and unnatural as, it may appear, he was again seized, and committed to destruction by his own parents!

"We have stated that the above sacrifices took place at Saugur, which Island is held to be peculiarly sacred from its being considered the termination of the Ganges, and the junction of that river with the sea. The spot where these rites are administered is described in Major Rennell's map under the title of 'the place of sacrifice.' Saugur is not the only place where rites of the above nature are performed; the same practice prevails at Allahabad, at Bannsbaria, in the Zillah of Hooghly, and at Chogdah, in the Zillah of Nuddea. We have reason to believe, however, that at those places it is become, for the most part, a mere ceremony, and that the children, though thrown into the Ganges in conformity to the vow of their parents, are generally, if not uniformly, rescued from destruction.

"It does not appear that sacrifices of this nature are sanctioned by any tenet of the Hindoo code. What, however, has nearly the force of a religious dogma is the vow itself, and usage, which, in the opinion of the Hindoos, is equally binding as a written law. The practice appears to be little countenanced by the religious orders, or by the great body of the people, who, on the contrary, think it a pious and meritorious act to rescue a child from destruction, and afterwards to adopt and maintain it at their own expense. Not having been in possession of any information regarding the sacrifices in the month of November last, the sacrifices took place at that period without any interference on the part of the police, when *the number of victims destroyed amounted to no less than thirty-nine.* In the past month we sent a party to prevent a repetition of these barbarous rites, and are happy that *the duty was effectually performed without any disturbance or opposition whatever.* In considering the means best adapted for preventing a practice so repugnant to nature and humanity, we observe that it would be consistent with precedents already established to propose a regulation for the prevention of such sacrifices in future. But, as we have no reason to suppose that the practice was authorized under the Mogul government, and as the parties concerned are liable to be punished according to the established law, we presume it would be sufficient to issue a proclamation, notifying that any persons who may be parties in such sacrifice will be tried and punished for the offence according to the general laws and regulations of the country. The foregoing remarks and suggestions are applicable only to the involuntary sacrifices of children. With respect to the self-devotion of the aged and infirm, in the Ganges, the practice prevails so generally, and is considered by the Hindoos, under certain circumstances, so instrumental to their happiness in a future state of existence, that we doubt whether any rules which could be adopted would prevent a practice rooted in the most remote antiquity, and sanctioned by express tenets in their sacred books."*

---

* Par. Papers, pp. 134, 135.

It is deeply to be regretted that the shield of British humanity and justice has not been thrown over the sick, the aged, and the infirm, who are frequently murdered by cruel exposure on the banks of the Ganges, and submersion in its waves.

The nature of these barbarities appears from the information and deposition of Charles Starling, a mate in the Pilot service, taken upon oath, before Charles Martyn, one of His Majesty's justices of the peace for the town of Calcutta, in Dec. 1801. He stated "that on the day of the full moon, in November last, this deponent, and Edmund Bartlett, branch pilot, went from the Philip Dundas schooner on shore to the Pagoda Creek on Saugur Island, where the people go annually to worship; that, after this deponent and the said Edmund Bartlett got on shore, they walked up to the huts of the natives, and after being on shore for an hour they saw the entrails, as they supposed, of a human body floating on the water; and at the same time they also saw about three thousand natives on the beach. This deponent further saith, that a fakeer was standing close to him and the said Edmund Bartlet; this deponent asked him, the said fakeer, the reason why a number of the natives were ordered to be put into the water; he answered that the head fakeer had ordered them to go to the water to be devoured by the sharks, for the prosperity of their respective families. The fakeer also informed this deponent that if a woman had four children she ought to put one of them into the water to be devoured by the sharks, with the hope that the other three children should live. This deponent further saith, that, while he was on the beach, during the time that he was in the boat going to the shore, this deponent saw altogether *eleven men, women, and lads, destroyed by the sharks.* This deponent further saith, that, while they were in the boat, they heard that a boy was to be put into the water to be destroyed by the sharks; they waited there with an intention to save the boy; but he was not put into the water while the boat was there. And this deponent is informed, and believes, that as soon as they returned to the schooner the boy was put into the water, and was destroyed by the sharks."*

Infanticide appears to exist in various parts of India. "The custom of Infanticide," says Sir John Malcolm, "ap-

* Par. Papers, p. 136.

pears to be confined to some Rajpoot Chiefs of high rank and small fortune, who resort to it to prevent their daughters contracting a marriage beneath their rank, and who despair of obtaining a marriage with their equals. The petty Thakore of Cherawul, a relation of the Amjerah family, married a daughter of the Rawul of Banswarrah thirty-four years ago (in 1821). The tribe of the Thakore's family was so inflated by this occurrence, that it was resolved no female should make an inferior match; and, in despair of obtaining such good fortune again, they kill every female child." Sir John says that "Suntook Ram, minister of Amjerah, told him, he was sitting with Puddun Singh, the present Thakore, when he heard the birth of a female infant whispered in his ear, and saw him preparing *the fatal pill of opium* (the usual signal): he implored that the child might live; his request was granted; and this little girl, added Suntook Ram, is always called my daughter."*

The Judge of Circuit in the Bareilly Division, in 1805, states to Government, "The number of persons convicted of wilful murder is certainly great. *The murder of children, for the sake of their ornaments*, is, I am sorry to say, common. For my own part, being convinced that under the existing laws we have no other means of putting an end to the frequent perpetration of this crime, I could wish to see the practice of adorning children with valuable trinkets altogether prohibited. A want of tenderness and regard for life I think very general throughout the country."†

"The crime of destroying illegitimate children in the womb is prevalent to a shocking degree in Bengal. In the family of a single Koleen Brahmun, whose daughters never live with their husbands, it is common for each daughter to destroy a child in the womb annually; this crime is very prevalent among widows, so numerous in this country. The pundit who gave this information supposes 10,000 children are thus murdered in the Province of Bengal every month!! (qu. every year?) Expressing my doubts of this extraordinary and shocking circumstance, he appealed to the fact of many females being tried for these offences in the courts of justice in every Zillah in Bengal. He said that the fact was so notorious that every child in

---

* Rep. of Cen. India, Asi. Jour. Jan. 1823. See also Ham. Hind. vol. ii. pp. 617—666. † Eclec. Rev. 1828.

the country knew of it; it had acquired an appropriate name. *petu phela* and *pet phelanee* is a term of abuse which one woman often gives to another. Many women die after taking the drug intended to kill the unborn child."*

The Rev. C. Lacey, the Author's Colleague in Orissa, in a letter, dated Cuttack, June, 1827, mentions the following interesting fact:—

"A human sacrifice has lately been offered near Cuttack; a few particulars respecting it will not be unacceptable. *Human sacrifices are more frequent than is generally apprehended.* Every possible precaution is taken to keep them secret, so that few are heard of. In the present instance the sacrifice was a young child, a boy, and his parents are of the Soodra caste. He was either bought or stolen from them by the sacrificer. It seems probable that the person who offered the sacrifice had made a vow to the goddess to offer a beautiful child in case of some favour granted; hence the boy chose, was of very respectable parents, about five years of age, and very handsome. How the ceremony was performed I do not know, but most likely by cutting off the head, as bodies and heads of human sacrifices have been found; and the goddess Kalee is represented as being pleased with the flow of blood. I have witnessed the sacrifices of goats and buffaloes to Kalee, in Bengal, and this was the manner of sacrificing them; it is therefore most probable that the blood and head of the child were carried immediately before the image and offered to her. The Brahmun, to conceal the murder, after offering the sacrifice, took the body of the victim and cut it into small pieces, and boiled it in a handy (a large earthen pot), in which it seems he intended to bury it. This was a most secure method, as the boiling disfigured the flesh, and no one here could suspect flesh being in a handy. It seems he was detected in boiling it. The perpetrator and the idol were brought before the Magistrate of Cuttack, and a minute investigation ensued; the evidence appeared clear against the Brahmun. We, however, condemn no one without oaths, and, the murderer being a Brahmun, not one of the witnesses would swear against him, as it would have taken his life. In this manner the murderer was acquitted of all charges, though it was evident he was guilty of the crime."

The following extract of a letter, on the neglect of children in India, from the Rev. A. Sutton of Balasore in Orissa, in Aug. 1828, shows that modern heathens, like those of old, are "without natural affection:"—

"The rains have commenced, and many deaths have occurred in consequence; several have died on and close to our premises. One case of peculiar distress came before me yesterday, which it may be interesting to record. As I was going in the evening to a neighbouring village to preach, I saw a Hindostanee woman with a child at the foot of a tree; on coming up to her I found her much exhausted with the cholera, and nearly insensible. I of course gave her medicines, and begged, long in

* Ward's View, vol. iii. p. 292. See also Asi. Jour. Feb. 1827, p. 269.

vain, of the hard-hearted villagers for a little milk to give the child. To-day I visited her twice, and she seems somewhat better, but there is little probability of her recovery; for, though she has money, yet no one will supply her with necessaries, and she cannot help herself; perhaps indeed the circumstance of her having a little money will induce them to behave worse towards her. I got a little milk to-day and fed the poor child, but it is painful work; any heart but that of a Hindoo must have been moved to witness the eagerness with which the half-famished infant devoured it; and, when she had drank it, the imploring look of the little creature made me think of Moses and Pharaoh's daughter. I tried every argument I could command to induce the villagers to take care of the child, and promised to pay any expense; but no, *it was a female child and nobody cared for it!* I tried what I could do with a fat wealthy Brahmun, and observed that the woman would die, and then what would become of the child? but his gentle reply was, 'Sahe murrebo now kee?—*It must die too, what else?*' Such are the mild and gentle Hindoo Brahmuns. 27th.—The poor woman and several others have been carried off during the day: we have taken the half-famished child under our protection. It is rather a pretty little girl, of perhaps about ten months old: the poor little thing seems determined to live; for she readily eats and drinks any thing we give her. Our present views are, if she should live for two or three years, to place her in Mrs. Marshman's or our Calcutta friends' Asylum for orphan children of native converts. It is more than probable that *many children are left as this little girl was, and of course perish in the most miserable manner imaginable.*"

Colonel Walker, in his letter to the Secretary of the Honourable Court of Directors, Aug. 1819, expresses his deep regret on the perusal of Papers relative to the present state of Infanticide. "It would," says the Colonel, "be a very painful task for me to enter into a minute and critical examination of those proceedings which have been held on Infanticide since I left India; some remarks are unavoidably necessary on a subject which cannot be viewed without emotion, and which, to a considerable degree, must involve the character of our country. *The policy and humanity of our Government are irrevocably blended with the success of the measures for abolishing this revolting crime.* After a careful perusal of the documents with which I have been favoured by the indulgence of the Honourable Court, I have found it impossible to suppress the conclusion that the subject has either been *forgotten for years together or that some imperious and uncontrollable circumstances had rendered our interference utterly impracticable.* From whatever resistless cause this has arisen, it is deeply to be lamented, and the consequences are far more formidable than even the immediate effects. The immediate effects are the loss of *so many thousand lives;* but the consequences are still more serious, as the enforcement of the engagement must now be infinitely more difficult by the long neglect and disuse of its provisions.

"At the time that I left India the subject was familiar to the Jahrejas; there was an impression of interest on their minds; a return had appeared of parental affection, and, above all, there was the necessity of obeying a legal enactment possessing their own solemn sanction, and for the enforcement of which the British and Guicowar Governments were pledged. Instead of this picture, the Jahrejas have now found out that the engagement, which was at first so reluctantly yielded, and strenuously urged, *means almost nothing,* since it may be eluded with impunity; may be violated without detection and without reproof. If they had imagined that there would be so little danger in its violation as they evidently, at present, believe to be the case, I should without doubt have found much less difficulty in obtaining their consent to discontinue the custom of destroying their daughters.

"The consequence at this moment operating in Kattywar is the impression of weakness and vacillancy on the part of the British Government, or that they are incapable of giving effect to their own measures. It may seem idle to trace out the nature and extent of the evil that remissness or accidents have produced. I am aware also that the truth cannot be stated in all its broadness and honesty to the Company's Government in India, as it might irritate instead of conciliate; yet it should be stated, though with as much delicacy as the nature of such truth will admit."*

The demoralizing influence of this inhuman custom must be evident. J. Duncan, Esq., in his communication to Government, Oct., 1789, speaking of the Rajkoomars and other disorderly tribes on the Juanpore frontiers, says, "Zalim Sing and Goordut, two of the principal of them, nave lately levied their forces with a design to fight each other on our borders. I have been obliged to warn the commanding officer at Juanpore to be on his guard against their possible inroads; and, although the appearance of peace between these men has since increased, yet we must not relax in our caution what may happen, for I cannot rely on their moderation; and what can be expected of men inured as they are by birth and education to the most atrocious

* Par. Papers, p. 121, 122.

deeds."* To the same effect is the following extract from the Judge of the Benares Court of Circuit to the Magistrate of the Zillah of Juanpore, Feb., 1816.—"The extreme prevalence of affrays, so much beyond the other Zillahs that I have passed through, seems to have existed for a long time; and although the aggregate annual number may be at present somewhat diminished, yet neither the propensities of the people, nor the facilities of prevention, seem to be essentially meliorated. The savage and quarrelsome spirit of the people in the Pergunnah of Unglee appears to originate a large and constant proportion of your business, as well as that of this Court. The jealous and hasty pride which induces them to become the murderers of their own female offspring has probably a considerable effect in blunting their feelings against a sympathetic sense of the pains they inflict upon one another on the smallest pretence of right or offence, and to render the dread of public justice of light or no collective influence."†

A more recent communication from W. Cracroft, Esq., Magistrate of Juanpore, May, 1819, expresses the same sentiments, equally applicable to every tribe or caste that practises Infanticide or any other sanguinary customs:—"It may perhaps not be advancing too much to say that *the practice of Infanticide is indirectly a very considerable cause of the insubordinate character and violent disposition of the Rajkoomars,* as it teaches them early to steel their hearts against the natural affections, and renders them familiar with inhumanity; the mere want of female companions and playmates, during the earlier part of adolescence, must have a material effect in preventing their manners and sentiments from being softened or civilized. Female Infanticide must also be a great check to population in a country which is far from having arrived at its greatest extent of cultivation. Indeed, a considerable number (I imagine as many as one-third) of the Rajkoomars are never married. *Considering the question either in a moral, political, or religious point of view, it demands the most serious attention of Government.*"‡

---

* Par. Papers, p. 6. † p. 13. ‡ p. 15.

CHAP. III.

Success of efforts, ancient and modern, for the suppression of Human Sacrifices and Infanticide—Difficulties of the entire abolition of Infanticide in India.

THE practice of human sacrifices, though so prevalent in different countries and distant ages, is opposed to the dictates of nature; and hence its partial abolition, by civilized states, long before the Christian era. Probably the earliest account of Infanticide is the destruction of the children of the Israelites in the Nile, by Pharaoh, king of Egypt. The first efforts to abolish it upon record originated in the divine command given by Moses to the Israelites, concerning the abominations of the Canaanites (B. C. 1490 years)—"Thou shalt say to the children of Israel, Whosoever he be of the children of Israel, or of the strangers that sojourn in Israel, that giveth any of his seed unto Molech, he shall surely be put to death; the people of the land shall stone him with stones. And I will set my face against that man, and will cut him off from among his people; because he hath given of his seed unto Molech, to defile my sanctuary, and to profane my holy name. And if the people of the land do any ways hide their eyes from the man, when he giveth of his seed unto Molech, and kill him not; then will I set my face against that man, and against his family, and will cut him off, and all that go a whoring after him, to commit whoredom with Molech, from among their people." Lev. xx. 2—5.

"The Carthaginians (says Rollin) retained the barbarous custom of offering human sacrifices to their gods till the ruin of their city. An action which ought to be called *Sacrilegium verius quam sacrum.* It was suspended for for some years, from the fear of drawing upon themselves the indignation and arms of Darius I., king of Persia, *who forbade them offering human sacrifices and eating the flesh of dogs.* But this horrid practice was soon resumed; since in the reign of Xerxes, successor of Darius (B. C. 484 years), Gelon, the tyrant of Syracuse, having gained a considerable victory over the Carthaginians in Sicily, made the following conditions, among other articles of peace granted them, *that no more human sacrifices should be offered to Saturn.* During the engagement, which lasted from morning till night, Hamilcar their general was perpetually offering to the gods sacrifices of living men, who were thrown on a flaming pile: but, seeing his troops routed, he himself rushed into the pile, that he might not survive his disgrace; and, says St. Ambrose, to extinguish with his own blood this sacrilegious fire, when he found it had not proved of service to him."*

The Romans exerted themselves with success in the same work of justice and mercy. "It is a very remarkable fact that the Romans (though heathens themselves) abolished human sacrifices in this country, at least *a century and a half before the introduction of Christianity among us.* The Romans conceived such an aversion to the Druids, the high priests of these abominations, whose inhumanities a reminutely described by *Diodorus Siculus* (Lib. 5), that contrary to the ordinary policy of that people, in their conquests, of invariably tolerating the religion of the country, they resolved upon an utter extirpation of these priests and their cruelties. It appears from Pliny (L. 30, c. 1) that human sacrifices were first forbidden at Rome, by a decree of the Senate, A. U. C. 657, but that, some persons still continuing them privately, the Emperor Augustus renewed the prohibition with effect. The Emperor Tiberius then suppressed them in Gaul, and Claudius, as appears from Suetonius (In Claud. c. 25), extripated the Druids as well as their sanguinary worship in that country. These sacrifices existed in our own country (as appears from Pomponius Mela *de situ orbis* L. 3 c. 2), until about the sixtieth year of the Christian era, when the Roman general Paulinus Suetonius, having reduced the Island of Anglesea, overthrew the Druids and their inhuman rites so completely that they never afterwards revived; but all this was considerably anterior to the introduction of Christianity itself. And will it be endured that our own heathen conquerors shall have actually done more for us than we are willing to do for our Indian subjects? Shall the mere natural principle of "*Homo sum humani nihil a me alienum puto*" have exercised an influence on idolatrous and pagan Rome? And shall Britain, acting under far higher sanctions,

---

* Ancient History, Vol. i. p. 109.—Vol. iv. p. 75.

and obliged by a more powerful responsibility, refuse to acknowledge the force of the same argument?"*

Christianity as a system of Religion, and by the principles it has diffused in the government of every people among whom it has been established, has accomplished the annihilation of every species of human sacrifice. Read the article of the learned Bryant, like the roll of the prophet, "written within and without with mourning, and lamentation, and woe," and taking the circuit of the western world, ask, Where are these horrid rites? They are all, with almost every relic of the idolatry connected with them,—

"Bury'd 'midst the wreck of things that were."

In various parts of India, by the progress of Christianity and the domination of the Mahometans, the practice of human sacrifices has become almost extinct. "Like the other temples in the Deccan (says Dr. Buchanan), the revenues of the temple of Ramisseram are wasting away. I saw no human bone in the island. Christianity in its worst shape has civilized the Deccan.†

"The law of Mahomed put a stop to the inhuman custom which had been long practised by Pagan Arabs, of burying their daughters alive. This wicked practice is condemned by the Koran in several passages, one of which, as some commentators judge, may also condemn another custom of the Arabians, altogether as wicked, and as common among other nations of old, viz. the sacrificing of their children to their idols, as was frequently done, in particular in satisfaction of a vow they used to make, that, if they had a certain number of sons born, they would offer one of them in sacrifice.‡

Colonel Walker adverts to the efforts of the Mahometans for the suppression of Infanticide in India, and shows the facility with which the British power may prevent this unnatural crime. "The subject was not overlooked by the former Government of India, to which the Company may now be considered as having succeeded. The author of the Acball Nameh relates that, in the route of the royal army from Cashmere to Lahore, they came to a village the

---

* Poynder's Speech on Human Sacrifices in India (Hatchard), p. 220.
† Life of Buchanan, Vol. ii. p. 49.
‡ Par. Papers, p. 58, 59. Sales Koran, Prelim. Dis.

inhabitants of which had formerly been Hindoo, 'where numbers of the poor people upon having daughters born to them, that instant secretly put an end to their existence.' This fact coming to the knowledge of the Emperor Jehanguire, he ordered '*that this barbarous practice should be discontinued; and enacted that whoever should commit it in future should be put to the torture.*' From this it would appear that Infanticide engaged the attention of the Mogul Government, and that it made an attempt to suppress the practice. It would be curious, as well as useful, to ascertain what has been the fate of the measures which were adopted for this purpose two hundred years ago. Have they been successful, or have they failed? The moral negligence which succeeded the decline of the Mogul Empire, and the impracticability, in the disordered state of the country, of enforcing a severe law, would be sufficient to discourage our expectations that the termination has been prosperous. Still it would be desirable to know the actual result, to discover the extent of the impression, and whether the attempt was only the effect of the feeling at the moment, or pursued as a system. *The extensive power and dominion which we now possess in India may be made subservient to this enquiry, and be directed to ascertain how far the practice of Infanticide prevails in any of the countries under the influence or control of the British Government.*"*

Modern efforts for the abolition of this inhuman custom have been various, and attended with some degree of success. J. Duncan, Esq., in a letter to the Governor General in Council, in December 1789, states, "I have been lately through that part of the country where the Rajkoomar tribe reside. I have conversed with several of them, and have found, from their own confessions, that the custom of female child-murder has long been and still continues very prevalent among them. I have prevailed on those situated within our frontier to agree to renounce in future this horrid practice, to which effect they have entered into the engagement which will be found in the accompanying extract of my proceedings; and, as there remain a few names to be yet affixed to this covenant, it is still circulating among the parties, and I shall hereafter mention the number of the names of the subscribers; to

* Par. Papers, 1824, p. 128.

increase which, and further to promote the salutary object in view, I have written concerning it to Lucknow. As this baneful habit is not confined to the Rajkoomars alone, but extends to the tribe called Raghevansa, who reside in our Pergunnah of Mongra, and Talooka of Chandwack, and in other parts, I have taken measures for their signing a separate similar engagement, from which I have very sanguine hopes that this system of Infanticide will be put a stop to, or be at least greatly lessened.

"The Rajkoomar renunciation of letting their daughters perish has been received, and is subscribed by all those of that tribe in this part of the country, including Zalem Sing, and Goordut Sing, the latter of whom is the *only one of the subscribers who disallows, by the words of his signature, of having been guilty of this crime.* I have sent a copy of the original engagement to the Amil of Juanpore, with directions to him to see it enforced, and to apprehend and send into Benares, to take his trial, any Rajkoomar who shall be guilty thereof hereafter: of all which I have apprized that body of men accordingly. I have circulated a similar subscription in this Pergunnah of Gurwarah, on finding that its inhabitants, who are all Doorgavansas, or descendants of one common ancestor, called Doorg, are addicted more or less to the same practice of destroying their female infants."*

The form of agreement entered into by the Rajkoomars :—

"Whereas it hath become known to the Government of the Honourable English East India Company that we of the tribe of Rajkoomars do not suffer our female children to live: and whereas this is a great crime, as mentioned in the Bretim Bywunt Pooran, where it is said, that killing even a fœtus is as criminal as killing a Brahmun; and that for killing a female or woman the punishment is to suffer in the nerk or hill called Kall Sooter, for as many years as there are hairs on that female's body; and that afterwards that person shall be born again, and successively become a leper, and be afflicted with the zukhma: and whereas the British Government in India, whose subjects we are, have an utter detestation of such murderous practices, and we do ourselves acknowledge that, although customary among us, it is highly sinful, we do therefore hereby agree not to commit any longer such detestable acts; and any among us who (which God forbid) shall be hereafter guilty thereof, or shall not bring up and get our daughters married, to the best of our abilities, among those of our caste, shall be expelled from our tribe, and we shall neither eat nor keep society with such person or

* Par. Papers, 1824, p. 6, 7.

persons, besides suffering hereafter the punishments denounced in the above pooran and shaster. We have therefore entered into this agreement; dated 17th of December, 1789."*

Colonel Walker, in a communication to the Governor of Bombay (dated Baroda, December 25th, 1809), specifies the Jahrejas of Kattywar who had preserved their female children to the amount of *thirty-two*, and suggested a distribution of 14,000 rupees in presents, which was adopted. He observes, "During the recent expedition into Kattywar I was not unmindful of enquiring into the success of the humane arrangements introduced under the influence of the Honourable Company's Government, for the abolishment of female Infanticide among the Jahreja Rajpoots; and I am happy to report that this reform has completely taken root. I have the honour to enclose a list of those Jahrejas who have preserved their female children, which fell under my own direct observance. On my halt at Dherole, I had all those in the immediate neighbourhood who were capable of attending brought to my tent, and many were too young to be brought from any distance. *It was extremely gratifying on this occasion to observe the triumph of nature, feeling, and parental affection, over prejudice and a horrid superstition; and that those who, but a short period before, would, as many of them had done, have doomed their infants to destruction without compunction, should now glory in their preservation, and doat on them with fondness!*

"I respectfully beg leave to submit to the consideration of the Honourable the Governor in Council a memorandum of a disbursement made in presents to those Jahrejas who had preserved their daughters, and who visited me at Dherole. The fund from which it is to be defrayed is from the Nuzzeranah, exacted from the Chieftain of Goondul, which the Honourable the Governor in Council is already apprized included an amercement for the destruction of the female infant of that Chieftain's son. This arrangement is in conformity to the instruction of the Honourable the Governor in Council, and I respectfully trust it will be honoured with their approval and sanction."†

---

* Par. Papers, 1824, p. 8. For the prevalence of just sentiments in the British Courts of Justice in India, see the Regulat. of 1795 and 1799. Par. Papers, 1824, p. 9—11.

† Par. Papers, p. 78, 79.

From the Register of the Jahrejas in Kattywar, June 1817, it appears that the degree of success attending the efforts to abolish Infanticide has been much less than might have been anticipated.

Captain Ballantine, in his laudable efforts to abolish this inhuman custom, proposed some very effectual plans, and presented to the Government a list of the families of the Jahrejas with the number of infants saved from 1807 to 1817. He observes, "In conformity with the commands of the Honourable Court, and those of the Governments in India, communicated in your several despatches, my attention has since been directed to obtain the best possible data to be procured on the humane and interesting subject of the Infanticide engagements contracted with the Jahrejas of the Peninsula by Colonel Walker in his first circuit in Kattywar. In presenting *the accompanying complete Register of all the Jahrejas known in Kattywar,* I have the satisfaction to think it will be acceptable, as I believe it is the first paper of the kind that has yet been obtained, and the more especially as it will form the best basis and data on which to watch, with better effect, the progress of an Institution which appears to have excited uncommon interest wherever its extraordinary history has reached; and at the same time the most decided attention of our Governments at home and abroad, so as to introduce, by every possible means, the best practicable prohibition to the practice of the most unparalleled crime,—the systematic murder by parents of their own children. It must be received as an indubitable testimony that *sixty-three female offsprings saved,* bear no proportion to the probable population of the Jahrejas in the Peninsula, during the long period of *ten years.* I much fear the object of our interference for the suppression of this singular custom has too generally failed, to select any individual party for the just vengeance of Government and offended nature."*

* Par. Papers, p. 108.

A complete List, or particular Register, comprising the Talookas, &c., *of all the Jahrejas at the present day in Kattywar;* together with *the Age and Number of their Female Offspring saved, or now living,* since the introduction of the Infanticide arrangement by Colonel Walker in 1807 and 1808.

TALOOKAS.	No.	AGE.
In Moorbee	1	7 years.
Ditto	1	4 do.
Villages belonging to the Moorbee.		
Madepoor, of Do.		
Surned, of .. Do.		
Lujyee.		
Beeralloo.		
Motana.		
Bhella Mota.		
Vowdey.		
Dyeesuroo.		
Rajcote	1	4 do.
Villages belonging to the Rajcote	1	3 do.
Rajcote of Do	1	1 do.
Kotarie belonging to the Rajcote	1	1 do.
Gurridur, of Do	1	4 months.
Ladhekoo, of Rajcote		
Wourey.		
Veerrva.		
Paal.		
Ghutgoo.		
Shapoora.		
Purgunnah Mingvey.		
Thora belonging to Do		
Endoo Do.		
Ambano Do.		
Purgunnah of Rajpoor	1	4 months.
Hunmuntijanoo, of Do	1	2 do.
Bhadwa, of Do.		
Kotedoo, of Do.		
Veerwal, of Do.		
Punch Tullow, of Do.		
Purgunnah Veerpoo.	1	2 do.
Kheyuryoo	1	3 do.
Kurreedee.		
Kheesurroo.		

TALOOKAS.	No.	AGE.
Gundol	1	5 years.
Bhyaud	1	15 do.
Loonewow	1	2 do.
Do	1	6 do.
Looneywow	1	2¼ do.
Hunmunteyalloo	1	5 do.
Ribra.		
Dhorajee	1	5 do.
Do	1	1 yr&6mo.
Do	1	1 do - 6do.
Draffa.		
Noanuggur.		
Surodhur, of Do	1	2 years.
Bhungore, of Do	1	5 do.
Momanoo, of Do	1	5 do.
Guvana, of Do.		
Khurba, of Do.	1	6 do.
Mokhanoo, of Do	1	11 do.
Paynehrura.		
Khurida a	1	6 do.
Do	1	7 do.
Khumbooroo	1	5 do.
Do	1	4 do.
Do	1	6 do.
Matta Moda	1	2 do.
Matta Moda	1	8 do.
Bebide	1	2 do.
Hunmunjoo.		
Vunthulley	1	5 do.
Khelsoo	1	7 do.
Choor	1	3 do.
Megpoor	1	20do. *
Chomdralloo	1	7 years.
Anundpoor.		
Vessamnoo	1	4 do.
Salpeperyoo.		
Munueet	1	2 do.
Maroodo.		
Jonu.	1	11 do.

* In the Bhull Pergunnah, and her husband is unable to feed her, therefore she returned to her father's house. Such a case of poverty is truly affecting, and will no doubt claim public attention. There are other instances where the parties in distress appealed for support, and said they would *lay their daughters at the Sirkar's door for the purpose!!*

TALOOKAS.	No.	AGE.
Jonu............	1	8 do.
Do............	1	6 months.
Joona............	1	2 years.
Satoodur............	1	1 do.
Do............	1	1 y.6 mo.
Rajpoora............	1	1 year.
Vaurey............	1	6 do.
Do............	1	1 do.
Do............	1	10 do.
Do............	1	4 months.
Do............	1	2 years.
Soosang............	1	1 do.
Do............	1	6 do.
Do............	1	2 do.
Vaurey............	1	6 do.
Chandley.		
Kurle Dhrole.......	1	2 do.

TALOOKAS.	No.	AGE.
Vunpurey..........	1	2 ys.6mo.
Do..........	1	3 years.
Sunuseera..........	1	10 do.
Leyalloa..........	1	14 do.
Rejeya..........	1	9 do.
Kheejeryoo..........	1	3 do.
Megpoor..........	1	3 do.
Sooltanpoor........	1	2 ys.6mo.
Bhakherdo.		
Bofueko.		
Gutko.		
Total....	63	Females saved.

N. B. This list inclusive of all the Jhamfa caste in the Peninsula Camp, Bullumba, June 20, 1817.

The Par. Papers on Infanticide, printed July, 1828, contain tables of infants preserved and stated to be alive belonging to the tribe of Jahrejas, in Cutch and Wagur in 1823, to the number of *ninety-one*. In 1824 was presented to Government a "Statement showing the number of Jahreja females born and preserved in the Western Peninsula of Guzerat. The total number shown consists of 266 *females:* sixty-three appear to have been in existence June 20, 1817; the remaining 203 have been born and preserved since; forty-seven of the whole number have died since their birth, twenty-five are married, and 194 are unmarried." H. Pottinger, Esq., Resident in Cutch, forwarded to Government a list of the female Jahrejas living in Cutch, Jan. 1, 1826, amounting to 143.* These important data, while they show the measure of success attending the efforts to abolish Infanticide, painfully demonstrate the continuance of the practice, and the necessity of more efficient means for its entire abolition.

The following extract of a treaty of alliance between the Hon. East India Company and his Highness Maha Raja Mirza Rao Shri Desserljee, Chief of Cutch, dated Oct. 1819, is interesting:—"The Hon. Company engages to exercise no authority over the domestic concerns of the Rao, or of those of any of the Jahreja chieftains of the country. That the Rao, his heirs and successors, shall be absolute

† Par. Papers, p. 110, 111.
* Par. Papers, 1828, pp. 7, 8, 11—14, 23—25.

masters of their territory, and that the civil and criminal jurisdiction of the British Government shall not be introduced therein.

"His Highness the Rao, his heirs and successors, at the particular instance of the Honourable Company, *engage to abolish in their own family the practice of Infanticide;* they also engage to join heartily with the Honourable Company *in abolishing the custom generally throughout the Bhyaud of Cutch.*

"Previously to the execution of the deed of guarantee in favour of Jahreja Byaut, according to the tenor of the sixteenth article, a written engagement shall be entered into by them to abstain from the practise of Infanticide; and specifying that, in case any of them do practise it, the guilty person shall submit to a punishment of any kind that may be determined by the Honourable Company's Government and the Cutch Durbar."*

The Papers on Infanticide, July, 1828, contain a translation of an agreement entered into by the Jahrejas of Santulpore for the suppression of Infanticide, dated March 3, 1827; a similar one was entered into by the Jahrejas of Charchut in June, 1827. For the form of this engagement see Par. Papers, p. 29, 30.

In the abolition of Infanticide at Saugur humanity and religion have obtained a noble triumph. The deposition, p. 161, shews the nature and extent of the evil; after due investigation of the subject, a proclamation was issued by the British Government, A.D. 1802, abolishing the practice.† In Dec. 1821, the Secretary to the Committee of Management of the Saugur Island Society reported to the Government that "*the practice of immolating children had entirely ceased.*" The following extract of an account of a visit to this place by a friend of the author's confirms the statement:—

"In the beginning of January, 1825, Mr. Williamson, with three of the natives, Gorachund, Rotun, and Tanin, went to Gunga Saugur to be present at the great annual assembly there. It is well known that the character of this assembly is greatly changed since the merciful and Christian measures of the Marquis of Wellesley have been in force. But still it presents a scene of the grossest superstition, and affords a favourable opportunity to missionaries of sending far and wide the news of salvation. While walking along the beach, they met a man with two

---

* Par. Papers, p. 115.

† See this interesting document Par. Papers, 1824, p. 137, 138. "Infanticide in India," by the Author, p. 64.

little boys, and asked him what he meant to do with them at Saugur, whether he intended giving them Gunga? He replied, *No no, but he had made a vow before they were born, that if Gunga would give him children, he would give their juta, that is their matted hair, to her as soon as they were able to accompany him.'* When it was told him that all this was useless, he said, it was agreeable to the shastras and the advice he had received from the Brahmuns.'

The following extract of a letter from Capt. H. Hall, Superintendent of Mhairwarra, to Sir C. Metcalfe, Baronet, Resident at Delhi, July, 1827, is interesting as showing the abolition of Infanticide in the north of India :—

" It is most satisfactory to be able to report *the complete and voluntary abolition of the two revolting customs, female Infanticide and the sale of the women.* Both crimes were closely connected, having had their origin in the heavy expense attending marriage contracts. The sums were payable by the male side, ever unalterable, equal to the rich and poor, without any abatement whatever in favour of the latter. What first established the payment is unknown, but it was so sacred, inviolable, and even a partial deviation so disgraceful, that the most necessitous of the tribe would not incur the imputation. Hence arose as decided a right over the persons of women as over cattle or other property. They were inherited and disposed of accordingly, to the extent even of *sons selling their own mothers!* Hence also arose Infanticide. The sums payable were beyond the means of so many, that daughters necessarily remained on hand after maturity, entailed immortal disgrace, and thus imposed a necessity on all female progeny of becoming victims to their family honour.

" On the establishment of British rule, both evils gradually diminished! Females were not allowed to be transferred, except for conjugal purposes, their consent was to be obtained, and their choice consulted; humane treatment was enforced, and the whole system of considering them as mere cattle was discouraged. *Female Infanticide was at once prohibited,* and though many, no doubt, still fell secret sacrifices from the great facility of undetected destruction, yet the danger, aided by improved feeling, increased the survivors so considerably as to force upon the Mhairs a due sense of the root of the evil, and a general wish for its removal, by a reduction of the regulated sum of contract; but they were *averse,* indeed declared their *inability* to alter their long-established custom themselves, and earnestly entreated *it might be effected by an order of authority,* *binding all to obedience by heavy penalties.* After the lapse of a few months, allowed for consideration, the whole was settled in public punchyte, and its resolutions were confirmed without the slightest alteration, so that the proceeding originated with, and has been carried through by, the inhabitants themselves; nor has there been a single petition against it, either pending or subsequent to adjustment. They have lowered the sum payable on marriage-contracts, abolished all right of subsequent sale, and fixed a year's imprisonment, or 200 rupees' fine, with exclusion from caste, as the punishment for deviation. The arrangement is calculated to give entire satisfaction, leaving nothing to be wished; and a more happy proof of general improvement could scarcely be adduced, embracing, as it does, in its very extensive bearings, the suppression of so much crime, immorality, and misery."*

The late Bishop Heber, speaking of the Ramayuna festival at Allahabad, mentions the following important fact:—"There was a hideous and accursed practice in 'the good old times' before the British police was established, at least if all which the Mussulmans and English say is to be believed, which shows the Hindoo superstition in all its horrors. The poor children, who represented Ram, his brother, and Seeta, who had been thus feasted, honoured, and made to contribute to the popular amusement, were, it is said, *always poisoned in the sweetmeats given them the last day of the show*, that it might be said their spirits were absorbed into the deities whom they had represented! Nothing of the sort can now be done. The children, instead of being bought for the purpose, from a distance, by the priests, are the children of neighbours, whose prior and subsequent history is known; and Ram and Seeta now grow old like other boys and girls."†

In Ceylon Infanticide has been abolished by the following Proclamation of the British Government:—"In the name of his Majesty George the Fourth, of the United Kingdom of Great Britain and Ireland, King, Defender the Faith, We, the Honourable Major-General Sir Edward Barnes, Knight Commander of the Most Honourable Military Order of the Bath, Lieutenant Governor and Commander-in-chief in and over the British settlements and territories in the Island of Ceylon, with the dependen-

---

* Par. Papers, 1828, p. 37, 38. † Journal, vol. i. p. 338.

cies thereof, do hereby proclaim, in order that no one may pretend ignorance of the law—That any person, whether being the parent or any other, who shall kill any child of whatever age, within the Kandyan Provinces, shall and will be equally punished with death as for the murder of a grown up person; and no plea will be admitted in any extenuation of any barbarous usage or custom of this description having prevailed, the same being wholly contrary to the ancient laws of the kingdom of Kandy. Given at Columbo, in the said Island of Ceylon, the twenty-fifth day of September, in the year of our Lord one thousand eight hundred and twenty-one."*

In the Island of Owhyhee, or Hawaii, the recent triumph of Christianity in the abolition of Infanticide and other inhuman customs presents a subject of the most grateful nature for the contemplation of the friends of humanity and religion. See Ellis's Tous through Hawaii (London), 1826, pp. 287—305.

The difficulties attending the entire abolition of Infanticide in India are considerable. We have seen the efforts of the Persians and Syracusans to destroy this cruel custom among the Carthaginians, yet Rollin observes—" It appears from Tertullian's Apology that this barbarous custom prevailed in Africa, long after the ruin of Carthage. ' Infantes penes Africam Saturno immolabantur palam usque ad proconsulatum Tiberii, qui eosdem sacerdotes in eisdem arboribus templi sui obumbraticibus scelerum votivis crucibus exposuit, teste militia patriæ nostræ, quæ id ipsum munus illi proconsuli functa est;—children were publicly sacrificed to Saturn, down to the proconsulship of Tiberius, who *hanged the sacrificing priests themselves on the trees which shaded their temples* as on so many crosses raised to expiate their crimes, of which the militia of our country are witnesses, who were the actors of this execution at the command of the Proconsul."†

The propensity of the Israelites to adopt the sanguinary customs of the original inhabitants of Canaan is frequently noticed in the sacred Scriptures. "Enflaming yourselves with idols under every green tree; slaying the children in the valleys under the clifts of the rocks." Isa. lvii. 5.—" In thy skirts is found the blood of the poor innocents; I have not

---

* Asiatic Journ. Sep. 1822.

† Tertul. Apol. c. 9, Rollin's Anc. Hist. b. i. p. 109.

found it by secret search, but upon all these." Jer. ii. 34.—"They have forsaken me and have estranged this place, and have burned incense in it unto other gods, whom neither they nor their fathers have known, nor the kings of Judah, and have filled this place with the blood of innocents; they have built also the high places of Baal, to burn their sons with fire for burnt-offerings unto Baal, which I commanded not, nor spake, neither came it into my mind." Jer. xix. 4, 5. So also the prophet Ezekiel: "Thou hast taken thy sons and thy daughters whom thou hast borne unto me, and these hast thou sacrificed unto them to be devoured. Is this of thy whoredoms a small matter, that thou hast slain my children, and delivered them to cause them to pass through the fire for them?" Ezek. xvi. 20, 21. This custom is found among the people who were transplanted to the cities of Samaria by the king of Assyria, and they continued the practice though in a strange land:—"Every nation made gods of their own, and put them in the houses of the high places which the Samaritans had made, every nation in their cities wherein they dwelt. And the men of Babylon made Succoth-benoth, and the men of Cuth made Nergal, and the men of Hamath made Ashima, and the Avites made Nibbaz and Tartak, and the Sepharvites burnt their children in fire to Adrammelech and Anammelech the gods of Sepharvaim." 2 Kings xvii. 29—31.

The Par. Papers on Infanticide show that considerable difficulties have been experienced in prosecuting the attempts for the abolition of this horrid superstition; and it is proper that these difficulties should be known, to chasten our sanguine expectation of success, and to arm to perseverance and fortitude. Lord Teignmouth, in a paper on the Customs and Practices of the Hindoos, justly observes:—

"A prohibition, enforced by the denunciation of the severest temporal penalties, would have little efficacy in abolishing a custom which existed in opposition to the feelings of humanity and natural affection; and *the sanction of that religion which the Rajkoomars professed was appealed to in aid of the ordinances of civil authority;* upon this principle, an engagement, binding themselves to desist in future from the barbarous practice of causing the death of their female children, was prepared, and circulated among the Rajkoomars for their signature; and as it was also discovered that the same custom prevailed, though in a less degree, among a smaller tribe of people, also within the province of Benares, called Rajebunses, measures were adopted at the same time to make them sensible of its iniquity, and to procure from them a subscription similar to that exacted from the Rajkoomars."*

"The practice," says W. Cracroft, Esq., Magistrate of Juanpore, May, 1819, "arises from the difficulty the Rajkoomars experience in procuring husbands for their daughters. The only tribes who will receive Rajkoomar females as wives are the Bisen, and Soreej Buns, of Goruckpore, and the Gurwars of Mirzapore, and the Boghel of Rewah; and these tribes, from an idea of their superiority, will not admit a Rajkoomar female, without receiving a very large dowry with her. They intermarry among each other, and feel no want of the Rajkoomar females to keep up their race. Until this obstacle can be removed, or some other means devised for providing husbands for the females of the Rajkoomar tribe, all efforts must, in my opinion, fail of checking the practice. No doubt can exist as to the propriety, indeed the necessity, of attempting to restrain it in some manner; but it appears doubtful whether severe punishment would have that effect. Hitherto no magistrate has ever apprehended or committed any individual on a charge of this kind; and I do not doubt that this has been avoided by design, for the instances are too frequent to admit the possibility of their evading proof, had a strict search been often made for that purpose. I wish to be favoured with your opinion, and to have the directions of Government previously to taking any steps in a case which involves so many difficulties."†

"I entered on this undertaking," says Colonel Walker, "with sanguine expectations of success, but which were *for a long time disappointed*; and I must own that the natives had formed much more just opinions on the subject, when they foretold the difficulties that would attend the attempt, which few of them thought could be overcome but by the Company making a conquest of the country. I conceived that reason and feeling would effect the relinquishment of a barbarous custom unconnected with the principles of society, and which all the passions of the human mind, and all the forms and maxims of religion, were combined

* Par. Papers, 1824, p. 9. Asiatic Researches, vol. iv.

† Par. Papers, p. 15, 16.

to destroy. As it was evident also that the most disinterested humanity had led the Honourable Company to interfere for the abolition of female Infanticide, I conceived that this reflection, and the respect due to their mediation, would have disposed the Jahrejas to comply with a request which it was scarcely to be supposed could be at variance with their own sentiments. *But sentiments of nature and humanity have no influence with the Jahrejas*; and I was soon, however reluctantly, obliged to relinquish the favourable expectations I had formed of success. The difficulties were many and formidable."*

The Governor of Bombay, the Honourable M. Elphinstone, expresses himself in the language of despondency, and unbecoming the high ground obtained by engagements and treaty with the abettors of this inhuman custom. "There is one point of great importance in which we are *already entitled to exercise the right of general superintendence*. This is in checking the crime of female Infanticide, and in imposing the fines authorized by Colonel Walker's agreements on those who may be guilty of it. It is greatly to be regretted that the difficulty of detection should secure the pepetrators of this crime so effectually from punishment as to render *the article against it a dead letter!* There has been no instance of punishment for Infanticide since the agreements were concluded; and this is so far from being owing to the diminution of the crime, that, from the best information Major Ballantine could obtain, it would appear that *not more than* 100 *females born since the agreement are now in existence*, and it is not easy to say how many of these might have been spared if the engagement had never been entered into. No effectual check can be imposed on this atrocious practice so long as it is so completely congenial to the general feeling of the people; unless, by employing hired agents, as proposed by Major Ballantine, whose duty it should be to detect offenders of this description; and such a measure would lead to so much intrusion into the most private and domestic proceedings of the superior castes (among whom alone Infanticide prevails), and would be open to so many abuses on the part of the informers, that I do not think the chance of success would compensate for the disaffection which it would create. It may also be doubted how far we have a right

---

* Par. Papers, p. 46. See p. 97.

to interfere to such an extraordinary pitch with the private life of a people with whose civil government and internal police we do not pretend to have any concern. We must therefore be content to follow the footsteps of our predecessors (without attempting to go beyond them) in their most meritorious endeavours to discountenance this enormity; and we may safely flatter ourselves, that, as the manners of the people become softened by a continuance of tranquillity and good order, they will gradually discontinue a practice which is not more inconsistent with reason than repugnant to natural instinct."* Jan. 1821.

The Par. Papers of 1828 contain the following remarks by the Political Agent in Kattywar, dated July, 1824:—"The principal obstacle to be overcome in rendering the engagements effectual is the difficulty in detecting those concerned in the perpetration of the crime; so long as the feelings and interests of the people render them disinclined to afford aid in discovering it, few are prompted to make it known by a sense of humanity, or even of interest. Though all classes are ready to admit the barbarity of the practice, still they view it with so passive a spirit that they feel indisposed to encounter the odium or animosity that the consequences of a disclosure might occasion. A constant intercourse with the Jahrejas, during my annual circuit, has given me opportunities of impressing on their minds the interest taken by the British Government in the suppression of this unnatural practice, and the guilt attached to the commission of it by the dictates of their own religion. I received continued assurances that they will discountenance it; but, *from the disproportionate number of females still existing, it is evident that, although this horrible practice may be somewhat subdued, it is still far from being relinquished.*

"The minds and opinions of the tribe do not appear to have undergone that change on the subject that will alone overcome the existence of a custom so unnatural. The effects of the penalties enjoined by the engagements entered into by the Jahrejas would operate in deterring from the commission of the crime, if the means of detection existed, or its discovery was not opposed by difficulties that defeat the utmost vigilance. Proving it is almost impracticable, unless some part of the domestic establishment of a Jahreja

---

* Par. Papers, p. 116.

betray him, a circumstance that seldom can be expected, as the domestic servants are generally the old adherents and dependants of his family."*

These various statements will prepare the reader to peruse with interest the concluding chapter of this book. The ancient Law of God to the Sons of Noah was, "At the hand of every man's brother will I require the life of man." If Infanticide be not punished in this manner, is it to be doubted whether or not, Britain should "make inquisition for blood?" How long is this feeble, temporizing system to continue? Are we "entitled to exercise the right of general superintendence," and shall we shrink from it, and thus be "partakers in other men's sins?" Let our motto be, "Be just and fear not."

CHAP. IV.

The necessity and propriety of adopting measures for the entire and immediate abolition of Infanticide—decisive steps requisite—objections answered—facilities enjoyed for its abolition—concluding remarks.

It is grateful to the friends of humanity, and confers a lustre on the British character, that *effectual steps have been taken to abolish some of the cruel customs of India.* It is, however, to be regretted that what has commenced so well has not been carried forward to the complete annihilation of every practice opposed to the natural dictates of humanity. "Usages," observes Lord Teignmouth, "originating in Hindoo superstition and customs of immemorial prescription have been discountenanced by the British Administration in Bengal; while the laws of the Mahomedans, which derive their authority from the Koran, have been modified, or, in effect, altered, in various instances. The financial system, which prevailed in Bengal when the East India Company undertook the exercise of the Dewanny functions, was a system of undefined exactions and

---

* Par. Papers, 1828, p. 10.

arbitrary oppression, supported by the most rigorous rules of practice; and the British are entitled to the merit of having annihilated it. The *corah*, or whip, under the Mahomedan Government, was considered a necessary appendage in the country courts, where the collections were made; and the application of it was incessant and severe. A practice adopted on the authority of these ancient rules would be severely punished by the Administration, which has wisely and humanely abolished them. Thus the former customs (particularly in the collection of the land revenue) have undergone a total alteration, to the great benefit of the community. Let it, however, be observed, that the Regulations, which, by deviating from ancient rules, have contributed so much to the happiness of the people, were in many instances, at the time of their establishment, considered as *hazardous innovations, repugnant to the feelings and prejudices of the natives of the highest class.*"*

Colonel Walker thus describes the steps so successfully taken by him for the abolition of Infanticide in Kattywar.

"I had been for several years in habits of friendly correspondence with Jehajee, the chief of Moorbee, and he had continually expressed a strong desire to cultivate the favour of the English Government. The artifices of this chief and his vakeel, who resided in camp, deceived and amused me for some time with promises which proved fallacious. I availed myself of the agency and influence of Soonderjee Sewjee, after his arrival in camp, but with no better success. At last Jehajee transmitted a paper, in which he offered to accede to my wishes by preserving his daughters, *provided I would reduce Mallia, and restore the village of Kuralla, of which he had been deprived by the Guicowar government!* The possession of this paper I conceived of importance, as it discovered the *selfish and mercenary motives* that attached the Jahrejas to Infanticide. I preserved it as a testimony which reflected on their pretences of the inviolability of the practice as a custom of the caste, and destroyed every argument which they had attempted to found on principle. When Jehajee perceived the disadvantage which attended the possession of this paper, he made several applications to induce me to restore it, with which I did not comply. It was also evident that it would be very difficult to awaken their natural feelings; and that the same motives of interest would have more influence in inducing them to relinquish the practice than any arguments derived from humanity, morality, or religion. It appeared likewise, from the communications of Jehajee and others, that the reproach of being the first to renounce an ancient practice operated as a considerable motive. The authority of this example could not be complete unless it were set by a chief of acknowledged rank and superiority.

---

* Considerations on communicating to the Natives of India the blessings of Christianity. Hatchard, 1808, pp. 23—38.

"The Rao of Cutch seemed to possess these qualifications from his family, and extent of territory. I was induced, therefore, to select this chieftain; but addressed myself principally to Futteh Mahomed, whose authority is paramount in that country, and from whom, as a zealous Mahomedan, I was led to expect the exertion of his influence for suppressing a crime against nature and religion. The answer, however, of Futteh Mahomed destroyed every hope of success from that quarter. This Jemader, who rose from the humble station of a goatherd, and is extremely illiterate, had the sentiments of his letter probably dicated to him, and by the hand of his writer transmitted, in an inflated and ostentatious style, an elaborate defence of the practice of Infanticide, such as could be expected to proceed only from a bigotted Jahreja. In the mean while every effort was continued to prevail on the Moorbee chief to abandon Infanticide, which the long detention of the detachment in the vicinity of that city afforded. It was the daily subject of letters, messages, and conferences.

"The humanity and tenderness congenial to the sex induced me to expect the assistance of the women of Jehajee's family. The preservation of their offspring appeared peculiarly their business. I conceived that my appeal to wives and mothers, and to women who came from tribes who rejected Infanticide, would be attended with every advantage. I was further led to entertain great hopes of this plan, on account of the high character of the mother of the chief of Moorbee for prudence, propriety of conduct, and a benevolent disposition. As this lady possessed considerable influence over her son, I expected that she would exert it in favour of a measure agreeable to her own feelings. The embarrassed state of Jehajee's affairs, and the countenance which he stood in need of from me for retrieving them, were circumstances which I conceived would occur to the discretion of his mother, and urge her to obtain from her son a concession which might give the family a claim to my support. My overtures to this lady were, at first, received with the feelings natural to her sex, and she seemed disposed, with the rest of the women, who held several consultations together on the subject, to unite their influence for the abolition of Infanticide. But these ebullitions were of short duration; the Jahrejas were alarmed, and the women contended for the ancient privilege of the caste: they were led away from the path of nature by the influence of their husbands. The mother of the chief of Moorbee requested that she might be excused soliciting her son on this head, and referred me for further information to Jehajee.

"At this period my prospect of success was very obscure and distant. Although these efforts, however, had failed of their effect, they were useful, and paved the way for success, by turning the attention of the country to a subject which had never before appeared to engage notice. *By discussiug the subject frequently in the public Cutcherry, and exposing the enormity of the practice, as contrary to the precepts of religion and the dictates of nature, every caste came to express an abhorrence of Infanticide, and the inveterate prejudices of the Jahrejas began to be shaken.*

"But, whatever influence these circumstances might produce, as Jehajee was the first chief whom I had addressed on the subject, it was of the utmost importance to make some impression on him. I bent every exertion, therefore, and tried various expedients to reclaim this chief, who had already destroyed two of his daughters, from the practice of Infanticide. At last I obtained from Jehajee a conditional writing to the following effect:—'From motives of friendship, the Honourable

Company have urged me to preserve my daughters: to this I consent, if the chief of Nowanugger and Gondul agree.' This was the first considerable step towards the attainment of this great object, and the writing appeared to reduce the question to a kind of point of honour, or respect for antiquity, in setting the example of sanctioning an innovation on a general habit. From the character and behaviour of Jam I could have no hopes that he would set this example; but, as the family of Dewajee of Gondul had already preserved several of their daughters, I was led to entertain the most favourable expectations from the general disposition of this chief, and his reputation for humanity. It may be proper to mention that Jehajee first proposed to insert the names of the Rao of Cutch, and Jam of Nowanugger in his writing; but I positively refused to take the paper unless it comprised Dewajee of Gondul. The compliance of Jehajee with this request it may be but fair to consider as a favourable indication of his sentiments; and that he was secretly, though not extremely, inclined to agree to the abolishing of Infanticide. It may be presumed that he was acquainted with the disposition of Dewajee, and of the general opinion that this chief, when pressed, would renounce the practice of killing his daughters. From Dessajee of Mallia I obtained a similar writing to that received from the chief of Moorbee. I had conceived great expectations from Dessajee, who had preserved a daughter, and had by his vakeel afforded repeated assurance that he was ready to renounce Infanticide; but it is remarkable that this chief used every evasion and delay to avoid executing a formal deed in renunciation of the practice.

"The narrative must now accompany the operations of the detachment which traversed the country of Jam, and arrived at Kundorera. I employed this time, as often as opportunity permitted, in favour of the design for abolishing Infanticide. Wassonjee Eswurjee, the vakeel of the Gondul chief, residing in camp, enabled me frequently to converse with him on the subject; and this respectable Brahmun was easily prevailed on to unite his influence with mine, in order to prevail on his master to enter into a formal obligation for abolishing Infanticide. During these events Wassonjee had occasion to proceed to Gondul on some revenue affairs, and before his departure he privately gave me such assurance as I conceived might be confided in, that he would obtain from Dewagee authority, on his return, to enter into any engagements which might be required for preserving the daughters of the Jahrejas residing in that part of the country. The mission of Wassonjee Eswurjee was entirely successful; and on his return to camp, after expressing the reluctance of his master to set an example which might bring on him the reproach of his caste, *a deed of the most solemn, effectual, and binding nature was executed, renouncing for ever the practice of Infanticide.*

"*The following is a translation of this instrument:—*

"Whereas the Honourable English Company, and Anund Row Guicowar, Sena Khaskel Shamsher Bahadur, having set forth to us the dictates of the shastras, and the true faith of the Hindoos, as well as that the Brimhaway Wurtuch Pooran declares the killing of children to be a heinous sin, it being written that it is as great an offence to kill an embryo as a Brahmun, that to kill one woman is as great a sin as killing 100 Brahmuns; that to put one child to death is as great a transgression against the divine laws as to kill 100 women; and that the perpetrators of this sin shall be damned to the hell Kule Sootheeta, where he shall be infested with as many maggots as he may have hairs on his body;

be born again a leper, and debilitated in all his members; We, Jahreja Dewajee, and Coer Nuthoo, Zemindars of Gondul (the custom of female Infanticide having long prevailed in our caste), do hereby agree for ourselves and for our offspring, as also we bind ourselves in behalf of our relations and their offspring for ever, for the sake of our own prosperity, and for the credit of the Hindoo faith, that we shall from this day renounce this practice, and, in doubt of this, that we acknowledge ourselves offenders against the Sircars. Moreover, should any one in future commit this offence we shall expel him from our caste, and he shall be punished according to the pleasure of the two Governments, and the rule of the shastras.

"The above writing is duly executed. With the exception of Jam, every Jahreja chief readily, and without offering a single objection, subscribed to a counterpart of this instrument."*

In the Bengal Presidency, the proceedings of Government were considered sufficiently explicit and authoritative to suppress this unnatural custom. The Sup. of Police addresses the Chief Secretary of Government, May, 1819. "Sec. 11, Reg. III. 1804, already provides for the punishment of Infanticide, and it is clearly inexpedient that the Legislature should interfere in any other manner; *the practice being declared a crime, it is the duty of the Magistrate to do his utmost to convict those who still persist in it*."† The prevalence of this custom in the Bengal Presidency, under such circumstances, is a source of deep regret, and demonstrates the necessity of some more efficient measures for its suppression; while it shows the defective moral influence of heathenism, in restraining from the perpatration of the most unnatural crimes.

More efficient plans have been proposed for the entire abolition of Infanticide in India. "His Lordship in council regrets to observe (says the Sec. to the Bengal Government, Aug., 1816), from the remarks contained in your Report, which are, in fact, confirmed by information received from your official sources, that the measures adopted by Mr. Duncan, when President at Benares, and the provisions of Reg. XXI. 1795, and Sec. 11, Reg. III. 1804, *have failed to prevent the inhuman practice which exists among the Rajkoomars, and some other tribes of Rajpoots, of destroying their female infants;* and that, although a greater degree of precaution is now observed to prevent detection, there is too much reason to fear that *the crime itself has not in any degree diminished!* The attention of the Nizamut Adawlut will be directed to the

* Par. Papers, 1824, pp. 46—49. † p. 16.

subject of the paragraph above specified, and they will be desired, after obtaining what further information the local authorities may be able to furnish, to offer such suggestions as may appear to them calculated for the more effectual prevention of this dreadful crime, and for the detection and punishment of those who may be guilty of it."*

"We are sensible (says the Honourable Governor of Bombay, in a Minute respecting Infanticide, in 1808) that it must require the vigilant and concurrent attention of the Government of the Guicowar and of the Honourable Company to ensure, especially during the first years, the faithful adherence of the several parties to the salutary stipulations to which they have thus been brought to subscribe: but we rely on the zeal of the Resident, who will not fail to stimulate the native administration of Baroda, and, through it, their officers in Kattywar, to attend to and make *periodical reports of the effects of the new system thus happily introduced;* which, if allowed to operate, must soon become manifest in the number of female children which every Jahreja house may soon be known to contain. On the other hand, the want of such indication will constitute engagements, which, *in the present instance, ought not to be treated with much indulgence, but rather punished by a moderate fine,* to be always imposed with the privity of the British Government, through the Resident; and the amount of which, to be applied to the relief of those among the more indigent classes of the Jahrejas who shall be known to fulfil and adhere to the letter and spirit of their engagements; or otherwise, by the infliction of such other penalty as the local authorities may deem the most impressive, and likely to ensure the attainment of an object so highly salutary and indispensable in all respects, as is the extirpation of the baneful practice of Infanticide from all the districts of Kattywar, with an ultimate view to the same humane object in Cutch. It is accordingly desired that the Resident will concert with the Guicowar government the best means for obtaining periodical notices of the operation of the obligations; making it also a rule to submit (exclusive of such intermediate reports as may become necessary) *one general statement on the last day of each year,* how far the amended system has been acted on and observed; what deviations are known or suspected

* Par. Papers, 1824, p. 14.

to have been made from its rules, and what measures pursued for their enforcement; the whole to be accompanied with an estimate of the number of lives that may, under the blessing of Divine Providence, be thus ultimately saved to the community."*

Captain Ballantine writes, July 1816,—"The increasing interest with which the entire abolition (of Infanticide) is viewed by the British Government, and community in general, suggests to me the propriety of offering for your consideration, and the sanction of the Right Honourable the Governor in Council, *a more efficient means of prosecuting, under our own immediate supervision, every possible channel by which to detect any deviation from these solemn engagements.* I have not relaxed on any occasion to impress on the minds of the Guicowar officers the common interest with which the entire abolition of the practice is considered; and, although my applications have not been successful, it is in justice to them to be observed that most of the principal Jahreja chiefs situated in Halaur, &c., have been amenable to the Paishwa's authority, which, combined with the causes above adverted to, is entitled to due consideration. *I have therefore to solicit permission to entertain such an establishment as may be considered equal to the full accomplishment of this interesting and humane object.* It is known to you that in the detection of any case of delinquency, as in those enumerated by Colonel Walker, a fine proportioned to the case, and the ability of the parties, is imposed; nor may it seem, I would respectfully observe, objectionable that the public expense on this account should be reimbursed from the same source.

"The means for detection must of course be by clandestine intercourse with the parties and surrounding inhabitants, and to which end persons so deputed must remain for some time on the spot. Guzurattee mehtas, or writers, are the proper persons to be employed on this duty; they were employed by the native Government in these duties, and the present number to be selected for this important duty should not be less than five at fifty rupees per mensem."†

The Resident at Baroda, in 1816, J. R. Carnac, Esq., accords with the propriety of these suggestions:—"The Jahrejas, though proud, are, like the other natives of India, very avaricious. The object which could not be gained by

---

* Par. Papers, p. 70. † Par. Papers, p. 98.

speaking to their feelings might be effected by working on their disposition. *The reward of a hundred rupees, to him who could satisfactorily establish in another the perpetration of Infanticide, might bring to light numerous circumstances of which we now remain in ignorance.* Nor would the expense of such remunerations fall on either the Native or British Governments. By the bond to which the Jahrejas have subscribed they have rendered themselves liable to punishment at the will of the Sircar; and it could not be considered a severe punishment to insist on the payment of a fine which would more than defray the charges attendant on receiving the information of their guilt. It may not be deemed irrelevant to furnish Government with what I conceive an adequate scale of rewards and punishments; an informer against the Jam should receive 1000 rupees; against the inferior Rajahs 500; against their near relations 250; and against a poor Jahreja 100. The Jam, if proved guilty, should be fined 30,000 rupees; an inferior Rajah 10,000; their near relations 2500, and a poor Jahreja as much as he could pay without ruin. The difficulty of inducing any one to come forward against so powerful a man as the Jam renders it necessary that his reward should be liberal; and, for the sake of example, it is desirable that a person in his high station should be detected and severely punished. The pride of the lower Jahrejas is to support the customs of their clan, and to follow the steps of their great relations in every act. We can never therefore expect the practice of Infanticide to be fairly laid aside till *the principal Jahrejas are either induced or forced to set the example;* I have therefore stated the reward of the informer against the Jam, and the punishment of that chieftain, at a high rate."*

The measures here proposed are desirable and necessary. The Honourable Court of Directors observe in a letter to the Governor of Bombay, March, 1816, referring to an enquiry of the Resident at Baroda, to ascertain and report whether the practice had been discontinued wholly or in part in Cutch, and whether it had entirely ceased within the province of Kattywar: "Most sincerely do we wish that that report may prove satisfactory; and we must again enjoin you, in the most serious and earnest manner, to be *unremitting in your endeavours to accomplish this humane*

* Par. Papers, p. 103, see p. 114, and Par. Papers, 1828, p. 15.

*object in the countries where the British influence can be felt or exerted."**

The Honourable Governor of Bombay, in Camp Jan. 1821, remarks :—"The three most probable points of difference with the Jahrejas are settling their disputes among themselves, enforcing the prohibition of female Infanticide, and compelling them to act against plunderers in their own districts. In the first, all danger may be averted by the prompt and impartial administration of justice; in the second, by caution and delicacy in the means of detecting guilt, and moderation in punishing it. The third is an object of great importance; it is more likely to be obtained by vigilance than severity, by explaining what is expected, censuring neglect, and compelling restitution, with the addition of a fine as the punishment of participation."† The prompt and impartial administration of justice towards the perpetrators of child murder, appears far more desirable and necessary than the caution of delicacy here enjoined. Why such tender treatment of acts of murder? Why such false delicacy to search out iniquity and make "inquisition for blood?" Surely this conduct is unbecoming the British and Christian character.

Colonel Walker, on returning from India, still deeply interested in the success of his humane efforts, addressed the Honourable Court of Directors, July, 1819, to the following effect:—

"In offering my opinion upon the means of suppressing female Infanticide in the West of India I must first observe that this object should be accomplished without violating the feelings of the natives, and without having recourse to actual coercion. I must also beg to refer to my own proceedings, which succeeded in obtaining the consent of the people to relinquish this barbarous and unnatural practice. It was accomplished, no doubt, with great difficulty, but it was so far a spontaneous act that it was solely effected by persuasion and reason. It is under this influence alone that the measure can ultimately be expected to prove successful; but, from the peculiar habits of the people of this part of India, the practice of destroying the children cannot be overcome by the mere dictates of natural affection. When this tie was once abandoned, it would be long before it could be again recovered; and it would be necessary that they should be continually watched, and urged to the performance of a duty which is seldom neglected even by the brutes! It was foreseen that the mere engagement which these people had contracted for discontinuing Infanticide, however solemn and authentic, would not be sufficient unless they were looked after with vigilance; unless they were frequently encouraged; and unless those instances in which they infringed their own voluntary engagement were detected and punished. This mode

* Par. Papers, p. 94. 99. † p. 117.

of punishment was provided by their agreement. I am persuaded that a system of this kind would have succeeded, and have preserved, in a great degree, the engagement inviolate for the abolition of Infanticide.

"It was under the influence of a similar train of reflection that I suggested to the Government, when I quitted India, to exact *an annual report of the progress of Infanticide*, and that it should be the object of continual care and solicitude. Before I rétired from the service I had the satisfaction to see that the principles for its abôlition had made no slight impression on the minds of the people, and in a short period they had saved a considerable number of infants. But, from the report which has now been received from India, it would appear that *the whole number saved in the course of* TEN *years is little more than* SIXTY! and perhaps not a third more than were presented by their parents to me in Kattywar with feelings of affection and delight.

"The first circumstance which requires attention is *to see the people often, and by a frequent intercourse to inspire them with sentiments more favourable to humanity*. It is scarcely to be expected that the Jahrejas will seek our society with greater encouragement than it is the habit of our countrymen, generally speaking, to afford to the natives of India, and we must therefore visit them in their villages. They must be sought out in their recesses, invited to attend the public Cutcherries, and the subject brought as often as possible under public discussion. In these situations opportunities would frequently arise of enforcing the heinous nature of the offence, of calmly discussing its tendency, of exposing its crime, and of contrasting the abominable practice with the universally contrary usage of the rest of mankind. By the effect of example, by the force of conversation, and by diffusing good and just notions of human nature, these men would be gradually alienated from their absurd and guilty conduct. In every attempt to arrest this crime, the Brahmuns, and; the precepts of the Hindoo religion, would be a powerful aid. That religion is directly opposed to the practice, and I always found the Brahmuns most willing coadjutors in this cause of humanity. It is not founded on religion; it is disavowed by the great body of the people, and prevails only among a single tribe.

"They would not withstand any *systematic exertion which might be directed to its overthrow*: and, in fact, did it not yield to an attempt which was made in a doubtful situation, amidst a multitude of other occupations, and which was not pursued for a long time? The same facilities, and greater, now exist to insure success. The Guicawar authority may be disposed more readily to co-operate with us, while our own is better established, and while we possess *an actual share in the government of the country*. The collector of the newly-acquired revenue in Kattywar would be a natural and an essential agent in this humane work. By means of the police, which is under his control, and by the frequent intercourse which his office obliges him to hold with the natives, he would have opportunities of communication superior, perhaps, to any other person. *Let the collector, the agent in Kattywar, the agent in Cutch, and the Guicawar authorities, heartily, and in concert, exert themselves, and they would be irresistible.* But I would not rest the success of this interesting measure on vigilance alone, and the active use of even all the agents in our power. I would employ other *stimuli*, and not neglect those that may be calculated to produce an effect on the grosser passions of those who persevere in the practice of Infanticide. I would not encourage the idea of an expensive agency, nor the direct and professed employment of spies, which are more likely to defeat than to promote the object; but there are, surely, means of ascertaining the result of a birth in a family, without either offending its delicacy, or requiring much expense. The fact of a pregnancy is always public, and the report of the neighbours would often be sufficient evidence. *A few detections would arrest the practice.* If the intercourse were as frequent as I have recommended, many things would be casually learnt, and little indeed could be concealed. In the course of this intercourse many acts of friendship, of courtesy and attention, could be conferred on the Jahrejas, which would be attended with little expense, but which they would highly value; they are both greedy and necessitous. The present of an inferior turban, of a deputta, of a snuff-box, of a pair of spectacles, or any other trifling article, would be prized by them as a mark of honour, and as a profitable acquisition. These little favours would be the means of bringing them together, of inducing them to come into our society, and finally of reconciling them to our views. *It is by association and constant attention that they are to be reclaimed.* The character and government of our country must suffer materially, should those people be allowed to resume a pratice which they had abandoned with all the formality of a regular and solemn compact. May it not be said that *we are more indifferent to the cause of humanity than in exacting a rigid and scrupulous compliance with the terms of a treaty which involved a paltry revenue, or some insignificant district?* We may by kindness and by patience bring them back to the path of their duty. The voice of nature, and the influence of the women, will unite in assisting us, and in this struggle against a deplorable practice we shall finally prevail, while our motives must be applauded, and cannot be mistaken. Were the power of Government never applied but in cases so obviously beneficial and disinterested the rudest minds would bless them; and the feelings of men, as well as their reason, would render them both agreeable and irresistible."* (London, July 1819).

To the adoption of the plans proposed to suppress Infanticide, several objections have been made; these relate to *expense—marrying the females saved—employing officers for detection—and the plans being opposed to the wishes of the people.* "The Governor in Council," it is said, "does not approve of Captain Carnac's entertaining an establishment forthe purpose of suppressing female Infanticide, which, even admitting its formation to be essential to effecting that desirable object, we are not at liberty to sanction without the authority of the Honourable Court; nor does it appear advisable to adopt the other proposition, of defraying the *expenses* of the marriage of the children of a Jahreja."† And in a letter addressed by the Governor to the Honourable Court of Directors, Dec. 1817, it is stated, "While we feel the strongest inclination to accede to any plan which would tend to its suppression, we are not aware

---

* Par. Papers, pp. 119—121. † p. 98.

that any can be adopted beyond the distribution among those who shall adhere to their engagements of the amount of the fines which may be levied on others, without incurring a very heavy charge on the public. To station spies in every town or village would be incurring a *large expenditure*, without, perhaps, securing the object desired; and the measure of authorising an establishment for that purpose is particularly objectionable in principle."*

To *marrying those saved* the Governor General in Council objects by saying,—" Captain Carnac must be informed that if the Honourable Court should undertake to defray the expense of the nuptials of the female children of one of the Jahrejas, the rest of the fraternity would expect the same consideration, to which they would be equally entitled with the Rajah of Moorvee: the introduction of such a practice, independently of the great expense attending it, would also be liable to be abused. The Governor in Council is desirous, however, to be informed what would be the probable amount of the expense attending the marriage of a female of this class, in case the Honourable Court should view the subject in a different light, and should authorize the incurring it on the present, or on any future occasion."†

Of *the officers for detection*, the Resident at Baroda, Sep. 1816, states:—" In 1812, during my employment in the negociations at Noanugger, Witul Rao, Dewanjee, in the hopes of satisfying my inquiries, established several mehtas in the principal Jahreja towns, with instructions to communicate the birth, preservation, or murder of female children, as soon as they received information of such occurrences; but the jealousy with which these men were regarded rendered their exertions almost abortive; and, while no Jahreja would himself communicate the condition of his wife, they found it in vain to ask for information from his neighbours. The duties of these mehtas were of that unquestionable nature that gives general dislike, and were likely to produce a feeling of opposition that would defeat all their inquiries. It was to the establishment of these men that Captain Ballantine alluded. They were withdrawn when the Paishwa resumed his rights in Guzerat, for the reasons stated in Captain Ballantine's letter. That gentleman probably supposes that, though such officers

* Par. Papers, p. 107. † pp. 99, 106.

could gain little information, their presence operated as a check, and made the fear of discovery tend to the abolition of female Infanticide; and it seems reasonable to think that it should have this effect. No better plan having yet been devised, Captain Ballantine has only done his duty, in recommending to the adoption of Government that which seemed to him the best fitted for the object in view."*

Objections to this judicious method of detecting the crime of Infanticide are urged by the Governor of Bombay, in Oct. 1827. "From Lieutenant-Colonel Miles's despatch, and the renewed agreements concluded with the several Jahreja chiefs, subject to the British government, your Honourable Court will learn with satisfaction, that although this barbarous practice has not, it is to be feared, altogether ceased, yet its frequency has greatly diminished. Lieutenant-Colonel Miles's exertions are very praiseworthy, and we have expressed our entire satisfaction with his humane intentions in checking Infanticide; at the same time we have apprized that officer that the measure he purposes adopting, of keeping carcoons to watch over births, was thought objectionable in Kattywar, as leading to an intrusion into domestic privacy very foreign to Indian notions. The chiefs of Chorin, with whom agreements have been concluded, are differently situated, and the measure may be less obnoxious among them; in which case, it would be a desirable experiment; but we have recommended that the greatest caution should be observed in its adoption, and to ascertain its probable effects by previous inquiry." †

As it respects the adoption of these plans *being opposed to the wishes of the people*, it is remarked by the Governor in Council, Dec. 1817, "Your Honourable Court will perceive, that since we had the honour of addressing you on the subject of female Infanticide, in our letter of the 16th of August, 1816, we have been unable to adopt any effectual means of extinguishing that inhuman practice; and we are obliged to add, that the propositions submitted to us for our consideration, with a view of discovering how far the Jahreja chieftains adhered to their engagements, have been abandoned, under the *persuasion that they would prove extremely offensive to their feelings*." ‡

---

* Par. Papers, pp. 102, 106. † Par. Papers, 1828, pp. 5, 6.
‡ Par. Papers, p. 106.

The Court of Directors express their approbation of this policy in a letter to the Governor General in Council in Bengal, Nov. 1822:—"We shall be much gratified to hear that the stipulations contained in the 17th and 18th articles, relative to the abolition of the practice of Infanticide, have been observed. We are not, however, very sanguine in our expectations on this head, unless these stipulations are enforced by interference on the part of the Resident, which would not be reconcileable with our engagement in the 10th article, 'to exercise no authority over the domestic concerns of the Rao, or those of any of the Jahreja chieftains of the country."*

The necessity and utility of these plans are ably advocated from the exceptions made against them. "The very alarm (says the Resident at Baroda, Sep. 1816) which the promulgation of the plan of rewarding informers would excite, might greatly tend to occasion the preservation of many female infants. Aware that no feelings of kindness, of religion, or of general interest for the caste, could induce the poor Jahreja to resist the temptation of a reward, every man would be afraid of his neighbour and his domestic; while there must be many, not of the Jahreja tribe, who are informed of the state of their families, and who can therefore gratify their avarice with less dread of censure. The advantages of this plan, however, are opposed by disadvantages; and these would grow into an evil of some magnitude to the whole body of the Jahrejas *unless provided against at the first outset*. The hopes of reward might induce many to bring forward false accusations, and also such as might have an appearance of validity, without being grounded on fact. The informer should therefore be bound to give proof for the specific information which he brings, under pain of being severely punished if his information should turn out to be false. The only accounts which it seems probable an informer could bring, appear to be that he knew of the pregnancy of a certain Rajpootanee, and that *the event was never published to the community*. Should the issue have been a female child, and it had died, it would require some discrimination on the part of the person investigating information to determine whether the child might not have been still-born, or died shortly after its birth. In either of the last mentioned cases the

---

* p. 115. Did they not stipulate to abolish Infanticide?

informer should receive no more than a third of the reward. But if it should so appear that the Jahreja's wife, against whom the accusation was preferred, had not been pregnant or had suffered an early abortion of her offspring, the accuser should be punished rigorously, or otherwise, according to the circumstances of the case. The evils of goindas in respect to the Jahrejas cannot, I presume, be felt in any degree to the same extent as they are in Bengal. The information which they are required to yield admits of circumstantial proof, and is not like that concerning robberies and murders frequently dependent on presumptive proof, and it is consequently not likely to be given but when there exists, or have existed, some undeniable, and in some measure, public grounds for its being true.

"I propose this plan with much deference to the wisdom of the Right Hon. the Governor in Council, sensible that it may appear better in theory than it may prove to be good in practice; but *I am at the same time hopeful that it may be better than no plan at all, in rendering the exertions of my predecessor a permanent benefit to the country.* But Government must be aware that *my success is entirely dependent on subordinate agents,* nearly as far removed from me, as I myself am from the seat of Government;* and that, whatever interest I may take in the subject, my individual exertions can be of no further use than in stimulating them to a zealous attention. I have every reason to believe that neither Captain Ballantine nor the Dewanjee has been less active than the most humane man could wish, but *the means in their power were not fitted to enable them to command success!*

"The expense of marrying the daughters of the chiefs of Kattywar would probably be as follows;—the marriage of the Jam would amount to 30 or 35,000 rupees; that of the daughter of a minor Rajah, such as the Rajah of Moorbee Goondul, and Rajcote, to 15 or 16,000; the daughter of one of the near relations of the Rajah would require from 5 to 7,000 rupees, and that of a poor Jahreja's daughter from 1,000 to 1,500 rupees. It would evidently be enormously expensive for any Government to defray the

* "Subsequently to Col. Walker's departure the public service rendered it expedient that the Resident at Baroda should remain at his station; which was 200 miles from the Province where the practice of Infanticide prevailed."—Debate on Suttees, in a general Court of Proprietors, March 1827. Asi. Jour. May 1827.—Auth.

charges of marrying even only one daughter in each family, and it might be impolitic to marry that of one person, and not of another. The Moorbee Rajah, however, might be made an exception, since it was he who first saved his daughter; and since it was by his means that Colonel Walker laid the foundation of the superstructure he afterwards raised. I conceive the Guicawar Government would willingly share with the British Government the expense and the honour of presenting a dowry to the first female child saved from the barbarity of an unfeeling parent."*

Captain Ballantine observes upon the same subject,—"I venture to repeat, the means I recommended were both desirable and eligible in many points of view, and, in my humble apprehension, calculated to have obtained us actual instances of individual criminality, and no doubt to have followed up with greater effect the prohibitory nature of the solemn compacts the Jahrejas entered into with us, to discontinue the systematic murder of their female offsprings. In regretting the cause of the apprehension submitted in the preceding paragraph, it is only necessary to recal to the recollection of Government, that we have hitherto, and have still, to depend on the native governments and authorities for the only information to be obtained, or essential attention to the enforcement of the stipulations of our engagements.

"From the voluminous papers before me, the British Government seems to desire the abolition of this singular custom with equal interest and solicitude; and that probably, through its wisdom and recommendation, *the Honourable Court will eventually sanction the adoption of measures better calculated to root out the evil.* For might not the expense and responsibility, and our active supervision, with deference I submit, be with strict policy and justice made chargeable to the Government who alone derive any pecuniary or real advantage from the country, and of course should be equally interested in the first dictates of humanity, and in the annihilation of customs offensive to all religions, and degrading to human nature in general?†

"I beg respectfully to remark," says J. R. Carnac, Esq., Resident at Baroda, Oct. 1817, to the chief secretary of the Bombay government, "that in no suggestions for the maintenance of an establishment for the discovery of those

---

* Par. Papers, pp. 103, 104. † pp. 108, 109.

Jahrejas who have immolated their female offspring, am I sensible of having recommended additional emoluments to my assistant, or in the most distant shape to combine the important objects of humanity with any personal advantages whatever. My desire has always been the adoption of *some effectual plan, hitherto entirely unheeded,* to give effect to the humane exertions of my predecessor, in the conviction of *the utter impossibility of preventing female Infanticide, where the means are confined to the personal influence merely of my assistant in Kattywar.*

"*The disappointment which has been experienced can be traced exclusively to* THE WANT OF A SYSTEM, *by which a detection of the guilty could be ensured, and not to any indifference on the part of the local officers to the enforcement of the engagements contracted by the Jahrejas.* I have had the honour on several occasions of bringing the subject in the most urgent manner to the attention of Government, and in submitting recommendations on the ways and means for an effectual abolition of Infanticide, have implored Government to devise any plan which in its wisdom might be efficacious. While my suggestions have been deemed objectionable, *no other plan has intermediately been prescribed, and doubtless the want of it is frequently affording the most melancholy evidence of an evasion of the excellent engagements contracted by the influence of Lieutenant Colonel Walker.*"*

The Governor of Bombay addressed the Honourable Court of Directors, Nov. 1827, in the following manner, which indicates a pleasing attention to the subject of Infanticide:—"The Chief of Rajcote applied to us for our guarantee to a mortgage of four villages, to enable him to raise a sum of money to defray the expenses of his marriage. The late Chief of Rajcote was one of the first who attended to Lieutenant Colonel Walker, in his settlement of Kattywar, and acceded to the advice and wishes of that officer, in his humane endeavour to abolish Infanticide, and the marriage of his daughter (himself a Jahreja) had involved the family, which had led to the mortgage of the farm of his talooka. It appeared to us, however, that instead of sanctioning this mortgage, which we were nevertheless disposed to do, under the peculiar circumstances of this chieftain's case, it would be more expedient to mark

---

* Par. Papers, p. 112, 113.

the high sense which we entertained of the conduct of this family, in renouncing Infanticide, to make the Takore a donation from the fund established for this purpose. A donation of the sum of rupees, 12,000, was accordingly made to him, to enable him to bear the expense of the marriage."* The beneficial effects of such measures are self-evident, and yet alone they appear inadequate to the suppression of this unnatural crime.

The facilities which Britain possesses for abolishing this horrid rite are very considerable. The whole civilized world naturally looks to her to do her duty in India, and suppress every sanguinary practice subversive of the principles of natural and revealed Religion.

"The influence," says the Honourable Governor of Bombay, Dec. 1817, "which the cession of the Paishwa's tribute from Kattywar will afford to the British Government over that part of Guzerat, will, we trust, enable us to secure a more rigid adherence to the engagements of the Jahrejas; and the Resident at Baroda has been directed to depute Captain Ballantine to inform them of our determination to enforce the penalties whenever a breach of their engagements can be established; and to withhold our countenance from those who shall continue to follow this inhuman custom."† In a letter to the Court of Directors, Aug. 1820, it is said, "Your Honourable Court will learn with satisfaction, that, by the 17th Article of the treaty with Cutch, *the practice of female Infanticide has been formally renounced in that Province.*"‡

The Guicowar Government, in Aug. 1825, expressed its approbation of Colonel Walker's suggestion, that "The sums levied and fines from disturbers of the peace and other offenders should, through the clemency of Government, be distributed in such sums as were suitable to the station in life of the parties concerned; to defray the marriage expenses of females who should be preserved." To which it was replied by the Cutch Government, "The case under consideration is one of charity and will procure the blessings of Heaven on both Governments; therefore, whatever sums have been realized as fines on offenders since Captain Barnewell was placed in charge of the Districts, or any extra revenue beyond the tribute, as fixed for perpetuity by Colonel Walker, may be appropriated as

---

* Par. Papers, 1828, p. 6. † Par. Papers, p. 107. ‡ p. 114.

above specified : the disposal being year by year duly communicated to us, and the arrangement is highly satisfactory to this Government." In Jan. 1826 the Resident in Cutch reported 143 female children being alive, and observes, "I have made an arrangement, in concert with the other members of the regency, for the birth of every child (male or female) that occurs in a Jahreja family being reported to the Durbar; and as all deaths are to be notified at the time, and in the same manner, I hope these precautions will effectually put a stop to any instances of Infanticide that may still be occasionally practised." The adoption of a similar check in Kattywar, if practicable, was considered by the Governor extremely desirable.*

The measures which should be adopted for the speedy and entire abolition of Infanticide are ably stated by the philanthropic Colonel Walker in a letter to the Honourable Court of Directors, dated London, Aug. 1819. The following extracts appear very interesting:—

"I shall turn with pleasure to the circumstances which are favourable to this cause of humanity, and which may encourage us to expect that this revolting practice will be overcome. The Court of Directors, the Government and its Assistants in India, appear at present to take great interest in the success of the measure. This is one favourable class of circumstances. Again, the prejudices of the Jahrejas with which I had to grapple, if not entirely done away, are at least suppressed and disavowed. They appear so far to move within the range in which nature acts, that they express no pride in the dèstruction of their offspring, and feel no shame in rearing them. It is evident that a very favourable change has taken place, since all the infants they have saved have been the consequence of their own choice; and, as some of their daughters have been reared within very recent dates, the principle of natural affection is even at this moment producing its effect.

"One of the principal objections to the remedial measures proposed to and rejected by the Bombay Government, *without the substitution of others*, is, that they uniformly consist of small details. They suggest to me the idea of a conqueror proposing to lay a vast region at his feet by merely disarming or taking captive a few of the videttes or outposts. It appears to me that there are two great principles, of which all the minor details must be merely ramifications. The first principle is *the maintenance of the authority of Government in connection with the solemn engagements of the Jahrejas*; and the second is *the adoption of that conduct towards the natives which I have endeavoured to illustrate.*

The authority of Government must be maintained, and the engagement, which has been mutually contracted, exactly fulfilled. We must show that we are serious, and that we are determined to be obeyed. This will be more difficult now than in 1808, but still it must be done. I would begin by sending to every Jahreja chief an authenticated copy of his engage-

* Par. Papers, 1828, p. 23—25.

ment, and apprize him in the most solemn and precise terms of the determination of the Company and the Guicowar to exact the performance of an obligation which has prescribed to all parties sacred and imperative duties. These *separate addresses* to the chiefs would soothe their pride, and prevent them from taking offence; but, that none may be able to plead ignorance of the intentions of Government, I would follow up the measure by a *public proclamation*, and give it as wide a circulation as possible. This should be addressed to the bosom and understanding of every Jahreja. It should declare the feelings and the intention of Government upon the subject. It should strongly mark the abhorrence of the crime, and explain the nature of his own obligations in consequence of his engagement to renounce Infanticide. That *where the monstrous inhumanity of Infanticide exists it is impossible that any good can exist*: that it involves a violation of good faith, as well as the recognized principles of Religion, and that no trust can be reposed in the perpetrators of this horrid crime: that, therefore Government are resolved to punish such outcasts of human nature by withholding from them every mark of confidence and regard, as well as by inflicting pains and penalties according to the nature of the case. That on the other hand those who give evidence of a sincere and hearty return to nature and the principles of Religion, shall be regarded with affection, and enjoy every mark of esteem, of favour, honour, and emolument, of which circumstances will admit.

"The servants of Government, Native or British, should have instructions *to watch over the operation of the engagements in their several districts, and to report upon every occurrence of a birth among the Jahrejas, or even the surmises of its consequences.* As they are not very rigid in the seclusion of their women, and as all those who are in the lower stations of life, who form the great majority in every society, must necessarily be employed in occupations which expose them to public view, a case of pregnancy can scarcely ever be concealed. There is no attempt made indeed to prevent it being known, and surely it would not require much discrimination of judgment, nor the exercise of a very officious impertinent curiosity, to ascertain a circumstance which is so notorious. But *there are other circumstances of less direct evidence, from which very fair and correct inferences may be drawn, and of which we may avail ourselves, in cases where stronger testimony may fail.* It is well known that among Hindoos of all descriptions the birth of a son is an object of congratulation and rejoicing. Whenever a birth in a Jahreja family was unattended by these cheerful and happy symptoms, where it was passed over in silence and without notice, we might, with very considerable certainty, conclude that the birth was a female!! Cases of a suspicious nature must occasionally occur, and come under our observation; but the miserable children of poverty must not become the victims of vengeance, while the more aggravated guilt of those who range in the higher ranks of life are passed over in silence and with impunity.

"Every servant of Government should have injunctions to ascertain the consequence of a birth by all the means that may be in his power; nothing should be too trifling for his notice which may bear on the point; he should collect even the rumours of the country upon the subject, and report to his superior; he again to another, if such there happen to be, and so on till each case reach the assistant of the Resident, and then the Resident himself, who should lastly report to the Government at Bombay. I would beg to recommend that the report of the Resident should be made at least *every three months for the first year or two,* or till it appear that the measure is proceeding so securely that an *annual report,* which must never be dispensed with, shall be deemed sufficient. *Quarterly Reports* for a time, indeed, would be highly beneficial, and, if they were mere blanks, still I think they should be punctually made. They would prevent the subject from falling into neglect, and by maintaining a spirit of inquiry make it manifestly appear that we are in earnest. I would even suggest, if it could be attained, *to engage the chiefs themselves to make returns of births, and not only of females but of males, which would be a check upon the evidence in regard to the former.* This would be gaining a step of decisive importance, not only to the cause, but might increase the small number of useful facts which we possess on the state of population in India.

" *It is evidently necessary that the whole system should be supported by rewards and punishments*; but a considerable diversity of opinion may prevail as to their nature and mode of application. The crime may be rendered more frequent by the severity of the laws which are enacted to prevent it; while there may be as much danger of encouraging it by too great tenderness in punishing. The offence is of such an odious description that it cannot be considered as a fit object for the exercise of clemency. At the same time it has been so long legalized by custom, and so common in its practice, that it may not be proper to inflict the last severity of the law on the first transgressors. Afterwards, however, and when the ordinance has been for some time generally observed, *the criminal may be prosecuted as a common murderer.* Cases of delinquency should, in every event, be punished by fine, and branded with infamy. The chiefs should be particularly held to their engagement, and punished with a pecuniary penalty to the extent of their means, and the degree of their offence. The poverty of many Jahrejas, however, must render the mode of amercement with respect to them impracticable, and the punishment of those who violate the engagement under such circumstances must be limited to disgrace, or ejection from caste.

" To this may be superadded, the displeasure of Government, the reproach and correction of society. I have said that I would not have recourse to coercive means, and if possible I would still adhere to this rule; but the authority of Government must at all events be maintained, and this gross departure from duty punished. If all other means therefore should fail, I would not hesitate to apply those of coercion, taking care to show that it is a matter of necessity, and not choice. Rewards and punishments always suppose something done to merit the one or incur the other; but it is generally a less difficult task to repay a good deed, than to discover the best means of punishing a crime so as to prevent its repetition. *Various marks of regard might be shown, at little expense, to the observers of the engagement.* They should have less the appearance of bribes than marks of honour; but at the same time instances may occur in which it may be necessary to display the generosity and liberality of Government. This must be particularly necessary in cases of extreme poverty, and inability to rear the offspring which has been saved. Such cases of extreme poverty and distress have actually occurred. Several instances are stated by Captain Ballantine to have happened, and an affecting appeal appears to have been made by the parties for pecuniary relief, which will not escape the humane attention of the Honourable Court of Directors. I would suggest the adoption of a Regulation, which, while it might serve as some check on the perpetrators of Infanticide, would be an encouragement to those who follow a different conduct. The latter should receive as much praise and publicity as possible. In this point of view it might be found useful *to publish in the Cutcherries and places of public resort, after a Report has been transmitted to Government, the names of those who have been faithful to nature and their engagement, and of those who have been proved to violate the dictates of both.* While one class would thus be marked as unworthy of trust or confidence, the other would be placed within the view of distinction and preferment. Might it not be a beneficial excitement to confer *an honorary medal on the Jahrejas who save their daughters?* The silver of a few rupees might answer the purpose; the medals would contain a suitable inscription, and the persons receiving them should be invested with them by the highest local authority of the District, and in as public a manner as possible.

"From the increased share and influence which we now possess in the revenue and Government of Kattywar we have proportionally increased means of binding the principles and directing the sentiments of the natives. Among the circumstances of which we have the command, is the power of employing in the transaction of public business only meritorious natives, and of selecting, especially for places of honour and trust, those Jahrejas who may have saved their children. The Company, in a great measure, possess *all those means of preferment and profitable appointment which formerly belonged solely to the native rulers.* The fines recovered from delinquents should constitute *a fund sacred to the benefit of those who have saved their daughters, which should be distributed by the Resident according to the merits and wants of particular cases.* The management and distribution of the fund in this manner would be one means of satisfying the country that the humanity of the Company's Government was quite disinterested. The accomplishment of this desirable object, ought to be considered as a prudent and legitimate measure for the consolidation and stability of our Government or influence in that quarter of India."*

From an attentive review of the various facts and observations contained in the two volumes of Parliamentary Documents on Infanticide, it is evident *that the unnatural custom of Infanticide still prevails to a lamentable degree in India.* In the first of these volumes the detail of its revival, after the efforts of Colonel Walker to suppress it, is peculiarly painful to every humane mind. The other volume presents a more pleasing scene, but shows that there is yet much to be done, before this custom will be annihilated—a few extracts will demonstrate this. The Governor in Council of Bombay writes to the Court of Directors, Nov. 1825:—" Mr. Gardiner, late Resident in Cutch, annexes to his Report a list of *ninety-one female infants* belonging to the Jahreja tribe, and now living in Cutch and Waugur. He appears to have satisfied himself of their

* Par. Papers, p. 123—127.

existence, and in any case, when it was practicable, had the infants brought to him. None of them appear to have exceeded the age of *seven years*, which marks the time when the abolition of this horrid practice first had operation under our influence. He adds his belief that among the chiefs the feeling is pretty general, that it has become their duty, as well as their interest, to preserve their female children; for, the penalty being undefined, any infringement of the agreement might be visited in the severest manner by a pecuniary mulct. On the other hand, the inferior byaud having nothing to lose, are not under the same apprehension, and *no doubt the practice is still continued to a lamentable extent among them.*"* "A constant intercourse with the Jahrejas," says R. Barnewell, Esq., Political Agent in Kattywar, July 1824, "during my annual circuit, has given me opportunities of impressing on their minds the interest taken by the British Government in the suppression of the barbarous and unnatural practice, and the guilt attached to the commission of it by the dictates of their own religion. I receive continued assurances that they will discountenance it; but, *from the disproportionate number of females still existing, it is evident that, although this horrible practice may be somewhat subdued, it is still far from being relinquished.*" †

"I was much surprised, (says the late Bishop Heber, speaking of Banswarra, in Guzerat,) to find, in such a situation, so large and handsome a place, of which I knew nothing before, except as one of those States which have been noticed in India for the wildness and poverty of their inhabitants; and for their abominable custom of murdering the greater part of their female infants. This cruel and most unnatural sacrifice, it has long been the endeavour of the British Government to induce its vassals and allies to abandon. Major Walker, when Resident at Baroda, thought he had succeeded with the greater part of them; but it is believed by most Officers on this side of the country, that the number saved was very small in proportion to that of the victims. Unhappily, pride, poverty, and avarice, are in league with superstition to perpetuate these horrors. It is a disgrace for a noble family to have a daughter unmarried, and still more to marry her to a person

---

* Par. Papers, 1828, p. 3. † p. 10.

of inferior birth, while they have neither the means nor the inclination, to pay such portions as a person of their own rank would expect to receive with them. On the other hand, the sacrifice of a child is believed, surely with truth, to be acceptable 'to the evil powers;' and the fact is certain that, though the high-born Rajpoots have many sons, very few daughters are ever found in their palaces; though it is not easy to prove any particular instance of murder, or to know the way in which the victims are disposed of. The common story of the country, and probably the true one, (for it is a point on which, except with the English, no mystery is likely to be observed), is, that a large vessel of milk is set in the chamber of the lying-in woman, and the infant, if a girl, is immediately plunged into it. Sir John Malcolm (who supposes the practice to be on the decline) was told that a pill of opium was usually given. Through the influence of Major Walker, it is certain that many children were spared; but, since that time, things have gone on very much in the old train, and the answers made by the chiefs to any remonstrances of the British officers is, '*Pay our daughters' marriage money and they shall live!*' Yet these very men, rather than strike a cow, would submit to the most cruel martyrdom. Never may my dear wife and daughters forget how much their sex is indebted to Christianity!"*

Its prevalence in certain parts of the Bengal Presidency has been stated by the Functionaries of Government. The Magistrate of Etawah, says,—"Murders have occurred respecting the division of land; we have no instance of real and deliberate homicide; but I fear that there is much reason to believe that *child murder is frequently perpetrated.*"† "There are (says Bishop Heber) among the Hindoos frequent instances of murder, but of a most cowardly and premeditated kind. They are chiefly cases of women murdered from jealousy, and *children for the sake of the silver ornaments with which their parents are fond of decorating them.* Out of *thirty-six* cases of murder, reported in the Province of Bengal, during the short space of, I believe, *three months, seventeen* were of children under these circumstances." "The number of children who are decoyed aside and murdered for the sake

---

* Heber's Jour. vol. ii. p. 88. † Par. Papers on Infan. 1828, p. 36.

of their ornaments, Lord Amherst assures me, is dreadful."‡

"The horrible practice of female Infanticide still prevails in some Districts in the Island of Ceylon. In the last general census, taken in 1821, the number of males exceeded that of *females* by 20,000!! In one District there were, to every hundred men, but fifty-five women, and in those parts where the numbers are equal, the population was almost exclusively Mussulman. The strange custom of one woman having two, or even more, husbands; and the consequent difficulty of marrying their daughters, in a country in which, to live single, is disgraceful; seem to be the causes of this unnatural custom. An astrologer is consulted on the birth of a female child, and, if he pronounce her to have been born under evil auspices, she is exposed alive in the woods, to be destroyed by beasts of prey or by ants; generally, I was happy to hear, without the consent of the mother."§

The adoption of a general law for India appears necessary.

J. Poynder, Esq., in his speech at a General Court of Proprietors, March, 1827, in which a resolution was carried that "*In the case of all rites involving the destruction of life, it is the duty of a paternal Government to interfere for their prevention,*" very forcibly observed; "It was on record, that, notwithstanding all that had been done by Col. Walker's meritorious exertions, the practice of Infanticide had again revived, in consequence of the apathy and indifference of that gentleman's successors. He might be told that practices of this description must of necessity go on. This however he must strenuously deny: if *positive laws were enacted and put in force* on this, as they had been on other subjects of less moral importance, such practices might and would be prevented. Let not Gentlemen content themselves with the exertions of individuals: it was not by the efforts of such excellent men as Col. Walker, succeeded as they might be by individuals who would not perform their duty, that the destruction of such practices could be accomplished. *It was only by a general law for India that a general reform could be expected.* Let them not lay 'the flattering unction to their souls' that partial efforts could remove the evil. Such efforts—

‡ Heber's Jour. vol. i. p. 82, vol. ii. p. 306. § vol. ii. p. 252.

"Will but skin and film the ulcerous part,
While rank corruption, mining all within,
Infects unseen."*

The conduct of the natives of the Society and Sandwich Islands is worthy of imitation. "In order to mark their sense of the enormity of Infanticide," says Mr. Ellis, "the very *first article in the code of Laws* proposed by the chiefs, and adopted by the people in most of the Society Islands, shortly after their reception of Christianity, is a prohibition of Infanticide, annexing *the punishment of death to its perpetration under any circumstances whatever*. In the Sandwich Islands, although not abolished, we have reason to believe it prevails less extensively than it did four or five years ago. The king, and some of the chiefs, since they have attended to the precepts of Christianity, have readily expressed in public their conviction of its criminality, and that committing it is in fact *pepehi kanaka* (to kill man) under circumstances which aggravate its guilt. Kairamokee, Regent of the Islands, has more than once forbidden any parents to destroy their children, and has threatened to punish with banishment, if not with death, any who shall be found guilty of it."†

The objections urged to the appointment of informers appear to arise from a false delicacy, and a destitution of that abhorrence of murder which in Britain we are taught to consider natural. Is blood to be secreted because intrusion into the haunts of murderers is unwelcome? R. Barnewell, Esq., in Kattywar, urging the Bombay Government to adopt more effectual means for the abolition of this practice, very justly observes:—"The only means to ensure further success is to persevere in discountenancing, as much as possible, this atrocity; but, so long as the force of pride and interest has a dominion sufficiently powerful to subdue in the Jahreja every principle of humanity and religion, this unnatural practice will be but slowly abolished.

"The effect of rewards for convicting the offender, and establishing the guilt of the parties, might be attended with some benefit; they might be offered to stimulate the activity of informers; to enforce the penalties prescribed by the engagement, and remove obstacles which now interfere to prevent the crimes being discovered. The fines levied for the commission of the offence might be expended

---

* Asiatic Journal, May, 1827, p. 699. † Ellis's Tour, p. 303.

partly or wholly in rewards to those actively engaged in enabling the British Government to give greater effect to the suppression of the crime; this appears the only temptation likely to induce an informer to come forward, that it would be politic or desirable to authorize, or that seems calculated to afford any increased facility in establishing the guilt of those perpetrating it."* "I should beg," says Lieut. Col. Miles, Political Agent, Pahlunpore, "to recommend that the cakoons (writers) in the Jahreja Talooks be instructed to keep a register of the births of female children, and use all vigilance in detecting any future violation of those solemn engagements."† The propriety of encouraging the detection of the crime of Infanticide appears evident.

It is the duty of the Honourable East India Company's Government, and, on their neglect of it, that of the British Nation, to promote the speedy and entire abolition of this, and every inhuman custom in India. The Government in India has been more attentive to the abolition of Infanticide than formerly. Some few fines have been levied, and donations given to defray the expense of the marriage of Jahreja females. Until Infanticide be punished severely it may be feared that it will not be annihilated. "Blood has a voice to reach the skies." It still cries to Britain for justice, and her apathy causes it to cry against her. British india is an "Aceldema, a field of blood." Infanticides—Suttees—the Exposure of the Sick—Pilgrimages (encouraged by British connection with Idolatry), in which thousands perish—the burying alive and drowning of devotees—prostrations under the wheels of Juggernaut's car, or that of his brother and sister—precipitation from eminences—actual human sacrifices, &c., defile the land. Why is not "inquisition made for blood?" Political expediency cannot justify palliation of crime and murder. No such expediency really exists. Let the inhabitants of the United Kingdom "relieve the oppressed, judge the fatherless, plead for the widow." Let petitions from every part of the land demonstrate the deep interest felt in the abolition of Infanticide, of Suttees, and every murderous practice in British India.

Societies and Corresponding Committees should be formed for the Abolition of Human Sacrifices in India.

---

* Par. Papers, 1828, p. 10. † p. 29.

They would diffuse information on the nature and extent of these sacrifices, and the propriety and facility of their abolition—originate Petitions—and press the subject constantly upon the attention of the British Government in this country and in India. Such have been formed in London, Birmingham, and Coventry. How long shall the exclamation of the Poet continue to be so just—

> "————— Hear it not ye stars,
> And thou pale moon, turn paler at the sound !
> Man is to man the sorest, surest ill.
> Heaven's sovereign saves all beings but himself !"

Why do not the British, the modern Romans, in arts, arms, enterprise, and extent of colonization, imitate the ancient Romans, who, says Montesquieu, "deserved well of human nature, for making it an article in their treaty with the Carthaginians that they should abstain from sacrificing their children to their gods?" Is Britain, once characterized "*Britannos hospitibus feros,*" by the benign power of Christianity recognised as the liberator of the slave, the patron of civil and religious liberty—the friend of the human race—Heaven's messenger of Gospel mercies to millions over whom she rules? Let the best influence of the British character be manifest wherever it is seen, and the sentiment of the Poet be regarded :—

> "————— Spread it then ;
> And let it circulate through every vein
> Of all your Empire ; that, *where Britain's power*
> *Is felt, mankind may feel her mercy too !"*
>
> COWPER.

JUGGERNAUT AND HIS BROTHER AND SISTER, FROM A HINDOO PAINTING. *Page* 213.

BOOK III.

BRITISH CONNEXION WITH IDOLATRY.

CHAP. I.

Origin, nature, proceeds, and appropriation of the Pilgrim Tax.—Traces of British connexion with Idolatry and Mahomedanism in various parts of India.

THE connexion of Britain with idolatry in India chiefly consists in the establishment of the Pilgrim Tax at the Temple of Juggernaut in Orissa, at Gya, and Allahabad; in the reception of the gains of Idolatry from certain temples, and in making annual grants of money for the support of this absurd and cruel system. The nature, extent, and injurious tendency of these proceedings are developed in this book, and the misery of the deluded pilgrims allured to the shrines of superstition (rendered more celebrated by these regulations and emoluments!) cry loudly to Britain, relative to the support of heathen temples, "Let them alone."

"*The origin of the Pilgrim Tax at the Temple Juggernaut* is thus stated in an interesting "Account of Orissa" by A. Stirling, Esq.:—"The Moguls (who gained possession of Orissa about the close of the sixteenth century) seem to have been actuated by peculiar rancour towards Juggernaut, and lost no opportunity of disturbing the Hindoos in the performance of their devotion at his temple. During these contests in and about Pooree the images,* so much

* Juggernaut, Bulbudra, and Subudra, his brother and sister.

venerated by the one party and abhorred by the other, were twice or thrice carried away across the Chilka Lake, and concealed among the hills until the times appeared favourable for again setting them on their thrones in the temple. This religious warfare was at last set at rest by the institution of the tax on pilgrims; which, if we may credit the author of the work translated by Gladwin, under the title of 'History of Bengal,' yielded the Mogul Government a revenue of 900,000 rupees. Under such circumstances religious antipathies, however strong on the part of the ruling powers, yielded gradually to the consideration of self interest."* The Mahrattas, who succeeded the Mussulmans in the Government of Orissa, levied the tax, and the British have followed the example of their predecessors.

"Before this place (Juggernaut) fell into the hands of the English, the King, a Mahratta Chief, exacted tolls from the pilgrims passing through his territories to Juggernaut. At one place the toll was not less than £1. 9s. for each foot passenger, if he had so much property with him. When a Bengalee Rajah used to go, he was accompanied by one or two thousand people, for every one of whom he was obliged to pay toll. The Hon. Company's Government levies a tax of from one to six rupees on each passenger."† Whether the origin of the Pilgrim Tax at Gya and Allahabad was the same as at Juggernaut is not certain; but it is probable that the rapacious followers of the prophet of Mecca established it in various parts of India.

The nature of the system will appear from the Government Regulations relative to the Pilgrim Tax, extracted from "Harington's Analysis of the Laws and Regulations of the Bengal Presidency," vol. iii. & vi.; and the Parliamentary Papers relative to Juggernaut, printed May 1813. The following compendious view of the system appears deserving of attention.

JUGGERNAUT.

"This is a celebrated place of Hindoo worship on the sea coast of Orissa, district of Cuttack, Lat. 19. 49. N.

---

* See Asi. Researches, vol. 15, 1825. p. 163—338. † Ward's View of the His. Lit. and Myth. of the Hindoos, vol. 2, p. 134.

and Lon. 85. 54. E., 300 miles from Calcutta. The population is estimated at 30,000. Possession was taken of the town and temple by the British, Sep. 18, 1803; *the sacred will of the Idol having been first ascertained through the medium of the officiating priest!* At Juggernaut there are thirteen annual festivals:—Chandan (sweet-scented powder), Snan (bathing festival), Rnth (car ditto), Bahura (returning ditto), Shayan (lying down ditto), Janma (birth ditto), Kojugara (waking ditto), Rasa festival, Urana (warm clothing ditto), Abhishaca (anointing ditto), Macura (sign of the zodiac ditto), Dole (swinging ditto), Ram Narami (Ram's birth-day ditto). Much the greater number of pilgrims are present at the Swinging and Car Festivals. The concourse of pilgrims to this temple is so immense that at 50 miles distance its approach may be known by the quantity of human bones which are strewed by the way."*

"Juggernaut is one of the most celebrated places in India. All the land within 20 miles is considered holy; but the most sacred spot is enclosed within a stone wall, 21 feet high, and forms nearly a square: two sides measuring each 656 feet, and the other two 626 feet in length. Within this area are about *fifty temples*, dedicated to various idols; but the most conspicuous buildings consists of one lofty stone tower, 184 feet high, and 28 feet 8 inches square inside, and is called the Bur Dewal, and two adjoining stone buildings with pyramidical roofs. The idol Juggernaut, his brother Bulbudra, and his sister Subudra, occupy the tower. The first pyramidical building, which is 40 feet square inside, is connected with the tower, and is the place where the idol is worshipped during the bathing Festival. Adjoining this temple is a low building on pillars (with a fabulous animal in the centre) which is intended as an awning to shelter the entrance from the rays of the sun; and after this is a second building, with a pyramidical stone roof, where the food prepared for the pilgrims, or others, is daily brought, previous to distribution. This latter building is said to have been removed from Kanaruck, or the black Pagoda, and is called the Beg Mundeep. The temple of Juggernaut was erected by Rajah Anung Bheem Deo, and completed in A. D. 1198. The roofs are ornamented in a singular style, with representations of monsters, which can only be understood by a drawing: but the walls

* Hamilton's Description of Hindostan. Vol. ii. p. 51—53.

of the temples, which are not visible beyond the enclosure, are covered with statues of stone. Several represent a famous Hindoo god, Mahadeo, with his wife Parbuttee, in attidues so grossly indecent that it seems surprising how any superstition could debase its votaries to such a degree as to make them introduce into their most sacred places such filthy and obscene representations! Each side of the boundary wall has a large gateway in the centre; but the grand entrance is in the eastern face.

"The idol Juggernaut is probably the coarsest image in the country. The *figure* does not extend below the loins, and it has no hands, but two stumps in lieu of arms, on which the priests occasionally fasten hands of gold, A Christian is almost led to think that it was an attempt to see how low idolatry could debase the human mind. The priests endeavour to account for the deformity by a strange legendary tale. Some thousands of years ago, in the Sutya Yuga, Maharajah Indradyumna, of Oojein, in Malwa, applied to the celebrated manufacturer of gods to make a new idol. This request was granted, on condition that the Maharajah should be very patient, and not interrupt the work, as it could never be completed if any attempt were made to see the process. This caution was not duly attended to. The prince endeavoured to see what progress had been made, and it became necessary that he should be satisfied with the imperfect image. When two new moons occur in Assaur (part of June and July), which is said to happen about once in seventeen years, *a new idol is always made.* A neem tree (*melia azodaracta*) is sought for in the forests, on which no crow or carrion bird was ever perched: it is known to the initiated by certain signs! This is prepared into a proper form by common carpenters, and is then entrusted to certain priests, who are protected from all intrusion: the process is a great mystery. One man is selected to take out of the old idol a small box, containing the spirit, which is conveyed inside the new: *the man who does this is always removed from this world before the end of the year!*"*

The first Regulations relative to Juggernaut's temple were adopted by the British Government Jan. 1806; these were afterwards rescinded, and others framed in 1809 and 1810. The following is a *summary of the Regulations*:—

* Col. Phipps' Account of Juggernaut.—Asi. Jour. March 1824.

The superintendence of the temple and its interior economy are vested in the Rajah of Khoorda. The Governor General in Council possesses the power of removing the Rajah or any of his successors from the superintendence, on proof of misconduct. The superintendent of the temple is authorized to punish instances of neglect or misconduct by imposing small fines, or by removing the offender (if not one of the three head Purchas) from his office: *the amount of fines is to be carried to the account of Government.* The three dewul Purchas are to be appointed by the Collector of Cuttack, subject to the confirmation of Government. In the event of orders being issued by the Rajah contrary to the recorded rules and institutions of the temple, a representation is to be made to the Collector of the tax for the orders of the Governor General in Council, if it appear necessary. The third dewul Purcha shall give account to the Collecter of the tax of *all offerings and presents made to the idol.* The collection of the tax is intrusted to an officer with the official designation of "The Collector of the Tax on Pilgrims," subject to the authority of the Collector at Cuttack; the general superintendence of the collections, and the control of the officers employed in the performance of that duty, is vested in the Board of Revenue at Fort William. The avenues for the admission of pilgrims shall be confined to two Ghauts, Attara Nullah on the North, and Ghaut Lokenauth on the south-west of the town of Juggernaut Pooree. The pilgrims liable to the tax shall be divided into four clases—*laul jattrees, nim lauls, bhurrungs, punj tirthees,* including the following persons of low cast who are not permitted to enter the temple.* The rate of tax payable by the different classes is as follows:—viz. pilgrims of the first class from the north, passing the Attarah Nullah, pay a tax of *ten rupees;* from the south, passing Lokenaut, *six rupees.* Pilgrims of the second class from the north pay *five rupees;* from the south *three rupees.* Pilgrims of the third class, from either the north or south, pay *two rupees.* Pilgrims of the fourth class, passing either Ghauts, pay *two rupees.* A pilgrim of the first class is allowed free access to the temple for thirty days, constantly attended by a punda. He may be exempted from the attendance of these officers by *a further payment of ten rupees* to the Collector; and by surrendering his pass shall be allowed to remain in the town as long as he pleases. Pilgrims of the second class, at the Car Festival, are allowed access to the temple ten days; at other festivals seven days only. Pilgrims of the third class, at the Car Festival, are allowed five days; at other times but four; and must be attended by a pun[illegible]. Pilgrims of the fourth class are *allowed to worship outside the temple* sixteen days. Pilgrims may enrol themselves in either of the first three classes on paying the prescribed tax. Printed certificates shall be procurable on the payment of the fixed tax, at the office of the Secretary to the Board of Revenue, the Collector of Cuttack and Ganjam, and at the two Ghauts. Form as follows:—

* These are kusbee (prostitutes), cullal (liquor sellers), machoowa (fishermen), numosooder (boatmen), ghooskee (private bad women), gazur (labourers who carry burdens on their heads), baugdee (fishers labourers), joogee (weavers), kahar bawry (bearers), raujbunsee (different cast of boatmen), chamar (shoe-makers), dhomee (washermen), paun (basket-makers), teor (another cast of boatmen), bhoinmalee (makers of garlands, &c., for marriages), haddee (maters). These sixteen casts are not suffered to enter the temple to worship Juggernaut.

"A. B., inhabitant of ——— in the district of ———, having this day paid into this office the sum of sicca rupees ———, is entitled to pass through the ——— Ghaut without further interruption, as a laul jattree to the cutcherry of the Collector of the tax at Jnggernaut. On producing this certificate to the said Collector, he is further entitled to receive a pass, and to have access to the temple thirty days."

Names or Designation of attendants.	*Amount of tax paid respectively.*	*Period for which to visit the temple.*

Forms No. 2, 3, and 4, differ only in the names of the class of pilgrims, the rate of tax, and the period of attendance at the temeple. A pilgrim of the first class, desirous of visiting the temple with his family and attendants, not exceeding twenty persons, these must first pay the tax of the second or third class, and then they may stop as long as their master. *The certificates shall be dated and attested by the official seal, the blank places filled up, &c.* A pilgrim presenting the printed certificate is to be allowed to pass without interruption. The molestation of such an individual by the daroga at the Ghaut shall be punished by a fine not exceeding his salary for three months and dismissal from office. The duty of the Collector of Juggernaut is to superintend the conduct of the darogas. Pilgrims of the first, second, and third classes, having passed the Ghauts at Juggernaut, are to apply to the Collector for *a license of access to the temple* in the following form :—

"A. B., inhabitant of ———, in the district of ———, is entitled to perform the customary ceremonies, under charge of ——— during ——— days, that is to say, from the ——— day of the month of ——— until the ——— day of the month of ———; and for that period you will afford to the holders hereof free access to the temple of Juggernaut. At the expiration of the period granted you will return the license into the office of the Collector of tax."

The fourth class, who are not allowed to enter the temple, receive a form a little differing from the above. In case of sickness the Collector is allowed to extend the period of a pilgrim's continuance in the town, but is to observe due caution in the exercise of this authority. Pilgrims are not to be delayed obtaining license to visit the temple, and therefore a sufficient number of blank licenses are to be prepared. The Collector of the tax shall keep a register of licenses granted, and every punda or purharee who neglects to return them shall be fined, in no case exceeding the amount of the tax paid by the first class of pilgrims. The attendants of the fourth class are to return their license or be fined, in no case exceeding one month's salary. *Pilgrims stopping in the town beyond the time prescribed, are to be expelled the town by the police daroga.* The following descriptions of persons are exempt from paying the tax : viz. byragees, sunyasees, dundies, brumacharies, mohunts, gosains, khomartees, and nagas, persons employed in carrying the water of the Ganges to Juggernaut and pouring the water over the idol at Lokenaut, and persons resorting to Juggernaut Pooree for trade (excepting for twelve days from the beginning of the Car Festival), or any other purpose except on pilgrimage. Persons professing to be carriers of the water of the Ganges are to be placed under the conduct of a punda ; and on refusing to do it are to be expelled the town, or to pay the tax. Persons intending to live in the town the remainder of life are exempted from the tax, if they are not able to pay it. All native military officers and sepoys on duty at Juggernaut are exempted from tax, but, *to obtain admittance into the temple, a pass must be received from the commanding officer at the station to the Collector of Tax*, who shall then admit them free. Servants of Europeans may enter the town without paying the the tax. The exemption from tax of persons born within the Byturnee river and Ganjam, having been found *detrimental to the public revenue*, and as under the Mahratta Government such persons were made to pay the tax, the following rules respecting the exemption of such persons are enacted : During the Ruth and Dole Festivals, the exemption in favour of these people is restricted to the residents within Pipley, to the north, and Manickpatam, to the south ; at all other times of the year they pass free. At the above festivals they have to pay a tax as follow : viz. Lauls, one rupee ; Nim Lauls, eight annas ; Bhurrungs, four annas. They are to receive the same attention as other pilgrims. Kungals or pilgrims in actual state of poverty, on declaring it, under *certain prescribed ceremonies*, are admitted free.* The Collector of the tax is required to give every attention to the religious opinions of the Hindoos, and the particular institutions of the temple.†

The Collector of the Pilgrim Tax at Juggernaut, in March, 1806, proposed to the Government in Calcutta the adoption of *a premium for the pundas who collect the pilgrims*. He stated, " As the pilgrims will never be well treated by their conductors, unless they receive a present from their own hands, I beg leave to propose that the fees of the pundas, &c., be publicly fixed, and collected by the pundas themselves, separate from the tax, as was formerly done under the Mahratta Government." To this it was replied :—" The Governor General in Council approves of your proposition for permitting the pundas to collect a fee from the pilgrims, exclusive of the tax payable to Government ; you will accordingly *fix the rates at which such fee should be levied, and publish the rates for general information at the temple, and in its vicinity*.—March 20, 1806."‡

Colonel Phipps, of the Bengal Native Infantry, stationed at Juggernaut in 1822, in an interesting article respecting the temple and worship of Juggernaut, gives the following information relative to the collectors of pilgrims, and the *premium* they receive :—" It having been decided that a tax should be levied, every precaution was taken to

---

* Numbers have perished from neglect, and disease, before they were admitted through the gates into the town. A correspondent, under date June, 1827, states that sheds for accommodating three or four thousand pilgrims, have been erected under the superintendence and at the expense of the British Government.

† Harington's Analysis, vol. iii. pp. 209—220.—Par. Papers, relative to Juggernaut, May, 1813, pp. 81—86.

‡ Par. Papers, May, 1813, p. 35.

make it yield as much as possible. Alterations were made in the Regulations from time to time. One of the principal was in the mode of rewarding the purharees and pundas. The purharees are a body of people who reside at Pooree, governed by four surdars; one of whom is their gomasta, or chief manager, who attends at the Attara Nulla, where the main barrier, or gate, is placed. They have a great number of subordinate agents, *who travel about in search of pilgrims, and bring them in companies to Juggernaut.* The pundas are the servants of the idol, and do the same duties as the purharees at the barrier. The Government at first authorized these people to collect at the barriers a fee from the pilgrims for their own benefit; but, this privilege having been abused, it was resolved that the British Collector should levy, *beside the tax for the State, an additional one, the amount of which he subsequently paid over to the purharees and pundas, in such proportions as they were entitled to, from the number of pilgrims which each had succeeded in enticing to undertake the pilgrrimage.* The pilgrims who attend the festival of the Chundun Jattra, and wish to remain in order to see the Ruth Jattra, are termed Lal Jattrees. They pay ten rupees to Government, and three rupees to the priests who have brought them, if they come from the northward; and, if they come from the southward, six rupees to Government, and three rupees for the priest. A great many pilgrims attend the Chaund or Snan Jattra; and those who then wish to remain a fortnight, and see the Ruth Jattra, are termed Nim Lauls. If they come from the northward, they pay to Government five rupees, and a rupee and a half to the person who brings them; if from the southward, three rupees to Government, and half that sum to the punda who brings them. Two rupees six annas is the tax for five days."*

"Some persons, on leaving this place, deposit with the Brahmuns of the temple one or two hundred rupees, with the interest of which they are to purchase rice, and present it daily to Juggernaut, and afterwards to dundees or Brahmuns. Deeds of gift are also made to Juggernaut all over Hindostan, which are received by agents in every large town, and paid to the mutdharees at Juggernaut Pooree, who by this means (though professing themselves mendi-

* Mis. Register, Dec. 1824, pp. 575—580. See Friend of India, Oct. 1825, p. 270.

cants) have become some of the richest merchants in India."*

Among the voluminous documents published by order of Parliament in 1813 there is no official estimate of the number of pilgrims resorting annually to this temple. "The following is a statement of pilgrims of all classes who attended for the last five years at *the three great festivals*, procured from the most authentic sources :—

YEARS.	PAYING TAX.	EXEMPT.	TOTAL.
1817—18	35,941	39,720	75,661
1818—19	36,241	4,870	41,111
1819—20	92,874	39,000	131,874
1820—21	21,946	11,500	33,446
1821—22	35,160	17,000	52,160"†

At the great Car Festival in July 1825 it was stated that the number of pilgrims was 225,000.

GYA.

Gya is the modern capital of Behar, lat. 24. 49. N., long. 85. E. Distance from Calcutta 322 miles. Population about 30,000. To procure the salvation of deceased relations, crowds of Hindoos here perform the shradda, or funeral ceremonies for deceased relatives.‡

"No printed regulations have been enacted relative to the tax levied at Gya, the duty of the Collector, and a European Superintendent, being simply to receive a fixed rate of tax upon licenses granted to the pilgrims for visiting the different places of worship and pilgrimage in the vicinity of the town. In a statement from the Collector at Gya, in July 1790, the rates of duty paid by pilgrims for permission to perform their religious ceremonies chiefly in honour of deceased ancestors, at the river Phulgo, or adjacent places, were stated to vary from *six annas to twelve rupees, eleven annas, three pie.* This duty of Government is independent of donations to the *gyawals*, or priests.

* Ward's View of the Hindoos. Vol. ii. p. 135.
† Stirling's Account of Orissa.—Asi. Reg. Vol. xv. p. 225.
‡ For a recent account of Gya, see Mis. Reg. Nov. 1827, p. 548.

Ever since the city of Gya became famous for its sanctity, it has been the custom of its Brahmuns to *travel through all countries where the Hindoo religion prevails in search of pilgrims*, whose donations are considered the property of the gyawal, through whose means they are brought. These contributions have ever been a source of considerable wealth, and are the property of those, *who, but for them, would probably never have visited Gya.* When a pilgrim arrives, his gyawal, or religious father, conducts him to the daroga, or superintending officer of the sayer collections, and explains to him the ceremonies which the pilgrim is desirous of performing; after which an order, specifying the names of the pilgrim and gyawal, as also the ceremonies, are made out *under the official seal and signature of the Collector*, authorizing the performance of the ceremonies. At the time of delivering this order, *the duty* (to Government) *is paid, which varies according to the number and nature of the rites performed.*"*

The nature of idolatry at this place is thus described:— " At Gya there is a particular stone on which Vishnoo set his foot, and a person by putting on this stone, in the form prescribed, a certain paste prepared there, and by repeating at the same time the name of a deceased friend, can transfer that friend from hell itself to supreme felicity: and this benefit he may extend, not to one friend only, but, by repeated applications of paste, to as many as he can recollect, even of his distant ancestors!!"†

" The British Government has an agent at Gya, who levies a tax on pilgrims, according to the magnitude of the ceremonies he means to perform. *One class visiting only one place, pay two $\frac{1}{8}$th rupees; another visiting two places, three $\frac{3}{8}$th rupees; a third visiting thirty-eight places, pay four $\frac{1}{8}$th rupees, and the fourth class, visiting forty-five places, pay fourteen $\frac{1}{8}$th rupees.* The duty to Government, however, is but a small part of the pilgrim's expense; for he is fleeced by the priests, not only of all the money he brings with him, but of *promissory notes* for future payments, which are sent to him when he returns home; the priests of Gya maintaining emissaries for this purpose in the remotest parts of India, which they also occasionally visit on speculation. The most numerous votaries are Bengalees and

* Harington's Analysis, Vol. iii. p. 207.
† Grant's Observ. &c., Par. Papers, June, 1813, p. 61

Mahrattas; and some of the great chiefs of the latter have been known to expend 50,000 rupees."*

ALLAHABAD.

"Allahabad is the capital of a province of the same name, situated at the confluence of the Ganges and Jumna. Lat. 25° 27″ N., Long. 81° 50″ E. Distance from Calcutta 550 miles, and from Benares fifty-three miles. Population in 1803, without the garrison, 20,000. By the Brahmuns Allahabad is called Bhat Prayag; or, by way of distinction, as it is the largest and most holy, is simply designated Prayag. The other four Prayagas (or sacred confluences of rivers) are situated in the province of Serinagur, at the junction of the Alacananda with other streams, and are named Devaprayaga, Rudraprayaga, Carnaprayaga, and Nandaprayaga. This Prayaga owes its celebrity to the junction at this spot of the Ganges, Jumna, and Sereswate. There is no such river as the last now visible in the neighbourhood, but the Hindoos assert that it joins the other two under ground, and that by bathing here the same religious merit is acquired as if the penitent had bathed in the three separately. Many persons renounce life at this confluence, by going in a boat, after the performance of certain solemnities, to the exact spot where the three rivers unite, where the devotee plunges into the stream, with three pots of water tied to his body.† When a pilgrim arrives, *he first sits down on the bank of the river, and has his head and body shaved, so that each hair may fall into the water, the sacred writings promising him one million of years' residence in heaven for every hair thus deposited!!* After shaving, he bathes; and the same day, or the next, performs the obsequies of his deceased ancestors."§

The following Rules are enacted by Regulation xviii., 1810, for the collection of duties on pilgrims at Allahabad, and for the prevention of abuses in such collections. The duties paid by pilgrims resorting to the conflux of the rivers Ganges and Jumna, at Allahabad, are levied at the following rates:—

---

* Hamilton's Hindostan, vol. i. p. 265.

† This is said to have been recently abolished by the British magistrate. Asiat. Journ. August 1827, p. 241. § Ham. Hind. vol. i. p. 300.

"On every pilgrim on foot, *one rupee*.

On every pilgrim with a horse, or palanquin, or carriage of any description, *two rupees*.

On every pilgrim with a camel, *three rupees*.

On every pilgrim with an elephant, *twenty rupees*.

All other duties or fees at the Ghaut, within the fort, or at any other place, are prohibited. Every pilgrim on application to the Collector of the Land Revenue at Allahabad shall be furnished with *a license to perform the usual ceremonies;* and no person shall be admitted to perform such ceremonies without a license. The inhabitants of the town and suburbs of Allahabad, and the Hindoos in the Honourable Company's Army, are exempt from duty; but every such person must be furnished with *a license of exemption from the Collector, before he can be entitled to perform the religious ceremonies*. No tax of any kind shall be imposed upon the shaving barbers attending at the conflux of the rivers; but they shall be required to register their names at the Collector's office, and execute an obligation to the Collector, under a penalty of fifty rupees in every instance of contravention, not to perform that part of the ceremony, resting with them, to any one without a license. Access to the place of ablution shall be restricted to a certain number of gates and avenues, fixed by a barrier annually established, on the subsiding of the rivers, from the palisades of the fort to the bank of the river: and no person shall be admitted through such barrier without the prescribed license. Such numbers and descriptions of native officers as may be approved by the Board of Commissioners shall be stationed by the Collector at the barrier, to prevent any person performing the ceremonies without a license. *A sufficient military force shall, on application of the Collector, be posted at the barrier during the mela or principal concourse of pilgrims in January and February, who shall prevent the people breaking through the barrier or otherwise forcing admission.* The licenses and exemptions, after being shown at the place of admission, shall be delivered up to the officers, to be returned to the Collector in order to their being cancelled. Persons, with a view to avoid the payment of the duty, attempting to cross over in boats from the opposite side of the river to the place of ablution, shall be liable to a fine of three times the prescribed duty: and, if any barber shall assist any such person in performing the ceremonies, he shall be liable to the penalty stipulated in his engagements. No barber, except such as shall have entered into the prescribed obligation, shall officiate in the ceremonies; and any barber contravening this prohibition shall be liable to the penalty of fifty rupees for every pilgrim shaved; and, if not able to pay, he shall be committed to jail for three months."*

The proceeds of this system, and the appropriation of them, appear from the notes appended to this section of the "Analysis."

JUGGERNAUT.

	Rupees.
Gross collection of Pilgram Tax for 1815—16 (including 72 rupees miscellaneous receipts) }	53,725

---

* Harington's Analysis, vol. iii. p. 222.

	Rupees.
Assessment of endowed lands	26,818
Sale of *holy food**	5,484
	8)86,027
	£10,753

Deduct charges for establishment and contingencies	17,143
Expenses of Juggernaut's Temple	56,372
English cloth for the three cars	1,365
	74,880
Net collection . . .	£11,147

Dr. Buchanan, in his "Christian Researches," states, from official accounts, the annual expenses of the Idol Juggernaut, presented to the English Government, as follows :—

	Rupees.		£.
Expense of the table of the Idol . . .	36,115	or	4,514
Ditto of his dress or wearing apparel .	2,712	—	339
Ditto of the wages of his servants . . .	10,057	—	1,259
Ditto of contingent expenses at the different seasons of pilgrimage . .	10,989	—	1,373
Ditto of his elephants and horses . . .	3,030	—	378
Ditto of his ruth, or annual state carriage	6,713	—	839
Rupees	69,616		£8,702

"In item 'wages of servants' are included the wages

* "With the consent of the Purchas I deputed an Aumeen to oversee and state the produce from the sale of holy food, the quantity and value of cloth presented for the purpose of being displayed on the wheel at the top of the temple, on which Government receives, from the person presenting, its full value as a fee, under the head of Dujja, exclusive of which he has also to pay the fee of the Purchas and others, for their ministry during the ceremony." G. Webb, Collector of Tax, Dec. 1807. Par. Papers, 1813, p. 65.

of the *courtesans*, who are kept for the service of the temple.*

"Item sixth—What is called in the official account 'the state carriage' is the same as the car or tower. Mr. Hunter (the Collector of the Pilgrim Tax) imformed me that three 'state carriages' were decorated this year (June 1806) with upwards of £200 sterling worth of English *broad cloth* and *baize*."

What a trifling sum is 11,147 rupees, about £1,393 sterling, as the clear gain of supporting idolatry at Juggernaut; a gain, doubtless, accompanied by the death of hundreds of unhappy pilgrims! The variation in the annual number of pilgrims is considerable; the principal cause is the early or late commencement of the most popular festivals. The mortality in the rainy season is great, and intimidates even the superstitious Hindoos from undertaking the pilgrimage. Mr. Harington states "the net receipts for 1814—15 at 135,667 rupees, and the number of taxed pilgrims, who were assembled from different parts of India at the Snan and Rut Jattra in May and June, to have been 77,323, inclusive of those exempted from the payment of duties. The attendance of pilgrims in June and July, 1815, who paid the established duty, was 5,444. The difference is partly to be ascribed to the lateness of the season of the principal festival, and the difficulty of travelling by land in Cuttack and the adjacent districts."

J. Poynder, Esq., in his interesting speech on "*Human Sacrifices in India*," at a General Court of Proprietors, in March 1827, gives the following statement relative to the temple of Juggernaut: p. 261.

* For the character of these persons see Heber's Journ., vol. ii. p. 283.

ANNUAL AMOUNT

OF THE TAX ON PILGRIMS ATTENDING THE TEMPLE OF JUGGERNAUT;

WITH AN ACCOUNT OF THE ANNUAL EXPENSES FROM 1812—13 TO 1824—25

(Estimating the value of the Rupee at 2s. 6d. English).

YEARS.	AMOUNT OF TAX COLLECTED.	COLLECTOR AND ESTABLISHMENT.	EXPENSES OF TEMPLE.	BUILDING, REPAIRS, AND CONTINGENCIES.	TOTAL CHARGES.	NET RECEIPTS.	SURPLUS EXPENDITURE.
	£ s. d.	£ s. d.	£ s. d.	£ s. d.	£ s. d.	£ s. d.	£ s. d.
1812–13	6,381 2 6	2,011 10 0	5,825 17 6	850 10 0	8,687 17 6	....	2,306 15 0
1813–14	10,895 0 0	2,011 10 0	5,522 7 6	425 5 0	7,969 2 6	2,925 17 6	
1814–15	26,065 0 0	2,877 7 6	5,979 0 0	845 7 6	9,701 15 0	16,363 5 0	
1815–16	6,714 17 6	1,826 5 0	6,502 0 0	9,757 17 6	18,086 2 6	....	11,371 10 0
1816–17	7,536 15 0	1,619 2 6	5,581 10 0	....	7,200 12 6	336 2 6	
1817–18	11,752 12 6	2,151 2 6	6,276 12 6	53 5 0	8,481 0 0	3,271 12 6	
1818–19	10,119 0 0	1,245 2 6	6,381 10 0	31 7 6	7,658 0 0	2,461 0 0	
1819–20	20,744 0 0	1,656 7 6	6,195 12 6	....	7,852 0 0	12,892 0 0	
1820–21	7,503 17 6	996 12 6	5,682 15 0	....	6,679 7 6	824 10 0	
1821–22	14,698 15 0	1,333 12 6	6,588 12 6	....	7,936 0 0	6,762 15 0	
1822–23	29,156 2 6	2,283 7 6	6,097 0 0	....	8,380 7 6	20,775 15 0	
1823–24	8,376 17 6	1,047 2 6	5,856 17 6	....	6,904 0 0	1,472 17 6	
1824–25	9,369 17 6	1,239 17 6	6,068 12 6	....	7,308 10 0	2,061 7 6	

GYA.

The amount of Pilgrim Tax at Gya appears more considerable than at Juggernaut; and is, with a small deduction, thrown into the Public Treasury.

	Rupees.
" Gross collections from May, 1815, to April, 1816,	229,805
Deduct charges of collections and 1 *per cent. to English Superintendent*	7,021
Charitable allowances to several individuals . . .	2,530
Donation to Native Hospital in Calcutta	11,300
Native Rajah, 10 per cent. on net collections . .	26,078
	46,929
	8)182,876
Leaving the net receipts . .	£22,859"

ALLAHABAD.

" The receipts and disbursements of the tax on pilgrims for 1815-16 were as follow:—

	Rupees.
Gross collections, including 695 rupees levied from pilgrims without licenses, who attempted to evade the tax	79,779
Charges and commission of 5 *per cent. to the English Collector*	6,726
	8)73,053
Net receipts to Government . . .	£9,131"

TRIPETTY.

" This is the most celebrated Hindoo temple south of the Krishna river, lat. 13. 46. N., long. 79. 24. E., eighty miles north-west from Madras. The temple is placed in an elevated hollow or basin, enclosed by a circular crest of hills, the precincts of which have never been profaned by Christian or Mahomedan feet, nor has even the exterior of it been seen but by a genuine Hindoo. The reciprocal interests of the Brahmuns, and of the different rulers under whose sway it fell, compromised this forbearance by the payment of large sums to Government, which, in 1758, amounted to £30,000 sterling. The incarnation of Vishnu, worshipped here, has a variety of names, as Vencata Ram, and Tripati; but, by the Mahrattas, he is named Ballajee, and his functions are considered to have particular reference to commerce. Crowds of pilgrims resort to it from all parts of India, who pour into it offerings of goods, grain, gold, silver, jewels, precious stuffs, horses, cows, and other articles, the aggregate of which, when converted into money, *not only yields a surplus revenue to Government, but serves to maintain several thousand persons performing the offices of an idolatrous worship, which is here conducted with extraordinary pomp.* The traders of the Banyan and Battia tribes of Guzerat are accustomed to present a per centage of their profits to the temple annually. The amount realized to the British Government at this temple was, in 1809, 60,791 star pagodas; 1810, 50,722; 1811, 50,722; or about £19,000 sterling."*

"It appears from the public accounts of 1815-16 that a small collection of tax is made from the pilgrims of Seetla Dabee at *Kasheepoor, Surkura*, and *Sumbul*, in the district of Moradabad; and from the pilgrims of Soru in *Itawa.* The amount received in the former district was 2592 rupees, and in the latter 3091 rupees in the year referred to. But I have not been able to obtain any further information relative to these collections." †

The following items show *the gain of this unnatural association with Idolatry*, the baneful influence of which, in supporting and aggrandizing it, is very considerable :—

		Rupees.
Net receipts of Pilgrim Tax at Juggernaut, for 1814-15		135,667
Ditto at Gya, ...	1815-16	182,876
Ditto at Allahabad	1815-16	73,053
Kasheepoor, Surkuru, Sumbul, and Itawa, 1815—16.		5,683
		8)397,279
		£49,659
Tripetty near Madras for 1811		19,000
	Total	£68,659

* Hamilton's Hind. vol. ii. p. 431, 432. † Har. Analysis, vol. iii. p. 208.

The following traces of British connexion with Idolatry and Mahomedanism, in various parts of India, are extracted from Hamilton's Description of Hindostan, 2 vols. quarto, dedicated to the late Right Honourable G. Canning, President of the Board of Control, &c., &c.

"*Dacca* is situated about 100 miles above the mouth of the Ganges, and 180 by land from Calcutta. The Nabob of Dacca has long been celebrated for the suavity of his manners, and his steady attachment to the British Government. In 1807 an allowance of 3000 rupees was granted to him for the repair of a Building devoted to religious purposes, not only on account of the uniform propriety of his conduct, and the respectability of his character, but also as a public indication of the disposition of the British Government to support the freedom of religious worship among all classes of their subjects."*

"*Bate Isle*. An island situated at the western extremity of the Gujerat peninsula. Shunkowar is its proper name, and is derived from that of a Hindoo demon, so named from his dwelling in a large shunk or conch shell, wherein he concealed the sacred Vedas, which he had stolen from Brahma. An incarnation of Vishnu, under the name of Shunk Narayan, cut open the shells and restored the Vedas to their lawful owner. The demon pleaded as his excuse that he hoped to have been put to death by Vishnu for the theft, which would have insured him future happiness. In consequence of this exploit, Shunk Narayan (Vishnu), or the destroyer of the shell demon, established his own worship on the island, where it continued paramount until the flight of another Hindoo deity, named Runchor, from Dwaraca, to escape the fury of a Mahomedan army; since which time Runchor has been supreme on Bate. In 1462 this place was taken by Sultan Mahmood Begra of Ahmedabad and Gujerat, who demolished the temples, broke the images, and gave up the country to indiscriminate plunder. In 1816 Colonel East advanced with a detachment towards the Isle of Bate, which quietly surrendered, on the promise of a suitable provision and complete security for their private property and religious establishments. An agreement was executed, by the conditions of which they engaged not to permit, instigate, or connive at any act of

* Vol. i. p. 186.

piracy committed by any person under their authority, and also to abstain from plundering vessels in distress. A free or open commerce to be permitted to all British vessels paying the regulated duties. *The British, by this treaty, undertook to afford the temple at Bate suitable protection and encouragement!*"*

"*Dwaraca.* A town and celebrated temple situated at the western end of the Gujerat Peninsula. It is the most original and sacred spot in this part of India. About 600 years ago the valued image of their god, Runchor (an incarnation of Krishna), by a manoeuvre of the Brahmuns was conveyed to Daccoor, in Gujerat, where it still remains. After much trouble the Brahmuns at Dwaraca substituted another in its stead; which unfortunately also took flight across a narrow arm of the sea, to the island of Bate, about 135 years ago, on which event another new one was placed in the temple here! Dwaraca is designated by the name of the island; and, having long been the residence of Krishna, it is a celebrated place of pilgrimage for the sectaries of that religion. At Muddee, near Dwaraca, the land thieves of Oka are named *Kaba,* a Sanscrit word which signifies a seeker or searcher, on account of the severe scrutiny all pilgrims and unprotected travellers undergo. The rags of the Byragee are carefully examined, and the ball of ashes, with which he besmears his body, is broken by these robbers in hopes of finding some small coin concealed in it! The pirates in this part placed great reliance on the power of their deity at Dwaraca, his priests and attendants being the strongest instigators to depredation. In return they (the priests, &c.) received a certain portion of all plundered property, as a recompense for the protection they (the pirates) receive from the Idol Runchor. Before embarking, it was a common practice for the pirates to promise a larger share than the god could claim by right, if he would ensure success to their trip. Many vessels were fitted out in the name of Runchor, as sole owner, and actually belonged to the temple, which received the plunder they brought back.

"The average number of pilgrims resorting annually to Dwaraca has been estimated to exceed 15,000, and the revenue derived to the temples about a lack of rupees (£12,500). The revenue derived from the holy places

---

* Vol. i. pp. 661, 662.

has been decreasing, as well as the number of pilgrims. In 1807 the chief of Dwaraca engaged not to permit or instigate any act of piracy, and the British Government engaged to *afford the temple every suitable protection and encouragement:* a free and open commerce was permitted to vessels paying the regulated duties. The depredations by sea renewed on British property, and the predatory system into the adjacent countries commenced by land, made the conquest of Okamundel the only effectual remedy for evils of such inveteracy and duration. Dhengee was captured by Colonel East in 1816, with inconsiderable loss; and, notwithstanding the treachery meditated by the Dwaraca chief, in consideration of the sanctity of the place,* he determined to attempt a negociation which was finally successful. In 1817 Okamundel, with its holy places of Bate and Dwaraca, was finally transferred to the Baroda Government.†

"*Puttan Somnauth* is a town near the southern extremity of the Gujerat Peninsula. Somnauth is one of the twelve images of Seeb, which are said to have descended from heaven to earth; and the great fame of its temple attracted the cupidity, while it stimulated the bigotry, of Sultan Mahmood, of Ghizni. According to Mahomedan authors, the image was destroyed, but the Hindoos assert that the god retired into the ocean! The symbol placed in the temple is deemed peculiarly propitious to those who desire offspring. It is visited by pilgrims from every quarter, who pay a trifling duty to the Nabob for permission to perform their devotions at this favourite shrine. In 1816, through the interposition of the Bombay Presidency with the Junaghar State, arrangements were effected, tending to secure *greater freedom of pilgrimage to Somnauth.*‡

"*Poona*, the modern capital of the Mahratta empire, is situated 100 miles from Bombay. The view from Parvate hill commands the town with all its gardens and plantations, the cantonments, and the British residency at the Sungum. At the bottom of the hill is a large square field enclosed with high brick walls, where the Peishwa used to assemble the Brahmuns, to whom he gave alms at the great feast, when the rainy season terminates; *who, on these occasions,*

---

* Why such respect for this idolatrous place—a den of thieves and pirates? † Vol. i. pp. 657—663. ‡ Vol. i. p. 671. Asi. Jour. Feb. 1827, p. 256.

begged their way from all parts of Hindostan. When all were assembled they were shut in and marked; and as they came out, one at a time, the gratuity was given to them. Something of the same kind is still continued by the British Government."*

"*Seringapatam* is the modern capital of Mysore. Hyder's palace occupies the east end of the island, and although built of mud displays considerable elegance, and is a very handsome native structure. Adjoining is the mausoleum of Hyder, where rests all that was royal of this Mahomedan dynasty, consisting of Hyder himself, his wife, and Tippoo, who lie under tombs covered with rich cloths, at the expense of the British Government; and *the establishment of priests to offer up prayers*, and of musicians to perform the Nobut (an instrument of music beaten five times a day), is retained as formerly. Hyder's palace is now the residence of a surgeon; his seraglio, a European Hospital. Tippoo's seraglio is a barrack for artillery; his private apartments are occupied by the Resident, and his public by European troops. How greatly degraded from their ancient dignity!"† Is not this establishment of priests supported by a Christian Government?

"*Colar* is the capital of a district of the same name, 40 miles from Bangalore. It was the birth place of Hyder. His son, Tippoo, erected a handsome monument for him; and near it a mosque and college of Moullahs, or Mahomedan priests (with a proper establishment of musicians), were endowed *to pray for his soul: the whole of which is still continued at the expense of the British Government.*‡

Of *the district of Tanjore*, it is remarked,—"The Mahomedans never having actually occupied this territory, or effected any permanent establishment in it, the Hindoo religion has been preserved in considerable splendour, and their ancient places of worship, with their vast endowments, remain untouched. In almost every village there is a temple, with a lofty gateway of massive but not inelegant architecture, where a great many Brahmuns are maintained, either by the revenues formerly attached to them, or by an allowance from Government. The Brahmuns are here the chief holders of land, and perform almost every office of husbandry, except holding the plough. They are all extremely loyal, on account of the protection they receive,

* Ham. Hind. vol. ii. p. 196. † p. 362. ‡ p. 374.

and also *for an allowance granted by the British Government of 45,000 pagodas (about £18,000 sterling) annually, which is distributed for the support of the poorer temples.*"* How much good would this sum do, if expended in supporting Christian schools, and the circulation of the Bible!

The temple of *Seringham* is situated in the district of Trichinopoly, under the Madras Presidency. "Pilgrims resort to it from all parts of Hindostan for absolution, and none come without an offering of value. Here, as in all great Pagodas, *the Brahmuns live in a subordination that knows no resistance, and slumber in voluptuousness that feels no want. At present the allowance made by the British Government for the support of the temple, and its establishment, amount to 15,600 pagodas per annum (about £6,240 sterling.)*"† It is to be lamented that voluptuous Brahmuns should be supported by a Christian Government, when Christianity would prove so great a blessing to the people of India.

"*Condatchy* is a bay in the island of Ceylon, and the most central rendezvous of the boats employed in the pearl fishery. *The superstition of the divers renders it necessary for the Government to employ two enchanters to charm the sharks*, in which they appear to be very successful, as, although they are seen, both from the boats, and while the diver is at the bottom, accidents rarely occur! These necromancers are all of one family, and possess the entire confidence of the natives. Two divers are attached to one stone, and go down alternately; and, when 300 boats are anchored on the banks, 1,500 divers may be supposed to go down every minute; and, probably, by their noise and numbers, assist the incantations of the shark charmers! These impostors receive ten oysters from every diver's share, and the *same number are allotted for the pagodas at Ramisseram and Nagore*, besides other privileges and emoluments of very ancient date, which have been continued by the British Government."‡

"*Serinagur* is the capital of the province Gurwal, thirty-eight miles from Hurdwar. On the opposite side of the river, at the village of Ranihut, is a temple sacred to Raja Ishwara; which is principally inhabited by dancing women. The initiation into this society is performed by

* Ham. Hind. vol. ii. p. 453. † 465. ‡ p. 518.

anointing the head with oil taken from the lamp placed before the altar; *by which act they make a formal abjuration of their parents and kindred, devoting their future lives to prostitution.** *Among the items of eleemosynary donations distributed to Brahmuns and others by the old Governments, and continued by the British, the principal in amount is 512 rupees, which is given to various tribes of religious mendicants, who frequent a mela or fair, held annually near Serinagur.*† Ought Britain thus to sanction and encourage obscenity? Would it be done were these things fully known? Happy day when British connexion with idolatry in India is dissolved, of whose temples, as well as those of ancient Rome, it may be said—

> " Nam quo non prostat fœmina templo ?—*Juv.*

" *Bhadrinath* is a town and temple, about eighty miles from Almora, in Kumaon. The principal Idol, Bhadrinath, is about three feet high, cut in black stone, or marble, dressed in a suit of gold and silver brocade, the head and hands only being uncovered. His temple has more beneficed lands attached to it than any sacred Hindoo establishment in this part of India. In 1808 it was said to possess 700 villages, which are all under the jurisdiction of the high priest, who holds a paramount authority, nominally independent of the ruling power. It was determined that the revenues of the purgannas, appropriated to temples and other religious buildings, should be continued, provided that the Commissioner was satisfied that they would not be diverted from their original purpose, and (as too frequently happens) converted to a source of individual emolument.

---

* " The worship of Brahma is constitutionally impure. There are temples of consecration for a life of impurity: these exist at Cambaya, Tivikarey, and other places of Hindostan. Tavernier mentioned the existence of the system. " From Cambaya you go to a little village, distant three coss, where there is a pagoda, to which all the Indian courtesans come to make their offerings. This pagoda is full of a great number of naked images. Among the rest there is a large figure of one that seems to resemble Apollo, all uncovered." Girls of eleven and twelve years old, who have been bought and educated for the purpose, are sent by their mistresses to this pagoda " to offer and surrender themselves up to this idol." (Tavernier's Travels in India, p. 37, 1678). See the Apocraphy, Baruch, ch. vi. ver. 43, and 2 Kings ch. xvii. ver. 30, respecting Succoth benoth. Is it possible that any man, whose mind has been cultivated under the influence of Christian principles, can wish such a system to be perpetuated?

† Ham. Hind. vol. ii. p. 640.

The repair of the road from Serinagur to Bhadrinath also appeared *an object of some importance as encouraging the resort of a greater number of pilgrims,* and thereby promoting the intercourse and traffic between the plains and the immense hills, whence springs the source of the Ganges."*

"In all the capital cities, principal towns, and districts, Mahomedan officers, known in this country by the title of *Cadis*, are stationed for the purpose of performing the religious duties and ceremonies prescribed by the Mahomedan law, and various other functions, at the public expense ; and their appointments are so far independent that they are only moveable for misconduct."†

"I cannot see," says C. Buller, Esq., M. P., in his letter to the Honourable Court of Directors relative to Juggernaut, May, 1813, "what possible objection there is to the continuance of an established tax, particularly when it is taken into consideration *what large pensions in land and money are allowed by our Government, in all parts of the country, for keeping up the religious institutions both of the Hindoos and the Mussulmans.*"‡

"*The temple of Deo Ghur* is situated on a rising ground, in the midst of a thick forest, and is attached to the Beerbhoom district. Thirty-two villages are allotted for the maintenance of the chief pundit or high priest of the temple at Deo Ghur, granted by Government at the settlement of the Jungleterry district. They are in a very flourishing state of cultivation."§

The conduct of individuals in India, especially when in authority, has too frequently tended to perpetuate idolatry. The following extracts from the late Bishop Heber's Journal appear very exceptionable :—"During my progress through the holy places (at Benares) I had received garlands of flowers in considerable numbers, which I was told it was uncivil to throw away, particularly those which were hung round my neck. *I now in consequence looked more like a sacrifice than a priest,* and on getting again into the gig

---

* Ham. Hind. vol. ii. p. 638.

† Teignmouth Cons. on Com. to the Nat. of India the knowledge of Christ. p. 62.

‡ Buchanan's Apology for Christianity in India, p. 162.

§ Francklin's Enquiry for the site of the Ancient Palibothra, part i. p. 88.

was glad to rid myself of my ornaments." "This being the great day of Hoolee, all my Hindoo servants came to pay their compliments and bring presents of red powder and sugar plums. The event was rather costly to me, as I was obliged to make presents in return. *But it is the "dustoor," and who in India can transgress that unwritten and common law of the land?"* "The Raja offered to return my visit next day; but knowing that Tuesday is, in the estimation of all Hindoos, *unlucky*, I named Wednesday in preference, telling him my reason. He answered, very politely, he should account every day lucky in which he had opportunity of cultivating my acquaintance, but was evidently well pleased."*

"The Grand Lama is an hereditary living deity, before whom millions prostrate themselves. When Captain Turner was on his embassy to this deity, *to gratify his votaries, he made an offering,* he says, *to the deceased Teshoo Lama*; and in addressing the same deity, who had entered the body of an infant eighteen months old, he said to the child:—'The Governor General, on receiving the news of his (your) decease in China was overwhelmed with grief and sorrow, and continued to lament his (your) absence from the world, until the cloud that had overcast the happiness of this nation was dispelled by his (your) appearance.'† Does such language comport with the dignity of the British and the Christian character?

Saugur Island, situated at the mouth of the Hooghly River, about 100 miles from Calcutta, is a well known place of pilgrimage. Infanticide was abolished here in 1802, during the administration of the Marquis Wellesley. The Madras Government Gazette, Jan. 13, 1827, contains an account of this pilgrimage; and observes, "According to the pundit an *impost* is levied by the officers of Government stationed here, of four annas per oar, besides a fee of one anna to the establishment: but the charge, if we are not misinformed, is *unsanctioned*, except as made by Byragees and Sunyasees, who assumed the right of levying four annas per oar, and eight annas to one or two rupees for each shop. This claim has been so far authorised that the right to levy any charge was withdrawn from the Saugur Society upon the petition of the religious mendicants. The

---

* Vol. i. p. 297. Vol. ii. pp. 84. 131.

† Ward's View of the Hindoos, vol. ii. p. 308.

temple of Kapila Muni, on the southern coast of Gunga Saugur, is under the alternate charge of a Byragee and Sunyasee. The latter presides at the Mela in the month of Kartik (Nov.), the former in Magh (Jan.) They levy a tax of four annas on each person who visits the temple, the amount of which is divided among five different establishments of Ramanandi Byragees, in the vicinity of Calcutta."*

It is hoped inquiry will be instituted into the conduct of these officers of Government, and that the various facts here stated will excite that attention which their importance demands.

CHAP. II.

The idolatrous Establishments chiefly supported by the System at Juggernaut, Gya, Allahabad, &c.

"It may be easily supposed," observes Colonel Phipps, "that a very large establishment of priests and others is attached to such a temple as Juggernaut. One of the head men stated the number to consist of 3,000 families, including 400 families of cooks to prepare holy food. The provisions furnished *daily* for the idol and his attendants consist of 220 pounds of rice, 97 pounds of kullye (a pulse), 24 pounds of moong (a small grain), 188 pounds of clarified buffaloe's butter, 80 pounds of molasses, 32 pounds of vegetables, 10 pounds of sour milk, 2½ pounds of spices, 2 pounds of sandal wood, some camphor, 20 pounds of salt, 4 rupees (10 shillings) worth of fire-wood: also 22 pounds of lamp oil for lights at night. *This holy food is presented to the idol three times a day!* the gates are shut, and no one but a few personal servants are allowed to be present. This meal lasts about an hour, during which period the dancing girls attached to the temple dance in the room with many pillars. On the ringing of a bell the doors are thrown open,

* Asi. Jour. Aug. 1827.

and the provision is removed. The food prepared for sale, or bespoken by the inhabitants, is not brought into the large tower, but collected in the Begue Mundeer, where it can be seen and sanctified by the idol from his distant throne!

"In addition to this food, a very considerable extra quantity is allowed for the great festivals: and, in order to make this superstition as profitable as possible, the priests have decided that nothing can pollute the food prepared in the temple—it may be conveyed to any place—it may be touched by a Mussulman, or a Christian, without becoming unfit for a Hindoo. Nothing can be more convenient than such a belief, as Hindoos in general must eat their food where it is cooked, and a thousand things may pollute it. The consequence is, that the cooks are employed to prepare food for most of the pilgrims, at a price which varies according to the demand, and is always highest during the festivals. It is said that a few days before the festival of the Ruth Jattra food is cooked within the court of the temple for at least 100,000 pilgrims; and it will easily be credited that, on these occasions, the 400 families of cooks have full employment. The potters make earthen pots of three sizes; the food is carried away in them, and they form a kind of standard measure: and, as none but new pots can be used, the consumption is very great, and supports a great many families. The only interruption to this cooking is during the time the idol is travelling in his car to the place where he was formed, and returning to the temple: nine days in all."*

The number of pilgrim hunters must be considerable; the same Gentleman stating,—"One of the principal natives related that a Purharee, in 1821, despatched 100 *agents* to entice pilgrims; and the ensuing year received the premium for 4,000 pilgrims! He was at that time busily employed in instructing 100 *additional agents* in all the mysteries of *this singular trade,* with the intention of sending them into the Upper Provinces of India."† This fact

---

* Col. Phipps' Account of Juggernaut, p. 6, 7.—Missionary Intelligence, March, 1823. (Published in Calcutta.)

† In the Parliamentary Papers relative to Juggernaut, May 1813, p. 80, an account is given of the establishment for collecting the Pilgrim Tax.—"Sudder Cutcherry, 19 Officers and servants, monthly salary 260 rupees; Ghaut Athara Nulla, Officers, &c., 26, salary 165 rupees; Ghaut Lokenaut, Officers, &c., 17, salary 111 rupees; at the temple 15, salary 89 rupees.—Total 77 Officers and servants, at 625 rupees per mensem.

Colonel P. related to the Author at Cuttack in 1822, and declared he would state it to the Marquis of Hastings on his arrival in Calcutta. A Missionary in Orissa, visiting Kontiloo (or Cooloo), about 90 miles from Cuttack, referring to the pundas, or pilgrim hunters, says—"I an informed there are *forty of these missionaries of idolatry* in Kontiloo. Nov. 1826." Another colleague in Orissa writes under date "Ganjam, Aug. 1826, I inquired how the pundas knew what to expect (of the pilgrims); and he said that some of them would come and stay *two or three months* in such a place as Ganjam, by which means they became acquainted with different people's circumstances. They subsist by bringing *maha presaud* (holy food), which they give to different persons, and get what they can in return. Some one says of the bad ones, 'What a curse to Christendom are the priests of Christendom:' surely one may say, 'What a curse to Orissa, and to a much greater extent of country, are the pundas and priests of Juggernaut."

JUGGERNAUT'S ESTABLISHMENT.

The following statement of the establishment of Juggernaut was extracted from Rennell's MS. account of Orissa.*

1. "*Maha Rajah Ram Chunder Dev*, honorary servant to the idol, to make ultkee chowr, sweep the ruts, and strew flowers on the idols. His son now officiates.

2. "*Mood Roth*, alias *Plenipotentiary*, in the absence of the *Maha Rajah* performs the above duties.

3. "*Naik Chattees Neejoy*, the head officer of *thirty-six* different orders of minstrel and other officers, who adorns the idol, and does all other personal services for it; and has full authority to superintend the attendance and performance of the duties of all the other officers.

4. "*Pundah* performs the ceremonies of the Bhoge (offerings).

5. "*Pussopaluk* adorns the idol.

6. "*Tulchoo*, in the absence of the Purchas, accom-

European Collector's salary 500 rupees per month, and 1½ per cent *commission on the amount of the tax collected.* The allowance to the Officers was fixed at 300 rupees per month and 2 per cent [on the net collections. Aug. 1809.

* See Friend of India, April, 1822. Asi. Jour. March, 1823.

panies the idol to the tank, and acts for them in the temple also.

7. "*Bhethurschoo* adorns the idol, and keeps watch in the time of the Bhoge, in order to prohibit any superfluous quantity of offerings being taken in.

8. "*Maha Soar*, head cooks.—Brahmuns who in the first instance take in the Bhoge.

9. "*Soar*, cooks and scullions.—Brahmuns who take in Bhoge after the *Maha Soar*.

10. "*Guarra Borro*, persons who give water to the *Poojah Pundas* at the time of their performing the ceremonies of Bhoge.

11. "*Puthree Borro* cleans the brass vessels, and takes flour, chundun, &c., in them to the *Poojah Pundah*.

12. "*Punthee Borro* are Brahmuns who put the kitchree in silver and golden dishes, and set them before the idol. *This is Sirkaree Bhoge, or the allowance by Government!! Alas!*

13. "*Soar Borro* is the office of distributing proper quantities of Bhoge to such other temples and officers as may be directed by the rulers of the temple.

14. "*Kheontiah* warns the idol and the Rajah of the time of festivals.

15. "*Mecaup*, masters of the wardrobe of two different descriptions; viz. *Mecaup* keeps the jewels, and *Changrah Mecaup* the wearing apparel in one department.

16. "*Dytah* removes the idols from the throne and puts them on the ruts, and replaces them again.

17. "*Puttee* are Brahmuns. After the Snan Jattra the idols are taken into a room allotted for the purpose of taking off the old clothes and swaddling them with new ones, which takes fifteen days, during which time the offerings in the room are made by these people.

18. "*Mahajona*. This description of officers convey the smaller idols to tanks and other places, and then put them in the proper room.

19. "*Hurrup Naik*. After the Bhoge is removed, these officers bring paun or beetle, and hot spices, and set the same before the idol, which (says the writer) *Juggernaut munches at his ease!!*

20. "*Aukund Mecaup*. Lamp-lighter.

21. "*Khaut Sage Mecaup*. Bed-maker.

22. "*Poohoree*. Watchmen at the time of Bhoge.

23. " *Pooran Pundah* reads the Pooran at certain times near the idol.

24. " *Mookpokhal.* A person who attends with a dantoon (used for a tooth brush) and water *to wash the idol's face in the morning !*

25. " *Austaun warns the idols of the time of ceremonies.*

26. " *Fanruk,* watchmen of the wardrobe.

27. " *Chathour,* a person who carries a chatta or umbrella.

28. " *Tauraseean,* a person who carries the tras, an ensign in the form of a half moon.

29. " *Deoreean,* a torch bearer.

30. " *Dondchuttur,* a person who stands by the throne with an umbrella at the Ekadusse and other particular festival days.

31. " *Kahaleah,* a trumpeter.

32. *Ghuntoah,* a person who sounds the ghunt or brass bason.

33. " *Ghutwaree,* a person who rubs sandal wood.

34. " *Lenka, Peons* (Soldiers).

35. " *Perdhanee,* persons who give the golden rods to the Purchas.

36. " *Dooarees,* door keepers.

37. " *Summuntah* grind kullaee and other kinds of grain.

38. " *Deb Dausee,* dancing girls with a band of Musicians."

A more particular account of this Establishment was procured for the Author, writtten on the leaf of a tree, by a native of Juggernaut; the following is a free translation of of it.*

1. " The *Moodeerut,* as the Rajah of Koorda's representative with Juggernaut, at all the festivals moves about the light, performs the daily service before him, and makes the offering of food.

2. " There are three head *Pundas,* who having poured clarified butter on the sacred fire, and worshipped the sun and the divine regents of the gates, present the sacrificial articles from the kitchen, to the three gods at three of the daily offices, until the period of Juggernaut's retiring to rest !

---

* See Friend of India, Oct. 1825.

3. "There are three *Pushoo-palas*, who perform worship between the periods of the regular service; and, ascending the throne of Juggernaut, clothe him in the three different dresses appropriated to the three services.

4. "The *Bheet-baboo* guards the sacrificial food before it has been offered, prevents the crowd pressing on it, and should the smallest blemish be found in it (such as a hair or an ant) he seizes and punishes the Pundas.

5. "The *Tulubu Pureechas* guard Juggernaut when he retires to rest. In their absence the *Pushoo-palas* act in their stead.

6. "The *Potee-mukapatra*, at the twelve periodical festivals, make the proper offerings, and move about the image of Sooda-buden; and at the great bathing festival, when Juggernaut moves out to the Neeladree beej, worship him during his progress, and during the fifteen succeeding days when *he is supposed to be ill, not having recovered from the effects of his bath!*

7. "The *Patree-buroo* arranges the sacrificial articles, and calls the Pundas to worship.

8. "The *Gora-buroo*, at the time of worship, places the water pot and presents the water to the officiating priest.

9. "The *Khootiya* calls the *Phashoo-paluks* who are appointed *to wake Juggernaut*, and bring forward the vestments and necklaces with which he is to be invested.

10. "The *Paneeya-mekab* presents the ornaments of Juggernaut to the *Pushoo-paluk*, and counts them as they come from Juggernaut's body; and likewise counts out to the *Pureechas* any new ornaments offered by pilgrims.

11. "The *Changro-mekab* carries the vestments of Juggernaut, and counts them out; and, when new vestments are offered by the pilgrims, he counts them out and puts them away.

12. "The *Bhandar-mekab* counts out the ornaments when taken off from Juggernaut by the *Paneeya-mekab*. The vestments presented by pilgrims pass into their custody after they have been worn.

13. "The *Suwar-buroo* sweeps the place, and places the sacrificial dishes before Juggernaut, presents odours to those who wake him, and distributes the sacrificial flowers among the servants and worshippers.

14. "The *Pureeksha-buroo* holds up a looking glass to Juggernaut during worship.

15. "The *Ukhundu-mekab*, or lamp-lighter, places lights and removes the lamps.

16. "The *Pureeyarees* watch at the gates and doors.

17. "The *Dab-khat* brings out Juggernaut's bed!

18. "The *Pureeyaree* of the southern gate cries out, 'the sacrificial food is coming.'

19. "The *Pureeyarees* of the gate watch the food; and, when Juggernaut moves out, carry with him the sweet smelling wood.

20. "The *Juya* and *Vijuya-pureeyarees* (or porters) allow no one to enter while Juggernaut is at his meals; and there are two watchmen at the door of the inner room where Juggernaut partakes of his food.

21. "The *Khurgu-nayuk*, at the close of the daily offices, presents the paun to the officiating priests to be given to Juggernaut; and, on the occasion of the last daily office, offers it himself.

22. The *Khatsuya mekab carries Juggernaut's bed to him at night for him to sleep on; and carries it back to its place in the morning!*

23. "The *Mook-pakhul pureeyaree* presents *the water and the tooth-pick* to Juggernaut, and inspects into every thing respecting the temple.

24. "The *Suwar-Kota* prepares the cakes, and delivers them to the *Maha-Suwar*.

25. "The *Maha-Suwar* brings the first service of cakes.

26. "The *Gopal-bullubha* distributes it.

27. "The *Bhatee-buroo* places food of a particular description before the idol.

28. "The *Rosh-payeed* lights the lamp in the kitchen, and expels the *suwars* when they become unclean; he accompanies the royal offering of food as far as the Juya and Vijuya gate.

29. "The *Beeree-buha-suwar* takes the articles of paun from the *Sumurthas*, and delivers them to the *Suwars*.

30. "The *Dhoa-pakhaliya* Brahmun washes and cleanses the kitchen.

31. "The *Unga-buha* Brahmun removes the ashes from the cook-room, and throws them away.

32. "The *Dita-suwaree* carries the image of Juggernaut when necessary, and prepares the image.

33. "The *Datya* paints the image, and fastens the flag on his carriage.

34. "The *Dwar-nayuk* is employed in openiug and shutting the door.

35. "The *Mahajhun* carries the image of Juya and Vijuya, the two heavenly porters.

36. "The *Beeman-buroo* carries the image of Juggernaut and fixes it in its place.

37. "The *Moodolee-bhandur* guards the door, puts the *chamura* into the hands of distinguished pilgrims who desire to fan Juggernaut; and locking, guards the door of Juya and Vijuya, the two heavenly porters.

38. "The *Chootar* holds the umbrella over the great god when he proceeds on a journey.

39. "The *Turasee* holds before him the *turas* (a large fan) when he goes on a journey.

40. "The *Meg-dumboora* proceeds with the *Meg-dumboora* when he goes on a journey

41. "The *Moodra* holds the lamp when an offering of flowers is made to Juggernaut.

42. "The *Paneeya-put* delivers the water pots to the *Buroo*, and washes them.

43. "The *Keehuleea*, at all stated festivals, during the service and during the offering of flowers, performs worship, and plays the *Kahulee*.

44. "The *Ghuntooa* rings the bell during Juggernaut's meals, and when he goes on journeys!

45. "The *Chumputee-tumukreeya*, at the time of *pusoowa* and during journeys, plays the tumuk.

46. "The head *Punda* calls all the servitors to their duty, gives the golden sceptre to the *Pureecha*, and gives food to the Brahmuns of the *Mooktee-mundupa*.

47. "The *Ghutuwaree* prepares the sandal wood and gives it to the *mekaps;* and, at one of the festivals, goes before the image with the incense.

48. "The *Buree Deega* supplies the water for cooking; and removes the remains of food.

49. "The *Sumundha* pounds peas of one kind, and grinds peas of another kind.

50. "The *Gruhu-mekap* cleans the dishes after the principal meal.

51. "The *Yogukuma* brings forward the articles of the principal meal.

52. "The *Tomabutee* accompanies the principal evening meal with a lamp, and brings the pots and cooking utensils.

53. "The *Chaulbacha* cleanses the rice and the peas.

54. "The *Elek* carries the Chukru or discus of Vishnoo before the Idol when he moves out, and is a general superintendent.

55. "The *Patrok*, having dismissed the attendants, cleans up the temples, and *there* retires to rest.

56 "The *Choonara* serves the image of Guroora (the bird god), has charge of the great standard of the temple, and lifts the great lamp.

57. "The *Khurga dhoaneeya* cleanses the space between the western part of the temple and the place called Jugunmohun.

58. "The *Nagadhya washes Juggernaut's linen, and hangs it up to dry!*

59. "The *Daree-ganee* sings the songs which precede the anointing of Juggernaut with sandal wood.

60. "The *Pooran-punda* reads the Pooranas in the gate of Juggernaut.

61. "The *Beenkar* plays the *beena,* a musical instrument.

62. "The *Tunubobuk* dances in the spot called Jugunmohun.

63. "The *Sunkhooa* sounds the shell during the offices of worship.

64. "The *Madolee* plays on the *madol,* a musical instrument, during worship.

65. "The *Tooree-nayuk* plays on the *tooree* or trumpet.

66. "The *Muhasetee* washes the linen of Juggernaut.

67. "The *Paneepaee mahar* removes all filth from within the enclosure.

68. "The *Hakeemeeshristar-buru-pureecha* is the great judge of all questions; he holds the golden cane."

Of the nature and regulations of the establishment at *Gya* no correct information appears to be extant, but the establishment must be considerable, as Mr. Harington observes, "The Gyawalas (pilgrim hunters of Gya) *travel through all countries where the Hindoo religion prevails, in search of pilgrims, who, but for them, would probably never have visited Gya.*" The number of pilgrims, and their attendants, in ordinary years, is not fewer than 100,000; but, in time of peace, when visited by the great Mahratta chieftains, the number exceeds 200,000, with many horses; nor will twenty lacks (two millions) of rupees defray their expenses, where many of them reside for three months.*

* Hamilton, supra, vol. i. p. 266, 277.

Of the establishment at the temple of Tripetty, near Madras, it has been remarked, " crowds of pilgrims resort to it from all parts of India, who pour into it offerings of goods, grain, gold, silver, jewels, &c., the aggregate of which, when converted into money, not only yields a surplus revenue to Government, *but serves to maintain several thousand persons performing the offices of an idolatrous worship, which is here conducted with extraordinary pomp.*"

At Allahabad the number of priests supported by the pilgrims must be considerable. Much hostility was manifested in 1815 to the introduction of a more efficient police. " The class denominated *Pragwals*, who perform the religious ceremonies at the junction of the great rivers, to the number of 4 or 5000, showed a determination to resist, threatened to cease to officiate, and withdraw altogether, which would have caused *a loss to Government of the pilgrim revenue.* Many other conspiracies to arrest the progress of the arrangements took place; but, by patience and firmness, they were ultimately dissipated and suppressed. The number of pilgrims in 1812 and 1813 was greater than had occurred for twenty-eight years, being 218,792.

	Rupees.
Amount of collections	223,563
Repaid to the account of Dowlet Row Scindia	175
Charges of establishment	3,407
	219,981
Fines on persons attempting to bathe without licenses	1,085
	8)221,066"
Net receipts . . .	£27,633

" The tax accruing to Government is three rupees* for

* This is a considerable sum to people who have to labour a month to obtain it. Hamilton, speaking of Bengal, says, "Notwithstanding the low price of the necessaries of life, the common labourers find it extremely difficult to subsist on their scanty earnings, which, in some places, are not more than from a *penny* to *twopence* a day." Vol. i. p. 100. This confirms the statement that *a rupee* to a poor Hindoo is

each person, but a much greater expense is incurred in charity, and gifts to the Brahmuns."*

The author of an interesting volume, entitled "Sketches of India," speaking of Allahabad, makes the following reference to the system of the Pilgrim Tax:—"On the small point of land at which the rivers the Ganges and Jumna join their waters sit numbers of Brahmuns, known by their distinguished flags, who receive the sums each pilgrim must pay for performing his ablutions, seal them, sell amulets, certificates, and Ganges water, to be conveyed many miles distant. A Sepoy sentinel, near the spot, boasted of the privilege he enjoyed, as being in the Honourable Company's service, he was exempted from the usual fine, paying a *smaller sum for permission to dip his body in the sanctifying stream at this place!* To prop superstitition, and countenance fraud, is surely a policy at once timid and impious: to benefit by the credulity of the poor plundered Idolater is a financial arrangement very little to our honour; and, perhaps, as little to our interest." The Constitutional Guardian remarks, "This account, that of Juggernaut, and the conduct of General Brownrigg, when Budhu was re-established in Ceylon, are parallel cases, that call for enquiry at the India House; and we may be sure they will redress such anomalies when they have time to investigate them."

---

equal to a *pound note* to a poor labourer in England. "It may show the poverty of the country," says Bishop Heber, "and the cheapness of the different articles, to observe, that having bought all the commodities which he wanted for a few pice, he was unable in the whole market to get change for a rupee." Journ., vol. i. p. 14. A missionary in Orissa, speaking of a country excursion (April 1827), observes, "Here at twenty or thirty miles from Juggernaut, there is little money circulating, and what there is is almost all cowries (shells), of which sixty make a farthing. A little rice comes into the market, but bartering is so common that an offer of cowries is rejected." The Pilgrim Tax is doubtless frequently very oppressive.

* Ham. Hind., vol. i. p. 299—301.

CHAP. III.

The Miseries resulting from this System, and its general Character.

"At the two annual fairs (held at Hurdwar, distant 1050 miles from Calcutta, a place of great celebrity for its numerous pilgrims), it is supposed, from 2 to 300,000 people are collected; once in twelve years, when particular religious ceremonies are observed, the number is computed to be almost a million: and in April, 1809, they were estimated at two millions. Owing to the precautions taken by the British Government, the fairs have lately ended at Hurdwar without bloodshed, to the astonishment of the vast multitude, who were before accustomed to associate the idea of bloodshed and murder with that of the fair. Those who come merely for bathing arrive in the morning, and, after performing their ablutions, depart in the evening, or on the following day. During the temporary Mahratta sway, a kind of poll tax and duties on cattle were levied; but all is now *free without impost and molestation, which considerably detracts from the merit of the pilgrimage.*"*

Of the new road from Calcutta to Juggernaut, Hamilton remarks, "This road was begun in 1813, and is still going on; but with respect to the pilgrims, *the merit of their peregrination being in proportion to the hardships they sustain, every arrangement tending to render the holy place more accessible, and their immediate sufferings less, in the same proportion diminishes the merits of the pilgrimage, and nullifies the contemplated expiation.*"† It is evident that the Pilgrim Tax enhances the supposed value of pilgrimages, and hence the celebrity of those places of idolatrous resort at which it is levied. But the poverty, exposure, sickness, mortality, and brutal treatment of the dead, consequent upon vast assemblies of pilgrims, demonstrate the pernicious tendency of a system which regulates, supports, and aggrandizes idolatry. From the united testimony of several eye witnesses, the miseries of pilgrimage (particularly to Juggernaut's temple in Orissa) are evident.

---

* Ham. Hind. vol. i. p. 451. † Vol. ii. p. 54.

A. Stirling, Esq., in his "Account of Orissa," describes the great car festival of Juggernaut, and adverts to the miseries of the pilgrims:—"On the appointed day, after various ceremonies are performed within the temple, the images are brought from their throne to the outside of the Lion-gate, not with reverence, seated on a litter or vehicle adapted to such an occasion; but, a common cord being fastened round their necks, certain priests, to whom the duty appertains, drag them down the steps, and through the mud, while others keep their figures erect, and help their movements by shoving them from behind, in the most unceremonious manner, as *if they thought the whole business a good joke!* In this way the monstrous idols go rocking and pitching along through the crowd, until they reach the cars, which they are made to ascend by a similar process up an inclined platform. On the other hand, a powerful sentiment of religious enthusiasm pervades the admiring multitude of pilgrims assembled without, when the images first make their appearance through the gate. They welcome them with shouts and cries of Jye Juggernaut! victory to Juggernaut! and when the monster Juggernaut, the most hideous of all the figures, is dragged forth, the last in order, the air is rent with acclamations. The celebrated Idols are nothing more than wooden busts, *about six feet in height*, fashioned into a rude resemblance of the human head, resting on a sort of pedestal. They are painted white, yellow, and black, respectively, with frightfully grim and distorted countenances, and are decorated with a head dress of different coloured cloths, shaped something like a helmet. The two brothers have arms projecting horizontally forward from the cars. The sister is entirely devoid of even that approximation to the human form. The ruths or cars* have an imposing air from their size and loftiness, but every part of the ornament is of the most paltry description, save only *the covering of striped and spangled broad cloth, furnished from the Export Warehouse of the British Government, the splendour of which*

---

* "The car of Juggernaut measures 43½ feet high; it has sixteen wheels, of 6½feet diameter, and a platform 34½ feet square. The Rut of Bulbudra is about 41 feet high, and has 14 wheels, and that of Subudra his sister is 40 feet high, 14 wheels, and 6½ feet diameter." The wood is annually provided by the Duspulla Rajah, but in 1806 he refused to send it farther than Cuttack. Par. Papers, 1813, pp. 35, 64.

CAR OF JUGGERNAUT, AND A HUMAN SACRIFICE. *Page* 250.

*compensates, in a great measure, for other deficiencies of decoration!** After the images have been lodged in their vehicles, a box is brought forth, containing the golden or gilded feet, hands, and ears of the great idol, which are fixed on the proper parts with due ceremony, and a scarlet scarf is carefully arranged round the lower part of the body, or pedestal. The joy and shouts of the crowd on the first movement of the cars, the creaking sound of the wheels as these pondrous machines roll along, the clatter of hundreds of harsh sounding instruments, and the general appearance of so immense a moving mass of human beings, produce, it must be acknowledged, an impressive, astounding, and somewhat picturesque effect, while the novelty of the scene lasts; though *the contemplation cannot fail of exciting the strongest sensations of pain and disgust in the mind of every Christian spectator.* In an unfavourable season, or when the festival occurs late, the proportion of deaths occasioned by exposure is very melancholy."†

Dr. Buchanan's visit to Juggernaut's temple, in June, 1806, is well known; a short extract or two from his "Christian Researches" may suffice:—"Numbers of pilgrims die on the road, and their bodies generally remain unburied. On a plain by the river near the pilgrim's Caravansera, at this place, Budruck (100 miles from Juggernaut), there are more than a hundred skulls; the dogs, jackals, and vultures, seem to live here on human prey. Wherever I turn my eyes, I meet death in some shape or other.—From the place where I now stand I have a view of a host of people like an army, encamped at the outer gate of the town of Juggernaut, where *a guard of soldiers is posted to prevent their entering the town until they have paid the tax.*—A pilgrim announced that he was ready to offer himself a sacrifice to the idol. He laid himself down in the road before the car as it was moving along, on his face, with his arms stretched forward. The multitude passed round him, leaving the space clear, and he was crushed to death by the wheels. How much I wish that the Proprietors of India Stock could have attended the wheels

---

* "The other evening a cart load of gay coloured English woollens passed me from the Company's Warehouse, to adorn the idols' cars. Alas! that the same country should, in so shocking a sense, send out both blessing and cursing. June 23, 1827."—Ext. Miss. Jour.

† Asi. Res. Vol. xv. pp. 321—325.

of Juggernaut, and seen this peculiar source of their revenue! I beheld a distressing scene this morning in the place of skulls; a poor woman lying dead, or nearly so, and her two children by her, looking at the dogs and vultures which were near. The people passed by without noticing the children! I asked them where was their home? They said they had no home but where their mother was. O there is no pity at Juggernaut! Those who support *his* kingdom err. I trust, from ignorance. They know not what they do."

Colonel Phipps, who witnessed the Car Festival in 1822, thus describes the miseries occasioned by it:—"The loss of life, by this deplorable superstition, probably exceeds that of any other. The aged, the weak, the sick, are persuaded to attempt this pilgrimage, as a remedy for all evils. The number of women and children, also, is very great. The pilgrims leave their families and occupations, to travel an immense distance, with the delusive hope of obtaining eternal bliss. 'Their means of subsistence on the road are scanty; and their light clothing and little bodily strength are ill calculated to encounter the inclemency of the weather. When they reach the district of Cuttack, they cease to experience that hospitality shown elsewhere to pilgrims; it is a burden which the inhabitants could not sustain: and they prefer availing themselves of the increased demand of provisions to augment the price! This difficulty is more severely felt as they approach the temple; till they find scarcely enough left to pay the tax to Government, and to satisfy the rapacious Brahmuns. The pilgrim, on leaving Juggernaut, has still a long journey before him; and his means of support are often almost, if not quite exhausted. The work of death then becomes rapid; and the route of the pilgrims may be traced, by the bones left by jackals and vultures. The country near the temple seems suddenly to have been visited by pestilence and famine. Dead bodies are seen in every direction. Parriar dogs, jackals, and vultures, are observed watching the last moments of the dying pilgrim, and not unfrequently hastening his fate."*

The late Rev. W. Ward has made a calculation of the number that are supposed to perish annually, the victims of superstition. He estimates that 4,000 pilgrims perish every

---

* Mis. Resigter, 1824, p. 578.

year, on the roads to, and at holy places, and a Gentleman whose opinion is of great weight, says, "I believe this estimate is far below the truth." "By fevers, by the dysentery, and other diseases, arising from exposure to the night air and the privations of a long journey, crowds are carried off in a few days. Sacred places, the resort of pilgrims, are spread all over Hindostan, and pilgrims travel to them from distances requiring journeys of three, four, and five months." An officer writing to his friends about the pilgrims at the gate of Pooree, detained for a time to make them pay the tax, says,—"I let above 100 out of limbo at Juggernaut: there were 1000 dead and dying:—all in limbo starving to extort money from them."*

The Rev. W. Bampton, Missionary at Juggernaut, in an account of the Car Festival of 1823, writes:—"July 11th. In front of one of the cars lay the mangled body of a dead man, one arm and one leg were eaten, and two dogs were then eating him: many people were near, both moving and stationary, but they did not seem to take any notice of the circumstance! I went to see the state of the pilgrims, who, either because they could not, or would not pay the tax, were kept without one of the gates. In the course of the morning I saw within a mile of the gate about six dead: the dogs and birds were eating three of them. Five or six lay dead within a mile of the gate; and it is generally admitted that there was not a *tenth*, perhaps scarcely a *twentieth*, of the pilgrims this year who attend sometimes; and, if there be the same proportion of dead and sick at all times, fifty or sixty dead might some years be seen, within a mile of this gate, and eighty or a hundred sick. A specimen of what is sometimes seen was given me by a military officer, who pointed out a piece of ground, perhaps scarcely an acre, on which he last year counted at one time twenty-five dead bodies."

The Rev. C. Lacey, the author's colleague at Cuttack, thus describes the car festival in June 1825:—"The mortality did not much appear before the 16th; on the 19th it was exceedingly bad, for the day before the rain began to fall, and more came on the 19th and 20th; and for the next three days it fell in torrents. At this time the scene had reached its height, and was truly shocking on every hand. In every street, corner, and open space,—in fact wherever

* Ward's View of the Hindoos. Vol. ii. pp. 126, 318.

you turned your eyes, the dead and dying met your sight! On the evening of the 19th, I counted upwards of *sixty dead and dying*, from the temple down to the bottom end of the hospital (about half a mile), leaving out the sick, that had not much life. At a corner opposite the hospital, on a spot of ground twelve feet square, I counted ten dead and five sick! This was the case, while there were several sets of men in active employ burying the dead! You will perhaps think, if the streets were thus crowded, what must be the various Golgothas! I visited but one, and that was between the town and the principal entrance, and I saw sights I shall never forget. The small river there was quite glutted with the dead bodies. The wind had drifted them altogether, and they were a complete mass of putrifying flesh!! They also lay upon the ground in heaps, and the dogs and birds were able to do but little towards devouring them." "Pages," says Mrs. L., "would not be sufficient to detail the miseries of the deluded worshippers of Juggernaut. The poor pilgrims were to be seen in every direction dead, and in the agonies of death; lying by fives, tens, and twenties. Mr. L. Counted upwards of 90 in one place, and in another Mr. Bampton counted 140. In the hospital I believe I have seen thirty dead at once, and numbers in the agonies of death, *and even the living using the dead bodies for pillows!*"

The Author, then residing at Cuttack, addressed a letter to the late J. H. Harington, Esq., Calcutta, relative to the miseries of the pilgrims, and the dreadful effects of the Pilgrim Tax, in taking the money which would procure them food, raiment, and medicine, and thus prevent premature death. Directions were immediately forwarded to Pooree, and some relief afforded to the pilgrims. About 400 rupees were sent to the Missionaries, and two of them undertook a journey from Pooree to Cuttack (a distance of fifty miles), to relieve the people. A few extracts from the journal of this work of mercy are of a very affecting nature. —"June 25, 1825. We left Pooree about five o'clock in the morning, with a few cloths, and a good quantity of medicine and money. We had brandy to prevent the effects of the effluvia from the dead bodies. For four miles from the gate, the dead were very numerous. O what a waste of human life was here! Some on the road among the mud, and some scarcely distinguishable from it: some under sheds into which they had crept from the rain; but mostly thrown into the narrow channel or grip on each side of the road. Here I saw them lie together by four, five, six, seven, eight, nine, ten, twelve, or more! I tried to keep account, but could not without detaining the palque bearers. Some of the bodies were carried beyond the grip into the fields and there lay, watched by the dogs and vultures. A great majority of the sick whom I relieved, on our first stage, were *females* deserted by their friends, who had left them not a pice (a halfpenny), and almost destitute of clothing."*

Of the number that perished it is impossible to form a correct idea. An eye witness of the scene writes, "The money received at the gate this year far exceeded that of others, being 260,000 rupees (£32,500). The number of pilgrims is estimated at 225,000. Captain F— estimates those who died at Cuttack and Pooree, and between the two stations, at 5000; but Mr. L— thinks this rather too high an estimate." How many of these miserable people must have died before they could reach their homes!—many of them coming 3, 6, or 900 miles. Mr. M—, the European Collector of the Tax at Pooree, estimated the mortality at 20,000!!

As the Author resided at Cuttack for nearly three years and a half, and has been at Juggernaut at the great festival in 1824 and 1825, he may be allowed to add his humble testimony to the above evidence of the misery of pilgrimage.—I have seen three persons measuring their way to the temple by constant prostration. At Cuttack and Pooree I have seen numbers of the dying and dead pilgrims; and one morning, near the temple, I counted between twenty and thirty skulls in one place. In the last stage to Pooree, in June, 1825, I counted thirty-seven bodies or skeletons. A few hundred yards from my residence at Cuttack (near the ford to Juggernaut), at the time of the great festival, the effluvia from the dead bodies has been very noisome, nor is there any allowance from the magistrate at Cuttack to inter the dead. Where the Suttee has slain its thousands, pilgrimage has slain its tens of thousands! The European who has visited Juggernaut at the great festival may be forcibly reminded of the appalling description:—

> " —— He saw the lean dogs
> Gorging and growling o'er carcase and limb,
> They were too busy to bark at him.

---

* See Report of the General Baptist Missionary Society for 1826.

From a pilgrim's skull they had stript the flesh
As ye peel the fig when the fruit is fresh;
And their white trunks crunsh'd o'er their whiter skull,
As it slipt through their jaws when their edge grew dull;
As they lazily mumbled the bones of the dead
When they scarce could stir from the place where they fed;
So well had they broken a lingering fast
With those who had fallen for that repast."

Some of the pilgrims to Juggernaut bring the water of the Ganges to pour over the idol Lokenaut; these are exempt from tax. The author while residing in Orissa has frequently seen these devotees. The devout go on pilgrimage from distant countries; but, to render this act meritorious, the pilgrims must previously visit the banks of the Ganges, lie on the ground and fast during the journey, and arrive laden with water to bathe the idol. To prove that the water was really brought from the Ganges, the bearers take the precaution to obtain a certificate to that effect from the officer of the place, who seals the vessel into which it is put with his seal. It is probable that this is done in all cases where the water is taken for idolatrous purposes. The engraving represents the mode in which both men and women carry the waters of the Ganges to a distance of several hundred miles.

HUMAN SACRIFICE UNDER JUGGERNAUT'S CAR. *Page* 257.

Of the Car Festival at Juggernaut, in July, 1826, Mr. Lacey writes,—"The festival took place late this year (July 9th), and was not numerously attended. A respectable man threw himself off from the front of the car, as it was moving forward, and the enormous wheels passed just over his loins, and nearly separated his upper from his lower parts! The blood and bowels were scattered and drawn about by the wheels passing over him!* There was very little mortality among the pilgrims this year; for, the numbers being so small, they were able to obtain food and shelter."

The Rev. A. Sutton of Balasore in Orissa, in an account of the great festival in 1827, remarks upon the oppressive and impure character of this idolatrous exhibition.—"The people at the outer gate of the town were admitted; they had been collecting for a long time, and were not allowed to enter because they would not or could not pay the tax. It was grievous to see the poor people (many of whom came from distant parts of India) with their little all tied up in a bundle, and suspended under their umbrellas, in some unguarded moment, rushed upon by the Pooree tigers, and their all taken from them. These villains of Juggernaut lie in wait, and when they see an old or disabled pilgrim, rush upon him, give him a blow upon the head with a large stick, and snatch the umbrella with the bundle out of his hand! I saw, perhaps, *fifty cases of this kind while I stood!*—The idols have been replaced on the cars to return. I cannot refrain from noticing the obscene gestures and lascivious songs which were again employed to animate the draggers, and spread an infernal enthusiasm through the gazing assembly. I asked a person near, what kind of worship that was, he replied, '*Kusbeeka bat*' (the language of prostitutes); but added, '*it gave Juggernaut pleasure!*' The following day a poor wretch threw himself under Juggernaut's car, and was crushed to death. Mr. B—— saw the horrid sight." The worship of Juggernaut is still the

---

* In 1828 "twelve persons had bound themselves to die a sacrifice under the wheels of the cars, but the under magistrate hearing of the circumstance placed them in confinement, and thus prevented the horrid deed. This was done at Pooree, at one of the largest festivals in Hindostan, and done on personal responsibility; and yet a poor woman, in circumstances of much less notoriety, is allowed to burn herself under pretence that we must not interfere with the superstitions of the Hindoos." (Cuttack, July, 1828.)

same. C. Buller, Esq., M. P., in 1813, endeavoured to palliate the sanguinary and impure worship of this idol,* but in vain.—" If you would know the character of the nation, look at the temple." When shall Britain cease to promote idolatry?—When shall Christianity abolish the miseries of heathenism?

The late Rev. J. M. Cropper, Missionary in Orissa, writes in Feb. 1828, " While we continued here (Pertubpore, near Midnapore), a number of jattrees passed us. On inquiry we found they had come from Nepaul, in a body of 500. They calculated that 200 would die by the way: about forty had died already! If this be the case in the cold season (the most healthy time in India), what havock must death make among the pilgrims, on their return from the Rut Jattra in the commencement of the rains?"

Of the effects of pilgrimage, in another part of India, Hamilton gives the following statement:—" The number of crimes that originate in the Behar District, of which *Gya is the capital, may in a great measure be attributed to the vast crowd of pious and superstitious pilgrims.* The wealth these persons possess generally consists of money, jewels, and other articles, which excites the cupidity of the unprincipled; while the defenceless condition of the greater part of these stragglers exhibits it to them as a prey of easy acquisition. Numerous affrays and breaches of the peace may also be expected where such a number of strangers, from all parts of Hindostan, are promiscuously congregated; nor will these votaries of superstition gain any addition to their prior stock of morals, by their intercourse with their spiritual guides at the sanctuary, who are in general both ignorant and dissolute, and do not affect even the appearance of any self denial or ascetism of conduct "†

The general character of the Pilgrim Tax System demands serious attention. It increases the celebrity of places of idolatrous resort. The tax on pilgrims at Juggernaut, while it encourages the emissaries of idolatry to wander to the distant parts of Hindostan, to collect its deluded votaries (a stipulated sum being received by them for each individual passed into the town), by its sanction of idolatry, not only adds to the celebrity of the pilgrimage, but confounds Christianity with Idolatry, in the sight of the

---

* See Buchanan's Apology for Christianity in India, pp. 33—38.

† Hamilton's Hindostan, vol. i. pp. 267—301.

TEMPLES OF BOBUNESWER, NEAR CUTTACK, ORISSA. *Page* 259.

Hindoos. A native inquired of a Missionary in Orissa, "*If Juggernaut be nothing, why does the Company take so much money from those who come to see him!*" "This tax," says Mr. Harington, in his "Analysis," referring to the sentiments of the Honourable Court of Directors, "is not to be considered a source of public revenue, but to be appropriated to *the repairs and other expenses connected with the place of pilgrimage,** *and convenience of the pilgrims.*" While the temples in general in India (as the Black Pagoda, Bobuneswer, Kalee Ghaut near Calcutta, &c., &c.,) bear evident marks of neglect and decay, the temple of Juggernaut has recently been repaired (it is said at the expense of a Bengalee); and its celebrity is very great. Of the numerous adjacent temples of Bobuneswer, (about twenty miles from Cuttack) Mr. Stirling, in his "Account of Orissa," remarks, "We have no particular account of the period and causes of the decline of the City of Bobuneswer and the worship of Maha Dah (Seeb). *Nearly all but the great temple have been completely deserted, and the establishment kept up there is on a very small and inadequate scale,* under the patronage of the Koordah Rajah, whose ancestors granted all the lands and endowments by which the Brahmuns now exist."

Of the conduct of the pilgrim hunters in extolling Juggernaut and promoting his worship, "The Friend of India" very forcibly observes, "We have *a body of idol missionaries far exceeding in number all the Christian Missionaries, perhaps, throughout the world,* going forth from year to year to propagate delusion, and proclaim for the sake of gain (what perhaps not one among them believes), the transcendant efficacy of beholding—a log of wood; and all these *through a perversion of British humanity, regularity, and good faith, paid from year to year by the officers of a Chritian and a British Government!*

"But that which most fills the mind with distress is the use which these ministers of deception make of the British name throughout the country. In proclaiming the greatness of Juggernaut, they of course affirm that he has now

* "The expense for the repair of the temple was formerly defrayed by an Abwaub. It appears not to be fixed in its amount, nor can I learn what the gross amount of the collection was; in future such repairs *as are necessary must be made at the expense of Government,* the Abwaub being consolidated as the land revenue." Dec. 1807. Par. Papers, respecting the Temple of Juggernaut, 1813, p. 66.

so fully convinced his conquerors of his divinity, that they have taken his temple under their own superintendence; and that, to provide him with an attendance worthy of his dignity, they expend thereon nearly 60,000 rupees from year to year, inspecting with care every department, and punishing any negligence in the service of the god. That, although the British so far surpass the Hindoos in knowledge, they are so fully convinced of Juggernaut's deity that they command a portion of food to be set before him! That they in reality worship him; and although, from their being *mleechas*, or *unclean*, the god cannot permit their near approach within his temple, yet that at his festivals they testify their veneration by sending the finest English woollens from their own stores in Calcutta to adorn his car. That they appoint officers to see that due order is observed in his worship; and that some great man, the representative of the Governor General, frequently attends to grace the solemnity with his presence. That, as they need money, convinced of the transcendent benefits to be obtained from beholding him, they levy a small tax on those who behold Juggernaut; which, however, on the richest, does not exceed ten rupees, while they permit the poorest to behold him gratis. That *they themselves are paid and sent forth by them to persuade all who wish for the full remission of sins to come and behold the god in all his majesty.*

"Although the whole of this is in reality a tissue of falsehood, yet when these victims to delusion come to Juggernaut's temple and see his car adorned with the finest English woollens, the officers of Government in attendance to keep order, and perhaps some English gentleman present, whom they in a moment transform into the Representative of the Governor General of India, they give credit to all the rest. Those who live to return home propagate this among their neighbours; and thus *the tax on the idol adds strength to the delusion, and increases from year to year those scenes of death at which human nature shudders.* That the British should be thus represented as in reality worshippers of this log, and as employing their superior knowledge in securing order in the service of its temple, and adding dignity and splendour to its public festivals, is sufficiently degrading: but that they should also be represented as employing a band of deceivers to beguile the ignorant and unwary—in so many instances to death! and persuade them to undertake this pilgrimage, that they may in reality enrich themselves by the tax they levy, before they permit the Hindoo to behold his idol, *is sinking the British name to the lowest pitch of degradation.*

"All this is proclaimed by the multitudes of agents who go forth from year to year to search for pilgrims. It is their interest to omit nothing, whether true or false, which tends to exalt Juggernaut and draw pilgrims to his temple. And even their being thus employed, with the express view of inviting all who are capable to undertake this pilgrimage, would serve as evidence in confirmation of all they advanced. Thus *a regularity, a splendour, an attraction, are given to the worship of this idol, and an impetus to the delusion it originates, which it never possessed under the former dynasty;* an impetus, too, which, fatal as it is in its consequences to so many of our Hindoo fellow-subjects, is increasing with the gain it produces, which knows no bounds but the number of persons they are able to deceive from year to year: and these have no bounds but the inhabitants of Hindostan itself."* Fr. of India. Oct. 1825. pp. 274—280.

Another feature of this system is, *it promotes the increase of pilgrim hunters and pilgrims.* "This tax, if originating in motives of humanity, has completely defeated its own end. While it has added that splendour and attraction to the worship of this idol which it never possessed before, it has created the means of urging persons in all parts of India to undertake this journey of death, which never previously existed in such regularity and extent. If this premium existed under the Mussulman Government, its payment was subjected to all the oppression which characterised that dynasty, as well as to all the evasions which are the natural offspring of idolatry. The British Government bring to all their proceedings with the natives *virtues the offspring of Christianity;* hence, on their faithfulness in paying this sum, the idol pilgrim hunter relies as safely as the peasant

---

* The author of a pamphlet published in Calcutta, on "The state of Protestant Missions in Bengal," speaking of Juggernaut and Hurdwar (at which latter place he supposes a tax is levied on the pilgrims), says, "The tax imposed by Government has been alleged to have the effect of leading the natives to suppose that the idolatrous festivals, held at these places, receive *the public sanction of the supreme authority.* To the extent to which this and similar laws are enforced, it would seem *to give the weight and authority of a political establishment to the popular idolatry.*"

who brings any article of sale to their factories. If he can search out a thousand persons, and persuade them to undertake this journey, he is as certain of receiving 300 rupees even if they be of the lowest class, 1,500 rupees if they be *nim lalls*, and 3,000 rupees if he can persuade them to enter themselves as *lall jattrees*, or pilgrims of the highest class, as though he delivered bales of cloth to that amount.

"This sum, paid with British fidelity to those who search out pilgrims, furnishes a fund so sure and so considerable that it would be no wonder if a number of agents were thereby stirred up to action, sufficient to traverse the whole of India, alluring those to undertake this pilgrimage of death who would otherwise never have undertaken it.*

Of *the increase of pilgrims at Gya*, Mr. Harington candidly acknowledges the fact, and refers it to the regulations of the Pilgrim Tax:—" He (Mr. Law) had the *satisfaction* of seeing that his efforts were not unsuccessful; while *great and progressive increase* in the amount of the *sayer collections*, under the circumstance of diminished rates, evinces the sound, and (with regard to the pilgrims) the attractive policy of the measure he adopted." A clergyman at Gya writes,—" I saw at Gya many poor creatures who had travelled 1000 miles, and who in their journey endured great privations. The well-meant intentions of Government have totally failed; for, instead of the tax having diminished the number of pilgrims, *it has greatly increased the multitude, rendered the Brahminical order respectable, and placed idolatry on a firmer basis than it ever was before!* The annual amount of revenue collected at Gya is only 250,000 rupees (£31,250 sterling); apparently a large sum, but nothing in comparison with what the Brahmuns receive from the pilgrims. As soon as Government know the inutility of their interference in these things, no doubt they will leave the system to stand or fall unsupported by authority. When that authority is withdrawn, we may venture to predict that in this place, as well as in other parts of the globe, idolatry will fall like Dagon before the ark of the Lord."†

"The introduction of the Brstish Police System so much confirmed the security of the pilgrims *that the num-*

---

* Friend of India, No. xiii. pp. 271—273.

† Miss. Reg. Nov. 1827, pp. 548—559.

ber of these wanderers has been gradually increasing, as will appear from the following statement of the number who received licenses to worship at Gya from the 1st of May to the 30th of April, in the successive years, viz.—

YEARS.	PILGRIMS.	YEARS.	PILGRIMS.
1798	17,670	1805	22,318
1799	21,659	1806	23,291
1800	14,560	1807	33,831
1801	22,732	1808	32,423
1802	18,964	1809	27,952
1803	23,334	1810	27,454
1804	14,190	1811	31,114

Amount of Collections of Tax on Pilgrims.

YEARS.	RUPEES.	CHARGES RUPEES.	NET RECEIPT.
1812-13	276,890	43,450	233,439
1813-14	226,291	41,472	184,819"*

From these remarks, and especially from these official documents, it appears evident that the Pilgrim Tax gives popularity to places of idolatrous resort, and induces multitudes to wander all over India to promote pilgrimages to them; unconcerned what misery they entail upon their devotees.

A third feature in this system is, *it occasions the death of many pilgrims, who die through want of what the Tax takes from them.* That hundreds die of want and disease in pilgrimage is evident. The sum which a poor pilgrim pays for admission to perform the ceremonies appointed at a holy place might be the means of saving his life on his journey home; but, as is frequently the case, having expended all, or nearly all, when he sets his face homeward, he soon finds the supply of the humane scanty; want is followed by disease, disease by the desertion of his companions, and death soon lays him by the road side,

* Hamilton's Hindostan, vol. i. p. 266.

unshrouded and uncoffined, to be the prey of birds and beasts. "Much reproach against the English is expressed by the Hindoos on account of the oppressive nature of the tax. Mr. Lacey, one of the Missionaries who went to relieve the destitute on the road to Cuttack, relates the following incident:—'You would have felt your heart moved to hear the natives say, '*Your preaching is a lie; for, if your Saviour and your religion are thus merciful, how do you then take away the money of the poor, and suffer them to starve?*' It is indeed no wonder that, when the natives see a poor creature dying for want, they should reflect that the two rupees he paid as a tax would have kept him alive; nor indeed is it a pleasing reflection to a European mind that *these two rupees form precisely the difference between life and death, to many who have perished for want on their road home.*"*

From the whole, it appears that the Pilgrim Tax and Premium System are *inhuman, impolitic, and unchristian.* The inhumanity which characterizes these pilgrimages is evident. Is it not impolitic to promote them? Do they not 'eternize the reign of poverty, superstition, and savage ignorance?' For Britain to legislate for idolatry, lest its institutions should grow into disuse—to stoop to the drudgery of superintending the collection of money from pilgrims, 'a painted, pagan, semi-barbarous race;' and, 'last, not least'—for the character of Britain to be associated with idolaters in their scenes of revelry, vice, and misery, is degrading to our national character,† and displeasing to Him who calls idolatry "*that abominable thing which I hate.*" The general features of this system are legislation for idolatry; paying monthly stipends to priests (from temple lands in the hand of Government); accumulating wealth (the Collector at Allahabad receiving 1 per cent, at Gya 5 per cent, and at Juggernaut, it is said, 10 per cent, on the amount of collections); defiling the revenue of the

---

* Friend of India, as above, pp. 283, 284.

† The Collector of Tax at Juggernaut addresses the Chief Secretary to Government, March, 1806:—"I have the honour to acquaint you that Ram Bukhsh and Ram Hutgur, pilgrims, presented a serviceable elephant to Juggernaut, and 200 rupees for its expenses, which last about six months. *The god's establishment is six elephants!* At or before the end of six months it will be necessary for Government either to order the elephant to be disposed of, or appoint some fund for its support, *should it be deemed advisable to keep it for Juggernaut's use!*" Par. Papers, 1813, p. 39. Who does not blush for his Country's shame?

country with the proceeds of a tax, in many cases "*the price of blood;*" and assimilating professed Christians with Idolaters, till the Christian character is scarcely distinguishable, even in the broad feature of abhorring idols. The Hindoos in Orissa have asked the Author, "*Is —— Sahab a Christian? Does Sahab —— read the durma Poostuk, or Holy Book? Do not the Sahabs go to Pooree to worship Juggernaut? Why should the Company destroy Juggernaut? he is their chakar, or servant.*" If Christianity be a blessing to India, this system is evidently opposed to its progress, and every principle of humanity and of Christianity demands its abolition.

CHAP. IV.

The facility and advantages of the repeal of the Pilgrim Tax—confirmation of the statements.

It is presumed that the abolition of the Pilgrim Tax System would be very easy, being unconnected with cast or any ancient prejudices of the Hindoos. It is not like the suppression of Suttees, Infanticide, and the murder of the sick by the Ganges, though the propriety of the abolition of these dreadful customs, equally with the system under consideration, is demonstrable.* The abolition of this system would be a very popular measure; and what humane, intelligent, pious mind but must rejoice to see the evils of pilgrimage disappear from the plains of India? Britain now uncon-

* The influence of British authority among the priests of Juggernaut appears from a letter of Archdeacon Corrie, written at Pooree, in 1823:—"On the occasion of a partial insurrection, about two years since, the priests gave out that Juggernaut would no longer suffer the English to remain in India, and would not return to his temple (on quitting it at the annual procession) till they were expelled; and mentioned a certain day for their overthrow. This was justly considered by the General commanding the District as an attempt to aid the insurgents against the Government; and he sent a private order to the officer in charge here, that, if the Idol were not carried back as usual on the stated day, he should replace it by force, and take military possession of the temple. The natives about the General no doubt gave notice to the priests, and *Juggernaut returned before his time.*" Miss. Register, 1824, p. 582.

sciously supports, regulates, and aggrandizes idolatry at some of the principal places of pilgrimage; Christianity in tears approaches her and says, "Touch not, taste not, handle not." O ye honoured men! at whose feet lie the destinies of millions, remove your countenance from idolatry, encourage the establishment of true religion in the East, and then, in these idolatrous establishments, will the sentiment of the Latin poet be verified :—

"Vis consili expers, mole ruit suâ." *Hor.*

The advantages of the repeal of the Pilgrim Tax (implying that the British entirely withdraw their connexion from Hindoo temples) are evident. The most prominent is *the reduction of idolatrous establishments.* Col. Phipps states, on the authority of a respectable native, that 3000 families are connected with Juggernaut's temple. Mr. Harington estimates the annual expenditure of the temple at 74,880 rupees. "During the Chundun and Ruth Jattras in 1822, embracing about two months, 40,000 rupees (£5,000) were collected and paid over to the attendants of the temple, who had brought the pilgrims." Estimating the annual premium to the pilgrim hunters at 50,000 rupees, *the sum requisite to support Juggernaut's present establishment would be* 124,880 *rupees;* to meet which, the endowed lands amount to only 26,818 rupees, leaving a deficiency of 90,062 rupees (£11,257). This sum has to be collected under the direction of a Christian Government, and to be paid to the attendants of Juggernaut,—who suffer their deluded votaries to die of want and neglect in the very precincts of the temple and the town, and then throw them out upon the sands, for their bones and skulls to whiten its arid plains.

The establishment of Brahmuns and inferior attendants at Gya and Allahabad must be considerable, the net receipts to Government in one year being according to Mr. Harington's statement,—at Gya 182,876 rupees, and at Allahabad 73,053 rupees. The annual proceeds of this system appear to be about £70,000 sterling. These are the bribes idolatry puts into the hands of Britain for legislating in its idolatrous establishments: but double, treble, ten-fold these sums are amassed by its priests in consequence of the celebrity of its services. Let Britain, consistently with her character, retire from these idolatrous and obscene establishments, and would their popularity continue? At first the attendance might be considerable, but the novelty would gradually cease; and though (as in other places unnoticed by the Government) the pilgrimages might continue, the inseparable attendants,—poverty, sickness, and death, could not be so great. The Author has been at Bobuneswer, Munchaswer, Puramunx, and Teenaturra, places of pilgrimage in Orissa; but he does not recollect seeing a sick person among thousands of pilgrims, or a skeleton on the journey. Why such a contrast between these places and Juggernaut? The former are unnoticed by Government, and no tax is levied. The latter has a vast establishment, supported and enriched at the expense of the lives of thousands!

"All my way from the Chilka Lake to Madras," says Dr. Buchanan, "I did not see one skull. *Like the other temples in the Deccan, the revenues of the temple of Ramisseram are wasting away.* But Juggernaut will fall before Ramacoil or Ramisseram. I saw no human bone in the island. Christianity in its worst shape has civilized the Deccan. All descriptions of people are more humane and intelligent than the Hindoos of Bengal."*

Let Britain retire from the temple of Juggernaut; let her obey the Divine command concerning papal Rome, equally appropriate to pagan establishments—"Come out of her my people, that ye be not partakers of her sins, and that ye receive not of her plagues." (Rev. xviii. 4). And what would be the happy effects? "The vast establishment of Juggernaut, founded as it is on delusion and unfeeling cruelty, would not long continue in its present splendour, when *it ceased to be upheld by virtues of Christian growth.* British regularity, activity, and faithfulness, are virtues which Juggernaut's worship is incapable of producing; and without these *the larger the establishment and the sum annually received, the sooner would the whole fall into ruin.* Selfish and rapacious, none of the pundas in the temple would trust one another.† Whatever might be the

---

* Life of Buchanan, vol. ii. p. 49.

† The late Bishop Heber, speaking of a public meeting of natives in Calcutta, for the relief of the sufferers by famine on the Coromandel coast, states a fact illustrative of this assertion:—One of the most liberal of the subscribers, Vomanundun Thakoor, said to him—"Ramaswame Pundit may be a very good man, but I took care at the meeting that all money subscribed should be lodged with the house of Palmer and Co. and be distributed at Madras by the English Committee there. *I do*

sum received one year (part of which they would probably conceal from each other), no punda would have the enterprize to expend sixty thousand rupees on the Idol's establishment as a speculation for the next year's profits, of which, after all, others might deprive him. No one of them would have the activity to see that all the attendants did their duty. One would neglect to prepare Juggernaut's food and perhaps sell the articles; others would neglect his wardrobe; and others the temple itself both within and without. As for the pundas being at the expense of adorning his car with the finest English woollens from year to year, this would be out of the qnestion. If they did it one year, they would neglect it the next; and *thus the temple, with all its apparatus, would gradually sink into neglect and contempt*."*

Another advantage would be, *a decrease of pilgrim hunters.* These men would not travel to collect pilgrims, as they now do, were they uncertain what they should obtain for their labour. Now they know the price set upon each individual, and British integrity ensures its payment; and hence the number of these people traversing the country with their miserable groups. Thousands of pilgrims execrate the oppressions practised upon them, and relate with horror the ravages of death: but the fascinations of the travelling pundas prevail with the credulous and superstitious, and every year produces multitudes of votaries, of each sex and of various ages, for this horrid pilgrimage.

---

not know the Madras Pundits, but I know that Europe Gentlemen have a character to lose." Vol. i. p. 74.

* Friend of India, Oct. 1825, p. 281, 282.—" The woollen cloths were formerly supplied by the Soobahs, and since by the Commissioners and Collectors, *the officers of the temple declaring themselves incapable of procuring them!!* The quantity required is 484 guz. (yards), of which one piece must be of superfine cloth. The colours are of no consequence, but there should be variety; *they can be best supplied from the Company's warehouses, and the charge is therefore omitted.* Owing to the want of an efficient control, I have every reason to believe *the internal affairs of the temple have not been properly conducted of late.* The Rajah attributes the improprieties to the conduct of the head Purcha, who he says refuses to obey his orders; the head Purcha attributes them to the Rajah's orders having been inconsistent with the recorded rules and established customs of the institution. There are complaints made that both parties have refused permission to opulent Hindoos to make valuable presents to the idol, unless a previous Nuzzuranna were paid, in one instance to the Rajah, and in the other to the Purchas, for permission."—Feb. 1809, C. Buller, Esq.—Par. Papers, 1813, p. 65—74. Auth.

"It appears," says Colonel Phipps, "to have escaped observation, that, under the present arrangement, THE ENGLISH GOVERNMENT COLLECTS A FUND, FOR THE SPECIAL PURPOSE OF SECURING TO THE ATTENDANTS OF THE TEMPLE OF JUGGERNAUT SO HIGH A PREMIUM AS TO STIMULATE THEIR CUPIDITY TO SEND AGENTS ALL OVER INDIA TO DELUDE THE IGNORANT AND SUPERSTITIOUS HINDOOS TO UNDERTAKE A PILGRIMAGE, WHICH IS ATTENDED WITH GREATER LOSS OF LIFE THAN ANY OTHER SUPERSTITION IN INDIA, AND WHICH ANNUALLY INVOLVES IN RUIN A GREAT MANY FAMILIES! This is the more extraordinary, as the President of the Board of Commissioners, in his correspondence with the Court of Directors, argues that the tax cannot be considered as introducing or tolerating the practice of idolatry. The arguments used on the spot are short and plain. The purharees and pundas will neither employ agents to entice pilgrims, nor will they treat them properly and kindly unless it is made their interest to do so. Hindoos will seldom come, if left to themselves; and, if the pilgrimage become unpopular, the tax will be so unproductive as not to be worth collecting. It is the opinion of the best informed persons in the Province that the dreadful scenes which occur annually, on all the high roads leading to Juggernaut, would soon cease, *if the temple were placed on the same footing as numerous other places of idolatrous worship, which are left without any kind of interference on the part of Government.*"*

A further advantage would be *the decrease of the popularity of places of pilgrimage, and consequently a diminution in the number and mortality of the pilgrims.* A decrease in the resort of pilgrims to any place, naturally lessens its notoriety. Let the Pilgrim Tax be abolished and few will be induced to collect pilgrims. Free ingress and egress as it respects holy places, long restricted by penal enactments, might, for a short time, increase the number of pilgrims, but the novelty would soon wear away; and, even while it continued, the pilgrims, having no tax to pay, could better support themselves than at present, consequently there would be less mortality. Of the temples of Bobuneswer, Mr. Stirling remarks, "A considerable num-

---

* Mis. Regis. 1824, p. 580.

ber are still in a state of preservation, though entirely neglected and deserted;" the Black Pagoda; Kalee Ghaut in the vicinity of Calcutta, &c., show that idolatry in India possesses the principles of change, decay, and dissolution, when unsupported by the ruling authorities. "Let the tax and the premium for bringing pilgrims be at once dropped; let all British interference with the idol and its temple be withdrawn; and it is certain their popularity cannot long stand. If it did, *the reproach and the guilt of blood would be for ever rolled away from the British nation.* It must in future stand through virtues of its own growth, or sink to ruin. Even the disappearance of all that regularity and splendour imparted to the worship of this idol, through British interference, could not be unnoticed by the natives; and would weigh in the most powerful manner. "Why have the British withdrawn themselves? What is there in the worship of Juggernaut which has made them choose to give up every idea of profit, rather than countenance it any longer? This cannot arise from veneration. It must arise from the reverse." Thus would a shock be given to this destructive delusion which it has not received for ages.

"Even the delusion attached to the spot, when it was no longer guarded by British power, would soon cease. At present the whole weight of the British authority is employed to support the deception that Pooree is a place peculiarly holy, by refusing admittance to any not authorized to enter by paying the tax, &c., and by *compelling them to leave the town as soon as their permission expires!* As the pundas would not be vested with magisterial power, they *would have no right to support this delusion by the arm of civil authority.* It must rest wholly on opinion; and, in spite of all their endeavours, people would both enter and prolong their stay contrary to their commands: and thus *by degrees the place itself would become too common to yield its present revenue.* Thus, when left to itself, this object of idolatry would naturally destroy itself. While its worship is delusion, the God of truth seems to have ordained that, in the very nature of things, idol worship should contain within itself the seeds of its own decay; and to attempt to counteract this natural tendency, and to support idolatry by virtue and wisdom the growth of Christianity, seems an act which, if continued, would make us fear more for the British empire in India, than from the combination of all its enemies."*

Finally, *the British character would appear in its true light, and the efforts of Christian benevolence for meliorating the state of India be more successful than at present.* Is it to the honour of Britain to collect annually about 500,000 rupees from the deluded followers of idolatry, while they are enriched who travel through the country to inveigle them from their business and their families, frequently never, never to return? Will not the heathen think Christianity similar to Idolatry, which amasses wealth at "the price of blood?" Does not the Hindoo think highly of his idolatrous rites, when he sees the solicitude of his Christian Rulers lest they should grow into disuse? It must appear incongruous to the Hindoos, to see some Europeans endeavouring to turn them from idols, and others engaged in their festivals as if they were concerned for the support of their establishments. The following anecdote shows the effect of European connexion with idolatry upon the native mind:—

Passing one evening the large temple of Seeta Ram at Cuttack (the endowed lands of which it is supposed are in the hands of Government, and an annual allowance made to the priests), I caught a sight of one of the idols, and exclaimed, "*pape! pape!*" (sinful, sinful). The native who was with me asked, "Sir, is that sinful for which the Company give thousands?" (meaning rupees). I felt confounded, and said, "Yes, it is sinful: but the Company are a long way off; they do not know every thing about this country, &c." "Some of the most common arguments employed in favour of idolatry," says a missionary in Orissa, in October 1825, "are conveyed in the following questions: '*If Juggernaut be, as you say, nothing, then why do so many people come so far to see him? If Juggernaut be nothing, then why do the Company take so much money of the pilgrims at the entrance of the town?*' I asked Abraham (the Hindoo teacher) what he said when the people talked about the Company taking the people's money: he said, he replied, 'So far from acknowledging Juggernaut, the English do it to punish the people! It would be too much trouble to *flog so many people*, therefore they set up a gate and fine them!' In the simplicity of his heart the

* Friend of India, No. xiii. p. 280—283.

poor fellow seemed to believe this was the case, and I did not undeceive him. As I cannot honestly defend it, I always say it is a sinful practice. As there is a Providence, I certainly think the British power has more to fear from its connexion with idolatry in this country than from any thing else. A man said to me a few days ago, '*If the Government does not forsake Juggernaut, how can you expect that we should?*' These arguments discompose me more than any others; and they are urged every day, and, perhaps, some days, several times." A late missionary in Orissa writes in April 1828, "This evening I met with a troublesome man who asked me several questions. '*If Juggernaut be nothing, why do the Company take so many rupees?*' I answered that was not my sin nor his. 'There are some of you (said the gooroo) who are not holy in all their conduct. *If your religion were true, then the Government would support it: but they do not.*'"

Confirmation of the above statements, showing the propriety and utility of the repeal of the Pilgrim Tax, and the discontinuance of British connexion with idolatry in India, appears important. The following facts it is presumed are deserving of serious attention.—

"About the close of the year 1801 a Civil Servant of the Hon. Company, holding the station of Collector in one of the southern Provinces of the Madras Presidency, sent his peons to the great Pagoda of the Province, with orders to break the car of Juggernaut in pieces and sell the wood, as it had been the property of a rebel chief. The Brahmuns remonstrated, claiming the car as the property of the god, and repulsed the peons. The Collector, however, apprized them that he should renew the attempt. On learning this, the Brahmuns sent him an intimidation, and caused it to be circulated through the province, 'That if he offered such a profanation to the car of the god, holy Brahmuns would cast themselves headlong from the lofty tower of the Pagoda.' The Collector sent a formal message, informing them he had heard of their vow to kill themselves, and that he and his family would attend to witness the spectacle. On the day appointed a great multitude assembled. The Collector and his family, his peons and retinue, attended. The tower over the gateway of the pagoda was the place from which the Brahmuns threatened to precipitate themselves. Within a full view of the tower, chairs were set for the Collector and his family. The decisive moment now arrived :—the Brahmuns appeared on the top of the tower, and the Collector gave the order for the demolition. The Brahmuns, with loud imprecations, and menacing gesticulations, endeavoured to intimidate him. They rushed repeatedly to the verge of the tower, and as often retired. But the officer was firm to his purpose: the car was broken, and the wood ordered to be sold; upon which the Brahmuns silently withdrew from the tower, and the crowd quietly dispersed."*

"A rare circumstance has occurred this year," says the Calcutta Missionary Herald, July, 1824, "in reference to the car of Juggernaut, kept at Chandernagore, which belongs to the French. This huge car, which is not much smaller than the one near Serampore, used to be dragged along the main road leading to Taldanga, where it used to stand for the space of a week, and was then brought back to its stand at Laldigghee. This road has lately undergone a thorough repair; and the French authorities sent word to the proprietors of the ruth that, as the wheels of the car would tear up the road, they could not suffer it to be dragged over it, unless they paid 500 rupees for its repair. The owners of it offered a sum considerably less than what was demanded, in consequence of which the ruth was not allowed to be drawn, in spite of the earnest entreaties of the Hindoos. Thus one of their most ancient customs has been laid aside by the peremptory orders of the Rulers of Chandernagore, without creating any spirit of rebellion among the Hindoos. A tax has been laid upon Juggernaut, and as he could not pay the mulct, and his votaries had not sufficient respect to pay it for him, he remains a monument of his impotency and subserviency to an earthly being."†

"A few years since there were two cars of Juggernaut at Bydpoor, near Culna, in the Nuddea district. They were kept at a short distance from the town, near an unfrequented road. From time to time several persons were missing, who were never heard of again. It was at length discovered that these cars were the nests of waylayers or footpads, whence they issued and knocked down solitary individuals for the purpose of robbing them: they almost invariably murdered them, and then took their bodies and concealed them among the wheels of the cars. The fre-

* Mis. Regis. 1814, p. 58. † Asi. Journ. May, 1825.

quent occurrence of these murders occasioned great trouble to the villagers, who were bound and examined by the police officers, and subject to great oppressions. It happily occurred to some Hindoos of the place that as long as Juggernaut's cars remained they should never escape the trouble brought upon them by the murders committed near them; they therefore came to the determination of setting fire to them, and burnt them to the ground. The place of concealment being removed, the murders have ceased."*

Great depredations are practised upon the pilgrims at Juggernaut's temple in Orissa. As they enter the town, the men employed to drag the cars have been seen to come from their encampment and seize their chattas, clothes, &c. In the town, as they lie asleep, their money is frequently stolen from them. Within the temple what oppressions are committed must remain unknown to Europeans, as no one enters it.† Hundreds, yea, thousands, die of starvation, exposure, &c., occasioned by the cruelty practised at Pooree. O that some of the Hindoos were wise and firm enough to destroy these cars! When shall the dreadful celebrity of Juggernaut cease for ever!

A. Stirling, Esq., in his "Account of Orissa," states what would be the result of leaving Juggernaut unconnected with the Government. "Generally, from two to three days are consumed in reaching the Gondicha Nour temple, where the images are taken out. Before even this period is elapsed, the curiosity and enthusiasm of the pilgrims have nearly quite evaporated; they steal off in numbers, and leave *Shree Jeo to get back to the temple as he may!* Without the aid of the villagers before described‡ and the population of Pooree, *who hold their*

---

* Asi. Jour. May 1826.—Mis. Herald, Aug. 1825.

† "Some captious persons became offended, and called out to the multitude, 'Worship Juggernaut, worship Juggernaut.'—Miss. Who is Juggernaut? He that sits on the blue mountains.—Miss. If that image be Durm Brumha, why does it decay? for you know it is renewed every twelve years. *If he were Juggernaut (the Lord of the world) would he permit his priests in his presence to tear away the silver and gold ear-rings and nose jewels of the jattrees? You know you can never come away from Pooree with a rupee, or pice, or cloth, or lota: could this, think you, be the case if Juggernaut were there?* It is all a trick of the Brahmuns to get your money to feed themselves."—Ex. Mis. Jour. 1827.

‡ "The inhabitants of the neighbouring Pergunnah, Raheng, Lumbai, &c., whose peculiar duty and privilege it is, conjointly with the inhabitants of Pooree, to drag the ruths."

ground free of rent, on condition of performing this service for the deity, the cars would now infallibly stick at the Gondicha Nour! Even the god's own servants will not labour zealously and effectually *without the interposition of authority; and I imagine the ceremony (the car festival) would soon cease to be conducted on its present scale,—if the Institution were left entirely to its own fate and to its own resources by the Officers of the British Government.*"

The following statement from a correspondent at Cuttack appeared in the Calcutta John Bull, July, 1821:*—"On account of the lateness of the Ruth Jattra this year, it was not expected that the assemblage of pligrims would be so great; but nothing like the falling off that took place was anticipated. Monsieur Juggernaut, in fact, was almost deserted; and Messrs. Brahmun, Pundit, and Co., threatened to remove his worship to a more central situation in India (in the neighbourhood of Mooradabad). We congratulate our friends in those parts on their good luck in the prospect of such a visit! We are sorry to state that from the epidemic, want, and exposure, the mortality among the few deluded wretches (comparatively) that did come was awful. We hope from the signs of the times that the reign of Juggernaut is drawing to a close, or is at least upon the decline. The pilgrims either could not or would not draw the ruth, and the priests of this vile superstition were obliged to call in other assistance. If the natives are not yet becoming Christians, we believe they are becoming less willing dupes to the Brahmuns. No devotee was found to pave the way with his blood for Moloch. The sight at the opening of the gates for the admission of pilgrims would have melted the heart of a savage; numbers of expiring wretches were carried in that they might die at the polluted and horrid shrine, instead of enjoying their domestic comforts in their native village. Who that witnesses or hears of such scenes, but must long for the time when these vile, degrading, and worthless rituals will pass away, and the pure, simple, exalting, and peace-giving religion of Jesus bless the benighted plains of Hindostan?†"

---

* No missionary or Chaplain had resided at Cuttack from its conquest in 1803 to this period. The author and his colleague arrived at this station Feb. 1822.

† Asi. Jour. March, 1822. On the decay of Idolatry see Francklin's 'Site of the Ancient Palibothra,' Part i. pp. 24, 25.

Let Britain discountenance idolatry, and Dagon will fall before the ark.

The Par. Papers respecting Juggernaut, May, 1813, abundantly show that the temple would gradually decrease in celebrity, but for the support of the British Government. References are made to the advance of money for the use of it. A petition from the chief Purcha, in May, 1807, states, " But, for the service of Shree Jeo, it is necessary that *some money should be given at present by Government* on charge of the dewal Purchas; and, if money is not given, *there will be the utmost difficulty in carrying on the affairs of the temple!*" p. 61. The Board of Revenue in 1806 suggested that the temple should be supported from the proceeds of its own lands, with fees levied on its account, and voluntary contributions; to which the Collector of tax replied, " *I suspect the priesthood will not willingly agree to continue the ceremonies of Juggernaut, in the present style, with the funds proposed to be assigned to them.*" pp. 50—53, see also pp. 58, 59, 60—65. Should a Christian people thus uphold idolatry?

The following brief extracts from the Calcutta Papers, previously to the Author's leaving India, in Nov. 1825, show the nature of public opinion concerning the propriety of abolishing the Pilgrim Tax :—

The India Gazette of Oct. 17, 1825, contains an article relative to Juggernaut; a brief extract is inserted.—" In the Weekly Messenger of yesterday there is a most harrowing account of the miseries suffered by the poor creatures who crowded to Juggernaut, to attend the Satanic festival of the Ruth Jattra. It is humiliating to read such things. They are degrading to us as men, and derogatory to our character as Christian masters of this country. And is it possible that yearly similar scenes occur? But do not the Brahmuns fatten? Do not the wily heartless priests, who squeeze the last rupee out of the hands of the poor victims, do they not profit by the system? Yes: and they will retort the charge that *they alone do not profit by it*. The abstraction of such vast masses of people must be very injurious to the general prosperity of the tracts whence they issue; unless India in general be considered too populous. When we remember the many places that lie waste, where a teeming soil would reward the efforts of the industrious, we cannot help thinking the population could be distributed more judiciously than by a long and deadly pilgrimage to

Juggernaut, were the journey merely dependent upon those convictions of necessity which lead to emigration, instead of the blind zeal of a flagitious superstition."

"We have perused with some attention," says the Editor of the Calcutta John Bull, November, the same year, "an article in the last 'Friend of India,' entitled 'Reflections on the incidents which occurred this year at the Ruth Jattra of Juggernaut in Orissa.' The subject is unquestionably of the first moment, inasmuch as the alleviation of human misery and the preservation of human life must be objects of the highest importance to every Christian and humane Government. The writer in the 'Friend of India,' adverting to the fact that the *tax humanely imposed by Government to discourage the practice has become the very means of perpetuating it*, and been even converted, by those who have a selfish purpose to answer in keeping it up, into a proof that the Christian Government of India recognizes *the divinity of Juggernaut, and believes in the virtue of a pilgrimage to his shrine as expiating sin:* he proposes (and we certainly concur with him) to *abolish the tax altogether*, and to leave the Hindoos free to go or not as they please on this pilgrimage. Nothing we are persuaded would tend more effectually to lessen the resort of pilgrims to this celebrated seat of superstition than *the total indifference of Government as to the practice.* The tax imposed upon the pilgrims, when found, as we believe it is, ineffectual as a check upon the practice, ought without delay to be abrogated. It has been imposed in ignorance of the native character; but now a better knowledge of this character is acquired,—and the natives themselves are undoubtedly beginning *to be influenced in their notions as to the value of their religious acts by their intercourse with Europeans*—it is time to change the system, and, at least, to try the effects of one directly opposed to the present, so far as levying a tax is concerned. The good people at home do not do justice to the Government of this country in the object they have in view by this tax. They maintain that it is a desire of revenue which has imposed it; and certainly, where the fact of its efficiency for that purpose is proved, this representation acquires strength by the continuance of the impost."*

* Asi. Jour. Feb. 1827, p. 270.

"We hesitate not," says the Editor of the Columbian Press Gazette, "to declare our concurrence in the sentiments expressed in the Bull, on the subject of the pilgrimage to Juggernaut. There can be no reason to doubt that the tax levied to promote the convenience of the pilgrimage, and to increase the revenue at the same time, is calculated to create an impression among the natives that *the British Government does countenance and believe in the efficacy of such pilgrimages;* while by the European world at large it is deemed satisfactory evidence that our chief, if not sole object, is to derive a profit from a source so polluted. The best method therefore of proving that we are not actuated by a motive so unworthy is *to repeal it at once.* It certainly has not been effectual in diminishing the number of pilgrims; and indeed, if we are rightly informed, it was never intended to produce such effects, being chiefly levied in the first instance to provide comforts for the pilgrims, and thereby (though humanely aimed at the diminution of human suffering) directly tending *to encourage the superstitious practices which caused it.*"

The Bengal Weekly Messenger, about the same date, contains the following paragraph:—"We believe now, though we hear it for the first time, that the English Government maintains, *by rewarding,* a set of men called pilgrim hunters, trained up by the various functionaries of the temple, to traverse the whole country, for the purpose of inducing the wretched inhabitants to undertake the pilgrimage, for what is confessedly not intended to form an item of our revenue, and almost the whole of which is expended *under British auspices,* in adorning and maintaining the Idol and its numerous establishment; thereby preserving a last refuge for that religion, which, in all other parts of our Indian territory, we are encouraging every proper endeavour to eradicate! We feel fully persuaded that *entire neglect of Juggernaut, on our part, would in a moderate time be followed by equal indifference on the part of the worshippers:* on this principle we conceive many places of ancient superstitious reputation have now fallen into decay, though once, perhaps, as great in sanctity as the Pagoda of Juggernaut. Let the tax then be abolished; desuetude will be the consequence at last, although the first succeeding year or two may produce a greater concourse of people. Let us not assist to keep up the mystery and priestcraft of the worship; let us not, by our authority, help to maintain the splendour of the Idol, nor his reputation of that abstergent holiness which is believed to wash away the sins of those who approach its residence, and the result will be found to answer the expectations which are so reasonably cherished."

The late Rev. T. Thomason, of Calcutta, in a letter to the Author in Aug. 1824, writes :—" The sad subject of the tax on pilgrims has been again and again brought forward. Before Mr. Harington was out of Council the subject was fully discussed ; minutes were written, opinions collected, and the whole is gone for the decision of the Court of Directors. Doubtless this and other abominations will give way at length, but politicians may protract their continuance for a season." In another letter, dated Calcutta, March, 1825, he says, " Every thing has been done here in the matter of *the Juggernaut abomination and of the burning of Widows.* For this also we must wait. Having done all we can only look to Him who can give prosperity."

" Every man who can afford it," says the late Dr. Buchanan, " is obliged to pay a tribute to the English Government for *leave to worship the Idol* (Juggernaut)! It will give me sincere pleasure if the further investigation of this subject shall tend, in any degree, to soften the shameful impression which the above statement must make on the public mind. What can be compared to the disgrace of regulating by Christian law the bloody and obscene rites of Juggernaut? The honour of our nation is certainly involved in this matter. But there is no room for the language of crimination or reproach ; for it is the sin of ignorance. These facts are not generally known, because there has been no official inquiry. In regard to the *Idol tax*, the principle of the enormity, it is said, has never been fully explained to the Government at home. The Honourable the Court of Directors will feel as indignant, on a full developement of the fact, as any public body of the nation."* In a letter addressed to the Hon. Court, respecting Juggernaut, May, 1813, he declares, " A writer may able, by the power of high embellishment, by noticing indifferent circumstances, and entirely suppressing others, to represent the Idol Juggernaut as one of the ' gay and elegant deities of Greece and Rome ;' but the substance of the facts, as stated by others, will remain the same. It will still continue true that Juggernaut is a fountain of vice and misery to

* The Eras of Light, 1810, pp. 41—44.

millions of mankind; that the sanguinary and obscene character of the worship is in the highest degree revolting, and that *it will be a most happy event when our Christian nation shall dissolve its connexion with that polluted place.*"

The editor of the Missionary Register, Feb. 1828, referring to the permission of Suttees and to the Pilgrim Tax, justly remarks,—"There are two topics of a very distressing nature, because they are putting to hazard the fidelity of this country in the discharge of that high trust which has been committed to it, in its delegated stewardship of India. The pilgrim Tax, levied by the Indian Government, on idolaters going on pilgrimage to supposed sacred places, whatever were its design, has had the acknowledged effect of sanctioning and legalising this destructive and wicked superstition." Adverting to the author's pamphlet on Pilgrim Tax in India, it is observed—"The author has collected abundant testimony to the duty, facilities, and advantages of the entire and immediate abandonment of this pernicious system."

The following remarks on '*Revenue from Hindoo Temples*,' by a public officer of high rank in India, appear very judicious:—"As the greater proportion of the pilgrims who present the offerings which constitute the revenue of Government are the inhabitants of the Honourable Company's territories, it becomes necessary to consider the effect of the payment of the tax. It will not, I conceive, require much argument to prove that the amount of collections drawn from them is most injurious to the general resources of the Government, more particularly with regard to the gifts made by landholders, from the richest zemindar to the poorest ryot. The offerings at the Pagoda tend to diminish their power of paying their rents, and that even to a much greater extent than if they were to pay a similar sum by a tax in any other mode; for the time and labour consumed in the journey, the extravagance and waste while the pilgrims remain, the actual detriment their cultivation and stock must suffer in consequence of their absence, are all to be considered: and this injury to their individual, and thus to the Government's interests, is entirely the effect of their being induced by their prejudices to proceed to so great a distance, to make an offering, that is, literally, *to pay an additional tax to Government above their assessments;* whereas, if no facility for so senseless a proceeding were offered to them, there is reason to believe that they would, with the sum expended in offerings, be either discharging their rents with greater exactness, or adding to their capital. I would submit, therefore, that *it would appear clearly to be most consistent with the best interests of Government to discourage the influx of their landholders as pilgrims to ———.*

"The remaining portion of the Company's subjects who visit the ———, and add to the revenues of Government by their contributions there, are the merchants, manufacturers, and artificers, with probably a small number of the idle part of the population. It is a well-established fact that, in the years of plentiful crops of grain, the Government dues are collected with the least facility, in consequence of the difficulty the ryots experience in disposing of their grain; it is plain they cannot sell to each other, as all have grain to dispose of—it follows the consumers and purchasers are the mercantile and manufacturing classes. As the quantity they can afford to buy, or the price they can afford to give, must of necessity depend on the earnings of their labour, should this class of persons be induced, by any facility not now possessed, to come in greater numbers to ———, the loss to the state must be very considerable; for they cannot follow their professions on their journey, but must be wasting their time and means; the value of the employment of their labour must be lost to themselves and to the Government. To put this in a clear light, suppose for a moment the circumstance of the whole manufacturing and mercantile population of the district of ———, leaving their employments and undertaking a pilgrimage to ———: we should at once see the bad effects of such a measure;—they would lose all their time and labour, thus greatly decreasing individual wealth; and the ryots would be suffering severely, there being no market for their grain. I do not imagine any person would think of encouraging such a movement of the population, and yet exactly the same effects follow in proportion from the absence of one or ten inhabitants of that country, or of any other of the Honourable Company's Provinces on a pilgrimage to ———, as in the case of the absence of the whole body. It is just as much the best policy of Government to discourage the pilgrimage in one or ten, as it would be their best policy on the supposition of the movement of the whole mercantile and manufacturing population."*

---

* Asi. Journ. May, 1822, p. 439. See some interesting remarks in the Ori. Her. vol. ii. p. 71.

"It was not attempted to be denied," says J. Poynder, Esq., "that the British Government not merely tolerates so much idolatry and crime, but derives an immense revenue from this polluted source. The gentleman who noticed external amendments (removing indecent emblems from the car, and the wall that surrounds the temple) has thought proper to produce only as much of the appalling account given by Colonel Phipps as was necessary to his own object;—but he has passed over every thing in that relation which proves the idolatry of Juggernaut to be most destructive to the Indian population, in its consequences upon human life, and most disgraceful to the British Government, in its continuance as a source of revenue. The public statement given by the Colonel* affords abundant proof that *the continuance of this national opprobrium is referrible to the Board of Control for India, rather than to the Court of Directors of the East India Company*."†

H. S. G. Tucker, Esq., in his "Review of the Financial Situation of the East India Company in 1824," disapproves of the tax levied on the pilgrims resorting to Juggernaut and other holy places: "he thinks *it does not harmonize with a great and liberal Government*."‡

G. Udny, Esq., Member of Council in Calcutta, in 1806, entered a protest against some parts of the Pilgrim Tax System. He suggested,—"If the revenue of the temple were insufficient for its support, a tax should be levied to meet the deficiency; but that Government should have no direct concern with what related to the maintenance of the temple, or the payment of the officers." The reason assigned was, "The making provision by law for such purpose, it appears to me, *would operate to sanction, and tend to perpetuate a system of gross idolatry, which Government is neither bound, nor does it seem becoming in it to do.*§" How much better that Britain should have no connexion with the temples of India, either in acquiring wealth from them, or in supporting or superintending their establishments!

"*It is evidently indecorous, if not inconsistent,*" says the late J. H. Harington, Esq., Member of Council in Calcutta, 1827, in the third volume of his "Analysis,"

---

* Miss. Reg. Dec. 1824.
† Speech on Human Sacrifices in India, March, 1827. (Hatchard)
‡ Asi. Jour. June, 1825. § Par. Papers, May, 1813, p. 41.

that the Government of a nation professing Christianity should participate in the offerings of heathen superstition and idolatry." In correspondence with the writer, in 1824, he stated the same opinion:—"I think, myself, a Christian Government ought not to derive a revenue from the allowance of this sin." And in a letter from the same Gentleman in June, 1825 (which contained the substance of the communication to J. Blunt, Esq., Commissioner of Orissa, relative to the relief of the pilgrims at the Car Festival), he observed, "The Court of Directors have recognized the Tax at Juggernaut as a Fund applicable to local purposes, not as a part of the general revenue of the State; and that *scarcely any purpose could be even worthy of Government, except that of mitigating the mischiefs which this miserable superstition occasions.*" Let the British withdraw from the temple of Juggernaut all possible connexion, the *eclat* of the pilgrimage will gradually cease, and its miseries disappear.

"We think," say the Board of Revenue in Calcutta, Sep. 1806, "the interference of the public officers, in superintending the general concerns of a Hindoo temple, so far from being calculated to promote economy in the expenses, to increase the reputation and prosperity of the temple, or to augment the public revenue, is likely to be attended with contrary effects. We would recommend the whole of the internal economy and management of the temple to be left entirely to the Hindoo priesthood; and that the interference of Government be confined to the levy of a duty from pilgrims, in like manner as is done at Gya and Allahabad. From the pilgrims resorting to Gya, Government derives *an annual revenue of about* 150,000 *rupees;* no interference whatever is had by the officers of Government with the priests of the temple. With reference to the *substantial benefits arising to Government from the tax upon pilgrims* resorting to Gya, and, on the other hand, to the inconsiderable receipts by Government from the temple of Juggernaut since it has been under the British Government, we consider ourselves fully justified in recommending that the rules respecting the concerns of Juggernaut's temple should be brought as near as possible to those visiting at Gya."*

---

* Par. Papers relative to Juggernaut, May 1813. Extract of a Letter to Sir G. H. Barlow, Bart.

In the correspondence of the Honourable Court of Directors with the Right Honourable the Board of Commissioners for the Affairs of India, in 1809, sentiments are expressed opposed to a considerable part of the present System at Juggernaut. "According to the Hindoo laws it may have been allowable for a Hindoo Government to interfere in the appointment of the ministers of that temple and the management of its affairs, but for our Government *to elect its priests and officers, to assume a control over the official conduct of those persons, to take the direction of its funds and the charge of preparing its annual car,* was, in the opinion of the Court, to furnish to the ill-intentioned pretexts for alarming the scrupulosity and superstition of the Hindoos in respect to their religion. The Court thinking the interference of our Government in these matters generally improper, *on the principles of the Hindoos and on our own,* and especially improper at such a time; judged it right, for the prevention of such interference in future, to express their disapprobation of it. The acts of interference disapproved by the Court were specified to be, 'electing the priests of the temple, controlling its ministers and officers, taking the management of its funds, or any other proceeding which would not leave the Hindoos in perfect possession of their religious immunities.' The Court beg leave respectfully to state that *they still deem it their duty to propose the prohibition of these things;* and if there be any points relating to the religious establishments of the Hindoos beyond the 'care of a police, the administration of justice, the collection of a tax requisite for the attainment of these ends,' that it would be proper to specify it to the Government, instead of leaving a universal interference in all matters without exception open to them, on the ground of securing the public tranquillity; because it is to be presumed there must be some point at which the interference of a Government not Hindoo, in the religious concerns of a people so remarkably separated and scrupulous in matters of that kind, must stop. The Court intend to provide for the maintenance of the public tranquillity; and humbly hope they have done so, by leaving to the magistrate 'the care of the police, and the administration of justice:' and they beg leave to offer it as their opinion, that instead of interfering by a direct exercise of the authority of Government in such matters as—*the contests between different priests and differents sects about the* *expenditure and provision of its funds, the possession and pre-eminence of particular images,** with other questions of that nature which have already arisen, and are always likely to arise in the internal administration of the temple: it will be better to refer all such questions to the judicial determination of our established Courts, which being done, the interference of the Government for the public peace can only be necessary should the parties proceed to acts of open hostility against each other."†

This chapter may be closed by quoting the sentiments of the Right Hon. the Board of Commissioners in 1808, in the correspondence already adverted to: they appear in strict consonance with the object here advocated. "It is undoubtedly desirable to avoid as much as possible the exercise of any control over the management and concerns of the temple; *as our interference in such matters cannot but be, at all times, disagreeable to the feelings and prejudices of the Hindoos; and may occasionally furnish ground of jealousy and misrepresentation, in regard to our views and intentions respecting their religion.* The revenue which may be raised, from any source of that nature, can never be an object compared with the high importance of consulting, on all occasions, the religious opinions and civil usages of the natives."‡

CHAP. V.

Objections to the repeal of the Pilgrim Tax System obviated—concluding appeal.

As the anomalous nature of the system under consideration has excited the attention of many highly respectable Gentlemen, both in England and India, it may be presumed that various objections to its abolition must exist among those who possess the power of performing this important service for the interests of humanity and religion in Hindostan.

---

* Par. Papers, May 12th, 1813. Extract of a Letter from W. Ramsay, Esq., Sec. to the Hon. Court of Directors, to G. Holford, Esq., Sec. to the Right Hon. the Board of Commissioners for India, Feb. 1809.

† Par. Papers, p. 19. ‡ p. 45.

The Right Hon. the Board of Commissioners, in the paragraph last quoted, proposes a common objection to the repeal of the Pilgrim Tax :—" Both the taxes above mentioned (those levied at Juggernaut and Allahabad) having been established during *the Nawaub and Mahratta Governments, there does not appear to be any substantial objection to the continuance of those duties, under proper rules for their collection.*"

In obviating this objection, the Author is happy in being able to use the language of the Hon. Court of Directors, to the Right Hon. the Board of Commissioners, in their correspondence relative to British superintendence of the temple of Juggernaut. " It is not our opinion, whatever the example of preceding Governments may have been, that the British Government ought to tax the Hindoos purely on a religious account; for instance, to make them pay merely for access to any of their places of devotion. We approve of the suggestion of the Board of Revenue, June 1806, to confine the interference of Government at Juggernaut to the levy of a duty on pilgrims, in like manner as is done at Gya and Allahabad; but the quantum of the tax ought to be fully sufficient to defray the expense incurred by Government for the establishment which it shall maintain at Juggernaut. With regard to imposing a tax upon the Hindoos for admission to a religious privilege, when the imposers believed, as the Hindoo Government did, that the privilege was a real good, it was, on their principles, for them to put a price upon it; but, *where the Government know the supposed privilege to be a delusion, the Court must question the propriety of its continuing the practice, though it may be ancient*; that reason not having been deemed by our Government, in other instances, sufficient to sanction customs repugnant to the principles of justice. And, with respect to the disbursing out of the Public Treasury any thing towards the support of religious establishments, Hindoo or Mahomedan, beyond what their own endowments furnish, the Court cannot but deem the principle objectionable, and the practice to be preferred which has lately been adopted by the Madras Government, who have determined not to receive into their hands the funds belonging to such institutions, nor to be concerned in the expenditure of them."* This reasoning appears very conclusive; and, when it is known

* Par. Papers, May 1813, p. 17.

that the Hindoos argue the dignity and even the divinity of Juggernaut from the attention of the British Government to his establishment, does not the impropriety of a Christian Government collecting a tax on the worshippers of a block of wood, irresistibly strike every intelligent and ingenuous mind?

The following incident shows that some of the Hindoos consider the establishment of the Pilgrim Tax by the British, and its consequent support of Juggernaut, as a proof of the Idol's interposition. The author's pundit related to him that "Juggernaut appeared in a dream to the General Sahab, as he lay upon his couch, and said to him, 'Why have not you given me my *konor* (food), as I used to have? If you do not give it, I will punish you.' The General was afraid, and gave orders that Juggernaut should have food set before him as formerly."

Another objection to the repeal of this system is, *its supposed protection of the pilgrims from oppression.* This was Mr. Udny's reason for adopting some kind of police establishment at Juggernaut's temple; as this gentleman expressed it, "to secure the pilgrims against every thing of a vexatious nature from the extortion and oppression of the officers of the temple." But is it possible to prevent the priests of idolatrous establishments from making a gain of their office? The present premium to the pilgrim hunters, being secured by Government, is claimed to its full amount; and, in addition to it, other demands are made upon the worshippers in the temple and at various places in the town:—"all the resources of superstition and priestcraft are brought into active operation; and every offering, from a sweetmeat to a lack of rupees, is grasped by the officiating Brahmuns with the most importunate rapacity."* At Juggernaut, it is said, the last act of worship (without which the whole pilgrimage is void) is performed under a tree in the enclosure of the temple, and, before the pilgrims are allowed to do this, certain sums are exacted from them according to the cupidity of the priests. Promissory notes are given at Gya, and pilgrims in general evidently lie at the mercy of their religious guides.

An extract from a communication of a correspondent in Orissa, dated Ganjam, August, 1826, shows that no system can be adopted to protect Hindoo pilgrims from op-

---

* See Ham. Hind. vol. ii. pp. 53, 647.

pression:—"Talking about Juggernaut, a man from the country asked the question so common in another place:—'*Why the Company had any thing to do with Juggernaut if his worship was wrong?*' And I said, as I always do on such occasions, that the Company did wrong. One of them told me that he had been to Juggernaut a few days ago; that his personal expenses on the road were two rupees. The tax was two rupees, six annas; two rupees went for food for the blocks (idols); three rupees were taken by the pundas, besides two pice here and two pice there in different parts of the temple. A man in another place told me that he did not pay the tax (pretending to be very poor); and that his last journey cost him about five rupees: *the expenses he said differed according to people's circumstances*, for the same journey would cost some *fifty rupees*. I inquired how the pundas knew what to expect, and he replied, some of them would come and stay *two or three months* in such a place as Ganjam, by which means they become acquainted with their circumstances."

The following facts may afford a specimen of the conduct of the immediate attendants of idols. "Krishnoo Vusoo gave to the temple of Juggernaut (near Serampore) an immense car, which could not cost less than 4 or 5000 rupees. He also added an allowance of six rupees a day for the expenses of the worship of this idol. Gourn Mullick, a goldsmith of Calcutta (who gave the interest of his mother's weight in gold to different temples!) added six rupees more to the daily offerings of this temple. These two benefactors, perceiving that *the Brahmuns of the temple, instead of expending these sums in the offerings to the god and in alms to strangers, applied the greater part of it to their private use, reduced the six rupees to one rupee four annas a day.* To extort more money from the donors, the Brahmuns at two succeeding festivals prevented the car proceeding to an adjoining temple, in which the donors were interested, pretending that the god was angry with them for their parsimony and would not go!"*

The late Bishop Heber, visiting two temples of Seeb, gave a rupee to two Brahmuns who had shown them to him, and observes,—"I thought one rupee was enough between them, and told the priests that they were to divide

* Ward's View of the Hindoos. Vol. ii. Intro.

it. No sooner, however, had it touched the threshold, than the two old men began scrambling for it in a most indecorous manner, abusing each other, spitting, stamping, clapping their hands, and doing every thing but striking; the one insisting that it belonged to him whose threshold it had touched; the other urging the known intentions of the donor. I tried to pacify them, but found it of no use, and left them in the midst of the fray."—Jour. vol. i. p. 94.

A Calcutta Paper, in Oct. 1822, contained the following relation:—"*Robbery at Juggernaut.*—Juggernaut has been in great commotion, and I suspect some of the followers of Juggernaut wlll be staggered in their faith. This morning, when the pundas went in to visit the idols, they found all the silver ornaments gone, to the amount of 5000 rupees. They say none of the doors had been forced. All the inside doors are locked, and the keys lodged with the head punda and several chokedars in the compound: the outside doors are likewise locked, and the keys lodged with the punda; and a sepoy sentry at each outside, as they are not allowed to go in dressed in their uniforms, or have any charge of what is inside. The Rajah and Collector's officers have had a meeting, and confined upwards of twenty attendants of the idol. On asking the sepoys what they they thought of it, they laughing replied, 'Thakoor must have robbed himself (that is allowed some one), as he would have struck a person blind who offered to take away ornaments of his, or his sister, or his brother!' It is a most curious circumstance altogether; for no one goes in but accompanied by pundas, and all the sepoys seem to say some of them must be the rogues. The Jacks do not seem to have much veneration for Juggernaut, as they seem to joke at the idea of his being robbed."*

A third objection to taking off the tax, and a vindication of its propriety, is, to use Mr. Harington's words in his "Analysis,"—"The Court of Directors (in a letter dated Oct. 1814) intimate that *they do not consider the tax on pilgrims a source of revenue, but merely as a fund for keeping the temple in repair.* The Vice President in Council, adverting to the probability of the net receipts exceeding the amount required for the repairs of the edifice,

* Asi. Jour. July, 1823. The author has seen the thief in the jail at Cuttack.

directed that the surplus should be applied,—*to the repairs of the temple and other local purposes; the completion and repair of a public road from the vicinity of Calcutta to Juggernaut Pooree, commenced on a donation for this purpose by the late Raja Sookmoy Roy; and to any other purpose connected with the temple of Juggernaut.*"

To this statement Colonel Phipps adverts in his account of Juggernaut.— "In the year 1814 the Court of Directors declared that 'they did not consider the tax on pilgrims as a source of revenue.' There is, however, some inconsistency in this: for what purpose is this tax levied?* Is it intended as *a fund to encourage idolatry?* The truth is, a small part, *one fourth*, or *one third*,† is appropriated *to purchase the holy food*, and to defray the other expenses of the temple, but the remainder goes into the Treasury. It is sometimes said that the surplus is employed for making a new road in the District. But nothing can be more self-evident than the fact that the Government must consider a good military road, connecting the Madras Provinces with those of Bengal, as a measure of primary importance, and which could not fail to be attended to, if there had never been a temple at Juggernaut Pooree. In 1810 Raja Sookmoy Roy offered to contribute 150,000 rupees towards making a good road to Juggernaut, to be designated by his name. This very liberal offer was accepted, and the road is now constructing; but this contribution would have been a sufficient inducement to undertake any public road, much more one so much wanted, if the Pilgrim Tax had never been thought of." The proceeds of the tax at Gya and Allahabad are, with some small deductions, put into the public treasury. The gross col-

---

* The Par. Papers, May, 1813, respecting Juggernaut, show that *gain was a principal object of establishing the Pilgrim Tax.* The Regulations were altered occasionally for the purpose (p. 48, 51, &c.). Satisfaction is expressed at the increase of pilgrims and produce of tax levied. To make but one extract, "The Governor General in Council has observed with satisfaction the increase of revenue stated to have been obtained at the present Jattra." Aug. 1809. (See pages 66, 68, 74, 81). Strenuous efforts are made to prevent pilgrims avoiding the tax. An expenditure of 10,000 rupees was authorized in 1812 for the construction of a wall, "for the purpose of preventing the pilgrims from forcing their way to the temple." p. 20. See also p. 39, 53, 73.—AUTH.

† This must refer to the seasons when the pilgrims are numerous. Some years the expense of the establishment nearly equals the proceeds of the tax.

lections at Gya in 1815—16 were 229,805 rupees, deductions (including 26,000 rupees to a native Rajah) 46,929, net receipts 182,876 rupees. At Allahabad, the same year, the gross collections were 79,779 rupees; deduct charges and commission, 6726; net receipts 73,053 rupees. It is devoutly to be wished that when the injurious tendency of this system, in perpetuating superstition and misery is known, it may be promptly abolished.

The most common and plausible objection to the repeal of this system is, *the supposed increase of pilgrims that would result from it.*

Dr. Buchanan, in his letter to the Honourable Court respecting Juggernaut, 1813, in reply to C. Buller, Esq., M. P., observes, "Mr. Buller would maintain the proposition that the imposition of the tax diminishes the number of pilgrims; but the events of the last year render this proposition very questionable. Mr. B. would place the policy of the tax on a *new ground*, namely, 'the diminution of the number of pilgrims, and the consequent prevention of famine and death.' Unhappily for this argument, it is a well-known fact that, while the temple was under the native dominion, when *the tax on admission was higher than it is now*, and when a discipline was observed among the people which we should not think right to exert, the concourse of pilgrims was yet immense; in peaceable times incredibly great; and the consequent evils were in the necessary proportions."*

"It has been thought by some," says Colonel Phipps, "that the tax which is levied on pilgrims would deter many from undertaking such a perilous journey; but it is perhaps inherent in any plan to obtain a revenue, from such a source, that steps will be gradually taken to render the tax more productive; and, however it may be disguised, it is obvious that this can only be done by increasing the number of pilgrims, or, in other words, by fostering and encouraging the superstition so as to render it more popular." In 1804 and 1805 the English Government levied no tax, the priests made every exertion to profit by this unexpected state of affairs, and the attendance of pilgrims was very great; the loss of lives, it is said, was very considerable, and there can be little doubt that something like a famine must have prevailed. On these circumstances Colonel P—— remarks,—

* Buchanan's Apology for Christianity in India, p. 35.

"This amazing number of pilgrims had evidently arisen from circumstances not likely to occur again; and it is probable that, if Government had persevered in avoiding all interference, *the novelty and great attraction would soon have worn off*, especially if the pilgrims had been protected from the rapacity of the priests; the trade of pilgrim hunters would have been unprofitable, and no man would have felt any inclination to employ hnndreds of agents to entice Hindoos to undertake such pilgrimage."*

"The interference of a Christian Government, in the worship of an idol temple, has unhappily *increased the fame of the Idol, and the scenes of death which inevitably follow the annual pilgrimage. A British Government levying any tax on access to a temple, or a place the sanctity of which is built wholly on opinion, must inevitably tend to raise the fame of these places of imagined sanctity, and increase the crowd of visitors, unless it be sufficiently heavy to operate as a prohibition.* While, to a rich Hindoo, *ten rupees* is a small sum when paid to obtain that sight of his god which is to obliterate the transgressions of a whole life; *two rupees* to a poor man, who has made up his mind to a two months' journey, only *enhances the merit of it by adding to its difficulty.* It by no means renders it impracticable; although to pay any thing for a sight of their god, to any one except to those who seal to them the unknown benefits of this act, they deem a species of religious oppression, which they had no right to expect from Christians, whatever they suffered under the Mussulman dynasty."†

The injurious tendency of the British Regulations relative to the Suttee in India has been acknowledged by many of the magistrates; and is not British superintendence of the temple of Juggernaut equally pernicious? "*The official attendance of the darogah stamps every regular Suttee with the sanction of Government; and I must humbly submit that authorizing a practice is not the way to effect its gradual abolition.*"‡ "The police officers are ordered to interfere for the purpose of ascertaing that the ceremony is performed in conformity with the rules of the shastras, and in that event to allow its

---

* Mis. Reg. 1824, p 578—581. See also Ham. Hind. Vol. i. p. 28.
† Friend of India, 1825, p. 270. ‡ W. Ewer, Esq., Act. Sup. of Police, Calcutta, Nov. 1818, Par. Papers, on Suttees, 1821. p. 229.

completion. *This is granting the authority of Government for the burning of widows; and it can scarcely be a matter of astonishment that the number of sacrifices should be doubled, when the sanction of the ruling power is added to the recommendation of the shastra.*"* "It can hardly be doubted but that *the necessary presence of the police officers of Government, at these immolations, stamps on them the character of strict legality*, and seems to afford that degree of countenance on the part of Government which must produce an evil effect."† "If this mode of issuing orders under the sanction of Government to regulate Suttees be continued, *the practice will take such deep root, under the authority of the supreme power, that it will be impossible to eradicate it.* The usage will be much more likely to fall into disuse under a total neglect on the part of Government."‡ The Honourable Court of Directors, in a letter to the Governor General in Council, dated June, 1823, declare, "To us it appears very doubtful (and we are confirmed in this doubt by respectable authority) whether the measures which have been already taken have not tended rather *to increase than to diminish the frequency of the practice*" (Suttees).§ Of these Regulations the Asiatic Journal justly remarks, "It is generally admitted that the Regulations hitherto adopted by Government, especially those by which a magistrate's order is required for the ceremony, and a police officer is directed to be present to prevent unfair practices, have really done more harm than good, by giving a sort of countenance and sanction to the custom. A precisely similar effect has attended the imposition of a tax on the ceremonies of Juggernaut: the votaries conceive they act under Government sanction."‖ From a parity of reasoning, it appears natural that British regulation of the temple Juggernaut, and connexion with other temples in India, must tend to promote their celebrity, and the evils connected with them.

A Missionary in Orissa writes, in May, 1827:—"The sound of the hammer and axe about the car wood excited my indignation, particularly as the workmen are paid by

---

* H. Oakley, Esq., Hooghly, Dec. 1818, Par. Papers as above, p. 236. † J. F. Petty, Esq., Southern Concan, Par. Papers, p. 218.
‡ C. Smith, Esq., Par. Papers, 1825, p. 148.
§ Par. Papers, June, 1824, p. 45.
‖ Asi. Jour. March, 1827, p. 358.

our government, and professed Christians are their superintendents and exhort them to make haste *(juldee kurro)*.—Called upon Mr. H——; he intended to exert himself to abolish the Tax, but the perusal of correspondence, &c., of the Court of Directors, determined him otherwise; and it seems—*we must still go on providing food, clothes, cars, missionaries, servants, and Christian superintendence, for the detestable idol!!* From some conversation with a long resident in Pooree, and a very creditable native, I ascertained that, within his knowledge, the population of Pooree has increased more than two-fold! I asked him the occasion of this increase, he answered, *under our administration Juggernaut had become popular, and so more people had taken up their residence there!* He moreover added, AS OUR CREDIT SOUNDED THROUGH THE FOUR QUARTERS FOR KEEPING JUGGERNAUT, IT WOULD BE A PITY NOW TO DESTROY ALL THIS GLORY BY LEAVING HIM TO HIMSELF! He concluded his speech by exhorting me *to regard their books, and become one with them!*"

The decay of idolatry, consequent upon the progress of Christianity in the south of India, is very evident:—"There is now (July 11, 1825) a great idolatrous feast at Tinnevelley. This day the car of the idol was to be drawn through several streets of the town. *The Collectors had refused to allow the Peons to force the people to come and draw the car as formerly.* When they were sent into the villages to bring the people together, they used to take bribes from many who did not wish to draw the car; this year, this source of income was cut off: and the people were far from coming voluntarily. Some rich natives, the principal patrons of these feasts, from which they derive emoluments, induced those people who were dependent upon them to come; but, as they were not sufficient to move the car, two Modeliars and a principal Gooroò seized the rope with a loud hurrah, which induced many to imitate their example. The ceremony was not begun at daybreak as usual; but soon after midnight: and they drew the car so quickly, that, instead of spending in this toil a day or a day and a half, as in former years, they finished it by sunrise! It being known that the Collector had taken the above step, considerably fewer people came from the country to attend the feast than at any former period; and the patrons of idolatry, instead of *forcing the carpenters and others to do the work gratis, were obliged to pay them this year more than their usual day's hire.* Some endeavoured to hide their disappointment, and to remove the dishonour thrown upon their god, by saying *the idol had shown its power by finishing its tour this year in a few hours, which had formerly taken a day or more!* Many said, before the drawing of the car, if the god would not move it without human help, they would not acknowledge him any more as a divinity."* "*The Brahmuns* (says Bishop Heber), *being limited to voluntary votaries, have now very hard work to speed the ponderous wheels of Balee and Siva through the deep lanes of this fertile country.* This is, however, still the most favoured land of Brahmunism, and the temples are larger and more beautiful than any which I have seen in Northern India."†

The probable increase of pilgrims, on the repeal of the present system, would be temporary. Let the premium for collecting them be discontinued, and their number would certainly decrease. This is Mr. Harington's opinion respecting the travelling priests of Gya, of whom he says, speaking of the pilgrims, "*Who but for them would probably never have visited Gya.*" This position—the natural influence of certain or uncertain gain inducing the pundas to seek pilgrims or not, is so evident, that it is presumed it must have been overlooked in the supposition that the repeal of the Pilgrim Tax would increase the horrors of pilgrimage. The existence and powerful influence of the premium for collecting pilgrims appears to be but little known, and it is presumed that, as soon as its injurious tendency is recognized, it will be discontinued. Supposing the number of pilgrims to be increased at Juggernaut, Gya, Allahabad, &c., on the British retiring from these idolatrous establishments (a very improbable circumstance, when so much of their present *eclat* would vanish), the poverty and misery of the people would not be so great; the tax must tend to beggar them, and sickness and death follow hard upon the heels of poverty. It is easy to confer this boon relative to the temples in India—"Let them alone:" yet it is very important. They cannot stand opposed by the progress of science and true religion, and shall Britain defile her hand by supporting their tottering ark? "Will ye plead for Baal? will ye save him? If he be a god, let him plead for himself." Jud. vi. 31.

---

* Miss. Reg. Nov. 1827, p. 559, see p. 564.

† Trichinopoly, April 1, 1826. Asi. Jour. April, 1827, p. 488.

In this concluding appeal, the author feels tremulously alive to its issue. So deeply is he convinced, from ocular demonstration at the temple of Juggernaut, of the evils of the Pilgrim Tax System, that might he be the unknown, yet honoured means of its repeal, he should rejoice on that account alone, to the latest period of his life, that he had been to India. How shall this service for the interests of humanity and Christianity be accomplished? Could it be obtained prostrate at the feet of the executive body of the Honourable East India Company, it should soon be done. But as Zeno said to Crates, "there is no retaining a philosopher but by his ears." Statesmen and Legislators must be convinced of the propriety of measures, strenuously urged for their adoption. This has been attempted in a temperate and respectful manner. Let the prominent features of the system under consideration be calmly considered, and the successful issue of this appeal appears certain.

The *miseries of superstition apparent in the pilgrimages of India are most appalling.* Probably half a million of people annually visit Juggernaut, Gya, and Allahabad (and in some years a much greater number), but how many hundreds, not to say thousands, of these unhappy people never survive the horrors of pilgrimage! The Author has seen the pilgrims of Juggernaut lie upon the sands of the river at Cuttack, a prey to dogs and birds. Like a pestilential stream the pilgrims carry disease, especially the cholera morbus, through the province of Orissa; and thus misery and death mark their course.* Can it be for the gain of this unhallowed system that it is continued? The annual revenue of Cuttack is stated by A. Stirling, Esq., to be 3,000,000 rupees, and the net revenue of Juggernaut's temple to the British Government, in 1815-16, was 11,147 rupees. For other years see the summary from Poynder's Speech (p. 227). In what view does such a sum appear when its source and the misery and death occasioned by its collection are considered? "We are fully convinced," says the Editor of the "Friend of India,"

* "The population of Ramnad (about 120 miles from Cape Comorin) was, in 1812, 13,481, of which number 2307 died of a fever between Dec. 1812 and Feb. 1813. This great mortality was by some attributed to *an infectious fever introduced by the pilgrims of Ramisseram:* by others to the remote and immediate effects of scarcity or rather famine." Hamilton's Hind. vol. ii. p. 475. Pilgrimages are a curse to a country.

"when all the effects arising from the close contact with this abominable idolatry, into which a misguided humanity has led the British nation, are thoroughly weighed; no one who reflects that the surplus of the tax from year to year applied to the completion of the great road in Orissa (the only public object to which this surplus is appropriated), on the yearly average, *can scarcely double in the number of rupees it contains that of our Hindoo fellow-subjects who perish annually in the course of the journey*, can refrain from wishing that Britain were completely disengaged from this scene of idolatry, deception, and death."

Consider the character of this system. Hamilton, in his account of Travancore, states, among the items of revenue, *a tax on Christian festivals*.* How do Christians approve of a Hindoo Rajah taxing their "solemn assemblies?" Can it be the love of wealth that perpetuates this system in India? The Calcutta John Bull spurns such an idea:—"We cannot for a moment imagine, as the India Gazette appears to do, that the practice is kept up at Juggernaut merely because it is a source of revenue to Government. *It is much too scanty to be worth the establishment necessary for the collection of tax on pilgrims;* and, were it *ever so prolific*, we do not believe that, on this consideration alone, such an office as Collector of the Pilgrim Tax would be one month in the Catalogue of Civil appointments. On this point we think two opinions cannot be entertained; for surely, in a Christian Government, having the means and satisfied of the policy of drawing its revenue *from no source that would perpetuate the horrors and cruelties of superstition*, the tax now collected at Juggernaut would not continue another day." (Oct. 20th, 1825). Why is this system continued? At Juggernaut it is stated to be *to keep the temple in repair and make a good road to it.* But this lies open to great opprobrium. Why tax is levied at Gya and Allahabad is not stated in Mr. Harington's "Analysis;" except it be that it was practised by the preceding Government. But can Britain in this manner follow the steps of the Mahrattas and Mahometans with consistency? The most common reason for the Pilgrim Tax is, its supposed discouragement of pilgrimages. But "On the very face of the subject it might have been seen that, unless such a tax by its weight amounted to *an entire pro-*

* Vol. ii. p. 310.

hibition, it must operate, as all opposition to religious opinions has done, *to bring its object into higher and more extended notice*. That this would be the case was the natural consequence. Among the Hindoos the British nation necessarily sustains a far higher character for knowledge than the Mahometan dynasty. Hence the moment *they* thought this imaginary benefit worth taxing, it acquired a value in the eyes of the Hindoos which it never possessed before."*

The conduct of the British Government in India towards Christianity has been censurable. "There are now," says the late Bishop Heber, "in the south of India about 200 Protestant congregations, the numbers of which have been vaguely stated at 40,000. I doubt whether they reach 15,000, but even this, all things considered, is a great number. The Roman Catholics are considerably more numerous, but belong to a lower caste of Indians, and, in point of knowledge and morality, are said to be extremely inferior. This inferiority, as injuring the general character of the religion, is alleged to have occasioned the very unfavourable eye with which all native Christians have been regarded in the Madras Government. If they have not actually been persecuted, they have been "disqualified," *totidem verbis*, from holding any place or appointment, whether civil or military, under the Company's Government; and that in districts where, *while the native Princes remained in power, Christians were employed without scruple*. Nor is this the worst; many peasants have been beaten, by authority of the English magistrate—*for refusing, on a religious account, to assist in drawing the chariots of the idols on festival days ! !* It is only the present Collector of Tanjore who has withheld the assistance of the secular arm from the Brahmuns on this occasion!" In the last letter which the Bishop wrote to his wife, he says, "Will it be believed that, while the Rajah kept his dominions (Tanjore), Christians were eligible to all the different offices of state—*while now there is an order of Government against their being admitted to any employment !*†

* Friend of India, Oct. 1825, p. 278.

† "The Zillah Judges shall recommend to the Provincial Courts the persons whom they may deem fit for the office of District Moonsif; but no person shall be authorized to officiate as District Moonsif, without the previous sanction of the Provincial Court, nor unless he be of the Hindoo or Mahomedan persuasion." Reg. of Madras Government.

Surely we are in matters of religion the most lukewarm and cowardly people on the face of the earth! I mean to make this and some other things which I have seen a matter of formal representation to all the three Governments of India, and to the Board of Control."* This hostility to Christianity under the Madras Presidency, and the countenance and direct support of idolatry, not to say amassing wealth from it, at Juggernaut, Gya, and Allahabad, are very inconsistent in a Christian Government. The God of nations abhors idolatry, and he has said—"*If ye walk contrary to me, I will walk contrary to you.*"

British connexion with idolatrous establishments in India must tend to perpetuate them. Is it desirable to see India for generations to come "bowing before her idols—trembling at the phantoms of her own imagination, and in the undisturbed possession of a religion of 'pollution and blood?'"† But shall Britain be seen supporting these temples; having presented *Sirkaree Bhoge*, or Government offering, to Juggernaut; giving a premium to pilgrim hunters; selling licenses to enter the temple of Juggernaut, and amassing wealth, cursed with the blood of the deluded pilgrims? Forbid it Heaven! Yet at this day the sun in India beholds this incongruous, inhuman, and unchristian procedure. These things should be known and felt. And can they be known without being abolished?

The impropriety of this system has of late excited much attention. The Marquis Wellesley, it is well known, would not consent to the taxation of Juggernaut's temple. In the succeeding administration Mr. Undy, as has been seen, objected to perpetuating this system of gross idolatry by legislative enactments. Dr. Buchanan, who visited the temple of Juggernaut in 1806, spoke in very strong terms of the anti-christian nature of this system. Before the author was compelled, by indisposition, to leave India in Nov. 1825, the subject had excited much attention there: and in a letter received from the Rev. T. Thomason, Aug. 1827, he says, "Nothing was done in the matter of Juggernaut when I left Calcutta. Certain discussions took place in Council, which terminated in no particular result: nothing was published, and the written documents could only be seen by calling at the India House and obtaining

* Journ., vol. ii. pp. 462—465.

† Grimshawe's Appeal in behalf of Hindoo Widows, p. 27.

the perusal of them from the Secretary." Surely these discussions will be renewed, and this injurious system abolished. Britain is doubtless a benefactor to India; let her ever act becoming her high character and responsibility to Him "Who ruleth in the kingdom of men, and giveth it to whomsoever he will."

The measure here advocated is of a popular nature. "In wiping away for ever this foul reproach from the British name there is every thing encouraging, relative to the natives. *Nothing could be more popular among them than the removal of this unproductive tax on their sacred places.* While they submit to it, they by no means approve of it. Let the tax be abolished and this scene of delusion left to its own authors for support; and, while the British name in India is for ever freed from one of its deepest stains, *this mass of idolatry and deceit will in time sink with its own weight!* We are well aware that nothing delays this step so much as the humane but groundless fear that this would increase the evil, by causing a greater influx of pilgrims. This fear, however, is without foundation. The influx might be greater the first year or two, but, in the present state of increasing light, this influx could not long continue. There can be no doubt that the removal of this tax would raise the British name among the natives of India. And that a measure which will remove a load of reproach unmerited, only because it was unforeseen, and give such general satisfaction to our Hindoo fellow-subjects, will not ultimately be adopted, with regret that it was not done sooner, we cannot bring ourselves to believe."*

The following letter from a Hindoo to a missionary in Orissa appears replete with important sentiments and deserving attention.—

A letter from Sundra das Bargee, to Christians in general.

"O ye favoured people, who are blessed with the Divine Spirit, ye have existed 1800 years, and what have ye done for this dark world? I am a Hindoo Boistub, poor and destitute, but ask of you neither land, nor elephants, nor horses, nor money, nor palanqueens, nor doolies: but I ask, what can be done to learn the people to obey the laws of God? O holy people this I ask!

"*Pooree is the heaven of the Hindoos*; yet there the practices of mankind are, adultery, theft, lies, murder of the innocent, whoremongery, eating fish with maha presaud, disobedience and abuse of parents, defil-

* Friend of India, Oct. 1825, p. 278, 284.

ing of mothers, defiling of sisters, defiling of daughters! *Such is the religion of Juggernaut!* For these crimes the people are visited with rheumatisms, swelling of the legs, leprosy, scrofulas, grievous sores, and acute pains, blindness, lameness, and such like! Such are the servants of Juggernaut!

"And now, holy people, hear the names of the gods of this people—gods which the people, when they have eaten, rise and worship—these are gold, silver, brass, cedar, stone, wood, trees, fire, water, &c., these be the names of their gods, and these be their servants. To serve these gods they burden themselves with expensive ceremonies and costly rites; they afflict their bodies and their souls with pilgrimages and many cruelties. The Brahmuns no longer observe the Vades, nor the devotees keep mercy. O ye Christian Rulers, ye feed the rich, the proud, and the great; while the poor and destitute are dying in want! O good fathers! good children! good people! hear the cries of the poor, O good people!

"The thief is judged, the murderer is judged, the perjured is judged, and all the wicked are punished according to their crimes. A large army is kept in obedience to your orders; *but why are not the people made to obey the laws of God?* Ye are the seed of the good, ye keep God's word; cause the subject to keep it. The Mahrattas were robbers, but they relieved the distressed. Europeans are faithful rulers, but in their Government falsehood abounds. Children, Fathers! the fate of all in the four quarters is in your hands! O good people! the subject has become wicked, having fallen into error, and in consequence get not food nor raiment.

"Rulers are the example of the people. O good people teach them God's commandments by your example. If ye will do this, then it will be well; if ye will not, then ye are stones to them. What more shall I write? Do as ye will, still religion is true, religion is true, religion is true!" *Cuttack, Nov.* 1827.

The author has conversed with many upon the subject of this pamphlet; and the circumstance of Britain supporting the dreadful superstition of Juggernaut, paying a premium to the collectors of pilgrims, and amassing wealth from idolatry, to use the expressive language of Scripture, has made "the ears of every one that heareth it to tingle."* What he has seen and heard he feels it an imperious duty to make known. May the subject excite that attention which it so justly demands, among those who hold in their hands the destinies of the millions of India! Let Britain stand at a becoming distance from idolatry; let her "shake her hands

* The horrors of idolatry at the temple of Juggernaut are thus described by an eye-witness:—"The shades of evening are now prevailing; the sun is sinking in the western waters and leaving me in darkness. A feeling of deep horror, which I cannot suppress, steals across my mind, and irresistibly drives me away. The jackals are leaving their jungles and repairing hither for their nightly repast—I hear them cry at a distance. The eagles are flitting to the neighbouring tree for the night,

from holding bribes," the gains of idols; let her facilitate the progress of Christianity in the East, till "the Idols He shall utterly abolish" and "there shall be but one Lord and his name one." "Thus India emancipated, through our instrumentality, from the yoke of a cruel superstition, and admitted to a fellowship in the peace and hopes of the Gospel, will recognize in Britain, no longer a conqueror, to whom she is bound by the terror of our arms, but a benefactor indissolubly endeared by the triumphs of our mercy."*

---

filled with the flesh of man. The din of idol pooja assails my ears from every direction, and the work of blasphemy commences. Farewell, ye mangled corpses! ye silent monitors! ye have read me admonitions I shall not forget. But, ere I retire, I breathe a wish for my country—*under who auspices such a system is tolerated and supported. By your sad fate, my fellow-creatures, may she be warned, led to repentance, and wash herself from your blood; and may her future conduct, regarding idolatry here, prove her sincerity,*" p. 36. Lacey's Reflections at the Temple of Juggernaut, in 1825. (Wightman and Co. London).

* Grimshawe's Appeal on behalf of Hindoo Widows, p. 28.

EXPOSURE OF THE SICK ON THE BANKS OF THE GANGES. *Page* 303.

BOOK IV.

GHAUT MURDERS.

CHAP. I.

Origin, nature, atrocity, and appalling scenes connected with the practice of exposing the sick on the banks of the Ganges.

THE exposure of the sick on the banks of the Ganges has been termed Ghaut Murder. A Ghaut is a flight of steps to a river, and at these places the acts of cruelty to the sick, described in this book, are generally perpetrated. The *origin of this practice* is probably to be traced to the absurd notion that the river Ganges is a goddess, and that to die in sight of it is beneficial. A Correspondent, who has resided several years in India, writes upon this subject:—"The origin of this practice is involved in great obscurity; but one or all of the following reasons may be assigned for its continuance. The veneration paid to the rivers. The rivers of India, like the Euphrates and the Nile, annually overflow their banks. The inundation continues for a considerable time, and covers the country; and its benefits are very numerous; the fields are covered with verdure, the soil is enriched, and vegetation proceeds with rapidity. Hence has arisen that idolatrous worship which has been paid to them; indeed the most extravagant and puerile rites are performed in the sultry plains of India, in honour of rivers; and the advantages supposed to arise from them are equally absurd. He that bathes in the morning, in the months of Magha, Voishakha, and Karteka, destroys the greatest sins. He who at the conjunctions of Naryunee bathes in silence, in the Koorootaya river, raises thirty millions of his ancestors to eternal bliss. The wish to get rid of a burthen is another reason. There is no public provision made for the old or infirm. All who are past labour become immediately dependent upon their relatives; and the consideration of the expense may possibly make them wish to rid themselves of an encumbrance; especially when it can be done in a way which, instead of appearing dishonourable or any proof of want of affection, is rather considered an act of kindness. It may also be encouraged by the doctrine of fate, which has generally prevailed in the Heathen world. Their gods, the general dispensations of Providence, and their private affairs, are all considered under the control of the iron-hand of necessity or gloomy fate, which, while it showers down upon earth calamities in abundance, cuts off every hope and every effort for the attainment of deliverance. Believing that every person's *kopol* (fate) is fixed by an unchangeable decree, they avoid using those means which a Being of infinite goodness has put into our hands for the recovery of the afflicted."

The nature of this cruel rite will best appear in the descriptions given of it by different writers, and eye-witnesses. "The Bengalee Hindoos," says Hamilton, "have generally a great terror of the dead, and will seldom venture to inhabit a hut or a house where a person has died. This seems connected with their custom of exposing the sick to perish on the banks of rivers; which tends to aggravate the last pangs of nature, and sometimes not only accelerates death, but exhausts that strength which might probably have enabled nature to overcome the disease. The practice also furnishes an opportunity of practising other horrid crimes."*

The late Rev. W. Ward, in his "View of the History, Literature, and Mythology of the Hindoos," states, "Thousands, yea millions, of people, are annually drawn from their houses and peaceful labours, several times in the year, to visit different holy places, at great expense of time and money, spent in making offerings to the goddess (Gunga). Expensive journeys are undertaken by multitudes to obtain the water of this river, or to carry the sick, the dying, the

* Description of Hindostan, vol. i. p. 111.

dead, or the bones of the dead, to its banks.* *What the sick and dying suffer by being exposed to all kinds of weather in the open air on the banks of the river, and in being choked by the sacred waters in their last moments, is beyond expression.*"† "A few years since a Rajah, living about 100 miles from Calcutta, sent for an English physician from that city. By the time that gentleman had arrived, his relations had brought the sick Rajah to the river-side, and in a short period, no doubt, would have killed him. The physician reproved them for their want of feeling, and ordered his patient to be carried home, where, in a few days, he recovered. Before the physician took his leave, he made the Rajah promise to give him the earliest information if he should be sick again. Soon afterwards, the disease having returned, he sent for his old friend; but, *before he could arrive, his relations had despatched him with the mud and water of the sacred stream!* The want of compassion and tenderness among the Hindoos towards the poor, the sick, and the dying, is so notorious, that European travellers are frequently filled with horror at the proofs of their inhumanity, merely as they pass along the roads or navigate the rivers in this country."‡

Dr. Johns, in his Pamphlet entitled "Facts and Opinions relative to the Burning of Widows, and other destructive Customs in British India" (Gale, London), refers to the practice of "*Exposing the Sick and Aged.*" "The Hindoo character is in many essential points defective, and led by deep-rooted prejudices, and barbarous customs, to the commission of *crimes which ought not to be sanctioned by any moral or religious code.* How often is the aged Hindoo parent deemed an encumbrance and an unnecessary expense by his family; and *carried a living victim, devoted to die on the margin of the Ganges, or some other holy stream: there his own children fill his mouth and nostrils with mud; and, thus cutting off every prospect of recovery, they leave the author of their being to be carried away by the stream, as food for alligators and vultures!* Although sanctioned by the Brahmuns, and perhaps sometimes voluntary on the part of the aged victim, no religion

* And yet "the broad stream sweeps by them guiltless of their impiety, and unconscious of their homage." Heber's Journ., vol. ii. p. 297. AUTH.

† Vol. i. p. 277. ‡ Vol. iii. p. 295.

should tolerate such a sacrifice; that it is not always voluntary we have many undeniable proofs. The fatal consequence of not submitting to this extraordinary viaticum, or of eluding its effect, by returning to his family in case of a rescue or recovery, is so provided for, by the brahminical laws, that death is far more desirable than the continuance of life on such terms. Many instances might be produced to confirm this assertion: I shall recite what Captain Williamson, in his '*East India Vade Mecum,*' from more experience than myself, has recorded on this subject. 'Many Hindoos in their old age, or when seriously ill, are removed to the banks of the Ganges, whose waters are held sacred: and, when about to resign their breath, are taken to the edge of the river on their beds; where a Brahmun attends to perform the religious ceremonies. *No doubt many, who might recover, are thus consigned to premature death.* The damp borders of the stream, with a burning sun, rarely fail, however favourable the season may be, to put a speedy termination to the sick person's sufferings; but it has often happened that the attendants become tired by the delay the poor wretch makes in shaking off his mortal coil, and, perhaps with the humane intention of finishing his pain, either place the bed at low-water mark, if the spot be within flow of the tide, or smear the dying man with the slime of the holy waters, and fill his mouth with the precious mud. When a person has been taken to the side of the Ganges, or other substituted waters, under the supposition that he is dying, *he is in the eye of the Hindoo law dead;* his property passes to his heir, or according to his bequest; and, *in the event of a recovery, the poor fellow becomes an outcast.* Not a soul, even of his own children, will eat with him, or afford him the least accommodation; if by chance they come in contact, ablution must follow. The wretched survivor from that time is held in abhorrence, and has no other resort but to associate himself in a village inhabited by persons under similar circumstances. There are but few such receptacles; the largest and most conspicuous is on the banks of the Smillah, which passes near Sooksaugur, about forty miles north of Calcutta.' "*

The late Rev. D. Brown of Calcutta, speaking of sick persons who are left on the banks of the Ganges, says,—"They are swept away by the returning tide. Some, how-

---

* Oriental Memoirs, vol. i. p. 220, 221.

ever, escape; and, as they can never be received again by their families, they associate with those who, like them, have escaped the jaws of death. There are two villages not far up the river Hooghly inhabited solely by these wretched fugitives. A gentleman told me, as he passed a place called Culna, a little above Calcutta, that he saw a set of Brahmuns pushing a youth, of about eighteen years of age, into the water; and, as they were performing their work of suffocation with mud, he called on them to desist. They answered calmly, 'It is our custom. It is our custom. He cannot live; he cannot live; our god says he must die!"

The Rev. H. Townley, in his *Address to the Society of Friends on behalf of Missions*, refers to this custom, and shows its unsatisfactory nature to support the mind of a Hindoo in the prospect of a future state. "I have conversed with a dying Hindoo on the banks of the Ganges, and the substance of his confession was—" I have no hope of heaven from the circumstance of my dying near the sacred Ganges; nor do I anticipate future happiness from the worship of the gods. I know of no mode whereby I can be saved; and I believe that after death I shall be cast into hell as the punishment of my many sins!" To the same effect is the following pathetic passage from the late Rev. W. Ward.—" Look at the heathen by the side of the Ganges, calling upon their dying relations to repeat the names of Narayun, of Gunga, of Ram, and of a whole rabble of gods; pouring the waters of this river down the throat of the dying, exposing them in the agonies of death to the chilling damps by night, and to the scorching beams of the sun by day; and listen to the cries of the dying—'Tell me not of works of merit, I have been committing nothing but sin. And now—where am I going?—What is there beyond this wretched existence? Am I going into some reptile or some animal body; or shall I at once plunge into some dreadful place of torment? I see the messengers of Yuma coming to seize me. Oh! save me—save me! O mother Gunga give me a place near to thee! Oh! Ram! Oh! Narayun! O my Gooroo (his spiritual guide) how dark and heavy the cloud which envelopes me—is there no certainty, no ray of light from any of the shastras to guide and comfort me in my departure? Must I take the irrecoverable plunge to be seen no more?' And, when they have seen and heard all this, let them look at the death of Krishna, the Christian, consoled by the addresses of his Christian brethren, by the hymns which they sing, by the words of the everlasting Gospel which they repeat; let them listen to the pleasant words which proceed from his dying lips: 'My Saviour has sent his messenger for me, and I wish to go to him:' and then let them say whether the Gospel be a boon worth giving to the heathen."

The Rev. W. Yates, in his Memoir of the late Rev. J. Chamberlain, missionary in India, describing what he witnessed while on the Ganges, remarks—"At the Ghaut, or landing place, are great numbers of persons bathing and performing their morning ceremonies; and among them a poor woman laid on a low bed, raised only a few inches above the ground, in dying circumstances, left exposed to the blazing sun, totally unheeded by all around her, with a young man, her son, sitting behind her waiting, to appearance destitute of all anxiety, to see her breathe her last." In the same Memoir an account is given of the death of a native Christian, and the conduct of his heathen friends. "We were informed that the relations of Seboo Roy, had made a great shradda for him, and buried him in the Hindoo manner; but I informed them he had believed in the Saviour, and that, when I last saw him, he said,—'They may persecute and reproach us, but we will rather lose our lives than forsake our Lord Jesus.' In the evening, on our return to Cutwa, we were accompanied by four persons who attended upon the instructions of Seboo Roy, and who related to us the following particulars:—'Soon after his return from Cutwa, he was taken ill of a cold and retching, and died on the second or third day. He requested that they would take him to Cutwa, saying, '*If I do not go thither I shall never be well.*' But his brother's son would not regard what he said. *When they took him out to carry him to Gunga, he said to them; 'It is all to no purpose. I am perfectly sensible; why will you take me thither?'* He requested to be buried; but they would not grant his request. They took him away and burned his corpse. After they had taken him out of his house he said nothing to any one. Those who used to meet with him on Sabbath days went to see him a few times during his illness, and he exhorted them not to forsake the assembling of themselves together, nor to cease publishing the glories of our Saviour. 'I am going,' said he, 'but we shall soon see each other again;' and with such sayings as these encouraged and comforted them.' Seeboo Roy used to speak very favourably of his wife; and, when he died, she did not beat her forehead and cry aloud, as is the custom in this country upon such occasions. Being asked why she did not, she answered, 'What use is that? I sit and think of what he said to me!' (p. 221.)

The Rev. S. Sutton, late of Moorshedabad, in a letter to the Author upon the subject of this book, observes, "The following are a few well authenticated facts to establish what I have advanced.—The late respected Mr. Ward of Serampore, recorded the following case in his diary in 1813. 'On March 18th, at nine o'clock in the morning, a sick man by the name of Beekenaut was brought by his relatives to the river side, and was laid on the wet sand in expectation of soon expiring. In this situation he remained, exposed to the scorching rays of the sun, till about four P. M., when he was immersed up to the breast in the river, and in this position one of his relatives vociferated in his ears, 'Hurree! Ram! Krishna! Ram!' After some time, finding that death was not so near at hand as they had anticipated, he was again replaced on the wet bank. The next morning the same ceremony was commenced of immersing and repeating the names of their deities, until five o'clock P. M., when the man expired, *being literally murdered by his own relations.*' In the second volume of the Friend of India, it is remarked that one very notorious trait in the character of the natives of India is their want of humane feelings towards *the brute creation, their own countrymen in distress, and even towards their sick relatives.* 'That this is really the case, needs no proof. The cruel manner in which they often treat the patient bullock, which they use as a beast of burden—suffering their cows, notwithstanding the veneration they pretend for this animal, often to perish in the winter for want of food, furnish a sufficient proof of their want of feeling for the brute creation. Their inhumanity towards their own countrymen is sufficiently evinced by their suffering one of them, in a state of want and disease, cruelly to perish before their eyes, if he should not happen to be one of their relatives or friends, or at least of their own division of cast; and, above all, by their seeing a boat full of their own countrymen, who perhaps a few hours before had been bowing before the same log of wood as themselves, sinking before their eyes without making the least effort to save them! But their unfeeling conduct towards their sick and dying relatives is sometimes shocking in the extreme. Of this an instance occurred some years ago in a village near Serampore. An aged father was brought by his children to the river side to die. After having been there for some time, contrary to their expectations, he recovered and went home again; but his unfeeling children, instead of rejoicing that he was spared to them a little longer, so tormented him by their jeers and scoffs, because he did not die when carried to the river side for that purpose, that, weary of his life, the old man at length went out and put a period to his existence, by hanging himself on a tree near the public road!'

"To the above statements, I will now add my own testimony. I lived upon the banks of the Ganges for six years. During the whole of that period scarcely a day passed without some circumstance occurring which strikingly reminded me of the language of the Psalmist, 'The dark places of the earth are full of the habitations of cruelty.' I have seen some held up in the river by two persons, while a third has incessantly kept pouring water down the throat until life has become extinct. I have seen others laid upon the wet bank with their feet in the water when in the act of dying; and I have observed others who have been suffered to lie upon mats at a little distance from the river *for several days before they have expired*; but during this time no means have been employed for their recovery. In short, it is a very rare occurrence for any sick person to be brought back to his home after he has once been carried from it to die,"

"One evening," says the Widow of a Missionary, "as I was walking with my husband by the river side, we saw two respectable natives carrying a woman in their arms. We asked them what they were going to do with her? They very coolly answered, 'We are going to put her into the water that her soul may go to heaven, for she is our mother!' I asked them if she was ill? They said, 'She is not very ill; but she is old, and has no teeth, and what is the use of her living?' I felt a great deal on hearing this, and said, 'What! have you no compassion on your mother? will you drown her because she is old?' The woman instantly fixed her eyes on me, and said, 'What sort of a woman are you?' I told her I was an English woman, and wished to prevent her children from drowning her; and, if they did, I would acquaint the Governor with it, and, have them both hanged. They said, 'Never mind;' and proceeded towards the river. Mr. R. then ran down the bank, and, taking hold of the woman, insisted upon their taking her home. They did so: but they brought her again the next evening, and Mr. F. Carey saw them throw her into the water, without performing the usual ceremony of giving her water in the name of their gods.

"A man who worked in the Paper-Mill at Serampore was bitten by a snake. His companions immediately took him to the river to throw him in, without knowing whether it was a poisonous snake that had bitten him or not. When Mr. R. and Mr. F. Carey got to them, they found the poor creature between two men; one had hold of his shoulders, the other of his legs, and they were about to throw him into the river. Mr. Carey said, he thought the man was not dead, and made them put him down. Medicine was sent for and a spoonful given to him. He had no sooner taken it than he spoke and said, 'It is very strong. I will sooner die than take any more!' Mr. C. well understood the nature of the bite, and said it would be necessary to repeat the medicine every twenty minutes all night. Mr. R. asked those around him, if any one would stay with the poor man all night. They all answered, '*No; we cannot lose our sleep. It would be much better for him to die than for us to be deprived of a night's sleep!*' My husband staid all night, and the poor man continued to get better. In the morning he was so far recovered as to be able to walk home. The next day he came to our house, and fell down at my husband's feet, and said, 'I am come to worship you, Sahab, for saving my life; and I will work for you as long as I live!' He proved a faithful creature; and was working on the Mission Premises when I left Serampore (in 1820). He attended preaching in Bengalee very regularly.

"The Mission House at Serampore has been, and still is, a refuge to the Natives. There they are protected from the Brahmuns at their swinging feasts—comforted when in trouble—have medicine administered when they are sick;—there they are relieved when in distress—there they are instructed how they can be saved without cutting themselves with knives, or running spits through their tongues, and other cruelties that their Gooroos require. Not only in the Mission House have they found protection, but in the house of our Native Christians. I have witnessed the death of two who died under the roof of a Native brother at Serampore, where they had taken shelter from the jackals and birds of prey; being cast out by their relatives when ill, forsaken by their companions in idolatry, and left to perish. One of them was an old woman covered with wounds. She had but little clothing on her, so that the birds had eaten nearly all the flesh off her back as she crawled along: but she soon died. Mr. R. had a coffin made, and with his own hands put her in, for he could get no one to assist him. Our dear Native brother and sister had fed and taken care of her while alive; but they were too much afraid of the disease to touch her when she was dead. The other was a young woman who worked in the Paper-Mill. She was left a widow when only ten years of age, and at this early period became utterly depraved. Her body was so maimed as almost to lose the appearance of a human being; but in this miserable condition she was spared eight months. She died praising God for his goodness to her, in sparing her so long to enjoy the privilege of worshipping the true God."*

The following extract of a letter from the same lady, dated Salisbury, May, 1828, is painfully interesting:—"While I am writing, I am feeling all the horrors I formerly felt respecting the sick in India. I once witnessed one of the scenes in all its aggravations. The sick person was a young woman who was not willing to go to the river. As they approached the Ghaut her screams were intolerable; crying, '*Ame morey jay na!*' (I am not dying!) But the men who had taken her were firm to their purpose, and would not listen to any thing that was said to them. They laughed at my entreaties; turned a deaf ear to my threats; and rushed forward into the water with their victim. Whether they were relations or not I could not ascertain. The poor creature had often said, '*I am not dying!*' but now she found herself in dying circumstances; a few cups of water poured down her throat in the name of their gods soon stopped her breath. I inquired whether it was a common case to take them to the river against their will. They said, 'Yes; or else a great many would disgrace their families by dying in their houses.' Many are carried thither at their own request; but in this case the conduct of the relatives was extremely cruel. Sometimes they leave them to perish by the river. I found a poor old man one morning by the river side, who had been left there all

---

* Youth's Mag. 1823, pp. 292—304.

night. Those who had taken him had rubbed his body with mud, and had left him quite naked, exposed to the ants; so that he was completely covered with insects! When I saw him move his head, I went to him; but, Oh! the horror that thrilled through me, to see a fellow-creature in his dying moments thus cruelly tormented with insects that were running over him in groups from head to foot. I ran for assistance, but the Natives refused to do any thing for him, unless I would allow them to put him a little nearer the water; saying, he was too far off for the tide to reach him. I said, 'Perhaps he may get better if he be cleaned and taken care of.' They shook their heads, and said, 'He was put there to die, and die he must.' My husband soon came with some wine for him; we put a little of it into his mouth, which he swallowed, and said it was very good. I then thought he would revive. But he had lain all night on the damp ground, and it was now eleven o'clock and the sun shining on him very hot, so that it had dried the mud that was on his body, which fatigued him very much. When we endeavoured to move him, he said he was very faint, and wished to remain where he was for a few minutes. Alas! it was but a few minutes indeed! for he soon expired. I could mention many more facts of horror, but I forbear."

The existence of this custom, and the inhumanities connected with it, were very fully discussed in the public papers in Calcutta before the author left India in Nov. 1825; a few extracts may be interesting. In the Bengal Hurkaru it is observed, "During the prevalence of Cholera, one of the symptoms of which is a sudden prostration of strength, leaving the pulse scarcely perceptible and the patient in an apparently lifeless state, it must frequently happen that individuals are carried down to the river in this state and murdered under the pretext that they are already in a dying state; when, if they had been properly treated, they might have been restored to health. We have heard that these unhappy victims of a demoralizing superstition are sometimes carried down expressing reluctance by every means in their power." (Aug. 27, 1825.)

The following letter, extracted from the Columbian Press Gazette, is given entire:—"I was informed a few days ago that numbers of sick Natives were daily brought to the Kidderpore Ghaut, to perform the last ceremony of dipping them in the stream, and forcing the mud and water of the

Ganges into their mouths. Curiosity led me to see this, as well as to try if I could be of service in persuading any to desist from this horrid act. On my arrival at the spot to which I was directed, I saw three individuals, two old men and a boy of about thirteen or fourteen years of age. The two old people were in a hopeless state, the boy however looked very well; but as he was lying on the *marshy ground on a bare mat*, not five yards from the water, and his body uncovered, his case seemed dangerous. I went up to him, felt his pulse, and perceived it beat well. I remonstrated with those around him for having brought the boy to such a place, and then leaving him in that condition. I inquired if a doctor had attended him. I was informed that the doctor attached to the Tannah was sent for, who gave him some English medicine, and promised to be back again very soon. Shortly after this the inhuman man (a Brahmun) appeared, but would give no medicine; saying, '*I have given* ONCE, *for which I have not been paid;* AND I WILL NOT *administer any more until paid for!*' I was struck with amazement at the words of this wretch, but all persuasions and promises were of no avail. Humanity led me to suggest that, if the boy were taken to his house and kept warm, I would pay any charge the doctor might make. This was not acceded to: and as it seemed useless to do any thing further so long as the boy remained in that damp place, exposed to the weather, I thought proper to go away. The doctor was still there; but whether he gave him any medicine after I left the place I cannot say. On inquiry the following morning I was informed the boy died about midnight. Can you inform me if the doctors attached to the Tannahs are paid by Government? This information from you, or any of the readers of your valuable Gazette, will much oblige C.

Tolly's, Nullah, Sep. 22, 1825."

"We are unable to satisfy our Correspondent on this point."—ED.

Would not this affair in Britain be justly looked upon as murder? "Ought not inquisition to be made for blood" thus shed in British India? Does not the humanity, even of the humane, in India, want elevating, which could leave a child thus to perish without using compulsory measures to have him taken care of?*

* See Bap. Mag. Sep., 1826.

A Correspondent, formerly resident in Bengal, writes in Oct. 1827:—"There are other customs practised in India as awful and abominable as that of immolating the innocent widow; among which may be reckoned that of *exposing the sick by the sides of their rivers.* If there be any period in human life in which man stands in particular need of the manifestations of friendship, it is in the hour of sickness and death. He looks to his friends to support his drooping head, to adjust his pillow, to administer the cordial, and to wipe away the dew of death; but, alas! these consolations fall not to the lot of the poor Hindoo. When he is overtaken by sickness, those around him, for a time, watch his bed; but, as soon as he is supposed to be in dangerous circumstances, he is hurried away to the banks of some holy river, and the ceremonies which then take place have a great tendency to extinguish life."

"We had not proceeded far," says the Widow of a Missionary who died at Digah, writing on the Ganges, Dec. 1826, "when we saw on a sand-bed a poor man and woman sitting by the water. The woman was busied in laving her dying son with mud and water, who was old and strong enough to be heard to say, 'I will not die! I will not die!' To which she was heard to say frequently, 'To die by Gunga is blessed, my son!' she at length stifled him; when the father assisted in pushing him into the river."

"In my way down from the Upper Provinces," says a correspondent in the Columbian Press Gazette, "my budgerow stopped at a Ghaut on the Hooghly river, in the vicinity of Moorshedabad. The crowd which was collected on the spot excited my curiosity to know what occasioned it. I accordingly went to the place and witnessed one of the most inhuman scenes that can be imagined. A poor helpless creature was stretched on a cot, the lower part of his body being immersed in water. In this posture *he was imploring his murderers in the most pitiful manner to let him go, declaring that he was yet far from death!* To hear his supplications, and observe the distressed and forlorn expression of his countenance, were enough to strike any heart with horror and pity. But these cruel wretches that were about him, unmindful of his entreaties, kept crying, 'Hurree bol! hurree bol!' and continued filling his mouth with water, till at length the poor creature became exhausted; his voice, which was at first loud, gradually sunk, and he fell an unwilling victim to superstition" (Aug., 1825.)

A Bengalee Newspaper, the Kowmoody, Aug., 1825, contains the following testimony to the existence of these atrocities:—"With a view to check the progress of the Cholera Morbus, the Government have, with their usual benevolence towards the natives, been pleased to appoint a native doctor to every Tannah, to afford medical assistance to the poor patients in the neighbourhood. We are happy to learn that a young man having been attacked with the Cholera, and his relations despairing of his life, took him to the river side, when suddenly his breath stopped and he appeared to be dead; his relations prepared a funeral pile, but to their great surprise they perceived him move, and approaching him, though with a degree of fear,* had recourse to some medicines, which restored him to life, and he returned home to the great joy of his whole family."

Another Bengalee Paper, named *Somachar Durpun*, Sep. 3, published at Serampore, states, "A respectable man of Sulkea, having been attacked with the Cholera, was taken to the river side; and on his becoming senseless, though not cold, every one thought he was dead; and, having prepared a pile, put him upon it and set it on fire. The poor creature, by imbibing a certain degree of heat, came to himself, and rose up. *One of his relations, who was close by, beat him on the head with a bamboo, and killed him on the burning pile.* This circumstance is not groundless; we have obtained the account from a European gentleman who was an eye witness of it. The perpetrator of this murder (says the Hindoo Translator), though it was prejudice that prompted him to act as he did, no doubt conceived with respect to the supposed dead man, what we have already stated. This instance corroborates our statement. Such absurd notions of evil spirits or supernatural beings are not handed to us by our ancestors, nor can we find any trace of them in our shastras, and hence we are at a loss to conceive how such groundless ideas could ever take root in the minds of modern Hindoos."

The appalling scenes presented to the humane, even in

* "If a Hindoo, after having been taken to the river, and supposed to be dead, moves himself or attempts to get up (as is frequently the case), his relations believe that some evil spirit possesses the body; and instantly beat it down with a hatchet, spade, or some iron weapon which they find close by; thus killing the poor creature who might otherwise have survived. Such is the cruel reign of superstition among this simple race of people." (NOTE BY THE TRANSLATOR.)

Calcutta, are such as show the character of the Hindoo and Mussulman, and the necessity that the mild dictates of Christianity should be propagated among the people. "It redounds little to the credit of the Magistates," says the Hurkaru, "or to their subordinates, that the Ghauts present spectacles both horrid and disgusting to every feeling mind. It not unfrequently happens that *twenty dead bodies* (and as many *living ones)* are brought to one Ghaut to be burnt. This Ghaut will admit of four or five only being consumed at one time. The rest are of necessity suffered to putrefy until an opportunity is afforded their relations to burn them; while the groans of the dying who are lying close by, and who inhale the smoke and smell, are calculated at once to excite both pity and horror. Sometimes also the relations are so poor that they cannot procure money sufficient to burn the body, in which case they leave it at the Ghaut, and go and beg for the necessary pittance to purchase the wood, and two days probably elapse before any charitable individuals are found to aid them! But why confine these remarks to Ghauts only? Turn towards the city; there we shall behold circumstances which excite our pity and our indignation. Several bodies of poor men are seen lying in the streets. Only last week a poor man, who was struck by the sun, fell down on the Circular Road and expired. His body was suffered to lie a whole day, while the effigies of Hussan and Hussein were exhibited by the Mussulmans; and the body must have been trampled on by the crowd which generally assemble on such occasions." (Sep. 1, 1825.)

"Since our last (says the India Gazette), we have had very heavy rains, and the sickness among the natives has, we are led to understand, somewhat abated. Dead bodies in rather considerable numbers may still be seen afloat, and even in Tolly's Nullah we have seen several. Indeed one remained two days near Allipore Bridge, and would, we suppose, have remained there to this hour, had it not been carried away by a rising of the water, owing to the heavy rains. It is quite horrible, close to a city like Calcutta, to see human carcases floating about or lying at length on the bank, a prey to dogs or carrion birds. The sight is degrading and brutalizing. It is no less so to see the *Dooms carrying the dead in a state the next to nudity, slung upon bamboos, and thus casting them into the river;* making, we may say, a nuisance of the stream! It would be a most desirable thing if such a scandalous mode of disposing of the dead could be obviated; for scandalous such spectacles certainly are to the eyes of Christians, in a city subject to Christian Laws and Government. The expense could not be very great of providing a stock of Mango coffins in different quarters of the town, to be available for the purpose of the Dooms, who ought also to be made to attach weights to the dead bodies they cast into the river. This would not prevent their being carried to the ocean, though it would keep them from floating on the surface of the water: perhaps, if the matter were properly represented to Government, such a suggestion would meet consideration."*

"We regret to state (says the Editor of the India Gazette), that the sickness and mortality have not abated. Among the natives the Cholera is not only prevalent but very destructive. The Mahometans also have suffered very severely. We have heard that no fewer than 158 Mussulmans, and from seventy to eighty Hindoos, died in Calcutta on Friday. This mortality may partly be attributed to the fatigue and dissipation of the Mohurrum festival. By dissipation we mean nocturnal watching, and wandering about in the heat of the day. *We would not willingly say any thing harsh about the solemn observance of any people; but convinced as we are that the Mohurrum is prejudicial to health and morals, and of no importance in a religious point of view, we consider it a nuisance which we should like to see abolished.* When we use the word nuisance, we trust we shall not be accused of intolerance, when the clamour and dissipation of the ceremony, and the unhealthy consequences are considered, and the inconvenience every way as it respects the families in which they serve. Perhaps our reference to

* "One of the first specimens of the manners of the country (says the late Bishop Heber) which have fallen under our notice has been a human corpse, slowly floating past, according to the well known custom of the Hindoos" (Jour. vol. i. p. 2). "The practice of throwing dead bodies into the river is, in many places, a dreadful nuisance; as in case a body should float to the side of the river, and remain there, it will continue to infect the whole neighbourhood, till the vultures, dogs, jackals, and other animals have devoured it. The throwing of dead bodies and other filth into the river makes the Ganges, in the neighbourhood of large towns, resemble a common sewer. Still the Natives drink it with the greatest appetite, bathe in it every day, to cleanse both their bodies and their souls, and carry it to an immense distance, as the greatest imaginable treasure!" Ward's View of the Hindoos, vol. iii. p. 276. AUTH.

what we deem morbific agents may be considered as grounded more on theory than fact. Let it be so. We deem it not less our duty to call attention to the subject again and again. We hesitate not to deliver it as our opinion that great unhealthiness may be expected from the accumulation of animal putrefactive vapour in and about Calcutta. *Dead bodies, in a state of putrefaction, are continually floating on the surface of the Hooghly, or stranded on the banks.* The Mahomedans bury their dead only *two feet* under the surface of the earth, and we understand, from this superficial mode of sepulture, the large Mussulman burying-ground in the Circular Road is covered with dead bodies, dragged out of their graves by jackals and dogs. Greater attention is necessary to the drains in and about Calcutta, which present an extensive surface for the evolution of putrescent matter. It is almost inconceivable how horribly filthy the densely populous parts of Calcutta are; the narrowness of the lanes, and the darkness of the alleys, of themselves constitute causes of filth, not only in the localities but in the inhabitants. The inhabitants of wide streets will, *a priori*, we imagine, be always cleaner, better dressed, more anxious about their appearance, every way more comfortable, and even moral, than those of lanes or gullies. In this idea we are in a measure supported by a saying of the philosophic and pious Paley, 'Want of cleanliness is want of morals.' We have reason to think our climate might be improved; and there are, we believe, several opulent natives who would support the plan, provided Government patronized it." (Aug. 25, 1825.)

From these various facts and observations, some idea may be formed of the dreadful nature of the practice of exposing the sick in British India, and the brutalizing and demoralizing influence of it upon the population. Does not the voice of humanity demand attention to these attrocities? Where are the tender sympathies of nature? Let Britain display her true character in India—let her abolish human sacrifices, and raise the tone of humane and moral feeling in society.

CHAP. II.

Extent of the prevalence of this inhuman practice.

On this subject it is impossible to speak with precision. The author hesitates to give an opinion; but it is presumed there can be no impropriety in presenting the statements of those who, from their residence in the vicinity of the Ganges, may be supposed best qualified to form some idea of the prevalence of this unnatural and destructive custom. "The immersion," says Dr. Buchanan, of half the body "of a person, supposed to be dying, in the water of the Ganges, must often occasion premature death. It is optional; not commanded. Though very common on the banks of the Ganges, it is reprobated in many places at a distance from it." The author never saw this practised during his residence in Orissa. It is hoped that attention will be awakened to this painful subject, and more correct information respecting it obtained.

"Every Hindoo," says the Rev. W. Ward, in his Farewell Letters, "in the hour of death, is hurried to the side of the Ganges, or some other sacred river, if near enough, where he is laid, in the agonies of death, exposed to the burning sun by day and to the dews and cold of the night. The water of the river is poured plentifully down him if he can swallow it; and his breast, forehead, and arms, are besmeared with the mud of the river; for the very mud of the Ganges is supposed to have some purifying properties. Just before the soul quits the body, he is laid on the earth, and then immersed up to the middle in the stream; while his relations stand around him tormenting him in his last moments with superstitious rites, and increasing, a hundred fold, the pains of dying. *Very often, where recovery might be reasonably expected, these barbarities bring on premature death. It is pretty certain that many private murders, in using these rites, are perpetrated.*" In a calculation, made by the same author, of the number of Hindoos who perish annually, the victims of superstition, he estimates that there are 500 sick persons whose death is hastened on the banks of the Ganges; and adds, "a gentleman, whose opinion is of great weight, says,—'I believe this estimate is far below the truth." Of the various kinds of Hindoo cruelties, it is remarked,—"There are a number of actions performed by Hindoos supposed to be meritorious in their nature, but which, in the opinion of a Christian, deserve punishment even in this life. The Hindoo widow burning with the dead body of her husband is promised a residence in heaven during the reign of fourteen Indras; yet no Christian doubts whether these are real murders or not. *The death of vast multitudes of Hindoos is procured, or hastened, annually, by immersing a part of the body, in a state of dangerous weakness, in the Ganges, and by pouring large quantities of the water into the mouth of the dying person: yet the Hindoos think it a work of great merit.* Many persons voluntarily renounce life in the Ganges, under the hope of obtaining immediate entrance into heaven; and yet a jury of Englishmen would pronounce it self-murder. Infatuated mothers devote their children to this sacred river, not doubting but they are sending them to heaven; yet *we* feel certain that every such infant is murdered."* Ought not Britain to exert her influence and abolish all these murderous practices? Is not this one great object of Providence in her supremacy over the millions of India? What a blessing would Christianity be to Hindostan!

A late resident in India observes, "With regard to the extent of the practice, every conjecture must be very uncertain. There are no registers of births and burials to which we can have recourse, and consequently we have no data upon which we can form any accurate calculation. The river Ganges rises in the mountains of Himmaleh. From this place it flows in the direction of Hurdwar. From Hurdwar, where it gushes through an opening in the mountains and enters Hindostan, it flows 1200 miles with a smooth navigable stream to the Bay of Bengal. In its course through these plains it receives eleven rivers, some of which are larger, and none smaller than the Thames. Through the whole of the course of the Ganges, and through many of its tributary streams, the custom of exposing the sick prevails. Nor is it confined to those who dwell near its banks: some are brought from a great distance that they may die near Gunga. If we consider the denseness of the population, and the number of villages,

* Ward's View of the Hindoos, vol. ii. pp. 127, 138, 173.

towns,—and cities, near which this river flows,—it is easy to be conceived that the loss of human life, occasioned by this custom, is of awful extent. Nor indeed have I heard of any Hindoos remonstrating against it, except Bruja Mohun, who wrote an excellent Tract on the present state of Polytheism in India. When this respectable and enlightened man was seized with the Cholera Morbus his relatives wished to hurry him away to the river, but he refused and n sisted on being left in his house."

The late Bishop Heber, when at Benares, stated,—"Fuel is extremely dear, and to this circumstance is imputed the number of bodies thrown into the river without burning. Suttees are less numerous in Benares than in many parts of India, but self-immolation by drowning is very common. Every year many scores of pilgrims from all parts of India come hither expressly to end their days and secure their salvation. They purchase two large kedgeree pots, between which they tie themselves; and, when empty, these support their weight in the water. Thus equipped they paddle into the stream, then fill the pots with the water which surrounds them, and thus sink into eternity! Government have sometimes attempted to prevent this practice, but with no other effect than driving the voluntary victims a little further down the river; nor indeed, when a man has come several hundred miles to die, is it likely that a police officer can prevent him. Instruction seems the only way in which these poor people can be improved, and that I trust they will by degrees obtain from us."† (Sept. 1824.) The success of the British magistrate at Allahabad, in suppressing this practice, shows that this and similar cruel customs in India might easily be abolished by the paternal power of Britain.

The late Rev. D. Brown bears his testimony to the appalling extent of this unnatural custom :—"The Brahmuns can, as may serve their interest, devote any sick branch of a family to death: and *incredible numbers are destroyed by this superstition*."* "It is my deliberate opinion," says the Rev. S. Sutton, late of Moorshedabad, "that, yearly, *thousands* of persons would recover from their diseases, if this absurd custom were abolished."

"The exposure of the sick and dying by the sides of the Ganges, and other sacred rivers, has been practised from

---

* Miss. Mag. vol. i. p. 117. † Journ., vol. i. p. 295.

time immemorial, and is extended to all the Hindoos residing near the rivers. At the hour of death, these poor creatures are brought from home, and exposed to the scorching heat of a vertical sun, even in the very agonies of death; or to the heavy dews and cold of the night. The body of the sufferer is besmeared with the mud of the river, and a large quantity of water is poured down him if he can be made to swallow it. *Hereby the most horrible cruelties are practised on the person of the dying, in the hour when suffering humanity, in every civilized country, receives the most soothing and unwearied attentions; and hundreds are hurried into a premature grave*."*

"I was much interested," says a correspondent in the Columbian Press Gazette, "with the perusal of your remarks on the practice of suffocating invalid Hindoos with *Gunga-jol*, or water of the Ganges. I have looked upon this horrid custom for years in the light in which you represent it, and in many instances I consider it *absolute murder. It is far more prevalent than the burning of widows.* Among the higher class of Hindoos, hardly any one is allowed to depart this life in peace at home, but is taken to the banks of the river, and there offered up a sacrifice to brahminical superstition. This indeed is such a crying and prevalent evil, among Hindoos, that it certainly deserves the serious consideration of those in authority."—August 24th, 1825.

Another correspondent writes,—"The perusal of a Paper called '*Brahminical Cruelties*,' and your observations upon it, induce me again to say something in defence of the cause of humanity which you have advocated. I entirely concur with you in opinion that the 'John Bull,' when speaking upon this subject, must have confined his view to the Bankshall and Chundpaul Ghauts, as the scenes of the barbarous acts; and am surprised he should be so ignorant of what is passing a little beyond Calcutta and its immediate environs. *I can confidently assert that such murderous acts as the one I described in your last number are of almost daily occurrence in the Province of Bengal.* Perhaps few of your readers are acquainted with a village called *Chakdah*: it is situated on the banks of the Hooghly, near Sooksaugur, a little above Bandel. When any of the unfortunate individuals who are carried to the river to receive the '*Gunga Labh*' survive the dreadful treatment

* Remarks on the Immolations in India (Parbury), p. 6.

of their murderers, by the physical strength of their constition, or other causes, they are generally expelled from their caste, torn from their relations, and sent to inhabit this village. After they are once taken out of the house to undergo this inhuman rite they are reckoned unholy and unfit for association. There they intermarry, and I suppose live as comfortably as any of the low caste Hindoos. I do not think that this village is inhabited by any but these people and their children. I deny not that, like other occurrences of life, the descriptions of this horrid custom are sometimes exaggerated; but this is no argument against the real fact; the most certain things are liable to exaggeration. Those who wish to have a correct idea of brahminical cruelties, in this respect, may pay a visit to Chakdah, and there learn, from the inhabitants themselves, the extent of tortures that each of them has suffered."

The following letter from a gentleman, in a Calcutta Paper, affords a specimen of the want of humanity and attention to the sick, so prevalent among the Hindoos:—

"I am a Mofussilite, and, in the absence of better society, I love to make companionship with a few faithful dogs, which have served me well ever since they had the happiness of having me for a master. The evening before last, having mounted my horse and whistled them about me, I started with the intention of running a fox if I could find one. I had scarcely proceeded a hundred yards from my house, when my horse started at something rolled up in a mat, lying under a tree by the side of the road. As there were numbers of people passing, who took no notice of it, I thought it could be nothing of consequence enough to require me to dismount, so I passed on; and, after having had my ride, and killed a jackal, I returned home. About ten o'clock next morning, my bearer informed me that a traveller, oppressed with age, overcome by hunger, and wearied with his journey, was lying under a tree a short distance off, and was just about to die: "*and,*" added he in a tone of the most perfect unconcern, '*he has been lying there for several days, without any thing to eat or drink, so he cannot live more than a day!*' Having put on my clothes as hastily as I could, I repaired to the spot, and to my astonishment found that what I had taken for a bundle of wood or grass was nothing less than a man. At first sight it appeared to me that he was totally stiff and dead; but, on turning him round, I found that life was not extinct, and that possibly something might yet be done to recal the parting spirit. I accordingly had him borne to my house, and with considerable difficulty I forced some medicine down his throat; by degrees he recovered so far as to make known to me that, having gone on a pilgrimage to the temple of Juggernaut, he was returning to his home at Moorshedabad, when he was seized with an illness which day by day increased: that, his money being all spent, he had been eleven days without tasting food; and that, not being able to advance farther than the place in which I found him, he had been left there by his *friend.*

(Mark the word, Mr. Editor). As to not having eaten any thing for eleven days, his emaciated state bore full testimony to the truth of his story; for I never could have believed it possible, without actually seeing it, that the human frame could be wasted to such a degree, and still have life in it.

"What a strange idea these people must have of religion, and what it requires! In this case, two persons set out together from Moorshedabad to Juggernaut. The one (my patient) is seventy years of age, the other a young man in full health. On their way back the old man fell sick; and, although his friend has been making this pilgrimage for the sake of his salvation, and trying to make his peace with his gods, yet he hesitates not to leave his sick companion to die as he may, and become food for dogs; and, when he returns to Moorshedabad, he, no doubt, thinks that he has washed away all the sins of his former life, by the merit of a pilgrimage to a shrine polluted with human blood! It is a comfort indeed to think that we profess a faith which points out a very different conduct on such an occasion. It is ours to act the part of the good Samaritan, and pour oil and wine into the wounds of the fallen and distressed, whether Christian, Jew, Pagan, or Mussulman; and I trust there are but few of my readers who would have passed by on the other side of the road, without heeding the miserable skeleton who now lies at my door. The Hindoos have a definition of the word 'neighbour,' but it is widely different from that given by the Author of our faith. They have no such precept as 'do unto others as you would be done by.' The fate of the poor wretch I hope to serve is the fate of thousands. Immense numbers of those who leave their houses in these pilgrimages, leave them never to return. Hundreds die by the way, and some are crushed to death by the ponderous car of Juggernaut. A description of the procession, by one of our best living Poets, may give an idea of the horror with which any spectator, but one of themselves, would view it. It is as follows:—

"A thousand pilgrims strain,
Arm, shoulder, breast, and thigh, with might and main,
To draw that sacred wain,
And scarce can draw along the enormous load.
Prone fall the frantic votaries in its road,
And, calling on their god,
Their self-devoted bodies there they lay,
To pave his chariot way:
On Juggernaut they call,
The pond'rous car rolls on, and crushes all;
Through blood and bones it ploughs its dreadful path;
Groans rise unheeded; the dying cry,
And death and agony are trodden under foot by yon mad throng,
Who follow close, and thrust the deadly wheels along."

"This is the religion of those who have been so often called the *mild Hindoos*: this is the religion of a people who shudder at the idea of killing a cow, but subject it to the greatest tortures when alive. This is part of a system which condemns the unhappy widow to be burned in the embrace of her putrid husband—which has found a merit in exposing a new-born child to the jaws of a voracious shark, or a greedy alligator—and which thrusts an iron hook into the back of its poor deluded votaries, and swings them in the air, with a savage satisfaction to the spectators! It is melancholy to think that one hundred millions bend the knee to innumerable gods, whose chief delight they conceive to consist in witnessing the agonies of a human being, expiring under tortures with a view to conciliate their favour! Give them education sufficient to see the errors of their religion and the presumption of their priests, and then some bold spirits must break through those fetters which have bound them for centuries. W.

Mofussil, July 5th, 1825."

The author's colleagues in Orissa unite their testimony relative to the existence of these acts of dreadful sacrifice to Juggernaut. The Rev. C. Lacey, under date July 9th, 1826, writes,—"This afternoon I had an awful subject for the foundation of my discourse,—the body of a poor man crushed to pieces by the car of Juggernaut. The wheels had passed just over his loins, and had nearly severed his upper from his lower parts; his bowels had gushed out, and presented a sight too shocking to look upon. It was one of the most horrid spectacles I ever beheld; and, while standing by it, I became quite ill with sickness, and every limb shivered with horror. The poor wretch threw himself from the front of the car, and so became a voluntary sacrifice. He seemed a respectable man, apparently a Hindostanee Brahmun. I felt very much indisposed this evening, but could not lose this opportunity of witnessing against the system which produced such effects. I felt my own mind in a serious frame, took my stand near the body, and spoke with some feeling of the nature of the Hindoo religion, and compared it with that of Christ; and, perhaps, I never had a more serious congregation. Some hardened wretches, pointing to the mangled body, said, 'See, Sir, the glory of Juggernaut!' I concluded with recommending them to look to Jesus Christ for mercy and salvation, which Juggernaut could never give." The Rev. A. Sutton adds,—"The people who assembled, while we stopped to look at him, exclaimed with approbation, 'burra bocte!' viz. great devotedness. Methinks that one scene like this would be sufficient to awaken the whole Christian world, could they but witness it; but is it less real because they cannot? Oh how long shall the blood, and skulls, and murders at Pooree, exclaim, with a voice that should almost harrow up our soul, and make our flesh crawl upon our bones, against the heartlessness and indifference which England manifests."

The Periodical Accounts of the Baptist Mission contain affecting statements of Hindoo cruelty. A passage or two only is given. "Do not send men of compassion here, for you will soon break their hearts.—Do send men full of compassion here, where many perish with cold, many for lack of bread, and millions for lack of knowledge. In England the poor receive the benefit of the Gospel, in being fed and clothed by those who know not by what they are moved. When the Gospel is generally acknowledged in a land, it puts some to fear and others to shame; so that, to relieve their own smart, they provide for the poor. But here (O miserable sight!) I have found the path-way stopped up by sick and wounded people, perishing with hunger, and that in a populous neighbourhood, where numbers pass by; some singing, others talking, but none showing mercy; as though they were dying weeds and not dying men."*

The late highly respected Bishop Heber, in the correspondence which closes the Narrative of his Journey through the Upper Provinces of India, declares,—"It is necessary to see idolatry to be fully sensible of its mischievous effects on the human mind. But of all idolatries of which I have ever read or heard the religion of the Hindoos really appears to me the worst, in the degrading notions which it gives of the Deity;—in the endless round of its burdensome ceremonies, which occupy the time and distract the thoughts, without either instructing or interesting its votaries;—in the filthy acts of uncleanness and cruelty, not only permitted, but enjoined and inseparably interwoven with these ceremonies;—in the system of castes, a system which tends, more than any thing else the devil has yet invented, to destroy the feelings of general benevolence and to make nine tenths of mankind the hopeless slaves of the remainder;—and in the total absence of any popular system of morals, or any single lesson which the people at large ever hear, to live virtuously and do good to each other. I do not say that there are not some scattered lessons of this kind to be found in their ancient books; but these books are neither accessible to the people at large, nor are these last permitted to read them; and, in general, all the sins that a soodra is taught to fear are killing a cow, offending a Brahmun, or neglecting one of the many frivolous rites by which their deities are supposed to be con-

* Vol. i. pp. 281, 281.

ciliated. Accordingly, though the general sobriety of the Hindoos affords a very great facility for the maintenance of public order and decorum, I really never have met with a race of men whose standard of morality is so low; who feel so little shame on being detected in a falsehood, or so little interest in the suffering of a neighbour not being of their own caste or family; whose ordinary and familiar conversation is so licentious; or, in the wilder and more lawless districts, who shed blood with so little repugnance."*

Hindoo cruelty to the sick is thus forcibly described by the same author:—" Their own religion is indeed a horrible one: far more so than I had conceived. It gives them no moral precepts; it encourages them in vice by the style of its ceremonies, and the character given of its deities; and, by the institution of caste, it hardens their heart against each other to a degree which is often most revolting. A traveller falls down sick in the streets of a village (I am mentioning a fact which happened ten days ago !†); nobody knows of what caste he is, therefore nobody goes near him lest they should become polluted:—he wastes to death before the eyes of a whole community, unless the jackals take courage from his helpless state to finish him a little sooner; and, perhaps, as happened in the case to which I allude, the children are allowed to pelt him with stones and mud. The man of whom I am speaking was found in this state, and taken care of by a passing European; but, if he had died, his skeleton would probably have lain on the road side till the vultures carried it away, or the magistrates ordered it to be thrown into the river! A friend of mine, some months ago, found a miserable wretch, a groom out of employ, who had crept, sick of a dysentery, into his court yard. He had there remained, in a corner on the pavement, two days and nights. Perhaps twenty servants had been eating their meals within six yards of him, yet none had relieved him—none had so much as carried him into the shelter of one of the out-houses, nor had any taken the trouble to tell their master. When reproved for this, their answer was, 'He was not our kinsman.' 'Whose business was it?' 'How did we know that the Sahab would like to be troubled?' I do not say these are every day instances: I hope and believe not. Nor would I be understood as de-

* Vol. ii. p. 384, 385.

† The letter is dated Tittygur (near Calcutta), Jan. 10th, 1824.

nying that alms to religious mendicants are given to a great amount in Bengal; or that several of the wealthy inhabitants, in what they consider good works, such as constructing public tanks, making roads to places of pilgrimage, building pagodas and ghauts, are liberal. I only mention these instances, because none of those that heard them seemed to think them unusual or extraordinary. In a Christian country I think they could not have happened; and they naturally arise from the genius of the national religion, which, by the distinction it establishes, makes men worse than indifferent to each other.*

Diego de Lonta, an early Portuguese writer, during his residence at Goa, speaks of hospitals for animals in India, but asserts the inhumanity of the Hindoos.—" One means of making atonement for their sins is by forming hospitals for birds. We have seen a remarkable one in the fortress of Cambayette, in which were very comfortable places provided for the birds which sheltered there, and persons were employed to take care of such as were sick. The revenues are derived from public alms. One hospital has persons in pay whose duty it is to walk the streets and fields to search for sick or infirm birds, and bring them to the hospital. They have also places for sick and aged beasts, where they are lodged and attended: people are kept to go in search of old buffaloes, horses, or mules, wounded or infirm, which are conveyed to the hospital and cured. If they see a lame *man* on the ground they will not lend a hand to lift him up, but let him be trampled upon by men and beasts, because they say he is reduced to this state by his sins. They buy birds merely to let them loose : but would not contribute to release a man from prison, even if it were their own father."†

Lord Teignmouth, in sketching the Hindoo character, confirms these statements. " If I were to describe the Hindoo character generally, allowing for individual exceptions, I should define it a compound of insincerity, servility, and dishonesty. Their master-passion is self-interest, which they pursue through all the mazes of cunning and duplicity. Their disregard for veracity is most striking; and the detection of falsehood excites no other sensation than that of regret for the failure of the purpose it was intended to answer. *Their charity has more of ostentation than of*

---

* Vol. ii. pp. 313, 314. † Asi. Journ. March, 1827.

benevolence. The apathy with which they see their fellow creatures suffering pain and distress is also very remarkable. Their boasted tenderness to the brute creation is a negative quality, extending no further than to the not depriving animals of life, without any effort to prolong it or render it comfortable. The most unerring index to the national character of any people is, to learn their own sentiments of each other; and no people show more reciprocal distrust than exists among the individuals of every tribe and family. In every country, where idolatry has obtained a complete establishment, we not only find a general debasement of the moral principle, and corresponding corruption of manners, but *even licentiousness, and the most shocking cruelty, deriving a sort of sanction from the religion itself, or from the authority of customs and practices founded upon it.*"*

These statements forcibly remind the humane and pious of the declaration of Scripture,—" Their sorrows shall be multiplied that hasten after another *god:* their drink offerings of blood will I not offer, nor take up their names into my lips." What a blessing would Christianity prove to the myriads of India, thus " seeking death in the error of their way." The dictate of the Gospel, which it is the imperious duty of Britain to give to the East, is " Do thyself no harm." May its blessings be extended as ' far as winds can waft and billows roll.'

CHAP. III.

The necessity and propriety of adopting measures for the prevention of these atrocities—utility of attending to the sick—confirmation of the statements—concluding remarks.

These appalling facts are submitted to the attention of the humane in Britain and India. That such atrocious acts, under the semblance of religion, are perpetrated, is

---

* See Considerations on Communicating to the Natives of India the Knowledge of Christianity, pp. 81, 82, 92.

beyond a doubt; but ought such infractions of the inviolable principles of justice and humanity to be tolerated? "Righteousness exalteth a nation." "Mercy and truth preserve the king, and his throne is upholden by mercy." It is not necessary for the preservation of the British power in India that these cruelties should be allowed. The God of nations is "a God of truth, and without iniquity, just and right is he;" and He will "make inquisition for blood." Can it be doubted whether Britain possesses the power to issue a proclamation, declaring that whoever is accessary to the death of an individual by the Suttee, Infanticide, or Ghaut murders, is a murderer, and as such amenable to the laws? In India "our will is our law." How great is the responsibility of the British Government! As the Poet declares:—

> "Hear it, ye Senates—hear this truth sublime;
> He who allows of murder, shares the crime."

The impossibility of detecting murder with the allowance of this custom is apparent.

The late Rev. W. Ward thus describes the dying circumstances of a heathen by the Ganges:—"Just before or after being immersed, they spread the mud of the river on the breast, &c., of the dying man, and with one of their fingers write on this mud the name of some deity; they also pour water down his throat, shout the name of different deities in his ears, and, by this anxiety after his future happiness, hurry him into eternity, *and in many cases, it is to be feared, prevent recovery where it might reasonably be expected.* Some persons who are carried down to the river side revive and return home again; but scarcely any instances are known of persons surviving after the half immersion in water. *In cases of sudden and alarming sickness, many are actually murdered by these violent means of sending men to Gunga.*" The difficulty of detecting murder, in the cruelties connected with this horrid rite, is evident. "Private murder is practised to a dreadful extent among the Hindoos, and is exceedingly facilitated, and detection prevented, by the practice of hurrying sick persons to the banks of the river and burning them as soon as dead. Many anecdotes on this subject might be given."*

Dr. Johns in his Pamphlet, before referred to, speaks of *a man drowned in sport.* "Some years ago, as Shivu

---

* View of the Hindoos, vol. iii. p. 269. 291.

Shiromee (the Brahmun who related the fact to the Rev. W. Ward) was returning from bathing, with Kashenaut, another Brahmun, they saw a poor old man sitting on the bank of the river, and asked him what he was doing there? He replied that he was destitute of friends, and was about to renounce life in the Ganges. Kashenaut urged him not to delay then, if he was come to die. But the man seemed to hesitate, and replied that it was very cold. The Brahmun (hinting to his companion that he wished to see the sport before he returned home!) reproached the poor trembling wretch for his cowardice;. and, seizing his hand, dragged him to the edge of the bank, where he made him sit down, rubbed over him the purifying clay of the river, and ordered him to repeat the proper incantations. While he was, with his eyes closed, repeating these forms, he slipped down and sunk into the water, which was very deep, and perished."* Was not this murder?

In the Circular Letters of the Missionaries at Serampore, accounts are given of the drowning of two lepers, at Futwa and Alumgung. "On hearing the people belonging to the boat say that a man was going to be drowned at Futwa, I looked out, and saw the poor creature without fingers or toes, but in other respects apparently healthy. He was eating very heartily, and surrounded by several people who appeared to have conducted him to the spot. The bank being high, I could not get out of the boat till we got to a considerable distance from the place where the man sat. As I was running towards the spot, I heard the people on the top of the boat call out, 'He his drowned! he is drowned!' His attendants, who appeared to be his relatives, had assisted him down the bank of the river; but whether they pushed him in, or whether he got into the water of his own accord, I cannot tell; but the bank was so steep at the place that he could not possibly get out again. He made great efforts to reach the side, but had he been a good swimmer he could not have got out, the stream was so rapid. I saw him struggle much, before he sunk to rise no more. I endeavoured to impress on the people who attended him the heinousness of the crime they had perpetrated; but they smiled at my concern, and said they had only complied with the wishes of the deceased, who had neither hands nor feet." (Nov. 1812).

---

* Facts and Opinions relative to the burning of Widows, p. 70.

"A Hindoo, of the writer cast," says the Rev. J. Moore, "informed me he saw a Hindoo carpenter drowned, because he had the leprosy. He was carried from one of the Ghauts at Alumgung in a boat, in the presence of a large assembly of people, and when in deep water put overboard. Two large earthen pots, one filled with sand, the other with barley, were fastened to his shoulders. The man sunk, but after some time floated on the surface of the water. The people in the boat rowed after him and took him up, but made sure work of it the second time." (Oct. 1813).

"The Kama Morun, or voluntary death, is when a person who is in distress or disgrace, or believes it meritorious to die in the Ganges, forms the resolution of parting with life in the sacred stream. Some of them abstain from food that they may expire in the holy place; but the greater number drown themselves in the presence of the surrounding multitude. Their children and other relations generally attend them. *It is no uncommon thing for a father to be pushed again into the river by his sons, if he attempt to swim back to land!*"* Are not these acts of murder? Must not India be greatly defiled with blood?

The Editor of the Bengal Hurkaru very judiciously and forcibly observes, on this subject, "We will make a remark or two on a topic that has been brought to public notice in the Columbian Press Gazette, and which has been attempted to be palliated on the ground of its being a Hindoo rite. It would be idle to waste words to prove that if it could be clearly made out in evidence that a sick man was put to death by his relations, by Brahmuns, or by any body else, when carried down to the river, or by any other means, and whether against the prayers of the sick man or not, at least within the jurisdiction of the Supreme Court, it would be murder; just as the performance of a Suttee would be murder.† *The pretence that the Hindoo rules and religion authorized such practices, would be equally unavailable in one case as in the other.* The fact that death is anticipated by violent means may be denied, and we certainly are in possession of no other proof than common report; but, *if such facts do exist, we do not con-*

---

* Burder's Mis. Anec. p: 37.

† The Suttee is not permitted in the jurisdiction of the Supreme Court of Calcutta; that is, within the Mahratta ditch or about the bounds of the circular road. Auth.

ceive that the presence of Police Peons is any protection at all against abuse; certainly not if they are Hindoos. We should be glad to know by what authority it is that dying persons are exposed by the river side; and would thank any of our readers, learned in the languages and customs of the Hindoos, to give us precise information; for without violence, and without the use of suffocation, the mere exposure on a muddy bank, under a burning sun, of a person dangerously ill, cannot be considered by any reasonable man but as an act approaching *very near* to murder, under whatever pretext it is done.

"There is a kind of fanaticism prevalent among Europeans in India, which is a melancholy proof of the force of habit, and of the puerile tendency to extremes that disgraces even intelligent men, who adopt theories that their self-love becomes interested to support. We allude not to fanaticism in the dogmas of Christianity, but a fanaticism that is ready to go all lengths in palliation and support of the most revoling doctrines of Hindoo superstition. This turn of mind, of which we have perceived many traces in the writings of Europeans who have been in India, naturally arises from a wish to dignify those things which have been the subject of their studies and investigation; and might be excused or pitied did it not lead to laxity of moral reasoning, and to sneers at real religion. *Their religion is one monstrous tissue of absurdity and cruelty—absurd in doctrine, cruel in practice; which no ingenuity in allegory, and no sophistry, can make reconcileable with common sense and humanity!* Prudence may induce us to tolerate, prudence may induce us to be silent, but it is too much to speak of such a system with respect. Such conduct cannot but excite indignation.

"There may be purposes to be served, and vanities to be gratified;—the Philologist, who has mastered the difficulties of Sanscrit, and explored with tedious care the occult meaning of Hindoo Mythology, may gratify the pride of a futile labour by a preposterous estimation of the value of his attainments:—the *cold Politician,* who looks only to the preservation of power, may be tremblingly anxious to prevent all alarm, and to throw discredit upon all attempts conversion:—and the concealed Unbeliever in Christianity may be delighted at an opportuity of instituting presumptuous and impious comparisons; or insinuating that, when once the order of nature is quitted, there is no rule of judgment, and one mystery and one miracle is *prima facie* as probable as another. But every candid believer, every friend to morals, to human nature, and to happiness, ought severely to examine his own mind, and deeply pause, before he is led away by literary zeal and vanity, by political interest and prejudice, or by polemical hate, to step forward the concealed or the avowed defender of *a system that is degrading to man, and has entailed slavery, wickedness, and misery upon millions of millions of men.*"

The inhumanity of the Native police shows the difficulty of allowing this custom to continue, consistently with the principles of justice and the well-being of society. On this subject it is remarked, in one of the Calcutta Papers, "In order to prevent the continuance of these inhuman practices, we deemed it right to call attention to them, and to suggest the necessity of adopting some regulations, making it incumbent on the Brahmuns to have the authority of a Native doctor, at least for pronouncing a fellow-creature so far past the hope of recovery as to justify, according to their own laws and customs, the administration of the inhuman ceremony adverted to. But we are told there is no necessity for this; and why? because the John Bull is persuaded that the cruel practices of Hindoism are, in many instances, exaggerated, therefore prevention and inquiry are unnecessary! We are told that police peons are stationed at the Ghauts to prevent such murderous scenes as are said to occur. These, it must be admitted by all who know their character, are bad securities against the perpetration of inhumanity: fellows who look on with the utmost indifference at any scene of cruelty, whether it be a widow burning, a man drowning, or a poor diseased creature suffocated by a Brahmun. As for their reporting to a Coroner any thing of the kind, even if they did so (which we believe they would not), he has no control beyond the *Mahratta ditch;* nor indeed have the police peons above referred to, for they are under the jurisdiction of the Zillah magistrates. We hope the Zillah magistrates will deem it their duty to institute some inquiry into this matter; for humanity loudly demands it." (Hurk. Aug. 25, 1825).

Palliation of the murderous nature of this rite appears absurd. A correspondent, in one of the public papers, proves that no dependence can be placed on the unprincipled Native officers. "The idea of chokedars interfering in this business appears ridiculous to those who are at all acquainted with the nature of the country. I have frequently passed a dozen villages and Ghauts without seeing or hearing of a single chokedar. How are these people to inform the Coroner, or any body else, of what is passing in these places, when they themselves are often ignorant of it? Unless there be a particular and strict injunction laid upon them by the higher powers (which I do not suppose is the case), it is absurd to suppose they would interfere in such cases. (A Subscriber)."*

The Calcutta John Bull thus attempts to palliate these evils:—"We feel at all times a satisfaction in being enabled to vindicate the Native, and particularly the Brahminical character, from the charges so often thrown upon it, as disfigured by all that is dishonest, selfish, and cruel; but we withhold not our assent to the assertion that there is much to lament over, after all that has been exaggerated has been reduced within the fair proportions of truth. We leave to the indiscriminate admirer of all that is Hindoo to speak his praises of a faith which is a disgrace to human reason, and a lamentable instance of human folly; and to arrogate to its priests virtues altogether incompatible with the doctrines and duties which, as ministers of this religion, they must teach and practice. But it is possible to err on the other side: and when the Brahmuns were represented as in the actual commission of murder, and that, as we are led to understand, within the very jurisdiction of the Supreme Court of Calcutta, we found that inquiry into the subject was due, if not to them, at least to the character of British justice itself. The fact of a person being stationed at the Ghauts within the jurisdiction, whose business it is, among other duties, to prevent the rights of Hindoo sepulture being given to any one bearing the marks of a violent death, until due investigation should be made, certainly seems to us altogether irreconcileable with the alleged occurrence of Brahmuns causing the death of Natives brought

---

* "When the father of a Hindoo family is ill, and conceived to be past hope of recovery, it is not unusual for the sons to take him to the side of a river, and suffocate him in the mud; and then, by way of preventing the widow from sharing in his property, they work upon her superstitious fears to induce her to burn herself with his body. Yet persons are not wanting who will talk of the innocence of a superstition that authorises children to smother their father and burn their mother." Wheatley's Letter to the President of the Board of Control on the latent Resources of India. Ori. Her. vol. i. p. 284.

to the river side to expire, before the disease was far from having overcome the vital energies.

"It is a question, not unaccompanied with difficulty, to say the precise moment at which death has assuredly made good his position, if we may so speak. And admitting that, in cases where this is clear, the practice referred to is not to be interfered with, as arising out of the religion of the Natives, some caution we think is requisite in affixing the stigma of murder to the acts of the Brahmuns. *We readily admit, however, that a practice, which on many accounts we should rejoice to see abolished, may be, and no doubt is, perverted to the most inhuman purposes.* The testimony supporting this is too strong to be denied; but we have as little doubt that where the proof is clear, that the officiating Brahmuns contributed in any way to hasten the death of the sufferer under disease, punishment would be awarded them both in Calcutta and in the Mofussil, where they persisted in extinguishing life against the entreaties and protestations of the sick man. The remark that, in the case of Natives being seized with the Cholera Morbus, there is an imminent risk that before the constitution can rally the cruel rites of Hindoism may have extinguished the only chance of life remaining, is highly deserving notice. It points to circumstances demanding a more than ordinary vigilance on the part of those whose duty it may be to prevent the violation of the laws, as they provide for the last rites that are to be performed by a dying Hindoo; and, if those officers are not clothed with sufficient authority to act in such cases, every humane and Christian motive concurs in demanding that they should."

To this it is replied, by the Editor of the India Gazette, —"The existence of the inhuman practice complained of is no longer denied: but the writer evidently labours under a very important mistake on the subject. He seems to think that the only danger of murder resulting from it is, that the Brahmuns may administer this inhuman rite to those who are not actually dead, owing to the difficulty, where great and sudden prostration of strength is a symptom of the disease, of ascertaining the precise moment when death 'has assuredly made good his position.' From this it would appear that the writer imagines that the Brahmuns never do administer this barbarous ceremony until their victim is pronounced dead, or until they actually think him so: but the fact is, that it is by no means necessary that the poor creature should be dead, nor do they wait for this. The moment he is pronounced in a dangerous state by any Native Doctor, or even by themselves, he is hurried down to the river, and subjected to a treatment, enough in itself, even in a disorder by no means dangerous, to bring on immediate death, as it no doubt often does. But if the writer wants a proof of the little reliance to be placed on the judgment or humanity of those who pronounce these miserable victims of a barbarous superstition to be past the hope of recovery, and therefore direct them to be treated as we have described, he will find it in a Subscriber's letter (p. 313). Was he aware that *many who have endured these brutal ceremonies, on the plea that they were dying, have actually recovered? that their recovery entails disgrace on them? and that whole villages of these degraded Hindoos exist within a day's journey of us?* We confess with shame that we were ignorant of the fact; but it speaks volumes as to the necessity of some regulation to prevent the unhappy victims of a dreadful disease from being, under false pretexts that they are in a state in which Hindoo superstition enjoins it, subjected to the cruelties we have denounced. If it should be deemed an unjustifiable interference with religious prejudice, to prohibit the application of Gunga labh to any but those who are actually dead, still it might be incumbent on the Brahmuns to have the sanction of the native doctors appointed by the Company, before they could perform the rite: and surely if it is illegal in the case of the burning of widows to use force, it must be equally so in that we are noticing."

"Since our last," says another public Journal in Calcutta, "the John Bull has put forth the following notice respecting the Ghaut Murders as denounced by us:—'A Correspondent has pointed out to us that the person (not properly speaking a Police Peon) stationed at the Ghauts, whose business is to superintend the burning, &c., of bodies, always prevents those that are brought there from being disposed of according to the Hindoo customs, should any marks of violence appear on them, until the same is duly reported to the proper authorities, with whose duties it would be obviously incompatible to permit the alleged murderous practice of the Brahmuns.' The absurdity of regarding any regulations like the above as a security against the cruelties we have stated must be sufficiently apparent to any one at all acquainted with the subject. If marks of violence appear, then it seems the circumstance is reported to the proper authorities by the Peons (not Police) at the Ghauts; but who ever heard of marks of violence being produced by suffocating a sick man with mud and water; and exposing him, while under the influence of a dangerous disease, to the heat of the sun and the vicissitudes of the weather, both before and after the administration of these destructive ceremonies? It is in this manner that the murders alluded to are perpetrated, and the fact has indeed been partly acknowledged to us by a Hindoo, and defended. He denied that any but OLD MEN were RELUCTANT VICTIMS of these cruelties; but with respect to them, he said, *however they might entreat or implore to be saved or be allowed to die at home, they were not listened to, but forced to the water side, to receive what is, with the Hindoos, deemed more important than the extreme unction of the Romish church.* But we disbelieve this; for we have since been informed by a friend, who witnessed a circumstance of this kind, that *old or young, willing or unwilling, are equally subjected to this inhuman mode of terminating their existence.* It is said that the Native Doctor employed by the family first pronounces the sick individual incurable; but it is needless to say that this is no sufficient security against the perpetration of these murderous rites, in cases where, but for them, the patient might recover. If it would not be going further than the Government might feel justifiable, *it would be a wise and humane Regulation, to prohibit the administration of Gunga jal* (Ganges water) *until the patient has actually expired.* In order not to shock the prejudices of the Hindoos, with respect to its importance as to future beatitude that they should die by the water side, it might still be permitted them to carry the sick who are dangerously ill down to the river side, provided they kept them there under shelter, and not exposed as they now are, without covering, to the noonday sun or a tropical shower; enough of themselves to produce a fatal termination of any disease, without the other barbarous aids; the application of which we would have prevented if possible. It would be well for those who profess Christianity, and would be thought as humane as their neighbours, to inquire into the subject of the evils to which we have endeavoured to call the notice of the Authorities, before they make light of them and deny the attempt to provide any remedy for them. They would not then betray their ignorance, by talking of Police Peons and the Coroner of Calcutta as the safeguards against inhuman practices, over which they have no manner of control.'' There appears, by the experience of the regulation and consequent legalization of Suttees in India, no intermediate measure really beneficial to society, between entire neglect of the practice and its abolition as murder. The dead body might be brought to the river, but if the sick lie at the mercy of Native Doctors, Darogahs, Peons, &c., there can be no security that they will not be murdered by this cruel rite. The prohibition of the exposure of the sick appears the dictate of justice and humanity,*

The propriety of adopting measures for the melioration of these evils, and even for the suppression of the practice, has engaged the attention of many. The opinion of the Editors of the India Gazette and the Calcutta John Bull has been given; the Bengal Hurkaru for Aug. 24, 1825, contains the following judicious remarks:—" *Ghaut Murders.*—From all we can learn on the distressing subject, the Cholera rages among the natives with unabated fury. It appears, from an expression in the John Bull, that regular reports are received from the different Ghauts (where, we presume, the bodies of the dead are consumed) of the extent of the mortality. If this be the case, we wish at the same time that reports could be furnished of the number of sick brought down to *these Ghauts to be murdered* by those legalized butchers of their fellow creatures, the Brahmuns, under the pretence that they are past all hope of recovery. In this state, we understand, many are brought to the river side, and their existence quickly put an

* "It is scarcely credible that so horrible an abuse of a superstitious custom should be allowed to exist in the presence of European residents and the vicinity of Magistrates, who have, in this case, nothing to do but to interpose for the preservation of life, without interfering with any Hindoo Law. What shall we think of that spirit of religious toleration which allows the young and strong, as soon as disease attacks them, to be carried down to the water's edge, and there stifled with mud, or maddened by the burning sun, or left at *low water mark* as night comes on? What shall we think of the liberal humanity of Magistrates, which, rather than meddle with a native custom, would stand by and see a struggling and imploring victim, whose health might be restored by a few hours' care, placed breast high in the advancing tide and overwhelmed with slime and water till his feeble cries are silenced for ever? Such scenes are witnessed by those who pass the ghauts or flights of steps which lead down to the Ganges." (See Review of India's Cries. 1st edit. Meath. Rep. Dec. 1829.)

end to by the administration of what is called *Gunga jal;* which means dipping the poor unhappy victims of a destroying superstition under water, and plentifully stuffing their mouths with the mud of the Ganges. The same policy which restrains the Government from any attempt to prohibit the burning of widows on the funeral pile, may possibly operate to prevent any attempt to put a stop to the cruelties we have described; but, at least, some means might be taken to ascertain the fact that the unhappy beings put out of the world, in a manner so revolting to humanity, are actually in *articulo mortis* when brought down to be submitted to this last inhuman ceremony: for unless they are, we understand, those engaged in putting a period to their existence would be liable to the penalty attaching to the crime of MURDER. In cases where the miserable victim is capable of showing any reluctance to be so sacrificed, and does evince it, interference to prevent it would surely be more than justifiable, *it would become a sacred duty, the neglect of which would not be merely cruel but criminal*. But how is this to be discerned? or who is to look after it? The people in authority about the Ghauts, which are the scenes of such sacrifices, the chokedars, &c., are generally, we believe, Hindoos, and by no means likely to discharge this duty faithfully, even if it be enjoined on them, which we greatly doubt. *Who then is to perform it?* This is a question which we presume the Zillah Magistrates can best answer; but humanity loudly demands that the matter should be investigated; and we hope it will attract their attention, Where are all the Native Doctors about whom we heard so much in former days when the Cholera prevailed? Many of these, we suppose, are Mussulmans, and, as they have no prejudice in favour of the inhuman practice we have adverted to, they might be very properly employed to prevent it, where interference is deemed justifiable. We imagine there could be no impediment to the promulgation of an order to this effect:—That before any poor unfortunate being should be dragged down to the Ghaut, to be suffocated by the Brahmuns, it should be incumbent on them to have the authority of the Native Doctor, in the same manner that they are compelled to obtain the sanction of a Magistrate to the burning of a widow. We hope this subject will receive the consideration it merits. We may be wrong in supposing there is a remedy for the evil, but we have felt it our duty to endeavour to bring the subject forward, in order that some means may be speedily devised to check the perpetration of these legalized MURDERS, if the entire prevention of them should be deemed impossible."

"The exposure of the sick by the side of the Ganges surely requires a regulation securing greater comforts to these dying persons. Such a regulation might easily be framed as would gradually put a stop to these dreadful cruelties inflicted on persons in the agonies of death, and preventing the recovery of others suffering under temporary maladies. Highly honourable as is the determination of Government not to interpose in the religion of their Indian subjects,—*yet cruelties and murders, not authorized by the Hindoo laws, have surely no claim to toleration.*"*

To legalize a cruel practice, pregnant with murder, is a highly exceptionable policy. The concession here made is very important, viz.—"*The chokedars, &c., are generally, we believe, Hindoos, and by no means likely to discharge this duty faithfully, even if it be enjoined on them.*" The preservation of life is the imperious duty of a well regulated Government,† and this cannot be accomplished with the permission of the practice. Hundreds and thousands have been murdered by the permission of Suttees. The perpetrators of these customs are guilty of murder—

"Murder most foul, strange, and unnatural."

The propriety and utility of medical attention to the sick in the circumstances here contemplated is deserving of particular regard. "The number of people in Calcutta who fell victims to the Cholera in the course of this week (says the Editor of the Somachar Durpun, Sep. 3, 1825) has been estimated at an average of *four hundred a day*. Many, we believe, attacked with a slight sickness, give themselves up to death, through fear; the more so when

---

* Remarks on the Immolations of India (Parbury), p. 23.

† "When the Russian Government caused to be conveyed back to Japan a number of its mariners who had been shipwrecked on the Russian coast, the Japanese Government thanked them; but observed, at the same time, that *they might either leave them or take them back as they might think fit*. These are the sentiments of an ignorant and barbarous policy, though they have sometimes been mistaken for greatness of mind. But no sentiment is great that is not humane, and no nation is civilized whose government is not solicitous for the safety of the citizens." Ori. Herald. Vol. ii. p. 194.

they are taken to the river, which makes them despair of life, and thus is their end hastened. We have known that those who immediately after the attack of the disease applied to European Doctors have been recovered by their medical assistance; it is indeed a matter of great pity that persons should not apply for medicine till it is too late. This disorder has also prevailed at Serampore and its neighbouring villages, but not with much violence. Those patients to whom we have given medicine in the early stage of the disease have recovered; and we are happy to say that, by *our appointing a Physician and rendering medical assistance, many lives have been saved.* Two days since a patient of the Boistub caste was found lying helpless on Joogul Uddies Ghaut at Serampore, and we immediately sent our Doctor to afford him relief; and on his giving the poor man some medicine he recovered on the third day."

The following circumstance shows the good effects of the friendly interference of Europeans in India, in preventing Hindoo cruelty to the sick:—"A bearer who had lived for a long time in a family was taken ill, and was on the point of being carried to the banks of the river, for the purpose of being given over to the care of the Ganges, to be conveyed to heaven. Before he was taken away, he requested to be allowed to speak to his old mistress; and, on being taken to her, he begged her to interfere to procure for him a respite of three days. On her speaking, some remarks were made by his friends, as *to the expense which would be incurred if they were to comply with this request!* His mistress promised to pay all the expense that might be incurred; and the result was, that the man who was so near death five or six years ago is now alive in Calcutta in the execution of his business."*

A missionary writes on the Ganges:—

"Two or three days ago, I witnessed a scene more shocking than any I ever saw in this place. A poor weaver was brought here, and cast into the river, with a pan full of water tied round his waist to make him sink; but the stream was shallow, and he was taken out, *after being in the water a day and a night.* Hearing of the circumstance, I went to him, and found the poor man only affected with rheumatic pains. I had him brought to my house, and I hope he will be restored to health in a fortnight. What

---

* Beng. Hurk. Aug. 1823. Asi. Journ., March, 1824.

adds to the horror of this narration, is, that the perpetrators of this intended murder were the mother and brother of the unhappy Hindoo!"

On this interesting subject, which has engaged the attention of humane gentlemen in India, and of which more will be seen in the appendix, it may be interesting to insert an extract from a communication of the Rev. A. Sutton, of Balasore, Orissa, March, 1827. "It is now a matter of conscience whether to attend to those who require medicine for the body, or to seek after those who will hear for their souls. Perhaps some will say, 'I think there is no room for hesitation when a person is dying, and you can possibly give him assistance which will save his life; it seems clear enough.' Perhaps if that individual could feel the responsibility which rests upon a missionary, to preach as far as he can among the Heathen the unsearchable riches of Christ, he would hesitate as I do. I have met with an instance of real gratitude to day. A poor fisherman whom I was successful in curing, not only expressed himself thankful, but brought a nice dish of fish for my breakfast, as the first fruits of his recovery. My fame as a doctor, of both bodies and souls, seems to be widely extending; for I have had people with all sorts of diseases and accidents to cure. With surgical cases I of course can do nothing, but refer them to the Doctor. Mr. B—— was surprised the other morning, while walking out for health, to see the people come to me as though I had been twenty years in the place. An old lady, who brought her child to be cured of cholera, gave as her reason that she had heard of my fame. I visited a young woman who was attacked with cholera, and just as she was recovering her husband was seized with it. The mother exclaimed, 'Oh, Sir, she is well enough! but save my son,' and instantly fell at my feet, with both hands joined, to entreat me. I was successful in both cases. The son is now fast recovering, and the old lady is the most grateful Hindoo I have met with. Calling to take some sago (which, notwithstanding caste, he ate), she fell at my feet, gratefully exclaiming, 'Ah, Sir, you have preserved my boy.'"

The following letter from a native was addressed to the Rev. W. Bampton, at Juggernaut, and shows the acceptableness of kind attention to the Hindoos in sickness. The original now lies before the author:—

"Most worth
Sir,
I have the honour to acquaint you that I am Sick by the fever this for cannot stand nor walk neither Rise from slip, but pass yesterday at Evening here did you order if will you go to-morrow then I will give you some physic, and I cannot go for my misfortune and did not Cure, therefore I pray before you I am very poor man and orphan So Gracious Grant me grace to aboid from this fever and always to be nourished as any Room. I am Sir your Most obedient humble Servant Fukeerchunder Doss."

"It is pleasant to my feelings," says a late resident in India, in a letter dated Salisbury, May, 1828, "that I have ever been made the instrument of delivering any of the Hindoos from such horrid deaths. It used to cost me about three rupees a month for medicine. I always found them willing to take it; and in many instances they came to our house for it, so that my husband has been called up twice in a night to administer medicine to the sick. When we have gone out an hour in the morning, we have frequently found three or four in the verandah waiting our return; but these natives had been accustomed to receive medicine from the Mission family. I think a missionary in another part of the country would find a little difficulty to get the natives to take medicine from a strange person; but he must act in that case as in all others, with patience and perseverence. The Mission House at Serampore has always been, and still is, an asylum for the sick and distressed. Mrs. M—— is quite a nursing mother to the natives. When I left India, our dear brethren had a fine boy under their care that was found by the river side, left there to perish, but was taken up by a Christian woman, and put into the Bengalee school. He has since been educated in the college, and is now preaching the gospel to his countrymen. I wish I had property, I would establish a Humane Society for the sick in India, and again administer medicine to them myself. I hope I shall meet many of them in a better world, where medicine will not be needed. My heart's desire and prayer to God for them is, that they may be saved."*

"In the course of this day's march," says the late Bishop Heber, when near Shahjehanpore, "a circumstance occurred which proves I think how much the people of this country look up to the English for help and counsel in all emergencies. I was going along a jungly piece of road, when I

* See also G. B. Repos. Ap. 1829, p. 157.

saw a little cluster of travellers of the lower class surrounding somebody on the ground. As soon as they saw me, they immediately ran up, saying that one of their friends was sick, and they begged me to look at him and give him medicine. What struck me was, the immediate impulse which led these men to suppose, on seeing a European riding along the road, that he was likely to help and advise them! Surely, if this opinion is general, it must be one of the best holds we have on our Indian empire."*

"At Broach," says the same intelligent traveller, "is one of those remarkable institutions which have made a good deal of noise in Europe, as instances of Hindoo benevolence to inferior animals; *I mean hospitals for sick and infirm beasts, birds, and insects.* I was not able to visit it, but Mr. Corsellis described it as a very dirty and neglected place, which, though it has considerable endowments in lands, only serves to enrich the Brahmuns who manage it. They have really animals of several different kinds there, not only those which are accounted sacred by the Hindoos, as monkeys, peacocks, &c., but horses, dogs, and cats; and they have also in little boxes an assortment of lice and fleas. It is not true that they feed those pensioners on the flesh of beggars hired for the purpose. The Brahmuns say that insects, as well as the other inmates of their infirmary, are fed with vegetables only, as rice, &c. How the insects thrive I did not hear; but the old horses and dogs, nay the peacocks and apes, are allowed to starve; the only creatures said to be in any tolerable plight are some milch cows, which may be kept from other motives than charity."†

The beneficial influence of Christianity, even in an indirect manner, appears in the real benevolence of the Rajah of Tanjore (Swartz's pupil), and forms a striking contrast to this attention to animals, and insects, when the human species are neglected. "Chatteram is a Hindoo charitable institution, established by the present Rajah, not merely for the maintenance of Brahmuns, but for the poor of every description. This charitable institution has saved many hundreds from perishing, when a severe famine and the cholera prevailed some years ago. There are also two hospitals attached to it, one for men, and another for women suffering by sickness."‡ On the necessity and utility of

---

* Journ., vol. i. p. 536. See also, p. 466.

† Vol. ii. p. 171. ‡ Vol. ii. p. 461.

efforts of this nature generally throughout India, see the Appendix.

These statements admit of abundant confirmation. When shall Britain bear the voice of reason and humanity, and above all of Christianity, demanding from her the suppression of every inhuman and murderous custom in India?

Colonel Dow, in his "History of Hindostan," has a section entitled "A Plan for restoring Bengal to its former prosperity," in which he says, "All religions must be tolerated in Bengal, except in the practice of *some inhuman customs, which the Mahomedans have already in a great measure destroyed. We must not permit young widows in their virtuous enthusiasm to throw themselves on the funeral pile of their dead husbands; nor the sick and aged to be drowned when their friends despair of their lives. These are particular usages, established by time into a law, which our humanity must destroy. Let no women burn themselves with their husbands, or dying persons be exposed by their friends.* To leave the natives to their own laws would be to consign them to anarchy and confusion."*

Dr. Buchanan remarks, upon the above suggestions,—"How many thousands of our subjects in Bengal have perished in the flames, and in the river, since the period when the above sentence was written! How many thousand lives would have been preserved, had the voice of this writer been attended to by the nation! So far from the Suttee being a voluntary act on the part of the widow, she is sometimes forcibly detained that she may not dishonour her family. Towns, as Nuddea on the Ganges, &c., are appropriated for the residence of such as have run away, and thus degraded themselves and lost their caste. The immersion of half the body of a person, supposed to be dying, in the water of the Ganges, must often occasion premature death. It is optional, not commanded. Though very common on the banks of the Ganges, it is reprobated in many places at a distance from it. The abolition of it would not be more difficult than that of the Sahamoron (Suttee)."†

"The removal," says the late Rev. W. Ward, "of the dying to the banks of the Ganges,—the voluntary immola-

* Vol. iii. pp. 128—143.

† Mem. Ecc. Esta. for British India, pp. 94.100. See also Grant's Obs. on the State of Society in India, Par. Papers, 1813, p. 60.

tions at places the resort of pilgrims,—and the burning of widows alive, entail so much misery on the Hindoos that *every humane heart is rent in pieces whenever these horrid practices are brought into public notice.* The great success which has attended the benevolent exertions of Government, in certain cases, encourages us to hope that the hand of mercy will, sooner or later, heal the wounds of a country bleeding at every pore from the fangs of superstition. These cruelties can have so little sanction from any form of religion, are so abhorrent to every humane feeling, and have in some instances been prevented with so much ease, that one can scarcely forbear wishing that *more may be done to prevent such plain violations of the duties men owe to themselves and to society.*"*

The Rev. J. H. Hough, Chaplain on the Madras Establishment, in his "Reply to the Abbe Dubois," demonstrates the facility of the suppression of Hindoo cruelties:—"I maintain the abolition of every practice that outrages the feelings and sympathies of human nature, and of which British law would take cognizance, would tend to confirm our political power in the East. It might alienate the minds of the interested few who profit by thesei mmolations; but it would conciliate the bulk of the Natives, and attach them more cordially to our Government. Remove every barbarous superstition that paralyses the affections of the soul, and you will instantly perceive the feelings of humanity begin to revive. Each cord entwined about the heart will soon vibrate to the sounds of parental, filial, and fraternal love; and even the Hindoo, no longer a misanthrope, or deaf and blind to the claims of society, shall own and rejoice in the relative ties by which man is bound to man. The heart-melting gratitude with which the Rajpoot mothers presented at the feet of Colonel Walker the children preserved through his humane perseverence;† the conduct of the widow, rescued from the funeral pile at Chicacole, towards her benefactress, and the subsequent behaviour of her relatives,‡ are alone sufficient to vindicate the Hindoos' claims to the feelings of humanity, and to show that these anticipations will, in all human probability, be realized,

* View of the Hindoos, vol. iii. p. 284.

† See Infanticide in India, p. 60; and Book ii. p. 173.

‡ A woman was rescued by a lady and afterwards received by her friends. Her gratitude was very great.

when the obstructions that now prevent the exercise of those feelings shall be done away."*

"As to the practicability of suppressing this wretched custom," says the Rev. S. Sutton, late Missionary in Bengal, "I am scarcely capable of giving an opinion. Every Indian custom appears so gigantic in its nature, and is so firmly imbedded in the affections of the people, that human means appear but little in opposing it. Two measures may be pointed out which are certainly lawful in themselves, and which can be immediately put into execution without the aid of the civil power. The first is, small pamphlets might be written on this subject, both in English and the native languages, and these should be extensively circulated among Europeans and Hindoos; by this means a spirit of inquiry will probably arise, and it will become a matter of public discussion. The second measure is the one you have alluded to, namely *a Humane Society.* I have known many cases where individual benevolence has been extended towards lepers, and others, who have been left to perish; but, if *a general Society could be formed for this object in the Metropolis of British India, it would soon extend its ramifications to all parts of the empire, and the victims snatched from the jaws of destruction by its influence would richly repay it for its labours.* And what is more consonant with Christianity than this? The Christian is fully taught by the Gospel to relieve distress wherever he finds it, without any regard to name or country."

The editor of the Christian Observer remarks, respecting the sanguinary rites of the Hindoo, "They are of a nature too criminal to be permitted under any regular government. It is impossible to regard without horror the murders and atrocities which are openly practised in India under the name of religion. These are practices which come under the designation of enormous crimes, and ought not to exist under a British Government, and which it might be proved that Government have it in their power easily and safely to suppress."†

The late C. Grant, Esq., in a letter dated Sep. 1811, thus expresses himself on this subject: "I would not be understood to imply that the British Government has done all that it might and ought to do, in relation to the horrid superstition (the worship of Juggernaut) in question. *I*

* Hough's Reply to the Abbe Dubois, p. 282. † March, 1813.

conceive that, as a Government, we might and should forbid all immolation of human victims, or sacrifice in any mode of human life; and that without using compulsion or violating the toleration allowed to the Hindoos. It might do far more than it has yet done for the safe and gradual introduction and diffusion of Gospel light in India—the only effectual cure for all the deplorable evils of idolatry and immorality which exist there. It has long been an interesting subject to me, and I regret I have not been able to render more service to a cause which, well understood, ought to be supported by the Politician and the Christian, since it is recommended by the soundest dictates of policy, as well as by the infinitely higher considerations of true religion."*

The late Hon. J. H. Harington, Member of Council, Calcutta, in a highly interesting document relative to the Suttee, justly observes, "As far as the New Regulation (enforced at Saugur by a military guard) opposed an established usage, originating in superstition, it may be considered a precedent for prohibiting and punishing other inhuman practices of a superstitious nature. As I have never heard of any resistance being offered, or objection made to the execution of the penal law above-mentioned, I cannot but think it affords some ground of presumption that other superstitious and inhuman practices, such particularly as the Suttee sacrifice, though sanctioned in a certain degree by the shastra and by popular opinion, might be suppressed by a legislative enactment with equal safety and success."†

Lord Teignmouth, in his interesting Pamphlet before quoted, shows the humane and beneficial influence of the British Government in India, in abolishing various customs opposed to sound reason and the true interests of the people.‡ Ought not Britain to prosecute this work of mercy, and abolish every inhuman custom that has originated in ignorance and superstition? "Usages originating in Hindoo superstition and customs of immemorial prescription have been discountenanced by the British Administration in Bengal; whilst the laws of the Mahomedans, which derive their authority from the Koran, have been modified, or, in effect, altered, in various instances.

"In trial for murder, the Mahomedan law officers are

---

* Review of Pilgrim Tax in India, Bap. Mag. April, 1828. † See Par. Papers, on the Suttee, July, 1825, vol. v. p. 8—18. ‡ P. 23—38.

required to deliver their opinions, according to the doctrines of certain learned expositors of the law named in the regulations; but, as these expositors admit many distinctions as to the mode of committing murder, the British Government has enacted (Reg. 9, A. D. 1793, S. 75), that no regard shall be paid to these distinctions; but the intention of the criminal, and not the manner or instrument of perpetration, shall constitute the rule for determining the punishment. The Mahomedan law considers *the religious persuasion of witnesses as a bar to the conviction or condemnation of a prisoner*, or, in other words, rejects the testimony of Hindoos. The British Government has most justly abrogated a distinction calculated to defeat the ends of public justice. A person deliberately intending to murder one individual, and accidently killing another, is not by the Mahomedan law held liable to the punishment of murder. The Regulations, in opposition to this rule, declare the homicide under such circumstances murder, and the punishment death. A murderer, though fully convicted, might escape the punishment due to his crime, by *obtaining pardon of, or from a compromise with, such heirs of the deceased as were entitled to demand retaliation.* According to an exposition of the Mahomedan law a father or mother, or grandfather or grandmother, wilfully murdering their child or grandchild, or any person of whom their child or grandchild may be heirs, cannot suffer death by the law of *Kissaas** or Retaliation; nor can such a sentence be passed against a master for the murder of his slave appropriated by his owners to the service of the public, nor against a person wilfully killing another at the desire of the party slain, &c. The Governor in Council has declared to all Hindostan 'the law of retaliation, in these and similar instances, repugnant to the principles of public justice.' In the year 1795 was adopted 'A Regulation for preventing Brahmuns, in the Province of Benares, establishing *koorhs*, wounding or killing their female relations or children, or sitting *Dhurna*;† and for

---

* The Mahomedan law considers the act as a private injury; not a public wrong.

† Hamilton, in his Description of Hindostan, thus describes the practice of *Dhurna*. "In 1807 a Rajghur Brahmun near Amran (in Guzerat), to deter his superior Kirjee kowas from depriving him of some land, led his mother to the gate of Amran and there cut off her head, which had the desired effect. Instances of this sort are frequent in Guzerat, and, on most occasions, the victim not only consents but glories in the

preventing the tribe of Rajkoomars, in that Province, killing their female children." Let Britain pursue the work of meliorating the state of society in India, until every custom opposed to the principles of humanity and justice shall be abolished. In what is here stated much has been done for the real welfare of India. "O si sic omnia!"

The influence of the British magistrate in India, in suppressing Hindoo cruelties, is very strikingly displayed in the abolition of self-murder at Allahabad.* The Asiatic Journal for August, 1827, contains the following statement:—"A horrid form of self-murder has happily been put down by a Regulation of the Government, and the wise and firm application of it by the present truly worthy judge and magistrate of Allahabad, Mr. Colvin, who said, he had not suffered any one to drown himself at the junction of the Ganges and Jumna. He has declared that, if any one aids another, either with a boat, or assists in tying on the earthen pots, or helps the individual to throw himself into the river, the person or persons so acting shall be regarded as accessary to the murder and dealt with accordingly. An instance of this self-drowning, Mr. C. said, had not occurred since he had had the government of Allahabad; nor will he suffer these or any other cruelties, which he has power to prevent. We rejoice to state that this is the judgment of all such judges and magistrates with whom we have had intercourse, in the different Districts; this, in connexion with the fact that the shackles of caste, and Brahminical domination, are much and obviously weakening, is a subject of sincere congratulation to the friends of humanity and piety."

The same respectable Periodical, referring to the cruelties

---

death inflicted. The person who is in many cases the innocent cause of the catastrophe is considered by the Brahminical code as damned for ever, while the wretch who for his own profit perpetrates the murder, is not only held innocent by his fellow citizens, but suffers no pang either of heart or conscience." Vol. i. p. 651. On the abolition of *Traga*, see vol. i. pp. 611, 691, 717, Evan. Mag. May, 1816, pp. 518. Of Hindoo ordeals disused by the British Government see Ward's View, vol. iii. pp. 54—58.

* The nature of this rite is thus described :—"Two Mahratta women had travelled to Allahabad from a great distance, to devote themselves to the Ganges. In vain did the missionary attempt to convince them of the delusion and wickedness of their purpose. After worshipping the river, these women entered a boat, with three others of the same caste; they most unfeelingly tied two earthen jars, filled with water, round the waist of each to make them sink, and saw them perish in the stream!" (Miss. Papers, 1823).

and indecencies of the Churuk Pooja, or Swinging Festival (rites acknowledged by the Brahmuns as not enjoined in their Shastra, and confined to the lowest castes), states that the magistrates in Calcutta are purposing to curtail and prohibit such infractions of the rights of civilized society, and that in actual accordance with the sentiments of the more intelligent Hindoos.

A friend in Calcutta in March, 1823, thus describes these barbarous customs:—"The places of the body which are pierced are, the back, the arms (generally above the elbow), the sides, and the tongue. But the piercing is the least part of what is endured by the sufferers. The tongue being pierced, an iron rod is thrust through it, sometimes carried by the individual himself, and sometimes by one of the group of his attendants. One of these sufferers had the point of a bayonet fixed upon a musket through his tongue and carried before him by the sepoy to whom it belonged, and thus he paraded the streets. Another had a live snake of five or six feet in length, the tail of which was thrust through his tongue, the head and part of the body remaining twirling in frightful shapes above his head. A singular instance of audacity was seen this year: among the numerous groups there was a man having the iron through his tongue with the upper part fastened to the leg of a woman of ill fame, who was carried upon the shoulders of bearers in a chair precisely even with the man's head, and he dancing and frolicking below! Some are so determined to excel, that, in order to insert a very thick rod, the tongue has been so far pierced as to leave merely a shred on each side; and it has happened that one side has given way, leaving the part of the tongue hanging on one side merely by a piece. The number of persons in Calcutta who thus torment themselves cannot, it is supposed, be less than a *thousand*, in all probability it is much greater. Europeans are not likely to hear the tenth, or even a hundreth part of the evil that occurs from these practices. The Natives are not sufficiently attached to each other to think *the maiming or death of their countrymen of importance sufficient to induce them even to relate the fact, unless it is elicited by some special circumstance, or inquiry should lead to the subject.*"*

"The celebration of the Churuk Pooja at Kalee Ghaut,"

* See also Heber's Journal, vol. i. p. 76, 77.

says the Asiatic Journal, "far from falling off becomes every year more revolting; and *the magistrates of Calcutta seem determined to suppress the disgusting exhibitions which take place at the ceremony every year, in the month of April.* Several persons, whose proceedings were more than ordinarily indecent, were taken up by the police and brought before the magistrates." A Native Paper, named *Timira Nasak*, says, "Such a celebration of this festival as was witnessed at Seebpore has never before been known there; many troops of Sunyasees came from different parts of the country, who, in the desperate tortures inflicted on themselves, seemed to partake of the nature of Seeb. One of them, ascending the swing, called out to the people below to whirl him round faster; and about thirty young men attaching themselves to the rope ran round with the utmost rapidity, in consequence of which, the hooks tearing the skin, he fell and would have been killed if he had not been caught by the bystanders. Others followed, but were thus disappointed in their expectation of distinguishing themselves." The subsequent sensible remarks in a Calcutta Paper in April, 1827, are signed *"A Hindoo:"*—"I have been informed that, on the 8th Choitra, a Native of the Western country, on account of some acquired or expected benefit, mutilated his tongue with a knife in the presence of the goddess of Kalee Ghaut; his whole body was covered with blood, and he himself became insensible. On hearing this circumstance I experienced such distress as I am unable to express. How is the folly of the person who cut his tongue to be communicated to the goddess? Such a circumstance has not occurred for a long time. Many people mutilate their little finger to propitiate the goddess; but this wretched man has defeated his brethren, and obtained the chief rank among them. How very grievous and distressing it is that he has lost the power of conversing for life, though he be deserving of punishment! *Howbeit, in consequence of the Honourable Company's possession of this country, similar acts of folly have been almost put an end to among the Natives; and, by analogy, it may be hoped, these diabolical transactions will be completely abolished in a short period.*"*

The following judicious observations, extracted from a Native Paper in Calcatta, prove how very acceptable the

* See Asi. Jour. vol. xxiv. 1827, pp. 768. 492.

suppression of the irregularities and cruelties of the Hindoo and Mohometan festivals would prove to many persons:—"During seven or eight days successively, the *Hori* men make it a constant practice to spoil, with a nasty dye discharged through a syringe, the clothes, and perhaps injure the persons, of passengers, whether respectable or otherwise; and abuse the latter by throwing nuisances against them; and some force a dye impression on the backs of women. If any of the sufferers are provoked, they fall upon them, drag them, or put strings of dirty shoes round their necks. It is no wonder that the cruel behaviour or ill-treatment of the votaries of this festival sometimes occasions bloodshed and loss of lives. At the festival of the *Mohurram*, in which the Mahometans are very apt to maltreat the Hindoos, the police have very judiciously made a rule to place sepoys at those parts of the streets which the Mahometans often frequent on those holidays, for the purpose of taking sticks and other offensive weapons from the people's hands, and prevent their picking quarrels. It is therefore hoped that the worthy magistrates will think it proper to adopt like measures during the continuance of the *Hori* festival, to keep the peace, and to prevent injuries being done to the passengers and the people at large. It may also be prohibited that no person should abuse men and women who are strangers to them; that they should play the Hori at home with their friends and their relatives, within their compounds, and not in the public streets to the annoyance of strangers. We hope that the authority who has the power vested in him will follow the same example."*

But to turn from India: it is highly gratifying to see the subject of the abolition of human sacrifices in Hindostan exciting that attention among the members of the Honourable East India Company which its importance demands.

The following extract is from "The Speech of J. Poynder, Esq., at a General Court of Proprietors of East India Stock, March, 1827," in defence of a Resolution to the following effect: "*That this Court, taking into consideration the continuance of human sacrifices in India, is of opinion that, in the case of all rites or ceremonies involving the destruction of life, it is the duty of a paternal Government to interpose for their prevention; and therefore recommends to the Honourable Court of Directors to transmit*

---

* Oodunta Martunda, March 13, 1827.

such Instructions to India as that Court may deem most expedient for accomplishing this object, consistently with all practicable attention to the feelings of the Natives." This Resolution was carried by a decided majority, only five Proprietors (four of whom were Directors) dividing against it. "The object of the motion (said the eloquent Gentleman) now before the Court, is,—To throw the ample shield of British protection quite as much over every deluded victim who may cast away life as a voluntary sacrifice, as over those who may be sacrificed by force or fraud. Wherever innocuous ceremonics terminate, and blood becomes necessary to the propitiation of 'them that are no gods,' there the motion I have the honour to submit will come into action; its broad principle being that, 'IN THE CASE OF ALL RITES INVOLVING THE DESTRUCTION OF LIFE, *it is the duty of a paternal Government to interfere for their prevention;*' precisely as it is the duty of a parent to save a *foolish* as well as a *wise* child from death, whenever it is in his power. God, in his Providence, having armed the British Government with *the power of saving life in India;* the point for which I contend is, that the Government has a better right to exercise that power, than the victim of superstition has to resist it; and that it is a greater duty in the Government to preserve its own subjects from destruction, than to suffer them to perish. I contend that the wretched victim of a sanguinary delusion has no more right over his own life, on the score of religion, than he has a right over the lives of his fellow-creatures, upon no better pretext. Aud that, therefore, the Government which consents to look on, while these deeds of darkness are doing, is in the eye of God and man, a partaker of the guilt of blood." (p. 233, 234.)* In accordance with these sentiments, the abolition of Ghaut murders is the paramount duty of Britain. "Blood has a voice to reach the skies." May it reach the ears of those who have power to save these victims of superstition, and induce them to suppress these cruelties.

---

* "It may not be generally known that, in consequence of this motion, the Court of Directors were desirous of transmitting such resolution to India; but, on submitting their letter of instructions to the late Board of Control, that Board determined that this resolution, adopted, as it had been, after two days' discussion, should not be sent to India; in consequence of which, the solemn expression of opinion thus recorded at the India House has not officially found its way to our Indian empire." (Bap. Mag. Dec. 1829, p. 521.)

The language of the Almighty to Cain is worthy the attention of all Legislators :—" And the LORD said unto Cain, Where is Abel thy brother? and he said, I know not: *Am* I my brother's keeper? And he said, What hast thou done? the voice of thy brother's blood crieth unto me from the ground." Gen. iv. 9, 10.

The numerous facts laid before the reader show that the practice of exposing the sick by the Ganges is of that inhuman and murderous nature which demands the attention of the Legislature. Its abrogation by a paternal Government would greatly promote the happiness of the people, and elevate the tone of natural and moral feeling among the Hindoos. The engraving (placed at the beginning of this book), taken from a Drawing by a Native Artist, shows a few of the superstitious practices connected with the Ganges. Some persons are bathing in its supposed sacred stream; and others are procuring and carrying away its water for holy purposes. But DEATH is the chief subject of the Engraving, which displays some of the miserable delusions under which the millions of our Hindoo fellow-subjects leave the world. The man on the couch has been brought down to breathe his last on the borders of the river, while a Brahmun is offering him its waters: the women are probably the wives of the dying man come to witness this scene—the more afflicting to them, as the barbarous superstitions of their country may require them to sacrifice their own lives on the funeral pile of their husband; and the very fire which shall consume the living parent with the dead, to be kindled by their own offspring. On the right hand is a Pagoda, before the door of which another miserable man has been laid, there to breathe out his soul in the presence of his Idol.*

Even the light of nature is opposed to the horrid practice of human sacrifices, and hence the abolition of them by certain civilized States before the Christian era. The Romans, prior to the establishment of Christianity, exerted their influence to abolish human sacrifices; and Britain is indebted to them, as the precursors of that civilization consequent upon the propagation of the Gospel in this country. And shall not Christian Britain emulate the humane example of Pagan Rome? Shall Gelon, the tyrant of Syracuse,† nearly 500 years before Christ, stipulate with the Car-

* See Mis. Reg. 1823. † Rollin's Ancient History, vol. i. p. 10.

thaginians, as an article of peace, *to abolish human sacrifices*; and shall not conquering Britain—

> "Whom grateful Afric worships; and whose name
> Poor crouching Asia dreads,"

proclaim liberty to the Slave, protection to the murdered Widow, comfort to the dying Hindoo, and life to the Infant devoted from its birth to destruction? Reason, consistency, and the experience of past ages, require this service for the common interests of humanity. The blood of Suttees—of Infanticides—of Ghaut murders—of Pilgrims led by British connexion with idolatry to its shrines—cry to Britain; and "their cries have entered into the ears of the Lord of Sabaoth." Britain, awake! "Put on judgment as a robe and a diadem;"—"do justly and love mercy."

The suppression of these cruelties is demanded of Britain.—They outrage "the inviolable obligations of justice and humanity."* Locke, in his Letters on Toleration, clearly defines the religious observances with which the civil magistrates can and cannot interfere.—"The magistrate ought not to forbid the preaching or professing of any speculative opinions in any church, because they have no manner of relation to the civil rites of the subject; for it does not belong to the magistrate to make use of his sword in punishing every thing indifferently which he takes to be a sin against God. His post is only to take care that the Commonwealth receive no prejudice, and that there be no injury done to any man in life and state. You will say, 'If some congregations have a mind to sacrifice infants, or practice any other such heinous enormities, is the magistrate obliged to tolerate them, because they are committed in a religious

---

* Bruja Mohun, a Bengalee, in his "Strictures on the present System of Hindoo Polytheism," has the following just remarks:—"With the view of obtaining Gunga you, at midnight, in the month of January, dip your aged and afflicted parents into the river and *thereby murder them*. The weather is then so cold, and the wind so bleak, that were you to submerge a healthful youth in the river his death would be no matter of surprise. You drink the water of a peculiar spot and anoint your body with dirt and mud brought from particular places, and esteem these acts holy—we do not. To burn defenceless women, *to murder an aged father and mother by immersing them in water*, you esteem holy;—we esteem these deeds unholy." (Friend of India, Dec., 1830, pp. 267, 290.) Thus correct ideas of the nature of the cruel customs of Hindoism are prevailing among the natives. Let not Britain fear to cast her shield over the wretched votaries of superstition, and "deliver them who are drawn unto death and ready to be slain."

assembly? No. These things are not lawful in the ordinary course of life, nor in any private house, and therefore neither are they so in the worship of God."* The abolition of human sacrifices of every kind would raise the tone of humane and intellectual feeling in India, and attach her to Britain, "no longer as a conqueror to whom she is bound by the terror of our arms, but as a benefactor indissolubly endeared by the triumphs of our mercy."

What is the state of Hindostan at the present period?—"Darkness covers the earth, and gross darkness the people."—"The land is full of idols:" and the people are "mad upon their idols." And "how are their sorrows multiplied that hasten after another god!" Idolatry is degrading to the human mind, inimical to the happiness of society, and incapable of supporting the soul in the prospects of a future state of existence. Its ceremonies are puerile, absurd, cruel, and murderous. Idolatry is cruel as the grave.†

And shall British India lie at the mercy of this merciless hydra; to whom thousands are annually sacrificed on its sanguinary altars? Shall no cry of "Murder! murder!" no cry of "Mercy! mercy!" be heard? Oh yes! a cry is heard—it increases—it is understood—and ere long the inhabitants of Britain, aided by other Christian countries, will be seen rising to rescue the victims of superstition, and direct them to the cross of Christ! Christianity is the only adequate remedy for the miseries of India, of the East, and of the World. Let the messengers of mercy, bearing "Good tidings of great joy to all people," be despatched to every part of India, saying, "Go, ye swift messengers, to a nation scattered and peeled, to a people terrible from their

---

* Locke's Works, vol. ii. pp. 368—370. See also Par. Papers on Hindoo Immolations, July, 1825, vol. iv. p. 21.

† What is the meaning of such sentiments as the following?

> "There's not a land on earth more fair
> Than that whose soil the Gunga laves;
> There's not a land *more blessed* than where,
> Through countless leagues, it rolls its waves.
> Land of the beauteous and the brave,
> Land of the Ganges holy wave."

(Forget-Me-Not, 1829, p. 129.—*Banks of the Ganges.*)

beginning hitherto; a nation meted out and trodden down, whose land the rivers have spoiled!" Isaiah xviii. 2. Let these efforts be accompanied with fervent prayer for the effusion of the Spirit of God, and his "way shall be known upon earth, his saving health among all nations." Thus true religion shall bless the plains of Hindostan; and its temples, idols, and cruel rites, be "buried 'midst the wreck of things that were." How numerous the blessings which follow in the train of Christianity! Behold the Hindoo "a new creature in Christ Jesus."

> "On Guilt's dark brow her glittering cross appears,
> His sullied cheek is washed with pious tears;
> And Ganges, hallow'd still for holier ends,
> *Death stream no more*, his wave baptismal lends!"*

To adopt the language of the late C. Grant, Esq., referring to the other European nations who have held possessions in India,—"It remains for us to show how we shall be distinguished from these nations† in the history of mankind; whether conquest shall have been in our hands the means, not merely of displaying a Government unequalled in India for administrative justice, kindness, and moderation; not merely of increasing the security of the subject and prosperity of the country, but of advancing social happiness—of meliorating the moral state of men,—and of extending a superior light, further than the Roman eagle ever flew. In success lies our safety, not our danger. Our danger must lie in pursuing, from ungenerous ends, a course contracted and illiberal; but in following an opposite course, —in communicating light, knowledge, and improvement, we shall obey the dictates of duty, of philanthropy, and of policy. We shall take the most rational means to remove, inherent, great disorders—to attach the Hindoo people to ourselves—to ensure the safety of our possessions—to enhance, continually, their value to us—to raise a firm and durable monument to the glory of this country—and to increase the happiness of the human race."‡

O Britain! my country! hear the glowing language of

---

* Wrangham's Poem on the Restoration of Learning in the East, 1805.

† Portuguese, French, and Dutch, in India.

‡ "Observ. on the State of Society among the Asiatic subjects of Great Britain." Par. Papers, June, 1813.

your poets ; and promote the work of the melioration and evangelization of India.

"Pursue thy glorious course. Be this thy art,
Not to corrupt, but meliorate the heart;
Where'er mankind in Gentile darkness lie,
Instruction's blessed radiance to supply;
O'er the oppress'd, soft mercy's dews to shed,
And crush with ruin the oppressor's head.
O haste your tardy coming days of gold;
Long by prophetic minstrelsy foretold!
Where yon bright purple streaks the orient skies,
Rise Science, Freedom, Peace, Religion, rise!
'Till, from Tanjore to farthest Samarcand,
In one wide lustre bask the glowing land:
And (Brahma from his guilty greatness hurl'd
With Mecca's lord) Messiah rule the world!"

"Then, while transported Asia kneels around,
With ancient arts and long lost glories crown'd:
Some happier bard, on Ganges' margin laid,
Where playful bamboos weave their fretted shade,
Shall to the strings a loftier tone impart,
And pour in rapturous verse his flowing heart.
Stamp'd in immortal light on future days,
Through all the strain his country's joys shall blaze;
The Sanscrit song be warm'd with heav'nly fires,
And themes divine awake from Indian lyres!"*

* See Wrangham and Grant on the Restoration of Learning in the East, 1805.

BOOK V.

SLAVERY.

CHAP. I.

Introductory Remarks — Origin, Nature, and Evils of Slavery in India.

A late highly respected writer on India states, respecting slavery in the East, "Though *no slavery legally exists in the British territories at this moment*, yet the terms and gestures used by servants to their superiors all imply that such a distinction was at no distant date very common. 'I am thy slave,' 'Thy slave hath no knowledge,' are continually used as expressions of submission and of ignorance." From this extract, and others of a similar kind which might be made, it is evident that the nature and extent of slavery in India are but imperfectly understood. A very voluminous collection of Papers on this subject, containing nearly 1000 folio pages, were "ordered by the Hon. House of Commons to be printed, March 12th, 1828," and it is important that their contents should be generally known. Of these papers it has been said, "An attempt to digest such a mass of documents into a narrative, or to reduce them into any symmetrical shape, is hopeless;" the author has not been thus discouraged in his investigation of them; but, being convinced that slavery in India is a subject of considerable interest, he has devoted much time to the perusal of these Papers, and hopes his labours may be beneficial to the interests of humanity in India. While so many works are published on West India Slavery, the author is acquainted with but one on Slavery in India,* and this a small pamphlet recently published. Whatever brings the real state of India before the British public must be productive of good; and, under this conviction, the author submits his feeble labour to the candid attention of his readers.

J. Richardson, Esq., judge and magistrate of Zillah Bundlecund, in his very valuable communication to the British Government in India, on the subject of slavery, in March, 1808, very justly remarks—" The humane abolition of the slave trade in England has added lustre to the enlightened wisdom of the British senate, and enrolled, to the latest posterity, the name of Wilberforce amongst the benefactors of mankind. That slavery should ever have been authorised, in any civilised community, is as astonishing to the mind, as disgraceful to human nature. The great Author of Creation made all men equally free. By what act then can that freedom be forfeited or given up? surely liberty can be forfeited by no act that does not militate against the general security and well-being of society, from which mankind acquire their happiness and protection. Nor has man more right to sell or give up the natural freedom of his person than he has to lay down his natural life at pleasure; much less can he have any title to dispose of the liberty of another, even of his child. That every human being should contribute by his labour, whether mental or corporeal, to supply the wants of his brethren in society, on principles of reciprocity and mutual advantage, is as natural as requisite; but that God should authorise the assumption of property and the absolute control of one human being over another, nothing inferior in form or organization, is surely an impious supposition, arraigning the justice of Omnipotence, and directly contrary to every benign attribute of the Deity, as delineated by reason and religion, and impressed upon our minds by the laws of nature and the use of our rational faculties.

" That *slavery is an infringement of the law of nature cannot be disputed.* The most respectable authority proves that, therefore, it is in its own nature and essence invalid. Blackstone, speaking of the law of nature, says, ' this law of nature, coeval with mankind, and dictated by

* East India Slavery by Saintsbury, 1829. See also East and West India Sugar, 1823. Hatchard.

God himself, is of course superior in obligation to any other. It is binding all over the globe, in all countries, and at all times; no human laws are of any validity if contrary to this; and such of them as are valid derive all their force and all their authority mediately or immediately from this original.' The most strenuous defenders of this horrid imposition of the powerful on the weaker part of mankind pretend not to maintain its propriety but on ideas of political utility. Impartial and minute inquiry into its effects would at once remove this specious veil, by which the diabolical principle is sometimes hidden; and the system, decorated in the eye of sensible and virtuous men under mistaken notions of human expedience, proves the uniform tendency of slavery to be depressive of every emanation of the mind, and highly destructive to our species."*

The origin of slavery in India, as it exists among the Hindoos at the present period, is involved in considerable obscurity. Its rise among the Mahomedans is evidently to be traced to the triumph of their arms. The following extract from the Papers on Slavery in India affords some information upon a subject painfully interesting to every human mind.

The Parliamentary Papers on Slavery in India commence with the following singular method of punishing decoits or robbers, and show one source of slavery in the East:—" That whereas the peace of this country hath for some years past been greatly disturbed by bands of Decoits, who not only infest the high roads, but often plunder whole villages, burning the houses and murdering the inhabitants: And whereas these abandoned outlaws have hitherto found means to elude every attempt which the vigilance of government hath put in force, for detecting and bringing such atrocious criminals to justice, by the secrecy of their haunts, and the wild state of the districts which are most subject to their incursions, it becomes the indispensable duty of government to try the most rigorous means, since experience has proved every lenient and ordinary remedy to be ineffectual: that it be therefore resolved, That every such criminal, on conviction, shall be carried to the village to which he belongs, and be there executed for a terror and example to others; and, for the further prevention of such abominable practices, that the village of which he is an in-

---

* Par. Papers on Slavery in India, 1828, p. 299.

habitant shall be fined according to the enormity of the crime, and each inhabitant according to his substance; and that *the family of the criminal shall become the slaves of the state, and be disposed of for the general benefit and convenience of the people, according to the discretion of the government*."*

On this subject it is stated:—"The decoits of Bengal are not like the robbers in England—individuals driven to such desperate courses by sudden want; they are robbers by profession, and even by birth; they are formed into regular communities, and their families subsist by the spoils which they bring home to them; they are all therefore alike criminal; wretches who have placed themselves in a state of declared war with government, and are therefore wholly excluded from every benefit of its laws. We have many instances of their meeting death with the greatest insensibility; it loses, therefore, its effect as an example; but when executed in all the forms and terrors of law, in the midst of the neighbours and relations of the criminal, when these are treated as accessaries to his guilt, and *his family deprived of their liberty, and separated for ever from each other*—every passion, which before served as an incentive to guilt, now becomes subservient to the purposes of society, by turning them from a vocation in which all they hold dear, besides life, becomes forfeited by their conviction; at the same time, their families, instead of being lost to the community, are made useful members of it, by being adopted into those of the more civilized inhabitants. The ideas of slavery, borrowed from our American colonies, will make every modification of it appear, in the eyes of our own countrymen in England, a horrible evil; but it is far otherwise in this country; here slaves are treated as the children of the families to which they belong, and often acquire a much happier state by their slavery than they could have hoped for by the enjoyment of liberty; so that, in effect, the apparent rigour thus exercised on the children of convicted robbers will be no more than a change of condition, by which they will be no sufferers, though it will operate as a warning on others, and is the only means which we can imagine capable of dissipating these des-

* Par. Papers on Slavery in India, p. 2, Plan for the administration of justice, Aug. 1772.

perate and abandoned societies, which subsist on the distress of the general community."*

"If we may judge (says the Editor of the Asiatic Journal, in a review of the contents of the Papers on Slavery in India) from a subsequent minute and regulation of the Bengal Government (1774), this proposal was not listened to; for therein, not only is the stealing of children or selling any Hindoo as a slave (without a regular deed) forbidden, but it is proposed to abolish slavery altogether, after the first generation then living, owing to 'the great increase of late years of this savage commerce, and in order to prevent hasty strides towards depopulation.' Further inquiry however seems to have convinced the Bengal Government that there were districts where slavery was in general usage, and the abolition of which might impede cultivation. The Government observes that the opinions of the most creditable Mussulman and Hindoo inhabitants condemn the usage of selling slaves as repugnant to the particular precepts both of the Koran and the Shaster."†

The Provincial Council of Patna, in Aug. 1774, address the Governor, Warren Hastings, Esq., on this subject as follows:—"We find that there are two kinds of slaves in this province, Mussulman and Hindoo; the former are properly called Mualazadeh, and the latter Kahaar. Slaves of either denomination are considered in the same light as any other property, and are transferrable by the owner, or descend at his demise to his heirs. They date the rise of the custom of Kahaar slavery from the first incursions of the Mahomedans, when the captives were distributed by the general among the officers of his army, to whose posterity they remained. All other slaves have become so by occasional purchase, as in cases of famine, &c. The Kaboleh must be signed by the mother or grandmother, and not by the father. Children also born of slaves are the property of the owner of the woman, though married to a slave of a different family."‡

The Collector at Trichinopoly, in the Madras Presidency, in reply to the inquiries of the Government addressed to a number of Collectors on the subject of Slavery in their respective districts, describes the origin of pullers or agricultural slavery as follows:—"It is, I apprehend, indisputable,

---

* Par. Papers on Slavery in India, p. 1, 2. † Asi. Jour. Nov. 1828, p. 559. ‡ Par. Papers on Slavery in India, p. 5.

that in the earliest ages of Hindoo government, agricultural and domestic slavery existed to a considerable and indefinite extent. The practice was sanctioned by prescription, and upheld by law; but it will be found that the terms of bondage, and the nature of the services required from the slaves, differed essentially in almost every district. No distinct information can be obtained at what period agricultural slavery commenced. It is now impossible to trace whether this establishment took its rise from the voluntary submission of the indigent to the wealthy, or whether the pullers were originally captives taken in war. But, as this species of bondage is generally the concomitant of barbarous governments, it must of necessity have been a very ancient institution of the Hindoos. Under their arbitrary government, the distinctions of caste were scrupulously maintained; and, adverting to the circumstance of the meerassidars in Trichinopoly being Brahmuns, it scarcely excites surprize that agricultural slavery should exist here unchanged and undiminished."*

The Lieutenant-Governor of the island of Java, in May 1812, gives the following information, respecting the origin of slavery in the Eastern Isles:—"Macassar and its neighbourhood may be considered as a principal source from which slaves have been exported; and without, in this place, entering into any discussion of the origin and causes of this state of society, which, in a general point of view, must be referred to backwardness of civilization and prevalence of native authority, it must be observed that, in consequence of its being the favourite source of revenue among those chieftains, it will require much delicacy and caution in attempting any measures to restrain where argument could be of no avail, and force would be inconvenient.

"In my instructions to Captain Phillips, on his proceeding to Macassar, I directed his attention in a particular manner to this interesting subject; but I regret to find from his report that at present there is little prospect of his favourable interference. In short, he seems decidedly of opinion that, "as men-stealers are very common over the country, if he prohibited their selling their stolen property at Macassar, they would still carry on the trade in the Boui territory;" where, though so immediately under the eye of the Resident, the Rajah would no doubt maintain his right

---

* Par. Papers, p. 892.

equally with that which he exercises at pleasure of life and death.

"The native laws, usages, and habits, regarding slavery, are in many instances so various and contradictory, and it is so difficult to trace them to any authentic source, that is universally admitted and acknowledged, that I am fearful but very little light will be obtained from them. Prisoners of war are in many cases considered as the property of the conqueror, and consequently sold as slaves. The families of criminals who may be executed for particular crimes become likewise a droit of the chief; and in many cases criminals are pardoned on condition of being sold into slavery. Throughout the whole of the Eastern Islands, debtors become responsible in their services to their creditors, and it does not appear that there is any generally acknowledged law among them to prevent the chief of a family selling his wife and children into slavery. The desperate manner in which the Bugguese prows are known to defend themselves at sea, is accounted for by the numerous crew, who are all separate adventurers on a borrowed capital, having left their families hypothecated for the debt, who become slaves to the creditor in the event of the debtor parting with the property under any circumstances without his life."*

"The Dutch law being blended with the Roman, and the colonial law founded on both, slavery has been fully recognised as legal by the European government, while the universal prevalence of Mahometanism renders it legal with every native administration, and as such it appears, without any occasional difference of opinion, to have been always considered.

"Slavery, however, on the island of Java, is to be considered as exclusively confined to domestic purposes, and may be viewed rather as a regulated domestic servitude than that detestable system which the legislature of Great Britain have, to the credit of humanity, so vigorously suppressed in the West Indies. *Slavery, however, under any shape, or if it bears only the name, is so repugnant to every principle of enlightened administration, and so inconsistent with your Lorship's† benevolent plans, that I fear I should not stand excused in my defence of such a*

* Par. Papers on Slavery in India,, pp. 154, 155.
† Lord Minto.

system under any modifications or circumstances whatever."*

The rise of slavery in the newly acquired island of Penang, or Prince of Wales Island, is described as follows, in a letter from the judge and magistrate in Jan. 1802, to the Marquis of Wellesley, then Governor General of India.—" My Lord Marquis:—In a case which lately came judicially before me, a question arose, 'Whether civil slavery, that is, a right in one man over the person and fortune of another, were to be considered as established at Prince of Wales Island.' I was not ignorant that slavery, limited and unlimited, had been here tolerated. I know that emigrants, both from the Malay Peninsula and from the Eastern Islands, who had become inhabitants of Prince of Wales Island, have been permitted to retain in slavery those whom they had brought as slaves to this place. Some of these, indeed, are in utter slavery, while others are only in limited servitude. The latter is the condition of those who are styled slave debtors, and these are people that voluntarily become slaves to their creditors till their debts are paid. But all this passed, *sub silentio;* for, after careful search, I have not found any regulation of the local government, or any order from the Governor General in council, authorising the establishment of slavery, limited or unlimited, at Prince of Wales Island. This right, if any such in fact exists, rests therefore *simply on a usage of fourteen years.* Thus circumstanced, having no authority to guide my judgment, my delicacy increased in proportion to the interests on which I was called to determine; and, in this case, subordinate to the question of civil slavery, arose two other questions. The first a question of fact, 'Whether the father of A. ever had been a slave at Quiddah?' The second a question of law, 'What was to be the condition of A. now resident at Prince of Wales Island, whether born of one parent, who was free, and of another, who was enlaved, or born of parents who were both slaves, and now resident at Prince of Wales Island.

" I was desirous of avoiding the determination of this case, and remitted it to the Lieutenant Governor; but, in deference to his particular request, I gave my opinion that

---

* For an account of the Slave Trade at the Island of Nias, near Sumatra, see an interesting article from the Singapore Chronicle, in the Imp. Mag. Jan. 1830, p. 48—54.

the evidence did not prove that the father ever had been a slave, but that it inclined to show that the mother had been a slave at Quiddah, and I thought *the son should follow the condition of his father.* I was led to this opinion from a consideration that it is the old law of villanage in England, and, although I know it was contrary to the maxim of the civilians, *partes sequiter ventrem,* yet the latter authority had no weight with me; first, because slavery had not yet been established by authority at Priuce of Wales Island; next, because I could not see any local circumstance requiring its establishment; and, lastly, because *a state of slavery is, in its own nature, bad, neither useful to the master nor to the slave, nor to the state under which they live.* The Lieutenant Governor, on the contrary, was of opinion that the evidence proved both parents of A. were slaves, and, under the regulations for the administration of justice on this islaud, ultimately decreed, that A., resident in this island, should be delivered up as a slave to Hakim Sullee, Captain Malay, resident also on this island.

"By this decree slavery is now recognised and established by the local government of this island, and therefore, in addition to the observations which heretofore I have had the honour of submitting to the consideration of your Excellency in council, I feel the necessity of representing that regulations are now requisite, in which the right that a master is to possess over the person and fortune of his slave, at Prince of Wales Island, should be explicitly defined; and I hope that your Excellency in council will take into consideration the case of the offspring of slaves, and particularly of those who are born of one parent who is free, while the other is a slave. Nothing can be presumed on the moderation or justice of Mahomedans who possess slaves. By their usages the virtue or honour of female slaves is at the mercy of their master. I could hope that the right of the master was by law expressly limited to the bounds of humanity. I have no other apology to offer than my conviction that the subject matter of my letter is of the first importance to the interests and prosperity of this rising colony."*

Of the nature of Slavery in India some idea may be formed from the following extracts. The Governor General, in March, 1775, transmitted to the Honourable Court of

---

* Par. Papers on Slavery in India, pp. 429, 430.

Directors extracts from a translation of the Hindoo Laws by N. B. Halhed, Esq. From this code it appears that slaves are divided into fifteen classes, viz.—

"1. Whoever is born of a female slave, and is called Gerhejàt.

2. Whoever is purchased for a price, and is called Keereeut.

3. Whoever is found any where by chance, and is called Lubdehee.

4. Whoever is a slave by descent from his ancestors, and is called Dayavaupakut.

5. Whoever hath been fed, and hath had his life preserved by another during a famine, and is called Enàkàl Behrut.

6. Whoever hath been delivered up as a pledge for money borrowed, and is called Abut.

7. Whoever, to free himself from the debt of one creditor, hath borrowed money from another person, and, having discharged the old debt, gives himself up as a servant to the person with whom the present debt is contracted; or whoever, by way of terminating the importunities of a creditor, delivers himself up for a servant to that creditor, and is called Mookhud.

8. Whoever hath been enslaved by the fortune of battle, and is called Joodih Peeraput.

9. Whoever becomes a slave by a loss on the chances of dice, or other games, and is called Punjeet; according to the ordinations of Perkashkar and Pareejaut, and according to the ordination of Chendeesur, it is thus that by whatever chance he is conquered, and becomes a slave, he is called Punjeet—approved.

10. Whoever of his own desire says to another, "I am become your slave," and is called Opookut.

11. When a Chebteree, or Bice, having become Sinassee, apostates from that way of life, the magistrate shall make him a slave, and is called Perberjabesheet.

12. Whoever voluntarily gives himself as a slave to another for a stipulated time, and is called Gheerut.

13. Whoever performs servitude for his subsistence, and is called Bheekut.

14. Whoever, from the desire of possessing a slave girl, becomes a slave, and is called Berbakrot.

15. Whoever of his own accord sells his liberty, and becomes a slave, and is called Bekreet."*

In the trial of the commander of a Danish trading-vessel for procuring native children, and exporting them as slaves, in Aug. 1789, Sir R. Chambers stated—"The only cases in which slavery was lawful under the Mahomedan Government. Infidels, taken prisoners in war, fighting against Mussulmans, were considered as the slaves of the captors, and the slavery extended to their children. In cases of famine, publicly declared, it was lawful for farmers to sell their children, and persons of more than fifteen years of

* Par. Papers on Slavery in India, p. 7.

age might sell themselves to obtain a subsistence. But that in these *four cases,* the only existing ones under the Mahomedan government, the condition of slavery was put under many legal restrictions, and that it was unlawful for a Mussulman to sell his slave. That the exportation of subjects of a Mussulman government to be sold to a state of slavery was unknown; and, he believed, that it was the first time such an offence had been committed under the British flag, and he trusted it would be the last. He wished it to be understood that, if a similar offence should ever unhappily be again tried before the court, the punishment would be more severe."*

The nature of slavery, both Hindoo and Mussulman, will appear by the following extract from the valuable communications to the Bengal Government by the magistrate of Bundlecund. This gentleman observes — "Previously to my submission of the draught of the Regulation directed to be submitted to the court of Nizamut Adawlut, I deem it of essential importance to the elucidation of the subject to offer a few remarks *on the laws of slavery as they now exist* in that part of Hindostan which it has pleased God to allot to the control and government of the British nation. For the sake of perspicuity, and to bring the subject at once under view, I shall transcribe the questions put to the Mahomedan and Hindoo law officers officially (for the purpose of procuring *a declaration of law on the subject of slavery,* according to their respective codes), insert their answers, and offer such remarks as present themselves to my judgment, or as seem applicable to the subject.

Questions put to the *Muftee by the Nizamut Adawlut.*

Questions and answers by the law officers.

First Question.—"*What description of slaves are authorized by the Mokomedan law?*"

Answer.—"All men are by nature free and independent, and *no man can be a subject of property, except an infidel inhabiting a country not under the power and control of the faithful.* This right of possession which the Moslems have over Hurbus (infidels fighting against the faith) is acquired by Isteela, which means the entire subduement of any subject of property by force of arms. The original right of property, therefore, which one man may possess over another, is to be acquired solely by Isteela, and cannot

* Par. Papers on Slavery in India, p. 21.

be obtained in the first instance by purchase, donation, or heritage; when, therefore, an Imaum subdues, by force of arms, any one of the cities inhabited by infidels, such of them as may be taken prisoners become his rightful property, and he has the power of putting them to death or making them slaves, and distributing them as such among the Ghazees (victorious soldiers), particularly when fighting against infidels; or he may set them at liberty in a Mussulman country, and levy the capitation tax; should he make them slaves, they become legal subjects of property, and are transferrable by sale, gift, or inheritance; but if, after captivity, they should become converts to the faith (Islam), the power of death over them is thereby barred, though they would continue slaves; for, slavery being the necessary consequence of original infidelity, the subsequent conversion to Islam does not affect the prior state of bondage to which the individual has been regularly rendered liable by Isteela, provided this be clearly established. From this it is evident that the same rules are applicable to slaves of both sexes. If slaves are afterwards sold, or given away, by the Imaum, or by the Ghazees, who shared at the distribution, or if they should become the property of another by inheritance, they then become slaves under the three different classes of purchase, donation, and inheritance.

"If a female should bear offspring by any other than by her legal lord and master, whether the father be a freeman or a slave, and whether the slave of the said master, or of any other person, in any one of these cases, such offspring is subject to slavery, and these are called Khanazad (born in the family); but, if the children be the acknowledged offspring of the right owner, they are then free, and *the mother of them* (being the parent of a child by her master) *becomes, at his decease, free also; and this rule is applicable to all their descendants to the latest posterity.*

"The practice among free men and women of selling their own offspring, during the time of famine, is extremely improper and unjustifiable, being in direct opposition to the principle above stated, viz. *that no man can be a subject of property, except an infidel taken in the act of hostilities against the faith.* In no case then can a person, legally free, become a subject of property; and, *children not being the property of their parents, all sales or purchases of them, as any other articles of illegal property, are consequently invalid.* It is also illegal for any free man to sell his own person, either in time of famine or though he be oppressed by a debt which he is unable to discharge. For in the first of these cases a famished man may feed upon a dead body! or may rob another; and a distressed debtor is not liable to any fine or punishment.

"We are not acquainted with the principal or detailed circumstances which led to the custom prevailing in most Mussulman countries of purchasing and selling the inhabitants of Zanguibar, Ethiopia, Nubia, and other Negroes: but the ostensible causes are, either that the Negroes sell their own offspring, or that Mussulman or other tribes of people take them prisoners by fraud and deceit, or seize them by stealth from the sea shores. In such cases, however, *they are not legally slaves, and the sale and purchase of them are consequently invalid.* But if a Mussulman army, by order of an Imaum, should invade their country, and make them prisoners of war by force of arms, they are then legal slaves, provided that such Negroes are inhabitants of a country under the government of Infidels, and in which a Mussulman is not entitled to receive the full benefit and protection of his own laws. With regard to the custom, prevailing in this country, of hiring children from their parents, for a very considerable period, such as for seventy or eighty years, and under this pretext making them slaves, as well as their produce also, under the denomination of Kharazad (domestic slaves), the following laws are applicable; viz. *It is lawful and proper for parents to hire out their children on service, but this contract of hire becomes null and void when the child arrives at the years of discretion, as the right of parentage then ceases;* a free man, who has reached the years of discretion, may, however, enter into a contract to serve another, but not for any great length of time, such as for seventy years; as this also is a mere pretext, and has the same object of slavery in view, whereas the said free man has the option of dissolving any contract of hire under either of the following circumstances:—It is the custom, in *contracts* of this nature, for a person hired on service to receive a compensation in money, clothes, and food, as the price of hire; any day therefore that a servant receives such a compensation he is in duty bound to serve for that day, but not otherwise. The condition of contract of hire requires that the return of profit be equal to the price of hire, and this cannot be ascertained but by degrees, and in course of time. The contract of hire, therefore, becomes complete, or fulfilled according to the services or benefit actually rendered in return for the price of hire received, and the person hired has consequently the option of dissolving the contract at any moment of the period originally agreed for.

"It is however unavoidable and actually necessary in contracts of a different nature, such as in rent of land, &c., that the lessee should not have this power; but reverting to contracts of hire for service for a long period, the nefarious practices of subjecting free men to a state of bondage and slavery, under this pretence, it appears expedient to provide against such abuses, and with this view to restrict the period for service in all contracts of hired freemen to a month, one year, or the utmost to three years, as in cases of Ijanawugh, a form of endowment. It is customary also among the Zanane Towaf (women who keep sets of dancing girls), to purchase female free children from their parents, or by engagements directly with the children themselves; exclusively of the illegality of such purchases, there is a further evil resulting from this practice, which is, that the children are taught dancing and singing for others, and are also made prostitutes, both of which are extremely improper and expressly forbidden by the law."

Remarks.—"From the reply it is evident that, by the Mussulman law, no man can have the right of property over another human being except a Mussulman, and even he can acquire that right over an infidel only, inhabiting a country not under the power and control of the faithful; and that this right which Mussulmans have over infidels fighting against the faith is acquirable by Isteela, which means the entire subduement of any subject of property by force of arms; the right of property, therefore, which one man may possess over another, is to be acquired, in the first instance, by "Isteela, and cannot be obtained originally by purchase, donation, or heritage, &c. It follows that all persons in a state of bondage, over whom the right of property has not been obtained by Isteela, or the offspring of parents over whom the above right was not acquired, are, by the Mussulman law, free; and that it is the duty of the Hakim, or persons claiming their freedom, over whom the right of property derived from Isteela cannot be legally established or traced, to declare such persons of either sex free by a legal recorded decision, which shall secure to them the future enjoyment of that freedom.

"It also appears, by this answer, that although legal bondage be established, the circumstance of subsequent conversion to the faith is a bar to the power of death, which the proprietor originally possessed over all slaves over whom the right of property was in fact obtained by Isteela; but that the above conversion does not affect the prior state of bondage, &c., &c. The same rule is applicable to slaves of both sexes.

"Slaves sold or given away by the Imaum, or the Ghazee (conquerors or victorious troops) who shared at the distribution, or if afterwards they become the property of another by inheritance, they continue slaves under the different rights of purchase, donation, and heirship. It appears by the Mussulman law that the offspring of a female slave, whether by a freeman or a slave of any description, except by her master, such offsprings are slaves, and are called Khanazad (born in the family). If, however, the offspring shall be acknowledged by the master, they shall be free, and the mother also, at the death of her owner, becomes free; *and this also emancipates their descendants to the latest posterity.* It may be inferred from the provision here noticed, &c., that, to entitle the child to freedom, and the mother to emancipation, on the death of her *lord, his acknowledgment,* and that he is the father, the offspring of the slave is *necessary* to give the law force. Here the principles pursued by European legislation are reversed, and there are many obvious motives that may induce the owner to deny his being the father of the child.

"The sale of their offspring by free men or women is declared to be *extremely improper and unjustifiable,* being in direct opposition to the fundamental and only principle upon which a Mussulman's right to a slave exists, viz. that no man can be a subject of property except an infidel taken in the act of hostilities against the faith. All sales and purchases of the above described offspring, as of any other articles of illegal property, are invalid.

"It is also declared by the Mussulman law, as here developed, that a *free man cannot sell his own person.* The law officer here states his unacquaintance with the circumstances which led to the prevalence of the custom in most Mussulman countries, of purchasing and selling the inhabitants of Zanguibar, Ethiopia, Nubia, and other Negroes, nor is the enquiry of any consequence to the British government: they are evidently not legally slaves by the Mussulman law.

"A free man, arrived at the years of discretion, may contract to serve for a reasonable, not a great length of time, such as seventy years; but it is here stated, that the said free man, so contracting, is to receive a compensation, and is compelled to serve for that day for which he has received compensation, but not otherwise; the person hired has consequently the option of dissolving the contract at any moment of the period originally agreed for. It is observable that this is contrary to the nature of all contracts, which are, or ought to be, specific and mutual; but the Mussulman law assigns reasons, in the subsequent paragraph of the answer on which I am remarking, explanatory of the causes which render this contract different from others, such as rents, &c., where the lessee has not this power, and those reasons are more enlightened, and show a greater anxiety for the personal liberty of the individual, than is commonly to be found amongst the laws of Mahommed.

"Here is stated a custom existing amongst the Zanane Towaf ("women who keep sets of dancing girls") of purchasing female free born children from their parents or others, or making engagements with the children themselves, to be taught the practice of dancing and singing for others, and also for the immoral and licentious purpose of being made prostitutes, both of which are allowed to be extremely improper and expressly forbidden by the law. *The extent of the above evil would be best ascertained by a few appropriate queries put to the several magistrates, but more especially to those of the large or principal cities; the result would at once open the eyes of government to an evil which loudly calls for the interference of the Legislature, on every principle of humanity, morals, and policy.*"

Second Question. "*What legal power are the owners of slaves allowed to exercise upon the persons of their slaves, and particularly of their female slaves?*"

Answer.—"The rightful proprietor of male and female slaves has a claim to the services of such slaves to the extent of their power and ability. He may employ them in baking, cooking, in making, dyeing, and washing clothes; as agents in mercantile transactions; in attending cattle, in tillage, or cultivation; as carpenters, ironmongers, and goldsmiths; in transcribing; as weavers, and in manufacturing woollen cloths; as shoemakers, boatmen, twisters of silk, water drawers; in shaving; in performing surgical operations, such as cupping, &c.; as farriers, bricklayers, and the like; and he may hire them out on service in any of the above capacities; he may also employ them himself, or for the use of his family in other duties of a domestic nature, such as in fetching water for washing on evazoo (religious purification), or anointing his body with oil, rubbing his feet, or attending his person while dressing, and in guarding the door of his house, &c. He may also have connexion with his legal female slave, provided she is arrived at the years of maturity, and the master or proprietor has not previously given her in marriage to another."

"There is nothing objectionable in the duties here stated to be lawfully demandable from slaves of both sexes. The obvious immorality, and the great impolicy and inhumanity of the licentious authority stated in this answer, requires no comment. The law officer, although he has stated in part the truth, has not embraced the whole truth: the Islamite has the power, by the Mussulman law, of exercising, with his female slaves, licentious intercourse, at the mention of which modesty recedes with blushes and humanity shrinks with horror."

Third Question.—"*What offences upon the persons of slaves, and particularly of female slaves, committed by their owners or by others, are legally punishable, and in what manner?*"

Answer. "If a master oppress his slave by employing him on any duty beyond his ability, such as insisting upon his carrying a load which he is incapable of bearing, or climbing a tree which he cannot, the hakim or ruling power may chastise him. It is also improper for a master to order his slave to do that which is forbidden by the law, such as putting an innocent person to death, setting fire to a house, tearing the clothes off another, or to prostitute himself by adultery and fornification, to steal or drink spirits, or to slander and abuse the chaste and virtuous; and, if a master be guilty of such like oppressions, the hakim may inflict exemplary punishment by Fazir and Ucqubut Shukool Illah: literally, the right of God, and *meaning* on principles of public justice.

"It is further unlawful for a master to punish his male or female slave for disrespectful conduct, and such like offences, further than by sadeeb (slight correction), as the power of passing sentence of tazeer and gizes is solely vested in the hakim. If, therefore, the master should exceed the limits of his power of chastisement, above stated, he is liable to tazeer. If a master should have connexion with his female slave before she has arrived at the years of maturity, and, if the female slave should in consequence be seriously injured, or should die, the ruling power may punish him by tazeer and Uquobut Hagool Jillah, as before defined.

"It will be allowed that the spirit which limits and enumerates the employments which a master is hereby forbidden to extort from his slaves, under the penalty of being liable to exemplary punishment by the hakim, on principles of public justice, is humane and proper, and might be sufficient for the purpose of good order and government, were it possible that the spirit of the law could be carried into effect. But that this is grossly the reverse must be obvious. To any man acquainted with the manners and customs of the natives, no argument is necessary to prove that the reverse is the case; and it is hardly necessary to remark on the degree of suffering that a poor, illiterate, wretched and desponding slave will submit to from his lord, whom, from infancy perhaps, he has been accustomed to look upon, with trembling anxiety, as the sole arbiter of his fate, upon whose whim or pleasure all the little happiness, or rather the absence of misery, which he hopes to experience, entirely depends. Is it likely that a slave under such circumstances should dare to apply to the ruling power for redress?

"If a master, excited by lust, unrestrained by shame, or by habit, shall have connexion with a female slave before she has arrived at the years of maturity, if the female slave should in consequence be severely injured or die, what is the consequence? The ruling power may punish him as before defined. Shall a British government sanction so horrid a law?

Fourth Question.—"*Are slaves entitled to emancipation upon any and what maltreatment, and may the courts of justice adjudge their emancipation upon the proof of such maltreatment? In particular, may such judgment be passed upon proof that a female slave has, during her minority, been prostituted by her master or mistress, or that any attempt of violence has been made by her owner?*"

Answer.—" If the master of male or female slaves should oppress or tyrannize over them by treating them unjustly, stinting them in food, or imposing upon them duties of an oppressive nature, so as to cause them affliction and distress, or if a master should have connection with his slave girl before she has arrived at the years of maturity, or should give her in marriage to another, with permission to cohabit with her in this state, such master sins against the divine laws, and the ruling power may punish him; but the commission of such crimes by the master does not authorize the manumission of the slave, nor has the hakim any right or authority to grant them emancipation. Adverting to the principle upon which the legality of slavery is originally established, viz. that the subject of property must be an infidel, and taken in the act of hostilities against the faith; and also to the several branches of legal slavery arising from this principle, as by purchase, donation, inheritance, and khanazadee; whenever a case of possession of an unlawful male or female slave should be referred to the hakim for investigation, it is the duty of the hakim to pass an order, according to the original right of freedom of such individual, to deprive the unjust proprietor of possession, and to grant immediate emancipation to the slave.

(signed and sealed)

Soorajoddeen Ullee, and
Mahomed Rashed."

"The purport of this question appears to be ascertained, whether on any and on what maltreatment a slave is entitled to emancipation on proof, and whether the courts of justice are entitled to pass such judgment, particularly on females being prostituted by their master or mistress during their minority, or on any attempt of violence being made. From the reply to this question, it appears that acts of oppression, and even violation of the person of a female slave, before she is at the years of maturity, by the master, or the crime of giving her at that age in marriage, are declared, as they truly are, crimes against the divine laws, and the ruling power may punish by stripes; but it is to be observed that, by the Mussulman law, the commission of these crimes by the owner does not entitle the wretched slave to manumission, nor has the ruling power the right to grant her emancipation!!

"Humanity, which is shocked at the idea of its being a question whether or not British legislation shall sanction so diabolic a law, under the impressions of horror which every humane mind must feel at the depravity of such inhuman laws, which cannot fail to debase the human mind to the injury of society, to morality, and religion, is relieved by the perusal of the next sentence. Adverting to the principle upon which the legality of slavery is originally established, viz. *that the subject of property must be an infidel, taken in the act of hostilities against the faith*;

and also to the several branches of legal slavery which shoot from this root or principle, purchase, donation, inheritance, and khanazeed; whenever a case of possession of an unlawful male or female slave, that is to say, who is not himself or herself under the original description of an infidel taken in the act of hostilities against the faithful under an Imaum, or descended from a person of the above description, over whom the right of property has not been obtained by one of the modes described, shall come before the ruling power, to pass an order according to the original right of freedom of such individual, and to deprive the unjust proprietor of possession, and to grant an immediate emancipation."

Questions put to the Pundit by the Nizamut Adawlut.

1st Question.—Answer. "There are fifteen different sorts of male and female slaves." See p. 372.

Remarks.—"Of the injustice and unreasonableness of the whole of the description of slaves sanctioned by the Hindoo law on the acknowledged principles of natural freedom, or on principles of expediency and humanity, few men I conceive will doubt; and to enter into argument to prove this self-evident perversion of the laws of nature and of God, which are written in the hearts of all enlightened men, would be a waste of intellect. I am confident such wide-spread degradation of the human race can never, on serious consideration, be authorized by an enlightened British Government."

2nd Question.—Answer. "The owner of a male or female slave may require of such slave the performance of impure work, such as plastering and sweeping the house, cleaning the door, gateway, and necessary; rubbing his master's naked body, *bunudome nehanu*, with oil, and clothing him; removing fragments of victuals left at his master's table, and eating them; removing urine and human ordure; rubbing his master's feet and other limbs, &c. In cases of disobedience or fault committed by the slave, the master has power to beat his slave with a thin stick, or to bind him with a rope: and, if he should consider the slave deserving of severe punishment, he may pull his hair or expose him upon an ass; but, if the master should exceed this extent of his authority, and inflict punishment upon his slave of a severer nature than above stated, he is liable to pay a fine to the hakim or ruling power, of a thousand puns of khar mahozrens, eight thousand cowries. This is declared by Munnoo, according to Patnakar Behbad, Chinta, Munnie, and other authorities."

"The facility and impunity with which power can tyrannize over a wretch in a state of bondage and absolute dependence requires no argument; and what is the punishment if, against all chance or hope, the tyrant is brought to trial, and even to conviction? A pecuniary fine!

3rd Question.—Answer. "A master has no right to command his male or female slave to perform any other duties besides those specified in the answer to the second question, or authority to punish his slave further than in the manner before stated; and if he should exceed this discretionary power, in either case, he is liable to the same penalty, viz. one thousand puns of cowries. This is declared by Munnoo and Beshie."

4th Question.—Answer. "The commission of offences of the above nature by the master does not affect the state of bondage of the slave; and the ruling power has not the right of granting his manumission; but if it should be established in evidence, before the hakim, that any person having stolen or inveigled away, by fraud, a child or slave, had afterwards sold him to another, or that any person had compelled another into a state of slavery by violence, the ruling power may then order the emancipation of such child or slave; and if a master, or any other by permission of the master, should cohabit with a slave girl before she has arrived at the years of maturity, and this fact be proved, the ruling power may sentence such offender to pay a fine of fifty puns of cowries, but cannot emancipate the slave girl!!

"Whenever a slave girl has borne a child by her master, *such slave, together with the child, becomes free, and the ruling power should sanction their emancipation.*

"This is the law declared by Jak Bulk Mannoo and Kutoobun, according to Mittuchora and other authorities.

(signed) *Chattoor Bhooj Necarutun.*
Chiterput Oapadhea."

"It does not appear that the commission of any, or all of the offences supposed in the fourth question, affect the state of bondage in the sufferings of the wretched slave, nor by the Hindoo law has the ruling power the authority of emancipating the injured bondsman, even under all the above maltreatment; but a treacherous inveigling away of a child and selling it as a slave, or the subjecting to slavery by violence, are declared illegal, and the ruling power may emancipate such child or slave. Should, however a master, or any other by permission of the owner, cohabit with a slave girl before she has arrived at the years of maturity, and the fact be proved, the ruling power may sentence the offender to fifty puns of cowries. Here a crime, most monstrous, by which the laws of nature are outraged, is punishable by a pecuniary fine! I suppose for the benefit of the ruling power."

"The foregoing being the Mussulman law, as expounded by the law officers, and the Mussulman law being that by which we govern in cases of life and limb, surely it ought to be extended to personal freedom; for from personal freedom alone can life or limb, the first gifts of nature, acquire their due value. The foregoing, I think, will be admitted, and investigation will render it evident that *at the present moment, of the many thousands male and female slaves held in bondage in the Company's dominions, and subject to the grossest usage, prostitution, and every other depravity, under the pretence of slavery being sanctioned under the Mussulman law, not a single man or woman exists to whom the right of property, on the principle laid down by that law, can possibly be proved and established!* The mode, therefore, of remedying the gross evils that do exist on this head, is as easy as it is obvious. Enforce the spirit and letter of the Mussulman law as it applies to slaves, and as far as that portion of the inhabitants of our Indian possessions are concerned;—you remedy the evil, and give the blessing of liberty to thousands, and that without infringing a particle of the Mahomedan religion; on the contrary, so far as this regulation is connected with the Mussulman religion, you only check a licentious deviation from the principles of Mahomedan law and religion on the point in question."*

The practice of kidnapping children, for the purpose of selling them as slaves, appears to have been very prevalent in various parts of India. Respecting a case of this kind at Midnapore, on the borders of Orissa, in 1794, the magistrate, R. Bathurst, Esq., thus expressed his indignation of the crime.—"To that part of the futwa which respects Shazaddee, equity and humanity alike prompt me to object in the strongest terms. Her crime is *of a nature to break asunder the tenderest ties, and to consign its innocent victims, either rudely torn, or cruelly seduced from their parents' home, to hopeless slavery, to experience in the course of it, too probably, no wages but stripes, no relief but death.* Such is the complexion of her guilt. What says the futwa, which, regulated by Mussulman justice, weighs, it would seem, in the same scale of moral turpitude, the stealing of a cur dog and the kidnapping of a child? Thirty-five strokes with a rattan and four months confinement, which if changed to hard labour and imprisonment for life, although still disproportioned to the extent of her

* Par. Papers on Slavery in India, p. 309—317.

offence, might, perhaps, operate to deter others from the practice of similar enormities."*

The nature of slavery in Canara, under the Madras Presidency, is thus described by J. G. Ravenshaw, Esq., Collector, in Aug .1801 :—" By far the greatest part of the slaves employed in agriculture are the Daerds, of whom there are various descriptions and properties; no order was ever given for their being included in the registers; the whole number of them, by the population statement, is 52,022, men, women, and children; of which number there are in the Baincoor talook 5,894; the number belonging to every landlord shall hereafter, as desired, be entered in the registers. There are three distinctions; the Moondaul, Mogare or Magor, and Mavey Daerd; the two former differ from the latter in the way of food,—neither of them will eat the flesh of a cow or bullock; or go near the place where one has died or been killed, till the carcase is removed; the Mavey Daerd, though he will not kill the animal, will eat its flesh after it is dead. If one dies at the house of a Moondaul or Mogare, a Mavey is sent for to remove the carcase. In the Moondaul and Mayer sects, property descends from uncle to nephew; *a father gives up his children to their uncle.* In the Mogare sects, property descends from father to son. A Mogare and Moondaul will eat together, though it is not common; if, however, they do, the form of taking away the dishes or pans they eat out of, washing and returning them clean to the party who gives the repast, is invariably observed. They never intermarry by consent; but if a Moondaul runs away with a Mogare, the latter sect assemble, call on the Moondaul, and, after reprimanding him for the crime he has committed, make him pay a fine for the offence, and give a repast to the whole party; when they have eaten of which, the Mogare is considered as having relinquished her caste, and being made over to the Moondaul by it, to become a member of her husband's sect. Neither of these sects associate with the Mavey Daerd.

" If a *Moondaul Daerd* goes to a landlord or other person, and says he wants to marry through his interests; if the person consents, he gives him from three to four pagodas to pay the expense of the ceremony; the Daerd, as soon as married, brings his wife to his landlord's house, and

* Par. Papers as above, p. 52. See also pp. 242, 243.

both are bound to serve him and his heirs as long as the husband lives. The landlord is considered as bound to give the man two cloths, each five cubits in length; and the woman two, each of eight cubits length, one to cover the lower and one the upper part of their frame, per annum; the estimated expense of which is one and a half rupees; the man is to receive one and a half, and the woman one hami of rice per diem, besides one mora of rice per annum between them; this last allowance is called 'mogu.' This couple have *no claim over any children they may have born:* they are the exclusive property of their uncle; but if he agrees to their remaining with their father till they are grown up, and their father consents to keep them, this may be done; and if, when grown up, their father's owners give the males money to marry, they are bound to serve him and his heirs as long as they live. If, however, their uncle does not agree to their remaining with their father when young, he takes them, and his master pays them according to the work they do. As to the daughters, if their uncle agree, they may remain with their father till some person comes with their uncle's consent to ask them in marriage; they are then given up and bound to serve their husband's owner. In the event of the husband's death, his master has no right whatever over the mother and children, who become the property of, or for whom the children's uncle is bound to provide, and they are bound to serve his master if he has work for them. If a man wants to marry a second time, his master supplies him with money; in consideration, however, of this extra expense, he stops the 'mogu,' or allowance of one mora of rice per annum. A man receives no daily allowance for himself and family during his master's harvest, but, in lieu thereof, he gets an *eleventh part of as much grain as is cut, threshed, and stacked, by the whole of them;* when this work is done, they receive their daily subsistence as usual. This sect may be called *a life property on the male side;* they are never sold, though they sometimes mortgage themselves. If a man who has no owner is distressed for money, he will borrow of some person, whom he will agree to serve till he repays the amount; their owners may also mortgage them in the same way.

"The *Mogare or Magor Daerds* are bought and sold, and thence *they and their male heirs are bound to serve their master and his heirs for ever.* Females remain with their fathers till married, after which their owners have no claim on them; they become the property of their husband's master. The average price of a man and his wife, if purchased together, is *from four to five pagodas.* These Mogairs receive the same daily allowance of rice and cloth as the Moondauls, but they get no annual allowance, the piece of land and the two trees they get are supposed more than to equal this; and in addition to it, if their master can afford it, he frequently gives them a bullock. The owner pays only as many of the family as work for him. This sect are sometimes mortgaged, as well as sold.

"If a person purchases a man and woman of the *Mauray Daerd sect*, and marries them, they and their male heirs are bound to serve him and his heirs for ever; the purchaser pays the expense of the marriage. If the man dies, and the woman marries again, the children she may have by her new husband are all the property of her owner, by reason of his having purchased the woman; but he has no claim whatever on the new husband. In cases when these people are not purchased, but merely bind themselves to service, on account of some person having paid the expense of their marriages, as the Moondauls do, the same rules are observed as with them; but there are many of these sects, who belonging, or being as it were an appurtenant to an estate, are bought and sold therewith; they enjoy the same privileges and allowances as those of the same sects who are purchased without an estate. The landlord can neither sell nor mortgage them, nor can they, without the landlord's consent, mortgage themselves or children.

"In many of the foregoing cases, an owner is only bound to give daily subsistence to as many of the family of his Daerds as he employs: if he has more than he requires, he may lend them out to other people, who pay him the mogu, or annual allowance of one mora of rice, as a sort of quit-rent or acknowledgment that the Daerd he employs belongs to him. Daerds cannot go to work for another person without their owner's consent, and they are bound to return whenever he may have work for them. This is the result of an inquiry I was induced to make into the customs of the people, in consequence of many complaints having come before me of Daerds being ill-treated by their masters. The little labour has been amply repaid, from a consciousness of my having done justice to many of them, which I should not have considered myself competent of doing without a knowledge of their manners and services.

"Exclusive of the Daerds, there were another sect of slaves in Canara, though I believe many of them are now free. Under the Biddenore government, all illegitimate children, save those by dancing girls, were considered the property of the Sircar, which took possession of, and sold them as slaves, to any person who would purchase them; the number of this sort now is about 722; there are also many slaves imported from Arabia."*

"The utmost to which the sale of slaves is tolerated in Malabar," says J. H. Baber, Esq., Judge and Magistrate in the North Zillah in 1812, "is domestic slavery, and this exclusively confined to those born in a state of bondage; formerly this degraded race of men were the exclusive property of the Hindoos of Malabar, but in course of time, from necessity and other causes, they were transferred and sold to the Mopillas, but never was it bargained that they were to be made proselytes. A Pooliar sold or transferred could not be removed out of the district, his place of nativity; in consequence the social tie among them was still preserved; even the women, though sold, are never separated from their husbands, whom they still follow, however often they may change their masters; the owner of the female, however, still maintaining his claim to her and to her offspring, whose right is thus perpetuated from generation to generation. In some districts *the offspring are divided between the owners of the father and the mother*, but they are never separated from their parents until adults."†

"The slaves in this part of India," says the Collector of Malabar, "may be divided into two very distinct classes; the one consisting of the slaves of Mussulmans, the other of the slaves of Hindoos. The former are exclusively *domestic* slaves employed in the house, and are commonly purchased whilst infants, and brought up in the Mussulman faith by their masters; many of them are females employed in the seraglio or haram of the richer Mussulmans to attend on their ladies; and, once there inclosed, they are seldom allowed egress from it, as they are viewed as part of that establishment, which it is the chief point of honour with a Mussulman to guard from the view of another. The men slaves are employed as menial servants, and having free

* Par. Papers on Slavery in India, p. 548—550. † p. 567.

communications with others, and means of complaint, are generally well treated; but none, except those who have access to the recesses of the haram, can judge of the treatment which the females receive. The Mussulman slaves, however, are comparatively few in number; the great slave population consists of the Hindoo slaves, of whom none are confined, and all of whom, with the exception of a very few, are employed in agriculture, and may be termed field slaves, though occasionally employed in domestic service."*

This state of society is very prevalent in the Indian Archipelago. See a description of Malay Slavery by the Acting President at Fort Marlboro in 1813.†

The evils of slavery are innumerable. "To remedy the evil," says one of the Judges in India, "it appeared to me highly necessary that it should be ascertained and acknowledged, and its extent fully understood."‡ The propriety of this appears from the want of information respecting slavery in India. The following extracts from the valuable Papers on this subject it is hoped will rouse the attention of Britain to the state of slavery in her eastern dominions.

"No progress in arts or science can be expected," says the worthy Judge of Bundlecund," from unhappy beings whose daily reflections reiteratedly press their forlorn condition upon their thoughts. The rudest cultivation of the earth is performed with sullenness and reluctancy, by wretches whose miseries know no end, but in the moments of repose. Perhaps exposed to the burning heat of a vertical sun, immerged to the knees in water, stagnate and unwholesome, respiring a vapour inimical to existence; perhaps buried alive in mines replete with noxious minerals and baneful air, which slowly consumes the human frame, they die by piecemeal.

"Or if (which is the summit of a slave's good fortune) they meet with a more lenient lord, still their comforts are embittered by the dread of a change. The stroke of death, or the pressure of misfortune, may transfer them with their former master's cattle or his lands to a less tender lord; devoid of any established mode of providing for, or bringing up a family, and fearful of entering into the marriage state, having no protection or security that their dearest

* Par. Papers on Slavery in India, p.897. † pp. 203,205. ‡ p. 308.

and most tender connexions will not be set at nought by the capricious lust of pampered power, population suffers.

"In Hindoston, slaves are kept for show, or employed in the meanest and most laborious offices of servitude. In ancient times, slaves were bred to trades; to cultivate the sciences and other philosophic studies; and accordingly some of this class distinguished themselves by their abilities, and contributed to enlighten mankind. But how much more speedily has general improvement increased since the establishment of freedom through the principal parts of Europe. The freest nations have ever been the first to dispel the clouds of error, and brighten the dawnings of knowledge into the meridian splendour of truth.

"If any thing can add to the horror which the idea of slavery raises in every human breast, it is the reflection that, by the Mussulman law respecting female slaves, the master is not only legal lord of their persons for purposes of laborious services, but for those of sensual gratification; even such as his perverted or unnatural passions may impel his brutality to indulge. The enormity of this diabolical law is shocking to humanity, and the horrors of such a wretch's situation are not calmly to be thought of.

"It is not less shocking to reflect that women, who have spent their youth and worn out their persons in the grossest debauchery, when their faded beauty no longer produces their wonted luxuries, and even their former paramours in guilt turn from them with disgust, purchase female children for the avowed purpose of the most licentious life. "These females, were such injurious practices prevented by *the abolition of all slavery*, would become useful members of the community, and add to the prosperity of the state, by the increase of their species. They would marry industrious labourers and mechanics, and numbers would escape being exposed to the venal and promiscuous intercourse of the sexes, which is highly prejudicial to population.

"The desperation sometimes occasioned by the unfeeling inflictions of cruel masters often incite to acts at which humanity shudders. "This spirit of sanguinary despair (for, in a state of slavery, it scarcely deserves the harsh terms of revenge or murder) had risen to such an alarming height, in the Roman empire, as to induce the sages of that early seat of arts and arms to sanction, by law, the most unreasonable and inhuman massacres; they cannot be called legal punishments, where the innocent and the guilty are equally involved in one undistinguished carnage.

"Under systematic slavery the minds of mankind are inevitably debased. Children being educated amongst, and attended by these wretches, imbibe their dispositions, and, having the example of their parents always before their eyes, learn to consider those under them as a distinct race, unworthy of the rights of humanity; consequently they tyrannize over these unhappy beings in mere wantonness, with as little remorse as they torture a fly. The first efforts of imitative cruelty are viewed by the parents without reprehension, their own minds having undergone the same perversion by the same tuition, and the practice of maturity having deadened their feelings; so that I fear not unfrequently this early discovery of vicious inclination is considered by the fond, but mistaken parent, as a sure presage of spirit and future greatness. View the manners of those nations who tolerate slavery, and say whether this reasoning is not warranted by reality."*

Sir William Jones, in a charge to the grand jury in Calcutta, June, 1785, thus describes the miseries of slavery existing at that period, even in the metropolis of British India. "I am assured, from evidence which, though not all judicially taken, has the strongest hold on my belief, that the condition of slaves within our jurisdiction is beyond imagination deplorable; and that cruelties are daily practised on them, chiefly on those of the tenderest age and the weaker sex, which, if it would not give me pain to repeat, and you to hear, yet, for the honour of human nature, I should forbear to particularise. If I except the English from this censure, it is not through partial affection to my own countrymen, but because my information relates chiefly to people of other nations, who likewise call themselves Christians. Hardly a man or a woman exists in a corner of this populous town who hath not at least one slave child, either purchased at a trifling price, or saved, perhaps, from a death that might have been fortunate, for a life that seldom fails of being miserable. Many of you, I presume, have seen large boats filled with such children, coming down the river for open sale at Calcutta; nor can you be ignorant that most of them were stolen from their parents, or bought,

* Par. Papers on Slavery in India, p. 298—300.

perhaps, for a measure of rice in a time of scarcity; and that the sale itself is a defiance of this government, by violating one of its positive orders, which was made some years ago, after a consultation of the most reputable Hindoos in Calcutta, who condemned such a traffic as repugnant to their shastra. The number of small houses in which these victims are pent makes it indeed very difficult for the settlement at large to be apprized of their condition; and, if the sufferers knew where or how to complain, their very complaints may expose them to still harsher treatment—*to be tortured, if remanded, or if set at liberty, to starve.* Be not, however, discouraged by the difficulty of your inquiries; your vigilance cannot but surmount it; and one great example of a just punishment, not capital, will conduce more to the prevention of similar cruelties, than the strongest admonition or severest verbal reproof. Should the slave-holders, through hardness of heart or confidence in their places of concealment, persist in their crimes, you will convince them that their punishment will certainly follow their offence, and the most hardened of them will, no doubt, discontinue the contest."*

In 1810 a claim was preferred before the court of Sudder Dewanny Adawlut for the restoration of some slaves who had escaped from the Nepaul territory, and sought an asylum in the British territory. Nine slaves were stated to have been purchased for 226 rupees. This sum was given by our Government and the slaves liberated. The depositions of two or three of them show the cruel nature of slavery in Nepaul.

"Jeewee acknowledged that he was a slave, but alleged that, being employed in cultivating, and receiving nothing from the prosecutor, he had run away. He represented that *if he should now return to the hills the prosecutor would cut off his ears as a punishment for his offence.*

"Dhunsree acknowledged that she was the slave of the prosecutor, saying, that she *having killed her own child was brought by the prosecutor* before Meer Singh Tuppa, who gave her to him to *keep as his slave*, that *this was the usual punishment for murder in the hilly country;* she added, that, having received nothing from the prosecutor to eat, she had run off.

"Joonhee and Lamee also acknowledged that they were slaves, and alleged the same reason for having run away from the prosecutor.

"Oodhree, witness, deposed that Meer Singh Tuppa had given Nathan and Dhunsree to the prosecutor's son as payment of his monthly allowance; that Nathee had formerly been the slave of Shoobur Suen, and that Dhunsree, having killed her own child, had been given

* Par. Papers on Slavery in India, p. 10. For an affecting account of a slave girl seized at Serampore, see p. 48—50.

by Meer Singh Tuppa to the prosecutor, whose slave she had now been for three years. With respect to the other four persons, the prosecutor not having given them any present, they had therefore run off He further stated that *it was the custom of the hilly country that, if any woman put to death her new born infant, she was reduced to slavery by the ruler; but, if she be able to give her value to her master, he may free her; and, in case of a dispute regarding the amount of the purchase money, it is to be settled on the oath of the master.*"*

It is further stated " that, if the slaves were delivered up to the prosecutor, *he would certainly put them to death on getting them to their own country.*"

R. K. Dick, Esq., Judge of Dacca, in 1813, justly observes—" Slaves, or others, sued under that denomination, labour under many disadvantages in contending against powerful and wealthy claimants, from their peculiar situations, the nature of the claim, want of friends, and their general ignorance and poverty. Their opponents contrive to obtain fraudulent possession, either by pecuniary rewards, or by the hope of better service; or entice them to desert their masters; or, by the same seductive influence, cause them to be inveigled away through the medium of their private agents, and often to be sold at such distant places as to prevent future discovery, or the return of the unfortunate being. I have known several instances of individuals having been happily rescued from this fate and restored to their families. The odious practice of trafficking in slaves has long subsisted in that zillah, and doubtless many and various abuses have been committed under the cloak of an authorized commerce, or at least of such mercantile transactions not specially prohibited. The trade is carried on to a considerable extent, as is universally acknowledged, and, from the best information on the subject, it is computed that *the number of slaves in the district amounts to about one-sixth of the whole population;* and this number *progresssively increases,* as their offspring are also born slaves. It is impossible to form a correct calculation of the number of slaves annually exported from the district, but it is believed to be much less considerable now than formerly."†

The misery of arbitrary servitude is depicted in a very affecting manner in the Par. Papers relative to thirty-five natives of Bengal, who, in 1813, were found in the service of Mr. W. Browne, at Sidney, New South Wales; they were discharged by the colonial magistrates, and restored to their

---

* Par. Papers on Slavery in India, pp. 119, 120. † pp. 243, 244.

native country, at the expense of the British Government in India. (See pp. 267—296). A few of their depositions before the magistrate are given.

" Chotee Lutchman, another servant of Mr. Browne—I complain of want of food; I sometimes got rice, sometimes ottar and wheat, and dhol and corn, the same as the rest; I have been ill treated while I was employed in the store: Mr. O'Brien *tied a rope to me to awake me in case of alarm;* I did not like it, and objected to it; Mr. O'Brien persisted in it, and then he gave me a rope's-ending. I used to do all sorts of work for him; I got a thrashing for throwing some straw out, which offended Mr. O'Brien, in consequence of which I went up to the farm; Mr. Browne ordered me back to Sidney, but as it rained he allowed me to remain till next day. I got drunk, for which Mr. P. Browne put me for three days on short allowance. I ran away in the bush; I was not flogged for it. I have worked on Sundays for myself; if the others go home I want to go also, but if they stop I will not. I had two bottles of rum charged to me; it was watered. I have lost my caste for eating victuals of Europeans, because I could get nothing else.

" Keereim, a table waiter of Mr. Browne's, sworn on the Koran, saith—I have to complain of bad and insufficient food. Mrs. Browne agreed I should be her table waiter, but, since I have been here, I have been put to the work of a groom and chamber-maid, and cooking the dog's victuals. I have often received a thump on the face and a box on the ear, on frivolous occasions. I was once sent for by Lieutenant M'Quarie to prepare his hookah for him. I was told by the ladies to go in my cap; Mr. Browne asked me why I did so, and gave me five or six blows with his fist; I ran behind a cask, where I was so severely beaten that two men came and lifted me up, gave me water, took me in the kitchen, and nursed me. I was so beaten that I lay behind the cask for an hour; Mrs. Browne called out of the window, "*Give the rascal two or three more kicks.*" Mr. Browne once gave me *fifteen strokes* with a horse-whip, because I did not get his breakfast ready in time; I still bear the marks; both Mr. Brownes were up at the farm, and I was ordered by Mrs. Browne to remove their *chamber-pot*; I refused to do so, and she made me do it, by which I have lost my caste. I applied for my provisions to the man who gives them out; he kicked me for asking for them. I came to Sydney to complain to Mr. Browne, and I was sent to the watch-house, brought before Mr. Wentworth, and by him discharged. Mr. Browne said he would investigate it; he came up, and gave the men a club to beat me with. I agreed for twenty seers of food per month; I have never received that quantity while I was in Sydney; I have received rice and ottar, but at the farm I had nothing but damaged corn; Mrs. Browne said, *shall I feed these hogs upon rice?* Sometimes we had butter-milk, but always three parts of water; Mrs. Browne said once, *you hog, you give me all the little potatoes, and keep all the large ones yourself.* I once received some good flour, but generally bad, I gave it to the dogs, and complained to Mrs. Browne, when she gave me some rather better. I want to go home, but, if I had been well treated, I would have remained twenty years. I have been employed in mixing rum and water for the servants, and it was equal quantities of rum and water; they were charged with it.

" The memorial of Chamine Dongrine, and of Charon Munny, respectfully showeth :—

"That both memorialists engaged with Mrs. Browne of Calcutta to serve her in New South Wales, and have both been employed on Mrs. Browne's farm; but, by reason of cruelty and ill-usage on their mistress's part, they pray humbly, but earnestly, to be released from such agreement. The former memorialist has to complain that she was employed at field labour, such as commonly is done by men in this colony; and, having been put to bed of a male infant, she was ordered to return to work by Mrs. Browne *on the fifth day after the child was born!* Upon remonstrating that she was not sufficiently strong, Mrs. Browne withheld her victuals, thereby compelling her to go reaping wheat, the infant lying on the ground of the store-room locked up, *which occasioned its death at twenty-one days old, for want of milk.*

"Your memorialist, Charon Munny, has to represent, amongst a continued length of ill-treatment, that, having been forced to carry a large brazen vessel of great weight, she then being heavy with child, miscarried; the next day Mrs. Browne ordered her to work, such as carrying large logs and other loads.

"Relying fully on the justice and humanity which distinguish every court under British administration, your petitioners submit their hardships to your consideration, should the same appear to require such redress as they ask."*

Of slavery in Malwa, in 1821, Sir John Malcolm observes, —"Male slaves are few in Malwa, and are generally treated more like adopted children than menials. The case is very different with females, who almost in every instance are sold to prostitution; some, it is true, rise to be favourite mistresses of their master, and enjoy both power and luxury, while others are raised by the success in life of their sons, but these are exceptions. The dancing women, who are all slaves, are condemned to a life of toil and vice, for the profit of others, and some of the first Rajpoot chiefs and zemindars in Malwa, who have from fifty to 200 female slaves in their family, after employing them in all the menial labours of their house during the day, send them at night to their own dwellings, where they are at liberty to form such connexions as they please; but a large share of the profits of that promiscuous intercourse into which they fall is annually exacted by their master, who adds any children they have to his list of slaves. The female slaves in this condition, as well as those of the dancing sets, are not permitted to marry, and are often very harshly treated; so that the latter, from this cause and the connexions they form, are constantly in the habit of running away. If discovered, they are always given up, provided the deed of purchase can be produced; which with them, above all others, must be

* Par. Papers on Slavery in India, pp. 274, 275, 276 281.

registered at the cutwall's chabootre at the period the slave is bought.

"It is not the habit of the native governments of Malwa to take any cognizance of the punishment which masters inflict upon slaves, except such extend to their life, when they are responsible; they are in some cases cruelly treated, but this is not general; it is indeed against the interest of the master to do so, when there are so many opportunities of escaping from his authority.

"The state of Malwa for the last thirty years has been favourable to the species of slavery described, and that province is filled with the mixed progeny of these unfortunate women. This traffic must however now decrease, as the Gwarriahs and others who carried it on, can no longer steal or conceal children with that confidence of impunity which they had long done. A few years ago no man dared leave his own district to inquire after his wife and daughter; the whole country can be now traversed in safety. From this cause, and the discoveries of guilt that have recently been made, the stealers of women and children have taken alarm; while the restitution to their relatives of slaves, bought by them at high prices, must deter future purchasers."*

The Committee appointed by the Government of Prince of Wales Island, in 1808, to report on the propriety of the abolition of slavery, advert to one of the many evils of this state of society in the following terms:—"Allowing that the abolition of slavery might have the effect to retard the increase of the population, by partially preventing the arrival of settlers, it would benefit the island in another respect most essentially—by effectually putting a stop to the infamous practice (still existing, notwithstanding every effort and regulation of government) of purchasing females for the purpose of hiring them, and compelling them to ply as public prostitutes, and enable many industrious Chinese and others to obtain wives, whom this infamous practice has hitherto prevented (the great gain resulting from it enabling the bawds to purchase these females at most extravagant prices); and consequently by connecting these Chinese and others more permanently, through the medium of families, with the settlement, will not only improve much the character of the community, but tend ultimately to afford

* Par. Papers, p. 415, 416.

a more certain source of increase of population than from casual residents."*

The evils of slavery in the Island of Nias, near Sumatra, are very forcibly depicted in an article from the Singapore Chronicle. "The circumstances that attend the traffic of slaves are no less revolting to humanity than those which marked it on the coast of Africa. The unhappy victims torn by violence from their friends and country, and delivered, pinioned hand and foot, to the dealers in human flesh, are kept bound during the whole course of the voyage—a precaution which is found necessary to the safety of the crew. Instances have occurred where the captives have seized a moment of liberty to snatch up the first weapon within their reach, stab all whom they encountered, and complete the scene by leaping overboard, and voluntarily seeking a watery death! The sudden change of diet to which they are subjected on board a ship, added to the confinement and dejection of mind, prove fatal to many. Of a cargo of thirty slaves, twenty have been known to perish before the conclusion of the voyage; and on a moderate calculation it may be estimated, that, of the total number purchased, *one-fourth* never reach their destination.

"On the scenes of violence that take place in the country itself, in the search of victims, it is needless to dwell; they can be better imagined than described. We shall relate one well authenticated instance, given by an eye-witness. A plan had been laid to attack a single insulated house, inhabited by a man, his wife, and children, and to seize the whole family. At the appointed hour the house was surrounded; the man no sooner discovered his situation, and saw that there was no escape, than he locked himself in the inner apartment, drew his kris, killed first his wife and children, and then plunged it into his own breast, preferring death to a life of slavery!

"Independently of the habits of cruelty and rapine, which the slave trade tends to infuse, the exorbitant profits it holds out create an aversion to the slower advantages of legitimate commerce and agricultural labour. In order to convey their produce to the sea-ports, the inhabitants of the interior are obliged to unite in parties of several hundreds, all completely armed, and, with their loads of rice on their backs, descend in order of battle to the shores to dispose of

* Par. Papers, p. 441.

it; such is the general insecurity and distrust, that the husbandman goes armed to his labour in the fields, they select the most difficult situations for their villages, and construct their houses with every precaution against surprises."* (See Imp. Mag. Jan. 1830).

Many pages of the Par. Documents on Eastern Slavery are occupied in detailing the state of the slaves in Malabar, especially in the investigation of the conduct of a Mr. Browne, of Anjarakandy, and his slaves (see pp. 560—790). A few extracts only can be given of the examinations of these slaves, taken by the magistrate of Zillah, North Malabar.

"I was with five children who were tending cattle, and while at play two mopillas seized me and took me that very night to Aloppi, where they gave me to Assen Ally, who sent me in a moonchoo to Mahé; thence I was sent to Anjarakandy, where they made me eat Pooliars' food; before, if I should be defiled by Pooliars, I must wash myself. I

---

* The misery of slavery in the Isle of France is thus affectingly described in a letter from that island. "Last night I heard a considerable noise in the yard in which we live, connected with another family. We went to the door, and saw a female slave with her hands tied behind her, and her mistress beating her with a club in a most dreadful manner. My blood ran cold within me, and I could quietly see it no longer. I went up to the mistress, and, in broken French, asked her to stop, and what her servant had done. I talked with her till her anger appeared to be abated; and she concluded her punishment with flinging the club she had in her hands at the poor creature's head, which made the blood run down on her garment! The slave continued with her hands tied behind her all night. They were untied this morning, and she spent the day in labour. This evening I saw a large chain brought into the yard, with a ring at one end, just large enough to go round her neck. The chain was as large and heavy as an ox chain, and reached from her neck to the ground. The ring was fastened with a lock and key. The poor creature stood trembling, while they were preparing to put the chain on her. The mistress' rage rekindled at seeing her, and she began beating her as before. I went to her again, and begged she would stop. She did; but so full of anger that she could hardly speak. When she became a little calm, I asked her if she could not forgive her servant. She made me understand that she would forgive her, because I had asked her; but she would not have her servant to think it was out of any favour to her. She told her slave that she forgave her, because I requested it. The slave came, knelt, and kissed my feet, and said, '*Mercy madum, mercy madam,*' meaning, Thank you madam. I could scarcely forbear weeping at her gratitude. The mistress promised me the chain should not be put on her, and ordered it to be carried away. I have felt very happy this evening, that this poor slave can lie down and sleep without that heavy chain." (Mem. of Mrs. Judson, p. 81. For an account of the misery of a Burmese slave girl, see p. 306.)

am not willing to return to Anjarakandy, if I can be admitted again to my caste; I wish to go to my country. My house name is Tekkadati.

"My tambooran is Panakada Canden; I was asleep at night when Panaparambil Pamikaree seized and brought me away, and gave me to Ayecagata Shuk Moidun, who gave me to a Sahib at Cochin; thence I was put in a moonchoo and landed at Chetwa; whence Coony Pareay and Bappen brought me by land to the Sahib, at the Bangsaul of Anjarakandy, twelve other polia s who were also brought with me are now here.

"I was at work, when, without the knowledge of my tambooran and poolian (husband), myself and two of my children, Dampan and Kanda, were seized by Eddacatta Vudeen, mopla and some others, and brought to Cochin, detained there eleven days, and then given to Walladara who brought us in a manchoo and landed us at Chitwa; besides myself there were eleven others, whence two moplas of Mahé, named Coony Parray and Bappen, brought us to Anjarakandy, and made us stay with a Sahib; those eleven that were brought with me are present here."*

"Nothing can be more abject and wretched (says J. H. Baker, Esq., Magistrate in Malabar) than the condition of that degraded race of mortals, the slaves of Malabar, whose huts (to use the words of Mr. Francis Buchanan in his Tour through Malabar, &c.) are little better than mere baskets, and whose diminutive stature, and squalid appearance, evidently show a want of adequate nourishment."†

"The slave alone (says Mr. Græme in his Report of Malabar, 1822) has his sieve of a hut in the centre of the rice lands; but on the coast at least he is an industrious, and not an unintelligent being, and in good condition, and nothing deficient in bodily frame. In the interior, he is a wretched, half-starved, diminutive creature, stinted in his food, and exposed to the inclemencies of the weather, whose state demands that commiseration and amelioration which may confidently be expected from the humanity of the British' Government, provided it can be shown that a change for the better can be effected without hazarding an evil of any formidable magnitude, without incurring the risk of general discontent, or exciting a worse feeling towards the objects themselves, by an unsuccessful endeavour to mitigate their ill treatment. The slaves of Malabar, known generally by the name of chermurs, are entirely prædial, or rustic, being engaged only in the cultivation of rice lands and plantations. I except, of course, the Mussulmans, who may be domestic slaves, and live in the houses of their masters, and partake of all the privileges of their religion. This kind of slavery is a social fraternity, and is

---

* Par. Papers, pp. 605. 609. 613. † p. 760, 761.

a step to the best comforts, and the highest honours of life among Mussulmans. It is totally dissimilar, in every essential point, to the servitude of the chermur, which is the most prevalent designation of the slaves of Malabar."*

"In the Calicut district, there is an anomaly in the general system among the Paliur, the Kulladee, and the Kunnakur, which are the only three castes of slaves residing there. There is a mixture of the two customs of mukkatayum and murroo mukkatayum, that is, the one or the other does not obtain separately in different families in the district, but in all the families throughout the district the inheritance partakes of the two modes, and *half of the children are considered to go with the mother, and consequently to belong to her proprietor, and half to be attached to the father, and therefore to be the property of his master. Where the number may not admit of an equal division, the odd number is reckoned to be the mother's!* The wife of a Palium, and of all the castes who observe the murroo mukkatayum, may be sold separately, and may therefore belong to a different master from the master of her husband, but she cannot be separated from her husband; she must be allowed to remain with him; she is purchased separately in consideration of her future offspring, which, by the custom of murroo mukkatayum, would become the property of her purchaser. In the other castes, the females are not separately saleable, neither the wife nor her female children. The daughters become the temporary property of the masters of their husbands; but this right of property ceases upon the death of the husband, and the wife returns to the house of her father. The rules of Malabar prescribe that a slave of the caste of Poleyan, Waloovan, and Brayen, shall remain seventy-two paces from a Bramin and from a Nair, and forty-eight from a Tean. A slave of the Kunakur caste sixty-four paces from a Bramin and Nair, and forty from a Tean; and the other castes generally forty-eight paces from a Bramin and Nair, twenty-four from a Tean! In the northern division these rules are deviated from in practice, in favour of the slaves, whilst in the southern division they are thought to be exceeded in strictness."†

One of the Magistrates, in 1823, suggested that, on account of "certain instances of cruelty practised on slaves by their masters, the forfeiture of the right of property over slaves

---

* Par. Papers, 914. † p. 920.

should be made the penalty for ill usage."—Slaves appear to have their noses cut off occasionally by their cruel masters. "Adverting (says one of the judges) to the facts elicited during the foregoing trial, *it will no longer be denied that cruelties are practised upon the slaves of Malabar*, and that our courts and cutcherries are no restraints upon their owners or employers; for whatever doubts may exist with regard to the exact period of the death of the Cherooman Koorry Noryady, or to the immediate cause of his death, there can be none as to the fact of *his nose having been amputated, as well as those of three other slaves belonging to the same owner;* and that, although the case had come before the magistrate, no steps have been taken to bring the perpetrators of such horrid barbarities to justice. Upon the latter head it may be argued that the slaves themselves preferred no complaint: but, if it is to depend upon the slaves themselves to seek for the protection of the laws, their situation must be hopeless indeed; for, having no means of subsistence, independent of their owners or employers, their repairing to and attending upon a public cutcherry is a thing physically impossible; and even though those provisions of the regulations that require all complaints to be preferred in writing were dispensed with in favour of slaves, and they were exempted from the payment of tolls at the numerous ferries they would have to pass, and though an allowance were made to them by government during their detention at the cutcherries and courts, unless forfeiture of the right of property over slaves was the penalty for ill usage, their situation would only become more intolerable than it was before they complained. I never myself entertained any other opinion, than that the treatment of the slaves in Malabar, particularly in the interior, was the very reverse of a mild description; and I have no doubt the late Commissioner, Mr. Græme, has, in his report upon Malabar, confirmed all I have written upon this most interesting subject, and suggested such measures as will, if carried into effect, be the means of improving greatly their condition, and of extending to them protection against, at least similar cruelties to those brought to light in the trial that has given rise to those observations."*

The last page but one of the Papers contains the following

* Par. Papers on Slavery, p. 928.

intimation of the misery of slavery in British India.—" The second Judge makes mention of two cases tried in Canara, wherein the accused were charged with causing the death of their slaves by severe chastisement, which, he states, induced him to make inquiry at Mangalore, regarding the prevailing custom in instances where the slave of one master marries the slave of another; and particularly whether their respective owners can prevent them from living together. The second judge remarks that the frequent absence from his ' master's work, which occasioned the deceased's chastisement in one of the above cases, was owing to visits to his wife, who resided at a distance on her master's estate, *who would not allow her to live with her husband*;' he was told that it is usual for the female slave to reside with her husband, and, if his residence be at such a distance as to prevent her from coming to work daily at her master's house, the master of the husband must indemnify her owner by the payment annually of half a moorah of rice; but, if the master should employ the female at his own house, he must employ also her husband, whose owner he must indemnify by the payment annually of one moorah of rice. The second judge offers his opinion that the magistrate should correctly inform himself on this point, and be required under the authority of government, after due notice given, to enforce the obligation on the part of the owners, to *allow their married slaves to live together*. The court of Foujdaree Adawlut are of opinion that the interference here proposed to be exercised by the magistrate could not be put in practice without the enactment of a Regulation for that purpose; and they are not prepared to suggest provisions with this view which would be free from objections; should, however, the Honourable the Governor in council deem it fit to give effect to the humane recommendation of the Judge, it may be in the power of the provincial court, in communication with the magistrates in the provinces of Malabar and Canara, to devise a mode of preventing the separation of married slaves, without any violation of rights, which the established usages in this respect confer."*

This chapter may be closed by contrasting " the effects of slavery with those of voluntary servitude under a system of liberty," as described by the Judge of Bundlecund.

---

* Par. Papers on Slavery in India, pp. 235, 236.

SLAVERY.	VOLUNTARY SERVITUDE.
"1. It is the interest and constant object of the master to get the greatest quantity of labour at the cheapest rate; consequently he stints the slave in food and raiment. It may be urged, by clothing and feeding well, the slave would be strong, and better able to endure fatigue, but it is the constant practice of avarice, by its short-sighted policy, to counteract its own wishes: a trifling immediate advantage being generally preferred to much more essential objects, if more remote.	1. The same object actuates the master here also, but, the servant being free to stipulate, his interest counteracts that of the other, and the contest reduces and establishes the price of labour at its just rate, that is, it allows the servant to provide for himself and family, and leaves the master a competent profit.
2. It is the uniform desire and endeavour of the slave to mitigate the hardship of his lot by evading toil, which brings him no advantage.	2. It is the general wish of servants to satisfy their masters, that they may not lose their employment; or, if their services are no longer requisite, to entitle them to a recommendation, not to insist on the greater quantity of work a servant will perform.
3. The slave, finding himself subject to capricious treatment and change of masters, will seldom add the cares of providing for a family of children to his other woes, and consequently avoids marriage.	3. A servant knowing he can dispose of his earning as he pleases, and being thus provided with an independent fund for the provision of a wife, &c., will marry; thus the state reaps benefit by the increase of population.
4. In their old age, it is the master's interest to get rid of the feeble, who eat but cannot labour; consequently the worn down wretch is neglected, and perishes more speedily for want of care, having no family or children to ameliorate and ease the pains of sickness, or prop the weakness of decline, by the soothing attention of filial duty and affection.	4. Under voluntary servitude, by the time old age approaches, many have saved a little from the rewards of their services, to assist in softening the hardships of sickness and debility, &c.; and almost all, having married and added to the general stock of industry and riches, have some family or children to soothe the evening of life. Though this may have little weight in the scale of political reasoning, it certainly ought to have some in that of humanity.
5. In times of scarcity and famine, the master must starve his slaves, send them to plunder, or emancipate them. The latter, his avarice will never permit.	5. In real scarcity, a servant is not harder to subsist than a slave; he will not eat more, and, having his stipulated wages, he is better enabled to evade the horrid effects of famine, by anticipating its approach, and making a timely provision.

6. When they can sell themselves or their children, numbers are induced to flock to great towns and cities, whereby many die from disappointed expectation, who would otherwise pick up a scanty subsistence in scattered villages.

6. Were slavery abolished, this evil could not happen: knowing they could not sell themselves or children, &c., they would not be tempted to cities in such numbers; having only a precarious charity to rely on, they would therefore substitute many modes of supplying a mere sustenance in the country, from berries, herbs, &c.

7. It would appear that it is the advantage of masters to promote *the rearing of their slaves.* This, like many other theoretic ideas, is found to be fallacious, and contradicted by fact. The expense of rearing, and the loss incurred by the indispensable attendance of the parents to their offspring, has always made proprietors prefer recruiting casual diminutions of their slaves by purchase, even in Rome, where slavery was universal. How much more will masters avoid such trouble and expense in this country, where I have seen, in a time of local scarcity only, a stout lad of fourteen or fifteen years old sold for the trifling consideration of *two rupees*, scarcely a month's wages for the meanest servant.

7. Were voluntary servitude substituted for slavery, avarice, real or mistaken, could not affect population.

8. Women of bad fame purchase females for the most public prostitution, which are thereby lost to the community.

8. Abolish the unnatural law of slavery, and the evil could not occur.

9. Children are sometimes sold to bondage by the fraudulent villany of others, in the cases of death or absence of parents, instances of which are not uncommon.

9. Nor this.

10. The sanction of slavery not many years ago gave birth to an infamous and most diabolical traffic, shocking to think of, and as injurious to our government as disgraceful to the wretches concerned, diminishing our resources, by depriving us of subjects."

10. Nor this.

"The effects of slavery are as plainly injurious as the benefits of freedom are obvious and undoubted."*

CHAP. II.

Nature and success of efforts for the abolition of the Slave Trade in India—melioration of Slavery by the Hindoos, Mussulmans, French, Dutch, and British.

THE abolition of the Slave Trade by the British nation was attended with very salutary effects in British India. It is pleasing to trace the influence of just and humane principles in the abolition of the Slave Trade in our Eastern dominions, and the nature of the efforts, though partial, to meliorate the existing state of slavery in those extensive territories.

" From a translation of the Hindoo Laws, transmitted by the Bengal Government to the Honourable Court of Directors in 1774, it appears that the Hindoos admitted various modes of enfranchising slaves."—

" Whoever is born of a female slave, and whoever hath been purchased for a price, and whoever hath been found by chance any where, and whoever is a slave by descent from his ancestors, these four species of slaves, until they are freed by the voluntary consent of their master, cannot have their liberty; if their master, from a principle of beneficence, gives them liberty, they become free.

" Whoever, having received his victuals from a person during the time of a famine, hath become his slave, *upon giving to his provider whatever he received from him during the time of famine, and also two head of cattle, may become free from his servitude;* according to the ordinations of Pachesputtee Misr, approved. Chendeesur, upon this head, speaks thus: That he who has received victuals during a famine, and hath by those means become a slave, on giving two head of cattle to his provider, may become free.

" Whoever, having been given up as a pledge for money lent, performs service to the creditor, recovers his liberty whenever the debtor discharges the debt; if the debtor neglects to pay the creditor his money, and takes no thought of the person whom he left as a pledge, that person becomes the purchased slave of the creditor.

" Whoever, being unable to pay his creditor a debt, hath borrowed a sum of money from another person, and paid his former creditor therewith, and hath thus become a slave to the second creditor, or who, to

---

* Par Papers on Slavery in India, p. 301—303.

silence the importunities of his creditor's demands, hath yielded himself a slave to that creditor, such kind of slaves shall not be released from servitude until payment of the debts.

"Whoever, by the loss of the chance in any game, and whoever by the fortune of war is enslaved, these two persons, *upon giving two others equal to themselves in exchange, are released from their servitude!*

"If the slave of one person goes to another, and of his own desire consents to be the slave of that person, in this case he must still be the property of the person to whom he was first a slave. The mode of release for every kind of slave shall take place according to the ordination laid down for each.

"A Chehtree and Bice, who, after having been Sinasses (religious mendicants) apostate from that way of life, and are become the slaves of the magistrate, can never be released.

"If a Brahmin hath committed this crime, the magistrate shall not make him a slave; but, having branded him in the forehead with the print of a dog's foot, shall banish him the kingdom.

"Whoever hath yielded himself a slave for a stipulated time, upon the completion of that term shall recover his freedom.

"Whoever performs a servitude for his subsistence, shall recover his freedom upon renouncing that subsistence.

"Whoever, for the sake of enjoying a slave girl, becomes a slave to any person, he shall recover his freedom upon renouncing the slave girl.

"Whoever hath become a slave, by selling himself to any person, he shall not be free until the master, of his own accord, gives him his freedom.

"If the master, from a principle of beneficence, gives him his liberty, he becomes free.

"If a thief, having stolen the child of any person, sells it to another; or a man, by absolute violence, forces another to be a slave, the magistrate shall restore such person to his freedom.

"If the master of a slave should be in imminent danger of his life, and at that time this slave, by his own efforts and presence of mind, is able to save the life of his master, *the slave aforesaid shall be freed from his servitude, and be held as a son;* if he choose it, he may stay with his former master, or, if he choose it, shall quit that place, and go where he will at liberty.

"Whoever is without a legitimate child, and hath a child from the womb of a slave girl, *that girl, together with her son, becomes free.*

"When any person, from a principle of beneficence, would release his slave, the mode of it is this: the aforesaid slave shall fill a pitcher with water, and put therein berenge-à-rook (rice that has been cleansed without boiling), and flowers, and doub (a kind of small salad), and, taking the pitcher upon his shoulder, shall stand near his master; and the master, putting the pitcher upon the slave's head, shall then break the pitcher, so that the water, rice, flowers, and doub, that were in the pitcher, may fall upon the slave's body; after that, the master shall three times pronounce the words, '*I have made you free:*' upon this speech, the slave aforesaid shall take some steps towards the east, whereupon he shall be free.

"Whoever hath become a slave to any person, *the master is proprietor of any property that slave may acquire, exclusive of the price of his own* *slavery, and exclusive also of any thing which may be given to him as a present.*"*

Lord Cornwallis, Governor General of India, in a letter to the Court of Directors in Aug. 1789, states his detestation of slavery and his purpose to suppress it as far as he was able.—"An infamous traffic has, it seems, long been carried on in this country by the low Portuguese, and even by several foreign European seafaring people and traders, in purchasing and collecting native children in a clandestine manner, and exporting them for sale to the French islands, and other parts of India.

"I have at different times taken steps to prevent the continuance of practices which are so shocking to humanity, and so pernicious to your interests. And, in order to deter all persons under the authority of this government from being concerned in that species of trade, I lately directed that a commander of a country vessel, who carried off some children last winter, should be *prosecuted criminally* before the Supreme Court; and I have likewise published a proclamation, to give notice that any person living under the Company's protection, or in any shape under the authority of this government, who shall be convicted of carrying on, or aiding or abetting the barbarous traffic that I have mentioned, will be certain of meeting with the most exemplary punishment.

"There are many obstacles in the way against abolishing slavery entirely in the Company's dominions, as the number of slaves is considerable, and the practice is sanctioned both by the Mahomedan and Hindoo laws.

"I have, however, a plan† under consideration, which I hope to be able to execute without doing much injury to the private interests, or offering great violence to the feelings of the natives, and which has for its object the abolition of the practice under certain limitations, and the establishing some rules and regulations to alleviate, as much as may be possible, the misery of those unfortunate people during the time that they may be retained in that wretched situation."‡

A Proclamation was made in the same year and was "published in the English and country languages." Referring to the period at which it was issued, this document

---

* Par. Papers on Slavery in India, pp. 7, 8.

"† No further notice of the plan here adverted to by his Lordship has been traced upon the records of the Bengal Government."

‡ Par. Papers as above, p. 13.

must be read with considerable interest. See this Proclamation at the foot of the page.

It is pleasing at this period to see the French authorities in India co-operating with the British in suppressing this trade in human beings. "We understand," says the Calcutta Gazette of Sep. 17, 1789, "Monsieur Montigny, governor of Chandernagore, has lately issued a proclamation prohibiting all persons within the jurisdiction of the French government from purchasing or transporting any of the Natives of these provinces as slaves; and, in order more effectually to prevent this infamous practice, a reward of forty rupees is offered to any person who shall give information of the offender, besides the sum of ten rupees to be given to each slave who shall be released in consequence. Both sums to be paid by the offender. The master attendant of Chandernagore is also directed to see that no Na-

---

"PROCLAMATION.—Whereas information, the truth of which cannot be doubted, has been received by the Governor General in council, that many Natives and some Europeans, in opposition to the laws and ordinances of this country, and the dictates of humanity, have been for a long time in the practice of purchasing or collecting Natives of both sexes, children as well as adults, for the purpose of exporting them for sale as slaves in different parts of India or elsewhere: and whereas the Governor General in Council is determined to exert to the utmost extent the power and authority vested in him, in order to prevent such practice in future, and to deter, by the most exemplary punishment, those persons who are not to be otherwise restrained from committing the offence: his lordship hereby declares that all and every person or persons subject to the jurisdiction of the Supreme Court, or in any respect to the authority of this government, who shall in future be concerned directly or indirectly in the above-mentioned inhuman and detestable traffic, shall be prosecuted with the utmost rigour, in the Supreme Court, at the expense of the Company, and, if British born subjects, shall be forthwith ordered to Europe; or, if such person or persons be not subject to the Court's jurisdiction, he or they, upon information being given to the magistrate of the place or district in which the offence shall have been committed, shall be apprehended by him and kept in confinement, to be dealt with according to the laws of the country.

"And also, that no one may plead ignorance hereof, the superintendents of the police for the town of Calcutta, and the magistrates of Adawluts in the several parts of the country, are hereby required to give immediate notice of this proclamation in such manner as shall render the knowledge of it universal to persons of all descriptions, and to repeat the same on the first day of January in every year; they are further directed to pay the strictest attention to the regulations contained in it, and to take the most active steps in their power to enforce them.

"And that all persons offending against this proclamation may be brought to punishment for the same, and the unhappy sufferers rescued

tive be embarked without an order signed by the governor; and all captains of vessels trading to the port of Chandernagore are strictly prohibited from receiving any Natives on board. Nothing can reflect greater honour on the humanity of Monsieur Montigny, and the liberal policy of the French government, than the above order; and we have no doubt this earnest co-operation with the measures already taken by our own government will put an effectual stop to this odious and detestable traffic."*

To the same effect is the following letter from the French governor of Pondicherry to the governor of Madras, March, 1798:—" I have taken notice of complaints made by you to my predecessor, respecting the continuance of the illicit

---

from misery, a reward of *one hundred sicca rupees* is hereby offered for the discovery of every offender, to be paid on his conviction before the Supreme Court of Judicature, or before the Magistrate of the district, and of fifty rupees for such person of either sex who shall be delivered from slavery, or illegal confinement, in consequence of such discovery. The money will be paid to the informer or informers on his or their application to the Secretary of government, and presenting to him a certificate of the conviction of the person or persons committing the offence, of which such informer or informers made discovery.

" The Governor General in Council further recommends to British commercial houses, and private merchants, to assist, as far as depends upon them, in carrying these regulations into effect, by taking the most effectual means in their power to prevent the commanders of their ships or vessels, or of ships or vessels consigned to them, or otherwise placed under their directions, from carrying away Natives of this country in order to sell them for slaves.

" The master attendant of this port is hereby forbidden to grant in future an English pilot to any ship or vessel, the commander of which shall not have previously declared upon oath that there are not then on board, and he will not, during his continuance in the river, consent to receive on board, any Natives to be exported as slaves, with an intent to dispose of them at some foreign place, or whom he (the commander) has any reason to imagine will be disposed of as such after they leave this country.

" And the master attendant is hereby directed to give notice to all the Native pilots that if they should pilot out any vessel having on board Natives of this description, knowing or believing them to be such, the privilege of piloting will be taken from them for ever, and their names and offence registered. And, that no one may plead ignorance of this order, it is hereby directed that it be placed constantly in view at the Banksaul, in the English and country languages.†

Proclaimed at Fort William, in Bengal, this 22nd day of July, 1789.

By order of the Governor General in Council,

(signed) *E. Hay*, Secretary to the Government."

* Par. Papers on Slavery in India, p. 22. See also in 1791, p. 34.

† Par. Papers, pp. 18, 19.

traffic in slaves, notwithstanding the orders of your government and of our own; my Lord Cornwallis has likewise addressed to me new complaints on this subject. I can only assure you that I will give fresh orders on the occasion, with an assurance, that those who deviate therefrom shall be arrested and prosecuted according to law. If your government, which I do not doubt, will readily second ours in that laudable intention, it will be difficult for the guilty to escape this double precaution. I am too desirous to see a stop put to so shameful a traffic, not to assure you of our efforts on that occasion, and to supplicate you to unite those of your government."*

Some free Natives of Bengal having been taken to St. Helena, and sold as slaves, the practice was prohibited by authority. The Honourable Court of Directors, in a Letter to the Governor General in Feb. 1793, observe—"It having been stated in the letter to you from the Governor and Council of St. Helena, dated 5th July, 1791, that they have heard of other complaints of the Natives of Bengal, who were entirely free, having been unjustly sold on that island, we direct that you cause an advertisement to be issued for the discovery thereof, and that you take the most effectual means for liberating such as may be under this unfortunate predicament; and, for putting a stop to a practice so disgraceful to humanity, reporting your proceedings thereon, for our information."†

To secure the return of Native servants, proceeding from Bengal to Europe, it was determined by the Government that a bond of 1000 rupees should be given for each individual. "The humane purpose of this bond," says the Hon. Court, in July, 1796, "is sufficient to ensure our approbation of the measure."

The murder of a slave, under the Bengal Government, is made a capital offence. In 1799 was issued "A Regulation for certain Modifications of the Mahomedan Law in cases of Murder." It enjoins—"In every case of wilful murder, wherein the crime may appear to the court of Nizamut Adawlut to have been fully established against the prisoner, but the futwa of the law officers of that court shall declare the prisoner not liable under the Mahomedan law

---

* Par. Papers on Slavery in India, p. 520. See pp. 487, 493.
† Par. Papers, p. 45. See the Proclamation p. 407.

to suffer death by *kissans* (or retaliation), solely on the ground of the prisoner's being father or mother, grandfather or grandmother, or other ancestor of the slain; or of the heirs of the slain, or one of the heirs of the slain, being the child, or grandchild, or other descendant of the prisoner; or of the slain having been the slave of the prisoner or of any other person, or a slave appropriated for the service of the public; or on any similar ground of personal distinction and exception from the general rules of equal justice; the court of Nizamut Adawlut, provided they see no circumstances in the case which may render the prisoner a proper object of mercy, shall sentence him to suffer death, as if the futwa of their law officers had declared him liable to kissans, or to suffer death by seazut, as authorized by the Mahomedan law in all cases of wilful murder, under the discretion vested in the magistrate, with regard to this principle of punishment, for the ends of public justice."*

In 1796 a communication was addressed to the Governor of Bombay from the Sultan and chiefs of the island of Johanna, praying for assistance against the incursions of the French and the Madagascar people, who destroyed and enslaved the inhabitants. They offer to "give these islands to the Company," and that "whatever shall be produced in this country, half shall be for you and the other half for us." In consideration of the friendly treatment which ships invariably received, at Johanna, some assistance was given to these islanders. (See the letters, which are very curious documents, pp. 82—84). In 1813 an application was made to Bombay by the Sultan of Johanna respecting some persons who had been carried from the island to the Mauritius by the French and there reduced to slavery. The Hon. Court of Directors very humanely remark, upon the proceedings of the Indian Government,—"With respect to the circumstance alleged by the king of Johanna, of certain persons, his subjects, having been carried by the French to Mauritius, and there made slaves, we entirely approve of your suggestion to the Governor of the Mauritius, for the purchase of such individuals, if in a state of slavery; and likewise of your further application to the Governor of Mauritius, respecting several natives of our Indian provinces of both sexes, being in a state of slavery

* Par. Papers on Slavery in India, p. 76.

on that island, and requesting his assistance in obtaining their release, or in purchasing their freedom, and charging the expense to your Government."*

In 1811 an important "*Regulation for preventing the importation of slaves from foreign countries, and the sale of slaves in the Territories immediately dependent on the Presidency of Fort William*," was passed by the Vice President in Council.† Copies of the regulation X. 1811, were ordered to be circulated to the officers of the

---

* Par. Papers on Slavery in India, p. 224.

† "Whereas instances have occurred of the importation of slaves from foreign countries into the British territories; and whereas such traffic is inconsistent with the dictates of humanity, and with the principles by which the administration of this country is conducted; the following Rules have been enacted, to be in force immediately on their promulgation throughout the territories immediately dependent on the Presidency of Fort William.

"The importation of slaves, whether by land or by sea, into the places immediately dependent on the Presidency of Fort William, is hereby strictly prohibited; and any person infringing this prohibition shall be liable to be prosecuted and punished for the offence by the courts of criminal judicature.

"Any person who may be convicted of the offence of importing slaves into the British territories, subsequently to the promulgation of this regulation, shall be sentenced to imprisonment for the period of six months, and to pay a fine to government according to his circumstances in life, not exceeding however the sum of two hundred rupees, commutable, if not duly discharged, to imprisonment for the further period of six months on the expiration of the former part of the sentence.

"Persons imported as slaves into the British territories shall be liable to be discharged or sent back to their friends and connexions in the country from which they may have been imported, according as may appear most advisable to the magistrate by whom the decision on the case may be passed.

First: For the more effectual prevention of the importation of slaves, at the port of Calcutta, captains or super-cargoes of vessels, with the exception of the Honourable Company's ships, importing at Calcutta, shall, previously to being permitted to land any part of their cargo or goods, execute a bond rendering themselves liable to the payment of a penalty of *five thousand rupees*, in the event of their disposing of any persons as slaves.

"Second: the bond mentioned in the preceding clause shall be taken by one of His Majesty's justices of the peace, acting in and for the town of Calcutta, who will of course cause it to be executed in due form.

"Third: It will be the duty of the collecter of government customs at Calcutta, to ascertain that the prescribed bond has been executed previously to permitting any part of the cargo or goods of any vessel, the Honourable Company's ships excepted, to be landed.

"Fourth: The following is the form of the Bond to be taken in the cases above stated:

Bengal Government, and also forwarded to those of Fort St. George, and Bombay. It was also resolved that this "regulation be sent to the political department, in order that a communication may be made to any of the Native States, which it may be deemed proper to apprise of the purport of the regulation."

The Resident at Delhi, in 1812, C. T. Metcalfe, Esq., most actively prosecuted the humane measures of the Government. He wrote to the Chief Secretary as follows:— "The slave trade, which has been prohibited for a considerable time in the other provinces of the British dominions in India, continued to exist in the district of Delhi subsequently to its abolition in other places, no local orders having been issued for its discontinuance; and, in consequence, the resort of slave merchants to this quarter was becoming more frequent than ever. Being convinced that it was not the intention of government that this iniquitous

---

KNOW all men by these presents, That I, *captain of the* *now lying and being in the river Hooghly in Bengal, am held and firmly bound unto the United Company of Merchants of England trading to the East Indies in the sum of five thousand sicca rupees of lawful money of Bengal, to be paid to the said United Company, their certain attorney, succcesors or assigns, for which payment to be well and truly made, I bind myself, my heirs, executors and administrators, firmly by these presents. Sealed with my seal. Dated the* *day of* *in the year of our Lord one thousand eight hundred and*

The Condition of this obligation is such, that if the above bounden *has made a just and true report in writing to the custom master of Calcutta, of the number of persons, male and female, imported by him into Bengal, in and on the abovementioned* *and if the said* *has not since his last arrival in Bengal, and shall not whilst the said* *or the said* *shall be or remain in Bengal, land for the purpose of selling, giving away, or otherwise disposing of, any person or persons imported on board the said* *as and for a slave or slaves, and if the said* *has not sold, given away or disposed of, and shall not in Bengal, or in any of the countries of or under the management of the said United Company, their governors or servants in India, sell, give away, or dispose of, any person or persons, male or female, imported on board the said* *on this her last arrival in Bengal, as and for a slave or slaves, then this obligation shall be void, otherwise the same shall be and remain in full force and virtue.*

"Sealed and delivered (where no stamps are used) in the presence of" Par. Papers on Slavery, pp. 99, 100.

traffic should be encouraged in any part of its territories; being satisfied rather that it was, and is, its earnest desire to abolish so abominable a commerce every where; I consider myself to be only fulfilling the manifest intentions of the Right Honourable the Governor General in council, *in putting a stop to the sale of human beings in the town and country of Delhi.* I have accordingly proclaimed the orders of government for the abolition of the slave trade."*

In 1811 the officers of the "*Nepaul* administration requested the co-operation of the British Government in their measures towards an amelioration of the situation of the inhabitants of the mountains." The following extract of a letter from the Agent at Bareilly, to the Chief Secretary to Government, at Fort William, shows the nature of the evil to be removed. "In my address of the 8th ultimo, I had the honour to communicate the application which had been made by the officers of the Nepaul government, to put a stop to the traffic in children, and the measures which, in compliance with that application, had been taken.

"To give some idea of the extent of this traffic, the manner in which it is carried on, and the abuses to which it is liable, I have the honour to submit, for the consideration of his Excellency the Vice President in Council, a copy of a correspondence which has since taken place with the magistrates of Bareilly and Mooradabad.

"From the letter of the magistrate of Bareilly, it appears that, a few days after the order was issued, several slave traders coming from the hills were apprehended with *forty-three of these children*; that none of these persons possessed any title under which they could be warranted to sell the children for slaves; that several of these children, who had attained an age of greater maturity, were very happy to get back to their hills, and that the remainder are now under charge of the magistrate until the Soobah of Almorah sends people to escort them back.

"The magistrate of Mooradabad sent to this office *twenty-three children* for examination, who turned out to have been purchased by individuals from the slave dealers, prior to the orders being issued, and not intended for a resale. Under these circumstances I did not consider myself authorized to interfere, without the sanction of government; for, *although the purchases are illegal, long usage has stamped*

---

* Par. Papers on Slavery in India, p. 101.

them with a degree of validity, which now calls for a law to abrogate or modify.

"These children had all been purchased at the towns of Nudgeedabad and Augunnah, which are established marts, where these children are collected *in hundreds*. The deeds of purchase, which were inspected, were not executed by the parents of the children, but by the slave dealers, and neither specified the names of the parents, or their places of residence, or where and how procured, or any circumstance by which they could be traced or identified; nor with these deeds was any prior title transferred, by which a presumed right in the slave dealers to make the sale might be inferred.

"From what I can learn, the greater majority of children brought from the hills are females, who are purchased for concubines to supply the brothels, and some as attendants in zenanahs. That the greater number are females is corroborated from the children here alluded to, out of whom *fifty-two were females*, and only fourteen males. The males are for the most part employed as domestic servants, who sometimes obtain comfortable establishments in the families by whom they were bought as slaves; this occurrence I believe to be rare, the greater number leading a laborious life for bare subsistence, and are often hardly treated. But the traffic, although divested of the enormities of the African slave trade, is still attended with circumstances of cruelty, which can only be put a stop to by the interposition of government. From the encouragement which the trade has hitherto met with in our provinces, kidnapping children has been introduced; nor are instances unfrequent of their being forcibly carried off. Men likewise are found, who, tempted by lucre, *sell their wives*; of this an instance was established in the cases before me. It has also introduced the practice amongst the more powerful inhabitants *to seize the children of their debtors, and to sell them in satisfaction of their demands*. These instances suffice to establish the dreadful system of oppression and cruelty which arises from this traffic,"* The co-operation, requested for the suppression of this trade, was cheerfully granted by the British Government.

The proceedings in India are particularly worthy of notice, as it respects the bearing of the Act of Parliament, passed in the fifty-first year of his late Majesty's reign,

---

* Par. Papers on Slavery in India, p. 115.

commonly called the *Slave Felony Act*, entitled, "*An Act for rendering more effectual an Act made in the forty-seventh year of his Majesty's reign, intituled, 'An Act for the Abolition of the Slave Trade.'*" Two hundred copies of this important act were printed in Calcutta, and duly circulated. A Letter to the Chief Secretary at Fort St. George, and a similar one to Bombay, show the sense taken of this act in India.* See the foot of the page.

---

* "The exact nature of the traffic in slaves, mentioned by you to be carried on from Travancore, not being stated in your letter, the Governor General in Council is of course precluded from forming a judgment, whether that traffic falls within the purview of the Act of the 51 Geo. III. c. 23, intituled, "An Act for rendering more effectual an Act made in the forty-seventh year of his Majesty's reign, intituled, 'An Act for the Abolition of the Slave Trade.'" With respect, therefore, to that particular point, his Lordship in Council can only observe that *he does not consider the provisions of the Act in question applicable to the importation or removal of slaves by land.* It having been deemed proper, however, to consider maturely the course of measures which should be pursued by the local governments of this country, with respect to the above mentioned statute, the following is the purport of the resolutions adopted by the Governor General in Council on that subject.

"The provisions of the Act being highly penal in their operation, and its object highly important, the Governor General in Council has considered it proper to order a copy of it to be published in the Calcutta Gazette, for general information. In like manner, his Lordship in council has directed copies of the Act to be forwarded to the local governments of Bombay, Java, of Prince of Wales Island, of Mauritius, of Ceylon, and the Residents at the Moluccas, and at Fort Marlborough. On the same principle, copies of the statute will be forwarded to the magistrates of Chittagong and Cuttack (the only sea ports, excepting Calcutta, in Bengal) in order that in their capacity of justices of the peace, under the law of England, they may aid in enforcing the provisions of the statute.

"The Governor in Council, at Fort St. George, is aware that a regulation was some time ago passed at this Presidency, for preventing the importation of slaves from foreign countries. Inquiries will be made, with the view of ascertaining whether the provisions of that regulation have been effectual in preventing that species of traffic; if not, a further regulation will be passed without loss of time, establishing severer penalties for the infringement of the prohibition now existing under the regulation above noticed, of the importation of slaves from foreign countries, in conformity to the spirit of the statute, to which the foregoing remarks allude. In like manner, the Governor General in Council begs leave to recommend that a regulation be passed, at Fort St. George, for preventing the importation of slaves by land into the territories subject to that Presidency, under such penalties as the Governor in Council may deem fully adequate to the prevention of that traffic.

"The foregoing remarks, it is presumed, will inform the Governor in Council sufficiently of the construction annexed by the Governor General in Council to the Act of the 51 Geo. III. c. 23, and of the mea-

In 1813 the Bombay Government issued a "*Regulation for preventing the importation of slaves from foreign countries, and the sale of such slaves, in the territories immediately dependent on the Presidency of Bombay.*"* A difference of opinion upon the application of this act to India was entertained; that of the Advocate General of Bombay, H. G. Macklin, Esq., is expressed in the following terms, in a letter to the Secretary to Government: "With great deference to the opinion of the Right Honourable the Governor General in Council, I think the Act extends *to importation by land as well as sea*. In the

---

sures which it has been judged necessary to adopt at this Presidency. It is scarcely necessary to add, that his Lordship in Council is of opinion that similar measures should be adopted by the government of Fort St. George, with such modifications as local circumstances may suggest, without of course departing from the principle on which the measures above detailed are founded.

I have, &c.

G. Dowdeswell, Sec. to Government Judicial Department.

Fort William, Sept. 26th, 1812.

* *Regulations respecting the importation of slaves.*

"Whereas the importation of slaves from foreign countries into the British territories is inconsistent with the dictates of humanity, and with the principles on which the administration of this country is conducted: and whereas it is fit that the slave trade should be effectually abolished, wheresoever it may be attempted to practice the same. The following rules have been enacted, to be in force immediately on their promulgation throughout the territories immediately dependent on the Presidency of Bombay.

"The importation of slaves, whether by land or by sea, into the places immediately dependent on the Presidency of Bombay, is hereby strictly prohibited, and any person infringing this prohibition shall be liable to be prosecuted and punished for the offence, by the courts of Criminal Judicature.

"Any person who may be convicted of the offence of importing slaves into the British territories, subsequently to the promulgation of this regulation, shall be sentenced to imprisonment for the period of six months, and to pay a fine to government, according to his circumstances in life, not exceeding, however, the sum of 200 rupees; commutable, if not duly discharged, to imprisonment for the further period of six months, on the expiration of the former part of the sentence.

"Persons imported as slaves into the British territories shall be discharged, and sent back to their friends and connexions in the country from which they may have been imported, at the expense of the person or persons importing them, or permitted to remain in the British territories, according as may appear most advisable to the magistrate by whom the decision on the case may be passed.

H. Newnham, Sub-secretary." †

† Par. Papers on Slavery in India, p. 216.

preamble it is recited, that it is fit such measures should be extended to the effectual abolition of the slave trade wheresoever it may be attempted to practise the same; and, in the enacting part immediately following, 'If any person residing or being in any of the Islands, &c., or territories under the government of the United Company of Merchants trading to the East Indies, shall, &c., carry away or remove, &c., as a slave or slaves, &c., any person or persons whatsoever from any part of Africa, or from any other country, territory, or place whatsoever; or shall import or bring, &c., into any island, colony, country, territory, or place whatsoever, any such persons as aforesaid, for the purpose aforesaid; then in every such case, &c., the persons so offending, &c., are declared to be felons.'

"This enactment is taken verbatim from the statute, and appears to me to comprehend every possible case of the importation (that is, the introduction) of slaves into British territories. The act is highly penal, and I have great satisfaction in observing that his Lordship in Council is resolved to lay before the Honourable Court the difficulties which attend carrying the penal part of the statute into execution in India, where slavery is of a much milder feature than in the western hemisphere. The manumission of the slave will be sufficiently provided for by the regulation, and the King's Courts may act upon the statute in cases of aggravation or enormity."* It is unnecessary to enlarge upon the importance of this view of the subject. It is evident that the abolition of the slave trade, either in the West or the East Indies, is not the abolition of slavery. It prevents the increase of slaves, but leaves those already in slavery nearly in the same state that they were.

A Proclamation against the slave trade was issued by the Government in Madras, in March 1790, similar to the one issued by the Marquis Cornwallis.†

It is grateful to see the Dutch authorities in India cooperating with the British in suppressing the detestable traffic in human beings. The following letter was addressed to the Governor of Madras, in March 1793:—"Favoured with your Honour's letter of the 26th inst., we cannot indeed emphatically enough express our indignation

---

* Par. Papers on Slavery in India, pp. 216, 217. On the melioration of Slavery in Java, in 1812, see Par. Papers, pp. 168, 169.

† See Par. Papers as above, pp. 469, 470.

and aversion, with regard to so horrible an event as the exportation of 180 natives from Bimlipatam, as slaves, in a French brigantine bound to the French islands; which, however, according to the declaration that came enclosed, was surprised and taken at Pedir by the Malays, who killed all those that were on board of her, and did not escape out of their hands.

"To show how much the exportation of the unhappy creatures merits our disgrace, we shall renew, in the strongest manner, our orders to our northern factories, to oppose such inhuman practice, not only in our subjects, but also with all possible diligence in strangers, in case they should think our territory a safe place for it, with a charge to deliver the unhappy creatures out of the hands of those who will not desist, but are refractory, either by good or forcible means, and to send them to one of your agents there, for the protection of their liberty, and the benefit of their support.

"We feel the propriety of your Honour's resolution, that such kidnapping may be prevented, to check it with exemplary punishment; and, in case any of our subjects transgress the orders instituted against it, they shall be seized and delivered over to the justice, to be punished according to the exigency of the case."*

These extracts show the efforts of the European powers in India, with the occasional co-operation of the Natives, to abolish the Slave trade. The success experienced in these humane efforts should have encouraged them to attempt more than has yet been done; not merely to meliorate but actually to abolish slavery in the East. In consequence of the active measures described, many slaves were liberated, and their importation into India, by sea, in a great degree annihilated. The subsequent extracts in this chapter will show *the prevalence of just and humane principles in India.*

"I make no scruple," says Sir W. Jones, in his charge to the Grand Jury in Calcutta, June 1785, "to declare my own opinion that absolute unconditional slavery, by which one human creature becomes the property of another, like a horse or an ox, is happily unknown to the laws of England, and that no human law could give it a just sanction; yet, though I hate the word, the continuance of it, properly explained, can produce little mischief. I consider slaves as servants under a contract, express or implied, and made

* Par. Papers on Slavery in India, pp. 537, 538.

either by themselves or by such persons as are authorized by nature or law to contract for them, until they attain a due age to cancel or confirm any compact that may be disadvantageous to them. I have slaves whom I rescued from death or misery, but consider them as other servants, and shall certainly tell them so, when they are old enough to comprehend the difference of the terms."*

In the province of Dacca many children were kidnapped, given away, or sold by their parents into slavery; a number of these were recovered and restored to their parents or relations. The Collector of Dacca, in Nov. 1787, addressed the Superintendents of Police, Calcutta—"I have the pleasure to acknowledge the receipt of your letter of the 1st inst. accompanying twelve boys and twenty-one girls belonging to this district, under charge of Churreemeulah and three other Peons, and which, in obedience to the wish of the Right Honourable the Governor General, shall be restored to their parents or relations in the same manner as those transmitted to me two years since."†

It appears to be received among the Mahomedans that murder may be atoned for by money or by giving a slave. In 1790 two persons, named Mungaly Khan and Assud Khan, were convicted of the murder of Nowaz Khan, and were ordered to make a pecuniary compensation to the plaintiffs, viz., Peranow the widow and the brothers of the deceased. In conformity with the Nowab's orders they were called upon to pay the "price of blood." The widow stated "Mungaly Khan, being unable to pay a pecuniary compensation, has *given up to me his son, to be my servant for life.* Assud Khan has given up to me, in satisfaction of the murder, his share of the village of Caympoor. The other plaintiffs declaring "in consequence of the poverty and distress of Mungaly Khan and Assud Khan they remitted their claim to a compensation." The Governor General, Earl Cornwallis, and his council, very justly disapproved of the proceeding, agreeing that—"The Naib Nazim be recommended not to admit of Mungaly Khan's making over his son as a slave for life to Peranow, and that he be requested to levy the amount of the compensation which it may be determined to exact from Mungaly Khan by the customary mode of process."‡

In 1791 an attempt was made by certain Frenchmen to

---

* Par. Papers on Slavery in India, pp. 9, 10, and 710. † p. 12. ‡ 27.

establish a traffic in slaves from Bengal to the French settlement of Pondicherry, which occasioned the loss of *thirty* lives; a cargo of slaves was also brought by some Frenchmen from the Andamans. The French Governor, Colonel Canaple, cordially co-operated with the British in suppressing this cruel traffic in human beings.

Ceylon has been a market of slaves from Bengal. In 1789 a " Captain Horrebow took on board at Fultah 150 unhappy children, whom, previously to his departure, he had purchased in Bengal; he transported them under English colours to Columbo, where they were sold as slaves. The Dutch governor, Mynheer Van De Grave, in terms most honourable to himself, refused to permit their being landed; but Captain Horrebow, not caring to lose the profit on a cargo so judiciously chosen, found means to elude the vigilance of the governor, and accordingly availed himself of an excellent market for his wares."* " Captain Horrebow was sentenced to be imprisoned for three months, to pay a fine of 500 rupees, and to give security for his future good behaviour for three years; himself in a bond of 10,000 rupees, and two sureties in 5000 rupees each."†

The state of slavery in Ceylon anterior to its subjugation by the British, and the mitigation of it proposed by the conquering power, are ably stated in a communication to the Marquis Wellesley, Governor General in India in 1800 (pp. 84--92). A short extract only can be given:—" The scandalous manner in which the unhappy persons, whom it is the principal object of the proposed regulations to protect, are treated in general by their masters and mistresses of every nation, caste, and religion, within these settlements, render it a positive duty of Government to delay as little as possible the adoption of strong measures for their relief. Those which I propose are taken chiefly from the statutes of Batavia, particularly from one published in the year 1770, and which was in force at the time of our occupation of this island (though never observed in practice). I have also recurred in some instances to the civil law, on which the jurisprudence of Holland is founded; and, as the principal class of proprietors of slaves are of the Mahomedan religion, I have adopted and made general some of the admirable regulations by which the *Khoran* and its commentators have

* Par. Papers on Slavery in India, p. 14. † p. 21.

softened the rigours of slavery, at the same time that they established its lawfulness.

"The principal point on which all codes which have allowed domestic slavery have universally insisted, *the clear and unequivocal definition of the slave, and of the means by which he or she may have been acquired*, was neglected in Ceylon, with the most barbarous indifference: out of more than a hundred cases that have been brought before me, the masters or mistresses of the beings claiming liberty have not in more than six or seven instances produced slave bonds properly authenticated, or such as a Dutch tribunal, acting according to the Dutch laws, would have received. In many cases no papers are existing; in others simple testamentary devices, proving the opinion of the defunct as to his power over the slave bequeathed, have been insisted on, not as a collateral but as a positive proof of the slavery of the person claimed under it; and, in the province of Baticalva, the assertion that a child was sold by his parents in a famine was urged before me as the right on which the greater part of the slaves in that province have been held for some time past, as well as their posterity. The practice of kidnapping, at Cockin, was for many years notorious, but the reception of slaves from that place was subject to scarcely any restrictions on this island; and those restrictions, I am afraid, were but ill observed. In short, *that institution, reprobated as it is by good policy, morality, and religion, exists here with all the aggravated horrors of uncertainty in its application and cruelty in its exercise.*"*

The final abolition of slavery in Ceylon is thus described by Sir A. Johnstone in a letter to W. W. Wynn, Esq.—"As the right of every proprietor of slaves to continue to hold slaves in Ceylon was guaranteed to him, by the capitulation under which the Dutch possession had been surrendered to the British arms, in 1794, the British Government of Ceylon conceived that, however desirable the measure might be, they had not a right to abolish slavery in Ceylon by any legislative act: a proposition, however, was made on the part of Government by me to the proprietors of the slaves in 1806, before trial by jury was introduced, urging them to adopt some plan of their own accord for the gradual abolition of slavery: this proposition, at that time, they unani-

* Par. Papers on Slavery in India, pp. 84, 85.

mously rejected. The right of sitting upon juries was granted to the inhabitants of Ceylon in 1811. From that period I availed myself of the opportunities which were afforded to me, when I delivered my charge at the commencement of each session to the jurymen—most of whom were considerable proprietors of slaves—of informing them what was doing in England upon the subject of the abolition of slavery, and of pointing out to them the difficulties which they themselves must frequently experience in executing with impartiality their duties as jurymen in all cases in which slaves were concerned. A change of opinion upon the subject of slavery was gradually perceptible among them; and, in the year 1816, the proprietors of slaves of all castes and religious persuasions in Ceylon sent me their unanimous resolutions, to be publicly recorded in court, declaring *free all children born of their slaves* from the 12th of Aug. 1816; which, in the course of a few years, must put an end to the state of slavery which had subsisted in Ceylon for more than three centuries."*

The valuable co-operation of the Rajah of Kotah with the Resident at Delhi, in May, 1808, in the suppression of the sale of children into slavery, shows how much Europeans in India may accomplish for the interests of humanity.†

While the Island of Java continued in the possession of the British, the abolition of the slave trade, and the improvement of the condition of the slaves, was considered an object of importance. The importation of slaves into the island, after the commencement of 1813, was prohibited by proclamation, and instructions on the subject were sent to "the islands depending on the Government." The Governor thus addressed Lord Minto in April, 1813:—"By a dispatch forwarded in January last your Lordship will have perceived that the importation of slaves into this island and its dependencies, after the commencement of the present year, had been entirely prohibited by an order of this Government, under date the 18th of November last; and it remained a doubt with us only how far it would be necessary to restrict the conveyance by sea, from one part of the island to another, of slaves which were not intended for sale, but were the domestic servants of the residents on this island. The arrival of your Lordship's dispatches having placed us

---

* Ori. Her. vol. xvi. p. 136.

† Par. Papers on Slavery in India, pp. 99, 100.

in possession of the sentiments of the supreme Government on the subject, we resolved that the Act of Parliament should be immediately promulgated and enforced throughout this island and its dependencies, which has accordingly been done; and, with a view to secure the neighbouring Eastern states, as much as possible, from any consequence that might arise from their being unacquainted with the Acts of the British Legislature, and being consequently liable to detention by His Majesty's ships, we have deemed it advisable to send a communication thereof to each of them.

"The constant use of slaves as private servants, and more especially in the navigation of trading prows in this part of the world, affords considerable grounds for apprehension, that unpleasant consequences might arise from an indiscriminate detention or capture of such vessels, which, though trading under their own flag, may be considered in some measure dependent upon the British Government. It has therefore been of great importance that they should be fully apprized of the consequences to which they become liable; and it is to be hoped that this public discouragement and communication on the part of this government, aided by a cordial co-operation and mild conduct on the part of His Majesty's cruizers, will, at the same time, prevent any of the unpleasant consequences that might be expected to result from a sudden and unexpected change, and will tend by degrees to abolish the employment of slaves entirely among the Eastern Islands."*

Previously to the transfer of Java to the Dutch the slaves were emancipated. Upon which the Hon. Court of Directors say—"We entirely approve of your proceedings, in emancipating the slaves at Java, previously to the transfer of that place to the Dutch, as we do of the option you gave to all the slaves, of being conveyed at the public charge to their native country."†

The slave trade appears to have been very effectually suppressed in most parts under the Bengal government by the humane and vigorous efforts before described. The magistrates of the Bareilly Court, Dec. 1812, state—"We have now the honour to submit attested copies of the answers received from *eight* out of the *nine* magistrates under our authority; from which it will be evident to Government that, since the promulgation of the regulation above specified, the traffic in slaves imported from foreign countries is

* Par. Papers on Slavery in India, p. 185. † p. 265.

almost, if not entirely, suppressed in the districts of Bareilly, Moradabad, Cawnpoor, Furruckabad, Etawah, Agra, Alligurh, and Seharunpore South."* "But, it should be understood, *the slave owners still disposed of those who were actually slaves as part of their real property*."†

The British Government in India has abolished *the duty levied on the sale of slaves* by the former Government of Kemaon, and suppressed the traffic in slaves in those countries bordering on Nepaul which were brought under its authority by treaty in 1815. This duty or tax was for every male and female slave *two rupees eight annas*. "We cannot touch on this subject," said the late Marquis of Hastings, "without adverting to a consequence of our having wrested the hill country from the Gholkas, in which your Honourable Court will feel the most lively satisfaction. A slave trade of great extent has been totally extinguished; and the hapless families, from whom the Gholkas used to tear away the children for sale, have now to look with joyful confidence on the security bestowed on their offspring by the British Government."‡

The Calcutta Journal in March, 1824, contained an article entitled the "*Slave Trade in British India*." This startling subject was introduced to the notice of the public and the Government as follows:—an extract or two only is given—"Our readers are of course aware that the nefarious traffic in human beings is equally forbidden by the letter and the spirit of British law in every portion of the British dominions, be their geographical position what it may, whether in the frozen regions of the north or the scorching climate of the torrid zone; wherever the British flag waves the disgraceful commerce is made criminal by British law; what, then, will the humane and enlightened community of this magnificent capital of our Eastern possessions say, when they are told that with all its glittering spires of the temples of a pure religion; all its splendid palaces, bespeaking the taste, the refinement, and the riches of their inhabitants; with all its colleges, and schools, and societies, to promote the propagation of knowledge, civil and religious; what will they say when they learn that, amidst all these signs of veneration for Christianity, the philanthropy, the greatness, and the refinement of Britons and British subjects in a British

* Par. Papers on Slavery in India, p. 140. † p. 141. ‡ p. 266 See Heber's Jour. vol. i. p. 492.

capital, it is disgraced by witnessing the lowest degradation of the human species?—that this great capital is, in short, at once the depôt of the commerce and riches of the East, and the mart in which the manacled African is sold like the beast of the field to the highest bidder. It is known, too, that the Arab ships are in the habit of carrying away many of the Natives of this country, principally females, and disposing of them in Arabia, in barter for African slaves for the Calcutta market!! Can it be possible that such degrading, such wicked scenes are passing around us, and that the actors are suffered to escape unnoticed and unpunished? We fear the fact is too true; but we hope that the publicity thus given to it will lead to the prevention of such gross violations of law and humanity in future. We can conceive the difficulty of detection in these cases; but let all those who are aware of the illicit practices of these followers of Mahomet remember that they are imperiously called on as Christians, and as British subjects in particular, to bring to punishment these violators of law and humanity. Nature shudders at the thought of the barbarities practised by these abusers of God's noblest creature, who are led by an accursed thirst of gold to brutalize the human species."* The Magistrates of Calcutta immediately addressed the Government upon the subject, acknowledging—"Under the provision of Reg. X., 1811, a bond is taken from the commanders of a certain class of ships previously to their being allowed to land their cargoes; and they are also required to give in a list of their crews and passengers. We must confess, however, that these are *very inadequate restrictions* to prevent the introduction of slaves into the town; the penalty could only be enforced by the detection of the offence, which is attended with much difficulty."† Translations in the Persian and Arabic languages were made of an extract of the 51 Geo. III. c. 23,‡ for circulation among the merchants. See the Extract of the Act at the foot of the page.§ These measures were certainly of a very decisive and praiseworthy nature.

---

* Par. Papers on Slavery in India, p. 378. † p. 377.

‡ By a more recent Act of Parliament, 4 Geo. IV. c. 17, the traffic in slaves has been declared to be an act of piracy, and all British subjects who may be concerned in it are liable to be dealt with accordingly.

§ "Be it therefore enacted by the King's Most Excellent Majesty, by and with the advice and consent of the Lords Spiritual and Temporal, and Commons, in this present Parliament assembled, and by the authority of

In Kumaon an extraordinary practice existed of *selling wives and widows*, which has been abolished. The Governor General, in Sep. 1826, writes to the Court of Directors—" We took measures to furnish the Commissioner, without delay, with the form of proclamation approved by us, prohibiting the *sale of wives and widows by their husbands or late husband's family.* We need not repeat the expression of our determination to put down so barbarous and hateful a custom."*

---

the same, That if any subject or subjects of His Majesty, or if any person or persons residing or being within this United Kingdom, or in any of the islands, colonies, dominions, forts, settlements, factories, or territories, now or hereafter belonging thereto, or being in His Majesty's occupation or possession, or under the government of the United Company of Merchants trading to the East Indies, shall, from and after the first day of June next, by him or themselves, or by his or their factors or agents, or otherwise however, carry away or remove, or aid or assist in the carrying away or removing, as a slave or slaves, or for the purpose of being sold, transferred, used or dealt with as a slave or slaves, any person or persons whatsoever, from any port of Africa or from any other country, territory, or place whatsoever, either immediately or by transhipment at sea, or otherwise, directly or indirectly, or shall import or bring, or aid or assist in the importing or bringing, into any island, colony, country, territory, or place whatsoever, any such person or persons as aforesaid, for the purposes aforesaid, or shall knowingly or wilfully ship, embark, receive, detain, or confine on board any ship, vessel or boat, any such person or persons as aforesaid, for the purpose of his her or their being so carried away or removed, imported or brought as aforesaid, or of being sold, transferred, used or dealt with as a slave or slaves, or shall knowingly and wilfully use or employ, or permit to be used or employed, or left or take to freight or on hire, any ship or vessel to be used or employed in carrying away or removing, importing or bringing, or for the purpose of carrying away or removing, importing or bringing, as aforesaid, any such person or persons, as a slave or slaves, or for the purpose of his her or their being sold, transferred, used, or dealt with as a slave or slaves, or shall fit out or cause to be fitted out, or shall take the charge or command of, or navigate or enter and embark on board any such ship or vessel, as master or captain, mate, supercargo, or surgeon, knowing that such ship or vessel is actually employed, or is in the same voyage for which he or they shall so enter and embark on board, intended to be employed in carrying or removing, importing or bringing, as aforesaid, any such person or persons, as or for the purpose of his her or their being sold, transferred, used or dealt with as a slave or slaves; then, and in every such case, the person or persons so offending, and their counsellors, aiders and abettors, shall be and are hereby declared to be felons; and shall be transported beyond seas for a term not exceeding fourteen years, or shall be confined and kept to hard labour for a term not exceeding five years, nor less than three years, at the discretion of the court before whom such offender or offenders shall be tried and convicted."†

* Par. Papers on Slavery in India, p. 416. † 380.

In 1815 several persons belonging to the settlement of Malacca were seized in boats, by pirates belonging to the neighbouring country of Perah, and were carried into slavery. The Governor of Prince of Wales Island dispatched the Honourable Company's cruiser, Thetis, with a demand for their liberation, with which the Rajah ultimately complied. These circumstances show the influence of the British in the East. The following was the letter to the Rajah of Perah. After compliments;—"It is with regret I find myself so soon again called upon to address my friend on the subject of fresh piracies committed by the bad men of Perah. My friend professes his inability to control the acts of his principal officers; but I cannot admit of this as a sufficient excuse, and unless unequivocal satisfaction be afforded to me of my friend's earnest desire to punish such, whensoever they are discovered, I shall be compelled to regard him as abetting their piracies, and must resent them accordingly.

"I desire, then, that without any delay the four persons named Kareem, Sie Adam, Sie Bamam (a lad), and Joakim, the three first Malays, and the last a Portuguese boy, all of Malacca, now in the possession of the Lacsamana of Perah, may be forthwith delivered to the bearer of this, Captain Reynolds, of the Honourable Company's cruiser Thetis. I also desire, peremptorily, that Nakooda Kooloop may be delivered up to Captain Reynolds, in order that a judicial investigation may take place, how far he may be guilty of the seizure of those people, and that he may meet with the punishment which his audacious atrocities merit."*

In 1821 the opinion of the Recorder of Prince of Wales Island was taken "as to the legality of apprehending and sending back to Malacca a runaway slave." This important question was answered in a Letter to the Secretary of Government. "I have the honour to acknowledge the receipt of yours of the 30th November, with a copy of a dispatch from the governor of Malacca. I am not acquainted with the Dutch language, and therefore if there should be any circumstance in that part of the dispatch which varies the question submitted to me, from the governor of Malacca's letter in French, I should wish to have a translation of it; but, as it is not probable, I do not delay my request, that you will communicate to the Honour-

* Par. Papers on Slavery in India, p. 456.

able the Governor in council, that, in the absence of any treaty, *I am of opinion that the slave in question cannot be legally secured and sent back to Malacca.*"*

A number of slaves, procured in the neighbourhood of Juggernaut's Temple in Orissa, were liberated and the captain of the vessel severely reprimanded, and threatened that, "on committing a second offence, he should be punished to the utmost rigour of the law and sent by the first conveyance to England."† Some slaves from Ganjam were also liberated, and the slave trader directed to be "fined the sum of 200 rupees (to be distributed amongst the natives liberated from the vessel under his command), imprisoned for three months, until he pays the fine, and that he be then publicly expelled the district."‡

The sale of slaves, under the Madras Government, for the arrears of the State was discontinued in 1819. The Secretary writes to the Collector of Malabar:—"The Board's proceedings on the general subject of slavery have been laid before the government, whose final orders will hereafter be communicated to you; but, in the mean time, am directed to disire that *the practice of selling slaves, for arrears of revenue, may be immediately discontinued.*"§

These extracts show the humane and vigorous efforts of the British functionaries in India to abolish the slave trade. The state of slavery at the present period next demands attention. The following chapter will show that much remains to be done before every British subject in India is free.

CHAP. III.

The present state and extent of Slavery in Hindostan.

The nature and extent of slavery in the British territories in India is a subject that cannot but be deeply interesting to every liberal and humane mind. The following extracts from the voluminous valuable Papers on Slavery

---

* Par. Papers on Slavery in India, p. 462. † p. 476. ‡ p. 494. § p. 873.

in India will cast some light on a subject upon which little information is possessed.

In 1812 the Resident at Delhi, C. T. Metcalfe, Esq., issued a proclamation prohibiting the Slave Trade altogether. On this subject the Governor General addressed the Court of Directors, in June, 1813:—"We observed that the Proclamation not only prohibited the importation of slaves for sale into the assigned territories, but the sale of slaves actually within those territories previously to its promulgation; *a measure which we were not prepared to sanction.* Odious and abominable as such a traffic is in any shape, although it must be admitted that the system of slavery in this country is infinitely mitigated, when compared with that against which the enactments of the legislature in England have been directed. *The laws which have hitherto been enacted to restrain it have been confined in their object to* THE TRADE IN SLAVES BY IMPORTATION OR EXPORTATION, *but have not been extended to the emancipation of persons already in a state of slavery, nor to the prohibition of their transfer by sale to other masters within the country which they inhabit.*

"We informed the Resident that for these reasons, and from other considerations of much apparent weight, our views were limited to the prohibition of the further importation of slaves for sale into the territories of the Honourable Company; and we accordingly directed that the terms of the proclamation might be modified, so as to correspond with the enactment contained in Regulation X. of 1811.

"The consultation of the annexed date contains the Resident's reply to the instructions, which, as stated above, were issued to him for the modification of the proclamation in question, submitting a statement of the motives and considerations which had induced him to suspend the publication of the modification required, until he should receive our further orders and instructions on the subject. The Resident stated that a general opinion prevailed, among the natives, that the total abolition of the Slave Trade had taken effect in the ceded and conquered provinces; that he had not found the prohibition of the sale of slaves had occasioned any surprise at Delhi; and that the people there were not aware that by the proclamation which he had issued greater restrictions were in force in the assigned territory than in any other part of the country; and that should it be published in that territory, *that slaves of a cer-*

tain description might continue to be sold, it would give a more formal sanction to the sale of slaves than that traffic was ever believed to possess. The effect of this erroneous belief, on the part of the natives, appeared to the Resident to be attended with salutary consequences; and he submitted that it was not desirable the delusion should be removed by the publication of a formal sanction for the sale of any description of slaves. We signified to the Resident our concurrence in the grounds on which he had suspended the execution of our instructions, and, having taken the subject of his dispatch last referred to into consideration in the Judicial Department, we resolved that the proclamation issued by the Resident should continue in full force and effect."*

But, though the sale of slaves is prevented, slavery is still continued. This is evident from the Resident's communication to Government:—" In issuing a proclamation for the abolition of the future importation and sale of slaves, I had no idea of infringing on the rights of the actual proprietors of slaves purchased or possessed heretofore. *All the proprietors of slaves in this territory, notwithstanding that proclamation, retain all their rights over their slaves, except that of selling them or making them the property of another.* This is perfectly understood, in consequence of the decisions given in the court of judicature in trials between owners and slaves. I have more than once embraced the opportunity afforded by such trials to explain publicly that *slaves are still the property of their owners,* though not (with reference to my former misconception of the views of government) as heretofore disposable property."†

The Magistrate of Bareilly in Nov. 1812, referring to the efficacy of the provisions of Regulation X. 1811, for preventing the importation of slaves from foreign countries, remarks, " This traffic has, I believe, suffered a very material check since the promulgation of the regulation, inasmuch as children are no longer brought down from the hills, and publicly exposed for sale, as formerly, within this district; but *children are still sold with in the Company's provinces by subjects of the British government, nor does the regulation contain any prohibition of such sale.* Parents, prevented by poverty from rearing a large family, will dispose of their children to an advantage, when offered, rather

* Par. Papers on Slavery in India, pp. 101, 102. See also p. 134.
† p. 104.

than allow them to starve; the feelings of nature will confine this traffic to cases of necessity only, and will act more forcibly than any legal prohibition in preventing abuses; it may be much doubted, indeed, whether the condition of children imported from the hills was not, in most cases, much ameliorated by such importation."*

A Mr. Browne, the proprietor of an estate at Anjarakandy, in Malabar claimed the right of a master over some slaves as a part of the Mahomedan law, under which he considered the provinces of the Madras presidency to be governed. "I cannot (says the Chief Secretary to the Government in Jan. 1813) agree to the proposition that these provinces are, so far as relates to British subjects, governed by the Mahomedan law. In questions of civil right they are governed by the different laws of the different nations to whom justice is to be dispensed. In criminal prosecutions, the Mahomedan law is, for what reason I do not know, established over all the natives in the provinces, but not over the British. They retain the rights of their birth, and ought also to retain all the relations connected with the British character, *to which it is equally abhorrent to be the master of slaves as to endure slavery*. It is expressly provided, in the several statutes, that our law shall not interfere with the authority exercised by the heads of families amongst the natives, who, from local residence at the Presidencies, are made subject in general to the British laws, but *no such provision is made for British subjects as the masters of slaves!*" The Advocate General expressed the same opinion; and this important position, that *a Briton in India could not be a slave-holder*, is thus definitely determined by a letter from the Chief Secretary to the Government, Fort William, March 1813, to the Secretary of the Madras Government:—"The Advocate General, having stated it as his opinion that it is quite impracticable, as the law at present stands, for *any British subject to support a claim to the person or services of any one residing within the limits of the British territories as a slave*, and that opinion corresponding entirely with the sentiments entertained by the Right Honourable the Governor General in council on the subject, his Lordship in council thinks that every case of that nature, which may be brought before the Governor in council of Fort St. George, should be regarded as an

---

* Par. Papers on Slavery in India,, p 141.

illegal and unauthorized assumption of power; and the legal measures should be resorted to, should circumstances appear to require it, against any British subject so acting in violation of the law."*

The difference between the state of public opinion, feeling, and, we may add, law, in the East and in the West Indies, cannot fail to strike the attention of every reader. It is very justly observed, in the communication first quoted, "the habitual exercise of the authority of a master over slaves is peculiarly destructive to the national honour and character."† When shall these just sentiments pervade the breast of every British subject!

Of Slavery in Dacca the Magistrate in March, 1816, observes:—"I have to state in reply, for the information of the Court of Circuit, that I have found in this court several prosecutions for inveigling away children and other persons with various intents, and they are generally females: such causes, however, in this city and district are not very numerous. The unfortunate persons who are sold for slavery are generally little children (females), or grown up girls that are enticed away from their parents or other relations in the Mofussil, and unconscious of their fate. Persons already in a state of slavery are seldom, as far as I can discover from the records of the court, or from other information, inveigled away with a view of being sold; but female slaves are often enticed away for other purposes, sometimes by men, and sometimes by women keeping houses of ill-fame. Both descriptions of offence are, I believe, *very prevalent*, especially the former, though few of them comparatively come officially to the knowledge of the magistrate."‡

The registration of slaves was proposed by the Government to the Nizamut Adawlut in May, 1816, which intimates that the prevalence of slavery is considerable. "In preparing the draft of the proposed regulation regarding slavery, the Governor General in council requests that the court will take into their consideration the expediency of requiring that *the future purchase or transfer of slaves shall be regularly registered*, and that any breach of the rules which may be framed for that purpose shall entitle the slave to demand and obtain his freedom."§

* Par. Papers on Slavery in India, p. 148. † p. 147.
‡ p. 248. § 249.

Inquiry was made from Bombay of the Supreme Government respecting the application of the 51st Geo. III. c. 23, relative to "the abolition of the slave trade, to domestic slaves, and the property of individuals in them; such slavery being known and legalized under the laws of both the Hindoos and Mussulmans, according to whose codes the courts are bound to administer justice." To which it was replied:—"On this point the Vice President in council observes, that none of the provisions of the Acts of Parliament passed for the abolition of the slave trade in any manner affect, or profess to affect, *the relation between master and slave, wherever that relation may exist by law.* Whatever therefore was the law, according to the Mahomedan and Hindoo codes (for those over whom they extend), on the subject of domestic slavery, before the passing of the Act of the 51st Geo. III., c. 23, continues to be the law still; more especially as those codes have been distinctly recognized and ordered to be observed by Parliament. At the same time it is not credible that any intention existed to abrogate those codes without reference to the established laws and usages of this country, and without repealing the Acts of Parliament by which the observance of them is guaranteed to the natives.

"The native subjects of the British government residing in the territories subordinate to the several Presidencies have, in fact, the same authority over their slaves, and the same property in them, that they would have had if the Act in question had never been passed; and the several zillah and provincial courts are bound to receive and determine all questions of that nature, which are respectively cognizable by them, under the existing regulations.

"The other points adverted to, in the documents now under consideration, relate to the conduct which should be observed on the occasion of applications being made by the subjects or governments of neighbouring states with whom we are in amity, for the restoration of slaves who have taken refuge within the Company's territories. On this point it may be remarked, that the construction which has been uniformly given by the Supreme Government to the Act of the 51st Geo. III., c. 23, viz. that it was only intended to apply to the importation or removal of slaves by sea, would not involve any alteration in the course of proceedings hitherto adopted in similar cases. *A slave, by entering the Company's territories, does not become free;*

nor can he, who was lawfully a slave, emancipate himself by running away from one country where slavery is lawful to another where it is equally lawful. The property in the slave still continues in the master, and the master has the same right to have it restored to him that any native subjects of our territories could have, supposing that right to be established in the mode prescribed by the local laws and regulations."*—Council Chamber, Sept. 9, 1817.

The permission of the sale of slaves in the Deccan appears from a letter dated Dhooliah, Aug. 1819, to M. Elphinstone, Esq., the Commissioner. "Application having been lately made to me for permission to purchase some slaves, I took the opportunity of investigating the circumstances, which I have the honour to report for your information.

"It appears that the slaves were young women and girls in the possession of some Mahratta Wunjarries, who, upon being questioned, state that they purchased them in Berar, from the Tandas of the Rajpoot Brimjarrias, who said they had got them during a late scarcity which took place in the Nirmut district. Upon further investigation, I understand that the practice of carrying off children from one part of the country, to sell in another part, *is not unusual with these people.* The women appear unwilling to be sold, though they complain of their scanty food, and of the treatment they experience from their present masters. Although your letter of the 19th Dec., 1818, in answer to a former application on this subject, informed me that no variation whatever was to be made in the existing laws regarding slaves, yet it appears to me possible that that may be intended to be applied merely to the proprietary right over slaves in actual possession, and of recovering such as may desert; I request to be informed, if the practice of *carrying slaves about for sale,* of which several instances have lately been brought to my notice, is still to be permitted. In the mean time I have prohibited the sale of the young women in question, till I hear from you."†

To which it was replied by the Commissioner:—"The sale of slaves, as described in the above-mentioned letter, is to be permitted, but all attempts to carry off young people by force will be punished in the severest manner."‡

---

* Par. Papers on Slavery in India, pp. 333, 334. † p. 339. ‡ p. 339.

"The mitigated kind of domestic slavery which prevails in the *Deccan*," says W. Chaplin, Esq., "and has prevailed from time immemorial in most parts of India, appears to be of a description entirely different from the foreign trade in slaves, which is proscribed by recent acts of parliament passed since the abolition of this traffic; and, although it may perhaps at a future period be necessary to introduce some regulations to prevent the stealing or kidnapping of children, *I conceive that any restrictive measure, that should at once put a stop to the sale of slaves, would be an innovation which would trench materially not only on long established customs, but on the rights of private property*. Whether this species of servitude, or rather of mild bondage, is eventually to be continued under certain modifications, or to be abolished entirely, is a question which is probably now under consideration; but as the importation of slaves from the Nizam's frontier, in consequence of the scarcity which prevails there, has of late greatly increased, the subject of your letter will be referred for the decision of the Honourable the Governor in council. Whatever eventual evil may result from the continuance of the traffic, it is certainly, I think, the means at the present moment of much actual good, inasmuch as it has the effect of preserving the lives of numbers of parents and children who would otherwise perish from famine."*—Poona, Dec., 1819.

The difference of opinion and procedure of some of the magistrates shows the difficulty of legislation in a society where slavery exists. This appears by some slave cases stated by W. Leycester, Esq., Second Judge of the Bareilly Court of Circuit in Sep. 1815.—

"In one case, Enayt Khaun is taken up by the police darogah of Bhudyke, and sent as a prisoner to the magistrate of Cawnpore, for importing two female slaves, and *the magistrate discharges him, and gives him the slaves*.

"In a seond case, Ooda is taken up for importing a woman named Mauncooer, by a police sowar, and delivered over to the police darogah of Bindrabun. Ooda says he bought her for twenty-one rupees in the Ranna's country, and she admits it, and adds, she understands he means to resell her. The acting magistrate liberates the woman.

"In a third case, Sabet Khawn is taken up by a jemmedar, and delivered over to the darogah of Koria Gunje. It would seem he had been sent by Assud Alee Cauzee of Jelaneh to purchase a slave in the vicinity of Cassepore and Roderpoore (*the markets for slaves imported from the*

* Par. Papers on Slavery in India, pp. 341, 342.

hills); but on coming to Bareilly he falls in with Besharut Khan, a slave-dealer, who from his stock in hand sells to him a woman named Zuhorun, twenty years of age; but the Cauzee, thinking her too old, leaves her on Sabet Khaun's hands. The assistant magistrate liberates the woman.

"In a fourth case, Nurotum is taken up by the darogah of Nudjeebabad. It would seem that he had purchased a woman named Anundee, for twenty rupees, of one Serya, an inhabitant of the hills. The assistant magistrate does not liberate the woman, but takes a recognizance from Nurotum to produce her, if any other claimant should appear.

"In a fifth case, Choonee, the head of a set of dancing girls, prosecutes Hyatt Alee Cutwaul of Amrooa, for detaining forcibly Munnuvur Jaun, one of her female slaves. Munnuvur Jaun says, she is not satisfied to remain with Choonee, and the magistrate liberates her. Choonee appeals, and produces a deed of sale for the slave, executed by Shumshere, an inhabitant of the hills. The opinion of the law officer of the court of Circuit is taken, who declares '*the sale of a resident of this country illegal*;' and the order of the magistrate was confirmed.

"The first case was submitted by me to the Nizamut Adawlut, with a recommendation that the said Enayt Khaun should be punished, and the slaves discharged or sent back as required by the 10th Regulation of 1811; and the court in reply adjudge that, under the construction given by the court to the provisions of the 10th Regulation, 1811, the case in question does not fall within the operation of that regulation; and, having referred to the court's orders of the 5th October, it would seem that on a representation from Mr. Blunt, the court had decided that the regulation in question was 'applicable only to the importation of slaves for the purpose of being sold, given away, or otherwise disposed of.' "*

It appears that when slaves have been imported their owners have endeavoured to evade the law against the Slave Trade, by not immediately disposing of them, on which it is very justly remarked—"Is not the keeping a person imported as a slave to be a slave, a disposal of him? and what is to be said to the notorious fact of female persons, so imported as slaves, being let out in retail for the purposes of prostitution, and any offspring they may have being sold, *agreeably to the daily practice regarding the indigenous slaves of the country, for the benefit of the slave master?* This surely is a disposal of them and of their issue."* —Is not this species of slavery equal in atrocity to the slavery of the West Indies?

"Slavery in Malwa," says Sir John Malcolm, "is chiefly limited to females, but there is perhaps no province in India where there are so many slaves of this sex. The dancing girls are all purchased when young by the nakins, or heads

---

* Par. Papers on Slavery in India, pp. 342, 343. † p. 344.

of the different sects, who often lay out large sums in these purchases; female children and grown up young women are bought by all ranks. Among the Rajpoot chiefs these slaves are very numerous, as also in the houses of the principal Brahmins; *the usage descends to the lowest ranks, and few merchants or cultivators with any property are without mistresses or servants of this description.* Male slaves are rare, and never seen but with men of some rank and property, with whom they are usually the confidential servants. There are a variety of ways in which slaves are procured in Malwa; numbers date their condition from a famine or scarcity, when men sold their children to those who were able to support them, with the natural view of preserving the lives of their offspring, at the same time that they obtained means of protracting their own. A great number of the slaves of Malwa are from Rajpootana, where the excesses of the Mahrattas drove the inhabitants to exile, and to such distress as to be compelled to part with their children. But, besides these sources of slavery, there are others of a more criminal nature. There are many instances of Rajpoots and men of other tribes, particularly Soandees, selling the children whom they have by their slaves, and who are deemed to be born in a state of bondage. This only takes place when the father is in distress, or when he is tempted by a large price. The sale, however, of the offspring of these women by other fathers than their masters is more common. The slaves bred (to use a term suited to their condition) in this manner are not numerous; but the further demand is supplied by the Binjarries, who import females into and from Guzerat and other countries, whom they usually pretend to have bought; and by the tribe of Gwarriah, who have been noticed as open and professed stealers of female children.

"When these slaves are bought, an inquiry is made as to their tribe, and the general answer (particularly from the Gwarriahs) is, that they are Rajpoots. The children are taught to make pretensions to high birth, and daily instances occur of whole families losing caste in consequence of their being too hastily credited. When persons of inferior tribes discover their daughters, or husbands their betrothed wives, in the houses of Brahmins, which often happens,—the latter are compelled to undergo long and expensive penances to recover the purity from which they and their family have fallen, in consequence of being defiled by intercourse with females so far below them. It is a remarkable fact, and one of the few creditable to the late community of the Pindarries, that among the numerous prisoners of all ages and sexes whom they took—though they employed them as servants, gave them to their chiefs, and accepted ransoms for them from their relations, *they never sold them into bondage, nor carried on, like the Binjarries, a traffic in slaves.* Females in Malwa, except in times of scarcity or general distress, from any cause (when they are very cheap), are sold from forty to fifty, to 100 and 150 rupees; the price is accordant with their appearance. They have been at times an article of considerable commerce, many being annually sent to the southward, particularly to the Poonah territories, where they sold high. This trade, which has of late years decreased, was principally carried on by the Mahratta Brahmins, some of whom amassed great sums by this shameless traffic."*

The Par. Papers contain more minute information respecting the state of slavery under the Madras Presidency than that of the other Presidencies in India.—"In Malabar and Canara, where the land is very generally divided, and occupied as separate and distinct properties, *the labourer is the personal slave of the proprietor, and is sold and mortgaged by him, independently of his lands.* In the Tamil country, where land is of less value, and belongs more frequently to a community than to an individual, the labourer is understood to be the slave rather of the soil than of its owner, and is seldom sold or mortgaged, except along with the land to which he is attached; but in Telingana, where it is difficult now to trace the remains of private property in the land, this class of people is considered free. There cannot, however, be a doubt, that the slavery prevalent among the lower classes of the Hindoos is of a very different and opposite nature from that so strongly and justly reprobated in England, inasmuch as foreign traffic or external commerce in slaves is quite different from domestic slavery. It has been stated by very competent authority, Mr. F. W. Ellis, the collector of Madras, that in the Tamil country, the parriyars and pullers, most of whom are slaves attached to the lands of the vallaler, as well as the pulli, who are generally serfs on the lands of the Brahmin meerassidars, sometimes claim meras, or *hereditary private pro-*

* Par. Papers as above, Rep. on Malwa, 1821, pp. 414, 415.

perty, in the 'incidents of their villainage;' and that 'it is generally allowed to them and their descendants, on proving their former residence in the village, however long they may have been absent from it.' On the other hand, the late magistrate in Malabar, in addressing government respecting the sale of men, women, and children of the Pollar, Cherumakul, Panian, Kanakan, Kallady, Yocallan, and Nacady tribes, submits that, 'if the general question of slavery, as recognised by the local usages of Malabar, or by the Hindoo and Mahomedan law, is not affected by the laws made to abolish the Slave Trade—adverting to the wretchedness and diminutive appearance of this description of natives—it still appears to be a subject well worthy the humane consideration of the Right Honourable the Governor in council, to enact such legislative provisions as will tend to ameliorate their condition, and prevent their being sold out of the talook, or, indeed, off the estate, the place of their nativity; and, above all, from being exposed to sale by public auction, in execution of decrees, or in satisfaction of revenue demands."*

It appears to have been common *to dispose of the slaves on an estate as a part of the real property*:—"The Hindoo law (says the Collector of Malabar), on the subject of transfers of property, speaks of 'land and slaves employed in the cultivation of it,' and evidently contemplates those two species of property as one and the same, and as not properly separable from each other; and we find that not only in this, but in other countries, it has been usual to transfer the slaves who were a 'descripti glebæ' with the land itself. Indeed the attachment of the Hindoos to the lands which they have always occupied, and to the village where they have always resided, is proverbial; and to separate them, therefore, from their native soil, might, under such circumstances, be considered an additional act of cruelty. A certain portion of the produce of the soil which they cultivate, is, in the Tamil country, allowed by the master for the maintenance of his slaves, whose duty it is to till the ground; and, unless they were transferred with the land, the new proprietor, when he obtained possession, might experience difficulty in carrying on the cultivation, and the former master might be deprived of the means of enabling him to afford subsistence to his slaves. The probability of being

* Par. Papers on Slavery in India, p. 817.

transferred with the land, moreover, gives them therefore on this coast a sort of property in their huts and little spots of ground, which they can thus occupy without any great fear of being turned out or transferred contrary to their interests, feeling, and comfort. It must, however, be observed, that on the other coast universally, and even generally on this coast, *slaves are not necessarily sold with the land*, although the convenience of all parts seems to have rendered the practice common."

The apathy manifested by the Collector of Calicut in 1819, on the sale of slaves for default of revenue, shows the influence of the slave system upon the most respectable of the European functionaries of Government. "In attempting to ameliorate the condition of these slaves, care must be taken that we do not increase them. The partial measure of declaring them not liable to be sold for arrears of revenue will be a drop of water in the ocean; though *why government should give up a right which every proprietor enjoys is a question worthy of consideration.*"* See also p. 435.

An extract of one of the *Rejected Police Regulations* refused Registration by the Supreme Court of Bombay, in 1826, affords some idea of the state of slavery in that part of India, at the period referred to.

"*Of the Slave Trade and Slavery.*

All importation of slaves into this island for sale is prohibited.

The petty sessions shall in such cases emancipate the slave and send him or her back to the family, or to the place to which he or she was brought at the expense of the importer. When the slave is desirous of remaining, the importer shall pay him the money which would otherwise have been employed in defraying the expense of his return. The petty sessions may inflict further punishments in aggravated cases, not exceeding the fine of 500 rupees, and imprisonment for six months in default of payment.

All children born of parents in a state of slavery in this island, after the first day of January 1812, shall be free.

The said court of petty sessions shall have power of summary conviction in all cases of persons enticing or conveying away any married females, or unmaried females under the age of thirteen years, out of the protection and against the will of the husband or father, or other person having the lawful protection and governance of any such female, for the purpose of her prostitution in any way, or for her disposal in marriage against the will of the person having such lawful protection or government as aforesaid; such offenders to be punishable by fine not exceeding 500 rupees; or in lieu thereof, as the case may seem to require, or in default of payment, imprisonment, with or without hard labour, as the case may seem to require, for any time not exceeding six months."†

---

* Par. Papers on Slavery in India, p. 846.

† See Ori. Herald, vol. 14, p. 515—533.

The following copious extracts from the reports of *ten Collectors,* to whom the Madras Government had addressed queries respecting the state of slavery in their respective districts, appear peculiarly interesting. The whole letter from the Secretary of Government in the revenue department contains fourteen folio pages, and bears date, April, 1819.

"In SALEM slavery does not appear to exist. The collector observes, 'I can safely state that, in the manner referred to in these communicatious, there is no vestige whatever of slavery in this collectorate, nor has any such practice obtained from the time the country came into possession of the Honourable Company. During the Mussulman government, there were a few slaves belonging to certain Nunjah lands in the vicinity of the Cauvery, and there are now some descendants of these people; but they are just as free as any other inhabitants. I have heard of one or two instances of a child being sold for the purpose of domestic slavery; but this is uncommonly rare, and otherwise such a circumstance as a person being sold as a slave has never transpired.'

"In MADURA and DINDIGUL slavery existed during the Mahomedan government. The slaves were sold at the pleasure of their masters, but they were not 'adscripti glebæ;' not necessarily sold whenever the land was sold. The collector's words are, 'When a puller or parriah was unable to gain a livelihood, he was accustomed to offer himself or his relatives as slaves to the cultivating inhabitants, for a sum of money, varying from one to ten cully chuckrums, when a bond of slavery was drawn out and signed. If they married, their children were considered the property of the owners; they were employed in the cultivation of land, and were maintained by the owners, who frequently, for their services, would grant them a soluntrum, or allowance in grain, in addition to other allowances. If the proprietor of land was obliged to dispose of the whole of his lands, he still retained possession of his slaves, and disposed of them as he pleased, as they were not considered attached to the land thus sold. If an owner was unable to maintain his slave, he could let him out to others, by which means he frequently derived a maintenance both for himself and slave; but the slave was obliged to return to his master whenever he required him, who could mortgage or sell him at pleasure. Since the assumption of the country, some slaves have continued with their masters; others have left them, and have even enlisted as sepoys. I cannot discover that any puller has sold himself as a slave of late years. Indeed, *slavery altogether seems gradually disappearing; which may be attributed to the knowledge that it is not encouraged in the different courts of justice.* Some pullers cultivate their own lands, and have their own puttiams. Those who cultivate the lands of others, and who are not slaves, receive a regulated hire.'

"In COIMBATORE slavery is reported to exist 'but in a very few villages.' The collector observes, 'From all that I can learn, it appears certain that *the owner has a right to sell his slave without the land; but that it is a right very seldom, if ever, exercised.* The highest price for a good slave is fifty rupees; the price, however, is seldom so high. The children of slaves are born slaves. On the birth of a child, the master presents the parents with clothes, and one or two rupees. The masters are supposed to be vested with despotic authority over their slaves, and with power to punish them. An apprehension, however, that the exercise of such authority is not permitted by the British government appears generally prevalent, and rather operates to prevent the merchandise of slaves, as *they are considered to be less valuable when free from the fear of punishment*. There appears reason for thinking that the slaves are, on the whole, better treated by their masters than the common class of free labourers. The master possesses a power, not only over the person, but over the property of his slave; and he may make use of the cattle reared by the slave for agricultural purposes! The slaves are sold with the land; but, if they should object to serve another master, they are not forced to do so. This, however, I take to be an indulgence of the master, not a right of the slave. The slaves have *a share of the produce allotted for their subsistence, about an eighth*. In some instances, land has been made over to the pullers, which they cultivate for their support. In many places, where slavery does not exist, a species of bondage is introduced, by the ryots undertaking to bear the expense of their puller's marriage, upon condition of the latter binding themselves to serve the ryots exclusively for life. Slavery may almost be considered as extinct in Coimbatore, as the epidemic has carried off many of the slaves, and the number was always inconsiderable.'

"In Tanjore slavery exists; but, as in Madura and Dindigul, it is founded, in the first instance, upon voluntary contract. 'The slaves are never seized or sold for arrears of revenue. The slaves here are of two castes only, the Puller and Pariah; the origin of their bondage arises in a voluntary agreement, on their part, to become the slave of some other man more powerful than themselves, upon whom they thus impose a more strict obligation to protect and maintain them and their families than if merely serving them as labouring servants. The Brahmins, in consideration of their caste, do not receive bonds of slavery directly in their own name, but have them generally drawn out in that of some of their soodra dependents. When a bond of slavery has been given, it ceases not with the life of the party, but is binding upon the descendants of the original giver, who continue bound by the conditions of it likewise. In return, the owner is obliged to find subsistence at all times, and under all circumstances, for the family of his bondsman, whom he can employ in any manner he pleases, although it is generally as a labourer in the fields. The bondsman does not reside in his master's house, nor form any part of his family, but has a house provided for him along with the others of his caste, to which a back yard of eighty goontahs rent-free is attached, the same as other labourers. *The master has the power of selling the slave, but he cannot sell him to any one who will carry him to a distant part of the country, without his own consent*. If the master, through poverty or other cause, fails or becomes unable to subsist and protect his bondsman and his family, he is at liberty to seek employment as a free labourer elsewhere, but is liable to be reclaimed at any time by his master, when he may be again in a condition to fulfil his part of the agreement. When lands are sold, in any way, it is always independent of the bondsmen, if any, upon it. If they are likewise to be sold, separate deeds of transfer are passed. If not, they continue attached to their former masters. No persons of this description have ever yet been considered as seizable property, or sold for an arrear of revenue; nor do I believe ever by a judicial decree in any civil cause; nor have I ever known this species of property recognized by the officers of government, although it is by the natives themselves, in their transactions with each other.

'On the part of the bondsman, his rights are subsistence and protection for himself and family from his master, with liberty to seek it elsewhere, as a free agent, if not found him, and the right of not being removed by sale to a distant country from the' place of his birth. With regard to himself, personally, his treatment from his master is the same as that of his other labourers, which is in general of a mild nature; but he is not more liable to personal punishment than others, in consequence of his state of bondage; and any cruelty or abuse of authority on the part of the master towards his bondsman would be complained against, and punished with equal strictness, as if committed upon a free man.

'Upon the whole, therefore, the Board will perceive that the condition of these people differs very little from that of the common labourers, and that the treatment of both is nearly the same. The disadvantage to the bondsman is *the power of being sold or transferred to other masters;* and this, I believe, is not very frequent, as it is the last property, generally, which is disposed of by a person in distressed circumstances. The advantages are the more effectually securing subsistence and protection to themselves and families, particularly in times of trouble or difficulty, than it is binding on masters in general to bestow upon common labourers; and this without rendering their condition in any degree intolerable, towards the amelioration of which, the equity and mildness of the British government have greatly operated, in respect to rendering the conduct of masters to their servants indulgent, forbearing, and kind. I do not find that the system of slaves attached to the soil, and transferrable by purchase as appendages to the land, obtains here.'

"TINNEVELLY. 'From all the information I have been able to collect, I understand it is usual in this district for slaves to be sold or mortgaged either with the land or separately, as the proprietor pleases, or his wants require; and that there is no particular rule, or general custom, by which the conduct between the master and slave, and between slave and master, is governed, further than that the master has at all times the command of his slave's labour, and that the slave cannot work for any other person without the permission of his master.

'In regard to the treatment of masters towards their slaves, it does not appear to be incumbent on them to afford a subsistence to their slaves, except when employed in their business, and then *it is on the lowest scale of allowance,* being generally no more than two measures of paddy per day. At other times their slaves are obliged to seek a livelihood at the hands of others, being bound only to return to their masters when the season of cultivation again commences. Besides this allowance, however, which the slaves receive from their masters on working days, they are entitled, when the crops are reaped, to a small deduction from the gross produce, called here 'Paroo,' which varies in different villages, but *amounts generally to about* 23·8 *per cent;* and it is usual, when deaths occur among them, for their masters to assist them in the necessary funeral expenses, and on marriages, births, and festival days, to grant them presents, according as their circumstances will admit; but these are acts quite voluntary on the part of the masters, and the slave, it appears, can claim nothing more than a bare subsistence while he works, and his soluntrum, as above described, at the time of harvest.

'All punishment of the slave by the master, if this power ever existed, and was recognized in former times, seems now to be at an end; and there is no instance, I am happy to say, within my experience in this district, of a slave complaining of ill-treatment from his master.

The fact, indeed, appears to be, that the slave is so necessary to the cultivation, and labourers are so scarce, that the proprietors find it their interest to protect and treat them well; and the slaves in time become so attached to the village in which they are settled, that they seem not to consider their situation, nor to show any desire to be free and independent.

'In calling upon the tehsildars for an account of a person's property, to know whether he is a fit security for another, it is usual, if he possesses slaves, to include them, a male slave being estimated in value from 3 to 15 C. Chuckrums (R 6 $\frac{93}{256}$ to 31 $\frac{209}{256}$), and a female from 3 to 5 C. Chuckrums (6 $\frac{93}{256}$ to 10 $\frac{155}{256}$); but I have always rejected them in the account as unavailable property by the Sircar, and none have ever been sold in this district for an arrear of revenue.'*

"South Arcot. 'The slaves in this collectorate are most of the Pully and Pariar castes, and the majority of them are chiefly devoted to the pursuits of agriculture.

'The number of slaves in this district, of both sexes, including children, amounts to upwards of 17,000; and they appear to have been generally born in a state of servitude, through some contract of their forefathers. The Hindoo code of laws, religious and civil, seems, however, to declare that the Soodra tribe are naturally born in a state of servitude; and, although some of the superiors of the sub-divisions of that tribe in modern days, have emancipated themselves from this degrading thraldom, yet the lower castes are always looked upon as natural slaves, the property of any person *who contributes to defray their marriage expenses, which is the ordinary way at present of constituting hereditary slavery.* Previously to the assumption of the Carnatic, the owners of slaves were empowered to punish them, either by castigation or confinement, for any misdemeanor or fault, at their discretion; but that power, subsequently to the British administration, has ceased to be exercised. The possessions and the acquisitions of slaves are generally considered to be the property of their masters, who, however, usually relinquish

---

* "The jemn *value of a good Parier*, as well as a good Addian (slave), is thirty rupees; Otty, twenty-seven and a half rupees; Kanom, fifteen rupees; and the jemn value of a less able one of either tribe is twenty rupees; Otty, seventeen and a half rupees; Kanom, ten rupees; and Paneyam, eight rupees. The jemn value of children (male) of those sects is twelve rupees. The jemn value of a female slave of any of the two tribes above-mentioned, as well as of their female children, is three rupees and eighty reas. The pattom of a good cherman of any of the two sects above-mentioned is three paddies of paddy; that of a less able one, two paddies; that of a boy, one paddy; and that of a female of those sects is also one paddy. The jemn value of a good slave of the Moopan and Naiken tribe is sixty-four silver fanams; Otty, fifty-two; Kanom, thirty; and Verroom Pattan, four silver fanams, but the females of those tribes are not given on Pattom or by sale. The jemn value of a good Poolean slave is twelve rupees; Otty, ten rupees; and Kanom, six rupees; and the jemn value of a less able one eight rupees; Otty, six rupees; Kanom, four rupees; and Verrom Pattom, one paddy of paddy. The value of a good Panian or Addian (slaves) might be said to have increased now by five rupees above the old price, but that of the Naiken, Moorpan, and Poliar, continues still the same." Par. Papers, pp. 852, 853.

them to the family of the slave. Slaves cannot enter into any matrimonial connexion without the consent of their owners, who, as they defray the expenses of the marriage, virtually revive the contract of hereditary bondage; for *the offspring of slaves are always regarded as the property of their father's owner.*

'It is stated that the slaves of this district can be sold by their owners to any person and to an alien village, and that no slaves are attached to any particular soil or village; but I am induced to believe that such a practice is at variance with the rights annexed to the state of real bondage; for in some Meerassi villages it is known that the Meerassidars have advanced pretensions to possess an equal proportion of the slaves with their share of the villages, and I also believe that such a practice is hardly ever resorted to. The price of a male slave and family, when sold by their owner to another person, varies considerably, and ranges from ten to *fifty pagodas.* The owners of slaves are required to provide them with food and clothing, to defray their wedding expenses, and to assist them on the births of children, and in their funeral charges. The food differs according to the opulence of the owner, but is always sufficient for subsistence, or the owner permits the slave to serve elsewhere during his poverty. The clothing is very scanty, except when the slaves are chiefly employed for domestic purposes; and I cannot discover that the apparel is designedly calculated to portray the class of the wearers. The duties of slaves are to attend the cattle and agriculture, and to assist in domestic services, connected with the house or person of their owners.

'It does not appear that *enfranchisement of slaves ever takes place;* yet as some owners have been reduced to indigence, and are unable to employ or subsist their hereditary slaves, those persons are ostensibly free, and labour for any person who will employ them. Cases of emancipation occur in the extinction of the owners' families; and from this description of Soodras, who still sacrifice their liberties, modern slaves are constituted; for they are mostly very needy, and consent to perpetual and hereditary bondage for about twenty or thirty pagodas, which the cultivator advances for the celebration of a marriage ceremony. In no instance, I believe, do engagements exist where a *labourer discharges such a loan by his manual labour.*'

"CHINGLEPUT. 'The slaves employed in the cultivation of the lands, and to which this report principally refers, have, for the most part, their allowances regularly rendered to them; so much grain being granted to each labourer, and a proportionate subsistence for each of his children or others of the family. They are housed and clothed; and, during the principal festivals, certain other allowances are made them both in money and articles required for their ceremonies. Their marriages are also performed at the charge of their masters; and, when reduced by infirmity, they are also supported by their proprietors. The condition of this description of people, composing the chief part of the Pariahs of the district, has of late years considerably changed. This may, in a great measure, arise from the vicinity of their situation to Madras, *where this system is known to be abrogated.* Many of them there obtain employment, and their proprietors would find it difficult to reclaim them; and the regulations have so far circumscribed the authority formerly exercised by the proprietors, over this description of their servants, that they cannot keep them under control as heretofore,—when the power was vested in them of inflicting very severe corporeal punishment, or confining them for the neglect of the duties assigned them: in former times the discipline exercised by the proprietors over their slaves was of a very severe description. The proprietors now finding themselves incapable of employing their services, or rather to control them as arbitrarily as heretofore, complain less of the loss of this description of property. The adami, or slaves, are also possessed by many of the Vellairs, &c., who are sookavasies, and who have long established themselves in the cultivation of particular villages; but their situation in such cases is similar to those in the service of other soodras. *The sale of adami* has been, I believe, of late years, *discontinued,* or of very rare occurrence; and in these parts no attachment of such property has, I fancy, ever been made on account of the dues of government.'

"TRICHINOPOLY.—'In the wet districts of Trichinopoly, the number of pullers may be stated at 10,000, including those employed for the purpose of watching and feeding the cattle. In the dry districts, there are about 600; but I must here observe that *pullers are only to be found in those villages where there is paddy cultivation.* The pullers of the dry districts appear to be liable to the same rules, and to possess the same rights, as those of the wet districts. The services they perform are chiefly confined to the irrigation of the land in its several stages of cultivation; but their services are also occasionally required by their masters in the menial offices of their household establishment. If a wall or pundall is required, *the pullers are obliged to erect it, without any further recompense than their usual and established emoluments.* The pullers are usually sold with the land; but there are many cases in which they may be purchased independent of the land. The price of a puller varies from *five to ten pagodas,* according to his age and qualifications. Their services are also occasionally mortgaged; a pullee, or female puller, is never sold; while it would appear that, *in Malabar, men, women, and children, are sold indiscriminately.*

'The pullers are supposed to be entirely supported by their masters in sickness and in health. Their marriages are made at the expense of the meerassidars, as well as the expense of their funerals. They enjoy some little gratuity at every birth, and receive a certain established sum at the principal Hindoo festivals. I have noted *a list of the yearly emoluments a puller is properly entitled to receive;* and these emoluments, though small, I have every reason to believe are scarcely ever withheld.* (See the foot of the page.)

* "The extent of cultivation to be made by a puller and by a pullee is 150 cullums of paddy.

Annual Emoluments:		ru.	an.
Warum of a puller culs.	–	8	5$\frac{3}{8}$
Do. of a pullee	–	6	6$\frac{3}{4}$
	–	15	$\frac{1}{8}$
Batta at the commencement of each fusly for ploughing	–	2	4
Soluntrums for sowing	–	–	6
Reaping share a' 5 per cent.	–	7	6
Thrashing do.	–	1	–
Pongal feast	–	1	–
Duparaly do.	–	–	–$\frac{1}{8}$
Gramadava do.	–	–	1$\frac{1}{2}$
Total annual	26	1$\frac{1}{8}$	5$\frac{5}{8}$ fs.

'I have examined the pullers themselves, on the subject of their being well or ill treated, and asked them what course they would pursue if ill used. They replied *they would seek other masters at a distance, who would treat them more kindly.* In corroboration of this fact I have never received a complaint, either in my fiscal or magisterial capacity, since my appointment to this district, from a puller against his master. The right of the puller is so distinctly defined by custom, and the interest of the meerassidar so substantially affected by the good conduct and health of the puller,—that it is hardly possible to suppose the meerassidars would be so blind to their own interest as to cause their pullers to abscond, or by harsh treatment reduce them to sickness. From what has been already stated it will be found that agricultural slavery has existed in this district from time immemorial.'

"CANARA.—'The origin of slavery in Canara is to be traced from extracts in an ancient book, called Sheehadry Pooranum, but by no means an authentic record. This treatise is stated to contain a fabulous narrative, which, when divested of its oriental imagery and metaphors, will be found to attribute the origin of slavery in Canara to the right of conquest.

'*The right of sale was, and is still, the master's exclusive privilege, either with or without the land.* The price varies, and is settled amongst the purchasers and sellers. The usual rates are as follow:—

'For a strong young man, from twelve to twenty-six rupees.

'Do. a strong young woman, twelve to twenty-four rupees.

'Do. a child, never under four rupees.

'It is customary to pass a bill of sale, on a bargain being made, or a mortgage bond. The transfer, by purchase or gift, is attended with a short ceremony, both between the seller, or giver, and receiver, and the slave. The slave drinks some water from his brass basin, and calls out '*I am now your slave for ever.*' The zillah court, I understand, has guaranteed this right by decrees, both on transfer of landed property, and on sale in execution of decrees. The master can lend his slaves out on hire. *He can sell the husband to one person, the wife to another!* This is not often done, because neither of the purchasers can be sure of keeping his purchase. Thus the great law of nature seems even in these humbled creatures to be acknowledged by their owners. Care is always taken in purchasing not to carry the slave to any distant estate; their attachment to the soil on which they were born being well known. *The master can sell the children;* but this is seldom done from the foregoing cause, the fear of desertion. The master, according to his means, feeds and clothes his slaves. He *never pays them wages in money,* but presents them on their marriages, or particular ceremonies, with a small sum. The quan-

---

	ru. an.
Proposed addition of warum a' 2 per cent. . . .	3 – –
	29 $1\frac{1}{8}$ $5\frac{5}{8}$ fs.
Contingencies estimated:	
For a marriage	4 – rs. 8
For a birth	– 2 fs. 2
For a death	– 2 fs. 2
	4 4 rs. 8 4
Total . .	33 $5\frac{3}{8}$ rs. 9 fs. $1\frac{1}{8}$"

tity of food and clothing to a slave varies in every talook. It does not seem to be *regulated by any rule,* although it would appear that some original quantum obtained. The average may be thus estimated :—

	FOOD.	CLOTHING.
A man . . .	½ Canara seer coarse rice, two rupees weight salt, a little beetel nut and leaf.	Two pieces of cauthey, six cubits. In some talooks, a coombly and roomal given.
A woman . .	1 seer.	1 do. seven cubits long.
A child . .	¾ do.	1 do. four do.

'The salt, beetel, &c., is optional. It is also customary to give them conjee from the master's house. From every inquiry I cannot learn that any want or cruelty is experienced by the slaves, the master being well aware that, on any ill-treatment, they will desert him; and that the trouble and expense attending their recovery would perhaps amount to the value of the deserters. *Slavery seems to be inconsistent with rights and privileges,* if I understand the correct meaning of the terms. On these points I can only generally state that the *dhers of Canara possess none.* The number of slaves of all descriptions, in Canara, has never been correctly ascertained; they may be estimated at 82,000.'

"MALABAR.—In Malabar (exclusive of Wynaud)* the number of slaves is estimated by the collector at 100,000. 'They are,' says the collector, '*slaves of the soil,* and are generally attached to the land of the proprietors of the ground on which they were born; but this is by no means considered an essential point, being frequently transferred by sale, mortgage, or hire. In Malabar, as in the West Indies, a man's wealth is as much appreciated by the number of his slaves, as by any other property he may possess! In one sect they observe what is termed makkatye; in another they observe the marra makka-tye; the former being the common laws of kindred, the latter similar to the customs among the Nairs, in which inheritance goes to the sister's son, and this constitutes the value of a female of one caste over that of the male, and *vice versâ,* a male being more valuable *where the progeny goes with him.* The marriage contract is made entirely among the parents of the parties, without any interference on the part of the proprietor; to whom, however, it is necessary to make known the proposed connexion.

'No valuable consideration is given by the male for the possession of the female to the owner. *The contract may be dissolved at the pleasure of the parties connected;* in which event the husband takes off the marriage necklace (commonly composed of shells or brass ornaments), which makes the dissolution complete, and each is at liberty to form new connexions; but whilst the contract lasts I have had opportunities in my magisterial capacity, when an assistant in the courts, of observing a wonderful degree of jealousy and tenaciousness of family honour, when contrasted with the general appearance, habits, and apparently brutish stupidity of these castes. *The measure of subsistence to be given by the proprietor is fixed,* and he is bound by the prescribed customs of the country to see it served out to them daily. A frequent failure on the part

* "The landed proprietors of Wynaud are torpid to a degree; all the field work is done by slaves called Paniers, who are held in higher estimation than the slaves of the lower districts. They are admitted to the threshold of their masters' houses, and they are even employed in grinding rice for the use of the temples!"

of the master to perform this duty is sure to be attended with desertion to another, from whom they expect kinder usage; and, when this does take place, the recovery of them is attended with difficulties that are not easily overcome; for, independent of being obliged to have recourse to courts of justice, *months and years perhaps elapse before they can discover to what place the slave absconded.* In short the proprietor feels it his interest to see them well treated, through apprehensions of the consequence of an opposite conduct. In former days the proprietor possessed the power of life and death over his slaves; but this was probably seldom or never had recourse to, and desertion only would, in all probability, have been one of the motives for so rigorous a measure; but there were many circumstances which would have operated as a check upon the gratification of this species of severity and revenge.

'I do not immediately recollect any instance of a churma having appealed to a court of justice for protection from the ill usage of his master; but instances are not wanting of persons having been brought to justice and to a severe account for the murder or wounding of a slave; and as it is universally known throughout Malabar that British justice considers the life of the lowest individual as valuable as the highest character in the country, and that as severe a measure of retribution would fall on the head of the murderer of a slave as of a rajah, we may consider them as well protected by the laws as any other race of beings. In some respects churmas may be considered in more comfortable circumstances than any of the lower and poorer class of Natives. An instance of a churma being a beggar is unheard of; they and their families are sure of having the means of subsistence, as, if the owner should be rendered unable to afford this, he will sell, mortgage, or hire, his churma to another, on whom would devolve the duty, as well as interest, of affording such subsistence as to enable the churma to go through the labours of the day. Contrast this with the situation of a free born but poor labourer, depending upon the labours of a day for his subsistence, unable, perhaps, to find employment, with a wife and family to support, and no one to whom he can look up for protection or subsistence.'* †

---

* "The churmas are *absolute property; they are part of the live stock on an estate.* In selling and buying land it is not necessary that they should follow the soil; both kinds of property are equally disposable, and may fall into different hands. The churmas may be sold, leased, and mortgaged, like the land itself, or like any cattle or thing. The feumokar may hire them for pattom or rent independently of this jenm land, or he may sell them altogether with his estate. The pattom on a churma is four fanams a year; if they are disposed of on otty, their price is thirty-two fanams; if on the attipit ola or jenmon, forty-eight fanams.

The jenmokar, by the ancient laws of Malabar, is *accountable to no person for the life of his own churma,* but is the legal judge of his offences, and may punish them by death, if they should appear to deserve it. The kolloonaven can neither put to death a churma nor sell him, but he may chastise him. In the same manner as the soil the possession of churmas was originally confined to a particular class. They were then employed entirely in the labours of agriculture; but, although they were the first and sole cultivators in Malabar, it is not to be imagined that this is the case at present, since there are many kuddians of all castes, who cultivate their own lands"—(Walker's Rep. on Malabar).

† Par. Papers on Slavery in India, pp. 887—896.

"The *Northern Division of* Arcot.—'The slaves in the district are not numerous; exhibiting a total of 688, inclusive of men, women, and children, and the practice of keeping them may be said to be confined to the five talooks of Arcot, Trevultoor, Cauvareeput, Poloor, and Suttawaid; for in Sholungar and Wondawash (the only two other talooks in which, according to the same statement, slavery prevails) their numbers are very small indeed.

'They are ostensibly employed in agriculture, and the pasturing of cattle, though they may occasionally do house work, and the persons in whose service they are principally engaged are of the Rajah, Brahmun, and Vellumwar castes; to this circumstance may perhaps be traced the practice of slavery in the above-mentioned talooks, where most of the head inhabitants and renters are of one or other of those castes.

'Children, born when their parents are in a state of slavery, become slaves also, and I would beg to be understood as speaking generally of the manner in which slavery, or the required number of slaves, is kept up; there are, it is true, instances of people having been slaves from their birth, but they are very few indeed; and in proof of this it may be mentioned, that it does not appear to be *accurately settled to whom the child of a slave belongs;* in one talook, it was said to the master of the male, in another to the master of the female slave; the question, perhaps, has never been agitated; for the people who keep slaves most likely *find it cheaper to buy than to rear them!* and the offspring, when left to their parents' charge, who have barely sufficient to support themselves, die of absolute want. They have not any particular marks whereby they may be distinguished, except it is their wretched appearance; they are fed and clothed and subsisted entirely by their masters; their food consists of raggy, the coarsest kind of grain, and their clothing is a common cumly. I cannot discover, though I was very particular in my enquiries on the point, that they have any rights or privileges, and they are not possessed of any property, neither can they inherit any.'"*

The latter part of the Papers refers to *the practice of stealing children,* which appears "very prevalent at Madras." "I beg (says the Magistrate at Tinnevelly in Dec. 1825) to bring officially to notice a custom which is, I believe, more or less prevalent throughout the Madras territories, and, as far as my own observation has gone, is more frequent in the district of Tinnevelly. The practice I allude to is the sale and purchase of female children by dancing women, for the avowed purpose of bringing them up to a life immorality. The custom is so notorious, and its abominable tendency so evident, that no comment can be necessary; but I am apprehensive that, unless it be specially excepted from those purchases of children which are now (under some circumstances) legal, an opinion maybe entertained that such dealings are countenanced by law. A

---

* Par. Papers on Slavery in India, pp. 873, 874

prohibition of such transactions could not be complained of as an infringement of any acknowledged rights; it would serve as a check upon child-stealing, which is occasionally practised under the pretence of purchase, and the public expression of the will of the government could not but have a beneficial tendency to promote morality. I offer these remarks, in the hope that, if they are submitted to government, the practice which I have mentioned may be prohibited by law."*

The reply to this communication, it is presumed, cannot be read without feelings of disapprobation. "It is understood, from your letter, that, in the opinion of the judges of the Foujdaree Adawlut, no new enactment is required upon this subject, because the selling or purchasing of children, for the avowed purpose of prostitution, may be punished under the law as it at present stands. The Governor in council entirely concurs with the judges in deeming any enactment unnecessary; and is further of opinion, adverting to the nature of the institution of dancing women, and to its connection with the ceremonies and observances, both religious and civil, of the great bulk of the people, that if it is at all expedient for the officers of government to interfere, for the purpose of preventing parents or guardians from assigning children in the customary modes to be brought up to this profession, the interference requires to be conducted with the greatest caution. The remarks in my letter of the 28th June, to which reference is made by the Foujdaree Adawlut, relate to the practice of selling children to be made slaves, and generally to the usages of the country with respect to slavery; and, it was observed, that that subject was one of much difficulty and delicacy. The subject now under consideration is of no less delicacy, and it seems to afford less inducement to interfere; for it is to be considered that loss of personal freedom is not among the consequences of being brought up to be a dancing woman, and that the species of immorality which the interference would propose to redress prevails, and is generally tolerated, in the most enlightened and most highly civilized nations of Europe, and it is much more closely connected with general depravity and with misery in England than it is in India."†—(J. M. Macleod

* Par. Papers on Slavery in India, pp. 934, 935. † p. 935. See also pp. 901—903.

Secretary to Government, Fort St. George, Jan. 13, 1826).

The *present state of the melioration of slavery*—for the abolition of it is not attempted—appears in an extract of a letter from the Honourable Court of Directors to the Governor of Madras, in April, 1824. "In the districts subject to your Presidency the rights and obligations of master and slave appear to be very indistinctly defined: and this obscurity of the law we apprehend to be favourable to the slaves; for, whatever the legal power of masters may be, their actual control over the liberties of those persons who are nominally their slaves appears to be but small. *We desire that you will be extremely cautious in making any regulation for defining the relations of master and slave. It is our wish to improve the condition of the latter to the utmost extent, and we fear that, in defining the power of masters, acts of compulsion might be legalized, which by custom are not now tolerated, and the slaves might be placed in a worse condition than before.* We shall defer making any further remarks on the subject, till we receive a further communication from you."*

To this, nearly two years after, the Governor in council refers with approbation. "The opinions and views stated in these paragraphs coincide with those entertained by us."†—Feb. 3, 1826.

Thus the state of slavery in India, which at one time is considered mild and scarcely needing attention, at another is considered of such a nature that the Government is afraid to touch the subject—even to "define the relations of master and slave." Is this the way to eradicate one of the greatest evils incident to mortal man? "Surely," says the late Bishop Heber, "we are, in matters of religion, the most lukewarm and cowardly people on the face of the earth; ‡ and is it not equally true of the interests of humanity in India as of religion?

The *actual extent of slavery in India*, it is presumed, cannot be ascertained by the Parliamentary Documents now before the public. No census or general registration of the slaves appears to have been taken; it is only, therefore, from occasional remarks by the Magistrates, or the more regular statements of some of the Collectors under the Ma-

* Par. Papers on Slavery in India, p. 901. † p. 901.
‡ Jour. vol. ii. p. 465.

dras Presidency, that any probable estimate can be taken of the extent of slavery in the British dominions in the East. By the publication of this first volume of Parliamentary Papers on Slavery in India, sufficient information is given to urge the full development of the nature and extent of this system, and to excite the friends of humanity to increased exertion, till Britain in all her dominions regards the divine injunction, "Let the oppressed go free, and break every yoke."

The second judge at *Dacca*, in 1813, states "The odious practice of trafficking in slaves has long subsisted in that zillah, and doubtless many and various abuses have been committed under the cloak of an authorized commerce, or at least of such mercantile transactions not specially prohibited. The trade is carried on to a considerable extent, as is universally acknowledged; and, from the best information on the subject, it is computed that *the number of slaves in the district amounts to about one-sixth of the whole population;* and this number *progressively increases*, as their offspring are also born slaves. It is impossible to form a correct calculation of the number of slaves annually exported from the district, but it is believed to be much less considerable now than formerly."*

Of *Sylhet*, and the zillah *Backergunge*, the Magistrate, J. W. Sage, Esq., in 1816, observes, "During the ten months I was at Sylhet, I often heard that some persons gained a livelihood by enticing boys and girls, whose parents were free, both from their houses in the district and from the adjoining territories of Kackar and Jynteah, by disposing of some to wealthy natives in the district, and carrying some for sale to other places.

"It is a common practice amongst the lower class of native women, on the loss of their husbands, or at the time of a scarcity of grain, both in Sylhet and this district (Backergunge), to sell their children, by which the mothers gain a livelihood, and the children are much better taken care of by their new masters, than if they had continued with their parents. It happens, frequently, that some mothers sell their female children to prostitutes; sales of that description are always made known to the police darogahs, whose duty it is to convey the parties instantly to the magistrate, that they may be punished for so nefarious a transaction. Some there

---

* Par. Papers on Slavery in India, p. 224.

are, whose families have been in a state of slavery for the last hundred years, and who, *when a sale of an estate takes place, are included in the purchase ;* as however many suits are instituted in the Sylhet district for slaves, and appeals are admitted by the court of appeal, I do not suppose Sir R. K. Dick had it in contemplation to draw the attention of government to that class of people. It might in some measure prevent illicit transactions, if every one purchasing a child was, under pain of a heavy fine and imprisonment, ordered to register such sale, and enter into an agreement at the court at the time of registering, binding himself to produce at the court the boy or girl he may buy, whenever the magistrate should call upon him."*

"There are (says the intelligent and philanthropic Judge of Bundlecund in 1808, J. Richardson, Esq.) districts under the Company's dominions wherein, to my own knowledge (particularly *Ram Ghur*), the greatest part of the cultivators and labourers are slaves. I have no scruple to avow I deem this one great cause of the wild and uncultivated condition of the country, and the barbarous and savage state of its inhabitants ; for what human being will labour with good will, or a desire of improvement, when another enjoys the sole produce?"†

This gentleman further observes, "By an enforcement of the spirit and principles of the Mussulman law, a total stop would be put to the horrid practice of slavery, which, wonderful and almost incredible to state, *exists contrary to law and reason throughout our dominions in India, to a degree scarcely to be believed ;* not a Mussulman family of even mediocrity that has not numbers both of male and female slaves. The people about their persons, and the female attendants on their women, are almost all slaves; and, to my certain knowledge, they have slaves for the purpose of cultivation and field labour."‡

Hamilton in his Description of Hindostan (two vols. 4to.) thus speaks of slavery in Bengal :—"Domestic slavery is very generally prevalent in Bengal, among both Hindoos and Mahomedans. More trusty than hired servants, slaves are almost exclusively employed in the interior of the houses for attendance on the members of the family, and in all the most confidential services. Every opulent person, every one raised above the condition of the simplest medio-

---

* Par. Papers on Slavery in India, p. 247. † p. 300. ‡ p. 317.

crity, is provided with household slaves, and from this class chiefly are taken the concubines of Mahomedans and Hindoos. In the lower provinces, under the Bengal Presidency, the *employment of slaves in the labours of husbandry is almost unknown.* In the upper provinces, beginning from Western Behar and Benares, the petty landlords, who are themselves cultivators, are aided in their husbandry by slaves, whom they very commonly employ as herds and ploughmen; landlords of a higher class have in a few instances the pretensions of masters over a part of their tenants long settled on their estates, and reputed to be descended from persons who were the acknowledged slaves of their ancestors. Their claims to the services of these hereditary serfs, who are scarcely to be distinguished from the rest of the peasantry, are nearly obsolete and scarcely attended with any practical consequences; but those employed in husbandry by the inferior classes of landlords are decidedly slaves. The employment of slaves in handicraft work is more rare, but not entirely unknown. It would be difficult to form a computation of the number of slaves throughout the country, and any steps towards the preparation of an accurate estimate would involve inquiries which cannot fail of exciting great alarm. Slaves are neither so few as to be of no consideration, nor so numerous as to constitute a notable proportion of the population. The slave is more usually a favourite and confidential servant than an abject drudge; and he is held superior to the hireling both in his master's estimation and his own."* †

Of *Penang, or Prince of Wales Island,* the Governor in 1807 very justly observes,—" Although domestic slavery, as practised by the Malays, meliorates in a great degree the situation of the slave, as hitherto permitted on this island, when compared with that of the same class of people in other quarters of the globe—still *slavery in its mildest form is degrading in the minds of Britons,* and hitherto only tolerated as a means of drawing population to an infant colony, which, from the now flourishing state of this island, is no longer necessary, therefore derogatory to our national

* Ham. Hind. vol. 1. p. 105—107.

† "Domestic Slavery (says the late Rev. W. Ward), which is very common in India, however mild, surely demands the reprehension of every individual who has a proper idea of the dignity of human nature. In some parts of India children are as much an article of sale as goats or poultry."—View of the Hindoos, 1820, vol. iii. p. 281.

character, and should in my opinion cease to exist: at the same time every reasonable consideration is due towards their proprietors, so as to remunerate the one without injustice to the other, or too suddenly interfering with ancient and authorized usages. This subject has, it appears, engaged the attention of the Honourable the Court of Directors, and they have more than once urged their government here to adopt the necessary measures for effecting so humane and honourable an object as the personal freedom of a considerable proportion of their subjects. I have consequently felt interested in the cause, and made such inquiries as enable me to state that there cannot be fewer than *three thousand, men, women, and children,* in a state of bondage on this island, and that of this number, the families of Tunka, Pootry, Seied Hussein, the Pangavas Heirs, Maha Raja Stra, and Noqueda Byan, together possess nearly one-third of that number."*

Of the Daerds, a description of slaves in *Canara,* the Collector of the Southern Division in 1801 states:—"By far the greatest part of the slaves employed in agriculture are the Daerds, of whom there are various descriptions and properties; no order was ever given for their being included in the registers; the whole number of them, by the population statement, is 52,022, men, women, and children; of which number there are in the Baincoor talook 5,894: the number belonging to every landlord shall hereafter, as desired, be entered in the registers,"† "Exclusive of the Daerds, there were another sect of slaves in Canara, though, I believe, many of them are now free. Under the Biddenore government, all illegitimate children, save those by dancing girls, were considered the property of the Sircar, which took possession of, and sold them as slaves, to any person who would purchase them; the number of this sort now is about 722; there are also many slaves imported from Arabia."‡

Some of the Daerds having enlisted in the Company's army, the collector of Mangalore requested the Madras government that they might be interdicted the service. The minute of government acknowledges the existence of slavery in this and other parts of India.—"The circumstances stated, by the Collector of the southern division of Canara, require, in the Board's opinion, particular consideration. He has represented that serious injury will be sus-

* Par. Papers on Slavery p. 436, see also p. 454. † p. 548. ‡ p. 550.

tained by the landholders of Canara, if their slaves are permitted to enter the sepoy corps, and desert the lands which they and their progenitors had cultivated for many generations. It is observed, by Mr. Ravenshaw, that, where these people do enlist, they seldom continue in the service, but almost invariably desert; in this point of view it appears ineligible that they should be allowed to enter the corps; but as it may be considered beyond the province of the Board to discuss the propriety of this measure in a military point of view, or the policy of emancipating this class of people, they will only observe that the encouraging these slaves thus to desert their masters would be *disturbing a property* sanctioned to them by the usages of the country, and the ordinances of their law; and, whilst it would be of no advantage to the army, *it would be of considerable detriment to the revenue; for not only in Canara, but in several parts of India, it is this class of people who cultivate the soil,* and on whose industry the landholder depends for the payment of the dues of the Sirkar government, and for the means of his own support."*

The Board of Revenue for the Madras government in 1818, in a very judicious minute on slavery, candidly acknowledge its prevalence:—"The provinces now subject to this government appear originally to have constituted several distinct Hindoo states, which are still to be traced by the difference of language, manners, and customs, that so strongly distinguish the inhabitants of one part of the country from the other. The five northern circars of Ganjam, Vizagapatam, Rajahmundry, Masulipatam and Guntoor, together with the districts of Bellary, Cuddaph, Paluand, and Nellore, or wherever the Telinga is the language of the people, may be considered one of these; the second may be said to include the district of Chingleput, the two divisions of the Arcot Soobah, Salem, Baramahl, Coimbatore, Madura, Dindigul, Trichinopoly, Tanjore, and Tinnevelly, or wherever the Tamil language is spoken; and the third comprises the provinces of Malabar and Canara, on the other coast of the Peninsula, where the Malayalam and Toolavo are the vernacular dialects of the country. In all these districts the labourer, who holds the plough, and performs the inferior offices of husbandry, is of the lowest, poorest, most ignorant, yet most numerons order in society; in general an outcast, or, at least, often of the degraded

* Par. Papers on Slavery, p. 552.

class of Hindoos, and therefore usually resident in the outskirts of his village; every where without any property in the land which he can transfer by gift, sale, or bequest; and receiving from his employer, the ryot, little more than food, with a scanty supply of raiment! It is almost superfluous to remark that, with this description of persons, the government officers have seldom had any direct communications; yet this may possibly be the cause that their situation has not yet received that consideration which it appears to merit; for it is not, perhaps, sufficiently known, that throughout the Tamil country, as well as in Malabar and Canara, *far the greater part of the labouring classes of the people have, from time immemorial, been in a state of acknowledged bondage, in which they continue to the present time.* It is, certainly, a curious circumstance, that in those provinces where the severe and arbitrary system of the Mussulman government was established at the most early and for the longest period, where consequently the public assessment on the land is the most high, and private property in the soil the most rare and least valuable, the labourer should also be the most free; while his condition is the most abject in those countries where the ancient institutions of the Hindoos have been least disturbed, where the public demand on the soil is the most light, and private property in the land is universal and of the highest value. It seems probable, however, that in former times slavery may have been as prevalent in the northern as it now is in the southern and western provinces; and the same circumstances that reduced the landlord of Telingana to the situation of a landholder may have tended gradually to weaken the power he possessed over his slaves, until they finally became altogether emancipated from his authority."*

As has been stated, no correct idea can be formed from the Papers of the actual number of slaves in British India. The slaves in Batavia in 1812, exclusive of those belonging to Government (which did not exceed 281), were as follows:—

"At Batavia and its environs, &c. . . .	18,972
In the Samarang division	4,488
In the Sourabaya division	3,682
	27,142"†

* Par. Papers on Slavery in India, pp. 816, 817. † p. 157.

The following are the only ***official number of slaves*** observed (with the exception of those in Amboyna, amounting to 1,613, now ceded to the Dutch) in a careful investigation of the Papers :—

"Penang	3,000
Arcot, S. Division	17,000
——, N. Division	688
Trichinopoly	10,000
Canara	82,000
Malabar	100,000
	212,688"*

These few items, producing more than 200,000 slaves, would lead us to suppose that their number in British India may be equal and even greater than that of the West Indies.—And should not this fact be known, and efforts made to meliorate the state of these degraded people and to elevate them to their proper place in society? When shall every subject of Britain be free as the air he breathes? How tardy, though encouraged by success, are our proceedings in this work of justice and mercy. But this will more clearly appear in the next chapter.

CHAP. IV.

Methods proposed for the melioration and abolition of Slavery in India—answers to objections to its abolition arising from the supposed kind treatment of slaves—the preservation of children and adults in famine by selling themselves for support—the indifference of the slaves to emancipation—decreasing the population of an Island or District—Mahomedan prejudices prohibiting any others than slaves attending on their women, and that they cannot dispense with slaves,—and the interest of the slave owners and the Government—concluding remarks.

The Madras Board of Revenue, in 1819, thus close their interesting letter, from which copious extracts have been given :—

* Par Papers on Slavery in India, pp. 436, 887—890.

"The Board are decidedly of opinion that slaves should not be sold for arrears of revenue; and prohibitory orders to this effect will be issued to Malabar, where alone it has occurred. In Malabar and Canara, alone, the number of slaves is calculated at 180,000; and the Board have now under consideration certain propositions from Mr. Græme, the Commissioner in Malabar, for the amelioration of their condition, and the gradual emancipation of slaves in that country. In the Tamil provinces the number of slaves is comparatively few; their condition is better, and any immediate emancipation of them would be attended by inconvenience, difficulty, and perhaps distress. This might therefore be at present deferred, until the practical remedy for the gradual abolition of slavery on the other coast shall have been fully considered and decided on. But, whatever may be the future decision respecting those who are already slaves, the Board think that a regulation ought to be published, to prevent the further extension of slavery, and to ameliorate in some degree, by a few general enactments, the condition of those who are already slaves. The further purchase of free persons as slaves should be declared invalid and illegal; *and all children hereafter born slaves should be declared free.* But any person should be still at liberty to contract for a given sum to labour for a term of years, or for life. Such contracts, however, should be in writing, and only binding upon the individual who executes it, not upon his wife or children.

"Slaves should be declared competent *to possess and dispose of their own property*, to the exclusion of any interference therewith on the part of their master. The Board further submit, whether it would not be proper to annex some penalty to the purchase of female children, for the purpose of being brought up as prostitutes, in the manner alluded to in Mr. Hyde's letter. It might also be provided that proprietors are to provide wholesome food and clothing for their slaves; that in sickness, in age, or infirmity, they shall not neglect them; that they shall not have the power of corporal punishment; that slaves, on being ill-treated by their masters, shall be allowed to claim the privilege of being sold to another; and that in breach of these laws, or refusal to comply with them, on the part of the master, the slave shall receive his liberty. It might further be provided *slaves shall have the power to purchase their liberty at the price for which it was forfeited*, and that slaves attached to lands or estates which may escheat to Government shall be liberated. Many of these provisions will be found to contravene those of the Hindoo law, which, with respect to Hindoos, is declared by the regulations to be in force; and the necessity, therefore, of a formal enactment of them in the code will be sufficiently apparent.

"The Collector in Trichinopoly has submitted a proposition for ameliorating the condition of the pullers in the District, by adding *two per cent.* to their warum, which is at present only *ten per cent.* By this, he observes, 'the situation of the pullers would be greatly benefited, and the expense to Government would be (taking the revenue of the wet districts in round numbers) not more than 2000 pagodas per annum. This sum would materially tend to the comfort of 10,000 people, by whose industry and manual labour the country is cultivated, and who, in point of fact, are the creators of revenue.' The Board are not aware of any objection to this measure, and it is accordingly resolved to recommend the adoption of it to Government. The Collector will hereafter report the result of it, and the effects which it may have on the condition of the people. Resolved, also, That the Collector in the other Tamil

Districts be desired to report whether a similar measure could not be adopted with advantage in their Districts; and, if so, the extent of remission proposed. In conclusion, the Board would remark that the subject discussed in these proceedings appears to them of great importance; that the suggestions which they have submitted should, therefore, be well weighed before they are adopted; and that any legislative enactment, that may be deemed requisite, be framed with great caution. It may also be for the consideration of Government whether the subject may not, as a general one, be referred in the first instance to the Supreme Government, in order to ascertain the state of slavery in the Bengal territories, and whether any restrictions are imposed on it there." *

The propriety of improving the condition of slaves in the East is stated and urged by different functionaries of the British Government. Mr. Græme in his Report on Malabar, in 1822, has the following judicious remarks :—

"Upon the occasion of the condition of the slaves of Malabar being brought into notice, it was lately suggested that slavery should be subjected to the rule of the Mahomedan law. This, if carried completely into effect, would indeed mitigate the severity of slavery, and render slaves in Malabar a very different race of mortals; but, strictly speaking, *slavery is not permitted by the Mahomedan law to be practised by any but Mussulmans, and even by them only as regards the inhabitants of countries not agreeing to become converts to Mahomedanism, and at the same time refusing to pay the tax imposed by Mahomed upon infidels, or to permit the free exercise of the Mahomedan religion.* Slaves made so by stealth, and not in open war, or an authorized occasion, are not recognized by the Koran; and the acquisition of slaves by purchase, as practised by the Moplar Mahomedans in Malabar, is equally irreconcilable to the Mahomedan law. Though it may be impossible to apply the minutiæ of the Mahomedan law to the peculiar kind of slavery existing in Malabar, it is nevertheless easy to borrow from the benevolent spirit of the law, or of the actual practice among Mahomedans. Ill treatment of slaves is with them punishable by the slave being emancipated, to the loss of the master, or being sold to another master, on convictions before the quazee.

"Though it may be allowed that slavery in Malabar is not intolerable, and not exercised to an excessive degree of active cruelty, the diminutive and squalid appearance, and the wretched hovels of a race of beings in the province, who by a census taken of the population in Fusly 1216 (A. D. 1809) were reckoned to amount to 94,786, sufficiently indicate that they do not enjoy that comfortable state of existence which every person should at least have it in his power to acquire by his labour. There are no doubt many freemen in the different ranks of society who are equally indigent with the slave. The slave is scarcely ever exposed to the extremity of actual starvation; and it has been stated by respectable public authority, and I understand with correctness, that a beggar of this caste is seldom or never to be found. But among the freemen there are too many, who are too proud from their former rank, too idle and too dishonest from habit, to work, and they have recourse to charity and fraudulent means to gain their subsistence; but it matters not that many worthless characters are in worse circumstances,—the question is, *whether slaves are as*

* Par. Papers on Slavery in India, p. 900.

*comfortable as they ought to be, and whether they acquire as much by their own industry in servitude as they would in a free state."**

It may be interesting to trace *the various steps proposed or adopted for the melioration of slavery in India.* The Bengal consultations as early as July 1774, in a letter to the Council of Dacca, contain the following judicious and humane observation:—" In those districts where slavery is in general usage, or any way connected with, or is likely to have any influence on the cultivation or revenue, which we are informed is the case at Sylhet, and may be so in the other (especially the frontier) parts of your division, we must desire you particularly to advise us what is the usage and every circumstance connected with it, and we shall then give such directions as we may judge to be necessary; but considering your reference, in the mean time, in the light of a general proposition, *we are of opinion that the right of masters to the children of the slaves, already their property, cannot legally be taken from them in the* FIRST GENERATION, *but we think that this right cannot and ought not to extend further, and direct that you do make publication accordingly."*†

This excellent suggestion does not appear to have been fully acted upon, as slaves are spoken of in Dacca many years after this period. The Bengal Judicial Consultations of Feb., 1817, contain a Report of the second judge of the Bareilly Court of Circuit, W. Leycester, Esq., who proposed the same rational and effective method of gradually annihilating slavery. " Many estates in the country are cultivated by indigenous slaves, but it is very desirable it should no longer be possible to transfer the African slave trade from the West to the East Indies, with only one proviso against it, that the slaves may not be resold ; and it is also most desirable that the present importation of females, for the purpose of breeding an hereditary race of slaves, should be put a stop to.—*Nothing, perhaps, is so revolting as the idea of hereditary slavery*—of a man's inheriting at his birth nothing but the misfortunes of his parents, without hopes of emancipation, without the possibility of rising in life through exertion or talent, and liable every moment to be taken to the market and sold, and transferred to the possession of another. I can hardly conceive, indeed, that there could be any objection to modifying the present sys-

* Par. Papers on Slavery in India, p. 922. † p. 4.

tem of slavery by an Act declaring *the children of slaves to be free; that, if men will have slaves, they should also have to pay for them, and not to rear and inherit them like the produce of a farm-yard!*"*

The reply of the Court of Nizamut Adawlut to this humane judge was—"The Court will only add, at present, that they fully participate in the sentiments expressed by Mr. Leycester, in abhorrence of hereditary slavery, and earnestly wish it could be discontinued, with regard to all children born under the British protection; but whilst it is allowed to remain, with respect to the progeny of existing slaves, born under the British Government in the West Indies and South Africa, the abolition of it, on general principles of justice and humanity, could not, the court apprehend, be consistently proposed for India, where it has from time immemorial been sanctioned by the laws and usages of the country, and where, it may be added, the state of slavery is not so injurious to the objects of it as in other countries where it is still maintained."†

The measures proposed by the Governor of Java, in June, 1812, for the melioration of slavery in that island, were cordially approved by the Governor General, Lord Minto, and his Council. For an account of these measures see Par. Papers, pp. 155—161.

The Governor of Prince of Wales Island, in May, 1820, entered a minute of some importance respecting slave debtors, and recommending the adoption of some regulations of a very beneficial tendency.—"I need not acquaint the Board," says the Governor, "that a custom obtains at this settlement which has always prevailed in every Asiatic country, and indeed sometimes extensively in Europe, of persons mortgaging their labour and services in consideration of a sum advanced, for which they become debtors to persons advancing the sum; but some recent instances which have come to my knowledge, of abuse on the part of the masters of such debtor servants, render me desirous of proposing certain regulations for the purpose of protecting and ameliorating the condition of this class of people, and of preventing a usage which we have sanctioned from becoming *a means of perpetuating and extending all the evils and horrors of slavery, only under a different appellation.*" Under these circumstances it was proposed and adopted that certain

* Par. Papers on Slavery in India, p. 345. † p. 646.

regulations be furnished to the Magistrate for his guidance in respect to debtor servants and their masters or mistresses. (See these judicious regulations, Par. Papers, p. 453).

The Board of Revenue under the Madras Presidency, in 1818, express their conviction of the necessity and propriety of improving the civil condition of the slave. "The right which the slaves in the Tamil country possess to continue attached to the soil where they are born, which, though not universal, is pretty general among them; their dependence rather on a community than on an individual; and perhaps the vicinity of some of them to the Presidency, where a general knowledge prevails that the spirit of our government is inimical to bondage, seem all, more or less, to have contributed to render their condition in some degree at least superior to that of their brethren on the other coast. It is by no means, however, to be understood that this is universally the case. Their treatment necessarily depends principally on the individual character of their owners; and *when we reflect on those evils that are inseparable from even the mildest state of Slavery, and consider how large a portion of our most industrious subjects are at present totally deprived of a free market for their labour, restricted by inheritance to a mere subsistence, and sold and transferred with the land which they till,—policy no less than humanity would appear to dictate the propriety of gradually relieving them from those restrictions, which have reduced them, and must otherwise continue to confine them, to a condition scarcely superior to that of the cattle which they follow at the plough.*

"While such, in the opinion of the Board, ought to be the policy to be pursued with regard to this class of people, it would be obviously unjust to interfere with *the private property*, which there can be no doubt that the Ryots at present possess in their slaves; and it might be dangerous too suddenly to disturb the long established relations in society subsisting between these two orders. For the present, therefore, it would seem sufficient, with the view to prevent oppression or abuse of authority, *to define, by legislative enactments, the power which may be lawfully exercised by a Ryot over his slaves;* but, as the revenue records do not afford information sufficiently minute and satisfactory for this purpose, it is resolved to call the particular attention of the collectors in Canara, Malabar, and the Tamil country to this subject, and to desire that they will take an early opportunity to communicate fully their sentiments thereon' for the consideration of the Board."*

The Collector of the southern division of Arcot very judiciously remarks, upon these paragraphs, "I take the liberty of suggesting that every labourer, who is now free, shall be declared *exempt from all possibility of slavery hereafter*; denouncing penalties against every person who may attempt to enslave any subject under our government. Rules calculated to abolish the general abuse of slavery, to provide for slaves in sickness and old age, to confine the transfer of slaves to the village of their nativity, and to interdict all corporeal punishment or imprisonment, would prove an alleviation of the miseries inseparable from bondage. As the continuation, or, I may call it, the revival of slavery, is dependent upon the assistance owners contribute to the propagation of slaves, by advancing money for the expenses of marriages, perhaps a rule might be enacted, *prohibiting the enslaving of unborn children*, by such a convention between the owners and their existing slaves."†

These extracts show some of the methods, for the gradual melioration or abolition of slavery, contemplated by those whose opinions are given in the Parliamentary Documents. The Philanthropist, who sighs, oh that all mankind were free! will rejoice to see a few proposals of more *immediate measures for the emancipation of slaves*. Upon "the practice of stealing children from their parents, and selling them for slaves," it is very justly remarked in a Minute of the Governor General, in May 1774,—"There appears no probable way of remedying this calamitous evil, but that of striking at the root of it, and abolishing *the right of slavery altogether*, excepting such cases to which the authority of government cannot reach; such, for example, as *laws in being have allowed, and where slaves have become a just property by purchase, antecedent to the proposed prohibition*. The opinions of the most creditable of the Mussulman and Hindoo inhabitants have been taken upon this subject, and they condemn the authorized usage of selling slaves, as repugnant to the particular precepts both of the Koran and Shastar, oppressive to the people, and injurious to the general welfare of the country."‡

The magistrates of Patna, in 1774, state to the Governor

---

* Par. Papers on Slavery in India, p. 818. See also, pp. 869, 870, 871. † p. 872. ‡ p. 3.

Warren Hastings, Esq.,—"Whole families of slaves were formerly sold together, but we do not find that the custom, though of old standing, and still in force, is now attended to, except in the Mofussil, where sometimes the survivor of an old family, retired on his altermga, cultivates his lands by the hands of these slaves, who also perform the menial offices of the house. To a person thus situated, the keeping of slaves may answer; the grain produced by their labour serving for their support. It seems that, on the sale of a slave who separately procures his own subsistence, only *one-half of the price is received by the owner, the other half going to the parents of the slave.* In the city, few people choose these Kahaar slaves, being indifferent to their business, and equally expensive with other servants. The female slaves, we are told, are of more use in families, none being without them. It is urged that a condition of this kind is consistent with the manners of a country where women are kept in continual retirement, and such privacy observed in regard to them as would be much affected by a frequent change of servants. On the whole, *we do not imagine that alterations, in the usage of slaves, will be attended with any consequences of moment to the cultivation or revenue of this province.*"*

In 1808 a Committee was appointed, by the Government of Prince of Wales Island, to report upon the state of slavery, and the propriety of its abolition. Three of the four European members express themselves as follows:—"After mature deliberation, the undersigned are of opinion that the views of humanity, and of the British Legislature, signified in the late Acts respecting the abolition of slavery in the British West India Islands, may be extended and adopted here, consistently with due attention to the political circumstances of this settlement. And, with all deference, they beg leave to recommend to the Honourable Board *the immediate and positive emancipation of slaves, in preference to relying on the accomplishment of it by the establishment of an annual tax, which, while the richer masters would be able to meet it, might have the effect only to induce the poorer to insist with rigour and inhumanity on greater exertions of service from their slaves, in order to enable them also to pay it.* Independent of the calls of humanity, and of the distinguished example afforded to the world

* Par. Papers on Slavery in India, p. 5.

by the British Legislature, the undersigned must allow that these considerations have also had much weight in inducing them to recommend *the immediate and positive emancipation of slaves;* though they at the same time are aware of the propriety and necessity of regarding, as far as is consistent with humanity, the *property* of the owner, and the prejudice of the natives of higher rank; but these they are hopeful may be nearly assimilated and combined, by adopting, as the basis of emancipation, a custom and usage which has been immemorially sanctioned and prevalent in the Malay countries, and on this island since the formation of the settlement, viz. that of *mortgaging labour and services in consideration of a sum advanced, for which the person or persons become debtor.* Originally in some degree resembling the feudal system which prevailed formerly in Europe, these services extended to accompanying their creditors or masters in all predatory expeditions, and obeying all their commands of whatever nature, the masters providing for their subsistence and clothing. In general the connexion was formed voluntarily by the debtor, uncompelled by pernicious necessities, with the view thereby of securing the interest and protection of the master, and occasionally by his own imprudence having involved him in debt, which entitled his creditor to his services till it was liquidated. On this island the engagement, of course, extends only to the use of his labour, and is generally made by a deed or bond in the Malay language."*

Governor Farquhar's plan for "annulling slavery in the shortest period in which that desirable object can be effected, without prejudice to individuals, or injury to the public interests in the settlement," is as follows:—

"I recommend slavery's being abolished at Prince of Wales Island. *It is the greatest of all evils, and the attempt to regulate such an evil is in itself almost absurd.* There was some excuse for using slaves in the West Indies, on account of the want of people, and Africa offered the readiest supply. But *there is no excuse for continuing the practice in India,—a country fully peopled, and where cultivation and commerce can be carried on by free men!* But, as slavery has in some degree been sanctioned by the government of Prince of Wales Island, it would be unjust, without an equivalent to the proprietors, to declare slaves free. Suppose then that a committee were appointed, and authorized to affix to each slave now on the island a value at which his master should be obliged to liberate such slave, on tender of the amount. Such as could not procure funds from their relations or friends, equal to the valuation, to be-

* Par. Papers on Slavery in India, pp. 440, 441.

come *debtors*, and serve the creditors, as now practised, under the following simple regulations:—The lender to find the borrower, in lieu of his services, meat, clothes, and lodging, good and sufficient. If in chastising a borrower for any fault (without the authority of the police) the lender bring blood, the debt to be cancelled. If the lender cohabit with any of the female borrowers, the debt to be cancelled. No idleness in the borrowers is to add to the debt: but, if dissatisfied, the lender may demand his money. Should the emancipated slave be unable to procure the money, the master may apply to the police, where the necessary enquiries will be made, and correction given accordingly. *The foregoing regulations would ameliorate the condition of those now slaves, and in time liberate the whole from debt, and give us from 4000 to 5000 good subjects in place of useless sufferers.* This is an object worthy of government's attention in every point of view."*

"My own ideas," says W. E. Phillips, Esq., the successor of Governor Farquhar in 1807, "are, that a Committee should place a value on each slave, as also a value on his annual labour, after deducting his maintenance; and, having done so, that the slave should continue in bondage till the estimated value of his labour has reimbursed the master for his original cost. Should the slave deem himself ill-treated, he may at any time sell the labour due to that master to one more mild, and who may be disposed to advance that sum to the original master. As the value of labour here is very high, and that of the slaves the reverse, I do not think I am sanguine in estimating that *the greater part of these poor creatures would be free in* TWO YEARS *from the date of their valuation.*"†

In these sentiments the Honourable Court of Directors, in February 1807, concurred. "As the toleration of slavery cannot be necessary at Prince of Wales Island, where the population is at present extensive and is daily increasing, we consider it a subject deserving of your serious notice, and direct that every means be resorted to for effecting its immediate abolition, provided the public interests of the settlement are not materially injured; but, even in that case, *we conceive an early period may be determined upon for the entire emancipation of slavery at your Presidency, from the date of which it ought by no means to be tolerated.*"‡ It is deeply to be regretted that these humane and judicious measures were not adopted. If they had been so, slavery might now have been unknown in this island.

It may be presumed that *various objections to the*

---

* Par. Papers on Slavery in India, pp. 434, 435. † p. 436. ‡ p. 435.

extensive melioration, and particularly the abolition of slavery, exist among the advocates of the slave system in India. It will now be our object, from the documents already adverted to, to notice the principal of these objections, and to reply to them—not with our own arguments or language, but that of gentlemen in India intimately acquainted with the subject upon which they have written. The official nature of these replies must add considerably to their importance and value.

One of the most common objections to the discontinuance of the present system of slavery, in many parts of British India, is—the *supposed kind treatment of the slaves.* The comparatively mild nature of Indian slavery (being frequently domestic) is often used as a reason for its continuance, and its abolition denounced as an evil. To this argument for slavery the following extract affords a very appropriate reply.—" The Madras Board of Revenue proceed to the consideration of that part of the letter from Government under reply, which desires them to state their opinion ' whether the practice which actually prevails,' with respect to the sale of slaves, ' should be permitted to continue as at present, or whether it ought either to be laid under such restrictions as would render it less objectionable, or to be altogether abolished, as productive of evils for which no adequate remedy can be devised.' Where ' in some respects churmas may be considered in more comfortable circumstances than any of the lower and poorer classes of natives.' Where ' no want or cruelty is experienced by the slaves.' Where the ' abolition of the puller system would be attended with the most serious and ruinous consequences.' Where they seem not to consider their situation, nor to show any ' desire to be free and independent.' Where the treatment of slaves by their masters ' is the same as that of the other labourers, which is in general of a mild nature.' Where ' the slaves are, on the whole, better treated by their masters than the common class of free labourers.' Where, finally, humanity on the part of the masters is encouraged by a sense of their own interest, and a disposition to personal cruelty and ill-treatment is checked and restrained by the establishment of the courts of justice, it does not appear to the Board that any immediate interference on the part of the government is particularly called for, or that any alteration in the existing state of slavery should be made, except by degrees, and after mature and attentive consideration has been given to the subject.

"But, because no immediate measures are urgently called for, it does not follow that the most useful, the most laborious, and one of the most numerous classes of our subjects in these territories, should, from generation to generation, continue the hereditary bondsmen of their masters, incapable of inheriting property of their own, deprived of that stimulus to industry which possession of property ever inspires; and, because they are fed and clothed, and reconciled to the present condition, it does not follow that the Government should confirm institutions which doom those who have thus fallen into this condition incapable of ever again recovering their liberty, or of rising to a level with their fellow men! Independently of those principles, hostile to any restraint on liberty, which are innate in every British Government, and which, as contained in our judicial code, without any express enactment on the subject, have operated to check abuses of masters towards their slaves; and independently also of those feelings, among free men, which naturally prompt them to extend to every one under their Government the blessings which freedom confers, it appears to the Board, on the mere calculating principle of self interest and policy, to be desirable that no one should be deprived of the means of acquiring property, or of diffusing those benefits among society which proceed from an increase of capital and wealth."*

A second reason urged for the perpetuation of slavery, and consequently an objection to its abolition, is the *preservation of children and adults in famine, by selling themselves for support.* On this view of the subject, which it must be confessed is one of considerable delicacy and importance, several Indian Magistrates have given their opinion. The Magistrate of Zillah Tipperah, under the Bengal Presidency, in 1816, writes—"Report states that, in the Mogul Government, slavery existed in the district of Sylhet to such a degree that persons would sell themselves as slaves to satisfy demands of rent; while others would, from similar necessity, dispose of their own slaves. Even at the present day it may be ascertained that some individuals, in order to supply the immediate wants of nature,

---

* Par. Papers on Slavery in India, p. 899.

voluntarily submit to a state of slavery, and dispose of their persons for determinate services, so long as they may be capable of performing them. Documents to this effect are executed in the customary manner with other written engagements; and the court may easily obtain them from the magistrate of Sylhet. Since necessity alone would compel any person to submit to a state of slavery, it may therefore, I presume, be inferred, that the slavery herein noticed originates in the extreme poverty of the lower orders of society, and that to tolerate it, under certain restrictions, would be preferable to exposing the poorer classes of the community to the risk of perishing for want, by depriving them of the only ostensible resource left to enable them to support existence."*

Relative to this state of things, it is judiciously observed, by W. Leycester, Esq., the second Judge of Bareilly—"I know it is argued that slaves in India are treated kindly; that they are comfortable; that in times of scarcity many must starve and die, if people who have the means of feeding them are not allowed to purchase them as slaves. Many, I believe, are treated kindly and comfortably in their places; but that they all are so, that there is not a great deal of ill treatment, nobody will, I believe, assert; and there is not a crime committed among mankind that has not, at one time or other, produced an incidental good, and it would be strange indeed if slavery were the only exception. But, at all events, it might be considered an adequate inducement to deeds of charity to compensate them by the labours of the object of it *during one generation, instead of aggravating the sorrows of accidental necessity by slavery through all generations.*"†

The Second Judge of Moorshedabad in 1814, and the Magistrate of Tanjore in 1825, recommend that in seasons of great distress from famine it should be allowed to sell children for a limited period. The latter gentleman says—"In seasons of great scarcity and distress it would perhaps be driving parents to greater extremities, more abhorrent to human nature, were any penalty attached to the sale of children by their own parents, or to the purchase of them direct from their parents; but the traffic should, in my opinion, be most strictly prohibited from extending any fur-

* Par. Papers on Slavery in India, p. 246. † p. 345. See pp. 300. 325, 484.

ther, and a *person purchasing a child from its parents should on no account have the power of disposing of it to another*."*

A third objection to the suppression of slavery in India is *the indifference of the slaves to their emancipation*. The Collector of the Southern Division of Canara, in describing the condition of the Daerds, advocates this sentiment :—" Several landlords of Canara having suffered considerable loss, from their Daerds and slaves having enlisted without their consent, it is in their behalf I bring this subject to the notice of the Board. Slavery has been defined to be, ' an obligation to labour for the benefit of the master, without the contract or consent of the servant, the master at the same time having the right to dispose of him by sale, or in any other way to make him the property of a third person.' The sect of the Daerds who are bought and sold, and who come nearest to the description of slaves, differ from them in the following respects : first, their service is *conditional;* a master, at the time of purchase, agrees to give them the usual allowance of rice, cloth, &c. ; if he fails, and refuses to do this, the Daerds are no longer bound to serve him, and can recover the balances of allowance due to them and their children. If the purchaser agrees to give the established allowances, the Daerds cannot refuse to enter his service ; but if, from any real cause, they have a dread of their man, the old master will generally, on being asked, keep them until he can get another purchaser. A master cannot make a traffic of them ; that is, he cannot put them up to public sale, or transport them, either by sea or land, to any place where there are not people of their own caste, which is confined to Canara ; they can never be sent out of the province ; they can even refuse to be sold out of the manganny in which they are born and bred. Such is their known strong and rooted attachment to the place of their nativity, that no person ever thinks of purchasing and taking one away to a distant place, even in the country ; it seldom indeed happens that they are ever bought or sold at more than twenty or thirty miles distance from the place of their birth. This sect of Daerds, therefore, and their children, may, I conceive, be truly called ' *conditional servants for ever*.' Those of the Maurey Daerds, who are attached to estates, have the same privi-

* Par. Papers on Slavery, p. 930. See also p. 325.

lege as those just mentioned, except that, in case of their landlord omitting to give them their regular allowance of rice, &c., they cannot quit his lands; but, on making a complaint, they can recover their right, with damages. All other descriptions of Daerds are 'conditional servants on the male side for life;' and in no case have they, so long as their master feeds and clothes them according to usage, a right to leave his service. Slavery is objected to, as being contrary to the fundamental principles of morality, because both men and women in that state, it is said, are tempted to commit and excite others to crimes they would not do in a free state. Supposing even that the service of the Daerds could be construed slavery, which in my opinion it cannot, the same objection does not apply to it, because, with them, it is merely the custom of their caste; and they are in general more constant and attached to their wives and families, who live with them, than most other sects. So far, therefore, from conceiving there can be any radical objection made to this kind of service, I am of opinion it is productive of very important political as well as moral good, and especially so, because it is one of the soundest and most necessary props to the support and even existence of that meritorious spirit of industry and agriculture of which the natives of Canara are so peculiarly possessed."*

Such sentiments appear very incongruous from a European, and would find few advocates in Britain. That the Daerds are slaves, that is, the property of others, cannot be denied. In this communication it is stated—"By the Daerds and slaves of other sorts nearly the whole cultivation of the country is carried on. *An estate indeed without a property in some of these people would be of little value*, because day labourers are not to be procured in this as in other countries." "Concluding, therefore," says the Secretary to the Board of Revenue, "that their right to the service of these people is good and legal, what would be the consequence of depriving them of it? Have we the right to do so? or would it be politic if we had? Daerds being naturally petulent and somewhat indolent,† frequently quarrel with their masters on most trifling occurrences, and leave them for a few days; in this state, and in the height of resentment, several of them have enlisted and their

* Par. Papers on Slavery in India, pp. 550, 551.

† When were slaves industrious?

owners been unable to recover them.—" If the recruiting of the Daerds or slaves, *the property of the landlords*, is allowed to be continued, it will be the cause of every possible mischief towards checking the prosperity of the country; it will afford those descriptions of people an asylum to fly to, whenever caprice or any trifling cause may tempt them to leave their master, who, as in that case they will never be able to command, to a certainty, hands to cultivate their estates, will foresee a train of new calamities coming upon them, which they were not even labouring under in the late government, and which all the advantages they have, or can gain by the present, will not recompense. The very fabric of their agricultural system will be undermined; if if this be the case, their attachment cannot longer be depended on, any more than can the troops raised by the property thus wrested from them."*

The interest of the slave proprietors, and not that of the slaves, is the great question in these remarks. But who can doubt whether slavery be better than freedom? The records of slavery, whether Eastern or Western, afford abundant proof of the dissatisfaction, the poverty, the misery attendant upon slavery, and, consequently, the desire of the slave to be free. The following extract from the Parliamentary Documents may suffice:—" It is a question," says M. Elphinstone, Esq., Resident of Poona, Mar. 1817, "how we are to treat slaves, subjects of his Highness the Paishwa, who fly from their masters, also subjects of his Highness, and take refuge in our camps. It is so obvious, that *we cannot open an asylum for fugitive slaves* within the Paishwa's territories, that I have hitherto directed persons in these circumstances to be refused leave to reside in our camps; but I shall be happy to be informed what is the proper course in such cases, and generally what is the law relative to the traffic in slaves, as far as is applicable to our forces in the territories of allied princes."†—That slaves generally are indifferent to freedom—to the acquisition of property—to elevation in society—will rarely be received by those at all acquainted with that system, which, to use the words of Earl Minto, " must be viewed as a violation of one of the first principles on which society is constituted."‡

Another objection to the abolition of slavery occurs in the papers relative to Prince of Wales Island, viz. *decreas-*

* Par. Papers on Slavery, p. 551, 552. † p. 332. ‡ p. 172.

*ing the population.** There might be some appearance of propriety in this remark as it respected the resort to the Island of Malays, Mahomedans, Chinese, and other nations who are favourable to slavery; but few of its advocates can be insensible that this system is inimical to the increase of population, and that its gains are consequently "the price of blood:"—"The great advantage to population (says the Judge of Bundlecund in 1808), derived from the emancipation of slaves, cannot be better illustrated than by quoting an example adduced by Mr. Coxe, in his tour through the northern countries of Europe. Speaking of the slavery of the Polish peasantry, he has the following remarkable and decisive instance of the benefit accruing from their manumission. A few nobles, however, of benevolent hearts, 'and enlightened understandings, ventured upon the expedient of giving liberty to their vassals. The event has shown this project to be no less judicious than humane; no less friendly to their own interests than to the happiness of their peasants. For it appears that, in the districts in which the new arrangement has been introduced, the population of the villages has been considerably increased, and the revenues of their estates augmented in a triple proportion.' The first nobleman who granted freedom to his peasants was Zamoiske, formerly great Chancellor, who, in 1760, enfranchised six villages in the palatinate of Moravia. These villages were in 1777 visited by the author of the Patriotic Letters, from whom I had the following information: on inspecting the parish registers of births from 1750 to 1760, that is, during the last ten years of slavery immediately preceding their enfranchisement, he found the number of births 434; in the first ten years of their freedom, from 1760 to 1770, 620; and from 1770 to the beginning of 1777, 585 births. By these extracts it appears that, during the first period, there were only 434 births; second period, 620; third period, 770 births. If we suppose an improvement of this sort to take place throughout the kingdom, how great would be the increase of national population!"† The argument against slavery arising from its depopulating tendency is used with great effect against the peculiarly destructive system of slavery existing in some of the West India Islands.

An objection to the abolition of slavery peculiar to the

* Par. Papers on Slavery in India, p. 440. † p. 301.

Mahomedans is made on the ground that the injunctions of their prophet prohibit *any other than slaves attending on their women, and that therefore they cannot dispense with slaves*. The nature of this objection, and the reply to it, are stated in the communication of the European members of the Committee formed at Prince of Wales Island, in 1808, to consider the propriety of the suppression of slavery in the Island:—" In support of this opinion (say the Committee), they adduce a passage in their Koran, which, on reference to Sale's translation of it (vol. ii p. 192), the Committee find translated thus:—'And speak unto the believing women, that they restrain their eyes and preserve their modesty, and discover not their ornaments, except what necessarily appeareth thereof; and let them throw their veils over their bosoms, and not show their ornaments unless to their husbands, or their fathers, or their husbands' fathers, or their sons, or their husbands' sons, or their brothers, or their brothers' sons, or their sisters' sons, or their women, or the captives which their right hand may possess, or unto such men as attend them and have no need of women, or unto children who distinguish not the nakedness of women; and let them not make a noise with their feet, that their ornaments which they hide may thereby be discovered.' The undersigned deem it unnecessary to state to the Honourable Board the import, in their opinion, of this passage, or to elucidate it by remarking how much the habits and manners of the Mahometan society, particularly of the poorer classes, are in opposition to the doctrine deduced from it. They beg leave to call the attention of the Honourable Board to the following passage only of the Koran (Sale's translation, vol. ii. p. 194): 'And unto such of your slaves as desire a written instrument, allowing them to redeem themselves on paying a certain sum, write one, if you know good in them, and give them of the riches of God, which he hath given you.' Which certainly not only directly enjoins the emancipation of slaves, but exactly in the manner suggested by the undersigned members. The undersigned, however, are far from wishing to recommend or advise the adoption of any measure which might be generally disagreeable or offensive to the Mussulman community here, whether their objections to it originate in ignorant prejudice, or proceed from a regard to interest and convenience; but they have good reason to believe that the opposition, even among the followers of the Mahometan

religion, to the emancipation of slaves, is very partial, and confined almost entirely to a few of the first rank."*

The Mahomedans further state on the general principle of this objection to the emancipation of slaves (to use the language of the European member of the Committee who, with the native members of it, dissented from his brethren): "By the law of their prophet, a Mussulman may have four wives, if he can afford to maintain so many, and he is not restricted to *any number of concubines*. His wives are generally chosen from among the daughters of free men of an equal rank with himself, but his concubines can only be taken from among his slaves. Now, say they, if all slaves are emancipated, or made simple debtors, our concubines will of course have it in their power to leave us, on paying the sum fixed upon as their value, which in most instances they will themselves be able to do, from the fruits of their master's generosity; and, in this infant and confined settlement, Mussulmans will find it difficult to meet with suitable wives. It is considered by all Mussulmans, but particularly among the higher class of Malays, a very great disgrace for a woman, with whom he has once lived, to go with strange men, or leave his house without his consent and permission, which their emancipation will enable them to do, even while they are with child by their master."† The precept of the Koran enjoins giving slaves "a written instrument, allowing them to redeem themselves on paying a certain sum." Why oppose the abolition of slavery with such a precept before them? Is it not evidently from other motives than those of respect to their religion?

But the greatest objection to the abolition of slavery, both in the East and the West, is that which arises from *the interest of the slave owners, and of the government*. On this view of the subject it is stated by W. B. Bayley, Esq., Secretary to the Bengal Government in Sep. 1817,—"With reference to the extent to which domestic slavery exists in India, under the established laws and usages of the Hindoos and Mahomedans, and to the known habits and feelings of the people relative to that point, the Vice President in council is of opinion that the greatest care should be observed to guard against the prevalence of an impression, amongst the natives, that any general or direct interference, in the existing relation of master and slave, is con-

* Par. Papers on Slavery in India, p. 443. † p. 444.

templated by government. Any impression of that nature might be expected to excite feelings of alarm and dissatisfaction; and on this ground it appears to be of importance that the government of Bombay should avoid, as far as may be practicable, the official revival and discussion of this question, after the deliberate consideration which it has undergone, in communication with the legal authorities at this Presidency."*

The Collector of Trichinopoly, in 1818, gives his views upon the difficulty of the question of the abolition of slavery, in the following terms :—

"I shall now submit my opinion, as to the policy, or otherwise, of abolishing this establishment. There is something so revolting and abhorrent to an Englishman, in the idea of slavery, that the advocates for its continuance *in any shape* must ever labour under the disadvantage of pre-judgment. Notwithstanding this, I shall endeavour to show that, so far as relates to *the revenue of this district* (and I trust my opinion will not be supposed to extend further), the abolition of the puller system would be attended with the most serious and ruinous consequences. It has been the custom to describe the pullers as the lowest order of society, involved in wretchedness and misery, and reduced to a condition 'scarcely superior to that of the cattle which they follow at the plough.' *In Malabar, it would also appear that the human form has even changed its wonted appearance, and that the slaves are distinguishable by their diminutiveness.* This theme holds out a fine subject for declamation; but, so far as it relates to this class of people in Trichinopoly, it is highly erroneous, inasmuch as there is no class of people generally so athletic or tall in stature as the pullers. It may *possibly* be urged that there is something degrading in a government being concerned in selling human beings, 'like to so many cattle.' It would, perhaps, be better if it could be avoided; but so long as the land continues possessed by Bramin meerassidars, who, by the immutable laws of caste, are prevented personally exercising the offices of agriculture, I see no posssible means of collecting the revenue, nor of cultivating the land, without the establishment of pullers (slaves). Divesting this discussion of national feeling, the most obvious inconvenience and evil which attend it are—that a man, for the sake of food and the other necessaries of life, is condemned to perpetual labour. I exclude all unreasonable rigour on the part of the master, because I have already shown that the ruling principle of human conduct, self interest, is conducive, in the present instance, to soften severity. But whether this obligation to perpetual labour, on the part of the puller, is not fully requited by a perpetual certainty of maintenance (for which those who work for hire are often at a loss) may, I think, be fairly doubted. It is, however, possible, that the advocates of freedom may think with Cicero, and the third judge in Malabar, 'Mihi liber esse non videtur, qui non aliquando nihil agit.'

---

* Par. Papers on Slavery in India, p. 335.

"For the sake of argument, however, I will suppose that, by proclamation of government, the establishment is directed to be abolished. In this case, I apprehend, the direct consequences would be, either an immediate desertion of the pullers in a body, or that they would remain in *statu quo*. The first would be the natural conduct of any class of society having experienced ill usage from their former masters; and the latter course would be adopted by the pullers, if they had no reason to complain. If the pullers absconded, it is clear that no revenue could be collected; for who is to supply their place? And, in this case, would government have any claim on the meerassidars? The latter would naturally say, you have taken away our means of paying; you have reduced us to poverty; you have abolished an establishment which has existed for ages, and have thought proper, at our expense, to emancipate our slaves, which prescription and our laws made as much our property as the houses we live in. By the laws of our caste, we are prevented tilling our land; and yet you ask us to pay a revenue which alone can be paid from its produce.

"On the other hand, should the proclamation have only the effect of leaving things as they are; if the pullers remained with their masters as heretofore, the only benefit resulting therefrom would be, that government had published a proclamation without any attention being paid to it. It would be at best a useless, if not a dangerous document. Hence to emancipate them entirely would be ruinous in its consequences, both to the revenue and the puller; for emancipation in India would confer no rights beyond what the puller at present enjoys. Though nominally emancipated, he and his children would remain the lowest order of society; he would either continue at the plough, possibly under less favourable circumstances than at present, or seek a livelihood by more daring means. In short, I have no doubt, as justly observed by the Board, that 'it might be dangerous too suddenly to disturb the long established relations in society subsisting between those two orders.'*

To these observations the Report of Mr. Græme on Malabar furnishes, it is presumed, a very satisfactory reply :—

"The most serious objections I have heard, against any active measure in favour of the slaves of Malabar, are the violation of the rights of private property which it would involve, and the necessity to which the proprietors would be subjected of paying more for labour, employed in the cultivation of their lands, and the difficulty which slaves would have of subsisting, if left to their own resources.

"It is not requisite to make such an abrupt innovation, upon established rites and customs, as to declare the slaves to be free forthwith; but a prospect should be opened of eventual but gradual emacipation, and proprietors should be indemnified by the payment of a *maximum price*, which should previously be ascertained for each district, and promulgated. To set the example, government might be disposed to sanction the occasional appropriation of small sums annually to the purchase of slaves, and to accept slaves in payment of arrears of revenue, which, from being too heavy, it might at all events be advisable to remit; but, in all these cases, the wishes of the individuals themselves should be con-

---

* Par. Papers on Slavery in India, pp. 893, 894.

sulted, and they should not be emancipated, unless they feel confident of being able to earn their own livelihood without assistance. Slaves should also have the power of redeeming themselves from servitude, whenever the exertions of their own industry may place them in a state of indemnifying their masters for the loss of their rights of property over them. The magistrate should have the power of fining or emancipating for ill treatment. It need not be apprehended that these provisions would bring about an emancipation too rapidly; but the knowledge of their future operation would in the mean time *act as a stimulus to the activity of the slaves, and it would insure better treatment on the part of the proprietors.* Slaves, thus cautiously emancipated, would not be likely to leave their usual places of residence as long as they afforded the necessary means of subsistence: and that in most cases they would, there can be little doubt; for there could be nothing to diminish the demand of their old masters for their services. They would therefore still be living on the old estates, but more comfortably and respectably, and probably less addicted to the petty pilfering of which their masters now accuse them. A great improvement might be expected to take place in the state of cultivation in the province; for not only would the old slaves work more cheerfully, and with more effect, but many proprietors in the southern division, who from indolence leave every thing to their slaves, would be inclined to betake themselves to manual labour, when they found that they were obliged to pay higher for it in others. Upon the principles of these observations, I have drawn out a Regulation respecting slaves, which I have submitted to government through the Board of Revenue. The cautious nature of the different provisions renders it easy to apply it to Canara as well as Malabar, without inconvenience; for, though in Canara slavery may be considered to exist in a milder form, its gradual supercession would be attended with benefit.

"Upon an assurance from themselves that they would earn a more liberal subsistence in a free state, I purchased and emancipated at Calicut, under deeds registered in the Zillah courts, a woman of about fifty-two years of age, her son of thirty-one, her daughter twenty-five, with an infant in her arms, and the husband of her daughter of thirty-five. They are of the Kalladee caste. They feel, I believe, some degree of awkwardness at not having some tambran, some patron to look up to; and their neighbours, who derived no pleasure from the example of emancipation thus commenced, endeavoured, and in part succeeded, in instilling into them the idea that they were purchased, with no other motive than that of being conveyed by sea to some distance on a good opportunity; but their alarm was not so great as to prevent their communicating the report to me on being asked. They were every day engaged out at work, upon terms which secured them a comfortable livelihood, so that I have little doubt that their freedom will promote their comfort and happiness."*

From these various documents it is evident that *slavery, though of a milder and consequently less destructive nature than that of the West Indies, exists to a considerable extent in British India.* This evil appears more prevalent under the Madras Presidency than the other

* Par. Papers on Slavery in India, p. 923.

Presidencies. "There are many estates in the country," says W. Leycester, Esq., cultivated by indigenous slaves, but it is very desirable it should no longer be possible to transfer the African Slave Trade from the West to the East Indies, with only one proviso against it, that the slaves may not be resold."* Under the Madras Presidency the number of slaves must be considerable. The following extract of a letter to the author, from a West Indian gentleman in London, in Aug. 1829, shows, in a clear and forcible manner, the difference between the nature of East and West India slavery :—

"I avail myself of ————'s intended reply to your communication to trouble you with some remarks on East Indian slavery. I have myself, with some considerable attention, gone through the Parliamentary Papers, and have made the same remarks as yourself relating to the meagre and unsatisfactory intelligence respecting Bengal, the sugar district of India. The information relative to Madras, without being very full, is precise on some very important points; such as the division of the produce of the soil between those bondmen who cultivate and those who possess it; that is, between the Marassidars and the Pullers—a feature which makes all the difference in the world between East Indian and West Indian slavery. I should premise that I am myself a West Indian, and somewhat recently from the West Indian colonies; therefore well acquainted with Colonial slavery there. And, being thus able to judge, I confess I see nothing in the details of East Indian servitude that can in any way identify it with that of our West India colonies.

"But, after all, the fact of the existence of Indian slavery will serve the West Indians very little—for the controversy is not about slavery, but the system of slave labour, and its moral and physical evils. Had the crying injustice of uncompensated toil, and the cruelties attending the system of coercion which necessarily grows out of it, not been made a part and parcel of West Indian slavery, I doubt whether the existence of slavery, as an abstract question of right and wrong, would have ever at all deeply interested the people of England; nothing, at least, could have existed, in connexion with it, to awaken the sympathies of the people into activity in behalf of those who were bound by its obligations.† I do not see in India that a case is made out at all analogous to the monstrous evils attending this institution in our Transatlantic possessions. Mr. Rickards, a writer decidedly unfavourable to the system pursued under the existing Government of India, expressly states that the lords of the soil are not vested with the power of tormenting the body; but that the happiness of the people was placed at their mercy, by the right of removing them from their native villages. This seems to be the greatest extent of the grievances established by the information in the Parliamentary Papers.—A great one, indeed, but seldom acted upon.

"In regard to subsistence, and reward for their labour, we have this distinct statement from Mr. Lushington, and other collectors of Madras,

---

* Par. Papers on Slavery in India, p. 344, 345.

† See Wilberforce's Appeal, pp. 53, 54.

that the pullers, besides certain gratuities at marriages, funerals, births, and festivals, have certain yearly emoluments arising out of the cultivated lands. Thus to each puller and pullee is assigned a cultivation of 150 callums of rice. Out of this their annual emolument is each man eight callums and a-half, and to each woman six and a half. As this for every man and woman gives the relative number of 15 to 150, the emoluments of a man and woman amount to a perquisite of 10 per cent. on their joint labour. Besides these they have certain fixed stipends for ploughing and sowing; they reap at 5 per cent. each; they thrash at 5 per cent.; and, the fixed gratuities to be paid at festivals being settled by long prescriptive custom, considerable addition is made to their income. Mr. Lushington estimates the emoluments of each cultivator at 19 per cent. on the proceeds of his labour.

"If a West Indian proprietor were compelled to apportion to each negro slave nearly one-fifth of the produce of his estate as the payment of their labour, and to take with the remaining four-fifths all the expenses and contingencies attending the capital invested, I think we should hear little of the obstinacy of the planter in not acceding to laws tending eventually to abolish the existing relations between the cultivator and proprietor.

"It is difficult to gather from the Parliamentary Papers what is the staple cultivation of the Madras Presidency besides rice. From what I can collect in the Oriental Herald for Sep. 1829, page 546, in some enquiries connected with the landed tenures and agriculture in Madras and Bombay, cultivation is almost wholly dependent on irrigation, and in Southern India rice is the great staple of agriculture. In regard to sugar, it is only necessary to attend minutely to the details respecting its manufacture, in the Eastern and Western World, to see that, cultivated by whomsoever it may, it is entirely divested of the evils attendant on the driving system with us in the West Indian colonies. There are certain papers laid before Parliament, entitled the East India Sugar Papers, which show this circumstance.—The facts will be seen in a pamphlet entitled *East India Sugar*, or an Enquiry, &c. (London: Hatchard. 1824.) It appears that the Asiatic sugar is grown in small fields, tilled by the Ryot, his family, and dependents; that the canes are cut, and the juice expressed, by moveable mills, and then boiled in earthen vessels in the fields in which the canes are grown. In this state it forms an unclarified and ungranulated mass, called *goor*, which is brought to market and sold to the sugar manufacturer. Beyond this process the cultivator has nothing whatever to do with the commodity. In all this there can be no driving system, because there is no extensive cultivation, no extensive capital invested, no working eighteen hours during crop, and no uncompensated labour, to render the profit as great as possible on a large capital, afloat in elaborating the article of commerce."

More particular information is requisite on the subject of slavery in India, relative to the actual number of slaves; 'the relations of master and slave;' the nature of the employment of slaves, their provision, increase or decrease, &c.

Though the Par. Papers contain 418 folio pages respecting slavery in the Bengal Presidency, not a single item appears which may furnish data on which to ascertain the number of slaves in this part of India. This must be considered a serious defect in this otherwise valuable collection of official documents. The same remark applies to the Presidency of Bombay; and as it respects Madras, with a few exceptions supplied by the Collectors, but little information can be procured of the real number of slaves. The absence of laws, to regulate the conduct of the owners of slaves, appears a very great evil in East Indian slavery. What can justify such sentiments as the following, before referred to:—"We desire that you will be extremely cautious in making any regulation for defining the relations of master and slave. It is our wish to improve the condition of the latter to the utmost extent, and we fear that, in defining the power of masters, acts of compulsion might be legalized, which by custom are not now tolerated, and the slaves might be placed in a worse condition than before."* Are uncertain customs better than law? How can the treatment of the slave be known, while there are no written and published laws to which he can appeal. Is not this procedure calculated to keep the degraded slave *in statu quo?* From the Madras papers some idea may be formed of the nature of the employment of slaves, and the provision allowed them; but more full information upon these subjects is desirable. Whether the slave population increases or decreases does not appear. The destructive influence of slavery in some of the West Indian islands is most apalling. "Into Jamaica alone, since the conquest (in 1655), when there were in it about 40,000 slaves, not less than 850,000 Africans have been imported; making a total of 890,000, exclusive of all the births which have taken place during that period. And yet, at the present moment, the slave population of the island does not exceed 345,000! No fewer than 545,000 slaves more than now exist there have been imported into this single island! It is for Jamaica to account for so great a waste of life."† It may be presumed, from the milder nature of Slavery in the East, that it is not so prejudicial to the increase, happiness, and civilization of the human race as the slavery of the West; but it appears that more particular information is necessary to form a correct judgment of its real nature and influence. Every friend of humanity

* Par. Papers on Slavery in India, p. 901.

† East and West India Sugar (Hatchard), p. 34.

must desire that the philanthropic advocate in Parliament of the abolition of Suttees in the East, and of slavery in the West, through whom the successive volumes of Par. Papers respecting the Suttee have been procured, and likewise the massy volume of Papers on East India slavery, may be enabled to procure that further information, respecting slavery in India, that may ultimately lead to its abolition in every part of the eastern dominions of Great Britain.

It is the duty of Britain to meliorate, and eventually to abolish slavery both in the East and the West. It is grateful to every philanthropic mind to see this sentiment increasingly prevail. It is not the author's design to touch the subject of West Indian slavery—nor is it necessary; so many valuable works having been published upon that subject. Slavery in the East may be greatly mitigated by the benign influence of the British Government; and the Madras Board of Revenue, in 1819, suggest "that the further purchase of free persons as slaves should be declared invalid and illegal, and all children hereafter born slaves should be free; that however any person might contract, in writing, for a term of years, or for life, such contract should be binding only upon the individual who executes it; that slaves should be held competent to possess property and to dispose of it without their masters' interference: that the purchase of female children, to be educated as prostitutes, should be prohibited: that owners of slaves should be bound to provide wholesome food for them, as well as clothing, and not to neglect them in sickness, age, or infirmity: that they should be deprived of the power of corporal punishment; that slaves ill-treated by their masters should be allowed to change owners; that a breach of the law should enfranchise the slave; that slaves should be allowed to purchase their liberty at the price paid for it; and that slaves attached to lands which may escheat to Government should be liberated. They recommend that these suggestions should be well weighed before they are adopted, and that the legislative enactment intended to carry them into effect, and which must contravene the existing Hindoo law, be framed with great caution."* In 1824 the Court of Directors express themselves as before stated, desiring the Madras Government to be "extremely cautious in making any regulation for defining the relations of master and

* Asi. Jour. Jan. 1829, p. 30.

slave." In Feb. 1826, says the Asiatic Journal, "the Governor in Council of Madras declares that the views and opinions above expressed coincide entirely with his own." This speaks little for the speedy melioration, we say not abolition, of slavery in this part of India. Why is Britain so timid, so tardy, in conferring upon her Asiatic subjects the blessings of freedom? It is important that the state of slavery in India should be more fully and generally known, and the practicability and utility of its entire suppression pressed upon the attention of the Legislature.

The adoption and encouragement of free labour is considered of great importance in promoting the abolition of slavery. Its utility in the cultivation of *indigo* in India is very apparent. The first few chests of indigo arrived in England in 1787: it is now estimated to employ nearly 500,000 free persons, and the article has ceased to be cultivated by slaves. "It is not known that there is any indigo whatever cultivated by slave labour, although from the nature of things it may be difficult to ascertain it with certainty; the quantity, however, if any, must be exceedingly small."* It is a question of much interest—Is East India sugar the product of slave labour or not? This has been asserted by some writers and positively denied by others. It is evident, from the Papers on Eastern Slavery, that the greatest number of slaves is found on the Malabar coast. No sugars are exported from Malabar, but it is stated, that sugar is imported for home consumption. In Bengal, the great sugar province of India, the number of slaves compared with other parts of Hindostan, appears comparatively small. The Bengal Board of Trade, in Aug. 1792, observe,—"In this country the cultivator is either the immediate proprietor of the ground or he hires it, as in Europe, of the proprietor; and uses his discretion in cultivating what he thinks best adapted to the nature of the soil or the demand of the market. One field produces sugar, the next wheat, rice, or cotton. The Bengal peasantry are freemen, and are in the usual course of nature replaced by their children. The Bengal peasant is actuated by the ordinary wants and desires of mankind. His family assist his labour and soothe his toil, and the sharp eye of personal interest guides his judgment. In the West Indies the whole labour of the ground is performed

---

* See A short Rev. of the Slave Trade, &c., Birminghan, 1827.

by hand, with the spade or hoe. Here the ox and plough, as in Europe, lessen the labour of man and facilitate the productions of the earth."* Slave labour is not an item in the different estimates given of the price of cultivating sugar. Mr. Udny, resident at Malda in Feb. 1793, writes, "The expense of cultivating one bigah (about 1600 square feet) is estimated at 8ru. 8an, whereof the particulars are,

	ru.	*an.*	*r.*
Hire of ploughs, oxen, &c.	1	12	0
Cooly (labourers) hire	0	14	0
Do. weeding eight times	4	0	0
Do. cutting and bringing earth	0	8	0
Do. tying canes four times	1	0	0
Petty charges	0	6	0
	8	8	0"†

This question must be acknowledged as one of some difficulty, and hence a powerful argument is derived, to promote the extirpation of slavery in the East:—"But we may spare ourselves the trouble (says the Anti Slavery Reporter for Sep. 1829) of confuting the elaborate misstatements of our adversaries on this question. The controversy is fast tending to its termination. The march of events will scarcely leave room, much longer, either for misrepresentation or misapprehension. The facilities already given in Bengal, by Lord W. Bentinck, to the investment of British capital, and the developement of British skill in the cultivation of the soil; the almost certainty that those fiscal regulations which have hitherto depressed the growth of sugar in Bengal, and prevented the large increase of its imports into this country, will soon be repealed; the prospect of an early removal of the other restrictions, which still fetter the commerce of our Eastern possessions; the rapidly increasing population and prosperity of Hayti; the official statements of Mr. Ward, as to the profitable culture of sugar by free labour in Mexico; and the rapid extension of the manufacture of beet root sugar in France (a prelude, as

* "Papers respecting the cultivation and manufacture of sugar in British India." 1822, pp. 51, 60, 146. See also pp. 32, 92, &c.

† For an ample investigation of this question see "A Letter to W. W. Whitmore, Esq. M. P., in reply to the erroneous statements of the late J. Marryat Esq. on the subject of slavery in the East Indies." Hatchard 1823. Oriental Herald, Oct. 1829. The Anti Slavery Reporter, Sep. 1829. East India Slavery by G. Saintsbury, Tilt, Fleet Street, &c.

we conceive, to its introduction into this country, and especially into Ireland); all these circumstances, combined, afford a promise which can scarcely fail of seeing a death blow inflicted on the culture of sugar by slave-labour."

Much encouragement may be derived, as it respects the abolition of slaverg in British India, from the just and humane sentiments on the subject frequently expressed by the functionaries of Government,—from the extent of our power,—and the general abhorrence in which slavery is held in Britain.

The author, while arranging the contents of the voluminous Papers on East India Slavery, noticed some of the excellent sentiments of the authorities in India on the nature and injurious tendency of Slavery; they are as follows:—

"It is impossible to think without horror of whole generations being born to slavery.*"—T. C. Metcalf Esq., Resident at Delhi.

"Slavery is a practice which is liable always to be attended with the greatest abuse; and which, however mild and unobjectionable it may sometimes be in its application, must still be viewed as a violation of one of the first principles on which society is constituted."†—Lord Minto.

"Slavery under any shape, or if it bears only the name, is so repugnant to every principle of enlightened administration, and so inconsistent with your Lordship's benevolent plans, that I fear I should not stand excused in my defence of such a system under any modifications or circumstances whatever."‡—Sir Stamford Raffles.

"Slavery is the greatest of all evils; and the attempt to regulate such an evil is in itself almost absurd. There is no excuse for continuing the practice in India, a country fully peopled, and where cultivation and commerce can be carried on by free men."§—Governor Farquhar.

"Slavery in its mildest form is degrading in the minds of Britons."‖—W. E. Phillips, Esq., Governor of Prince of Wales Island.

"Nothing, perhaps, is so revolting as the idea of hereditary slavery. It might be considered an adequate inducement to deeds of charity to compensate them by the labours of the object of it during one generation, instead of aggravating the sorrows of accidental necessity, by slavery through all generations."¶—W. Leycester, Esq. Judge of Bareilly.

Let such sentiments as these become general among those who hold in their hands the destinies of India, and it may be justly anticipated that slavery at no very distant period will be annihilated.**

---

* Par. Papers on Slavery in India, p. 105. † p. 172. ‡ p. 157. See p. 303. 317. § p. 434. ‖ p. 435. ¶ p. 345

** "These different public establishments (the Botanic Gardens at Calcutta) used to be all cultivated by the convicts in chains. In the Botanic Garden their labour is now supplied by peasants hired by the day or week, and the exchange is found cheap, as well as otherwise ad-

The influence of the British Government in India is great, and may be safely and successfully exerted in abolishing slavery and every inhuman custom. It was justly remarked, by the late Bishop Heber, that in India "our will is our law." To the same effect is the sentiment of C. Smith, Esq., one of the Calcutta magistrates, in 1821, respecting the abolition of Suttees.—"They have no idea that we might not do so with the most perfect safety. *They conceive our power and our will to be commensurate.*"* Let Britain sincerely will the good of India, and much will be accomplished. The present time is eventful for India; may it be improved. To use the language of Mr. Græme's Report on Malabar, in 1822,—"It matters not that many worthless characters are in worse circumstances than the slave; the question is—*whether slaves are as comfortable as they ought to be, and whether they acquire as much by their own industry, in servitude, as they would in a free state?* Their condition is undoubtedly improved considerably under the Company's government; for the British law has extended its protection to them in common with all, against injury to their lives or limbs, or any great severity of ill usage; but British justice and humanity are not satisfied till they have accomplished, by rational means, all the good that is capable of being done. *The general tranquillity which prevails, through the British empire in India, seems to present a favourable opportunity for commencing the work of amelioration, and to withhold it would be to sanction the perpetuity of slavery.*"†

Slavery is justly held in abhorrence in Britain; and, as the nature and prevalence of this evil in British India is known and lamented, measures will be proposed and urged upon the attention of the Legislature for its abolition.‡ This

---

vantageous and agreeable; *the labour of freemen here, as elsewhere, being infinitely cheaper than that of slaves.*" (Heber's Journ. vol. i. p. 43).

* Par. Papers relative to Suttees, vol. ii. p. 267.

† Par. Papers on Slavery in India, p. 922.

‡ "In the British Parliament, Slavery, and the questions relevant to it, will always be the object of serious discussion. Orators, not less distinguished by the brilliancy of their talent than by the solidity of their virtue, seconded from without the walls of the senate by the writings of men gifted with the same qualities, will continue to raise their voice in favour of justice and Christian charity. These accents, repeated by the periodical press, will at length resound through each hemisphere, and prove the knell of Slavery." (Ori. Herald, vol. xiv. p. 96. "On Nobility, of Skin."—See also "The Death-warrant of Negro Slavery," 1829. p. 23.)

state of society is inimical to human happiness and opposed to the improvement and elevation of our species. The author trusts he may adopt the language of the Judge of Bundlecund, whose proposed judicious Regulations on the subject of slavery appear to have been disregarded.—" I have endeavoured to point out some of the inconveniences of systematic slavery, and aimed at displaying the future advantages of abolishing so inhuman an institution.

" Aware of the great importance, and convinced of the caution with which innovation should be attempted, or the ancient laws, customs, or prejudices of a people infringed, I presume not even to sketch out the mode or to fix *the period of general emancipation ;* and perhaps the sudden manumission of those now actually in a state of bondage, though abstractedly just, might be politically unwise ; but *there can exist no good reason, either political or humane, against the British government prohibiting the purchase or sale of all slaves, legitimate or illegitimate, after a specified time, and likewise ordaining and declaring that all children, male and female, born of parents in a state of slavery, shall from a like date be free.*

" Should my humble arguments on the subject draw the attention of men possessed of more ability to investigate and determine the propriety of establishing personal liberty on the British model, throughout the Company's provinces, as well as invested with power to extend relief to the objects of my regard, so as to promote a mitigation of their miserable situation, I shall deem myself well rewarded, having no end in view but the honour of my country, and the happiness of my fellow creatures."*

But Britain has a greater boon than personal liberty to bestow upon her enslaved and superstitious subjects in the East :—

" ——— There is yet a liberty unsung
By poets, and by senators unpraised :
'Tis liberty of heart, derived from heaven—
Bought with His blood who gave it to mankind."—

This liberty is revealed in the Gospel—" If the Son shall make you free, ye shall be free indeed." For what purpose is India subjected to Britain, by His fiat who " ruleth in the kingdom of men, and He appointeth over it whomsoever he will ?"—Is it not to make his glory known, and

---

* Par. Papers on Slavery in India, p. 303.

hasten the period when it shall be sung in heaven—"The kingdoms of this world are become the kingdoms of our Lord and of his Christ, and he shall reign for ever and ever?" O Britain, my beloved country, consider thy high destiny, and labour by the messengers of heaven's mercy to man to make "His way known upon earth, his saving health among all nations."

"Britain! thy voice can bid the dawn ascend;
On thee alone the eyes of Asia bend.
High Arbitress! to thee her hopes are given
Sole pledge of bliss and delegate of heaven;
In thy dread mantle all her fates repose,
Or bright with blessing, or o'ercast with woes;
And future ages shall thy mandate keep,
Smile at thy touch, or at thy bidding weep.
Oh! to thy godlike destiny arise!
Awake and meet the purpose of the skies!
Wide as thy sceptre waves, let India learn
What virtues round the shrine of empire burn.
Let gentle arts awake at thy behest,
And science soothe the Hindoo's mournful breast.
Be thine the task, his drooping eye to cheer
And elevate his hopes beyond the sphere,
To brighter heavens, than proud Sumeeru owns,
Though girt by Indra and his burning thrones.
Then shall he recognize the beams of day
And fling at once the fourfold chain away;
Through every limb a sudden life shall start,
And sudden pulses spring around his heart;
Then all their deadened energies shall rise
And vindicate their title to the skies.
Be these thy trophies, Queen of many Isles!
Yes, it shall come! E'en now my eyes behold,
In distant view, the wish'd for age unfold;
Lo, o'er the shadowy days that roll between,
A wandering gleam foretels the ascending scene.
Oh! doom'd victorious from thy wounds to rise,
Dejected India, lift thy downcast eyes,
And mark the hour whose faithful steps to thee,
Through Time's press'd ranks, bring on the jubilee."*

---

* Grant's Revival of Learning in the East. 1805.

RELIEVING THE SICK ON THE BANKS OF THE GANGES. *Page 491.*

APPENDIX.

HUMANE HINTS

FOR THE

MELIORATION OF THE STATE OF SOCIETY IN BRITISH INDIA.

On the connexion that exists between Britain and India, and the consequent duty of this country to promote the welfare of the superstitious and degraded inhabitants of the East, Lord Teignmouth very justly observes,—"Were the same superstitions, or the same barbarous and licentious rites, which are now exhibited on the banks of the Ganges, to be practised on the banks of the Thames, or even in the remotest part of the British Islands, they would excite the strongest possible feelings of horror, and stimulate our efforts to substitute a purer and more benign system in the place of Hindoism,—this compound of cruelty and crime. But surely, to the eye of reason, the distance of that part of our dominions, in which this system prevails, makes no real difference. It is equally a portion of our empire; subject to our rule, and contributing largely to our prosperity. May we not still further consider the natives of Hindostan in the relation of tenants, to whom we are bound by the obligations and duties of landlords? If these circumstances are attentively weighed, they will exhibit a most extraordinary phenomenon.* The most enlightened, im-

*"Even in a cultivated and Christianized man, the disposition to sympathise in the woes of others is in proportion only to the distance, and not to the qualities of the sufferer, or the degree of his agony. And this feeling seems to be in the *inverse ratio*, both of distance and of

proved, and (may we not say?) most religious nation upon earth, standing for many years in the closest of all social relations to a people bowed down under a dark and degrading superstition—might it not be very naturally supposed, by those who in the varying fortunes of nations acknowledged the hand of a superintending providence, that it had been the design of heaven,—in bringing these vast countries under the dominion of a nation enjoying the purest of all systems of religion,—that their benighted and depraved inhabitants might thus receive the light of Christian truth, and the blessings of a sound morality? They who might hesitate to accede to this, would readily acknowledge that it is at least our duty to endeavour, in every way, to promote the well-being and happiness of our Oriental fellow-subjects."*

"As far as cruelty (cruelty of any kind) is tolerated in a state, its pretensions to civilization may be questioned, and its views must be considered proportionably contracted." The Quarterly Review for Jan. 1828, justly observes,—"Superstition, ignorance, and delusion must be dispelled; *new rights and new duties must be inculcated; motives, charities, affections, hitherto unknown, must be imparted:* mountains must be removed, a moral reformation must be wrought in the character of the people of India." 'Must new rights and new duties be inculcated;—motives, charities, and affections hitherto unknown,' be imparted to the inhabitants of India? Where can they be originated so well as in the mother country, and then assisted and matured by the humane and pious in every part of India? Philanthropic exertions, to improve the state of society, would

---

number. That which would excite inexpressible solicitude, and produce a most prompt, if it could possibly be a successful interposition, if transacted within the precincts of our city, or at the length of a street, loses almost all its power to interest when it is done in another country and another hemisphere; as if geographical space altered the very character of moral delinquency: while again the greater the multitude that suffer, the less appears to be the amount of sympathy—the individual has more of human commiseration than the mass of the dying or oppressed. Let a man burn his mother at our door, from any cause, and the nation would cry out with horror; but let ten thousand mothers die upon the funeral pile, by the same unnatural instrumentality, and scarcely has the world one tear to shed—one sigh to heave."—Review of India's Cries, 1st edit. World Paper, July 24th, 1829.

* Considerations on the Practicability, Policy, and Obligation of communicating to the Natves of India the Knowledge of Christianity, Hatchard, pp. 92, 93.

greatly facilitate the progress of Christianity, and enable Britain with greater ease to discharge the debt she owes the eastern part of her empire. The author has for some time desired to present these documents to the notice of a humane and Christian public, and particularly to the friends of Humane Societies. The Reports of the Royal Humane Society, instituted in London, 1774, are highly interesting, and display the humanity and magnanimity of the Christian character. The cities of Calcutta and Madras are enrolled among the number of Foreign Humane Societies; but what are these two Institutions for the whole of Hindostan? What influence can they exert for the elevation of the Native character? A Humane Society, embracing various philanthropic objects, at every principal station, would be highly beneficial to society. British India needs the efforts of such Societies to raise the tone of sympathetic and heroic feeling in the preservation of human life. In India 'dying men are no more regarded than dying weeds.' What a perfect contrast is formed by the apathy and cruelty of the Hindoos—as seen in suffering a boat full of people to drown without trying to assist them, in their Pilgrimages, Ghaut Murders, Infanticides, Suttees, &c.—and the noble efforts of Britons for the rescue of their fellow-creatures from a premature grave. (See the various Reports of the Royal Humane Society).

The following miscellaneous articles, it is hoped, may form *humane hints* calculated to promote the welfare of British India. It is a Syrian Proverb, "A glance is enough for the intelligent." The institution of the Royal Humane Society is attributed to Dr. Hawes, of whom it is stated,—"To the persevering efforts of this gentleman, and especially to his disinterested early efforts, the English Nation is indebted for the formation of a Society which, whether we reflect on its purposes or success, does honour to our country, and exhibits most impressively the power of a single mind to accomplish objects of the most benign character and extensive utility." May the perusal of these pages stimulate some humane and energetic minds to commiserate the miseries of India, and, in connexion with the general diffusion of Christianity, promote among its inhabitants the adoption of those various philanthropic measures, for the alleviation of human misery and the preservation of life, which confer so many blessings upon the British Isles.

(1.) Attention to promote *the salubrity of the Presidencies, and of the Cities and Towns in India,* is very important. Of the insalubrity of Calcutta, a correspondent in the Columbian Press Gazette, Sep. 20, 1825, thus writes :—

" It is very lamentable to notice the great supineness which prevails in Calcutta with regard to any attempt to improve its healthiness, or even to inquire into the causes of the dreadful mortality which, year after year, visits the poor natives of this city; especially when we view examples of the most praiseworthy energy in every other part of the world, and in every other town in the Company's possessions. At Madras we lately saw orders issued for the cutting down the hedges, which it was agreed prevented the proper ventilation of the place. At Bombay the improvements in new roads, and proper attention to cleanliness, have made the Island, which was before much below Calcutta in salubrity, now full five per cent. superior to it. In every large town in our provinces the alterations taking place are most judicious and very extensive, under the superintendence of local Committees, composed of all the Civil Officers, with the assistance of the resident Engineers and Executive Officers ; *the whole of the town duties of the respective places being appropriated, I believe, to these purposes alone.* In Calcutta we have the Lottery Committee making a gradual progress in improving *the centre of the town ;* but in all the vast extent of *the suburbs,* with a population thrice that of Calcutta, we see no measures whatever adopted either to drain the stagnant tanks, to remove filth, to cut down weeds and jungle, to make roads, or to preseve them. While the suburbs remain in their present close and pestiferous state, it is impossible but we shall always have to record the same scenes of misery, the same *daily deaths of hundreds,* both in and out of Calcutta, with which the Papers have for the last two months been so plentifully and alas! so vainly filled. *Why is nothing done to prevent this periodical destruction? Why are the Natives allowed to die by thousands without any attempts to remove the causes of this devastation?* The answer to these questions is obvious enough, but I may not venture to give it."*

* " I know not from what singular fatality it has arisen," says the late Bishop Heber, " that almost all the principal establishments of the English in India have been fixed in bad situations. The reason which I have heard given is the unwillingness of Government to interfere with the comforts of their subjects, or to turn out people from their farms and villages, which has compelled them to fix on spots previously uninhabited and untilled; which, of course, in an anciently peopled country have generally been neglected in consequence of some natural disadvantage. But it would be so easy at a moderate rate to recompense any Zemindar or Ryot, whom a new cantonment inconvenienced, and the bad effects of an unwholesome or otherwise ill-situated station are so great, that this is a reason which, though it was gravely given, I could hardly hear with gravity. The fact however is certain; Secrole, the cantonments at Lucknow, nay, Calcutta itself, are all abominably situated. I have heard the same of Madras, and now the lately settled cantonment of Nusserabad appears to be as objectionable as any of them."—Jour. Vol. i. p. 582.—See Hamilton's Hindoo, Vol. i. p. 49. "The attention of the Medical and Physical Society of Calcutta has been directed

From the following recent information it appears that attention is excited to this subject. "The roads in the eastern suburbs of Calcutta are undergoing a thorough repair; some of them are to be widened, and other improvements are to be effected, which will be conducive both to the comfort and health of the inhabitants; in particular, all the superfluous vegetation is to be removed. A canal from the northward to Chitpore, by that adjoining the Salt Water Lake, and terminating at Entally, is commenced; and a still more important improvement, with a view to diminish the causes of malaria, is in contemplation, namely to drain the Salt Water Lake."*

(2.) A suggestion in the India Gazette, in Sep. 1825, for *the erection of Porticos at the Ghauts in Calcutta*, appears worthy of notice.

"You would permit the Hindoos to be carried to the side of the river to die, 'provided they were kept there under shelter, and not exposed without covering to the scorching of a noon-day sun, or the drenching of a tropical shower.' Unfortunately there is no shelter at any of the Ghauts, which appears a great oversight on the part of the Lottery Committee. There should be a handsome Portico, or double Colonnade, erected at each Ghaut, along the Strand. Every person who has had to embark or land at either of the Ghauts during the heat of noon-day, and to wait for a boat or carriage, must know how desirable such a shelter would be; and how much more so would it be to those whose occupation keeps them for hours or days in attendance at the river's side, and to the unfortunate creatures forced down thither, by a lamentable superstition, in the extremity of sickness! The only Ghaut that is so covered in, that I recollect, is at Cossipore; the work, not of the Government, but of a rich native gentleman, who also made at his expense the road from the Ghaut to Dum Dum, which has so greatly improved that part of the suburbs.—A Subscriber." "The Lottery Committee," says the Editor, "are necessarily limited in their useful labours to the improvement of the city, and it is not at the Ghauts of Calcutta that these cruelties (of exposing the sick) are practised. We agree with our Correspondent on the importance and necessity of the improvement he suggests; which, while it would adorn the view of the city from the river, would be invaluable in point of utility, and greatly add to the convenience of the inhabitants and of all persons resorting to the Capital of British India."

---

to an Essay on Public Health in India, by Dr. Ranken, applying especially to the choice of situations for the establishment of Civil Stations and Military Cantonments. The greater part of the diseases that prevail in India are ascribed by Dr. R. not so much to the extreme heat or atmospherical vicissitudes, as to the presence of noxious impregnations in the air, exhaled during the decay of vegetable and animal matter. In proportion as these abound, situations will be unhealthy, and salubrity of site will be found exemption from their influence."—Asi. Jour. Aug. 1827. * Ori. Herald, Sep. 1829.

(3.) ***The necessity of some humane efforts in India, on behalf of Sailors of the various Countries employed by Britain,*** **appears from the following simple appeal, extracted from a Calcutta Paper, in Sep. 1825:—**

"There is no situation in the whole round of human sufferings which appears so dreadful to encounter, nor so awful to contemplate, as that of a *shipwrecked sailor;* nor is there any humane person who would not stretch out his hand, at the risk of his own life, to rescue him from the grasp of death. Falconer has indeed given us an able description of their situation and sufferings; but who can paint the feelings of the mind when the perils and troubles at sea are past;—We arrive at the entrance of our destined haven with hearts elated with joy at the prospect of meeting our wives, our children, and our friends. All, in a moment, is blasted: for the approach to this Port (Calcutta) is dangerous beyond all the toils of our voyage. *On the coast of Bengal there is no assistance, in any part, to render us relief.* No Life Boats; *no enterprising men to venture their lives for us, and no chance of escaping death.* If we should reach the shore the mouths of ravenous tigers are open to receive us. How dreadful to every feeling mind must be the situation of every sailor wrecked upon this coast; and of late we have had examples sufficient to call the attention of Government to the lamentable truth—that no life boats—no light houses—nor any means of saving the shipwrecked sailor, exist on this coast. Looking to the coast of our own country; the coast of America, and almost all the coasts of the civilized world, we find them more or less provided with the means of saving from death the shipwrecked mariner. I would fain hope to see something of this kind on this coast: such as life boats stationed at Saugur; one on Light-house Point, another at Point Palmira, with some beacon to attract attention. Their establishment would encourage the efforts of a sailor's perseverance. There is no danger insurmountable in the mind of a British tar; who is the bulwark of our Country, the maintenance of our rights by sea, the slave of our trade and commerce, and deserving the fostering hand of every Government and the consideration of every mercantile body. I am, Sir, A Bit of a Sailor." The Editor of the John Bull remarks—"We have heard that it has been determined to station boats permanently at Edmonstone's Island, with a view to afford assistance to vessels that, like the Lotus, are so unfortunate as to suffer shipwreck on the sands, at the mouth of the Hooghly. We shall be glad to find that this measure has been really determined on. Such boats as those spoken of might have saved *the whole crew of the Lotus, and probably not a little of the stores,* besides affording shelter and sustenance until the men could be taken off."

How far the deficiency here complained of by a sailor is now supplied, for the relief of our valued seamen, the Author is not informed; but it is presumed the insertion of this short article may awaken attention to their claims on British humanity.

(4.) The following letter, on *the difficulty of obtaining suitable medicine in seasons of great sickness,* written in Calcutta, and published in the Bengal Hurkaru, Sep. 1825, demands the attention of the humane both in India and Britain:—

"This dreadful scourge of the human race, the cholera morbus, seems to continue with little if any abatement. There are, I believe, few families who have not suffered, and are not daily suffering, the loss of one or more of their domestics; for, notwithstanding the prevailing sympathy, few, comparatively speaking, possess the means of affording relief. I am one of this class, and I know a great many others thus situated: they would most willingly contribute all in their power, by strict attention in administering medicines, did they possess or could they purchase them; but there are many, like myself, who cannot afford to do so. *I know of no public or private Dispensary that will, in a direct way, gratuitously supply them.* I have been informed that a direct application from a private person (as the master of a family), to the Hon. Company's Dispensary, cannot be complied with, being against the rules;—the signature of a medical man is necessary; to obtain which a favour must be craved, obligation incurred, or compensation made. I do not mean to insinuate any thing unfavourable against an institution which confers its benefits with the most liberal hand; or any thing prejudicial to an honourable and humane profession, every individual member of which, probably, if applied to, would give the requisite signature or recipe; and many, probably, the medicine itself, without remuneration. But private practitioners are frequently, for hours together, from home; and I hope I may be excused, in these times of dreadful visitation, *where delay is death!* for urging the expediency of *a more direct and ready access to the Dispensary*, which it is conceived should be somewhere available.

"I am informed that native doctors are in attendance at the several thannahs, but from what cause I know not—whether for want of proper attention in these officers, or their too general failure in the cure; and, perhaps, a consequent despair in the sufferers and their friends,—I believe applications are seldom made in these quarters. I almost daily hear of dozens cured by individuals who afford a proper supply of medicines; and who, with a tender feeling of humanity, far above all praise, assiduously watch the progress of the disorder, and carefully attend the suffering patient. My object, in calling public attention to this state of things, is *to obtain a more direct access to medicine*, to be offered to those who have the desire patiently to attend to administering it, for the preservation of their suffering fellow creatures. Should you think proper to suppress my letter, submitting something of your own for the attainment of an object so desirable, the saving of human life, what more can be desired by—HUMANITAS."

(5.) ***The establishment of a Dispensary at each civil and military station in India, and at the principal Towns in the tributary and allied states,*** supported by subscription and the assistance of Government, would be highly beneficial to society. The late Rev. W. Ward observes, in his View of the History, Literature, and Mythology of the Hindoos, "The imperfections of their medical system, and the ignorance and rapacity of the quacks who bear the character of physicians, greatly add to the general misery. It would be an act of philanthropy to improve the medical knowledge of the Hindoos; and this might easily be done by instituting a college at Calcutta for the instruction of the medical class; and by disseminating, in the native languages, European ideas on the nature of diseases and their remedies; showing, at the same time, the absurdities in the Hindoo practice."* The establishment of such institutions in different parts of the country would be attended with the most grateful results. The Marquis of Hastings gave some attention to this subject, and established a native medical school in Calcutta. Dr. Breton, the Superintendent, has published translations of several tracts on medical subjects in the Bengalee and Hindostanee languages. They amount to fifteen in number.† The general circulation of these pamphlets, and the adoption of this medical system in the country, is highly deserving the attention of the philanthropic and liberal both in Britain and India, and especially of a Government desirous of the melioration of the state of society among the Natives.

(6.) The following letters, on *the treatment of cholera morbus*, were addressed to the Editor of the India Gazette; and, if known generally in India, especially among the natives in their different dialects, would be beneficial.

"During my residence at the Isle of Bourbon, I observed the good effects of distilled or strong vinegar on the natives afflicted with the cholera, when rubbed in all parts of the body, and more particularly on the parts where *the circulation of the blood appeared suspended*. Immediately after the vinegar is applied, the patient is to be rubbed with flannel, as it is of the utmost importance he should be kept warm. In the hospital at Batavia the patients were put into warm baths of a high degree of temperature, and frequently bled until the spasms ceased, and then mercurial preparations,‡ &c., were administered, according to the violence of the disease or constitution of the individual: by which means numbers were saved.

"But if it be useful to administer remedies to the sick, it is not less necessary to ascertain the causes of the disease, and to warn those who expose themselves to their fatal effects. The attacks of cholera in India generally occur during the change of seasons, but more particularly in the rainy season, when the evaporation of the waters on the surface of the ground occasions a considerable degree of damp. The sudden change of temperature is one of the causes of the sickness. During these variable seasons the body should be preserved in a uniform state of heat; a free perspiration being kept up without producing a profusion

---

* Vol. iii. p. 282. † Asi. Jour. Feb. 1826, p. 223.

‡ In Orissa, pills, each containing six or seven grains of calomel, and one grain of opium, were given with effect. One pill was sometimes sufficient; at other times, a second, third, or fourth, at intervals of half an hour, were requisite to arrest the progress of the disease. An aperient was afterwards administered. AUTH.

of sweat, as the debilitating causes (independent of the insalubrity of the air) are already sufficiently great. To prevent other weakening causes, violent exercise should be avoided, particularly at night, as it is attended with serious consequences. Long walks at night, exposed to the rays of the moon, are more pernicious than those taken during dark nights, although the beauty of moonlight tempts many people to walk. Perhaps the excesses committed by the Bengalees during the night of the late festival have caused so great a mortality among them, as their customary food is very simple and not alecholic. The following should be avoided:—Exposure to the dew at night, which falls in great quantity when there are no clouds to intercept the radiation of the sky. Excess of exercise. Excess of eating and drinking, &c. Some persons of strong constitutions can commit excesses in all seasons, and even bear the pernicious influence without sustaining any bad effects; but delicate or sickly persons, and particularly those not seasoned to the climate of hot countries, should avoid any thing that may cause an alteration in the state of their health. Woollen clothes should be worn; gin and brandy in water are recommended by skilful physicians, but great quantities are to be avoided. Any acid substances, fruit, &c., which may occasion weakness, must be avoided, and in these seasons stimulants and tonics must be taken.

"If, in awakening the attention of some people to their own preservation, I succeed in preventing sickness, I shall have attained the object of publishing this advice.

"*Calcutta, Sept.* 16*th*, 1825. B. BOURET."

The following letter was addressed to the Editor, with the hope that its publication might cast light on the treatment of cholera in peculiar cases:—

"The wife of my Khansama, a woman of about twenty years of age, was attacked with cholera morbus, with all the usual symptoms, but more vomiting than purging. About half an hour after the commencement, her husband applied for medicine. I gave her the cholera mixture, sold by Messrs. Bathgate and Co., Calcutta. This was rejected three times successively in the course of about three-quarters of an hour; a cataplasm of pounded chillies, warmed, was applied to the stomach, and the feet and hands, which were cold, were rubbed with cloths. Finding the cholera mixture would not remain in the stomach, I tried laudanum and æther, but these too were twice rejected; the patient sinking very fast with strong spasms, and being nearly senseless. I almost began to despair of her life; but, having heard that *calomel had frequently been found effectual in desperate cases*, I gave her eight grains of it with the usual quantity of laudanum and æther (thirty drops of each); this remained on the stomach a short time, and vomiting again took place. A large worm of the common Teres or round sort, about the size of a small quill, and eight or nine inches long, was thrown up, and in a short time another. I then gave her two grains more, which in a short time brought off two more. The woman then rapidly recovered, and is now perfectly well. She was a Mousalmanee; I saw her twice, and my writers and a Christian servant saw her also. The symptoms were exactly those of violent cholera, of which I have seen many hundred cases; but the pulse was stronger than is usual in that disorder.

"*Neemtullah, Sept.* 19*th*, 1825. H. P."

"The plan for the treatment of cholera pursued with most success, (says Dr. Graham) consists in bleeding from the arm, to the extent of sixteen or twenty-four ounces, and immediately afterwards administering calomel with opium in very free doses, of from fifteen to twenty grains of the former in a dose, with one or two grains of opium, which is to be repeated, if necessary, every two or three hours, till the urgency of the symptoms subside. To these should be added a most liberal use of the most diffusible *stimuli*, as the sweet spirit of nitre, carbonate of ammonia, hot arrack and water, &c. The hot bath is also proper, and stimulating embrocations to the abdomen and limbs."

Dr. Anslie's treatment was by anti-acids, and he generally gave preference to the subcarbonate of *magnesia*, in a full dose; seldom less than two drachms and a half, or three drachms dissolved in water. By this means he saved many hundred lives in India, and since his return to England it has been ordered with equal success.

A happy blunder.—" By mistake, twenty grains of calomel, six minims (equal to 120 drops) of laudanum, were given at an interval of less than half an hour. The patient was inclined to sleep; nothing more was done; and in two hours and a half he was as well as ever he was in his life."—Oriental Herald, vol. xii. p. 529.

The Asiatic Journal for January, 1828, contains the following method for treating the cholera:*—

" Here I am most sorrowfully interrupted by the melancholy news of the sudden death of our good Governor, Sir Thomas Munro, who died of the cholera on the 5th of July, 1827. We have been free from this epidemic plague for many years. I was attacked with it, and given over, having had the common last symptoms, of a general cramp over the whole body, with sinking of the eyes, when I was cured by a powerful medicine, prescribed by Mr. Gay, an able medical practitioner, though only a sub-assistant surgeon. A number of people have been cured by taking that medicine.

" We have been furnished with the prescription for the above medicine, with a request that it may appear in this journal; it is as follows:—

Anticholera Drops, No. I.

Take of Daffy's Elixir (with a larger proportion of Senna)	2 oz.
Aromatic Spirits of Ammonia	$2\frac{1}{4}$oz.
Oil of Cloves (made an essence of with Alcohol) . .	$0\frac{1}{2}$oz.
Oil of Juniper	6 drops.

* " Dr. Kennedy, of the Bombay establishment, has published, at Calcutta, a Tract on the epidemic cholera. Dr. Kennedy's plan consists of bleeding, with reference to the state of the patient; promoting the vomiting in the early stages by simple emetics or warm water, and when more advanced administering castor oil with laudanum; giving camphor and opium to allay spasmodic action after the vomiting has ceased; and finally exhibiting exciting but not intoxicating or acrid stimulants, as cordials to support the sinking strength of the patient. These measures, according to Dr. Kennedy, were extensively useful." Asi. Journ., Dec. 1827, p. 757.

Oil of Peppermint	8 drops.
Oil of Cajuput	10 drops.
Sweet Spirits of Nitre	3 drams.
Camphor Mixture	10 drams.

Make a mixture and take 1 oz. or two table spoons full.

No. II.

"The same, leaving out the camphor mixture, and adding half an ounce of the compound tincture of camphor.

"Should repeated doses of this mixture not check the watery motions, ten drops of laudanum may then be added to each dose, increasing it five drops each time, till it composes the bowels; an hour or two after which, if the patient be not very much exhausted, six grains of calomel, with a scruple or fifteen grains of rhubarb, ought to be administered in a little ginger tea, and the latter to be made use of pretty freely after the bowels have been opened by the medicine.

"Should the cholera commence with evident acidity at the stomach, the cure ought to be commenced with eight grains of calomel and a drachm of prepared chalk, with a little ginger powder; after which, mixture No. I. should be persevered in till the stomach is composed.

"Mr. Gay attributes the success he has experienced, from the use of the Anticholera Drops, to "their powerful action on the digestive and urinary organs, which by some mysterious cause become so greatly affected as to encourage (it is believed) the congestion of the blood, which, being reduced into a congee-water-like fluid, is evacuated in large quantities, and necessarily produces that prostration of strength and restlessness, which are ever attendant on cholera. The symptoms in this formidable disease strongly point out the necessity of stimulants to keep up the circulation of the blood; which the Anticholera Drops are admirably calculated to effect, particularly when assisted by stimulating frictions of cajuput oil, or (which is better when spasms come on) a mixture of a cajuput oil, æther, and laudanum, in equal parts.

"He recommends the patient's thirst to be quenched with small, but repeated, doses of strong ginger tea, prepared with toast and water."—See *Evan. Mag., April,* 1828.

(7.) As India is much infested with serpents, the following account of *the virtues of the Guaco plant, and the propriety of its cultivation in the East, appears deserving**

---

* The following singular account is from the India Gazette, and the circumstances occurred in 1810:—'Morza Jannee told Col. Palmer that he had brought the root he had formerly mentioned, as that which the Munghoore (Ichneumon) runs to when bitten by a snake, and his hurkarus were in attendance to exhibit its powers. These men were accordingly called in, and they produced some root in fibres about the thickness and colour of the largest end of common *kus-kus.* They had no serpents, but had supplied themselves with a number of scorpions, with which experiments were made to the satisfaction of all present, that, while in contact or connexion with the root, the scorpion was helpless and innoxious. A lively scorpion, having a piece of the fibre on its back, presently became torpid. The people having a piece of the root on the palm of the hand readily handled the scorpions, and allowed them to lie on their

the attention of all who are interested in the welfare of its inhabitants. The cultivation of this plant in India by liberal individuals, or by Humane Societies, appears important. The account is extracted from "The Colonial Journal," March 1817.*

"It is an observation made by Pliny (Nat. Hist. lib. 7) that nature has, in one sense, been more liberal to brutes than to man, by providing the former with natural clothing, and gifting them with sufficient sagacity to know and defend themselves against their enemies; whereas man is destined to seek the same advantages by dint of labour and reflection. The fact certainly does exist, nor can it be proved by any instance more remarkable than the one that forms the subject of this article.

"Among the most valuable discoveries made in the tropical regions, in favour of suffering humanity, certainly we may rank that of the preservative and cure for the bites of venomous serpents; a virtue subsisting in the *Bejuco del Guaco*, a species of bind-weed. The secret is understood to have been long known to some of the Indians in the tropical parts of South America; but, ever mindful of the injustice and cruelty of their conquest, this, as well as the knowledge of many other important facts, preserved by tradition, they have uniformly refused to communicate to their intruders; even the Missionaries sent among them, in whom they placed the greatest reliance, and held in profound veneration, were unable to wrest the secret from them. The virtues of the plant in question were, however, recently discovered, almost in an accidental manner, as will be seen by the following details.

"The Negroes in the province of Chocó, dependent on the kingdom of Santa Fe, were the first who observed a bird, called the Guaco, pursue and fight with serpents; and, on closer examination, they discovered that these were the common food of this animal. This bird must not be confounded with the one belonging to the species of herons, mentioned by Buffon, in the last volume of the Natural History of Birds, which he calls Guaco or Souaco, the name commonly given to it on the shores of Boulogne. The American Guaco might rather enter into the class of carnivorous birds, under the head of hawks, as Catesby calls the Serpent-hawk (*Expervier serpent*), from that reptile's being its food and object of destruction: and may deserve the name in the same manner as does the sparrow-hawk, &c. The negroes perceived that the Guaco, when wounded in its severe battles, always recurred to a certain plant, and never appeared to receive material injury. When unable to kill its enemy, they also noticed that it availed itself of the leaves of the same plant to lay him asleep, and he then became an easy prey. Pushing their discoveries and experiments still further, they eventually ascertained that this plant, to which they afterwards gave the name of Guaco, in reference to the bird which had taught them its virtues, not only, in all

---

fingers. All this speaks as to prevention, not to cure; yet as the natives dared not to touch the scorpions without this root, and as the Munghoore, when bitten by a snake, instantly ran to it, a presumption may be a drawn from analogy."—Asi. Journ. Jan. 1826, p. 64.

* See Philosophical Mag. vol. 12. Methodist. Mag. 1818, p. 41—47. India Gazette, June 20, 1825. Weekly Messenger, June 19, 1825. See also Asi. Jour. Jan. 1826, p. 55.

cases, cured the poisonous bites of the above reptiles, but also operated as a preservative against their destructive powers, when taken with a degree of frequency.

"Mutis, the celebrated botanist of Santa Fe, previously to the above discovery being properly known, had been astonished at the facility with which the negroes, inhabiting the borders of the river Magdalena, caught serpents, and carried them about in their hands and bosoms, without any dread of fatal effects; and, ever active in that spirit of research for which he was so much distinguished, the following experiments were made in his presence, and that of several other botanists:—

"A negro was obtained, well versed in the above dangerous trials, who brought with him a venomous serpent, known to the Spaniards by the name of *Taya*, in consequence of the white spots it has on the back, something resembling the letter X. The negro handled the serpent in every way he was desired, and gave it several blows, without its appearing roused or attempting to bite him. It was at first imagined that the serpent was not of the most venomous kind, or that the negro had extracted its teeth; but, on causing it to open its mouth, the rows of sharp teeth were found in perfect order, and ample assurances were given that it was of the most deadly species known in the provinces of Santa Fe. No further doubt was entertained of the efficacy of the preservative, and *one of the Gentlemen resolved to undergo the same experiment the negro had just performed.*

"For this purpose, the negro pressed the juice of a handful of the leaves of the guaco-plant into a glass, and caused the person to drink two table spoonfuls, after which he inoculated some of the juice into the skin. He made eight small incisions; one in each foot; one in each of the fleshy parts of the hands; again between the forefinger and thumb; and, lastly, on each side of the breast. On the appearance of blood, some of the juice was poured on, and well rubbed with the pounded leaves of the plant; which operation being fully performed, the person, if bitten, is considered as perfectly cured, and, besides, prepared to handle any serpent of the worst kind at pleasure. Various experiments were then tried, both by Mutis and his companions, and all proved the evident powers of the juice. Several questions were also proposed to the negro, respecting other plants; but he assured the bye-standers that he knew of no other as equally efficacious, and that this plant was always eaten by the guaco or serpent-hawk, when worsted by the serpents it attacked in search of food; moreover declaring that he had frequently witnessed the circumstance, and always noticed that the bird uniformly recurred to the same remedy.

"The guaco-plant is found indigenous in the neighbourhood of Maraquita, as well as in the hot and temperate parts of the vice-royalty of Santa Fe; and it thrives singularly well on the margins of rivulets and in damp places. The plant has been called guaco, a name that was found preserved by tradition among the negroes, from whom the communication was received; but its genus is not yet determined in botany. Its root is fibrous, and extends in every direction. It is a species of creeper or bind-weed, and its climbing and adhering shoot is round when young, but angular when old, and set with opposite leaves. These are green, intermixed with purple, smooth below, rough above, and somewhat hairy. The flower rises like a crest, is yellow, flosculous, and four petals are seen in each calix. In the inside of the tassel of the flower, which is dented, are five stamina, united to the apices. These, which are cylindrically shaped, surround the style, and contain long and bristly seeds.

"Although, as a preservative, it was at first supposed unnecessary to inoculate with the juice of the guaco-plant, under an impression that its effects on serpents arose out of the disagreeable smell the plant emits, it was nevertheless found that the mode usually practised by the negroes possessed some peculiar advantages, and that as the virus of the small pox, introduced by the smallest orifice into the system, affects the whole mass of the blood, this also might have some strong communicative properties which rendered the inoculation more safe and efficacious. The juice operates as a powerful anodyne, and creates in the patient a copious perspiration. When the cure has been performed, the native empirics nevertheless say that it is advisable to continue the dose five or six times during the successive month, lest any of the venom should be left lurking behind. The repetition of the process tends constantly to maintain in the humours of the body the strong effects of the herb, which operates as a shield against future poison, even though at the time of being bitten the plant should not be at hand to rub the wound and renew the dose. They further add, that the curative virtues of the plant subside if the same precaution is not used at the next increase of the moon, when it becomes necessary to be inoculated by the hands of the empiric. This, however, is held out from no other than interested views, as the curing of serpents' bites among the negroes is still a kind of trade; and distinguished botanists and physicians have had ample proof, that the antidote is permanently efficacious. By way of experiment, serpents have been handled long after the monthly period of inoculation had passed, though it is strongly recommended, in cases of trial, that the person should prepare himself half an hour before the serpent is taken into the hand, *by a dose of the fresh juice, and previous rubbing his hands with the leaf*, a practice that has been frequently followed with success.

"The experiments made on this subject have not clearly pointed out whether it is the effluvia of the plant which acts on the reptile by creating a kind of disgust, or whether an agreeable sensation is communicated, that lulls it, and makes it forget its natural malignity. It has, however, been noticed, that, on spittle impregnated with the juice, being cast on the head of the serpent, it appears to become drowsy, notwithstanding it was before in an irritated and restless state; whereas, when handled by the person who has been previously prepared, it is uneasy and evinces a wish to escape. A considerable quantity of the juice being poured on two serpents, it was observed, that the sensation of stupor was not very durable; for, after the lapse of a short period, they recovered their accustomed vigour, and were as active as before they had been sprinkled.

"The guaco-plant is now applied, as a cure for the bite of all kinds of serpents, by the Spanish physicians in the tropical provinces of South America. In those of the Venezuela and Caracas, its use is become so general that it has been planted and reared on all the large estates; and every morning, when the labourers go out to work in the fields, a small calabash of the juice is carried with them, in case a misfortune happens to any of the people. This example is worth following in the West India Islands, where the plant may be easily obtained; and with this view the present details are given, chiefly taken from what has been written on the subject by eminent persons of the faculty in Lima and Santa Fe.

"The guaco-plant, although not in use for more than twenty-five years, has been found to possess sovereign virtues, and to counteract the poison of all the snakes and serpents peculiar to the Spanish main; and experiments to this effect have been made on the *taya;* the *coral*, or coral-snake, so called from its red colour; the *cascabal*, or rattle-snake; and a green one found near the city Giron.* Indeed, no greater proof of the powerful effects of the plant in question can be brought forward than the case of the rattle snake. The bite of the latter is both violent and grievous, nevertheless this remedy has proved efficacious to persons in the agony of death. It is proper to remark, that, to proceed safely in the cure of persons bitten with serpents, the fresh leaf of the plant is necessary, and its juice by itself, or mixed with a small portion of warm water, is to be given to the patient in any period of the disease, and without any previous preparation. The chewed or bruised leaves are applied to the wound and the parts affected; and, if the swelling has not gained the farthest extreme of the limb, the plant ought to be bound round the part to which the poison has not reached, in order that its progress may be stopped. The dose must be repeated several times, and the patient may then throw aside his dread, and resume his customary occupations.

"This plant has been found so efficacious as a remedy, in the tropical regions of the New World; the various experiments, made on both man and dogs, in the way of preventatives, have been so completely successful, that, besides the West Indies, it might be of *the greatest service in Europe*, where the plant also deserves the notice of the rational philanthropist, and the experiments of the public schools of medicine. Its virtues, once established, would render the plant an object of trade, and from this an essential relief might be derived to the ills of the human frame. The inhabitants of North America annually export a considerable quantity of snake-root; and it is to be hoped those of the Southern Continent will, ere long, be enabled to turn their attention to the number of herbs and gums with which their forests abound; and that then the guaco-plant may be reckoned in their list of exports.

"If brought to this distance, perhaps the best method of conveying it would be, by extracting the juice, bottling it carefully, and packing it in a state of good preservation. This article might be abundantly supplied from Santa Fe, as well as many other parts of the main continent, and by a further chemical analysis it undoubtedly would be found to possess other qualities, hitherto unknown. Even experiments already made have proved that it is an excellent vermifuge, and the peculiar bitterness of the plant strongly corroborates the fact. It is also stomachic and tonic.

"A species of creeper, or bind-weed, of partly a similar kind, is said by Father Gamilla to exist in Guayaquil; but its exact affinity with the

---

* Vallemont, in his Dictionairé Raisonne of Natural History (verb Serpent), observes, that in Martinique a species of serpent is found, and there called the coule-sang, owing to the blood gushing from every part of the person bitten. It is a small species of serpent, inclining to the viper; the eyes glaring, the skin transparent, and spotted with white and black. The body is thin, and the tail very small. As the effect of the poison of this reptile is different from that of any other serpent, which rather tends to coagulate the blood, possibly the guaco-plant might not be more successful than alkalies, which, in this case, have been tried with less effect than acids; but, perhaps, this is the only instance that can be mentioned as an exception.

Guaco-plant has not hitherto been traced. There is also another, mentioned by Mr. Jaquin, in his History of American plants, possessing properties not unlike those of the Guaco-plant, though different in genus and classification. This he describes under the name of *aristolochia anguicida, stipulis cordatis*, which answers to the description of the one called *carate*, in South America, of which the flower is denominated in Carthagena *flor de alcatraz*, or pelican-flower, from its resemblance to the bill of the pelican; and its virtues, though by no means equal to those of the Guaco-plant, have an affinity.

"Besides serpents, it is well known that there are several other animals whose poison is more or less active and deadly, against which the antidote in question might be rendered extremely valuable. Among the most terrible is that of the blood and froth of a certain species of lizard, *found in the island of Java, and used by the Natives to poison their arrows.* In order to obtain it they suspend the lizard by the tail, and irritate it till it emits from the mouth a yellow viscous matter, which is received in an earthen cup, and fermented in the sun. Afterwards their arrows are steeped in it, and the wounds they inflict are of a deadly nature. In these cases the Guaco-plant would undoubtedly answer the end desired, and certainly it is on that account highly deserving *the attention of the physicians attached to the British armies in the East Indies, where the soldiers are alike exposed to the ills of war and reptiles of the woods.* This specific is now well known, and easily found on almost all the margins of rivulets, and in damp places; and it can also be readily transplanted, or propagated by means of seed."

Cure for snake bites.—"Strong diffusible stimulants prove the most effectual antidotes; and it is probable that they all act in virtue of that stimulant quality alone. Ammonia, hartshorn, eau-de-luce, or whatever its form or name, has proved eminently successful, solely as a stimulant, not (according to the old idea) as a corrector of poisonous acidity. But this valuable medicine has disadvantages; it varies exceedingly in strength, according to age, preparation, &c. I believe its use to have been attended with fatal consequences, and which finally determined me to try the strongest *narcotics*—of these the most convenient is laudanum and ardent spirits (brandy I have constantly used)—and they have answered my warmest expectations. Without a single auxiliary, besides external heat, they have cured at least *nine cases within the last six months.* My patients were nearly all sepoys of the Goruckpore light-infantry, on duty with the different guards, and, as the poor fellows were generally bitten at night, some minutes necessarily elapsed before I could see them. I have had opportunities of watching the effects of the remedies in all stages of the symptoms, even to spasms of the back, total insensibility, and cessation of every pulse but that of the heart; and in every instance I have to attribute the cure to these two remedies, given internally, and rubbed on the throat and chest. Only one man died, and he was pulseless, and of course incapable of swallowing ammonia, æther, &c.

The natives in India hardly ever use the simple but effectual precaution of *tying the limb with cord above the wound.* Several of the towns-people have this year died of snake-bites. It is obvious that the doses given must depend on the age, sex, and apparent constitution of the patient, and on the degree in which the venom has acted. None of my patients had less than 100 drops of laudanum and two glasses of brandy, given in two or three doses, with a little peppermint, sugar, and water, (warm, if it could be had), and many of them had double that quantity. Except one man, every one of the patients was at his duty next day, a circumstance which powerfully corroborates the idea of a direct sedative action, and consequent expenditure of the vital principle; for what sepoy could otherwise bear unharmed that quantity of stimulant?

"It is proper to keep the patient walking about, if he can use his limb: and the ligature should not be removed till the medicine has unequivocally shown its action by the returning pulse and heat, which, in my experience, has always happened in less than an hour. I have used no applications to the wound, as they are apt to degenerate into troublesome ulcers when irritated by caustics, &c."—Asi. Jour. Oct. 1824.

(8.) *A Humane Society to attend to the sick and dying at the Ghauts, or landing places of the Ganges, &c., as suggested in a Calcutta Paper, would be very beneficial.*

"As you are ready to give a place in your pages to the remarks of your Correspondents that are of general utility, I trust the following, upon a subject which has much engaged my attention, will meet with a ready insertion:—Having understood that many people were brought to the Ghauts in this town, in the early stages of the attacks of cholera, and there suffered to die without proper attention, a friend of mine stationed a person at the principal Ghaut (with direction to pay some attention to another belonging to the village of C——, where the cholera has greatly raged):—by the timely application of suitable medicine, in *one day, eight out of twelve*, who were brought to the Ghauts, were restored to their families. The detail of other days was encouraging. With these circumstances before me, I could not forbear to call the attention of a humane public in general, and the Government in particular, to the importance of *stationing persons with medicines at the principal Ghauts of the towns and villages where the cholera at any time prevails.* By this expedient many may be rescued from premature death, and the benevolent spirit of Christianity will appear in influencing the authorities and humane individuals to promote the welfare of the people, when exposed to one of Heaven's most dreadful scourges! Would it not be practicable and highly desirable to establish *a humane society for the relief of the sick* in different places, and thus regular, permanent, and suitable means would be in existence to meet the ills of life arising from sickness, with all its train of sorrows? Hoping some of your correspondents will take up the subject, I subscribe myself, PHILANTHROPOS.

Sep. 9, 1825."

The engraving, p. 491, represents the exposure and relief of the sick.—Messrs. Yates and Pearce relate the following facts in an account of an excursion on the river Ganges:—

"On Sabbath morning, at breakfast time, we reached a small village, where we went ashore. Here, under a large tree, we found a poor woman, about fifty years old, brought to die by the side of Gunga. She complained of no pain, but seemed labouring under great weakness. Having unhappily no medicine, we gave her a little brandy and water, and dispatched her relations into the village to make her some gruel. At this time was brought to the same spot an interesting young woman, about twenty years old; and on the other side we found lying on the ground, deserted by her friends, a third, about twenty-five. *All these* *could speak without difficulty, were free from pain, and would probably in a short time have perfectly recovered if properly attended*: but yet we fear are doomed to perish, through the neglect and superstitious cruelty of their relatives. We got a promise of nutritious food for them all from their friends, and, having no medicine with us, after giving the two latter likewise a little brandy and water (which they would take as medicine), left them with a heavy heart. Well may it be said that the dark places of the earth are full of the habitations of cruelty."*

The Friend of India, for Sep. 1825, contains a letter, by the Author, upon the subject of *Humane Societies in India*, which he should rejoice to hear were extensively established, and assisted by contributions from this country.—

"I should be happy, through the medium of your pages, to present to the Christian public the following interesting paragraphs from an American periodical, entitled The Friend of Peace, for April, 1825, and a few remarks relative to the establishment of humane societies in India. 'The Royal Humane Society was formed in London in 1774. By its Annual Report, in 1821, it appears that this institution had been instrumental in restoring to society 5,020 persons in the metropolis and its vicinity; and that within forty-seven years it had rewarded 20,320 *persons* for their exertions in saving the lives of men exposed to untimely death. To a philanthropic mind it must be a pleasing thought that 5,020 persons have been rescued from sudden death by one Humane Society in the course of forty-seven years. There are other Humane Societies besides this in England. What their success has been we know not; but we may suppose that the persons saved by them in this period, added to 5,020, will make the aggregate 15,000. This is a goodly number to be saved by a few societies; and the promoters of these institutions are entitled to great respect as saviours of their species.'

"'The liberal deviseth liberal things and by liberal things shall he stand.' Is there not great necessity for similar benevolent exertions in such a country as India? Are there not many at the Presidencies, and the various stations throughout the country, disposed to promote humane exertions for the recovery of the sick in cholera, epidemics, &c.?—to rescue from premature death those who are exposed to die on the banks of the Ganges, or who find a watery grave through the apathy of their countrymen? To the honour of Britain and of Christianity an affirmative to these inquiries may be given. Permit me to suggest the establishment in Calcutta, and at different stations of ——, of *A Humane Society, to promote attention to the recovery of the sick, and to those brought to die on the banks of the Ganges,—to reward the preservation of people exposed to drowning, or the resuscitation of those apparently drowned, and any humane and efficient exertions for the benefit of individuals exposed to death. The object* of such an institution immediately commends itself; and it would not lack funds to carry it into effect. The *means* of accomplishing it appear specific and simple;—providing a stock of suitable medicines;—supporting a few Native doctors or Portuguese to administer it in the streets, lanes, ghauts, &c.; and awarding a premium for every well-authenticated instance of the preservation of human life. The *officers* of such a society would be few. Medical gentlemen would be eminently

* Ghaut Murders, p. 9.

qualified to direct and aid its operations. A few humane individuals might, with little trouble, direct the truly charitable donations of many into a useful and highly commendable channel.

"'Within the last few weeks, at Serampore, of the number of sick brought to some Ghauts, *a great many have been restored and sent to their families by the timely application of Cholera Medicine.* How much such exertions tend to promote the happiness of all ranks of Society, and endear man to man! At the Annual Meeting of the Royal Humane Society, in London, some who have been restored to life in the past year, through the exertions of the Society, are presented for the gratification of its friends. Might not such a scene soon be presented before the friends of humanity in Calcutta and other places? Such exertions must have an important bearing upon the interests of the infant cause of Christianity in India. To give life to the dead (as in the case of resuscitation)—to raise from affliction the dying and miserable sons and daughters of adversity—and to have, annually, numbers bearing their testimony to the kindness of Christians, must have a most beneficial tendency in society.'"

The Editor, in his remarks upon the above, says, "It is a happy circumstance that the most effectual remedies for the Cholera (the great scourge of India) are both simple and cheap. We have had the gratification of *saving a considerable number of lives this season,* by the following easy prescription:—Drop into a wine glass thirty or forty drops of laudanum, add one-third of a glass of brandy, an equal quantity of water, and four or five drops of essence of peppermint.—Repeat this dose every half hour till the vomiting and purging cease. If the stomach cannot bear the sudden addition of so much liquid, the patient should slowly sip it from a tea spoon. The following prescription is from high medical authority, and has been very successful:—Take laudanum twenty drops, diluted sulphuric acid (in which there are ten parts of water to one of acid) ten drops, oil of peppermint three drops, and mix them with a little water.* Commercial houses have much in their power; and we believe that in many cases their factories, so extensively scattered over the country, are known as refuges for the sick and the needy. *Judicious grants from Government of me-*

---

* The following treatment of Typhus Fever has been very successful:—"Take the root of butter bur washed clean and sliced thin, two ounces; pour upon it one quart of boiling water, in an earthen vessel, and stop it close; let it stand till cold; then pour the clear liquor off, and to a bottle of this liquor add a quarter pint of mountain wine, and a little lump sugar. Take one-quarter pint every four hours; let the patient's feet be put in warm water before going to bed. It operates by perspiration, and care must be taken not to take cold. When the patient is brought into a strong perspiration, discontinue the medicine.—Auth.

dical stores, or the sale of them at cost price, would much facilitate the work of benevolence. If such can be had, according to existing regulations, it would be well to make it more generally known;—if not, we would pray for a new regulation on the subject." After giving a just tribute to "the humane attention to the sick extensively displayed in British India, by public authorities and private individuals," it is acknowledged,—"We confess we are not at all sanguine in the expectation of it (the letter) giving rise to any public measure; but we do trust that it will induce many private individuals to do more than they yet have done in relieving the sick and forsaken." It appears therefore that, if India enjoy the numerous blessings conferred by active *Humane Societies*, seconding and directing the benevolent efforts of the Government,—a stimulus must be given from the philanthropic in Great Britain. In reference to this subject, and to every effort for the good of India, may its friends remember the sentiment of Dr. Buchanan: "There are some sanguinary practices which affect human life, and demand the early interference of a humane legislature. It is right indeed to look forward to the future benign effects of our religion; but *human lives are taken away* while we are waiting for the promulgation of Christianity. *The delay of another year will seal the death of thousands, the premature death of thousands, of British subjects.*" (Col. Esta. p. 126.)

(9.) It has long appeared very desirable, to the Author, that there should be established, in this country, *British India Humane Societies*, or *Humane Funds for British India*, attached to the various Missionary Societies. The following is the substance of a letter addressed to the Editor of a Periodical in London, which was returned as unsuitable for insertion. When shall the miseries of our fellow subjects in India obtain that attention they merit from our hands?

"While a resident in India, and an eye witness of the state of its inhabitants, I have often been reminded of the well-known sentiment of Dr. Thomas, the colleague of Dr. Carey:—'Don't send men to India destitute of feeling, for they will do no good: don't send men of feeling, for they will soon die!' One cause of this singular dilemma, of the humane and pious in India, is the frequent scenes of misery and death that they witness. For the moral miseries of the people, the Missionary has an antidote,—in the diffusion of the knowledge of the Gospel, which 'giveth life to him that hath it;' but from their natural miseries he must often turn away and steel 'the tender visitings of nature.' A '*British*

India Humane Society' established in London, with auxiliaries in Britain and India, might raise funds that would enable benevolent gentlemen, the medical profession and missionaries of different societies in India, to supply perishing myriads with medicine, food, &c., who for want of these pine in all the wretchedness to which Hindoo and Mussulman apathy doom the aged, the sick, and the dying. Should the establishment of such a general society be thought impracticable, something could be done by *each mission to India having a humane fund,* the proceeds of which would gladden the heart of the missionary, and cause the blessing of those who were ready to perish to come upon their kind benefactors.

" *The necessity of such a fund must strike every feeling mind.* A missionary in Pooree, at the temple of Juggernaut, wrote in June, 1825,—" We have relieved many a child of misery by administering medicine to the sick, clothing to the naked, food to the hungry, and money to the destitute; but what we have been able to do falls short indeed of the wants of the miserable. Many a heart-rending scene we have been called to witness where we could afford no relief;—many poor creatures we have dismissed with partial assistance, under a full persuasion they would soon want again and die: and many a scene of death have we endured; and turned away with a heavy overflowing heart from many a dying fellow creature, without God, and without hope, the victims of a wretched superstition." The distribution, here referred to, was from funds humanely supplied by the Government to relieve the miseries of the pilgrims to Juggernaut at the great Car Festival. A representation was made by one of the missionaries in Orissa, which was very promptly regarded;—but the supply arrived too late, and but little could be done for the miserable multitudes. It is evident that it must be highly desirable for missionaries to be furnished with means to alleviate the miseries they witness, that both temporally and spiritually, like their compassionate Lord, they may " go about doing good."

" *The manner of applying the proceeds of this fund is easily conceived.* Resources are wanted for " *entertaining strangers," clothing the naked, food for the famished pilgrim; medicine* (especially when the cholera morbus prevails in the district or country), *relief for the beggars* (aged, lame, blind, leprous, &c.), who look up to a Padre Sahab with confidence, and may be regularly assembled to obtain a little support and instruction; and, it may be added, the occasional employment of *a native Christian, a poor Portuguese, or a Native doctor*—to visit the sick, and carry medicine where the cholera or any other disease is known to prevail. Can a missionary do all these without assistance from his benevolent friends in Britain? and can they be neglected, or but partially regarded, without a poignancy of regret, alike injurious to body and mind, to character and usefulness?—A few incidents may confirm these statements. The Rev. C. Lacey of Cuttack, speaking of relieving the pilgrims at Juggernaut, says, " A great majority of the sick that I relieved on our first stage were females, almost without exception, deserted by their friends, who had left them not a pice (a half-penny) and no good cloth, and sometimes none; and many of them hundreds of miles from their home. I was frequently obliged to *clothe the helpless female with my own hands.* The bystanders when this was the case would generally say,—how holy is this!" On another occasion he writes, " The cholera morbus is raging in the country. I have sent the Pundit out with medicine, and to day he returned with the following account. At Janocotto gave to two persons, both recovered; at Mutagogapore, to three persons who recovered; at Dowanpatna to four, two recovered and two died, &c. The Pundit said they enquired who had sent him, and, being told the Padre Sahab, they pronounced many blessings and called it holy work. O may it prove to the furtherance of the Gospel, and may they be led to the physician of souls and live!"

"*The utility of a humane fund is evident.* The wise man says, "Every man is a friend to him that giveth gifts." In India, where a missionary has so much to oppose his progress, how desirable it is to have the benevolent character of that great man of the East, Job :—"When the ear heard, then it blessed me; and, when the eye saw me, it gave witness to me; because I delivered the poor that cried, and the fatherless, and him that had none to help him. The blessing of him that was ready to perish came upon me: and I caused the widow's heart to sing for joy.—I was eyes to the blind and feet was I to the lame. I was a father to the poor: and the cause which I knew not I searched out." Job. xxix. 11—16. What a pattern this of the amiable religion of Christ! what a contrast to Heathenism and Islamism! and how certain, under the blessing of its Divine Author, to bless the suffering and benighted sons and daughters of the East!

"*Humane efforts in India are attended with encouraging results.* The writer has found a young Bengalee female pilgrim left to die, but by suitable medicine, lodging, and food, had the pleasure to see her restored to health. A native servant recovered from a violent attack of cholera, by the pills (part of them given to him for the relief of others), returned with the grateful language—"*Ha Sahab amba au junmu pielu!*"—O Sir, I have got another birth. The Rev. Mr. R.——, a missionary at Calcutta, in a letter to a friend in September, 1825, states that "not one had died out of *sixty*, to whom he had administered medicine* for the cholera, except one individual, who had previously received some native medicine very prejudicial to her." Another missionary, in the vicinity of that city, said to the writer, "You saw that poor woman waiting on Mrs. T——: she was taken down to the Ganges to die, but was restored by some medicine that we administered." Where the attention of the Government is directed to the melioration of the miseries of the Natives, much good is done. In Orissa, a few years since, 3000 cholera pills were sent from Cuttack, for the relief of the salt manufacturers then suffering by the cholera, and several hundred lives were saved. A writer in the Friend of India (Sept. 1825), states, "We know that, when the cholera first began its ravages, one gentleman obtained from Government forty or fifty native doctors to supply his district, and medical stores to what extent he chose; and the gratifying result was that *medicine was adminis-*

---

* This medicine was, "eighty drops of laudanum, a wine glass of brandy, and two table spoonfuls of castor oil, mixed and given if possible at once; if not, one desert spoonful after another, until all is taken. This is the dose for a man; for females, girls, and boys, sixty drops of laudanum, the brandy and oil the same quantities as before. Should this be ineffectual, give a second dose of forty drops of laudanum, a wine glass of brandy, but no oil. In case of this failing, a wine glass of *Drogue a mere* may be effectual. This medicine may be administered in almost all stages of the disease. After the vomiting ceases give warm rice water, and after that boiled sago or soogee (flour). The patient should be kept on a dry place and warm." (Asi. Journ., March, 1826, p. 386.)

tered to upwards of 20,000 *persons, of whom more than* 17,000 *recovered!!* —It must be evident that the Government in India cannot do all that humanity requires, and hence the necessity of the humane exertions in Britain here advocated. A missionary speaking of a school examination, January, 1826, says, "At our last examination, all the boys who could read the Scriptures, read and repeated the whole of Watts's Catechism in Oorea, and were rewarded with *cloths;* and the next class with a few pice, from a *donation by a friend in England.* These cloths not only rewarded and encouraged the children, but will prove a real blessing to them, as they are most of them very poor and the season is cold. If any friend could be induced *to contribute a little to be spent in such rewards,* he would render most effectual help to our Mission, and bestow a great blessing upon many poor indigent children and parents." Surely this appeal to British humanity and liberality will not be in vain.* To state but one more circumstance: a colleague observes, "When endeavouring to do something for the sick, those around will exclaim, Ha durma Aubitar! Sutya Aubitar!" &c. &c.—'O holy incarnation, true incarnation!' Some would fain worship us, and bowed their foreheads to the very dirt; of course we objected to this, and taught them to look to God and give him all the praise. Some observed, *This would occasion our religion to be talked about far and wide!* It certainly has given us favour in the sight of the people, and they often manifested an expression of it." Let Britain pity and alleviate the spiritual and temporal woes of India, and she will be instructed and animated to promote the diffusion of the knowledge of Christ, and the exemplification of every humane and Christian trait that adorns the human character."

Idolatry is cruel as the grave; but Christian benevolence imparts, as it is said of Solomon, "largeness of heart, even as the sand that is on the sea shore."

> "Friend, parent, neighbour, first it will embrace,
> Our country next, and next the human race."

The importance of the humane efforts here recommended, viewed in connexion with the preservation of the British power in India, may be shown by the following extract from the speech of Lord Erskine on Cruelty to Animals, in the house of Peers, May 15, 1809.—"The times in which we live, my Lords, have read us an awful lesson upon *the importance of preserving the moral sympathies.* We have seen that the highest state of refinement and cultivation will not secure them: even in struggles for human rights and privileges, sincere and laudable as they may occasionally have been,—all human rights and privileges have been trampled upon, by barbarities more shocking than those of the most barbarous nations: because they have not merely

* Two ladies, sisters, at St. Ives (Hunts), were so affected in reading the Report of the General Baptist Mission for 1826, that they sent £10 for the relief of the Pilgrims to Juggernaut.

extinguished natural unconnected life, but have destroyed the social happiness and independence of mankind; raising up tyrants to oppress them all in the end, by beginning with the oppression of each other. *All this has arisen from neglecting the cultivation of the moral sense, the best security of states, and the greatest consolation of the world.* The cruelties which we daily deplore, in children and in youth, arise from defect in education; and that defect in education from the very defect in the law which I ask your Lordships to remedy. From the moral sense of the parent reanimated, or rather, in this branch, created by the law,—the next generation will feel, in the first dawn of their ideas, the august relation they stand in to the lower world, and the trust which their station in the universe imposes on them; and it will not be left to a future Sterne to remind us—when we put aside even a harmless insect—that the world is large enough for both. This extension of benevolence to objects beneath us, become habitual by a sense of duty inculcated by law, will reflect back upon our sympathies: so that I may venture to say, firmly, to your Lordships, that the Bill I propose to you, if it shall receive the sanction of Parliament, will not only be an honour to the country, but an era in the history of the world."

(10.) *The necessity and importance of societies to promote the abolition of human sacrifices in India appear evident.* By them, information upon the nature and extent of every species of human sacrifice, may be extensively circulated in the united kingdom and in India, petitions to Parliament promoted, and the subject pressed upon public attention till these evils are no more. Such societies, or corresponding committees, have been formed in London, Birmingham, and Coventry.* The following regulations of the Coventry Society were adopted at the first general meeting of the Committee, Dec. 1828:—

I. Its *designation* shall be "The Society for Promoting the Abolition of Human Sacrifices in India."

II. Its *object* is to circulate information respecting the nature and extent of human sacrifices in India, by the burning of Hindoo widows, Infanticide, river murders, pilgrimages, &c.; to awaken general attention to the subject; and to promote the speedy abolition of these horrible practices.

III. The *means* by which this important object may be promoted are

* In July, 1829, a proposal was inserted in a Calcutta newspaper, for the establishment of a Society in that city, for the abolition of Suttees.

—procuring information upon the above subjects,—circulating it among persons of influence in this country and in India,—and originating petitions to Parliament from every part of Great Britain and Ireland.

IV. Every person subscribing not less than 5s. a year shall be considered a member of the Society.

V. Every member shall, on application, be entitled to half the amount of his subscription in the publications of this Society, and the privilege of purchasing at prime cost for gratuitous circulation.

VI. The publications adopted by the Society at its formation are—"The Suttees' Cry to Britain,"—"Pilgrim Tax in India,"—Ghaut Murders, or an Appeal to British Humanity and Justice relative to the Exposure of the Sick on the banks of the Ganges; to which is added, Humane Hints for the melioration of Society in British India,"—and "Claims of British India, or an Appeal to the Society of Friends for their co-operation in promoting Christianity in India.* A Pamphlet on the Present State of Infanticide is intended to be published. The Society would be happy to promote the circulation of what has been published on the Suttee by Dr. Johns, J. Poynder and R. Jackson, Esqrs., and the Rev. T. Grimshawe.

VII. The Society, anticipating the establishment of similar Institutions in various parts of the country, proposes to supply them with its publications at prime cost, or Societies may reprint them.

VIII. The business of the Society shall be managed by a Committee, of which the Treasurer and Secretary are members *ex-officio*.

IX. From January to June, inclusive, the Committee shall meet monthly, on the first Monday of the month, at eleven o'clock in the morning; and the remainder of the year, every two months, on the same day of the month: and the Secretary shall be empowered to call a special meeting when necessary.

X. An Annual Report shall be presented at the close of the year, stating the proceedings of this and similar Institutions, and the progress made towards the attainment of the object of their establishment.

The following Petition to Parliament was unanimously adopted at a public Meeting in the County Hall of the City of Coventry, the Mayor in the Chair, Feb. 17, 1829, and may suggest an appropriate form for general adoption :—

To the Honourable the Commons of the United Kingdom of Great Britain and Ireland, in Parliament assembled.

The humble Petition of the Inhabitants of the City of Coventry, and its Vicinity,

Sheweth,

That your Petitioners learn with the deepest regret that the burning of widows with the bodies of their late husbands, the destruction of female children, the exposure of the Sick on the banks of the river Ganges, and other customs by which human life is cruelly sacrificed, continue to be practised in British India; and particularly that Pilgrimages to certain Temples in that country, are superintended by the British authorities, as sources of revenue to the Honourable East India Company's Government.

---

* In addition to these "*The Suttees' Cry abridged, and the Appeal of the Society*," are presented to subscribers.

That it further appears to your Petitioners that the practice of burning Widows is unauthorised by the institutes of Menu, the great Legislator of the Hindoos, who enjoins various precepts for the future conduct of Widows, which of course are inconsistent with the existence of such sacrifices; that the British Government in India is able to abolish these appalling practices, in its own dominions, apppears from the testimony of many of its Functionaries, as stated in the six volumes of Parliamentary Papers on Hindoo Immolations; that the existing regulations adopted by the Bengal Government respecting Suttees, by which the permission of the Magistrate is granted, and the attendance of the Police appointed, have unintentionally promoted the celebrity and increase of these Immolations; that other cruel practices continue their ravages in society, unawed by British humanity and justice; and that the system pursued by the British Government, which allows a premium to the Pundas who collect Pilgrims for the worship of the idol Juggernaut at the great Temple in Orissa, occasions an increase of the native superstition, contrary to the purport of a resolution of your Honourable House in One Thousand Eight Hundred and Thirteen, recognising it as the duty of this Country to introduce among our fellow-subjects in India the blessings of Christianity.

That your Petitioners, therefore, most earnestly implore your Honourable House to adopt such measures as may be deemed most expedient and effectual, for the suppression of such atrocious practices, and the discontinuance of the support of a sanguinary idolatry, soopposed to the real welfare of our Indian possessions; and thus to remove the stigma which attaches to our national character, and relieve the Inhabitants of British India from the effects of their deadly superstitions.

And your Petitioners, &c.

A similar Petition was presented to the House of Lords.

"We are astonished (says a writer in the Evangelical Magazine, Aug. 1828) that Britain, so justly famed for humanity, does not more powerfully plead for the widow, and that petitions, more numerous than those against the sacramental Test, do not flow into Parliament from all quarters." Let the favourable impressions of an Honourable East India Proprietor be justified, expressed on the Suttee question March, 1827.—"The people of England and the Legislature should know of *the hundreds of murders annually committed under British authority, and the public should be invoked for their suppression.* He had not the least doubt, the call would be answered, and the *tables of the Houses be covered with petitions against a custom so obnoxious to every moral and religious precept and so disgraceful to the national character.*" (Jackson's Speech.) And let the continuance of various efforts for the good of India, be in full accordance with the eloquent language of the philanthropic Wilberforce, before the British Parliament in 1813.—"I feel Christianity to be the greatest boon we can confer upon the Natives of

India. Let no man think that the petitions which have loaded the table of this House have been produced by a burst of momentary enthusiasm, or that the zeal which actuates the Petitioners will soon be expended. *No, Sir, it will be found to be as steady as the light of heaven! While the sun and moon continue to shine in the firmament of heaven, will this object be pursued with unabating ardour, until the great work be accomplished.*"

Behold the cruelties of Hindoism seen in its unnatural rites; and what power can bind the Hindoos, but the uncertain influence of self-interest? "Would not the British dominion in India," says Lord Teignmouth, "acquire additional solidity, by the accession of a body of Natives, united to us by the bond of a common faith? Major Scott Waring foresees no danger in the operation of bigotry, superstition, and prejudice, which, while they exist in their present force, must oppose a bar to the cordial union between the Natives of India and their European Rulers. I see the subject in a different light; and, without wishing to circumscribe the limits of that toleration which has been hitherto adopted, feel the necessity of introducing a principle of counteraction and melioration, by implanting among them the doctrines of Christianity."* The efforts of the philanthropic and Christian public in this country and India, under the blessing of God, may do much for the welfare of Hindostan. *A British India Humane Society in London*, aided by Societies in other parts of this country, would stimulate our philanthropic countrymen in the East to second their exertions. Can it be doubted whether there be a necessity for such Institutions? In what country under heaven is there so much misery as in India? View the shipwrecked mariner—the poor widow hurried to the funeral pile—the murdered infant—the sick exposed by the Ganges—the thousands of miserable pilgrims—the degraded slave—numbers drowning in the rivers in stormy weather, without any assistance being afforded—myriads dying in epidemics for want of medicine and attendance; and, to crown the whole, the distress frequently so great as to defy individual exertion to alleviate it, and hence occasioning an apathy, inhuman and unchristian, even in the European character.

---

* Considerations on diffusing the knowledge of Christianity in India, p. 89.

A Humane Society in Calcutta, and other cities and towns, aided by funds and correspondence from Britain, would do much to remove these miseries—rescue numbers from a premature death—do honour to humanity and to the British people—and commend Christianity to the acceptance of the Heathen and the Mahometan. And as it approaches them let mercy attend the steps of its messengers. Humane exertions, either by the Legislature, by individuals, or by Humane Societies, must be beneficial. It is written, " Mercy shall be built up for ever." Let these pages be attentively perused, and it is hoped the humane and liberal spirit of Britain, will devise " liberal things" for the temporal and spiritual welfare of India. " When we consider that so many millions of the population of India are our fellow-subjects, what a stimulus to seek their good! What an imperative, what a paramount duty! Is it not manifest that, in the mental and moral improvement of this vast empire, Great Britain has a work of benevolence before her, which, in national glory, will eclipse all other achievements as much as the meridian sun exceeds in splendour the morning star? *Know then, the country of the Howards and the Wilberforces, thy high destiny! Never were such miseries to be removed—never was such a mighty good put within the power of one nation—the raising a population of sixty millions to a rational and happy existence, and through them the illumination and civilization of all Asia!*"*

---

* Ward's View of the Hindoos, Vol. iii. pref. p. 54.